Practical Intelligence an

Practical Intelligence and the Virtues

Daniel C. Russell

CLARENDON PRESS · OXFORD

OXFORD
UNIVERSITY PRESS

Great Clarendon Street, Oxford OX2 6DP

Oxford University Press is a department of the University of Oxford.
It furthers the University's objective of excellence in research, scholarship,
and education by publishing worldwide in

Oxford New York

Auckland Cape Town Dar es Salaam Hong Kong Karachi
Kuala Lumpur Madrid Melbourne Mexico City Nairobi
New Delhi Shanghai Taipei Toronto

With offices in

Argentina Austria Brazil Chile Czech Republic France Greece
Guatemala Hungary Italy Japan Poland Portugal Singapore
South Korea Switzerland Thailand Turkey Ukraine Vietnam

Oxford is a registered trademark of Oxford University Press
in the UK and in certain other countries

Published in the United States
by Oxford University Press Inc., New York

© Daniel C. Russell 2009

British Library Cataloguing in Publication Data
Data available

Library of Congress Cataloging in Publication Data
Data available

Typeset by Laserwords Private Limited, Chennai, India
Printed in the United Kingdom by
Lightning Source UK Ltd, Milton Keynes

ISBN 978-0-19-956579-5 (Hbk)
ISBN 978-0-19-969844-8 (Pbk)

For Mark LeBar

Acknowledgments

It first occurred to me to write a book on practical intelligence during a seminar on Aristotle's ethics at Wichita State University in 2005, and so I would like to begin by thanking my students in that seminar for their participation and discussion. Thanks also to the students in my 2006 virtue ethics seminar at Monash University, where we discussed many of the issues I cover in Part I.

For support both philosophical and moral during the writing of this book, I would like especially to thank Julia Annas, Joachim Asscher, Dirk Baltzly, Monima Chadha, Fiona Leigh, Neil McKinnon, and David Soles. Thanks also to Benjamin Miller for his comments on Part I.

I find that here, as so often, I am especially indebted to Mark LeBar, who patiently, faithfully, and carefully read the entire manuscript, usually in rather awkward drafts. His comments have been invaluable, as has my correspondence with him about innumerable half-formed ideas. (So any of those ideas that still remain only half-formed, not to say half-baked, are my own fault.) Above all, he was a good friend throughout the whole process. Thanks, Mark.

It gives me great joy to acknowledge my many personal debts. Most of all, I wish to thank Gina Russell, my wonderful wife, and our daughters Jocelyn, Grace, and Julia. I also thank our families, Dan and Eileen Russell and Roger and Joyce Butz.

With respect to individual chapters, I owe thanks to the following parties:

Chapter 2: Thanks to the audience at Macquarie University, where I presented an early version of this chapter in 2006, and thanks to Tim Bayne and Catriona Mackenzie for organizing the talk. A portion of this chapter was expanded and published as 'That "Ought" Does Not Imply "Right": Why it Matters for Virtue Ethics' in the *Southern Journal of Philosophy*, 46 (2008), 299–315. I thank the editors of *SJP* for permission to use that material here.

Chapter 3: Thanks to the audience at La Trobe University, where I presented an early version of this chapter in 2006, and thanks to Tim Oakley for organizing the talk. A version of this chapter was published as 'Right Action and Virtuous Motives: What is Wrong with Agent-Based Virtue Ethics?' in the *American Philosophical Quarterly*, 45 (2008), 329–48. I thank the editors of *APQ* for permission to use the article here.

Chapter 4: Thanks to the audience at Sydney University, where I presented a predecessor of this chapter in 2006. Thanks especially to Luke Russell for organizing the talk, and to Mark Colyvan for comments and correspondence that radically altered my approach.

Chapter 5: Thanks to the audiences at Wichita State University and Monash University, where I presented predecessors of this chapter in 2005. Thanks to Laura Schroeter for organizing the talk at Monash.

Chapter 7: Thanks to the Melbourne Area Society for Ancient Philosophy, where I presented an early version of this chapter in 2006, and to the organizers, Dirk Baltzly and David Runia.

Chapters 8–10: Thanks to the audiences at the University of Otago and the University of Auckland, where I presented a paper summarizing these chapters in 2007. Thanks especially to Rosalind Hursthouse, Alan Musgrave, and Koji Tanaka for organizing the talks, and the trip.

Chapter 12: Thanks to the audiences at the Monash Conference on Free Will, the University of Melbourne, and the Australasian Association of Philosophy, where I presented various predecessors of this chapter. Thanks to Nick Trakakis, who organized the Monash conference, and to François Schroeter for organizing the talk at Melbourne.

Last but certainly not least, I owe thanks to various anonymous referees, at OUP and elsewhere, for their often invaluable comments. I shall acknowledge my many other debts as they arise in the course of the book.

D.C.R.

Wichita, Kansas
July 2008

Preface

One of the most important developments in moral philosophy over the last half century has been the resurgence of virtue ethics, an approach to moral philosophy based primarily on the notion of virtue and vice, rather than primarily on moral duties or the consequences of action. Virtue ethics is now a central feature of the contemporary philosophical landscape, and work on the virtues has proceeded at an increasingly rapid pace. Not surprisingly, work critical of virtue ethics has proceeded just as rapidly, and in particular it has long been clear that the biggest challenge facing contemporary virtue ethics is to demonstrate that it is 'action guiding', that is, that it can serve as a general approach to thought about how one ought, morally, to act. Work on the virtues in both normative and applied ethics since the 1980s has now, I think, won virtue ethicists the right to be confident about their prospects of offering distinctive and interesting action guidance.

More recently, though, this challenge has taken two more specific forms: one, the challenge of giving a more formal virtue-based account of what makes an action 'right', and two, the challenge of defending an empirically adequate psychological model of the virtues. Ultimately the guidance that we want is guidance to action that is *right*, so if virtue ethics were not to meet the first challenge, then it could not claim to be a complete, self-standing moral theory, but could be at most a complement to other theories. And if it were not to meet the second challenge, then any guidance it may offer about how we should develop morally would be moot—perhaps appropriate for creatures with a very different kind of psychology from our own, but not for us. Therefore, to be action guiding, virtue ethics must be both complete as a *normative* theory and adequate in its *empirical* presuppositions. I argue in this book that both challenges can be met, but only by focusing on the role of practical reason in the virtues, and in particular on the role of practical intelligence.

This book comprises three broad tasks: addressing the relation between virtue and right action, addressing the empirical presuppositions of virtue theory, and defending my view against certain objections. I shall briefly sketch each of these below.

Before we go any further, though, there are two things about my subject matter that I should clarify. One is that this book is sometimes about virtue *ethics*, sometimes about virtue *theory*, and sometimes about both. Following

Julia Driver (1996, 111 n.) it has become somewhat common to distinguish these: roughly, a virtue theory is a theory of what the virtues are, whereas virtue ethics holds the virtues to be central to a theory of the ethical evaluation of action. Virtue theory thus falls under the umbrella of moral psychology, and virtue ethics under normative ethics. To be sure, every virtue ethic must build on a virtue theory, but no virtue theorist—no one with a theory about the nature of the virtues—need for that reason be a virtue ethicist. This terminological distinction is far from universal, but it will be useful to employ it here, and I do so throughout the book.[i] It will be particularly useful for my purposes since I focus on virtue ethics in Part I, consider both virtue ethics and virtue theory in Part II, and shift my focus even further to virtue theory in Part III.

The other point has to do with what sorts of theories we mean by 'virtue ethics'. I shall say more about this in Chapter 2, but for now I should note that by 'virtue ethics' I mean a family of theories all of which take the virtues as primary in their account of right action. I understand this 'primacy' in Gary Watson's (1990) sense: roughly, that right action is defined in terms of the virtues, but not vice versa. Clearly, many ethical theories with a serious interest in the virtues will not count as 'virtue ethics' in this sense. I am open to the idea that there may be other ways, felicitous for various purposes, of sorting what we wish to consider under a common umbrella of 'virtue ethics'. But this is what I shall mean by 'virtue ethics' here, and it is a fairly standard way of demarcating the field (cp. Adams 2006, 6).

Virtue and Right Action

The challenge of giving virtue-based accounts of right action is the focus of the first two parts of this book, where I concentrate on two more specific issues, respectively. First, while various virtue-based accounts of right action, and various critiques of these accounts, have been offered, there is at present no common base of agreement as to the formal constraints on an adequate virtue-based account of right action, what counts as a fair (vs. question-begging) objection to such an account, or even what exactly makes an account of right action a distinctly virtue ethical one in the first place. It is therefore sometimes

---

[i] This is important since, if we take having a virtue theory to be a sufficient condition for being a virtue ethicist, rather than only a necessary condition, 'virtue ethics' will seem like a very odd category indeed—as in fact it does to Nussbaum 1999. See also McAleer 2007, 210 for discussion.

difficult to tell, given present philosophical resources, when such accounts succeed or fail. So although many varieties of virtue ethics are currently on offer, what virtue ethics now requires is not yet another theory of right action, or another round of replies to critics, but a more general framework for determining both what makes an account of right action a 'virtue ethical' one, and what counts as an adequate specimen of such an account.

And second, it seems to me that virtue ethicists have largely failed to notice an important tension between a necessary feature of virtue ethics, on the one hand, and an unnecessary but increasingly commonplace feature, on the other. The necessary feature is that for virtue ethics a right action must be virtuous in an 'overall' way, that is, in accordance with the virtues, in the plural. The commonplace feature is that, on many of the approaches to individuating the virtues currently on offer, the virtues would turn out to be infinitely many. For instance, it is tempting to individuate virtues in terms of the special contexts to which they seem particularly relevant—one for ordinary generous giving, say, and one for large-scale philanthropic giving (see Aristotle, *Nicomachean Ethics* [*NE*] IV.1−2)—but of course there is in principle no limit to the number of 'special contexts' for which one could require a virtue. In that case, it would be impossible to know on such an account when an action was overall virtuous—virtuous in accordance with infinitely many virtues—and therefore when it was right. Nor could such an account make sense of the idea of being an overall virtuous person. It is time, therefore, for virtue ethicists to pay much closer attention to the individuation of virtues than they have done so far.

In both cases, I argue that meeting the challenges surrounding virtue-based accounts of rightness requires a conception of the virtues on which practical intelligence is a crucial part of every virtue. The conception of practical intelligence I develop is an Aristotelian one, on which it is an excellence of deliberating not merely about the *means* to virtuous ends (e.g. how to carry out a generous act) but also about the specification of the very *content* of virtuous ends (e.g. what would in fact be, in these circumstances, a generous act), as well as the reasons to *adopt* those ends in the first place.[ii] I argue in Part I that there can be an adequate tie between the notion of a virtue and that of a right action, but only if phronesis is part of every virtue, since reliably finding a right action requires deliberative skill and excellence. And I argue in Part II

[ii] My Aristotelian approach to practical intelligence is also reflected in my choice to call it simply 'phronesis' from this point on. By now I think that 'phronesis' has become part of the philosophical lexicon, and has the advantage that it is perhaps less likely than 'practical intelligence' to mislead by suggesting inactive contemplation, say, or special intellectual sophistication. See Annas 1993a, 73; Owens 1987, 6ff.

that we can individuate the virtues in a principled and economical way by individuating them according to the particular kinds of reasons to which each virtue is responsive. After all, it makes sense to say that one can respond to the same reason across a wide range of different contexts; in that case, virtues as forms of reasons-responsiveness would not have to multiply as contexts do. Once again, then, the virtues must all involve phronesis, since a virtue must involve responsiveness to reasons that is practically intelligent if it is to respond appropriately.

My view therefore stands in stark contrast to the trend towards increasing indifference to the notion of phronesis in recent thought about the virtues of character. Some virtue theorists argue that phronesis is important for some virtues, but certainly not all (Swanton 2003); others that while phronesis is part of the virtues, this requirement is soft enough that even the 'kindheartedness' of an 'imperceptive' person, fragmentary and deficient in phronesis, still counts as a virtue (Adams 2006, 187); others that phronesis and even deliberation are unnecessary if one's motives are virtuous in a 'balanced' way (Slote 2001); and yet others that the virtues require no particular underlying psychological attributes at all, much less phronesis (Driver 2001). My approach therefore has implications not only for defending virtue ethics against its critics, but also for rethinking the nature of the virtues in terms of which right action can be understood. Consequently, I distinguish between two basic varieties of virtue ethics: those on which phronesis is part of every virtue, which I call 'Hard Virtue Ethics', and those on which it is not ('Soft Virtue Ethics').[iii] The argument of Parts I and II, then, is that this distinction is a *fundamental* one, as only the former is viable.

Virtue and Social Psychology

The next part of the book takes up a mounting challenge not just to virtue ethics but to any theory of the nature of the virtues, a challenge stemming from certain apparent discoveries about personality and character in empirical psychology. Whereas all accounts of character take character to be important in explanations of what people do, the so-called 'situationist' paradigm in social psychology suggests that even the apparently minor details of one's situation have far more to do with behavior than one's alleged dispositions do. If that is right, then there would seem to be rather little evidence

---

[iii] On this 'hard'/'soft' terminology, cp. DePaul 1999, 150.

supporting disposition-based conceptions of personality and character. Several philosophical psychologists have therefore concluded that theories of the virtues are moot, on the grounds that they involve normative assessment of certain features of human psychology whose existence is totally unsupported by our best empirical evidence about the causes of behavior. In other words, there is no more point to theorizing about the moral qualities of character traits than there would be to theorizing about the moral qualities of 'phlegmatic' and 'choleric' personalities.

Situationism is therefore at the center of one of the hottest controversies in philosophical psychology today. And perhaps not surprisingly, virtue theorists have been quick to question and even to reject outright the apparent findings of situationist research in social psychology. By contrast, I think—and indeed I argue—that the best interpretation of the findings of researchers in personality theory is precisely the interpretation that situationist social psychologists give them. The problem lies neither in the empirical research nor in its interpretation by social psychologists, but in the more recent translation of that research for a philosophical audience. In particular, situationism has been presented to philosophers mainly as the negative thesis that there is no evidence for behavioral dispositions and thus no evidence for character, full stop. But what situationism rejects, more precisely, is the notion that personality and character are causes of behavior that operate in relative isolation from situations; it does not reject the notions of personality or character themselves. In fact, situationism also offers a positive theory of the nature of personality, little discussed by philosophical psychologists, on which personality consists of an individual's various cognitive and affective processes—seeking certain goals, attending to certain features of situations, attaching certain meanings to one's experience, placing value on certain outcomes, etc.—in virtue of which one adjusts one's behaviors to one's situations.

In that case, I argue, the personality theory suggested by situationist social psychology *leads naturally* to a certain philosophical theory of the virtues. On such a theory, character is understood as personality considered from an ethical point of view, and a virtue as some set of interrelated cognitive-affective processes whereby one seeks appropriate goals, attends to appropriate features of situations, etc. Since I think that situationism offers the best understanding of personality currently available, a virtue theory that conceives of the virtues as involving certain skills and excellences of practical reasoning and deliberation would be an empirically formidable theory. In other words, the empirical adequacy of virtue theory depends on making phronesis a central feature of every virtue. Given our best evidence, therefore, an empirically adequate virtue theory must be a form of what I shall call Hard Virtue Theory. As is the case between Hard and Soft Virtue Ethics, so too the distinction between Hard and Soft Virtue Theory is a fundamental one.

Defending the View

In the final part of the book, I defend Hard Virtue Ethics and Hard Virtue Theory against two main sorts of objections. First, the idea that phronesis is part of every virtue is commonly, and correctly, associated with the thesis that to have any virtue is to have every virtue (on the grounds that having any virtue means having phronesis, and having phronesis means having all the virtues). But of course it is obvious from our everyday experience that while many people are virtuous in some ways, no one is virtuous in every way; so this thesis—the so-called 'unity of virtue' thesis—is simply untrue to experience. I argue that the unity of virtue thesis need not be a claim about the necessary conditions for anyone's having any virtue at all. Rather, I offer it as a claim about how the virtues are such as to include one another's perspectives in an increasing way as one matures in the development of virtue.

And second, the idea that phronesis is part of every virtue suggests that virtues would have to have tremendous rational 'depth': one's virtues are among the very deepest parts of one's character, identity, and rationality, so that one must be the 'author' of one's virtues, in some sense, rather than merely a bearer of them as one may be of one's purely physical characteristics. However, some philosophers have argued that, on our best understanding of human development, one is no more the 'author' of one's virtues, or of any other features of one's psychology for that matter, than one is the 'author' of the face one is born with (Strawson 2003). I argue that the intuitive 'depth' of character requires not self-authorship, but the capacity to engage in the sorts of reflection and practical reasoning about one's character by which persons take ownership of their character, turning simple motivations into ends they can endorse in rational reflection.

I think that these challenges all show that virtue ethics is on the verge of a crucial new stage in its future development. The main task for virtue ethics today is both to demonstrate that some form or forms of virtue ethics can meet the normative as well as the empirical demands on it, and to demonstrate even in broad outline what such a form of virtue ethics would be like. This book is my attempt at answering that challenge.

Contents

1. Practical Intelligence and the Virtues: An Aristotelian Approach   1

    1.1 Deliberation   4
    1.2 Phronesis   13
    1.3 The Phronesis Controversy   31

Part I. Phronesis, Virtue, and Right Action   35

2. Right Action for Virtue Ethics   37

    2.1 Right Action and Serious Practical Concerns   39
    2.2 Two Constraints on Right Action   44
    2.3 *Must* Virtue Ethics Accept the Act Constraint?   46
    2.4 *Can* Virtue Ethics Accept the Act Constraint?   65

3. Right Action and Virtuous Motives   72

    3.1 The Structure of Agent-Based Virtue Ethics   74
    3.2 Virtuous Acts and Virtuous Motivations   77
    3.3 Why Virtues are Virtues   86
    3.4 Reasons for Virtue   95

4. Right Action and 'The Virtuous Person'   103

    4.1 Doing Without 'The Virtuous Person'   104
    4.2 'Virtuous Enough'   112
    4.3 Ideals and Aspirations   123
    4.4 Virtues, Persons, and 'The Virtuous Person'   130
    4.5 Representing 'The Virtuous Person'   135

Part II. The Enumeration Problem   143

5. The Enumeration Problem   145

    5.1 The Enumeration Problem: An Introduction   145
    5.2 Enumeration and Overall Virtuous Actions   161
    5.3 Enumeration and Overall Virtuous Persons   166
    5.4 Enumeration and Naturalism   172

6. Individuating the Virtues   177

    6.1 From Individuation to Enumeration   178
    6.2 'The Same Reasons'   188
    6.3 Reasons, Individuation, and Cardinality   196
    6.4 Implications for Hard Virtue Ethics   204

7. Magnificence, Generosity, and Subordination   209

    7.1 Magnificence as a Virtue   212
    7.2 Subordination, Specialization, and Cardinality   217
    7.3 Alternatives to the Subordination View   221

Part III. Situations, Dispositions, and Virtues   237

8. Situations and Broad-Based Dispositions   239

    8.1 Situationism and Dispositionism   243
    8.2 Situationism and Personality   252
    8.3 Idiographic Predictions of Consistency   263

9. Situations and Dispositions: Examining the Evidence   268

    9.1 How to Test Broad-Based Dispositions for Cross-Situational Consistency   269
    9.2 Putting Dispositions to the Test: Four Representative Experiments   273
    9.3 Interpreting the Findings   278

10. From Situationism to Virtue Theory   292

    10.1 Situationism: From Empirical to Philosophical Psychology   295
    10.2 Situationism and Virtue Theory: Normative Adequacy   304
    10.3 From Common Sense to Virtue Theory?   306
    10.4 Out-Sourcing the Empirical Work?   314
    10.5 A Cognitive-Affective Approach to the Virtues   323

Part IV. Defending Hard Virtue Theory   333

11. Phronesis and the Unity of the Virtues   335

    11.1 The Unity of Which Virtues?   339
    11.2 What Unifies the Virtues?   355
    11.3 Attributive and Model Theses   362

12. Responsibility for Character 374

    12.1 Depth, Self-Construction, and Responsibility 374
    12.2 On Responsibility and 'Ultimate Responsibility' for Character 380
    12.3 What is Critical Distance? 388
    12.4 From Critical Distance to Responsibility 392
    12.5 Objections to the Critical Distance View 404

Works Cited 415
Index Locorum 429
General Index 433

1

Practical Intelligence and the Virtues: An Aristotelian Approach

There was a time, not long ago, when people would say things like, 'Virtue ethics is concerned with character rather than right action'.[1] Times have changed. In fact, it is difficult to think that the slogan 'character instead of right action' has ever been true of virtue ethics.

It certainly is untrue of Aristotle, from whom the modern revival of virtue ethics has most often drawn inspiration. For one thing, Aristotle famously dismisses the idea of the 'inactive virtuous' as simply ludicrous (*NE* I.5). More important, although Aristotle says that the virtues are unlike skills in aiming at 'doing' rather than 'making' (VI.5, 1140b1–4), and that a person's actions cannot be evaluated in the same way that a craftsman's wares are (II.4, 1105a26–33), he is also impressed by the fact that the virtues, like skills, are learned through practice, and for the sake of practice (I.3; II.1, 4). Likewise, he takes practical reasoning about virtuous action to parallel reasoning about skill, in at least two ways. One, as a doctor must know how best to treat a patient—what procedures and medicines to use—so too a virtuous person must know how to execute virtuous plans and, as we say, how to 'get things done'. And two, before a doctor can execute a planned treatment, he or she must first formulate that plan—the general end of healing the patient must be made specific, as what it would be to heal *this* patient in *these* circumstances. Likewise, virtuous aims like acting generously or fairly must also be made specific in the same sense. The former, executive sort of reasoning

---

[1] See Hursthouse 1999*a*, 25ff for discussion. See also Louden 1984, 229: 'It has often been said that for virtue ethics the central question is not "What ought I to *do*?" but rather "What sort of person ought I to *be*?" However, people have always expected ethical theory to tell them something about what they ought to do, and it seems to me that virtue ethics is structurally unable to say much of anything about this issue.'

about virtuous aims involves what Aristotle calls 'cleverness' (*deinotēs*), and the latter, planning sort involves practical intelligence or phronesis. Phronesis is of particular importance in Aristotle's account of the virtues, because, he says, actions done with praiseworthy aims but not with phronesis can be as likely to go wrong as right (VI.13; see also Hursthouse 1999a, 82; 2006a; Foot 1978a, 5f, 11f). And famously, Aristotle defines the virtues as aiming at the 'mean', understood as what is 'fitting' or 'appropriate' to the circumstances at hand. This is why phronesis is so important to the virtues, since it is phronesis that ascertains what is fitting (II.4, 6; VI.1). Clearly, Aristotle thinks that being virtuous has rather a *lot* to do with 'right action', although that is a phrase he lacks.

Contemporary virtue ethics is also marked by a clear focus on action and the rightness of action. In recent years, there has arisen a large and growing literature on distinctly virtue ethical conceptions of and approaches to right action. As I write this, three such approaches have proven most notable. Rosalind Hursthouse (1999a, chs. 1–3) has argued for an understanding of right action that begins with a model of the patterns of deliberation, feeling, and practical reasoning that are characteristic of persons with the virtues, and Christine Swanton (2003, ch. 11) has approached right action through a rich discussion of the complex aims, or 'targets', that are characteristic of the virtues. Michael Slote (2001, ch. 1) has taken an even more radical approach to right action, which he understands purely in terms of the virtuousness (and in particular, benevolence) of the motives from which an act is done.

Virtue ethics has also had a profound effect on thought about action in various fields of applied ethics, offering fresh and distinctively virtue ethical approaches to bioethics, professional ethics, environmental ethics, the treatment of animals, and sexual ethics, among many others. In fact, although virtue ethics has sometimes been criticized as offering no practical guidance, its strong entrance into the field of applied ethics suggests that it may be in the area of action guidance that virtue ethics shines brightest. Perhaps the failure of that criticism is not too surprising, since it was largely fueled by the now-hackneyed slogan about 'character instead of action'. Virtue ethicists have paved their way into practical ethics by defending a new conception of what it is for a theory to be 'action guiding', pointing out the naivety of expecting an action-guiding theory to produce solutions to ethical problems by itself, and thinking of action guidance instead as modeling those features of agents that make deliberation and choice ethically responsible and, in a word, done well. On this view, theories guide action not so much by telling agents what to do as by directing their development into ethically mature agents who are better able to tell for themselves what to do (see Hursthouse 1999a; Watson

1990, 453; Louden 1990; Broadie 2007, 130; Annas, 'Virtue and Nature', unpublished).

At the same time, though, a second trend in recent virtue ethics and virtue theory is gaining ground. Some philosophers have argued recently that phronesis is important for some virtues but not others, and some that phronesis is actually redundant to an account of virtue altogether. Many of these have felt that a more robust, 'Aristotelian' view comes at the cost of being too strict, pointing out that none of us shall ever have such a thorough, all-encompassing understanding of the human good as phronesis seems to involve, and worrying that tying phronesis to the virtues will imply that only an intellectually sophisticated elite will be capable of being virtuous. And some have argued that making phronesis indispensable to virtue has no benefits with respect to action guidance, anyway. The upshot of this trend seems to be a common supposition that phronesis is either a merely optional feature of an account of the virtues, or perhaps best dispensed with altogether (see Annas 2006, §B.1 for discussion of this trend).

My argument in this book is that virtue ethics cannot survive without a robust commitment to phronesis, pretty much as Aristotle conceived of it, as a crucial part of all the virtues, and that such an account of the virtues is not only defensible but downright attractive. And a central focus will be on right action: virtue ethics cannot establish an appropriate connection between having a virtue and doing what is right unless every virtue includes phronesis.

Given these two recent trends, it seems a good time to look carefully at phronesis and the indispensable role that Aristotle takes it to play in the virtues. That is what I do in this book, and so I begin in this chapter with Aristotle's conception of phronesis. My aims are philosophical rather than scholarly—to defend a view that is Aristotelian, rather than to interpret Aristotle's view. However, since the conception of phronesis I shall employ in this book is Aristotle's, it follows that even though interpreting Aristotle is not my aim, still a fair measure of interpretation is required by my aim. This is so for three main reasons. First and foremost, making Aristotle's understanding of phronesis explicit will serve to clarify the conception of phronesis that I shall employ throughout this book. Second, many of the issues that arise in piecing together Aristotle's view will come back as we consider, on more purely philosophical grounds, the role of phronesis in an account of the virtues, and it will be useful to highlight some of these early. And third, many of the difficulties that Aristotle encounters in constructing a theory of phronesis are interesting and instructive in their own right within a project like mine, although I shall try to keep them from becoming a distraction.

In this introductory chapter I examine Aristotle's conception of phronesis by discussing first his account of the practical deliberation of which phronesis is the excellence (§1.1), and then the nature of that excellence itself (§1.2). I conclude with a brief sketch of the main contemporary controversies surrounding the view that phronesis is necessary for virtue (§1.3).

1.1 Deliberation

1.1.1 Deliberation and Decision

In Aristotle's ethics, phronesis is a virtue concerned with deliberation and decision. Unlike the particular virtues of character—generosity, courage, etc.—phronesis is a virtue of the intellect, broadly speaking, and concerns the human good in general. It underlies all of the virtues of character, guiding the exercise of each to its characteristic 'mean' in a way that is virtuous overall.[2]

For Aristotle, 'deliberation' (bouleusis) is a form of practical reasoning specifically concerned with what to do (as opposed to idly speculating about what one might do, say), and so Aristotle first approaches deliberation by discussing 'choice' or 'decision' (prohairesis), which he argues is the terminus of deliberation. Decision, he says, is decision to act, so it is not 'wish' (boulēsis): we can wish for the impossible, but of course we cannot decide to do the impossible; and we can also wish for an end, but we cannot decide to achieve an end (e.g. we do not decide to find, only to seek) (NE III.2, 1111b19–30; cp. Eudemian Ethics [= EE] II.10, 1226a6–17; Magna Moralia [= MM] I.17). Decisions are not beliefs, either, since we can have beliefs about things we can do nothing about, and since we decide to act but do not believe to act (NE 1111b30–1112a1, 3–5; EE II.10, 1226a1–17). Aristotle also says that decision reveals a person's character—his reasons for acting—far more than bare descriptions of actions do (NE 1111b4–11, EE II.10, 1226a11–13). This is another reason why decision is not a kind of belief, Aristotle says, since beliefs do not reveal character (NE 1112a1–13),[3] and because decisions concern

---

[2] Contrast this usage of 'phronesis' with the Stoics', for whom 'phronesis' is one of the four cardinal virtues of character, albeit one that concerns 'appropriate acts' in general; see Arius Didymus, in Stobaeus, Anthology II.5b–5b2.

[3] I do not think this is to say that our beliefs have nothing to do with character. After all, our belief-forming processes are activities we engage in like any others, and the way we train ourselves to acquire beliefs affects the beliefs we actually come to have. And surely there are beliefs, even of a non-evaluative sort, that are important parts of one's ethical outlook and one's character; see Hursthouse 1999a, 187–91.

what we take to be good, all things considered, while belief is broader than this (1112a7–13). Furthermore, people do not always do what they decide to do, since incontinence sometimes interferes; so decision is not the same as appetite, either, since appetite can oppose decision (1111b13–16). Likewise, decision is not a kind of emotion, since the things we do purely from emotion 'seem least to be from decision' (1111b18–19; EE II.10, 1225b24–31),[4] presumably because action in the 'heat of passion' often conflicts with our more considered values. (On deliberation and decision, see also EE II.10.)

Aristotle concludes tentatively that decision seems to be that at which deliberation arrives (NE III.2, 1112a13–17), and supports this conclusion by showing that deliberation is practical in just the same way that decision is (III.3, 1113a9–14). For one thing, no one deliberates about what he cannot change (1112a21–7; cf. VI.2, 1139b5–11; VI.5, 1140a31–b4; VI.7, 1141b8–12; EE II.10, 1226a20–6). For the same reason, deliberation concerns what *one* will do, since one can determine only one's own agency (NE III.3, 1112a28–34; EE II.10, 1226a28–30). We deliberate only about 'the things that depend on us and are doable' (NE 1112a30–1), where these involve outcomes that require careful judgment, rather than simply following rules, as is especially clear in cases where we ask others for advice as we deliberate (1112a34–b11; MM I.17; cp. EE II.10, 1226a31–3). So Aristotle concludes that decision just is the determination of one's agency through deliberation (NE 1113a2–7); decision is a 'deliberational' species of desire (1113a9–12; EE II.10, 1226b13–20; MM I.17), or is perhaps 'intelligence qualified by desire' (NE VI.2, 1139b5, cf. 1139a32–3). 'What we deliberate about and what we decide on are the same', Aristotle says, adding a very important proviso: 'except that what is decided on is, as such, something definite; for it is what has been selected as a result of deliberation that is "decided on"' (III.3, 1113a2–5). Deliberation works towards a definite, particular action that one decides on.

Deliberation, like decision, is about what to do, but does it also reveal character? If I deliberate about what road to take to work, this concerns what to do, but surely it does not reveal my character. Yet if deliberation did not reveal character, why would Aristotle think it is so intimately tied to decision, which reveals the reasons for which one acts? This question is tied to perhaps the most controversial feature of Aristotle's discussion of deliberation, namely his claim that 'we deliberate, not about ends, but about what forwards those ends' (NE III.3, 1112b11–12, 33–4; cp. EE II.10, 1226b9–12, 1227a5ff).

---

[4] Throughout I rely on the recent translation of the NE by Broadie and Rowe 2002, with occasional minor modifications.

How can deliberation reveal character, if it is 'not about ends'? Answering this question will be crucial for understanding what role phronesis might play in practical reasoning both given one's ends and about one's ends themselves.

1.1.2 'The Things Towards the Ends'

There is no denying that 'what forwards the ends'—more literally, 'the things towards the ends' (*ta pros ta telē*)—includes means to ends, but it also seems clear that it must include constituents of ends as well, as when a golfer plans to play golf during a holiday not as a means to having a pleasant holiday, but as a way of having a pleasant holiday. (The example is from Ackrill 1980, 19.) Likewise, virtuous acts are chosen for their own sake (*NE* II.4, 1105a28–33); so 'the things towards the ends' should be taken as 'for the sake of' the ends, revealing what the agent sees as worthwhile in the action (McDowell 1998, 108f).[5]

About that much there is little doubt. But what else do 'the things towards the ends' include? On a narrow reading, these are restricted to means to and constituents of ends, in one of two ways. A 'quasi-Humean' version of this view holds that our grasp of ends is non-rational, practical intellect working out means and constituents of ends that motivate from outside the intellect.[6] On the other hand, a non-Humean version of this view holds that while we do not grasp ends through deliberation, it is nonetheless the practical intellect that grasps them. The non-Humean version seems preferable: although Aristotle holds that we acquire the virtues through habituation of emotion and desire, such habituation results in a rational recognition of the appropriateness of the actions and ends desired (Sorabji 1980, 216; Price 2005, 274).[7] However, we must note that both versions hold that ends are not grasped by deliberation

---

[5] There is general consensus that 'the things towards the ends' include constituents; see Annas 1993a, 88; Dahl 1984, 76f, also citing Greenwood 1909, 46–8; Irwin 1985, 318; Kakoliris 2003, 190; McDowell 1998, *passim*; Reeve 1992, 82, also citing *Metaphysics* 1032b18–29; and Sherman 1985, 89f, also citing *De Motu Animalium* 7.

[6] See McDowell 1998, 113f, 120 for discussion, tracing this view to Walter 1874. William Fortenbaugh defends the quasi-Humean view by observing that for Aristotle a person displays true courage only if he springs into courageous action straightaway, that is, without first weighing up prudential considerations, unlike the person who acts 'courageously' only because he already knows that the odds of staying safe are in his favor (1117a17–22). Fortenbaugh 1975, 71–8 takes this to mean that good conduct is a matter of moral virtue—a sort of emotional disposition—and not of deliberation, which is only about finding means to the goals set by virtue. See Fortenbaugh 1991 for further discussion of this sharp division between practical reason and moral virtue.

[7] See also Burnyeat 1980, 73, who notes that for Aristotle 'practice has cognitive powers, in that it is the way we learn what is noble or just'. For defense of this non-Humean view, see Tuozzo 1991.

and are already determinate in content. So both versions agree that we do not deliberate about ends.

By contrast, a broader reading of 'the things towards the ends' holds that those ends are not always already determinate, and that deliberation also involves *specification* of ends. For instance, Aristotle's examples of deliberation include a doctor aiming at making his patient healthy, a public speaker at persuading his audience, and a statesman at governing well (*NE* III.3, 1112b12–14; cp. *EE* II.10, 1227a18–21), and clearly these ends are not already determinate (see also Pakaluk 2005, 137–40; Price 2005, 269f). It is equally clear that the aims of virtue—to act generously, say, or justly—are indeterminate in just the same way. Deliberation about 'the things towards the ends', then, must include deliberation about what generosity or fairness would amount to in one's present circumstances. And that seems to be one reason that Aristotle thinks virtue requires phronesis: it takes excellence in deliberation to recognize that sometimes the courageous thing, say, is to forgo a project, rather than push it through; simply aiming to do 'the courageous thing' is not enough (Urmson 1988, 85; Annas 1993*a*, 88f; McDowell 1998, 114; Hursthouse 2006*a*, 288f, citing Woods 1986, 157).

Furthermore, Aristotle insists that there is no moral virtue without phronesis, and no phronesis without moral virtue (*NE* VI.12–13). This is easy to square with the broader view of 'the things towards the ends', on which phronesis is a kind of thought about what virtuous action amounts to in particular circumstances; by contrast, on the narrow view it seems perfectly possible that a person could have moral virtue without phronesis, and vice versa. Likewise, Aristotle says that phronesis is practical reasoning about realizing virtuous ends, whereas 'cleverness' is a kind of practical reasoning about good and bad ends alike (VI.12, 1144a23–8). On the narrow view, phronesis would seem to be identical to cleverness about means, where the ends are good, and so Aristotle's distinction would be gratuitous (Urmson 1988, 83); on the broader view, phronesis unlike cleverness grasps the very nature and content of virtuous ends. And on the broad view, deliberation reveals character because specifying one's ends reveals the reasons for which one acts; on the narrow view, it does not.[8]

Considerations such as these have led most of Aristotle's commentators, myself included, to a broader reading of 'the things towards the ends' as truer to Aristotle's thought and indeed as the more philosophically plausible

---

[8] A further problem for the narrow view would arise from the thesis, defended by Broadie 1991, 191ff and Wiggins 1980, 246, that productive skill, unlike phronesis, involves seeking an outcome that is already determinate in advance of reasoning about how to bring it about. However, I am not convinced that the ends of productive skill are always (more) determinate in this way.

one.[9] And this view may suggest that we can deliberate even about our ends themselves. But before we get to that, two things about this view must be noted. One, Aristotle goes on in *Nicomachean Ethics* III.3 to say that deliberation about 'the things towards the ends' is a matter of finding the best way to realize one's end (1112b14–31), and some take this to suggest a narrower reading. But as Nancy Sherman observes, 'best' here can mean either the best way to achieve a goal considered in isolation, or the best way to achieve a goal given one's overall aims and beliefs. As we have seen, Aristotle says that incontinent people do not act in accordance with what they decide is best, and it seems clear that this means that they do not follow their decision about what is best all-things-considered; incontinence is not a matter of being mistaken about means (Sherman 1985, 96f; see also Anscombe 1967, 56–63).

And two, it is possible to take too broad a reading of 'the things towards the ends'. An extremely broad view would hold that the intellect determines a virtuous person's motivational orientation, whereas moral virtue consists in the habituation of the emotions and desires to obey the intellect.[10] Of course, for Aristotle habituation of the emotions does prepare them for obedience to reason (e.g. *NE* I.13, 1102b30–1), but again, the virtues that result from habituation have their own appreciation of the appropriateness of their ends, and do not merely go along with ends whose appropriateness is grasped by something else (McDowell 1995*b*, 214f).

So it is best to understand 'the things towards the ends' as including specifications of the content of ends that one's moral character finds appropriate. On this 'specificatory' view, when Aristotle says that virtue makes one's end the right one, and phronesis makes right 'the things toward that end' (*NE* VI.12, 1144a7–9; cp. *MM* I.18), he means that virtue supplies the right general end, and that phronesis gives that end the right sort of specification.[11] Phronesis, then, is the excellence of practical reasoning whereby one specifies the contents of one's ends well—and not just any ends, but the ends of the various virtues, the ends that are ends not just for this or that person, but without qualification (*NE* VI.9, 1142b28–33).

Consequently, on the specificatory view there is no sharp division of labor between having an end and deliberating about how to achieve it; deliberation is

---

[9] Proponents of this view include Hardie 1968, 216, 226f, 235; Irwin 1985, 346; McDowell 1998, 110; Sherman 1989, 87–9. See also Monan 1968, 60ff, who agrees with Allan 1953, 1955 on this point, against Jaeger, Walter, and Burnet.

[10] For discussion, see McDowell 1998, 120, who attributes this view—the polar opposite of the quasi-Humean view—to Cooper 1988. See also *EE* II.2, 1220b5ff.

[11] See also Irwin 1985, 348; Broadie 1991, 239f. The label 'specificatory' comes from McDowell 1998.

a single process in which habituated character and practical reasoning construct an end together (Sherman 1989, 88; Broadie 1991, 239ff; Broadie and Rowe 2002, 49f). And so on this view there is a sense in which we *do* deliberate about ends after all. To deliberate about the content of an end, of course, just is to deliberate about what one's end *is*, that is, what determinate end one will pursue. Moreover, such deliberation may lead one to change one's ends—as when one cannot do the would-be generous thing one had intended, since it turns out, upon deliberation, to involve doing injustice to someone else—and may even lead one to abandon an end altogether, as when there turns out to be no way to specify its content without making unacceptable compromises (Broadie 1991, 241, 245; Broadie and Rowe 2002, 50; Price 2005, 270). This seems consistent with Aristotle's claim that 'we deliberate, not about ends, but about what forwards those ends': on the specificatory view, this is the claim that because deliberation specifies the content of an indeterminate end, deliberation can proceed only in relation to some end. Consequently, for the purposes *of any given deliberation*, some indeterminate end must be taken as given—in any given deliberation, we deliberate about that end only in the sense of specifying its content.

In fact, I think an even more radical version of the specificatory view is also possible, since it seems that sometimes to specify the content of one end just *is* to decide which further end to adopt. For instance, one may have the end of having a meaningful career, and deliberate about 'the things towards' this end. That end is indeterminate, so deliberation must specify a content for it; but to specify its content just is to decide upon a particular career that one will pursue as an end.[12] This more radical version of the specificatory view, then, seems to follow from the less radical version, once we recognize that sometimes to specify one end is to choose another end.

Now, we should note that Aristotle is quite clear that deliberation is concerned only with 'particulars', and many take this to mean that deliberation occurs only where it can result in a decision to do a particular action, here and now; in that case, deliberation can shape the ends we have, but it cannot say what ends to adopt (Broadie and Rowe 2002, 45f; cf. Sherman 1989, 87).[13] However, it is clear that Aristotle's universal/particular distinction is different in different contexts (Devereux 1986, 485–91). For instance, Aristotle says that

---

[12] For an excellent discussion of ends of this type, see Schmidtz 1994, who, incidentally, does not attribute the specificatory view to Aristotle.

[13] This is not to deny that we engage in practical reasoning about what ends to adopt, but that whatever such practical reasoning is, it cannot be deliberation. However, deliberation is the only form of practical reasoning of any sort dealing with ends that Aristotle discusses, so it is not clear what that practical reasoning might be if it is not deliberation.

mistakes in deliberation can arise due to ignorance either about the universal (e.g. that 'heavy water' is unhealthful) or about the particular, that is, that *this* water is heavy (*NE* VI.8, 1142a11–25).[14] Yet just over the page Aristotle says that good deliberation about wholesome food requires grasping both the universal, such as that white meat is healthful, and the particular, that is, that poultry is white meat (VI.7, 1141b14–22). This time, the 'particular' involved in deliberation is not an individual, but a more specific *type*.

That the 'particulars' of deliberation can be more specific types is very important, for at least two reasons. One, it means that decisions need not be decisions to act *right now*. It is obvious that sometimes I decide to do this very thing, at this very moment, but it is equally obvious that sometimes I decide to do this sort of thing, at some other time—first thing in the morning, say, or as soon as the time is right (Sherman 1985; see also Sorabji 1980, 208f). There is an isomorphism between deliberation that results in a decision to act now and the practical reasoning that results in a decision to act later, so the latter sort of practical reasoning is also deliberation. And two, it is also clear that if I can decide as a result of deliberation to do a type of act as soon as the time is right, then surely I can decide as a result of deliberation to do that type of thing as a kind of 'standing order', that is, as something to do *whenever* the time is right. But of course, that just is to decide as a result of deliberation to adopt engaging in that type of action as one of my *ends*.

On this more radical version of the specificatory view, then, we deliberate about 'the things towards the ends', rather than the ends, only in the sense that we cannot *simultaneously* deliberate about how to specify an end *and* whether to adopt it; rather, we deliberate about how to specify an end on the assumption that the end is adopted, *even though* the specification of the end in question may be the adoption of some other end. Likewise, the end assumed as adopted here may itself be the specification of yet some other end, so that we can deliberate about it, at another time, as well. If this is correct, then Aristotelian deliberation does concern ends, in several ways: it concerns their content, how to pursue them, the conditions under which they must be changed or abandoned, *and* their very adoption. This view is attractive, I think, since Aristotle says that 'it is thought characteristic of a wise person to be able to deliberate well about the things that are good and advantageous to himself, not in specific contexts, e.g. what sorts of things conduce to health, or to physical strength, but what sorts of things conduce to the good life in general' (*NE* VI.5, 1140a25–8). Of

---

[14] See also *Metaphysics* 981a12–24, cf. *NE* 1112b34–1113a2, discussed by Devereux 1986, 488f, who rejects (486–91) the view of Cooper 1975, 22–58 that the distinction is generally a distinction within types. Louden 1991, 165–7 goes too far in the other direction, denying that types of acts are ever 'particulars' for Aristotle.

course, 'living well' is an indeterminate end, and one that we achieve only by adopting and pursuing other ends. For Aristotle, then, deliberation should include practical reasoning about what ends to adopt.[15] Nonetheless, Aristotle's text is far from direct on this point, so while this more radical specificatory view is, I think, a real Aristotelian possibility, and further reveals the great richness an Aristotelian view of deliberation can have, it is not clear whether it is Aristotle's own view or not. But what is clear, I think, is that we can understand phronesis as an excellence of deliberation concerned with the very specification of determinable but as yet indeterminate ends. I happen to think that this is Aristotle's view; but for present purposes what matters more is that this specificatory role shall attach to my conception of phronesis in this book. This point will become especially important when, for instance, we consider in Chapter 3 whether having a virtuous end is all that we need to consider in assessing the virtuousness of an action.

1.1.3 Deliberation and Time

That question leads us to a further, final puzzle about deliberation, a puzzle concerning time in another way: does deliberation always take clockable time, or are some instantaneous actions also done from deliberation? After all, it seems likely that many virtuous actions will be automatic, and will not involve any 'stopping and thinking'—indeed, Aristotle himself underscores the habitual nature of the virtues. But in that case, if deliberation takes time, then presumably deliberation will play no role in very many virtuous actions, and neither, then, will the deliberative excellence of phronesis. Simply put, tying phronesis to the virtues may conflict with the habitual nature of virtue.

This is a difficult issue, and it is far from clear that Aristotle had made up his own mind about it. On the one hand, when someone jumps up immediately to help someone else lift a pram onto a train, it seems clear that there is *some* sort of practical thought involved in the act. In this way, such an immediate action is unlike pulling one's hand from a hot stove or jumping from a spider;[16] it makes sense to ask in the pram case 'What were you thinking?' but not in the stove or spider case. To be sure, it does not take phronesis to see that helping with the pram is the thing to do, only common sense (see Hursthouse 2006a, 287f). But calling it 'common sense' is to say that it is practical thought that any ordinary adult should find obvious; it is not to say that it is no practical

---

[15] This model would render moot the view that Aristotle says that we do not deliberate about ends because the end he has in mind is *eudaimonia*—living well or flourishing—and we cannot deliberate about adopting that end; see Reeve 1992, 84f; Wiggins 1980, 227.

[16] Some virtuous actions are of the latter sort, e.g. a parent's affectionately ruffling his child's hair; see Swanton 2003, 132; Hursthouse 1991; see also Broadie and Rowe 2002, 44f.

thought at all. Yet on the other hand, deliberation does suggest, at least in the usual case, a kind of careful 'weighing up' and thoughtful 'working out' that seems just as absent in the case of helping with the pram as in the case of jumping from the spider. So construing such practical thought as a kind of deliberation seems to capture the structure of that thought, since such a construal reveals one's reasons for acting, but it also seems hard to square with the instantaneousness of the action.

Aristotle is unclear on this issue. He does say that 'things done on the spur of the moment we say are voluntary, but not done from decision' (NE III.2, 1111b9–10), but it is unclear whether he has in mind cases like helping with the pram or jumping from the spider. He also says that it is characteristic of deliberation that 'one deliberates for a long time', but he says this only to distinguish deliberation from mere guessing, which never needs time. So he need not mean that deliberation *always* needs time, and in fact he goes on in the same passage to say that where some take a long time to deliberate, others arrive at their answer straightaway (VI.9, 1142b2–5, 26–7; but see Irwin 1985, 345 on 1142b2 and 1117a20).

Perhaps there is some stronger evidence that Aristotle thinks of deliberation as taking time. For instance, he says that deliberation involves 'searching' (*zētein*, NE III.3, 1112b20–3; VI.9, 1142a31–b15), which strongly suggests a sort of 'stopping and thinking'. However, such a view conflicts with Aristotle's claim that even sudden acts of daring are decided for (III.8, 1117a17–20; see Sorabji 1980, 204f). Likewise, Aristotle also says that 'in the case of what is clearly foreseen, one can decide also as a result of calculation and reasoning about it; with what comes suddenly (*ta d' exaiphnēs*) one decides according to one's disposition' (1117a20–2). A 'disposition' or *hexis* is how Aristotle usually refers to a character trait, which is a feature of habituated character, not of practical intellect. This suggests that 'calculation and reasoning' take time, but it is not clear how decision can result from disposition rather than practical intellect.

So we seem to arrive at an inconsistent triad: (1) it takes deliberation to arrive at a decision (cp. EE II.10, 1226b5–9, 13–17; MM I.17); (2) deliberation always takes time; and (3) some decisions are reached in no time. One way to extricate Aristotle from this complication is to soften (3): the actions in question are from a sort of thought that is like deliberation, but involves no 'searching', so such actions are not decided for, strictly speaking. But it seems a mincing of words to say that helping with the pram involves practical thought but not decision. Alternatively, we could soften (2): central cases of deliberation take time, but not all do; deliberation is a broader sort of practical thought, and not all forms of it involve 'searching' (Broadie 1991, 252). Or we could soften (1): decision stems from practical thought that reveals the reasons for which one acts, and that thought does not always involve deliberation (McDowell 1998, 107; see also Broadie 1991, 212). However, each of these latter two options appeals to some sort of practical thought (which either is deliberation, or is a genus of which deliberation is a species, respectively) that is broader than the sort of thought Aristotle discusses. These readings are not impossible, but they do leave Aristotle's discussion with a rather unsettling lacuna.[17] So it seems clear that every way of making out Aristotle's point involves, as one commentator has put it, giving Aristotle 'a pinch of salt' (McDowell 1998, 107).

My own view can be stated more directly, and involves a more nuanced understanding of the idea that deliberation takes time. While it is true that it takes deliberation to arrive at a decision, and that deliberation takes time, we should distinguish between the act of deliberating, to which these claims apply, and the deliberative structure of an act, to which they do not apply. When someone helps a parent with a pram out of kindness, he makes a decision and acts, and the decision has a deliberative structure—that is, one could reconstruct the ends for which he acted, and of which his act was a determinate specification. But that is not to say that he had to stop and search over that specification; he did not have to, since certain patterns of end-specification have already become habitual. Simply put, deliberation takes time, *until* a deliberative pattern becomes habitual. Surely there is nothing special about practical ends that should prevent specifying their content from becoming habitual. In that case, there is no tension after all between the habitual and spontaneous nature of much virtuous action and the requirement that virtue involve deliberative excellence. I shall return to this point in Chapter 3, when we consider the role of phronesis in virtuous action; and indeed much of Parts II and III can be seen as further unpacking the notion of the deliberative structure of actions done for the sake of ends.

Now that we have addressed deliberation, we can move on to the intellectual virtue of deliberating *well*, that is, phronesis.

1.2 Phronesis

1.2.1 Passional, Theoretical, and Practical Virtues

Phronesis is a virtue—not one of the more familiar virtues of habituated character, but a virtue of practical reasoning. The character virtues are stable

---

[17] And in any case, what about the suggestion at *NE* III.8; 1117a20–2 that there can be decision without practical thought?

dispositions to react emotionally at the appropriate times, about the appropriate things, to an appropriate degree, and so on, and to desire and aim at the appropriate kinds of ends or targets (*NE* II.4, 1105a26–33; II.6, 1106b18–1107a8). Emotions and desires are not forms of practical reason themselves, Aristotle says, although habituation brings them into agreement with reason (I.13, 1102b13–1103a3). This is genuine agreement, and not mere conformity, because both passion and practical intellect 'possess reason': the latter possesses reason 'in the proper sense and in itself', and the former 'as something capable of listening as if to one's father' (1102b25–33; see also *EE* II.1, 1219b25ff, 1220a5ff).[18] And more generally, Aristotle understands the passions as all involving judgment, often of rather complex sorts.[19]

Aristotle attributes the character virtues and the virtues of practical reasoning to two broad 'parts' of the soul, the rational and the non-rational (setting aside the soul's purely biological functions, *NE* I.13, 1102a32–b12). Caution is needed here. While talk of 'parts of the soul' initially recalls Plato's rather sharp tripartition of the soul in the *Republic*, the similarity soon fades as Aristotle makes it clear that by 'parts' he has nothing special in mind. He takes no position on whether the soul has literal, distinct parts, or whether these 'parts' are merely like different sides of a single coin (1102a28–32, b25); Aristotle seems more interested in distinguishing psychic functions than in literal parts of the soul. Notice too that Aristotle distinguishes passion and practical reason by the difference in the *senses* in which they 'possess reason', not in *whether* they possess reason. To be sure, passion and reason can pull in different directions, as in continent and incontinent persons (1102b14–25); passions are not part of decision, but are among the things that we make decisions about (III.2, 1111b10–19). But Aristotle's separation of reason and passion is motivated neither by the thought that passions are not cognitive, nor by the thought that reason lacks motivating force (cf. Cooper 1988, 32).

Aristotle further subdivides the rational soul into a part that is theoretical, scientific, and contemplative, and another that is calculative and practical (*NE* I.13, 1102a26–1103a10; VI.1, 1138b35–1139a17; cp. *MM* I.34). These differ in terms of how they reason about their objects (*NE* VI.1, 1139a6–11): we reason about things like the circumference of the earth, as well as about how to vote in the upcoming election and how to repair a car, but there is nothing we can *do* about the circumference of the earth, so there is no *decision* to make about it, only a discovery. Aristotle himself makes the point by saying

---

[18] On the distinction between agreement and conformity between reason and emotion, see Russell 2005a, ch. 7.

[19] See esp. *Rhetoric* II.1–11. See also Reeve 1992, 71f: for Aristotle emotions are 'ways we perceive situations as problematic, as requiring deliberation and action'.

that the contemplative intellect grasps principles that 'cannot be otherwise', whereas the practical intellect—the reasoning that deliberates about what to do—grasps 'variable principles', since the former is concerned with eternal, theoretical truths whereas the latter is concerned with particular decisions.[20] For the practical intellect, then, the task is to determine what to do, broadly speaking.[21]

Interestingly, Aristotle says that the intellectual virtues are all capacities by which we reason correctly and arrive at truth (NE VI.2, 1139a21–31; see also MM I.34). Truth is a clear enough notion in the case of the theoretical virtues: philosophic wisdom (sophia, NE VI.6–7) is the complete mastery of a science, the conjunction of demonstrative scientific knowledge (epistēmē, VI.3) and theoretical intelligence (nous, VI.6–7), the latter being a settled grasp of the first principles from which demonstrations proceed.[22] But what is truth in the case of practical reasoning? Aristotle says it is 'truth in agreement with the correct desire' (VI.2, 1139a29–31). Some suggest that truth here is the truth of belief about the most effective means to an end (e.g. Hardie 1968, 224f), but as we have seen, deliberation, as Aristotle seems to recognize, concerns much more than means.[23] On the other hand, some have argued that phronesis grasps universal moral principles, and others that it grasps true propositional statements of the mean in particular circumstances.[24] However, against the former view, Aristotle repeatedly denies that ethical reasoning deals in universals (e.g. II.9, 1109b1–7), apart from such moral truisms as that murder is always wrong (II.6, 1107a8–27); and against the latter, note that it makes gratuitous Aristotle's

[20] This characterization of scientific knowledge as grasping principles that 'cannot be otherwise' recalls, of course, Aristotle's philosophy of science in the *Posterior Analytics*.

[21] Con. Bostock 2000, 78, who argues that since theoretical reasoning involves 'evaluation of particulars, i.e. particular observations and experiments', there is no real contrast with practical reasoning in this respect, and thus no reason to distinguish theoretical and non-theoretical parts of the intellect. But for Aristotle, virtues of theoretical intellect have as their subject matter invariable, necessary, and universal truths, whereas virtues of the practical intellect have as their subject matter particular actions. Even a superficial similarity between these virtues in terms of their working with 'particulars' stretches the imagination. (See also Owens 1987, 9, who argues that 'theoretical knowledge is required for wise action', since e.g. one must know about road conditions in order to make a wise decision about driving on a stormy night. But of course facts about road conditions are not invariable truths.)

[22] For a discussion of the shift in Greek thought from *sophia* as technical to theoretical intelligence, as it is in Aristotle, see Owens 1987.

[23] It may also be suggested that practical judgments are true in the sense that they are proper specifications of *eudaimonia*, but this requires not only that such a conception of *eudaimonia* should guide one's selection of goals, but also that it be determinate enough to yield concrete decisions in particular situations—that is, that it be a sort of grand blueprint of *eudaimonia* and how all of one's actions fit into it. I shall consider this general view of practical reasoning, and its problems, in §1.2.5. See Price 2005 for discussion of this view as a way of understanding practical truth.

[24] For discussion of the former view, see Gómez-Lobo 1995, 17f, who himself advocates the latter.

claim that the mean is in accordance with 'right reason', if right reason is just a grasp of a true statement of the mean. Alternatively, it could be that practical truth is the success of one's practical judgment according to standards for such judgments resting on social consensus and convergence, although this of courses raises questions about the status of such convergence (see Price 2005, 264, 272–8).

An attractive alternative, it seems, would be to understand 'truth' here not as a semantic property of propositions, but as a property of an intellectual faculty when it stands in its best relation to the objects of its inquiry (Broadie 1991, 220–3; Broadie and Rowe 2002, 362; see also Broadie 2007, 121). Put another way, 'truth' describes the state of the theoretical intellect when it apprehends what there is most reason to believe, and the state of the practical intellect when it decides in accordance with what there is most reason to do.[25] That state of the practical intellect Aristotle calls 'right reason' (*orthos logos*), which is crucial to making appropriate choices and, in the case of the character virtues, hitting the 'mean'—indeed, it is this point that brings Aristotle to his discussion of the intellectual virtues in the first place (*NE* VI.1, 1138b18–25; cp. *EE* II.5; *MM* II.10). Decision, Aristotle says, is a 'desire informed by deliberation' (*NE* VI.2, 1139a23, cf. 31–3; III.3, 1113a9–11), and so for a decision to be appropriate 'what issues from reason must be true', and 'reason must assert and desire pursue the same things' (VI.2, 1139a23–6).

This brings us to skill. Like phronesis, skill (*technē*) belongs to practical intellect, since it is concerned with 'what can be otherwise' and thus with questions of what to do. But skill concerns what to do in the specific sense of what to *make* (*NE* VI.4, 1140a10–16; *MM* I.34), whereas phronesis is concerned with *action*, rather than making a product that is distinct from the agent's bringing it into existence (*NE* VI.5, 1140b4–7).[26] Furthermore, a craftsman can excuse his having made a poor artifact by saying that he made it that way on purpose, but one cannot excuse one's bad actions in this way (1140b21–4). Appraisal of action is an overall appraisal, involving intentions

---

[25] I leave aside the difficult question whether truth of the latter sort obtains independently of the exercise of the practical intellect.

[26] Aristotle's target seems to be Plato, who suggests in a number of dialogues that virtue is a kind of skill, and who himself is puzzled as to what virtue's distinct product would be, taking it to be the business of every skill to yield such a product. See *Euthydemus* 288d–293a, esp. 291d–293a; for discussion, see Annas 1993a, 397ff; Annas 1993b, 63–6; Broadie 1991, 206f; and Irwin 1985, 342 and references. Interestingly, the Stoics would later resuscitate the idea that virtue is a skill, avoiding Plato's pitfall by pointing out that skills such as those involved in the performing arts make no distinct product; see Cicero, *de Finibus* III.23–5. Broadie 1991, 208 argues that such examples are of no help, because we can still evaluate the performance as an event apart from the performer. But while that is true, there is still no difference between such an 'event' and the bringing about of the event, as there is in productive skills.

and character, in a way that appraisal of production is not (II.4); unlike skill, then, phronesis cannot be directed at just any goal, and cannot be misused (Bostock 2000, 82; Broadie and Rowe 2002, 369).[27] Skill aims at some particular kind of goal, such as physical health in the case of medicine, whereas phronesis deliberates about 'what sorts of things conduce to the good life in general' (VI.5, 1140a28, cp. b4–6), its aim being 'doing well' (*eupraxia*, 1140b6–7) through 'forming a clear view of what is good for themselves and what is good for human beings in general' (1140b7–10). And so, Aristotle says, 'the person who is without qualification the good deliberator is the one whose calculations make him good at hitting upon what is best for a human being among practicable goods' (VI.7, 1141b12–14). Consequently, one can be a good or a bad craftsman, but one cannot be a bad *phronimos*, that is, a person with phronesis (VI.5, 1140b21–2; see Broadie and Rowe 2002, 369).

Phronesis also differs from skill in the kind of value it has. The goal of production is not the producing but the product, whereas the very exercise of phronesis is its own goal: 'here, doing well (*eupraxia*) itself serves as an end' (*NE* VI.5, 1140b7).[28] So even though we can say that phronesis 'produces' happiness or flourishing (*eudaimonia*), still it does so not as the physician produces health but as health 'produces' health: being in a state of health constitutes being healthy, and likewise to be active in phronesis is a constituent part of flourishing (VI.12, 1144a3–6). Now Aristotle also argues that phronesis is indispensable for right conduct, that is, for turning good intentions into appropriate actions (VI.13, 1144b1–17), but even apart from such results, phronesis is part of flourishing because it is the excellence of the practical intellect, and thus of a crucial aspect of the human person (VI.12, 1144a1–3; VI.13, 1145a2–6).[29]

For all these differences, though, practical skills supply Aristotle's favorite examples of the sort of practical reasoning involved in phronesis, as we have already seen.[30] This is because Aristotle finds phronesis to be very much like skill in the structure of its reasoning: both involve 'true rational prescription' (*NE* VI.4, 1140a10, 20–1), and book VI even opens with an analogy between right reason in the case of the virtues and in the case of

---

[27] Plato makes a similar point about justice (*dikaiosunē*) at *Gorgias* 456c–461b.

[28] I return to the relation between phronesis and *eudaimonia* in §2.5.

[29] For an excellent discussion of this point, see Korsgaard 1986, esp. 278; see also Broadie and Rowe 2002, 380f.

[30] As Broadie 1991, 181 observes, 'For [Aristotle], as for Socrates and Plato, the craftsman is a favourite paradigm of practical rationality'; and 'It is because craft involves deliberation that craft resembles practical wisdom enough to have to be distinguished from it' (203).

medical skill (VI.1, 1138b25–32). It is important to remember that, as one commentator has said, 'It is not the object of the skill but the structure and unification of the skilled reasoning that is the crucial point of analogy for ethical reasoning' as far as Aristotle is concerned (Annas 1993a, 71). Aristotle also likens phronesis to political skill for its generality: as political skill is a master skill that unifies and oversees all the particular skills pertaining to the maintenance of the state, so phronesis is concerned with all the various pursuits of life, because we need to 'do well' not just in this respect or that, but in an overall way (I.2, 1094a22–b11; VI.5, 1140a25–31, b4–11). In fact, Aristotle says that phronesis and political skill are the same disposition, although they differ in their definitions (VI.8, 1141b23–4).[31] This suggests that political skill is unlike the *productive* skills in the same ways that phronesis is unlike them. Why these observations do not lead Aristotle to reconsider his claim that all skills are productive is not clear. But what matters for our purposes is that since phronesis is like a skill in the structure of its reasoning, phronesis is no mysterious faculty but of a piece with intellectual abilities we already find familiar—even, as one philosopher has put it, mundane (Hursthouse 2006a).

1.2.2 Phronesis and 'Right Reason'

Aristotle opens *Nicomachean Ethics*, book VI by reminding us that virtue aims at the 'mean'—that is, what is appropriate and fitting in action—and that the mean is in accordance with 'right reason' (*orthos logos*) (VI.1, 1138b18–25). Some have thought that right reason is a body of rules or principles, and phronesis the knowledge of these rules and their application in particular circumstances: Aristotle's account of the virtues, the thought goes, would be incomplete and lacking in action guidance unless the virtues involve a grasp of codified rules of conduct. But Aristotle would surely find such a suggestion extraordinary, since he says that we find the notion of right reason in medicine and carpentry as much as in ethical decision-making (1138b18–34). And as in the case of medical skill, phronesis is needed most when one's end is not already fully determinate, and thus where such rules would not help. Furthermore, as John McDowell points out, such a deductive, rule-based model of deliberation would require ethical principles 'formulable in universal terms', but Aristotle denies that ethics deals with such universal truths (e.g. I.3, 1094b11–27; II.9,

---

[31] He even employs this observation to work out a certain puzzle: although phronesis is about both general, abstract principles and dealing with particular circumstances, his focus on the latter is not off the mark because political deliberation also takes both general and particular forms, but it is to political deliberation about particulars that we give the generic name 'political skill', recognizing that deliberation concerned with particulars is the central kind of deliberation (VI.8, 1141b24–33). See Broadie and Rowe 2002, 373.

1109b12–23), beyond such truisms as that adultery and murder are always wrong (II.6, 1107a9–12). Such a model also conflicts with Aristotle's claim that phronesis is more like a perceptive ability than a deductive, discursive one (VI.8, 1142a23–30; VI.10, 1143a5–b5; see McDowell 1998, 110–12; see also Gómez-Lobo 1995, 17f; Pakaluk 2005, 209–14).

The point of Aristotle's discussion of right reason, then, seems to be to say what is distinctive of such reasoning in the ethical case, not to codify it (Broadie 1991, 189, 199; see also Louden 1991, 162f). This is fortunate, since Aristotle's discussion of phronesis is sure to disappoint any expectation of codifiable rules.[32] So there is now general consensus that right reason is a reasoning capacity that a *phronimos* has, rather than a set of principles that a *phronimos* knows (Hursthouse 2006a, 284; Urmson 1988, 86; Pakaluk 2005, 209–12; Broadie 2007, 127–9). This view is further supported by Aristotle's treating phronesis and right reason as interchangeable (*NE* VI.13, 1144b25–30; see Natali 2001, 55f).[33]

Aristotle believes it is right reason that enables one to hit the 'mean' in action, so for Aristotle phronesis is intimately linked with the notion of appropriate and fitting conduct, or what we nowadays call 'right action', broadly understood. Aristotle illustrates the importance of phronesis for right action by contrasting a person with phronesis on the one hand and a person with decent dispositions and habits but without phronesis, on the other.[34] Aristotle therefore allows that there are virtues without phronesis, as common thought supposes, as when we say that an adult is naturally disposed to be courageous, say, or temperate about food, or that a child is naturally generous or compassionate, or even that certain animals are naturally brave or loyal (*NE* VI.13, 1144b1–9). Such virtues Aristotle calls 'natural' virtues, and they are fairly stable character traits (*hexeis, ēthē*) by which we are disposed to certain behaviors (1144b3–6; *MM* I.34, II.3; see also *Rhetoric* II.12, cited in Sorabji 1980, 214). The natural virtues need not be robotic and mindless dispositions, but without phronesis they lack the practical reasoning by which to 'unify and reflect on the reasons' for being

---

[32] See e.g. Urmson 1988, 79, 85, who understands VI.1 as proposing to set out 'principles' that determine the mean, which he regards as a false start or poor editorial choice. For discussion of some rule-based interpretations of Aristotelian deliberation, see McDowell 1998, 110–12, citing Allan 1953, 1955; and Cooper 1975.

[33] Surprisingly, Gómez-Lobo 1995, 32 also draws attention to this fact, even though he holds right reason to be 'a particular practical proposition which identifies the intermediate to be chosen in the given circumstances' (15).

[34] Hursthouse 2006a argues persuasively that this is a more relevant contrast than that between the *phronimos* and the vicious person; the difference between the latter pair, after all, is not a difference in practical intellect, but in simple decency. And as we shall see, some of the intellectual capacities of the *phronimos* are shared by the vicious as well.

so disposed and caring about such things (Annas 1993*a*, 74; Hursthouse 2003, §2);[35] consequently, a person with such virtues may be well meaning, but unreliable about acting well and appropriately in an overall way. Likewise, as we have seen, it takes phronesis to recognize that sometimes the courageous thing is to give up or step aside, a point that takes the sort of discernment that is characteristic of phronesis but not of natural virtue. Indeed, this seems to be why phronesis is not based on codified principles, since a common weakness of the natural virtues is too great a reliance on generalizations and stereotypical cases (Hursthouse 2006*a*, 288–90; Annas 2005*c*).[36]

By contrast, Aristotle says that virtue in the strict or primary sense must be something more than this, since natural virtues are just as likely to go wrong as right (*NE* VI.13, 1144b6–9). Character virtue in the primary sense, then, must include phronesis, because such virtues are the *excellences* of passion and character (1145a2–6).[37] It is this sort of consideration that shall be our concern in Part I of this book.

1.2.3 Parts of Phronesis

It is important to note that phronesis is not a monolithic virtue of the practical intellect, but includes an array of more particular practical capacities. The difference that phronesis makes where deliberation and action are concerned can therefore be made clearer still by considering these various capacities.

Phronesis concerns deliberation, which necessarily results in a decision to act, but phronesis includes another virtue of practical intellect, 'comprehension'

---

[35] Telfer 1989–90, 38f, 44f argues against Aristotle here, pointing out that continence can suffice for good conduct, and that while a virtue in isolation from the others may be precarious, it may nonetheless be a virtue. However, the issue for a theory which understands the notion of good conduct or right action primarily in terms of the virtues is to establish a regular, stable, and reliable general connection between action done from the virtues and action that is right. Such a connection does seem to require phronesis; see also Irwin 1988*a*, 70f.

[36] It is therefore a mistake to suppose, with e.g. Dahl 1984, 88, that virtue in the strict sense is simply natural virtue with the addition of phronesis. Virtue in the strict sense may, of course, develop out of a natural virtue, but it seems that, for Aristotle, phronesis makes an intrinsic difference to the virtues as dispositions to act, feel, and think.

[37] When Aristotle says in II.1, 1103a18–23 that none of the virtues arises by nature, he presumably means that none of the virtues in the strict sense arises by nature. For an alternative reading, see Bostock 2000, 86.

There is some disagreement over the extension of the naturally virtuous. Some have restricted these to animals and children, on the grounds that such traits turn into virtue or vices in the strict sense by the time of adulthood; see Hursthouse 1999*a*, 104f. But most commentators broaden the class to include adults as well; see e.g. Broadie and Rowe 2002, 383, and indeed Hursthouse 2006*a*. Aristotle's text seems to underdetermine the issue: he says both that many character traits in 'us'—his adult readers, presumably—are there 'from the moment we are born', and on the other hand that the natural dispositions belonging to children and animals become (always?) 'harmful' if phronesis does not develop (VI.13, 1144b8–9), perhaps suggesting that such traits are not natural virtues in adults.

(*sunesis, eusunesis*), which is also about what to do, in general and not in some special area, except that comprehension exercises 'judgment in order to discriminate about the things wisdom deals with, when someone else is speaking' (*NE* VI.10, 1143a11–16). This could be clearer, but Aristotle's point is that comprehension, unlike phronesis, is not 'prescriptive' (*peritaktikē*) but only 'discriminatory' (*kritikē*) (1143a8–10). He also thinks that comprehension involves something like being 'quick on the uptake', as we say, and he compares it to 'comprehending' in the case of grasping some point in the sciences (1143a12–18). It seems, then, that although comprehension does not itself result in decision, it is a crucial part of deliberation, since it is a sort of discriminatory ability to 'read' a situation, as it were, so as to recognize what is salient, to assess how trustworthy one's information is, whether one's situation really does involve a dilemma, and so on.[38] Comprehension also seems to concern thought about the actions of others; a person with comprehension must therefore be 'a very good listener and a perceptive critic', and thus have keen discriminatory abilities (Louden 1997, 112f, also citing Urmson 1988, 81). Likewise, it seems that comprehension must also involve discrimination of the advice and moral pronouncements that are given by others (Dahl 1984, 46).

Another discriminative virtue of the practical intellect Aristotle calls 'sense' (*gnōmē*), which in English as in Greek is cognate with both 'sensible' and 'sensitive', in the sense of 'reasonable' and 'sympathetic', respectively (*NE* VI.11). Again, Aristotle has rather little to say about this virtue: it is concerned with 'making correct discrimination of what is reasonable', or appropriate (*epieikeia*) (1143a19–20). Aristotle emphasizes that a person with 'sense' has sympathy (*sungnōmē*), and as Robert Louden has remarked, this suggests an ability to see things from another's point of view in deliberating about what is reasonable or appropriate.[39] Comprehension and sense seem plausible as aspects of phronesis: it would be extraordinary if someone with an excellence of deliberation nonetheless lacked the ability to reflect intelligently on what to do in a more general way, and from multiple perspectives.

Another part of phronesis is a practical virtue that actually shares its name with the theoretical virtue of 'intelligence' (*nous*) (*NE* VI.11). In fact, Aristotle

---

[38] Hursthouse 2006a, 291–8. It is worth pointing that comprehension, Aristotle says, is no different from comprehending well (*eusunesia*, VI.10, 1143a10–11, 16–18). Whether this means that comprehension is always a virtue, or that it is always a capable sort of discrimination, is unclear. The latter view would be preferable, since as Hursthouse 2006a points out, such discriminatory facility seems to be shared by *phronimoi* and con-men alike.

[39] External evidence for this point, Louden 1997, 114f says, is the practice of Athenian jurors swearing to decide according to 'their most equitable sense' (*gnōmē hē dikaiotatē*).

suggests that it may even be the same as that theoretical virtue, despite his rather sharp division between the practical and theoretical virtues. In both cases, Aristotle says that intelligence always grasps 'what is last': in demonstrations, the principles of which demonstration is not possible, and in deliberation, the point at which the determinacy of one's end makes further deliberation redundant (1143a32–b5; see Broadie and Rowe 2002, 378f).[40] In any event, intelligence for Aristotle seems to be that element of phronesis by which deliberation correctly adjusts one's grasp of what one must do in particular circumstances as regards a general end, such as acting generously or as a good friend. In that case, it is that aspect of phronesis by which one gives one's ends a determinate specification that is appropriate to them (Sherman 1989, 44).

Aristotle devotes rather a lot of his discussion to the idea that *nous* or intelligence appears in both theoretical and practical reasoning. Unfortunately, he devotes much less space to a direct discussion of intelligence in deliberation, and relies too much on a comparison of intelligence to visual perception: those with intelligence have acquired through experience a 'perception' of what it is appropriate to do in particular circumstances, and so 'because they have an eye, formed from experience, they see correctly' (*NE* VI.11, 1143b13–14). This metaphor has led some to suppose that Aristotle held the intuitionist view that moral rightness is a primitive property of actions that can be known only by being immediately perceived; in fact, *nous* has sometimes been translated 'intuition'.[41] But as we have seen, Aristotle thinks that, with respect to the structure of its practical reasoning, phronesis is rather like productive skills, but surely Aristotle does not suppose that carpenters and physicians 'intuit' the right way to raise a wall or treat a fever. Furthermore, theoretical *nous* is not intuition, either: *nous* is a settled grasp of the first principles of a science that results from induction, not a process of arriving at those principles intuitively (Barnes 1975, 267f). Likewise, in practical intellect *nous* is not the process by which one knows how to solve problems here-and-now—that process is experience and practice—but is rather the developed problem-solving ability resulting from experience, and is no more 'intuitive' than the analogous problem-solving abilities of builders, physicians, and other technical experts (see also McDowell 1997, 142).

Still, even what little Aristotle does say about intelligence is instructive for our purposes. In particular, it is clear that phronesis involves certain

---

[40] In theoretical reasoning *nous* is built up by induction from experience of particulars (VI.4, 1139b29–31, *Posterior Analytics* II.19), so in both theoretical and practical reasoning, *nous* bridges particular instance and general principle.

[41] David Ross' translation is a noteworthy example. For a recent intuitionist reading of Aristotelian deliberation, see Slote 2001, 5–7.

problem-solving abilities that are built up over time through experience. Such abilities are analogous to those that differentiate an experienced builder from an apprentice, say. It would seem, then, that intelligence is the particular aspect of the virtues of character that accounts for the fact that with proper experience and practice, a person can progress from imitating just or temperate persons to being a just or temperate person himself in a reliable and self-directing way (*NE* II.4). It would also seem to account for the fact that, typically, good ethical judgment is something that takes time to develop, and is thus rarely to be found in the young or immature, and cannot be obtained simply through reading books or listening to lectures (I.3; see also Annas 2004; Annas 2006, §A.3.; Pincoffs 1986, 59f; Hursthouse 1999*a*, 59ff).

This account of intelligence also has three more specific implications for our understanding of phronesis. One, phronesis turns out again to be nothing mysterious, but a settled ability that we can both understand in its own terms and compare with very familiar and everyday skills. Two, it lends further support to the idea, suggested earlier, that good patterns of deliberation can become habitual and automatic. After all, skills that require complex reasoning and deliberation, such as carpentry or medicine, can with experience take the shape of settled problem-solving abilities that function automatically. We can say, then, that such skills both have a deliberative structure and can do their job without clockable deliberation; and just such a skill phronesis seems also to be. And three, it suggests something that is very near to the virtue ethicist's heart, namely that it is a mistake to think that good ethical reasoning can be codified and broken into rules which one can grasp and apply correctly, regardless of one's particular character and if only one is a quick enough study. As with other skills, *nous* comes about only through a pattern of doing acts of the appropriate sort, and only if that pattern leaves one with an understanding of what makes them appropriate. Such an understanding need not be philosophically sophisticated, but it must be sufficiently deep—it cannot be separated from one's own set of values and convictions.

Aristotle says that we attribute sense, comprehension, intelligence, and phronesis to the same people, because each of them concerns 'what comes last' in the order of deliberation, that is, 'what to do', and since they involve discrimination and wisdom (*NE* VI.11, 1143a25–32). The idea seems to be that phronesis is a suite of practical virtues, and although it is primarily concerned with deliberation, and deliberation is about deciding what one shall do, the aspects of phronesis by which one ascertains what there is reason to do can be applied also to reflection on practical matters that does not (or does not directly) terminate in decision. Each of these particular practical virtues is a crucial aspect of phronesis, but phronesis is more than the sum of them, since phronesis grasps a broad conception of human goods and ends, and is prescriptive rather than detached (Louden 1997, 107, 116).

Since phronesis is a virtue of deliberation, it involves what Aristotle calls 'deliberative excellence' (*euboulia*) (*NE* VI.9). Although one can deliberate about bad ends as well as good, 'deliberative excellence is correctness as to what one should achieve, and the way in which, and when, all in accordance with what is beneficial' (1142b27−8; cp. *MM* II.3). Deliberative excellence therefore grasps beneficial ends and how to take the right steps towards them (*NE* 1142b20−8). However, deliberative excellence need not always involve the architectonic grasp of the human good characteristic of phronesis (see Louden 1997, 110f); so Aristotle distinguishes deliberative excellence 'in relation to some specific end' from 'deliberative excellence without qualification', which is successful deliberation with respect to what is 'the end without qualification', all things considered (see Broadie and Rowe 2002, 42),[42] and this just is phronesis (1142b29−31). 'So if it is characteristic of the wise (*phronimoi*) to deliberate well', Aristotle says, 'deliberative excellence will be the sort of correctness that corresponds to what conduces to the end, of which phronesis is the true grasp' (1142b31−3).

The final virtue of practical intellect that Aristotle discusses is 'cleverness' (*deinotēs*), which is a certain acuity at finding the best means at hand for doing what one has decided to do, and thus is a practical ability that the wicked also can share (*NE* VI.12, 1144a26−8; cp. *MM* I.34; Hursthouse 2006a, 300−3). Aristotle says that cleverness is necessary for phronesis, but it is less clear whether it is also *part* of phronesis in the way that comprehension and the others are. Some hold that phronesis is simply the same thing as cleverness, when cleverness is conjoined with praiseworthy goals (e.g. Bostock 2000, 89; Natali 2001, 53), but such a view takes a very narrow view of deliberation, and as we have seen, it makes the difference between phronesis and cleverness gratuitous. It seems rather that phronesis and cleverness are different forms of practical reasoning, phronesis having to do with 'planning' in a broad sense, including the specification of one's ends, and cleverness only with 'execution' of plans made through deliberation (Urmson 1988, 82f): 'the decision is made correct by excellence, but the doing of whatever by the nature of things has

---

[42] It seems likely that *euboulia* always involves some grasp of good ends, even when that grasp is not architectonic, otherwise the difference between it and mere cleverness about means would be gratuitous; see Dahl 1984, 66.

to be done to realize that decision is not the business of excellence but of'
cleverness (*NE* VI.12 1144a21–2).

It is clear enough that cleverness can be found without phronesis, but less
clear why Aristotle thinks that phronesis cannot be found without cleverness
(*NE* VI.12, 1144a28–9). He offers little by way of argument, but the idea
is a reasonable one. For one thing, Aristotle observes that phronesis cannot
exist without the character virtues: phronesis arrives at a correct decision by
making an appropriate goal determinate in one's particular circumstances, and
such goals or 'starting-points' are liable to corruption by badness of character
(1144a29–b1). And as we have seen, phronesis is able to arrive at good
decisions because it involves the sort of 'intelligence' that long experience
brings. Now it is difficult to imagine a normal adult with virtues of character,
and whose experience of the world suffices for the sort of intelligence that is
characteristic of phronesis, but who *nonetheless* is little more than a 'bungling
do-gooder' (Foot 1978*c*, 165f; Hursthouse 1999*a*, 148f, 118; Russell 2005*b*;
Swanton 2003, 27). It is therefore this combination of phronesis, with its
suite of practical virtues, and nuts-and-bolts cleverness that makes phronesis so
important for the idea that there is a regular connection between the character
virtues and right conduct.

The distinction between phronesis and cleverness will be important for our
purposes. For as we shall see in Chapter 3, it may be tempting to suppose
that taking care to find the best means to one's virtuous ends is all that
virtuous action requires, and thus that phronesis is redundant. But once we
take seriously the distinction between cleverness and phronesis, we can see that
such a line of thought misses out an all-important step in virtuous deliberation
and decision: specifying and making determinate a virtuous end—finding not
just how best to do a benevolent act, but determining what would constitute
benevolence in the case at hand. Excellence at the latter determination is what
phronesis is all about.

1.2.4 *The Unity of Virtue*

As we have just seen, Aristotle argues that there is no phronesis without the
character virtues (*NE* VI.12, 1144a29–b1). And as we saw in §1.2.2, Aristotle
argues that although it is possible for the so-called 'natural' virtues to exist
without phronesis, this is not possible for the virtues in the strict sense (VI.13,
1144b1–17). It is also clear that this phronesis must be the same one for each
of the virtues, if it is to perform its role of balancing and integrating them so
as to produce action that is good in a complete, overall way; 'departmental'

wisdoms would render virtuous action more like skilled production, which can be good only in one respect at a time, rather than without qualification (Broadie 1991, 259; Annas 1993a, 78). From these theses it follows that the character virtues are, so to speak, a package deal:

It is clear, then, from what has been said that it is not possible to possess excellence in the primary sense without wisdom (phronesis), nor to be wise without excellence of character. But this conclusion also offers a means of resolving the argument one can employ, in a dialectical context, to show that the excellences can be possessed independently of one another—i.e. that the same person is not best adapted by nature to all of them, so that at a given moment he will have acquired one, but not another; for this is possible in relation to the 'natural' excellences, but in relation to those that make a person excellent without qualification, it is not possible, since if wisdom, which is one, is present, they will all be present along with it.   (1144b30–1145a2)

If there is no virtue without phronesis, and no phronesis without the virtues, then there is no virtue without *the virtues*.[43] This thesis is nowadays known as the 'unity of virtue'. Needless to say, this thesis is a very controversial one, but I shall not say more about it just now. I mention the unity of virtue here only to point out how and where it arises from an Aristotelian conception of phronesis. I shall return to the unity of virtue thesis in §3, and indeed I shall defend a robust version of that thesis in Chapter 11.[44]

---

[43] This conclusion would seem to follow as well from Aristotle's claim that phronesis is incompatible with continence and incontinence, which reflect a lack of unity in aim and thus interfere with practical reasoning. See Drefcinski 2000; Woods 1986, 150–2.

[44] Surprisingly for us, Aristotle devotes relatively little space to defending the unity of virtue, and does not seem to find it a particularly controversial view. Rather, he devotes much of his discussion of the unity thesis to distinguishing it from the even stronger thesis that all the virtues are the same, because they are all forms of phronesis (NE VI.13, 1144b17–18).

Socrates, Aristotle says, had believed that all the virtues were knowledge of 'right reason', whereas Aristotle holds instead that the virtues are dispositions in accordance with right reason, and thus accompanied by right reason—that is, phronesis—but not identical to it (1144b18–30; MM 1.34). But although Aristotle dispatches Socrates' view fairly quickly, his stated grounds for doing so seem somewhat shaky. Aristotle may be placing rather a lot of weight on the idea that a virtue is 'in accordance with right reason', rather than a form of it. Originally, 'in accordance with right reason' had merely distinguished primary from natural virtue, but he now seems to interpret it as distinguishing primary virtue from right reason, with no further argument. Alternatively, he may be relying on the distinction between the respective parts of the soul to which phronesis and the character virtues belong, but of course Aristotle professes indifference about the sense in which there are 'parts' of soul in the first place (not to mention his view that 'intelligence' straddles both parts of the intellect). And in fact it is arguable that the difference between phronesis and the character virtues is little more than the difference in their respective definitions (Broadie and Rowe 2002, 50–2; cp. McDowell 1995b); just as phronesis is a suite including many intellectual skills, so too a character virtue seems to be a suite including excellences both of passion and of intellect (see also Irwin 1978, 263). The stronger Socratic thesis, I think, is also worthy of serious consideration, but I shall not take it up here.

1.2.5 Phronesis and Ends

One of the hottest areas of controversy over Aristotle's conception of phronesis has to do with the nature of the ends for the sake of which phronesis chooses actions. Broadly speaking, some commentators argue that phronesis decides upon actions in particular situations *qua* components of the ultimate end of happiness or living well (*eudaimonia*), while others argue that phronesis decides upon actions in relation to more local or proximate ends, such as doing something generous in a particular situation.

Views of the first kind hold that phronesis chooses actions *qua* local implementations of a grand blueprint for the good life. Such 'blueprint' views, as I shall call them, see phronesis as beginning with a correct and comprehensive blueprint of the human good, and choosing actions that realize this blueprint—achieve *eudaimonia*—in particular circumstances.[45] Of course, for Aristotle *eudaimonia* belongs to a life considered only as a whole, from beginning to end (see e.g. *NE* I.9–10), so we would need to explain what it would mean to achieve *eudaimonia* on particular occasions.[46]

On this sort of view, deliberating about what to do here and now is deliberating about different courses of action as fitting into one's blueprint of the good life. For instance, phronesis may enable one to determine what, say, generosity would require of one in present circumstances, in some way (what way?) that is steered directly by one's more general blueprint of the good life. We might say that such a blueprint guides deliberation about particular cases by supplying a picture of one's ideal sort of person and conduct (Wiggins 1980, 223–5, 236f), or that one's blueprint involves a number of ordering and weighting principles that extend all the way down to one's particular ends (Cooper 1975, 96f).[47]

However, every kind of blueprint view faces at least three serious problems, apart from the general problems infecting all narrow views of 'the things

---

[45] See Broadie 1991, 198 who does not accept this view, and Reeve 1992, 69 who does.

[46] Broadie 1991 in particular has done an excellent job of bringing the 'blueprint' debate to the fore in modern scholarship. Nonetheless, I find that she tends to run together the thesis that phronesis implements a conception of the good life in particular circumstances, and the thesis that a *phronimos* must have a conception of the good life, calling each a 'grand end view' of deliberation. So too, I think, does Kraut 1993 in his otherwise excellent discussion of Broadie's view. (Hence my preference of the label 'blueprint views' over 'grand end views'.) I shall return to the difference between these theses below.

[47] Sorabji 1980 also embraces some sort of blueprint view, but is unsure exactly how the blueprint provides guidance in particular cases, suggesting (206f) that the blueprint must be influential in deliberation but not necessarily the subject of conscious contemplation; see Gómez-Lobo 1995, 27f for discussion. For other versions of the specificatory blueprint view, see Hardie 1968, 233; Irwin 1975, 570; Kakoliris 2003, 192; MacIntyre 1988, 131–3.

towards the ends' (§1.1.2). One is that Aristotle assumes that the basic structure of ethical deliberation is already familiar from everyday practical reasoning, including the productive skills, but blueprint views of phronesis make it a decidedly *unfamiliar* sort of reasoning. Of course, the actions about which we deliberate ethically can be set within a larger blueprint: I help the parent with the pram because of my end of being kind; and if you ask why I am no fool to have the end of being kind, the answer can trace that end all the way up to the end of living a *eudaimōn* life, if you insist on going that far up. And the same is possible with the productive skills as well: the carpenter places the walls here or there so as to make the building sound; and we can explain the end of having sound buildings by going all the way up, if you insist, to an account of the roles that shelter plays within our lives, the living of which is such a great concern to us. But the blueprint view says much more than this, namely that the deliberative structure of my decision to help the parent with the pram has this grand structure—that what has become habitual here is my ability to see how the act of helping this person, here, now, fits within the grand scheme of my living well. In that case, such deliberation is quite unlike what happens in the other skills. Skills like carpentry and medicine do fit within grander schemes and bigger blueprints, but the deliberations that lead the carpenter to put a wall just here or the doctor to prescribe just this drug are nothing like as grand as that.[48] On the blueprint view, then, the structure of reasoning must be very different indeed between phronesis and other practical skills. But why should we accept that there is any such difference?

A related problem is that such a view would restrict phronesis to the very philosophically sophisticated, who must have such a determinate and structured conception of *eudaimonia* that it makes clear what decision, in the light of it, one should make in particular circumstances (Broadie 1991, 199f). And finally, because Aristotle explicitly rejects the idea that deliberation can proceed from codified practical principles, much less from ranked and weighted ones, the precise connection between grand blueprint and particular decisions, for Aristotle, would have to remain an utter mystery.[49] Put another way, dispelling the mystery introduced by the blueprint view means codifying

---

[48] See Broadie 1991, 198f; see also Wiggins 1980, 226, who bites the bullet and portrays deliberation in the productive skills as of the 'blueprint' sort.

[49] See also Broadie 1991, 200. Broadie 1991, 193, 200 also makes the further objection that such a view would render Aristotle's account of phronesis circular, since the exercise of phronesis is part of Aristotle's conception of *eudaimonia* (see *NE* VI.12, 1144a1–3, VI.13, 1145a2–6, discussed above) and the blueprint view would include *eudaimonia* in the definition of phronesis. But see Kraut 1993, 368f, who argues that such circularity would only be problematic if neither concept had any independent content, which is not the case.

ethical reasoning; but that is to put the account of ethical reasoning in tension with the fact that developing ethical wisdom takes time, experience, and practice. It is to take the guts out of phronesis.

The alternative is that phronesis concerns deliberation about local ends, such as acting generously in one's present circumstances, without choosing one's actions as components in a grand, overall design or blueprint (see also Broadie 2007, 123–6). However, even though phronesis is not about implementing some grand scheme of *eudaimonia* in particular circumstances, might it nonetheless be the case that a *phronimos* needs to *have* a conception of the good life as a whole in order for phronesis to function properly? Aristotle seems to think so: 'it is thought characteristic of a wise person', he says, 'to be able to deliberate well about the things that are good and advantageous to himself, not in specific contexts, e.g. what sorts of things conduce to health, or to physical strength, but what sorts of things conduce to the good life in general' (*NE* VI.5, 1140a25–8; see Bostock 2000, 84). A conception of the good life is important for phronesis, which balances different ethical concerns with one another: sometimes courage involves standing and fighting, and sometimes it involves stepping down; one can know the difference in a particular circumstance only by understanding what is worth fighting for, and at what cost, and this means having an overall conception of the good (Annas 1993*a*, 75f; Woods 1986, 163).[50]

Likewise, for Aristotle the character virtues are not simple dispositions to stereotypical behavior, but are also characteristic forms of responsiveness to reasons to act, feel, and choose in certain sorts of ways (Annas 1993*a*, 75–7; Kraut 1993, 362). This fact suggests that part of having the virtue of courage, say, is to understand why courageous action makes sense, and in particular why it makes sense that such action should have a place in one's life. This seems to be why actions that one deliberately decides to do are especially revealing of one's character: they are especially revealing of the sorts of reasons for acting that one takes there to be, and to reveal such reasons is to reveal, ultimately, some sort of view about how one ought to live (McDowell 1998, 109). Moreover, a conception of the good life just *is* an appreciation of what sorts of things one has reason to do. In that case, to grasp (as comprehension does) what one should do 'in relation to the end without qualification' is to grasp what reasons there really are, and this involves accepting those sorts of reasons as reasons of one's own (see McDowell 1998, 109; Woods 1986,

---

[50] Con. e.g. Bostock 2000, 86–8, who argues that the unity of virtue requires a blueprint view, on the grounds that resolution of potential conflicts between virtues requires an overall conception of how each fits into happiness. I agree that the grounds are true, but they are not sufficient to ground the blueprint view.

160, 164).[51] So it seems that while phronesis is not about implementing a true conception of the good life on particular occasions, still phronesis requires that one have a true conception of the good life.

1.2.6 Phronesis and the Mean

Aristotle's discussion of the virtues of intellect began with a question about hitting the 'mean' in action, that is, to act and feel 'when one should, at the things one should, in relation to the people one should, for the reasons one should, and in the way one should' (NE II.6, 1106b21–3). It is in terms of this mean or 'intermediate' that Aristotle defines character virtue (1106b36–1107a6), and it is the difficulty of hitting it that prompts Aristotle to devote a book to the intellectual virtues (VI.1, 1138b18–25). So how has Aristotle's discussion of phronesis illuminated his notion of finding the mean?

Aristotle identifies two ways in which phronesis finds the mean. First, hitting the mean with respect to some virtue—benevolence, say—involves determining what it would in fact be benevolent to do in the circumstances at hand, such as something that would be genuinely helpful to another, rather than merely well intended. It is because people with 'natural' virtue lack phronesis that they are unreliable about hitting the mean in this respect; as Aristotle says, virtue gives us the right goal, while phronesis enables us to do right in realizing that goal (VI.12, 1144a7–9; cp. EE II.11).

Second, and consequently, no virtue can function in isolation from other virtues, since it is not clear that an act can hit the mean of any virtue if it also fails with respect to some other virtue. For instance, consider the 'justice' of Jauvert in Les Misérables, whose insistence on strict conformity to principle is not tempered by mercy or sympathy. Jauvert, we should say, does not know what justice is for—he does not understand how the ends sought by justice fit into a larger scheme of goods and ends—and so Jauvert does not have the virtue of justice at all, if justice as a character trait is an excellence (see also Wolf 2007, 139f). Becoming expert at hitting the mean with respect to any virtue—that is, acquiring that virtue—requires the integration of that mean with the means of the other virtues, and therefore requires phronesis, which deliberates about ends from a more panoramic perspective of good ends (NE VI.5, 1140a25–31, b4–11). And as John McDowell has observed, this fact yields substantial motivation for the idea that the virtues are a unity, that is, that 'the specialized sensitivities which are to be equated with particular virtues ... are actually not

---

[51] This observation also explains, I think, why Aristotle both thinks that phronesis requires a conception of the good life and does not state the content of that conception in detail; on the latter point, see Broadie 1991, 192f.

available one by one for a series of separate identifications' (McDowell 1997, 143). Once again, please notice, we come back to the idea that the virtues must form some sort of unity, in order for any of them to count as a virtue at all. We shall revisit this point in Chapter 11.

Phronesis illuminates the notions of the mean and right reason, then, because phronesis is a virtue of the practical intellect that plays the twin roles in deliberation of guiding one's decisions towards the 'mean' of a virtue, and balancing that decision among the demands of the various virtues (see also Foot 1978a, 5–7). Simply put, to have phronesis is not just to have a virtue, but to understand what a virtue is for. At various points in this book, I shall recall this point by simply referring to the 'twin roles' of phronesis.

1.3 The Phronesis Controversy

So far I have tried to make clear the Aristotelian conception of phronesis that I shall employ in this book. I do not pretend to have shown more at this point than that that conception is a plausible one, although I do believe I have shown that much. A fuller defense of that conception, and of the thesis that phronesis so understood is a necessary part of all virtue, is the job of the rest of this book. So I want to end this first chapter with a discussion of the obstacles that I shall face in defending that thesis.

The idea that phronesis is a necessary part of all virtue is a very controversial one. For the sake of simplicity, for the moment I shall call this thesis 'Φ' (the Greek letter *phi*, the first letter in the Greek word '*phronēsis*'). Put most simply, the thesis of this book is that Φ is true. So I want to conclude my discussion of Aristotle's conception of phronesis with a sketch of some of the main objections that have been brought against Φ. On the one hand, some philosophers have argued recently that the virtues do not or need not (all) include phronesis. And on the other, some have argued that virtue ethics and virtue theory would be better off without Φ anyway, on the grounds that Φ makes for an account of the virtues that is elitist, intellectualist, or perilously demanding, or that Φ entails the very implausible thesis that to have any virtue is to have them all, that is, the so-called 'unity of virtue'. Let's briefly consider these issues in turn.

1.3.1 Is Phronesis Necessary?

Aristotle says in *Nicomachean Ethics* VI.13 that there is no virtue—that is, no virtue in the strict sense—without phronesis, and there are two broad reasons for this. One of these is that phronesis is the excellence of our nature as practically rational creatures (1145a2–4), and therefore is a necessary part of any virtue that is a genuine human excellence (1144b12–14). However, some philosophers have rejected Aristotle's view of human excellence, on various grounds. For instance, Nietzsche argued that the 'heroic' virtues of people of exceptional creativity and zeal are profound human excellences, but only if they are unfettered by practical intelligence, even if this leads to excess.[52] Such virtues do not fall short of phronesis, but *transcend* it. And in any case, is it really so bad to fall short of phronesis? Julia Driver (2001, 38) asks exactly this question:

> A diamond may be made more brilliant by a chip or a crack. One could say of this diamond that it has the virtue of being cracked in just the right way, although under one description the crack can be viewed as a flaw. Thus, the criticism of some Aristotelians that these traits, while 'good' in some imperfect sense, are not good enough to count as virtues misses the point. In what way are they not good enough?

There is something comforting about the thought that we may all have virtues, even if only virtues of 'being cracked in just the right way'. But Driver's query raises an even more serious point: in what way is a virtue, sans phronesis, not good enough?

This brings us to Aristotle's second broad argument for Φ: virtues that lack phronesis, he says, cannot be relied on to act well or rightly (1144b8–12). This is not necessarily to say either that phronesis is necessary for right action (even fools can do the right thing sometimes) or that it is sufficient (even a *phronimos* can meet with bad luck), but Aristotle's point seems to be that without phronesis, the connection between virtue and good conduct would be far too loose. However, Michael Slote has argued recently that, in a fully virtuous agent, the right decision stems immediately from virtuous motivations themselves, without the sort of deliberation or 'searching' that Aristotle describes. Not only will such decisions hit the 'mean', but Slote (2001, chs. 1–2) argues that they will also do so in a way that is 'balanced' with all other considerations of virtue, so long as one's overall motivation is virtuous. So even if we agree that the virtues must be closely linked to good conduct in order for the virtues to be excellences of practically rational beings, perhaps that link does not require that Φ be true after all, despite what Aristotle says about it.

---

[52] The ideal philosopher, Nietzsche says, 'is a "free spirit" who lives "unphilosophically" and "unwisely", above all *imprudently*', *Beyond Good and Evil*, §205, p. 132, cited in Swanton 2003, 171. See Swanton 2003, 27f, 82–4, 135, 142, 171f for discussion of Nietzsche's view. For discussion of such 'heroic' virtues in Gauguin and Gandhi, see also Slote 1983, ch. 4 and Pincoffs 1986, ch. 7, respectively.

1.3.2 Is Phronesis Problematic?

Perhaps it would be just as well if Φ were false, since some worry that Φ would restrict the virtues to a philosophically sophisticated elite. As Driver puts the point, Φ seems to imply that '[o]nly the *phronimoi*, the wise, are virtuous', but of course 'these people are few and far between' (Driver 2001, 53; see also Driver 2001, ch. 3). Such a view would also seem to make moral disagreement with a *phronimos* a sure sign of moral failure, reducing moral disagreements between reasonable persons to intimidation and posturing (Driver 2001, 12; Schneewind 1997, 200). Aristotle makes a point of distinguishing practical from theoretical wisdom (see esp. *NE* VI.7, 1141b3ff), and arguably this is due to his own distaste for an elitist and intellectualist conception of practical virtue (Broadie and Rowe 2002, 46f). On the present line of objection, Aristotle fights a necessarily losing battle.

A further worry is that even if we can live with falling short of Aristotle's ideal of the *phronimos*, still the very attempt to approach that ideal may prove perilous. As Christine Swanton argues, a person that one emulates may have strengths of character and intellect that enable him or her to be virtuous beyond one's own ability; by emulating that person, then, one may in fact push oneself beyond the breaking point, ending up a worse person rather than a better one (Swanton 2003, ch. 9 *et passim*; see also Wolf 1997). Perhaps, then, it is better to do without the rather idealistic conception of virtue and practical intelligence that the *phronimos* seems to embody.

A proponent of Φ also has the burden of showing that phronesis is the sort of intellectual virtue that humans could have. One worry in this regard stems from the fact that Aristotle's conception of phronesis seems quite clearly to entail the unity of virtue. Perhaps the most common statement of the unity thesis is that no one may have any virtue without having every virtue (e.g. Telfer 1989–90, 35). But of course that is an extraordinary claim: who could possibly be virtuous *in every way*? And why should we think that anything less is incompatible with being virtuous in *any* way? Consequently, some philosophers have moved towards a more 'departmental' conception of the virtues, where these can operate fully in some contexts without doing so in others (Badhwar 1996; Hursthouse 1999a, 155f; Swanton 2003, 229f). However, although some proponents of such a modified unity thesis are also proponents of at least some version of Φ, it is not entirely clear how phronesis can play its role of balancing these departmental virtues without leading back to a stronger form of the unity thesis after all. Yet if phronesis does not play that balancing role, then we may worry that the connection between virtue and right action would seem to fall apart.

Yet another worry is that phronesis may not be the kind of virtue that humans could have, because human psychology seems not to be made up of traits or virtues in the first place. A massive body of research in empirical psychology suggests that the situation one is in has more to do with one's behavior than do any alleged 'dispositions' or traits one has. In that case, looking to phronesis as a source of good behavior or right action may seem to have less point than simply getting one's environment right. And of course, if there is little evidence for the existence of character traits, then *a fortiori* there is little evidence supporting the traditional notion of the virtues, including deliberative virtues like phronesis.

Finally, we have seen that phronesis involves not only specifying the content of virtuous ends, but also the maintenance and (I have argued) the very adoption of such ends. And since such ends are among the deepest parts of one's character, Φ would seem to commit us to the idea that having a virtue involves maintaining and indeed constructing one's character. However, Φ would therefore seem to commit us to a kind of self-construction and responsibility for one's character that humans may well be incapable of, highly dependent creatures that we are.

These and other controversies are what this book is about. I discuss a number of issues surrounding right action and the virtues in Parts I and II, where I also consider the role of the *phronimos* in virtue ethics and what that ideal demands of virtuous persons. In Part III, I consider questions about the empirical adequacy of an Aristotelian theory of the virtues and of phronesis. Finally, I consider the unity of virtue and responsibility for character in Part IV. Throughout I argue not only that virtue ethics and other virtue theories can survive if they take phronesis seriously, but indeed that they cannot survive otherwise.

PART I

Phronesis, Virtue, and Right Action

2

Right Action for Virtue Ethics

One of my favorite Bollywood films features a group of drought-stricken villagers in Victorian India facing a tax burden they are unable to meet. When they ask their British rulers to forgive the tax, a mean-spirited officer challenges them to a game instead: if they win, he will forgive their tax, but if they lose he will triple it. Even worse, the game they must play is cricket, a favorite pastime among the officers but completely foreign to the villagers. In wonderful Bollywood style, the villagers (eventually) accept the challenge, form a rag-tag team and, of course, win the game and are forgiven their tax.[1] This makes the film great fun to watch, although—or perhaps because—we know that in real life there is usually little hope of winning at someone else's game, and usually it is just stupid to risk it.

The situation is far less melodramatic for virtue ethicists, but in a sense their increasing efforts to offer theories of right action are not unlike being made to play someone else's game. For most of the twentieth century philosophers held by and large that whatever right action is, considerations of character, virtue, and the inner states of agents must be simply irrelevant to it, and claimed that this was just part of the very concept of right action itself. One result of this tendency was that, when virtue ethics began to resurface, it was widely assumed that it could be only a theory of self-improvement, say, but not of right action, and so not a self-standing ethical theory, although perhaps a complement to one (e.g. Louden 1984, 229; see Hursthouse 1995a and 1999a, 25ff for discussion). Times have changed, not because virtue ethics has changed, since virtue ethics has always been keenly interested in right action, as even a passing familiarity with Aristotle reveals. Rather, I think that this is because virtue ethicists have stepped up and offered just the sorts of theories that virtue ethics was supposed to have been 'structurally unable' to give, in Robert Louden's phrase. And so today, although objections to those theories abound—abounding is what objections do in philosophy, after all—yet they

---

[1] I am glad that thoroughly entertaining films like *Lagaan* (*Tax*) are still being made somewhere.

rarely take the form any more of saying that virtue ethics has simply changed the subject.

Even so, virtue ethics can be seen as a sort of 'protest' against traditional ways of thinking about rightness and ethical theory (Louden 1990, 94), and since those ways of thinking have dominated for so long, it is little wonder that, as one philosopher has put it, virtue ethics offers an account of right action only 'under pressure' (Hursthouse 1999a, 69). In a way, then, virtue ethics tries not so much to win at the old game as to find a new way of playing. Dropping the metaphor, we can say that virtue ethics offers not only a different account of right action, but indeed a different conception of it, and unless we appreciate what is different about it we risk simply begging all sorts of questions against it, wondering why the new account does not fit the old conception. What we need at this moment is not yet another battery of familiar criticisms of virtue ethics, but a more general framework for evaluating virtue ethical theories of right action while taking those theories on their own terms.

My aim in this chapter, then, is to explore carefully the basic shape of virtue ethical approaches to right action (at least as they are represented in the literature we now have) and to develop a framework for assessing them for adequacy without begging any questions against them. Thinking carefully about this framework is something that I owe the virtue ethicist. My argument in this first part of the book, after all, is that the demands of offering an adequate theory of right action require the virtue ethicist to take phronesis to be a part of every virtue. I had better be sure that those demands are fair. Nonetheless, even though my aim *per se* is not to defend virtue ethical approaches to right action, I think it is inevitable that as parts of the framework I develop take shape, we shall also see what is wrong with many recent critiques of virtue ethics.

I focus on two main issues: one, whether we should take seriously the idea that the virtues have anything to do with rightness, and two, the role of consequences and outcomes in a virtue ethical theory of action. Two other important issues, of course, are the difference between acting from duty and acting from virtue, and what it means to think of right action or obligation in terms of what 'the virtuous person' would do. But I shall leave these aside for now, since the relation between virtue and duty has been much discussed already, with largely conciliatory results, and since the question of 'the virtuous person' is a thorny enough issue to require separate treatment (I take it up in Chapter 4).[2] I begin, then, with a discussion of the notion of right action,

---

[2] Although I should say, as a 'heads up', that I do not see 'the virtuous person' as a problem-solving heuristic.

arguing that that notion is broad enough that virtue ethics can indeed have something to say about it.

2.1 Right Action and Serious Practical Concerns

The first thing we should say about 'right action' is that there is no theoretically neutral concept of right action. When the idea of an 'ethics of virtue' was still new, philosophers would often insist—usually with an air of perfect self-evidence—that an action's rightness depends not at all on its agent's motive or other internal states, but only on what the action 'does' or 'brings about', say (e.g. Frankena 1980, 48; Smart and Williams 1973, 45–9; Gorr 1999, 586f, 589; for discussion see Garcia 1992, 237; Schneewind 1997). Many philosophers still take some such view as this, but philosophers who disagree on this point are not simply confused, or talking past each other, or working with different concepts. Defenses of such a view cannot simply appeal to 'the concept' of right action, but must argue for a particular understanding of what moral philosophy is about. This is because, as Christine Korsgaard (1995, 1168) has observed, philosophy—and moral philosophy in particular—is a practical enterprise, one that begins not from a premise but from a plight. We are interested in a theory of right action in the first place because we have serious concerns of a very practical nature—deciding how to act, assessing what we do, thinking about outcomes, having good reasons, and so on—and philosophical reflection can perhaps yield insights on these concerns that we could not have gotten just as well anywhere else. Differing views of what 'right action' is about rest on differing views about which of those concerns we think a theory of right action should cast light on, and how such a theory should do so. In this respect, theories that focus on external outcomes and theories that focus on internal states are all on an equal footing.

The lack of any such theoretically neutral concept of right action is nowhere clearer than in those stock objections to virtue ethics that profess to appeal to it. One such objection is that it is part of the meaning of 'right' that only an action, understood in terms of what one brings about, can be called right or wrong; agents and their motives may be good or bad, and may make an action good or bad, but have no place in a theory of rightness (see Garcia 1992 for discussion). Such talk of 'meanings', though, serves only to conceal a number of substantive assumptions about the subject matter of moral philosophy: action understood in one way rather than in another.

Another sort of objection holds that what is right is a matter of what one ought or is obligated to do, and this involves just acting, not acting from a particular inner state.[3] But that view cannot be simply 'read off' the concept of right action, but again merely voices a particular view of what moral philosophy is about—our obligations, what we ought to do. On that view of moral philosophy, to find what one ought to do just is to find what it is right to do; but virtue ethics denies this, precisely because it thinks that a theory of right action is about more than just obligations. (I shall say more about this below.)

Now consider a different type of objection that, so far from masking a view of what a theory of right action is about, appeals to that very view as its first premise: i.e. that 'rightness' applies only to actions in the sense of what one brings about, because that is what the notion of rightness is *for*, namely the suppression of harmful behavior.[4] This is a view that no virtue ethicist will accept, but at least it approaches virtue ethics on its own terms by recognizing that a theory of right action is to shed light on *some practical purpose* for the sake of better understanding which we turn to moral philosophy. Such an approach is a sensible one, at least insofar as arguing about the very concept of 'rightness'

---

[3] This idea is familiar from philosophers like Prichard and Ross, who argued that there can be no obligation to act from a certain motive; see Frankena 1970 and Gorr 1999, 583f for discussion. The underlying assumption seems to be that one has little or no control over what motives one has, or from which motives one acts. But it seems clear that one can have some such control over time, as is illustrated by Iris Murdoch's (1970, 17) famous example of the mother-in-law who takes steps to become more lovingly disposed to her daughter-in-law. This points to a fundamental difference between virtue ethics, which views actions within the history of an agent, and other sorts of approaches that tend to focus on actions one at a time.

[4] French 1979, 47–9, cited in Garcia 1992, 240. See also Louden 1984, 72, discussed in Garcia 1990, 85. And see also Gorr 1999, 588, who argues for the weaker thesis that the desire to suppress harmful behavior explains why rightness concerns behavior much more than it does motive. This sort of view of right action reveals a 'legislative' conception of rightness. Indeed, note that Gorr's argument (1999, 590–5) appeals to the fact that certain laws pertaining to less serious forms of harm such as nuisance, can regard some non-serious harms as permissible or pardonable, when its motive is innocent (e.g. creating a nuisance as the result of a desire to express oneself artistically). See also Taylor 1988, who takes it to be the 'basic meaning' of right and wrong that something is wrong just in case it is forbidden by some principle or law, and right otherwise; he concludes that ancient virtue theorists therefore believed that ethics has nothing to do with right and wrong. The fact that such a position appears to be supported by such jurisprudence is of course unsurprising—and indeed ironic—given Elizabeth Anscombe's 1981*b* complaint that the notion of legal obligation has skewed the moral notion of rightness to favor precisely the sort of view advocated by philosophers like Gorr and French. This complaint is also a major theme in Pincoffs 1986. Still, the influence of this legislative conception is apparent in the die-hard view of morality, and of the concept of right, as necessarily pertaining only to matters of the interpersonal effects of action. See e.g. Milo 1995, and Scanlon 1982, 110: 'An act is wrong if its performance under the circumstances would be disallowed by any system of rules for the general regulation of behaviour which no one could reasonably reject as a basis of informed, unforced, general agreement'; cited in Williams 1985, 75. See also Russell 2005*b* for critique of such views; and see Pincoffs 1986, 46, who queries how we could imagine a person whose moral life 'is confined to minimal public standards'.

gets us nowhere,[5] and although it rejects the virtue ethicist's view, it does have the advantage of allowing that such a view is at least an *intelligible* one about right action. It also suggests the sort of reply that it expects the virtue ethicist to make, namely to argue for a different view of the serious practical concerns we should want a theory of right action to cast light on.

Thinking of right action in terms of serious practical concerns, as I have suggested here, gives different theories of right action a common ground on which to meet, and this is because our serious practical concerns are not immovably fixed. For one thing, we can argue with each other about what those concerns are. It is widely agreed that our serious practical concerns include the intentions and motives of people who act, but philosophers have disagreed about whether 'moral motivation' should be understood in terms of rules, principles, duties, and 'conscientious' motives, or rather in terms of practical intelligence and discernment, say (McDowell 1997; Hursthouse 1999a, 56–9), and benevolence (Slote 2001; Foot 1978c), inner strength (Swanton 2003), or other such notions. Many moral philosophers outside virtue ethics—and in particular many neo-Kantians—have also argued convincingly that moral motivation need not be understood in terms of rigidly 'conscientious' motivation, rather than in terms of love, benevolence, or humane concern (see Hursthouse 1999a, ch. 4 for discussion). This has also been an important theme in those forms of feminist ethics that emphasize notions of caring rather than duty or obligation (see Slote 2001, ch. 3). What all this shows is that our concern that agents' motivations be 'morally right' is one that can be transformed as we continue to reflect on the nature of moral motivation.

Likewise, we can also change our minds about which of our serious practical concerns we think a theory of right action should address. There is no denying that we do care about suppressing harmful or otherwise troublesome behavior, and about the 'upshot' or consequences of actions, and I shall say more about how virtue ethics cares about them. But we also care about people's reasons for acting—and according to virtue ethics, they are among the concerns that we want an account of right action to tell us about. Such concern is clearest in the actions of people 'near and dear' to us. As Alasdair MacIntyre (1981, 192) has observed, what action an agent has done is not independent of why the agent has done it: if my friend passes me in the corridor, for instance, and walks by despite my greeting him, whether his action is one of 'snubbing' or

---

[5] As Williams 1985, 128 says, 'the theorist, in trying to sort out the relevant uses of [general ethical terms], brings to the inquiry presuppositions that are not only already theoretical but already ethical. The results are usually bad philosophy of language.'

'being lost in thought'—and thus whether or not I take offense—depends on why he did it. And so actions do not happen merely within relationships, but define and shape those relationships: if someone is honest with one friend but dishonest with another, what he 'cannot then intelligibly claim is that he stands in the same relationship of friendship to both ... By telling the truth to one and lying to the other he has partially defined a difference in the relationship'.[6] (See also Garcia 1992, 240f.) Since inner states are part of how we treat one another within relationships—since they are *themselves* important ways of treating one another—we should not be satisfied with any general ethical account of action that left them out, as simply off-topic.

Our reasons for acting define not only close relationships in this way, but also our ties to other members of our community, or 'social union', more broadly. As John Rawls has argued, in a social union participants share ends and value their common institutions and activities as good for their own sake, and such a union exists in a society when its members have a common aim of realizing their own and one another's good according to a shared sense of justice. Since it is part of a person's good to adopt a regulative sense of justice, which is to have the virtue of justice, this speaks in favor of what Rawls calls a 'well-ordered society', in which 'being a good person (and in particular having an effective sense of justice) is indeed a good for that person' (Rawls, 1971, 577; see also §§79, 85, 86). Be that as it may, Rawls' argument rightly emphasizes the fact that part of every human's good as a social creature is to live with others who do more than suppress their antisocial behavior, and who indeed act from a shared sense of justice and a shared commitment to the practices of social union.[7]

Inner states also matter crucially from the agent's own perspective on his or her actions. Often what one wants in addition to an outcome of one's action is that one should produce the outcome oneself—and more than that, that one should produce it for certain kinds of reasons (Williams 1985, 56; see also Frankfurt 2003). This is so especially where those reasons bear on one's action as expressing one's conception of the good, and a 'coherent scheme for a life', in John McDowell's phrase (1995b, 214). Reasons for acting that are nearest to our sense of our deepest selves, I think, are those reasons to which we are committed to making our characteristic reasons for acting, that is, reasons that we want to make part of our character.

---

[6] We shall consider further questions about of how agents' inner states shape and even identify their behaviors in Chs. 8–10.

[7] Unfortunately, Rawls himself seems to have been kept from the thought that inner states should be a part of an account of rightness, apparently because of his independently over-simplified view of 'right' and 'good' as disjoint concepts; see Watson 1990, cf. Hursthouse 1999a, 37f.

For all these reasons, it seems clear that our reasons, motives, and indeed characters should be central among the practical concerns we look to moral philosophy to understand. Do these sorts of considerations also show that an agent's reasons for action are part of the concept of 'right'? I do not know, but in any case that is the wrong question. The real question is whether agents' motives and reasons for action matter to us in such ways that we want a theory of right action to address reasons for action, in addition to what outcomes actions yield. And it seems clear that reasons for action matter in just that way. We can assess the merits of a conception of right action only by reference to the serious practical concerns that lead us to inquire about right action in the first place.[8] Those concerns clearly focus not on mere events, but on actions—things that people do, which include such 'distinctively human aspects' as why people act (or fail to act) as they do (Garcia 1992, 242).

In any case, what is clear is that there is a way to demand a theory of right action from virtue ethics without begging any questions: this is to frame such a theory not as analyzing a concept—a bad move anyway—but as addressing our serious practical concerns. And it also seems clear enough that when the demand is put in those terms, virtue ethics does seem quite reasonable in making motivation and character central among those concerns. Now, I want to make it clear that this is *not* to argue for virtue ethics against alternatives—as if what sets virtue ethics apart were this broader way of thinking of right action, or as if virtue ethics were simply uninterested in principles, rules, or outcomes. Surely it is not. On the contrary, for all its surrounding air of conceptual self-evidence, the very narrow focus on duties or principles or outcomes to which virtue ethics protested was a fairly recent, and fairly temporary, blip in the history of moral philosophy (see Nussbaum 1999, esp. 170).[9] Rather, my point is only to reject the idea that virtue ethics, by emphasizing character and

[8] As Williams 1985, 115 has put the point, 'How can we come to see the weaknesses of a theoretical concept except by reference to the everyday distinctions it is supposed to replace or justify, and by a sense of the life it is supposed to help us to lead?' Williams (1985, 127) attributes the co-opting of the concept of rightness by narrow conceptions of what ethics is about to 'the linguistic turn in moral philosophy', whose 'prevailing fault, in all its styles', he says, 'is to impose on ethical life some immensely simple model, whether it be of the concepts that we actually use or of moral rules by which we should be guided. One remedy to this persistent deformation might indeed have been to attend to the great diversity of things that people do say about how they and other people live their lives.'

[9] However, Nussbaum 1999 argues that there is in fact *no* very substantial commitment among virtue ethicists that either sets them apart from others or unifies them with each other. Nussbaum is entirely correct, I think, to point out both how many significant points of overlap there are between virtue ethics and other sorts of views, and how many significant points of difference there are between different forms of virtue ethics. Ultimately, though, I think that there *is* a way of demarcating virtue ethical theories which, though abstract, is nonetheless substantial rather than 'thin', in Nussbaum's phrase. I consider this issue in §2.4.

motivation, cannot be one of our alternatives for thinking about right action. There is every reason to suppose that virtue ethics can join the conversation about right action.

Even so, we are left with at least two main questions about some of our other practical concerns. One, what does it mean for a theory of right action to do justice to our serious practical concerns? Is it a criterion for an account of right action that the account consider right *only* those actions in which *all* of our serious practical concerns are met, including our concerns about outcomes? Must virtue ethics, in other words, address our serious practical concerns about outcomes and consequences by making the rightness of action contingent on the states of affairs that actions result in or consist in? Can any account of right action that does not meet such a criterion be said to take those concerns seriously enough? And two, how far can a purportedly virtue ethical account of right action go in taking seriously our concerns about consequences, outcomes, and upshots, before it has merely smuggled in some prior view about rightness? If virtue ethics does give states of affairs an important role in determining whether an action is right or not, then does it covertly rely on some sort of outcome-based conception of rightness, and thus fail to be genuinely virtue ethical after all?[10] Sorting out these issues will yield a framework for sizing up virtue ethical accounts of right action, and so in the rest of this chapter I consider these two issues in turn.

2.2 Two Constraints on Right Action

Our first question is how far virtue ethics must go in taking the outcomes of action seriously. We should begin by distinguishing two ways of addressing our serious practical concerns in an account of right action:

> *Account constraint*: An account of right action is adequate only if that account takes sufficiently into consideration all of our serious practical concerns; and

> *Act constraint*: An account of right action is adequate only if that account holds that an action is right only if that action sufficiently meets all of our serious practical concerns.[11]

---

[10] These two issues correspond more or less to what Ramon Das (2003, 324) has called the 'insularity' and the 'circularity' objections to virtue ethics, respectively.

[11] We can also distinguish a stronger version of the act constraint—an action is right only if things go *sufficiently well* (e.g. Aristotle, *NE* IV.2; Swanton 2003, 229f, 232)—and a weaker version—an action

Virtue ethicists such as Michael Slote, who accepts the 'account constraint' but not the 'act constraint', hold that it is enough that an account of right action should build careful consideration of outcomes into its model of virtuous motivation or deliberation, and then understand right action as arising from such motivation or deliberation. On the other hand, virtue ethicists like Philippa Foot, Rosalind Hursthouse, and Christine Swanton accept the stronger act constraint and therefore hold that acting in a virtuous way is necessary for right action, but not sufficient for it.

As I just said, the act constraint is stronger than the account constraint. The account constraint says only what all accounts of right action are supposed to do—address our serious practical concerns—while the act constraint requires addressing those concerns *by* making rightness of action contingent on all of them. So on the one hand, for virtue ethics to accept the account constraint is not to smuggle in any prior conception of right action (*pace* Das 2003, 328), but only to set about constructing one. To accept the account constraint is to join the conversation about right action. And on the other hand, while the account constraint is a minimal constraint on any account of right action, the act constraint will be far more controversial, and once the distinction is made it is not immediately obvious that any theory will have to meet it. That is what we must determine here (in the very next section, actually).

It is therefore significant to note that this distinction is seldom made (Garcia 1992, 250 seems an exception). Indeed many objections to virtue ethical accounts of right action (including, I suspect, some by other virtue ethicists) assume that virtue ethics as such is beholden to the act constraint, as if by default. The objections I have in mind take the following form: 'Theory *T* counts action *A* as right; but *A* does not meet some of our serious practical concerns; therefore, *A* is not right, and so *T* is inadequate'. For this reason, some critics have argued recently that virtue ethics must rely on some sort of 'ideal observer' theory, since virtuous agents lacking certain information can make mistakes, and it is simply taken as given that actions involving such mistakes cannot count as right (Kawall 2002, 207ff; Copp and Sobel 2004, 549; Hurka 2001, 225, 229, discussed in Copp and Sobel 2004, 545f). Likewise, several philosophers have objected that even if virtuous persons carefully consider the consequences of their actions, there is no guarantee that they will always succeed in achieving their aims (Stohr and Wellman 2002, 53; Hurka 2001, 224f; Swanton 2003, 230f). However, these sorts of objections simply assume without argument that every account of right action must accept the

is right only if things do not go *seriously badly* (e.g. Hursthouse 1999a, chs. 2–3, esp. p. 79; Hursthouse 1995a, 62).

act constraint: A fails with respect to some of our practical concerns, so A cannot be right.

Here, then, are two broad ways of taking our serious practical concerns seriously: by building them into the account of the virtues and virtuous practical reasoning, and by making their satisfaction a necessary condition on an action's rightness. So our first question from the end of §2.1 now becomes this: *must* virtue ethics accept the act constraint, or is the account constraint enough? And our second question becomes: *can* virtue ethics accept the act constraint, without changing into an outcome-based theory of right action? Is either way of taking our concerns about outcomes and states of affairs seriously a legitimate option for virtue ethics? I take up the first question in §2.3 and the second in §2.4. My argument, simply put, is that adopting the weaker or the stronger constraint is something that virtue ethicists can disagree about; the stronger constraint is neither required nor precluded.

2.3 *Must* Virtue Ethics Accept the Act Constraint?

Should we take seriously any account of right action that rejects the act constraint? Before we can answer this question, we must be more precise about what an 'account of right action' is an account *of*, since 'right' has the twin roles of pointing to an action as something to do, on the one hand, and as something praiseworthy on the other (see Hursthouse 1999a, ch. 2). The first role concerns action *guidance*—roughly, helping us decide what to do. The other concerns action *assessment*, or what it is reasonable to approve and disapprove about what one does. Now, an account of right action must touch on both of these issues, so although virtue ethicists disagree as to whether an account of right action is subject to the act constraint, we must ask whether they disagree about that constraint as touching on an account of action guidance or of action assessment (or both). So my aims in this section are as follows. One, I argue that the disagreement between virtue ethicists over the act constraint does not concern action guidance, where virtue ethicists are correct in rejecting that constraint (§2.3.2). Rather, two, that disagreement concerns action assessment, but I argue that there is nothing about virtue ethics *per se* that requires the act constraint here, and indeed that an at least *prima facie* plausible account of action assessment can be given without that constraint (§2.3.3). In that case, it would be prejudicial to require virtue ethical accounts of right action to accept the act constraint, without further substantial argument. But first, I must defend the distinction between guidance and assessment, and I want to show how doing so will allow us to consider, and answer, a prevalent objection to virtue ethical accounts of right action which, I argue, does not take that distinction seriously enough (§2.3.1).

2.3.1 Right Action: Guidance and Assessment

Let's begin with the objection, and then see how the distinction between guidance and assessment fits in. The objection I have in mind targets the idea that a right action is what a virtuous person would do, characteristically, in the circumstances, pointing out that it may make no sense to ask what a virtuous person would do in my circumstances at all, because no virtuous person would be in my circumstances in the first place. In particular, the objection goes, there may be actions that it would be right for me to do precisely because I am *not* virtuous, such as acts involved in compensating for or remedying my vicious tendencies. In that case, decision procedures aside, being 'what a virtuous person would do' cannot be a necessary condition of right action, and so it must be a mistake to analyze right action in terms of the actions of virtuous persons. For the sake of simplicity, we can call this the 'right but not virtuous' objection.

The 'right but not virtuous' objection is fast becoming a new standard or textbook objection to virtue ethics.[12] Gilbert Harman made such an objection explicitly in a 2001 paper. Citing Rosalind Hursthouse's soundbite thesis that 'An action is right iff it is what a virtuous agent would do in the circumstances' (1997, 219), Harman (2001, 119 and n. 6) states that this version of virtue ethics holds that 'what one ought morally to do in a particular situation is to do what a virtuous person would do in that situation'. An 'obvious objection' to such a view, Harman (2001, 120, 121) says, is that

sometimes a nonvirtuous person will be in a situation that a virtuous person would never be in.... For example, a person who has done something wrong often ought morally to apologize to those affected by his or her action. However, an ideally virtuous person would not have done the wrong thing in the first place, and so would have nothing to apologize for.

More recently, Robert Johnson (2003, 811) has reminded us that 'however an ethical theory combines its account of the virtues with its account of

---

[12] As Copp and Sobel (2004, 546 n. 74) have noticed, the form of this objection is parallel to a different objection that Williams (1995b, 190) makes against analyzing the notion of a reason to act in terms of what a good deliberator would do. The problem, Williams argues, is that if a given agent is not a good deliberator, then perhaps what he or she has reason to do in some situation is to control some wayward desire, say, that no good deliberator would have had in the first place.

right action, it must make room for a genuine moral obligation to improve your character and to act in other ways that are appropriate only because you could be a better person than you are'. He then considers a chronic liar who undertakes a course of 'remedial' actions to reform his character, such as keeping an account of his lying, reminding himself of the importance of truth-telling, and so on. Such actions would be the right ones, but no virtuous person would do them:

> Common sense would regard these kinds of things as what he morally ought to do in circumstances such as these, at least insofar as they will improve his character. Yet all are utterly uncharacteristic of completely virtuous agents....But surely he ought to do things of this sort, things over and above simply 'deciding to tell the truth from now on.' This would in large part consist in behavior that a completely virtuous person would not characteristically engage in. That he ought to do such things goes directly counter to the claim that right conduct is conduct characteristic of the virtuous. (Johnson 2003, 817f)[13]

Not surprisingly, this objection also found its way into David Copp and David Sobel's recent review article on the current state of virtue ethics. They observe that

> there can be actions that would be morally good, or even morally required of a person who is not virtuous, that no virtuous agent would do precisely because she is already virtuous. A person with a tendency to lie to save herself embarrassment might need to remind herself of the importance of truth telling, but no virtuous person would need to do this.   (Copp and Sobel 2004, 546)

This they interpret as a particularly damaging objection to any analysis of right action in terms of what a virtuous person would do.

Perhaps one response to this objection would be to point out that virtue ethicists need not—and indeed most do not—think of virtuous persons as morally perfect persons (see e.g. Swanton 2003, 24f *et passim*; Hursthouse 1999*a*, ch. 7; Badhwar 1996).[14] However, the objector has a plausible reply to this: even if virtuous persons may be imperfect, it is surely not *qua* imperfect that the notion of a virtuous person is employed in the analysis of right action. It would, after all, be rather surprising if the right action turned out to be some act of incontinence, say, on the grounds that some virtuous persons sometimes succumb to incontinence (see also Louden 1984, 229). And this is, I take it, at least part of the reason that Hursthouse (1999*a*, 28) analyzes right action in

---

[13] Johnson (2003, 816–25) also considers a case in which one ought to take steps to avoid giving in to one's frequent tendency to break promises, and a case in which one ought to seek the guidance of others given one's own moral immaturity.

[14] I thank an anonymous referee for the *Southern Journal of Philosophy* for suggesting this.

terms of 'what a virtuous agent would *characteristically* (i.e. acting in character) do in the circumstances'. So even though virtuous persons are imperfect, I think that this fact offers little help for the virtue ethicist here. In any case, I shall concede to the objector on this point and take a different tack.

Rather, I think that the strongest response to the 'right but not virtuous' objection lies elsewhere. In particular, it lies in distinguishing what one 'ought' to do from what action would be 'right', a distinction that some virtue ethicists have already made in other contexts. By contrast, the 'right but not virtuous' objection makes no distinction between the claim that the reforming liar (say) ought to do such-and-such and the claim that his or her doing such-and-such would be right. So I turn now to the distinction between 'ought' and 'right', and show how the 'right but not virtuous' objection assumes, without argument, that 'ought' implies 'right'. I then turn to the further objection that virtue ethics is too stingy in its assessment of the rightness of remedial acts, that is, acts of making up for one's own shortcomings of character. I conclude this subsection by demonstrating the importance of the right/ought distinction in another way, arguing that it can clarify a recent debate in virtue ethics over the thesis that 'ought' implies 'can'.

The difference between guidance and assessment is perhaps clearest in certain kinds of dilemma. As Hursthouse puts the point, in an irresolvable dilemma all of the courses of action open to one may be so awful that none of them is happily described as 'right', yet it may still be the case that there is something one ought to do. Hursthouse (1995a, 62) herself says that in such cases 'I think of the virtuous as, rather characteristically, saying, … after their decision in a particular case, "No, of course I didn't think it was the *right* [thing]; how could either have counted as the right [thing] in such a terrible set-up?" '[15] So suppose that some person, Smith, is faced with such a dilemma, and in the midst of his deliberations asks a friend, 'Whatever I do will be an awful thing; but help me do the right thing anyway.' What exactly is one to seek in making such a plea? Since Smith is (*ex hypothesi*) in an irresolvable dilemma, we should not see 'the right thing' in this case as a praiseworthy action. In this sense, a 'right action' is one that warrants the 'satisfactory review of [one's] own conduct', in David Hume's phrase, or as Hursthouse (1999a, 46f, 50) puts it, one that warrants a 'tick of approval'.[16] On the other hand, sometimes we say 'Smith did the right thing' where the focus is not on Smith's *action* itself, but on his *decision* to act: even though what he did was an awful thing for

---

[15] 'Thing' here replaces 'decision' in Hursthouse's text, since the context makes it clear that 'decision' here means the action decided upon. See also Hursthouse 1999a, chs. 2–3; Swanton 2003, 229f.

[16] Consequently, as we shall see below, Hursthouse goes on to qualify the initial, simple thesis that an act is right just in case it is what a virtuous person would characteristically do.

anyone to have to do, he successfully recognized that it did have to be done. It is in this second sense, I think, that we should understand Smith as seeking help to 'do the right thing'. Identifying an action as a praiseworthy one is a matter of action *assessment*, whereas identifying an action as the (or a) thing to do is a matter of action *guidance*.

Although the distinction between assessment and guidance is an important one in virtue ethics, it certainly is not confined to virtue ethics. For instance, William Frankena (1970, 6)—as staunch a critic of virtue ethics as one could hope for—also distinguished between what he called 'direct moral judgments', which concern what to do, and 'indirect moral judgments', which concern the assessment of action. Of course, the difference between assessment and guidance is not always obvious: usually when I do what I ought to do my action gets a tick of approval. Yet it is clear that there is a difference between recommending or enjoining a certain course of action, and giving approval of the actions entailed by that course (Hursthouse 1999a, 49ff).

Unfortunately, in everyday English we usually talk about these two things with just the one term, 'right'. That is an ambiguity that we should watch carefully. Hursthouse herself avoids that ambiguity with a technical distinction between 'right' as a matter of action assessment, and 'ought' as a matter of action guidance. This is what is meant by the right/ought distinction.

Granting that distinction, we must still ask how action assessment and action guidance—'right' and 'ought'—are related to each other. For virtue ethics, anyway, enjoining an act is neither necessary nor sufficient for giving it a tick of approval. On the one hand, 'right' does not imply 'ought'. That an action is 'right' and gets a tick of approval does not entail that the action is also obligatory or what one 'ought' to do, at least on certain views of 'ought' common among philosophers. For one thing, the idea that one ought to do such-and-such often tends to convey uniqueness—that such-and-such is '*the* right thing to do'—but there may be open to one multiple courses of action equally deserving of approval (Hursthouse 1999a, 66f; Geach 1956, 41; con. Garcia 1992, 244ff). 'Ought' can also convey universality—'what *anyone* ought to do in the circumstances'—but virtue ethics holds that the goodness of a decision may depend on the peculiarities of an agent, so that to hold an action 'right' is not necessarily to enjoin it as the thing, or even a thing to do, *simpliciter* (Pincoffs 1986, 20ff; Hursthouse 1999a, 70). But even on a sense of 'ought' more amenable to virtue ethics, 'right' still need not imply 'ought'. For instance, it may be the case that it would indeed be a fine action if I were to do such-and-such; nonetheless, perhaps what I ought to do—and what would perhaps be more virtuous—is to step aside and give someone else the opportunity to do this fine thing instead (Aristotle, *NE* IX.8, 1169a26–34).

And more generally, as Christine Swanton (2003, 241) has put the point, 'an action may be right without being obligatory'. So for virtue ethics, 'right' need not imply 'ought'.

On the other hand—and this is the important point for our purposes here—'ought' does not imply 'right', either. For instance, as I said above, there may be dilemmas in which there is an option that one ought to choose—to advocate heroic and precarious life-saving measures for one's comatose mother, say, or to allow her to die—even though each option may be apt for regret rather than celebration. Alternatively, bad luck may interfere so that despite doing what one 'ought' to do, things turn out very badly anyway, and thus one's action is not 'right' (Swanton 2003, 229f). Furthermore, some virtue ethical theories of right action base the rightness of an action solely on the motives from which the action is done (Slote 2001; Garcia 1990). On such theories, one may do what one 'ought' to do—do what it is one's duty to do, say—but do so from an inappropriate motive, and thus not act rightly. (I shall return to this point below.)

That 'ought' does not imply 'right' can be seen in another sort of case as well, viz. when what one ought to do in one's circumstances results from one's own prior wrongdoing. In such a case, doing what one ought to do may not be the same as doing a right act or 'good deed'. In fact, the same prior failure may both increase one's level of obligation to do a given act now, *and* decrease one's level of praiseworthiness for doing it. To borrow an example from Hursthouse (1999a, 46f, 50f), suppose that a philanderer has irresponsibly impregnated two women, and now can marry and fully support only one of them. Now suppose that one of these women, fortunately, has another suitor who is happy to support her and help her raise her child. In that case, the philanderer ought to marry the other woman, since abandoning her would be worse and more callous than abandoning the first woman. But of course in doing so, he still abandons the first woman, and the fact that someone else is willing to support her makes him lucky, not praiseworthy. He should feel shame and regret for what he has done, rather than enjoy the 'satisfactory review of his conduct'. In such a case, 'right' and 'ought' actually pull in opposite directions: the prior irresponsibility that makes so strong the sense in which he 'ought' to do such-and-such is also what makes whatever he does so much less than praiseworthy or 'right'.

So for virtue ethics, 'ought' does not imply 'right'. I now want to consider the 'right but not virtuous' objection in two ways, focusing in each case on Johnson's version of the objection. First I consider it as implicitly assuming that ought implies right. Then I consider the 'right but not virtuous' objection as a more radical rejection of the virtue ethicist's right/ought distinction itself.

I think there can be no disagreeing with Johnson (2003, 811, 817) when he says that virtue ethics 'must make room for a genuine moral obligation to improve your character', and that steps so taken are what one 'morally ought to do' in such circumstances. The problem, I think, comes in the unargued assumption that such actions are therefore right, in the virtue ethicist's sense (Johnson 2003, 818). As we saw above, this is one legitimate common usage of the word 'right', viz. what one ought to do. But that is not the sense in which 'right' is used in the thesis that an action is right just in case it is what a virtuous person would characteristically do. In that thesis, 'right' is functioning as an action assessing concept, not an action guiding one.

We can make this point clearer in the following way. The 'right but not virtuous' objection has the form of a *reductio ad absurdum*, and can be reconstructed as follows:

1. An agent with a serious moral shortcoming ought to take steps to remedy or make up for that shortcoming.
2. Therefore, for such an agent the right action is to take those steps.
3. No virtuous person has such a shortcoming, and so no virtuous person would take such steps.
4. Suppose that an action is right just in case it is what a virtuous person would characteristically do in the same circumstances.
5. In that case, taking steps to remedy or make up for a serious moral shortcoming would not be the right action, contra premise (2).
6. But since premise (2) is clearly true, the supposition in (4) must be false.

There is no disagreement about the first premise, so the crucial step in this argument is the step from the first premise to the second, since it is the second premise that drives the *reductio*. Notice that whereas the first premise talks about what a non-virtuous agent *ought* to do, the second moves to talk of what would be a *right* action for a non virtuous agent. If we take seriously the difference between guidance and assessment, then premise (2) admits of two different readings:

2a. For such an agent, the right *decision* is the decision to take those steps; or
2b. For such an agent, those steps themselves would be right *actions*.

We can set aside (2a) straightaway, because it focuses on action guidance, whereas the targeted account in premise (4) is about action assessment. Hurst-house makes this clear when she offers a fuller statement of her account:

[A] An *action* is right iff it is what a virtuous agent would, characteristically, do in the circumstances, [B] except for tragic dilemmas, in which a *decision* is right iff it is what such an agent would decide, but the action decided upon may be too terrible to be called 'right' or 'good'. (And a tragic dilemma is one from which a virtuous agent cannot emerge with her life unmarred.) (Hursthouse 1999a, 79, italics added)

We see in this passage that Hursthouse's original, soundbite statement of her view, which I have labeled [A], is about the assessment of actions, since she distinguishes this from guidance about decisions in the proviso that I have labeled [B]. So in premise (4) of the *reductio*, 'right' must be understood in its action-assessing sense, and so (2a), which concerns action guidance, would not generate the *reductio*.

So the virtue ethicist will accept premise (1) only if it is a claim about action guidance, and the targeted virtue ethical thesis in (4) is one about action assessment. Therefore, in order for the *reductio* to get off the ground, the argument must somehow shift from a first premise about action guidance—what such an agent ought to do—to a second premise about action assessment, that is to (2b). But on this reading of the crucial second premise, it no longer follows from the first—*unless* we assume that enjoining an action implies a positive assessment of that action, that is, that 'ought' implies 'right'. Interestingly, one other recent critic of virtue ethics is far more forthcoming about the necessity of this assumption, stating as the first premise in his critique that 'We can characterize a right action as that action (or one of a set of equally acceptable actions) which an agent morally ought to perform, all things considered' (Kawall 2002, 198). But whether it is explicit or not, such an assumption merely begs the question against virtue ethicists who deny that 'ought' implies 'right'.

Is that denial restricted to just an odd minority of virtue ethicists? I do not think so. At any rate, the denial that 'ought' implies 'right' goes back at least to Aristotle (*NE* IV.9, esp. 1128b29–31), who argued that one ought to feel shame (*aidōs*) if one has acted disgracefully, but that feeling shame will be 'right' at most in a highly conditional and qualified way.[17] That is why virtue ethics begins its account of right action not with the concept of obligation, but with central cases of right action—actions that are right in an unconditional, unqualified way—and thus with virtues that are good full stop, rather than only conditionally so, as in the case of shame. (I shall return to this point below.)

---

[17] See also *NE* II.9, where Aristotle notes that those of us who struggle to hit the mean in certain areas of life often would do well to veer in the direction of one extreme rather than the other, depending on the nature of our struggle. Note, however, that Johnson and Aristotle alike reject an understanding of *wrong* action as what a virtuous person would not do; con. Zagzebski 1996, 233 *et passim*.

Consequently, it would seem that proponents of the 'right but not virtuous' objection face a dilemma: either the objection overlooks the distinction between guidance and assessment, i.e. between 'ought' and 'right', or it begs the question against virtue ethics by assuming without argument that 'ought' implies 'right'. However, although Johnson does not argue that 'ought' implies 'right', he does argue that there are good reasons to think that the sorts of remedial actions he describes should be assessed positively as right actions, full stop, and therefore that virtue ethics is implausible for withholding such an assessment. (Put another way, why should we allow the virtue ethicist to insist on reading the first premise of the *reductio* as a claim about action guidance rather than assessment?) So understood, the 'right but not virtuous' objection is an objection to the right/ought distinction itself, or at least an argument that in cases of remedial action, the distinction does not make the difference that the virtue ethicist supposes. So let's take up this second issue now.

As we have seen, a commonplace of virtue ethics is the denial that 'ought' implies 'right': enjoining an action (action guidance) need not give the action a tick of approval (action assessment). But why should we think that remedial actions do not warrant a tick of approval? Virtue ethics seems committed to the view that such actions are, in Johnson's phrase, 'second best', since they are not the sorts of actions that virtuous persons characteristically do. But as Johnson (2003, 825) points out, 'acting to improve oneself, both morally and naturally, seems not to be merely acceptable. There is, or at least can be, something truly excellent in a moral respect about the reformations of the liar.' I agree, and in fact I think that most virtue ethicists would agree, too; what is more, many virtue ethicists openly resist casting assessments in terms of the good, the bad, and the merely permissible or acceptable (Hursthouse 1999a, 69, 74). But how can virtue ethics reconcile the idea that such actions can have something excellent about them with the idea that action assessment is tied to what a virtuous person would characteristically do?

I do not think that the issue is best understood in terms of what is 'first best' and what is 'second best', as if action assessment were like judging a contest. Rather, the issue for virtue ethics, I believe, concerns what sorts of acts are *central* cases of excellent action, and what sorts are less central cases. This is an important point. To say that remedial actions are not right actions is not to deny, full stop, that remedial actions can be morally praiseworthy or excellent. After all, to 'turn over a new leaf' is an excellent thing. Rather, the question is whether a remedial act is excellent in exactly the same way that right actions are, that is, actions that are the central cases of morally praiseworthy or excellent actions. The virtue ethicist can, I think, make 'what a virtuous person would characteristically do' a necessary condition of right action, without denying for a moment that other sorts of action can be morally excellent as well. What the virtue ethicist does, rather, is to identify certain cases of morally excellent action as central cases, and restrict the account of right action to these.

Should we say, then, that remedial actions and fully virtuous actions are not only excellent but excellent in just the same way and to the same extent? Johnson (2003, 825) says that we should, complaining that the only way to deny it is merely to dig in one's heels and insist that 'morally excellent' just means 'characteristic of a virtuous person': 'there are no grounds other than these on which to hold that self-improving actions and the like are not every bit as morally excellent as any actions that would be characteristic of the virtuous'. This seems an extraordinary thing to say, as it suggests that summoning the continence or shame to avoid telling the malicious lies one so desperately wants to tell is exactly on a par with speaking with straightforward honesty. Perhaps this claim is based on the common notion that difficult actions require greater effort of will, and that this makes them all the more morally excellent. Fair enough, but surely it makes a difference where the difficulty comes from—from one's own appallingly mendacious character, say, or from the fact that one is poor and hungry, and lying would make procuring one's next meal so much easier (Foot 1978a, 11).

As a matter of common sense, therefore, there seems to be a difference between more and less central cases of morally excellent action. But why should the virtue ethicist suppose that being 'characteristic of a virtuous person' is a necessary feature of the central cases? The answer, I think, lies in the virtue ethicist's grounds for finding remedial actions to be excellent in any sense, in the first place. First, the virtue ethicist conceives of certain rules or standards of the virtues, such as 'Be honest' and 'Do what is charitable'. Of course, these rules cannot be codified into an algorithm for decision-making; they are too general, and require specification through practical wisdom (Hursthouse 1999a, 36–9 et passim; McDowell 1998). Rather, on this view moral development and improvement, and thus excellent remedial action, consist not in learning determinate rules and how to apply them, but in the task of adopting these rules as standards of one's own. To adopt these standards is to recognize that one ought to act in accordance with them, to accept that one is reasonably to be measured, praised, or criticized by reference to them, as the case may be, and to accept the task of growing into a mature understanding of what being honest or charitable amounts to.[18] Now on this view the excellence of

---

[18] This notion of 'accepting standards as one's own' is of a piece with a similar point that Donald Davidson makes about accepting standards of practical rationality as one's own. As Davidson (1985) says, to accept such standards is to accept, say, the rationality of all-things-considered judgments as a

remedial action consists in the fact that in turning over a new leaf, one begins to accept the standards of virtue as standards of one's own. In fact, in that respect there can even be something *virtuous* about remedial actions: taking steps to overcome habitual lying is an expression of one's commitment to the idea that honesty is a virtue, and is therefore a sort of 'first step' in honesty. And the same will be true of self-improving actions that are not remedial of an already distorted character, since those actions also express a developing acceptance of virtuous standards as one's own.[19]

We can now see why the virtue ethicist both treats some cases of excellent action as central, and restricts these cases to those that are characteristic of the virtuous. As we have just seen, for the virtue ethicist some cases of excellent action are actions that express a wholehearted or unqualified commitment to the standards of the virtues, such as honesty and charity, as standards of one's own. Remedial actions, then, are assessed in terms of the extent to which they approximate to a commitment to such standards of the virtues. Therefore, we need to understand the excellence of unqualified cases of excellent action before we can understand why certain remedial actions count as *improvements*, and thus as having any sort of excellence at all. However, we do not have to have a view about remedial actions in order to understand why the unqualified excellent actions are excellent. Consequently, it seems clear both that the unqualified cases of morally excellent action are central cases of morally excellent action, and that those cases are necessarily characteristic of the virtuous. And this is why it makes sense for the virtue ethicist to restrict right actions to those that are characteristic of the virtuous, since to do so is to restrict right actions to the central and unqualified cases of morally excellent action.[20]

However, one may still object that by restricting right action to these central cases, virtue ethics cannot give an adequate account of what is excellent about other sorts of cases, such as remedial actions. But I trust that by now such an objection will have lost much of its force. There is no reason to deny that remedial actions can be excellent, in some sense, but there is good reason to deny that they are *central* cases of excellent action, namely right actions. The same account that shows why remedial action is no central case of excellence

principle of one's own; the charge that one has violated that principle cannot be met with the response 'So I have broken your rule; who says I should do things your way?' By accepting the standard, one has made the 'rule' or principle a principle to which one sees oneself as bound.

[19]   Here I am in broad agreement with Valerie Tiberius (2006) that the way to approach this issue is to focus on the reasons for which the virtuous person acts, since the virtuous and the non-virtuous can act for the same reasons in very different contexts. (I take up the notion of 'the same reasons' in Ch. 6.)

[20]   It is worth repeating that although what a virtuous person would characteristically do is treated as a central case of right action, this is not to say that virtuous persons must be conceived as *perfectly* virtuous persons.

also shows what is excellent about it. It is therefore possible for virtue ethics to deny that such actions are on a par, without having to restrict all morally excellent action to 'what a virtuous person would characteristically do'. Instead, virtue ethics can take 'what a virtuous person would do' as a necessary feature of any central case of moral excellence, expressing full commitment to standards of virtues, and extend its analysis of excellent action based on such central cases to less central cases, such as remedial and other self-improving actions. The substantive issue here is whether virtue ethics can give a plausible account of what is morally excellent about actions of this latter sort, and it seems clear that it can.

So although Johnson maintains that the moral excellence of a remedial action is no 'second best', the real issue is that for virtue ethics such remedial actions are not excellent without qualification, and therefore cannot play a central role in an understanding of excellence. On the contrary, any excellence of a remedial action would be posterior to the excellence of virtuous action, and qualified accordingly. Not all *bona fide* cases of excellent action are central cases.

It is clear, therefore, both that the virtue ethicist's distinction between 'ought' and 'right' is plausible and defensible, and that given that distinction the 'right but not virtuous' objection does not go through. So much for that objection. I now turn briefly to a further issue in virtue ethics on which I think the right/ought distinction should be brought to bear.

While some critics of virtue ethics have not paid sufficient attention to the possibility that 'ought' may not imply 'right', I think that even some proponents of virtue ethics run into trouble by overlooking this possibility. I want to suggest that the denial of 'ought implies right' can ground a defense of a controversial point in Michael Slote's virtue ethics—a point about whether 'ought' implies 'can'—which I think is much more effective than the defense that he himself offers.

In *Morals from Motives*, Slote understands right action entirely in terms of virtuous motives, so that an action is right just in case it expresses a motive that is in fact virtuous, such as benevolence. Slote is aware that one difficulty for such a view arises from the fact that there can be cases in which one is obligated to do a certain action, even though one's motives for doing the action are vicious. For instance, in a well-known case of Sigdwick's, a prosecutor is obligated to prosecute a person for whom he feels great personal malice and ill-will. Slote's view seems to entail that whether the prosecutor prosecutes or not, he will act wrongly: if he prosecutes, then he acts maliciously, and therefore wrongly; and if he does not prosecute, then he neglects his obligation, showing insufficient concern for the duties of his office, and thus again acts wrongly. (For the sake of argument, set aside the possibility of the prosecutor's recusing himself.) As Slote (2001, 16) recognizes, such a case seems to force him to deny that 'ought' implies 'can', since 'if badly motivated people have obligations but everything they can do counts as wrong, they have obligations they are unable to fulfill'. The problem, Slote says, is not that the prosecutor is unable to *prosecute*, but that he is unable to do anything that is *right*. Since 'ought' implies 'can', the worry goes, there can be no 'ought' where all of one's options are wrong acts, and yet the prosecutor does seem obligated.

One way out of this problem, of course, is to deny that 'ought' implies 'can' (as some philosophers do), but Slote does not do so, and I too shall leave this more drastic approach to the side. Rather, Slote (2001, 17) proposes to solve this problem by maintaining that although 'one cannot simply change one's motives or character at will', still it is within the power of a person with a malicious character to refrain from acting from malice on some occasions. So, Slote argues, there is something the prosecutor can do that would be right, after all, namely to prosecute but not from malice. However, as Daniel Jacobson (2002, 59ff) is surely correct to point out, even if it is possible for the prosecutor to set aside his personal feelings of malice on some occasions, it does not follow that he must be capable of setting aside his personal feelings on *this* occasion.[21] So the problem stays put.

Jacobson himself suggests that Sidgwick's case shows that the evaluation of an act as right must remain a separate matter from the virtuousness of the agent's motives, *pace* Slote (see also Hurka 2001, 225; Stohr and Wellman 2002, 53f; Das 2003, 238). However, I think that this conclusion can be avoided if we do not suppose, as both Jacobson and Slote seem to do, that 'ought' implies 'right'.

How does the idea that 'ought' implies 'right' drive the prosecutor case? Let's take a closer look at the argument. We begin with the idea that there is something that the prosecutor ought to do, viz. to prosecute (perhaps because not prosecuting would express even worse motives). So there is a certain decision that the prosecutor ought to make. Now if we suppose that 'ought' implies 'right', then to say that there is something that the prosecutor *ought* to do is to say that there is something it would be *right* for the prosecutor to do. Consequently, if there is no right course of action open, then the prosecutor ought to do something that he cannot do, viz. a right action, and this result violates the principle that 'ought' implies 'can'. So, since either course of action

---

[21] Consider also that the motivation for policies guarding against conflicts of interest, for instance, is not only the fact that some people are not good enough to set aside personal feelings when they conflict with professional duty, but also that for each one of us there may be circumstances in which we would simply find it too difficult to set personal feelings aside, however good we may be.

would express a bad motive, and would therefore be wrong, there seems to be an 'ought' in this case, but no 'can'.

Now if we drop the assumption that 'ought implies right', it is not difficult to reconcile Slote's view with the principle that 'ought implies can'. To say that the prosecutor ought to prosecute is to say that the decision not to prosecute would be even worse, but we need not suppose that prosecuting would be a right action, either. Clearly, the prosecutor *can* prosecute the case, so the principle that 'ought implies can' remains intact. Of course, what he may well be unable to do, despite Slote's suggestion, is any action that can be assessed as 'right', that is, a good deed that gets a tick of approval and warrants the satisfactory review of his conduct. But that is a separate matter from whether or not there is something that the prosecutor ought to do, because 'ought' does not imply 'right'.

Having clarified the difference between action guidance and assessment, we can now move on to consider each in relation to the act constraint—that is, whether 'right action' must be subject to the act constraint in either of the twin senses of 'right'—beginning with 'right' in its action-guiding sense.

2.3.2 Action Guidance and the Account Constraint

Our serious practical concerns entitle us to an account of rightness that takes those concerns as seriously as they deserve. That is what both the account constraint and the act constraint say, although they differ over what 'taking seriously' comes to. But since an account of right action is actually an account of two things—of action guidance and of action assessment—we should ask whether meeting the account constraint is sufficient for an adequate account of those two things.

Put that way, I trust it is clear that meeting the account constraint is all that is needed for an account of action guidance. For instance, Michael Slote (2001, 34, cf. 17f *et passim*) argues that so-called 'agent-based' forms of virtue ethics, which derive rightness exclusively from motives and thus reject the act constraint, nonetheless

do take consequences in account because they insist on or recommend an overall state of motivation that worries about and tries to produce good consequences. Someone genuinely concerned with the well-being of another person wants good consequences for that other (for their own sake and independently of any ulterior motive).[22]

---

[22] I am therefore puzzled by Hurka's 2001, 224 claim that, on Slote's view, 'To determine what is right, [one] must examine the desires her actions would spring from rather than their objective qualities or likely effects'. Stohr and Wellman 2002, 52 argue that Slote's account is not action guiding in cases in which one's motive is to act rightly, since right action arises instead from motives of benevolence.

Likewise, consider Philippa Foot's (1978*c*, 167, 170) image of moral agents as an 'army' of benevolent people guided only by 'hypothetical imperatives'.[23] In such a world, awful things would still happen, of course, and would even result at times from the acts of benevolent people, since benevolence is not omniscience, even when backed up by phronesis. But from the perspective of our concerns about practical deliberation, it is difficult to see what more we could want from creatures remotely like ourselves, for whom omniscience is impossible anyway. In the sort of world that Foot describes, all our serious practical concerns are accounted for—not in the sense that they are all met in each benevolent act, but in the sense that the deliberation of right-acting agents, as modeled in the theory, takes those concerns as seriously as any deliberating agents can. What guidance could do better, given what we have to work with?

On this point even virtue ethicists who accept the act constraint are agreed. Indeed, it is a defining characteristic of virtue ethics that it denies that the task of such an account is to *solve* ethical problems. Instead, virtue ethics affirms the task of *modeling* deliberation about ethical problems, and is quite explicit in refusing to offer guarantees that actions chosen on that model will themselves satisfy all of our serious practical concerns. (I return to the modeling/solving distinction in Chapter 4.) As Robert Louden (1990) observes, in this respect virtue ethics departs from several traditional conceptions of the task of ethical theory as aimed primarily at solving ethical problems (see also Hursthouse 1999*a*, 39f, 53ff). On such views a theory aims not only to 'help agents decide what to do when they are faced with a moral problem', but indeed to guarantee good decisions, so that 'agents who correctly apply [such] theories will be able to *resolve* moral quandaries' (Louden 1990, 95, my emphasis, citing Brandt 1959, 1). Even more than that, ethical theory is sometimes aimed at solving agents' problems *for* them. This thought stems from the traditional expectation that ethical theories will give a 'decision procedure',[24] as well as from the expectation that such procedures be such that anyone can apply them correctly, regardless of their character, so that 'anyone who employs [such]

However, Slote does say that such conscientious motives, while not right, may nevertheless be 'all right'; see 2001, ch. 2.

[23] I shall return to Foot's view in the next chapter.

[24] As Louden 1990, 96 describes this expectation, 'Ethical theories are designed to solve moral problems rationally by providing agents with a step-by-step decision procedure. Theorists assume that agents who apply their decision procedures correctly will always reach correct answers. The steps to be taken can all be laid out discursively, thus eliminating guess-work, bias, subjectivism, and all other non-rational factors from moral deliberation.'

methods correctly will arrive at correct moral answers' (Louden 1990, 97; see also Hursthouse 2003, §3).[25]

As Louden rightly observes, here virtue ethics is a sort of 'protest' view. Hence the virtue ethicist's characteristic focus on moral dilemmas: as Foot points out (1983; see also Hursthouse 1999a, 66f; Hursthouse 1995a, 62f), there can be cases in which one's options are all equally *attractive*, with no moral concerns deciding between them, so why suppose that there must always be deciding moral concerns when one's options are all *unattractive*?[26] The startling optimism of traditional 'ethical theory' about dilemmas seems more an artifact of its commitment to a problem-solving decision procedure than a motivation for such a commitment. Virtue ethicists have also protested that such views reduce moral deliberation to following a set of prescribed steps, as when one fixes one's computer (Annas 2004; Annas 2006, §A.3.; Pincoffs 1986, 59f). Not only does such a model seem a gross over-simplification of moral life (Hursthouse 1999a, 59ff), but it also implies that the agent's decision-making should be detached from her conception of the good, and thus from herself, considered as an agent with a 'practical identity', in Christine Korsgaard's phrase. On such a model, ethical theory if successful has already solved the problems for the agent; she need only follow the steps.

When we consider a theory of right action as offering action guidance, virtue ethicists of all stripes accept the account constraint and reject the act constraint: our serious practical concerns entitle us to an account of rightness that takes those demands as seriously as they deserve, but they do not entitle us to an account of rightness that will guarantee that the actions it recommends will meet all of our concerns. Instead, virtue ethics—like many other normative theories—is an attempt to offer the best guidance that philosophers can offer in a world without guarantees. Consequently, disagreements among virtue ethicists over the act constraint must concern not action guidance but action assessment, so I turn to that now.

2.3.3 Action Assessment and the Account Constraint

Action guidance concerns the rightness of decisions, and action assessment the rightness of actions; but what is it to assess an 'action'? Consider a case that

---

[25] '[T]he theory of morality', Alan Donagan says, is 'a theory of a system of laws or precepts, binding upon all rational creatures as such, the content of which is ascertainable by human reason.' Donagan 1977, 8, cited in Louden 1990, 96.

[26] Not surprisingly, Louden 1990, 97 notes, ethical theory has traditionally held that all moral problems are solvable, and that no real dilemmas exist.

appears both in Hursthouse (1995a, 62–4; 1999, 71), who accepts the act constraint, as well as in Slote (2001, 39f), who does not: one's mother is dying, and one must decide whether or not to advocate heroic measures to keep her alive without any clear hope of pulling through. Whatever one does in this sort of case, the resulting state of affairs can only be described as very awful. Of course, someone in such a difficult situation can still act virtuously, both in how she decides what to do and in how she then goes about what she has decided to do—there can be a 'right' decision and thus action guidance (Hursthouse 1999a, 69–74, cf. 48; Hursthouse 1995a, 64f). Nonetheless, as we saw above, from the awfulness involved in the action (or, if you prefer, in what the action entails) Hursthouse concludes that the action cannot be right. But Slote (2001, 35, 5) denies this: in such a case, when one has been fully virtuous in one's deciding, 'the moral acceptability or rightness of action is insured by having good overall or total motivation'. This is so, because an 'agent-based approach to virtue ethics treats the moral or ethical status of acts as entirely derivative from independent and fundamental aretaic [roughly, virtue-based] (as opposed to deontic) ethical characterizations of motives, character traits, or individuals'.[27]

This disagreement about rightness is not a disagreement over the assessment of the resulting *states of affairs*, which all agree may be awful, but over the assessment of *actions*, which can be not only awful but also (unlike states of affairs) right or wrong (cf. Garcia 1992, 239). This disagreement about action assessment is more than a verbal issue, since it rests on a deeper disagreement about exactly what we are to assess when assessing an action. Both sides accept a distinction between two aspects of action that we might call an 'exercise of will', on the one hand, and an 'extension of the will into the world' on the other. For instance, 'acting mercifully, thoughtfully, and courageously' can be one description of an action that can also be described as 'allowing one's mother to die'. The former is a matter of how one deliberates, reasons, conducts oneself, and is motivated—in a word, how one exercises one's will—while the latter is a matter of one's action seen in terms of the repercussions it has out in the world.[28]

One source of this disagreement could be a radical disagreement over what action really is: we might say that allowing one's mother to die can be a right action because an action *is* only an exercise of the will. The view that action just is exercise of will is not new; the Stoics, for instance, held that even actions

---

[27] I discuss Slote's notion of 'fundamental aretaic concepts' in the next chapter.

[28] Of course, on Kant's view the determination of the will just is what constitutes agency; so this distinction is hardly peculiar to virtue ethics. See also Hursthouse 1999a, 46f, 79, who distinguishes between 'right decision' and 'right action'.

like walking should be seen in the first instance as a particular kind of exercise of soul.[29] And of course some virtuous actions, such as acts of moderation or 'determination',[30] seem to involve only exercises of the will, and we may suppose that an analysis of such actions could be extended further even to more outwardly tangible ones (and notice that even an act of determination is often an act of trying to do something out in the world).[31] Nonetheless, the view that allowing one's mother to die can be a right action does not require such a radical view of action as this.

A more plausible explanation is that this disagreement over action concerns the *range* of 'right action': on the one view, 'right action' ranges over only that element of an action that is the exercise of the will, while on the other, 'right action' ranges over the lot.[32] And it is not entirely obvious what the range of 'right action' has to be; we certainly cannot tell just by inspecting the concept. One reason for saying that the act of allowing one's mother to die cannot be right is that 'right' conveys the notion of a good deed, whereas allowing one's mother to die is a very regrettable act (Hursthouse 1999a, 44ff). But regret is not the same as repentance: one can experience sorrow that one's mother has died, even that it was through one's decision and action that she died, without repenting of one's action, and one may even give one's action—one's exercise of will—a 'tick of approval', in this sense.[33] After all, we have seen that there *is* a sense in which even such an action can be 'the right thing to do', namely when we focus on 'action' mainly as a decision.

Another reason to make 'rightness' range over actions as extending into the world is that we (English-speakers) often speak of doing 'the right thing for the wrong reasons', and of doing 'the wrong thing for the right reasons'. But of course, 'the right thing' can be reinterpreted as 'the outcome that a well-motivated person would try to bring about', as when we say (perhaps carelessly) that a novice chess player whose desperate move is in fact the most strategically advantageous move available, has made 'the right move'. Perhaps we should say instead that what *he* has done is to act desperately, even if in

---

[29] Seneca (*Letters* 113.23) reports that the Stoics Cleanthes and Chrysippus, while disagreeing about the details, agreed that walking is to be defined as an act of the 'leading part' of the soul; see Annas 1992, 99f.

[30] Swanton 2003, 235 considers a virtue of 'determination' to demonstrate that sometimes the aim or target of a virtue is internal to the agent, a kind of exercise of the will.

[31] Swanton 2003, 237 considers a similar conception of action, I think, when she says that the act of poisoning opossums, when done with regret and in order to save endangered trees, is not a *cruel* act, despite its effects on the opossums.

[32] Consider Slote 2001, 170: 'for all practical purposes choices *are* actions' (italics in original).

[33] See also Copp and Sobel 2004, 546. Note too that since all actions have opportunity costs, regret is a common feature of decision-making, in a way that repentance is not; I thank Mark LeBar for raising this point.

doing so he moved in just the way that a good chess player would have done (Garcia 1992, 243f).[34] In each case it is reasonable to expect a theory to preserve the basic, underlying idea and distinction behind the original expressions, but it is not reasonable to expect it to do so in the same (prejudicial) terms in which it is stated.

Likewise, we may point to the common practice of differentiating between, say, murder and attempted murder, as meriting different punishments, and conclude that rightness and wrongness must be understood, at least in part, in terms of an action's (actual) consequences (Gorr 1999). However, such a difference in punishment need not depend on a difference in wrongness between murder and attempted murder, but may depend instead on the difference in what one is responsible for—perhaps what 'debt to society' one has incurred—when a murder attempt is successful and when it is not (Garcia 1992, 248f; Garcia 1990, 84f).

Now it is beyond our present task to argue for one or the other of these two views. I mean to point out only that this is a *reasonable* disagreement: there is something to be said for each of these perspectives, and in any case neither is more 'virtue ethical' than the other.[35] Nor is this disagreement a simple one to settle; as we have seen, it cannot be settled by a simple appeal to common sense. Since these commonsense intuitions can be so readily reinterpreted, and since the disagreement need not be over the basic idea behind those intuitions anyway, there must be a deeper issue on which reasonable persons can take different sides, or even be unsure which side to take. The disagreement over the range of 'right action' discussed here is a disagreement over exactly that sort of deeper issue—over what aspect of action it is that we mean to assess with a theory of right action.[36] And of course disagreement over that issue *just is* a disagreement over the appropriateness of the act constraint. Consequently, neither plain common sense nor the special nature of virtue ethics requires a commitment to the act constraint for purposes of action assessment. Since the act constraint also has no place in virtue ethics for purposes of action guidance,

[34] Garcia (1992, 239, cf. 251) argues that rightness and wrongness, like virtue and vice, are what he calls 'input-dependent concepts' whose application 'depends on what goes into the action—beliefs, desires, intentions, reasoning, deliberation, etc.' See also Garcia 1990. Geach 1956, 41 reports a similar view in Aquinas. And, importantly, Hursthouse 1999a, 125 herself turns out also to have considerable resistance to the idea of doing the right thing for the wrong reasons.

[35] See Irwin 1990 for discussion of disagreement over this sort of issue between Stoic and Aristotelian virtue ethicists.

[36] Perhaps it may seem that, if rightness and wrongness of action depend only on the inner states of the agent expressed in action, then what is wrong with cruelty, say, has to do with the perpetrator of the cruelty rather than with its effects on the victim. But this does not follow, since one who rejects the act constraint could still maintain that what makes cruelty a bad inner state is its indifference to the reasons there are not to be cruel. I shall return to this issue at the end of the next chapter.

it follows that the act constraint is not a necessary constraint on virtue ethics, certainly not just as such, and certainly not by default. Therefore from the bare fact that some virtue ethical theory counts as right some act that does not satisfy some of our serious practical concerns, it does not follow that that theory is inadequate. The act constraint is not compulsory for virtue ethics, just as such, but only for virtue ethics plus further controversial premises about which different virtue ethicists can reasonably disagree.

This is a major step towards a framework for criticizing virtue ethical theories of right action, since it shows that any fair request for a virtue ethical account of right action must allow for different positions on the act constraint. However, even if virtue ethics as such need not accept the act constraint, the question remains whether it *can*.

2.4 *Can* Virtue Ethics Accept the Act Constraint?

By accepting the account constraint, virtue ethics takes outcomes and states of affairs seriously in its account of right action, without presupposing any conception of rightness that is based on states of affairs rather than on virtues. But the act constraint takes states of affairs seriously in a much deeper way: the rightness of action is actually contingent on states of affairs. This may well lead us to suppose that a virtue ethics that accepts the act constraint thereby smuggles in a prior conception of right action: can virtue ethics give such an important place to consequences and still retain its distinct identity? I argue that it can, but first we must look at what makes a theory distinctively 'virtue ethical' in the first place. Here we can build on work already begun on this question by Gary Watson and Rosalind Hursthouse.

2.4.1 *The VE Constraint*

It has become something of a standard formula that virtue ethics thinks of right action in terms of what 'the virtuous person' would do (Oakley 1996; Hursthouse 1999a; Stohr and Wellman 2002, 64f), although recently there has been a move away from it.[37] But whether or not that formula is necessary for a theory to be a virtue ethics, what concerns us at present is that it certainly is not sufficient. A moment's thought reveals that this is so because one may simply define rightness entirely independently of the virtues, and then characterize the virtues as dispositions to do actions that are right in that sense. For instance,

---

[37] I return to this issue in Ch. 4.

Rawls (1971, 436) glosses 'the moral virtues' as 'the strong and normally effective desires to act on the basic principles of right', where the specification of those principles themselves is entirely prior to the notion of the virtues (Watson 1990, 449; see also Louden 1984, 227). Likewise, Jeremy Bentham (1973, 89, cited in Louden 1984, 227) understood a virtue as a 'tendency to give a net increase to the aggregate quantity of happiness in all its shapes taken together' (see also Annas 2002, 1f and references).

Such accounts of right action are not virtue ethical because they involve background accounts of the virtues on which right action is prior to virtue. Rosalind Hursthouse (1999a, 30f; see also McDowell 1997, 141) makes the point by observing that Rawls' and Bentham's ways of tying right action to the virtues are 'truisms': right action is antecedently defined independent of the virtues, the virtues are conceived as dispositions to do such right action, and so it is not only true but a truism that actions done from the virtues are right actions.[38] So more generally, as Gary Watson has argued, what sets a virtue ethical account of right action apart from these other sorts of accounts is the fact that virtue ethics (a) makes the notion of a virtue prior to right action, in the sense that a virtue can be understood apart from a formula of right action, and (b) holds that right action cannot be fully understood apart from an account of the virtues.[39]

---

[38] It is possible to generate this truism because it is possible to use 'virtuous action' or 'virtuous person' merely to speak of good or praiseworthy actions or persons, in whatever sense of 'good' or 'praiseworthy' one likes; see Slote 1992, 10 and references. I shall return to this issue in Ch. 10, where I argue that the very attempt to define the virtues in terms of a prior conception of right action is in fact highly problematic.

[39] See Watson 1990, 451f: (a) 'virtue must be intelligible independently of the notion of right conduct', and (b) 'the basic moral facts are facts about the quality of character. Moral facts about action are ancillary to these'; likewise, 'the concept of proper or right conduct will be well understood only if the concept of virtue is' (1990, 454). This 'priority' does not mean that an account of the virtues develops in a vacuum, apart from any antecedent ideas about what kinds of actions are right. e.g. Aristotle observes that becoming virtuous involves learning things like, 'Just people do things like this, and do not do things like that' (see Hursthouse 1997, 220n., citing Aristotle, NE III.1, 1110a22; see also Hursthouse 1999a, 38f, 60f; cf. Copp and Sobel 2004, 519). Das 2003, 331–3 has recently objected that a view like Aristotle's must therefore rely upon 'an unexplained concept of right action'. And in a sense, of course it does; but in the same sense, every ethical theory begins with some 'concept' of right action, and moves back and forth between some fixed ideas (provisional and otherwise) about what sorts of actions are right and what sorts wrong, on the one hand, and a set of more theoretical ideas that attempt to organize and inform our understanding of what one should do, on the other.

Likewise, it is important to notice that Watson's criteria do not rule out defining virtue in terms of certain sorts of action or conduct, but only defining virtue in terms of a prior conception of the rightness of action. We can, with e.g. Aristotle, understand the virtues as fundamentally active traits, i.e. traits which are such as to express themselves in actions of particular sorts. Con. Santas 1993, 11–15 who argues that Aristotle does not have a virtue ethics, on the grounds that Aristotle understands virtue not merely as an inner state, but primarily as the exercise of a disposition in activity, and that Aristotle

I shall call Watson's two-part condition the 'VE constraint' for short (although I shall modify it in a moment). The VE constraint is important for understanding what makes virtue ethics—as diverse as that category is—a distinctive kind of ethics; surely it is not distinctive just for taking the notion of virtue and character seriously, say, as if other approaches had not done this (see Nussbaum 1999, 163–7). The VE constraint also reveals, I think, a common ground among otherwise very disparate virtue ethicists, one that represents a substantial and distinctive commitment in ethical theory (*pace* Nussbaum 1999). Now it is clear that the VE constraint is a necessary condition on a theory of right action counting as a kind of virtue ethics. It is also clear that virtue ethical theories that accept the act constraint can also meet the VE constraint: even if the rightness of action is dependent on outcomes, it can still be the case that right action cannot be fully understood without an account of the virtues, whereas the virtues can be understood without an account of right action. But is meeting the VE constraint also *sufficient* for a theory's being virtue ethical? Or does the act constraint effectively smuggle in a prior conception of right action, after all?

2.4.2 Is the Act Constraint a Smuggler?

Consider two things. One, given the act constraint, the notion of a good outcome or state of affairs is prior to an account of right action in exactly the same sense that virtue is supposed to be: right action cannot be fully understood without an account of good outcomes, whereas good outcomes can be understood without an account of right action. And two, so far from reducing ethical concepts to the virtues, virtue ethics holds that the notion of a good outcome is prior to virtue in this sense, as well (Hursthouse 1999*a*, 81–3; Watson 1990, 451).[40] This does not mean that a virtue is simply defined

therefore violates Watson's criteria by rejecting 'the priority in definition of states of character over conduct'.

[40] McAleer 2007 reads Watson as holding that for virtue ethics, virtuousness must be prior not only to rightness but also to goodness. I do not read Watson this way; but in any case, that is not my view here, with which I think McAleer (see 216) would probably agree. See also Annas 1993*a*, 9: 'In [ancient virtue ethics], the notions of the agent's final end, of happiness and of the virtues are what may be called primary, as opposed to basic. These are the notions that we start from; they set up the framework of the theory, and we introduce and understand the other notions in terms of them. They are thus primary for understanding.... However they are not basic in the modern sense: other concepts are not derived from them, still less reduced to them.'

It must be noted, though, that Hursthouse 1999*a*, 82 says that virtue ethics requires 'some sort of reduction' of right action to virtue, and Copp and Sobel 2004, 547 and n. 76 make much of this. This contrasts sharply with Hursthouse 1995*a*, 72: 'a common misunderstanding of virtue ethics ... [is] that virtue ethics, in being agent-centred rather than act-centred, in starting with the virtues and vices rather than right or wrong acts, is committed to a sort of reductionism'. However, Hursthouse 1999*a*, in terms of the production of good outcomes,[41] but notice that the virtue of mercy, say, cannot be fully understood without an account of the goodness of freedom from suffering, whereas the latter good can be understood without any account of the virtue of mercy.[42] Now if good outcomes are prior to rightness, *and* if the rightness of a virtuous action is contingent on the goodness of outcomes (given the act constraint), should we conclude that the act constraint smuggles in an outcome-based conception of right action?

I do not think that this conclusion follows.[43] On the view in question, a bad outcome upsets rightness of action only indirectly: a bad outcome keeps the action from being virtuous, and *for that reason* keeps it from being right. Let me explain.

Given the act constraint, a benevolent person's registering the awfulness of the upshot of her action involves her refusing to assess her action as 'right'. So, for instance, failing to protect consumers or the environment through one's policy-making, or killing opossums in order to save endangered trees (Swanton 2003, 229f, 237), are as much a part of one's action as the good intentions with which one decides upon and carries out one's action, and on the view in question, just as much within the range of 'right' and 'wrong'. Now part of having a virtue is to have what Williams (1995a) and Hursthouse (1995b) have called 'virtue reasons', which are the sorts of aims that it is characteristic of virtuous persons to have, such as preserving the truth, establishing fairness,

---

82f speaks of the 'reduction' of one concept to another, where in fact she seems to mean the priority of the latter concept to the former, and I think that her remarks about the 'reduction' of right action should be interpreted in the same light.

[41] Watson 1990, 459: although a virtue ethical account of right action appeals at several stages to 'several notions of good... at no stage need there be an essential appeal to the idea of a valuable state of affairs or outcome from which the moral significance of everything (or anything) else derives.... To put it another way, it will follow from an ethics of virtue that virtuous people care about certain things (and outcomes) for their own sakes (as final ends in themselves). There is no further requirement, however, to the idea that these concerns are virtuous ones *because* their objects are inherently valuable or desirable for their own sakes.' (Emphasis added.) For a theory of the virtues that does accept the latter idea, see Hurka 2001, 11–23; see also Copp and Sobel 2004, 515f for discussion.

[42] Likewise, as I argue in the next chapter, we cannot understand genuine benevolence or benevolent acts, for instance, without understanding what someone's being helped (as opposed to merely being the object of someone's good intentions) consists in; yet we can understand the latter without the former. See also Hursthouse 1999a, 81f; Hursthouse 1995a, 72–4. Con. Kawall 2002, 217, 'the virtues will lead us to value certain outcomes, etc., but the value of the outcomes is derivative from the virtues'.

[43] One way to avoid such a conclusion, which I shall mention but not pursue here, is to deny that goodness is prior to virtue after all. e.g. virtue ethicists could hold that 'good' and 'bad' are properties of states of affairs in virtue of how persons with the right sorts of reasons would respond to them—that is, that such properties are 'response-dependent'—and that such a notion of right reasons makes virtue prior to goodness and badness of states of affairs after all. I thank Mark LeBar for this suggestion. Con. Copp and Sobel 2004, 546f, who present a dichotomy between the view that 'a rightness or a goodness... is already there in the action to be detected' and the view that 'acts are right or good because virtuous persons would perform them'.

saving what is of value, and so on (see also Audi 1997*b*, 180; Zagzebski 1996, 99; Swanton 2003, ch. 11). To be benevolent, then, is (among other things) to have the characteristic aim of making others' lives better, to protect others from needless danger, to protect the environment, to avoid causing suffering in others, and so on.

In that case, we might say that when a benevolent person must instead concede defeat and allow another to die, or must kill opossums to save trees, her benevolence has been *frustrated*: benevolence does not do in this case what one, *qua* benevolent, has a *pro tanto* reason to do. In a word, here benevolence does not do what benevolence characteristically aims at doing. This is, I think, why Hursthouse makes the point by imagining how a virtuous person would assess *her own* action in such an awful situation: such a person does not count her action as right, because she recognizes that, among all the ways in which her benevolent *exercise of will* may extend into the world, there is none that is a really *benevolent thing* to do. She has not done the 'wrong thing', since she has acted well, but the benevolent person may well hold that there simply was no benevolent thing, and therefore—precisely because of her benevolence—that there was no right thing to do in that situation.[44] On the other hand, someone who harms or fails to protect consumers or the environment despite his best efforts may be said to have done 'the wrong thing for the right reasons', where the notion of 'the wrong thing' is understood as 'what virtue reasons would have one not do'.[45]

In all of these sorts of cases, the rightness of action is contingent on outcomes, but only in the sense that in such cases *virtue itself* is frustrated and hindered in its characteristic sorts of aims where states of affairs are concerned, and it is *for that reason* that the action is not right, that is, fails to warrant the satisfactory review of one's conduct. So the VE constraint must be understood in greater detail: the notion of virtue's priority to an account of right action must be understood as also including virtue's priority, not necessarily to the notion of good outcomes, but *to the notion that outcomes can bear on the rightness of*

---

[44] Indeed, Hursthouse 1999*a*, 74ff holds that in very awful situations a person with the virtue reasons may find his or her life marred by having had to do what, being virtuous, he or she cannot bear the thought of doing. Hursthouse (1999*a*, 33) also points out the falsity of the idea that deontology is indifferent to consequences, noting that 'many actions we deliberate about only fall under rules or principles when we bring in their predicted consequences'; I think that a similar point holds for virtue ethics: an action's consequences matter for whether it can properly be classified as merciful, say, or fair.

[45] The notion of 'what virtue reasons would have one not do' is clearly connected to what Foot 1983, 396 describes as 'the inevitable loss involved ... when one really good thing which the man of virtue must cherish has to be sacrificed for another'. It is therefore difficult to understand Louden's (1984, 230f) influential objections that virtue ethics cannot correctly assess the outcomes of actions that go wrong despite the agent's excellence of character, that virtue ethics cannot 'recognize the wrong in Oedipal behavior', that virtue ethics cannot say why intolerable acts are intolerable, etc.

action. Notice also that this understanding of what is meant by 'virtuous action' does not make the connection between virtue and right action a truism: it is hardly a truism that having a certain kind of excellent character trait—a form of practical wisdom, or attunement to the mean, or type of psychic health, or type of inner strength—consists in (among other things) adopting just such-and-such sorts of characteristic aims.[46]

Furthermore, it is now clear that meeting the VE constraint is not only a necessary but also a sufficient condition for an account of right action to be a virtue ethics. As we have seen, the VE constraint entails that the bearing of outcomes on rightness must be understood in terms of the failure of an action to be virtuous, considered not merely as an exercise of will but as an extension into the world. In that case, the VE constraint holds that virtue must be prior to *any* conception of rightness in action assessment, and so satisfying the VE constraint is sufficient for an account of right action to be a virtue ethical one. Therefore, a virtue ethics that accepts the act constraint can also satisfy the VE constraint. So there is no smuggling.

Conclusion

It has not been my primary aim to forestall objections to virtue ethical theories of right action, but only to call for a recess from objecting just long enough to ask where the boundaries are. This involves considering carefully just what is required of a virtue ethical account of right action, and what sorts of options are available to virtue ethicists within those requirements. Nonetheless, doing even that much does reveal that many common objections against virtue ethics are not nearly as compelling as at first they seem.

These steps towards a more general framework for right action for virtue ethics have put us in a better position to size up virtue ethical theories of right action on their own terms. It has also revealed a minimal formal constraint on any such theory, namely what I have called the 'account constraint'. Ultimately, our aim is to determine whether virtue ethics must make phronesis part of all the virtues if it is to yield a credible account of right action. Such an account need not hold that acting from virtue is sufficient for right action, necessarily, but it should at least show that acting from virtue is reliable in bringing

---

[46] Indeed, virtuous agents need not have the same sorts of aims, even relative to the same virtue, such as benevolence: some benevolent persons will have benevolent aims that are cautious and risk-averse, some guardedly optimistic, some full of unflagging hope, and so on. Cf. Hursthouse 1999a, 70; Pincoffs 1986, 20ff.

about right action, and is considerably more likely to bring about right action than not. Wouldn't it be something if it followed from the minimal account constraint that virtue ethics must do so! In fact, I argue in the rest of Part I that that is precisely what does follow. In the next chapter, I argue that the account constraint entails not only that virtuous deliberation must take seriously all our serious practical concerns, but also that such deliberation must involve good specifications of virtuous ends, and that in order to account for right action in terms of virtues, the virtues must make such good specifications reliably and intelligently. In that case, forging a credible link between virtue and right action means understanding virtue as involving excellence in deliberation, that is, phronesis. And I argue in Chapter 4 that phronesis, so far from being the unattainable ideal it has been supposed to be, is such that being '*phronimos* enough' is sufficient for being *phronimos* indeed, and that a virtue ethical account of right action must hold that virtuous deliberation must also involve 'phronesis enough'. If I am correct, then real virtue ethics just is Hard Virtue Ethics.

3

Right Action and Virtuous Motives

In his recent book *Morals from Motives*, Michael Slote has given his most complete statement to date of a view he calls 'agent-based virtue ethics'. This view consists of two theses, one about the nature of rightness and one about the nature of virtuousness. The thesis about rightness is that a right action is right solely on account of the virtuous motivations that produced it. And the thesis about virtuousness is that, on the one hand, actions become virtuous only on account of the virtuousness expressed by the agent in doing the action, and on the other that the virtuousness of an agent and an agent's motives is a 'fundamental' notion and not grounded in anything else.

Notice, then, that the first thesis of agent-based virtue ethics rejects what I have called (in the previous chapter) the 'act constraint' on right action, and accepts only the weaker 'account constraint': 'in an important sense agent-based moralities do take consequences in account', Slote (2001, 34) says, 'because they insist on or recommend an overall state of motivation that worries about and tries to produce good consequences. Someone genuinely concerned with the well-being of another person wants good consequences for that other (for their own sake and independently of any ulterior motive)'. As we saw in the previous chapter, such a view is certain to be controversial, but for all that I think that it is a view that the agent-based virtue ethicist is surely entitled to take; at the very least, it offends against neither virtue ethics *per se* nor plain common sense, so I shall be content to let it stand.

However, to date the literature critical of Slote's view has focused almost exclusively on the thesis about rightness. This is rather surprising, since although both theses are controversial, it is the thesis about the fundamentality of virtuousness that seems the more ambitious and indeed problematic one. It is that second thesis that is the sole focus of this chapter.

More specifically, Slote's thesis about virtuousness entails the rejection of two important and prominent ideas about the virtues. First, most virtue ethicists have seen the virtuous person as characteristically engaged in deliberation in order to find what would be, say, a benevolent action in the circumstances at hand, and then choosing that action because it is a benevolent one. Slote, however, rejects such a picture of the virtuous person's choices, arguing instead that virtuous persons do not choose virtuous actions, but make the actions they choose virtuous by the very act of choosing them from their virtuous inner states. Consequently, Slote rejects the notion of deliberative excellence or phronesis, arguing that phronesis is redundant if one really is virtuous. Whereas Aristotle, say, would see the benevolent as relying on phronesis or practical wisdom in their efforts to do good for people, Slote argues that the benevolent person's goodness of heart does the work of wisdom already. For instance, it is a virtue in a parent to balance his love and attention among his children, but, Slote argues, such balance does not require wisdom—or even, apparently, deliberation—since genuine parental love has built into it the disposition to give affection and attention to each of one's children anyway.

And second, whereas many virtue ethicists ground their account of the virtues in a prior conception of the human good, as is perhaps clearest in the case of classical eudaimonism, Slote takes the notion that benevolence, say, is a virtue to be fundamental and grounded in no other account. The fact that benevolence is a virtue is clear, on his view, from the fact that people just do find such a trait to be an admirable one and its absence deplorable. Slote therefore rejects any form of naturalism as grounding a theory of the virtues.

I think that the thesis of the fundamentality of the virtues raises three major types of problems for agent-based virtue ethics. One concerns the agent-based model of virtuous practical reasoning, which I argue turns out to require precisely the sorts of deliberations that it professes to reject in the Aristotelian model. The second problem is that although agent-based virtue ethics could be modified to allow that model of deliberation, it must nonetheless hold that the deliberative excellence of virtuous persons—their responsiveness to real reasons—is *not* what explains why such persons count as virtuous. Instead, agent-based virtue ethics explains virtuousness only in terms of such concepts as admirability, and I shall argue that such explanations of virtuousness render the agent-based account of the virtues both parochial and a form of intuitionism. And third, if virtue concepts are fundamental, then we can give no answer as to why a person ought to be benevolent, unless they happen to have reasons to want to be 'admirable' rather than 'deplorable'. Let me begin by briefly laying out the basic structure of agent-based virtue ethics and distinguishing it from other types of virtue ethics, and then I shall explore these three objections.

3.1 The Structure of Agent-Based Virtue Ethics

3.1.1 Classification

Slote says that 'an agent-based form of virtue ethics...treats the moral or ethical status of actions as entirely *derivative* from independent and *fundamental* ethical/aretaic facts (or claims) about the motives, dispositions, or inner life of moral individuals' (2001, 7, italics in original, see also 5).[1] So agent-based virtue ethics proceeds along two dimensions. One dimension concerns *rightness*: the rightness of an act is entirely derivative from the virtuous motive the agent expresses in doing the action. The other dimension concerns *virtuousness*, and breaks into a further two issues. One, the virtuousness *of action* is derivative from the virtuousness of the agent in doing it: there is no such thing as the 'courageous thing to do' apart from what a person does in expressing a courageous inner state. And two, the virtuousness *of agents* is fundamental: what makes an agent virtuous must be expressible exclusively in 'aretaic' terms, such as 'admirable' or 'excellent'.[2] We can summarize these two dimensions in this way: rightness derives from virtuousness, and virtuousness is fundamental.

These two dimensions allow Slote to classify different versions of virtue ethics, and thus to isolate what is distinctive about agent-basing. One alternative to agent-based virtue ethics is the sort of Aristotelian view we briefly sketched earlier, which holds both that the rightness of an action is not entirely derivative from virtuous motives, and that the virtues are not fundamental. A virtue ethics of this sort Slote calls 'agent-focused virtue ethics'. Second, a less radical alternative to agent-basing would agree that rightness of action derives entirely from virtuousness of motive, but deny that virtuousness is a fundamental concept. This sort of view Slote calls 'agent-prior virtue ethics', and one such view, he says, is Plato's, who he says assesses actions 'by reference to the health and virtue of the soul', but bases the virtuousness of souls in their appreciation of the Form of the Good, which 'represents a level of evaluation prior to the evaluation of souls' (2001, 7, see also 20f).[3] Finally, the third alternative is to deny that rightness of action derives entirely from

---

[1] Jacobson 2002, 55 formulates 'Slote's account of right and wrong' thus: 'An act is right if it expresses (or "reflects" or "manifests"—Slote uses these terms interchangeably) a virtuous motive, and wrong if it expresses a vicious (or "inferior") motive'. See also Garcia 1990, 75: it is the viciousness of acts 'as expressions of vicious attitudes in the agents that determines their moral wrongness'. Moreover, Garcia 1992, 247 also agrees that 'The moral duties we owe one another all derive from and center on forms of benevolence.' However, unlike Slote, Garcia 1992 holds that the goodness of the agent's motive or intention is necessary but not sufficient for rightness of action.

[2] Slote does not make the notion of 'aretaic' concepts much more precise than this, but hopefully the idea is clear enough for the purpose of discussing his view.

[3] This classification simplifies Slote's own use of these terms. Slote uses 'agent-focused virtue ethics' generically to describe all types of virtue ethics as having a 'focus' on the agent. But on

virtuousness of motive, but agree that the virtues are fundamental. Slote does not consider this sort of view in *Morals from Motives*, although his view in his 1992 book *From Morality to Virtue* seems to have been a version of it (see esp. 1992, 89f). Otherwise, though, this view seems unattested, and in that case, it is the second dimension of agent-based virtue ethics—the fundamentality of virtue—that makes agent-based virtue ethics unique. So now I want to consider the fundamentality of virtue in greater detail, since it is here that I think the most serious problems lie for Slote's attempts to make phronesis redundant.

3.1.2 The Fundamentality of Virtue

What does the fundamentality of the virtues amount to? Slote's discussion of this idea is indirect, and he focuses mainly on various alternatives to the fundamentality of virtue that he rejects. As Slote (2001, 5) reads Aristotle, Aristotle holds that the virtuousness of agents is explained in terms of the reliable ability to identify and do what would be, say, a courageous or just action, where the latter notion 'is treated as in some measure independent of agent-evaluations'.[4] On an interpretation of Aristotle he attributes to Rosalind Hursthouse, the virtuousness of agents is explained in terms of 'judgments about, a conception of, *eudaimonia*', or human flourishing (Slote 2001, 6). In each case, Slote refuses to ground virtuousness in any 'level of evaluation prior to the evaluation of souls' or agents (2001, 7), which is also his basis for rejecting the apparently Platonic view that virtuousness is grounded in recognition of the Form of the Good. Slote (2001, 8) also rejects the Humean view that the virtuousness of motives is based, to some extent, on the utility of such motives, as well as a type of Christian ethic, perhaps to be found in Augustine, that grounds the virtuousness of *agape*-love in the duty to obey God, who enjoins such love (2001, 9).[5]

---

this usage, we must describe a virtue ethical view that rejects both dimensions of agent-basing as, somewhat awkwardly, 'agent-focused, but neither agent-prior nor agent-based' (2001, 8). Slote also treats agent-prior virtue ethics as generic at the next level down, such that an agent-based view is also agent-prior, but not necessarily vice versa. Not surprisingly, some of Slote's commentators have taken to restricting these categories to a specific rather than a generic use, and I have followed this practice. Cp., e.g., Zagzebski 1996, 78ff and Das 2003, 325; Stohr and Wellman 2002, 49, on the other hand, are scrupulously faithful to Slote's own use.

[4] According to Slote, Aristotle holds that one can do a right action without having a virtuous motive (for instance, one may do a right action merely under the direction of another), and also 'characterizes the virtuous individual as someone who *sees* or *perceives* what is good or fine or right to do in any given situation' (2001, 5). Slote describes this view as 'intuitionistic' (p. 7), but con. Hursthouse 2006a.

[5] Slote also considers two versions of Christian ethics that he finds consistent with agent-basing: one that grounds the virtuousness of *agape*-love in its moral goodness and praiseworthiness, and one that grounds it in the notion of gratitude to God (2001, 9).

Likewise, Slote rejects the idea that an action can be virtuous in any other sense than that an agent has done that action from a virtuous inner state. By contrast, Slote (2001, 5) says, Aristotle 'implies that the virtuous individual does what is noble or virtuous because it is the noble—for example, courageous—thing to do, rather than its being the case that what is noble—or courageous—to do has this status simply because the virtuous individual actually will choose or has chosen it'. On Aristotle's view, an action can be virtuous if it conforms to certain standards of appropriateness—a notion that Aristotle calls *to prepon*, 'the fitting' or 'the appropriate', which is a central feature of his thesis that a virtuous action lies in a 'mean' that is discerned by 'right reason' (*orthos logos*). Slote's position on the virtuousness of action is tied to his position on the virtuousness of agents:

[I]n the case of Aristotle, choice lying in a mean between vices is according to (what is sometimes translated as) 'right reason', and a rational and virtuous individual has a disposition to make such choices. But here (as analogously elsewhere in Aristotle's ethics) the disposition seems to be virtuous or good because of the way it leads to rational, virtuous, or 'noble' choices, so rather than in agent-based fashion understanding the rationality of choices in terms of independently characterized rational motives or dispositions, the status of the latter would appear at least partly to derive from the former, so that the theory isn't agent-based.   (Slote 2001, 171)

Since the disposition to make such choices cannot be understood as a disposition to make choices that are virtuously made, on pain of circularity, the virtuousness of those choices must be understood in some other terms, and thus is not fundamental (see 2001, 5f).

What precisely, then, does the fundamentality thesis reject? One interpretation of that thesis would be that all other ethical or evaluative concepts must be derived from aretaic concepts, but Slote (2001, 197) rightly denies this; in fact, Slote allows that aretaic concepts and claims about human well-being can be 'fundamental and occupy the ground floor together' (1997, 210). Another interpretation would be that the virtue status of certain traits and persons can be explained in terms of no other concepts at all, but Slote allows that such status can be explained in terms of concepts like 'admirable' and 'morally good'.[6] For Slote, the key is that such concepts are other *aretaic* concepts, that is, concepts that are in the same fairly tight circle as our virtue concepts, so that the concepts that explain the virtuousness of certain motives are all concepts at the same level as the virtues themselves.

---

[6] Slote also says (2001, 18) that the 'fundamental admirability of certain motives' can be called into question if they lead to actions that are 'intuitively unacceptable'; it is difficult to know what this claim means, and I shall return to it later.

Consequently, it seems clear that agent-based virtue ethics makes virtue fundamental in the relatively weak sense that the status of a virtue as a virtue is to be explained only in terms of concepts that are themselves also in the sphere of aretaic concepts—concepts like 'admirable', most notably. Moreover, the fundamentality thesis is therefore also the thesis that aretaic concepts can be understood as underived. Treating that thesis as a thesis about explanations also jibes with Slote's claims that we distinguish 'ethical theories by which of the main ethical concepts—the good, the right, and virtue—they make explanatorily primary, and only agent-based forms of virtue ethics *do* treat virtue (claims/facts about what is admirable or morally good in people) as explanatorily primary' (2001, 7, italics in original). Of course, as Gary Watson (1990, 454) points out, all virtue ethics, as such, make the concept of virtue 'primary', in the sense that 'the concept of proper or right conduct will be well understood only if the concept of virtue is', and Watson has in mind specifically forms of virtue ethics that ground virtuousness via ethical naturalism. So Slote must mean that only agent-based virtue ethics makes virtue 'primary' in the sense of not grounding it in or deriving it from any non-aretaic evaluative concepts (including naturalistic ones).

Having clarified Slote's conception of fundamentality, I want to examine now the first half of the fundamentality thesis—namely the view that the virtuousness of an *act* is entirely derivative from virtuousness of motive—before turning to the second half about the virtuousness of *motives* and *agents* themselves.

3.2 Virtuous Acts and Virtuous Motivations

It may seem obvious that benevolence—Slote's Ur-virtue—requires judgments about the good, but such judgments play a remarkably small part in Slote's theory of virtuous practical reasoning, and perhaps this idea is not so obvious after all. Indeed, even in heart-wrenching cases such judgments may be redundant, as they seem to be in Slote's case of a woman who must decide how to care for her elderly mother who has suddenly developed a life-threatening condition. Assuming that this woman is benevolent, Slote (2001, 18) says, she 'must be open to, seek contact with, and be influenced by the world around her—her decisions will not be made in splendid causal/epistemic isolation from what most of us would take to be the morally relevant realities'. This is so, on an agent-based view, because the absence of such appreciativeness is 'deplorable'—demonstrating 'indifference or callousness' toward others (2001, 40). Since this benevolent woman must decide whether or not to advocate heroic life-extending measures, she will—because benevolent—seek to 'find out more about her mother's condition and prospects, as regards quality and duration of life and certainly as regards future suffering and incapacity' (2001, 40). Assuming (with Slote) that all these facts

> have emerged and assuming they are fairly clear-cut and point to horrendously painful and debilitating prospects for her mother, the woman's decision is ... plausibly derivable from morality as benevolence. At that point, it would be callous of her to insist on heroic measures and benevolent or kind not to do so and the proper moral decision can thus be reached by agent-based considerations.   (Slote 2001, 40; for another case involving 'obvious facts', see 105f)

So it would seem that once the woman knows the relevant facts, there is no further deliberation required—the very structure of her benevolence determines what to do next. As Slote (2001, 40) puts it, her decision is 'derivable from morality as benevolence'. Slote does have a point: if one has the benevolent wish to save one's mother from suffering, and it becomes clear that allowing her to die peacefully is the best way to save her from suffering, what is there to deliberate about? (See also Herman 1993, 145f.) On this model, one does not find the benevolent act, but is, so to speak, naturally drawn to a particular act by one's very benevolence, and it is choosing and doing the act from *that* sort of motivation that makes the act benevolent.

Thus while Slote (2001, 27) suggests that benevolent persons need some 'conception of human well-being' or other, deliberation about human well-being plays virtually no role in his account of virtuous practical reasoning. Instead, the role usually assigned to phronesis is replaced by Slote's notion of 'balance'. Slote illustrates balance with the example of a loving father of two children, one of whom suffers from a serious disability. While this father will invest more of his time and resources in the disabled child, he loves his other child too, and that very love *just will* strike an appropriate balance in his treatment of his children. On this view, 'balance' results not from phronesis and deliberation, but simply from letting one's love and benevolence have its own way. In fact, Slote (2001, 67) says, striking a balance by deliberating would show a lack of love, because balance is woven into the very fabric of love. And this is just what the fundamentality of the virtuousness of action requires, since that thesis holds that the virtuousness of an act consists in its being benevolently chosen. In that case, the virtuous person cannot be seen as deliberating about what act would be virtuous in the case at hand. There is therefore no room for phronesis.

Perhaps agent-based virtue ethics is a sort of 'benevolent intuitionism': the choiceworthiness of an act is immediately apparent to an intuitive faculty, in this case, 'a good heart that seeks to do good for and by people' (Slote 2001, 42). Of course, such judgments are not made in isolation from the relevant particular facts. But as H. A. Prichard pointed out, taking such facts into account does not make judgment any less intuitive, but only gathers the material on which one's intuitive faculty is to work (1912, 27–9). Still, I think this charge of 'benevolent intuitionism' is too quick, because, as I argue now, the very idea of a benevolent motive involves deliberation that goes beyond bare intuiting that benevolence, as a primitive property of acts, holds of a certain act.[7] However, this defense of agent-based virtue ethics will remove the distance that Slote sees between himself and Aristotle regarding deliberation; and what is more, intuitionism will reappear for Slote's view elsewhere.

3.2.1 Benevolence, Balance, and Wisdom

Recall from Chapter 1 Aristotle's model of virtuous deliberation and practical reasoning, which includes three main elements (NE VI.12). One of these Aristotle calls the 'aim' or 'target' or 'mark' (Greek skopos), and Aristotle says that virtue makes one's aim the right one. Another element Aristotle calls 'cleverness' (Greek deinotēs), which is 'such that, when it comes to the things that conduce to a proposed mark, it is able to carry these out and do so successfully' (1144a24–6). The notion of the 'mark' corresponds to wanting to do what is best for one's mother, say, or wanting to give one's children plenty of attention, while 'cleverness' would include finding out relevant facts about one's mother's situation, and clearing one's schedule to make room for activities that one's children enjoy.

The third element in Aristotle's model is phronesis, which also concerns hitting the 'mark', but in a different way: 'Virtue', Aristotle says, 'makes the mark right, and phronesis makes right the things towards this mark' (NE VI.12, 1144a7–9, my translation). Cleverness finds the most effective means to fulfilling one's end, but phronesis determines what fulfilling one's end amounts to. To borrow an analogy from Aristotle, the physician does not deliberate (obviously) about whether her mark is to heal her patient, nor, yet, about what medicines or procedures to use, but first about what constitutes healing in the case at hand (cf. III.3, 1112b11–20). Likewise, phronesis determines what

---

[7] I shall say more about intuitionism in §3.3.3.

hitting the 'mark' of justice or courage is, by exercising an understanding of what is worthwhile, beneficial, and 'what sorts of things conduce to the good life in general' (VI.5, 1140b5−6).

The distinction between cleverness and phronesis points to a more general difference between two kinds of practical reasoning: one that has to do with the *execution* of one's plan, and one that has to do with the *formulation* of plans with an eye on what is good for human beings. The former, then, concerns questions like 'How can I best do what is benevolent in this case?', and the latter concerns questions like 'What would be benevolent in this case?' To say the least, it is controversial whether a virtuous person must have phronesis—that is, of course, the controversy at the center of this book. And it is clearly false that a person must have phronesis in order to have a virtuous or benevolent motive, which does not even require that one have the virtue in question, considered as a durable and excellent trait of character. My question is a more modest one: is it a necessary condition of having a benevolent motive that one rely on good-faith judgments about questions like 'What would be benevolent in this case?' I argue that it is.

Clearly, Slote recognizes that it is part of having a benevolent motive that one take care to make the right decision. But does this care also involve the second, 'specificatory' kind of practical reasoning—namely, the formulation of plans by discerning what constitutes one's goal, i.e. what act would be a benevolent one—or only the former 'executive' kind?[8] Given Slote's fundamentality thesis, he must restrict such reasoning to the executive kind. And that is why he argues that one's benevolence naturally moves one to do certain things, making judgments of the specificatory kind redundant and leaving one to reason only about the execution of the plans provided automatically by one's benevolent motives. And indeed his case of the woman looking after her mother would seem to support him in this. However, the case seems very carefully chosen. So I begin by looking at a more difficult case, in which the importance of such specificatory judgments is clearer, and then determine whether such judgments are at work even in Slote's simpler cases.

Consider the Nukak, hunter-gatherers living in Colombia's increasingly violent forests. In 2006 a tribe of Nukak people emerged from the forests, apparently pushed out by guerilla warriors; consequently, Colombian authorities are treating these Nukak as displaced persons, and are thus legally required

---

[8] For the idea that practical reasoning of the former kind is 'specificatory', see McDowell 1998.

to provide them with aid and assistance. How would a benevolent person help the Nukak? As Slote (2001, 18, 34; cp. 105) correctly observes,

> If one is really benevolent or wants to be socially useful, one doesn't just throw good things around or give them to the first person one sees. Benevolence, for example, isn't benevolence in the fullest sense unless one cares about who exactly is needy and to what extent they are needy, and such care, in turn, essentially involves wanting and making efforts to know relevant facts, so that one's benevolence can really be useful.... [S]omeone who has the fullest concern for the well-being of another won't be slapdash or heedless.... This is not an empirical claim, but arguably points to a criterion, a constitutive element, of genuine concern ...

The reality and extent of the Nukak's need is obvious, as is what they need: shelter, food, clothing, and, eventually, a place of their own. But they also need something more, something that is very much on the minds of those providing that aid, eager to avoid repeating the mistakes of 2003, when another Nukak group had similarly emerged. As Juan Forero reported in the *New York Times* (11 May 2006),

> [E]ven as the aid arrives, the donors are well aware that the largess could well doom the Nukak to a life of dependency, ensuring not only that they never return home but also that they never learn how to live in their new world. 'People want to protect them' [said Xismena Martínez, who oversees aid to the Nukak for San José]. 'To help them, we give them food and clothes. That doesn't help them at all in the long term.' What everyone agrees on is that the [present] Nukak...must avoid the fate of the Nukak who came here in 2003 and now live in a clearing called Barrancón. Now in their fourth year in the area, the Nukak in Barrancón lead listless lives, lolling in their hammocks awaiting food from the state. They do not work, nor have they learned Spanish. They also have no plans to return to the forest. 'I think we will be here always', said Martín, a young man who is considered a leader.

Notice that the long-term failures of 2003 did not stem from failures in fitting means to benevolent ends—as if workers had sent the wrong goods, or sent them to the wrong people. Ms. Martínez herself says that they failed to help, but this failure was not caused by a lack of cleverness. Rather, it stemmed from faulty or perhaps missing judgments about what their benevolent ends amounted to, that is, about what really would count as helping these people. Those failures do not show that aid workers in 2003 did not have benevolent aims, but it seems clear that real as opposed to naive and child-like benevolence necessarily involves at least good faith efforts to form judgments about such matters of wisdom as they bear on the case at hand. As Aristotle observes (*NE* VI.13), a good-hearted disposition without wisdom, much less without even the attempt to be wise, is as apt to go wrong as right, and it is a criterion of benevolence that one care deeply that things do go right. That aid workers did not get their judgments right in 2003 does not show that their motivations were not benevolent, but an indifference about such judgments would show exactly that; and that is why benevolent aid workers are now thinking even harder about very difficult and philosophically weighty issues of what is worthwhile, beneficial, and in general what is good or bad for people (and for these people). Nor is such reasoning made redundant merely by pointing out that some means of helping others may create dependence in them. This is because the question whether dependence is to be created or avoided is also one requiring specificatory deliberation. After all, as David Schmidtz has pointed out, reasonable people have disagreed, and continue to disagree, about whether dependence on the state is good for people (see Schmidtz and Goodin 1998, 18; see also Goodin 1998).

Cases like this one, where it is far from obvious where the mean of benevolence lies, reveal that people with benevolent motives do, necessarily, deliberate about that mean. Now, as I said in Chapter 1, we must not let the fact that benevolent decisions can sometimes be made straightaway trick us into thinking that they are not deliberative. To say that a decision is deliberative is not necessarily to say that the decision was preceded by 'stopping and deliberating' about what to do. As Aristotle noted, and as we noted in Chapter 1, virtue involves habituation, and such habituation will make 'stopping and deliberating' redundant on very many occasions. Indeed, some of the best examples of phronesis are cases of instantaneous action, done 'without thinking', as it were (see Foot 1978a, 4f; Hursthouse 2006a, 300−5). Phronesis is a virtue of deliberation, but we must not confuse a model of choice in accordance with phronesis, with a narrative about a particular, explicit deliberative process (see also Audi 1997b, 176f). My claim, rather, is that it must be possible to model the decisions of benevolent persons as emanating from good-faith judgments of a specificatory kind.

And it should now be clear that benevolent persons rely on specificatory judgments about the mean even in cases where there is little question what to do. If the woman caring for her dying mother finds it only common sense to advocate against heroic life-saving measures, this is only because she finds it common sense that it would do her mother no good to prolong her suffering without hope of relief. Likewise, the loving father will find it a matter of common sense that he should make the time to share activities with the children he loves (see also Slote 2001, 89f), but only because he finds it common sense that shared activity with parents is a crucial good for children. That a judgment is one of common sense makes it easy not to notice it, but it does nothing to prevent it being of a mean-specifying kind. Perhaps benevolent motives are such as to lead towards balance, but if so, this is *only* because they involve judgments about what is worthwhile, beneficial, and good—in short, about finding the benevolent act. Such judgments are clearer in the hard cases than in the more obvious and clear-cut ones, but they are never redundant.[9]

So we must make a friendly amendment to Slote's view, and say that acting from a benevolent motive involves judgment of a specificatory type. As such, agent-based virtue ethics now looks nothing like the intuitionist view that moral properties like rightness are primitive properties that can be known only by being immediately perceived. Intuitionism, as I understand that view here, is a view about the process by which one assesses an action or agent: because the predicate to be assessed holds immediately and primitively, there can be no explanation of and no discursive reasoning about its holding; the process by which one finds the predicate to hold of an action or agent is therefore a sort of immediate apprehension or perception. But even when the benevolent person recognizes straightaway the thing to do, this is not a leap of intuition but a judgment that can be unpacked into a number of finer background judgments of both specificatory and executive types. Such judgments involve no mysterious intuitive faculty; they are the sorts of 'good sense' characteristic of practical intelligence and people who know, in Philippa Foot's phrase, 'what's what' (1978a, 6; see also Hursthouse 2006a).

However, such a modified agent-based model of virtuous practical reasoning also looks rather a lot like the very sort of Aristotelian model that Slote set out to replace. It seems hard to avoid the conclusion, then, that the virtuousness of an action is not conferred upon it by virtuous choosing, but is there for the virtuous chooser to deliberate about after all.

3.2.2 Finding the Benevolent Act

Slote's fundamentality thesis presents him with a dilemma. If he denies that benevolence involves practical reasoning of a specificatory type, then benevolent motives will regularly fail to hit their benevolent marks, or even to deliberate about them adequately. And if he makes such reasoning part of benevolence, then he would seem to agree with Aristotle, after all, that benevolent persons choose their acts because those acts are benevolent ones. Slote has another card to play, though: agent-based virtue ethics rejects the

---

[9] This should not be surprising, since it is the difficult case that reveals the practical reasoning of the virtuous; the clear-cut cases reveal only the practical reasoning of those who are not downright wicked or idiotic. See Hursthouse 2006a, 300.

Aristotelian thesis (*NE* II.4) that a person acting without an actual benevolent motive—say, one who is simply following the example of another—can nonetheless do a benevolent act (2001, 5). The Aristotelian view implies that the virtuous person is simply 'in the best possible position to know/perceive what is fine or right', whereas Slote holds that the virtuous person's actual motive is what confers fineness and rightness upon the action chosen from that motive. But as shall become clear now, this dispute turns out to be only a verbal one.

As we have seen, Aristotle and Slote both think of virtuous motivation as involving a virtuous 'aim' or 'mark'. Robert Audi has captured this point with his notion of the 'characteristic targets' of the virtues, 'such as the well-being of others in the case of beneficence' (Audi 1997*b*, 180; see also Zagzebski 1996, 99). As Slote (2001, 28) puts the point, 'benevolence involves not only the desire to do what is good or best overall for the people one is concerned about, but also the desire that no one of those people should be hurt or suffer'. Doing what is best overall for people and avoiding their harm are targets characteristic of the virtue of benevolence.

It is in terms of these 'targets' that agent-focused and agent-prior versions of virtue ethics describe an action as 'virtuous', such as courageous, just, temperate, or benevolent. For instance, when Aristotle says that we learn to be just by doing just actions, he means that we learn to be just by aiming at the sorts of targets that just people aim at. Following Aristotle, Christine Swanton, who advocates an agent-focused virtue ethics, has defined a 'virtuous act' as an act that hits the characteristic target of the virtue in question. Likewise, Swanton and Aristotle distinguish a 'virtuous act' in this sense from an 'act from virtue', for instance a just act that is done by a just person acting justly (Swanton 2003, 231–3).[10] In this respect, the notion of 'just action' is like the notion of 'grammatical utterance': in each case, what one does conforms to standards of appropriateness relevant to the state or ability, and one can do things conforming to those standards—do something just or say something grammatical—without having the full-fledged state or ability already. This is important, Aristotle says, because it is by doing just acts, and by making grammatical utterances, that we develop the full-fledged virtue of justice, or linguistic fluency (*NE* II.4).[11] The sense in which one's act can be a just act,

---

[10] See also Zagzebski 1996, 248, who defines an 'act of virtue' as involving both of these aspects.

[11] There is, I think, cause for reservation about Aristotle's model of how the virtues are acquired (see Johnson 2003, 818–20), but the important point for our purposes is that thinking about the targets of a virtue gives us a very plausible way of understanding what agent-prior and agent-focused virtue ethics mean by a 'virtuous action'.

even when not done from the virtue of justice, is defined in terms of the characteristic 'targets' of that virtue.

Now return to the agent-based thesis that only a benevolent agent can do a benevolent act. This cannot mean that only a person acting from a virtue of benevolence can do an act from benevolence, since that is a tautology. Nor can it mean that only a person acting from a benevolent motive can do an act from benevolence, since that is the unsurprising claim that acting from benevolence implies acting from a benevolent motive. But if it means that only a person acting from a benevolent motive, or only a person with the virtue of benevolence, can act so as to hit the target of benevolence, then the claim is clearly false. Yet that would seem to be Slote's meaning, if he really means to reject Aristotle's view that 'nonvirtuous individuals can perform good or virtuous acts under the direction of others' (2001, 5). After all, it has become clear that Slote agrees, and must agree, that benevolence *has* certain targets, namely doing what is best overall for people and avoiding their harm. And of course a person *can* hit these targets—do something genuinely helpful to another, say—and hit them for their own sake, even if she must rely on the judgments of others about those targets (as in Aristotle's account of acquiring the virtues). To be sure, Slote will correctly deny that an act can be virtuous *regardless* of motive; but so too will agent-focused virtue ethicists.[12]

It is also important to note that choosing an act because it is courageous or just, say, is not the same as choosing it for merely 'conscientious' reasons. As Aristotle says (*NE* II.4), just persons choose just actions for their own sake—not for some ulterior motive, or (more to the present point) for the satisfaction of knowing one did 'the courageous thing', but for the sake of that mark or target at which one aims and about which one deliberates.[13] Quite rightly, Slote both rejects a picture of virtuous motivation as conscientious motivation, and finds this no point of disagreement between agent-based and

---

[12] See Swanton 2003, 234f, who points out that the target of a virtue includes, and in some cases just is, certain sorts of inner states, such as proper respect. And see Aristotle, who holds that virtue is about both action and feeling (*NE* II.6), and that virtuous persons choose virtuous actions for their own sake (II.4).

[13] See Hursthouse 1995*b*, and Williams 1995*a*, 17, who notes that on Aristotle's view, the generous person (say) chooses the generous action not in a '*de dicto*' sense, but in the '*de re*' sense that such a person does 'the generous thing because it [is] the generous thing to do, and we understand what this means because we understand what it is about the situation and the action that makes this action in this situation something that would seem to a generous person the appropriate thing to do'. See also Audi 1997*b*, 176, 179ff; Stocker 1981.

other forms of virtue ethics. Again, then, it is difficult to see exactly what the disagreement about virtuousness of actions is supposed to be about.

What, then, of Slote's denying the Aristotelian thesis that a person without a benevolent motive can do a benevolent act, and thus that acts themselves can be benevolent, and do not derive their benevolence entirely from the agent's motive? This dispute is without substance. As has become clear, virtuous motivation necessarily includes good-faith judgments specifying what would constitute hitting the target of one's virtue. But that is all that agent-focused virtue ethics means by a 'virtuous action'—an action that hits that target—so the only difference between that view and agent-based virtue ethics is that the former calls such actions 'virtuous', while the latter does not. When Aristotle says that one can do a just act under the guidance of another, then, Slote would seem to object to the words, but he cannot object to the ideas. Furthermore, once deliberation about targets of virtues is part of an account of virtuous motivation—as of course it must be—it becomes clear that just and benevolent agents do choose the actions they do *because* they are just and benevolent actions. To advert to those features of the action that prompted one to do it just is to reveal the reasons for which one acted (see Davidson 1984, ch. 11; Davidson 1980, ch. 1); there is no difference between doing something from a just motive and doing it because one thought it was the just thing to do.

So much, then, for the thesis that the virtuousness of actions is fundamental. Acting from a genuinely virtuous motive, or from a virtue, requires good faith mean-specifying judgments. (I shall come back to the question whether and how phronesis fits in.) But what about Slote's claim that the virtuousness of *agents* is fundamental? And what about the idea that the virtuousness of personal character traits like benevolence is to be explained in purely 'aretaic' terms—in terms of their 'admirability', say?

3.3 Why Virtues are Virtues

3.3.1 Agent-Basing vs. Naturalism

Return to the Colombian aid workers: if they are motivated by benevolence, then we can say that they are responsive to benevolent reasons, in two respects. One, they are responsive to the reasons there are to offer aid in one way rather than in another, since the one really is helpful while the other only seems to be. They are responsive to these reasons in the sense that they are doing their best to be wise about them. And two, they are responsive to the reasons there are to be benevolent in the first place, because they have already responded to them. With all of this, agent-based virtue ethics can readily agree; what makes agent-basing distinctive, though, is its view of the relation between such reasons-responsiveness and the status of benevolence as a virtue.[14]

One account of that relation would be that the reasons-responsiveness of the workers explains why their virtuous traits and motives count as virtuous (and thus as admirable). Such an account grounds aretaic concepts of virtue and admirability in the non-aretaic value of reasons-responsiveness, which is part of the good for humans considered as rational creatures. This is a form of ethical naturalism: virtues are those traits which actualize our nature as reason-seeking creatures, where what we have reason to do 'depends on essential features of specifically human life' (Foot 2001, 14; see also Swanton 2003, ch. 3; Pincoffs 1986, 152f.). For instance, Aristotle argued that it is our nature to live directed and guided by our sense of what is reasonable (NE I.7), and so benevolence is virtuous—an excellence in us—because it is one kind of realization of our nature as reason-seeking creatures.[15]

As Gary Watson has observed, ethical naturalism holds that living 'a characteristically human life (functioning well as a human being) requires possessing and exemplifying certain traits', and that these traits 'are therefore human excellences and render their possessors to that extent good human beings' (1990, 459). Now perfectionism understands actualization of our nature as an intrinsic good that it is right to promote, and thus uses the notion of actualization to forge the link between the virtues and right action. Virtue ethical naturalism, by contrast, uses that notion only to forge the link between a given trait and the virtuousness of that trait (see also Hursthouse 1999a, ch. 1).[16] For the naturalist, then, benevolence is a virtue because the reasons to be kind and

---

[14] I shall return to reasons-responsiveness in Chs. 6–7.

[15] On this argument see Korsgaard 1986. See also Korsgaard 1996a, 93 for the idea of reasons-responsiveness as central to human nature. I return to the notion of virtues as excellences in Ch. 11.

[16] To be sure, virtue ethical naturalists give very different accounts of that link: for some, nature plays a foundational role, itself determining what reasons there are on the grounds that the good involved in the things we do by nature requires certain virtues; for others, reasons can be determined only within an ethical outlook as a whole, and a conception of our nature is not the foundation of that outlook but an ineliminable part of it. For instance, the former view holds that (say) fidelity is a virtue because our nature is such that good depends on our ability to trust those who make promises, while the latter holds that fidelity is a virtue because promising is a practice which we find we have good reason to endorse, within our overall ethical outlook (including our conception of our nature). For the former view, see Foot 2001 and Anscombe 1981a, 18f. Following Anscombe, Foot considers the virtues as 'Aristotelian necessities': things that are necessary in the sense that good depends on them. Notice that on this view, 'by nature' and 'natural' are not necessarily opposed to 'by convention', since some of the conventions we devise—such as promise-making—we devise because it is our nature to do so. For the latter view, see McDowell 1995a, esp. 154, 172, 176f; McDowell 1998, 117f; Hursthouse 1999a, chs. 8–11. My

helpful, the reasons to which the benevolent are responsive, are real reasons.[17] The agent-based fundamentality thesis, by contrast, rejects such an explanation of virtuousness, since the notion of 'real reasons' is not an agent-based notion. For agent-based virtue ethics, benevolent motives are virtuous because they are admirable, and they involve reasons-responsiveness because its absence would be deplorable. Virtuousness, then, is explained in terms of other aretaic concepts, like admirability, and together those concepts form a fundamental cluster; it is in this sense that agent-basing 'treats benevolence as fundamentally and inherently admirable and morally good' (Slote 2001, 16).

This contrast can be made clearer if we consider some of the broadly naturalist approaches to the virtues that Slote explicitly rejects. For example, Slote says of Aristotle's virtue theory that 'since the character evaluations are not regarded as fundamental and are supposed to be grounded in a theory or view of *eudaimonia*, the theory is not agent-based' in Slote's sense (2001, 6). Likewise, Slote considers Nel Noddings' view that caring for particular others is a constitutive part of central human goods, goods we have reason to embrace and that are possible only in loving, caring relationships, and *therefore* that caring is virtuous. In this respect, Slote says, 'Noddings does veer sharply from agent-basing' (2001, 31). Rather, caring (which Slote considers a type of benevolence) is virtuous because it is admirable, and that admirability is fundamental, requiring no explanation. Indeed, agent-basing holds that that admirability can *have* no explanation.

Furthermore, Slote considers many different conceptions of benevolence—aggregative, universal, and partialistic—and what is for us more interesting than which conception he prefers is the basis for his preference.

own view is that only the latter sort of naturalism is viable, but I cannot pursue the point here. (See also Adams 2006, 51f, whose criticism of naturalism seems to overlook the latter, non-foundationalist sort.)

Christine Swanton 2003 also defends a kind of non-foundationalist (and non-eudaimonist) naturalism, resting as it does on a conception of our nature: 'A correct conception of the virtues', Swanton says, 'must be at least partly shaped by a correct conception of healthy growth and development which in part constitute our flourishing' (2003, 60). Swanton derives a conception of healthy growth and development largely from work in analytic psychology (drawing especially on Karen Horney, Alfred Adler, Abraham Maslow, and others), a conception which, to be sure, is itself part of an overall ethical outlook. See esp. Swanton 2003, chs. 5–6. (It is therefore surprising that Slote thinks that Plato's view that virtue is a kind of 'health of the soul' is consistent with agent-basing. What could a notion of the health of the soul be grounded in, if not in a conception of human nature? Yet such a conception is independent of and prior to agent-evaluations, every bit as much as the 'Form of the Good' is.)

Finally, see Annas 2005a for a distinction between views that take our nature as determining what we can and cannot reasonably think we have reason to do (e.g. Foot 2001, 115), from views that take our nature as itself up for reworking (e.g. McDowell 1995a).

[17] On the foundationalist variety of naturalism, notice, aretaic concepts are not fundamental because nature is; and on the non-foundationalist view, aretaic concepts are not fundamental because nothing is—rather, all ethical concepts are part of a nexus that has a holistic and 'Neurathian' structure.

Many virtue ethicists have argued against certain impartial conceptions of benevolence on the grounds that they would, if widely adopted, undermine some of our most cherished goods, such as certain intimate relationships, perhaps so much so that humans could never widely adopt them in the first place (Hursthouse 1999a, 224ff; Annas 2005a).[18] By contrast, Slote considers different types of benevolence instead in terms of what we admire or have a 'high opinion' of—whether 'we truly admire the love we feel for some people rather than others', say (2001, esp. 76, 117, 137). Other issues that Slote refers to our intuitions about admirability include the ethical status of self-concern and selflessness (77f), of patriotism and an interest in the national good (94f), and of paternalism (132), as well as what makes courage or inner strength in the face of difficult facts a virtue (21, 158); and so on (see also Slote 1983, ch. 4). Slote is true to his word, since 'agent-based views', he has said,

don't bring in claims about what constitutes human happiness or well-being in order to ground judgments about the aretaic goodness of inner traits.... Rather, claims or theories about human well-being are themselves derived from claims about virtue and rightness ... or (perhaps more plausibly) treated as partly or wholly independent of such claims. In the latter case, aretaic evaluations of the inner life and claims about what constitutes human well-being *both* count as fundamental and occupy the ground floor *together*.... [A]gent-basing can proceed with moral evaluation separately from any particular theory of human well-being ... (Slote 1997, 210, italics in original)[19]

Now it seems awkward at best that agent-based virtue ethics should agree, as indeed it must, that deliberation about the targets of the virtues is essential to virtuous motivation, and *then* assert that the consequent reasons-responsiveness of such motivation is *not* what explains its virtuousness in a human being. Humans are, after all, reason-seeking creatures by nature; perhaps this is why Slote takes such pains to marginalize that sort of deliberation in the first place. We can put the point into sharper relief by returning to the idea that benevolence requires good-faith judgments specifying the targets of virtues. As we have seen, such judgments—for instance, about whether one helps others by making them perpetually dependent rather than self-sufficient—take

---

[18] See also Swanton 2003, who argues (as did Nietzsche) that whether a certain form of benevolence is a virtue depends on its underlying psychology in humans and in particular agents.

[19] In 2001, ch. 8 Slote returns to and defends the view that claims about well-being are derived from claims about virtue—a position he calls 'hyper-agent-based virtue ethics', which holds further that the goodness of each personal good depends on its connection to the virtue which makes that good possible for an agent. (Cp. Zagzebski 1996, 210: 'In motivation-based ethics all moral judgments—those about motives, virtues, acts, and the impersonal good—are derived from the goodness of the motivational component of virtue.') None of my remarks will assume so strong a position, however.

place only within an ethical outlook, even when they seem to be no more than common sense.[20] And Slote is correct to point out that benevolence is not consistent with just any such judgments: 'If someone has a perverse sense of what is good for people—for example, thinks that pain is in itself good for you and acts accordingly—then the benignness of their motivation is questionable, and they are presumably self-deceived as well' (2001, 27). So benevolence requires not only an ethical outlook, but an ethical outlook that is to some extent a correct, a reasonable outlook. But here our question comes back: can the correctness and reasonability of the ethical outlook so central to benevolence really be redundant to the explanation of why benevolence is a virtue?

The idea that aretaic concepts are fundamental is an awkward one at best, but its most serious problems are still to come, as I now argue: if the admirability of benevolence is 'intuitively obvious and in need of no further moral grounding' (Slote 2001, 38), then our understanding of the virtues will be parochial, as well as intuitionistic after all.

3.3.2 Fundamentality and Parochialism

Slote leaves what is 'admirable' a matter of common sense, but it hardly needs to be said that what is admirable and virtuous admits of wide disagreement. For instance, Plato's Meno has a sexist view of the virtues, admiring traits in men that he would find deplorable in women. Some have disagreed about whether there is a virtue of temperance with respect to sex or whether this is an impossible ideal, about whether the same state of character is a virtue of benevolence or a vice of paternalism, and so on (see Hursthouse 1999a, 244–7).[21] And of course Nietzsche denied that such apparent forms of benevolence as charity and pity are virtues at all, deploring what most others admired. Furthermore, even when we agree in admiring benevolence towards loved ones and benevolence towards more distant others, say, there will be disagreement about which of them is more admirable—and, consequently,

---

[20] Such judgments concern facts that are not 'evaluative', strictly speaking, but nonetheless can be appreciated as facts only from within a particular ethical viewpoint: facts about, as Hursthouse 1999a, 189 puts it, 'who can and cannot be relied on, about whether you can fool most of the people most of the time, or whether they can easily be manipulated, about what can be discerned to be a pattern in life, what is to be attributed to good or bad luck and what is "just what is to be expected"—about, in short, human nature and the way human life works'. Likewise, Aristotle says that although cleverness can be shared by the wicked and virtuous alike, the same is not true for the things that phronesis grasps, since, as Hursthouse 2006a, 304 points out, the 'wicked do not know what love and trust, for example, can do for people, and couldn't set about using the knowledge if they had it'.

[21] See also Zagzebski 1996, 88, who notes Aristotle's skepticism about the virtuousness of humility, as well as some feminists' rejection of such so-called virtues as honor and civic pride.

what counts as an admirable 'balance' (Copp and Sobel 2004, 520). Likewise, although Slote rejects agent-based views that make virtues of benevolence derivative from virtues of inner strength, it is not clear that inner strength is to be only a derivative virtue, either, so there is sure to be disagreement about what is more 'basically' admirable, too (see 2001, 21−3; Copp and Sobel 2004, 520f).

Such disagreements are difficult, but they need not be intractable. For instance, as Socrates realizes, Meno's sexist virtue theory must be addressed by considering whether human nature and character differs between the sexes. And in general, such issues call for thinking about human nature and what one has reasons to endorse, since it is from there that such disagreements arise in the first place. Skepticism about virtues of temperance with respect to sex, for instance, begins with a different picture of human psychology and sexuality, and Nietzsche's deploring of charity and pity stemmed not only from an (often alarmingly insightful) diagnosis of their underlying psychology, but also—and crucially—from his deeper views about 'what constituted a good life for a human being' (Foot 2001, 112). I suspect this is why Slote says that Nietzsche offers 'resistance to being interpreted' as an agent-baser (2001, 9).

Such tractability is possible because 'admirable', like 'good', is an attributive adjective. We may say that a cactus is 'good' because it suits our tastes in cacti, and therefore a 'good ornament', say, but we can say that it is a 'good cactus' only if it is as a cactus should be (Geach 1956; Foot 1978b; Hursthouse 1999a, 195ff).[22] A similar point holds, it seems, for 'admirable' (see also Richardson 1994, 705). It is one thing to say that Fred is an admirable horseman, say, and another that he is an admirable mountaineer. (Notice that that would no longer be so if one substituted 'blonde', a predicative adjective, for 'admirable'.) Consequently, to the claim that Fred is, simply, 'admirable', one must respond, 'An admirable what?' For purposes of virtue ethics, saying that Fred is admirable is to say that Fred is an admirable agent, perhaps overall or perhaps in some respect, but in any case as someone who forms intentions and acts for reasons. Now the discussion about Fred's admirability (or otherwise) has a point from which to begin. Of course, this way of addressing disagreement leads back to naturalism. In fact, it is worth noting that at one time Foot had also suggested understanding morality in terms of such concepts as 'despicable', 'contemptible', 'low', 'admirable', 'glorious', and 'honorable',

---

[22] See also Thomson 1997, 277−9, who seems to me far too quick in concluding from the fact that a banana may be a good banana to eat, say, or a good banana to look at, that there is no such thing as a good such-and-such, full stop. Not all goodness is relative to some extrinsic interest, or such that people's wants, a thing's 'design functions', or various features of a thing's surroundings 'fix what is good for' the thing in question, as Thomson 1997, 292−4 has it.

but hastened to point out that since such concepts are deeply social and rooted in 'language games', morality can be understood in their terms only if there is some non-parochial way of addressing 'what is really worthy of admiration and contempt' (Foot 1981, 311f). More generally, as Henry Richardson observes, 'Traditional virtue theory constrains what is to be admired by developing a conception of the human good in terms of which true virtue is to be specified' (1994, 705).

Now Slote recognizes that our aretaic concepts sometimes need revision, but he has a very different approach to revising them: 'If judgments about the ethical status of motives ground claims about right and wrong action, then the claims about right and wrong action that a given agent-based view yields can be used to test the validity or reasonableness of its grounding assumptions' (2001, 18). So if a certain motive is *prima facie* virtuous, but action from it turns out to be (systematically) inept, say, then we can reassess that motive. Fair enough, but ineptitude stems often from failures about targets of virtues, and that sort of ineptitude can be recognized *as* ineptitude only within a broader ethical outlook. In that case, such adjustment of our aretaic concepts proceeds from our other, non-aretaic concepts, upsetting the agent-based thesis that those aretaic concepts are fundamental.

Furthermore, as Stephen Darwall (1994, 696) has pointed out, it is unlikely that aretaic concepts are independent of moral concepts in the first place: 'we should ask, not what traits and acts do we now think are admirable or deplorable, but what would we think were we to come to believe that there is no such thing as moral right or wrong, moral obligation, or moral goodness?' This is a serious problem for the idea that the admirability of the virtues is fundamental. The question is not what character traits are admired now, but what character traits would be admired if somehow non-aretaic ethical concepts were bracketed, such as those about human flourishing and reasons-responsiveness. To avoid parochialism, one must look *somewhere* to explain why one trait is virtuous or admirable while another is not, but of course to give any such explanation is to concede that aretaic concepts are not fundamental.

The fact that the fundamentality thesis rules out explaining the virtuousness of certain character traits by opening a wider ethical outlook, also means that an agent-based account of the virtues is not a normative account, in an important sense of that term. As John McDowell has argued, the normativity of a concept must be based on what we have reason to endorse, and not merely on a recognition of what we do happen to endorse. Part of being a rational creature is that one can go beyond noticing that one is a certain way or does a certain thing, and is vulnerable to 'coming unstuck' from what one is or does

(McDowell 1995a).[23] To come unstuck from some practice is to recognize that one needs a reason to go in for it, and when one is unable to find such a reason, one can no longer find that practice normative. On the other hand, one can find the practice to be normative if it is supported within an ethical outlook as a whole.

McDowell's thesis is extremely attractive, and in that case reasons for practices are found via a Neurathian process in which grounding relations can flow in any direction, depending on which parts of one's outlook keep one afloat while other parts are repaired, as it were. Now, given Slote's fundamentality thesis, grounding relations can flow only from our aretaic concepts to the other parts of our ethical outlook.[24] But then aretaic concepts cannot be *supported* by an ethical outlook as a whole, and so we cannot find them to be normative. If we come unstuck from the idea that benevolence is a virtue and admirable—as many do in Plato's dialogues, not to mention Nietzsche—then we shall be simply left adrift, if that idea really is fundamental in the agent-baser's sense.

Therefore, no concepts that are fundamental in the agent-based sense can be normative concepts, and since aretaic concepts are normative, they cannot be thus fundamental. And once those concepts are supported within an ethical outlook as a whole, the fundamentality thesis falls, and with it what is agent-based about agent-based virtue ethics.

3.3.3 Virtue Intuitionism

The fundamentality thesis, then, leaves one with a parochial theory of the virtues. And it will become clear now that it also leaves one with an unattractive intuitionism about the virtues. Now, intuitionism about *rightness* is perhaps most familiar from H. A. Prichard's seminal paper, 'Does Moral Philosophy Rest on a Mistake?', where he argued that the concept of rightness is fundamental: 'The sense of obligation to do, or the rightness of, an action of a particular kind is absolutely underivative and immediate' (1912, 27). Agent-based virtue ethics rejects intuitionism about rightness: agents do not *find* the right act, intuitively or otherwise. For the same reason, agent-based virtue ethics rejects intuitionism about virtuous acts, as well: one does not intuit the benevolent act, but makes the act benevolent by choosing it benevolently. And even with

---

[23] See also McDowell 1995b for the idea that reflection on something entails putting that something 'at risk'.

[24] Recall Slote's view (1997, 210) that aretaic concepts and other ethical concepts must either be independent of each other, or (as Slote now holds, 2001, ch. 8) the latter must be derived from the former.

the revision of that view so that agents do find the right or the virtuous act, they do so through good judgments about 'targets', not by intuition.

However, because agent-based virtue ethics holds that the virtuousness of benevolent agents derives not from their reasons-responsiveness—or anything else, for that matter—but is fundamental and primitive, it *is* a form of intuitionism about the virtuousness *of agents and motives*. The fundamentality of virtue amounts to the view (modifying Prichard) that 'the virtuousness of an inner state of a particular kind is absolutely underivative and immediate'. Or, as Slote says, 'the moral goodness' of benevolence 'is intuitively obvious and in need of no further moral grounding' (2001, 38).[25] Agent-basing is a form of virtue intuitionism precisely because it holds that grounding could flow only from aretaic concepts to the rest of our ethical outlook. Of course, this is not to say that agent-based virtue ethics detaches intuitions about virtues from the world, but that wherever aretaic evaluations come from, they are immediately obvious once all the facts are in. And in this, there is no difference between intuitionism about virtuousness and that about rightness (see Prichard 1912, 27–9).

It is the intuitionism of agent-basing that makes for its problems with parochialism. For one thing, disagreements about intuitions, once the facts are in, are intractable. John Maynard Keynes reports the *de jure* and *de facto* methods for resolving such disagreements among the British intuitionists. *De jure*, differing intuitions were to be traced to a difference either in the focus of the observers or in the quality of their perceptions. *De facto*, the victory typically went to 'those who could speak with the greatest appearance of clear, undoubting conviction and could best use the accents of infallibility', complete with incredulous gasps, head-shaking, grim silences, or even shrugs (see MacIntyre 1981, 16–18). And no surprise, since intuitionism isolates its fundamental ethical judgments from grounding in the rest of our ethical outlook, but it is only within that outlook that we can go beyond parochialism in our ethical judgments at all.

---

[25] Likewise, Zagzebski 1996, 83f says that we can 'see the goodness of a person' in a 'rather direct way': 'She may simply exude a "glow" of nobility or fineness of character, or … there may be an inner peace that can be perceived to be good directly'. In such persons, she says, we could 'simply see' that certain feelings and motivations are themselves good, or that in virtue of which the agent who has them is good. I think that this captures our experience of finding someone good, on many occasions anyway, but virtue intuitionism offers such a view not merely as an account of our experience, but indeed in place of a theory of goodness.

Note that intuitionism about (say) the status of benevolence need not imply that benevolent persons choose actions conscientiously, as 'benevolent' rather than as, say, simply relieving suffering; see Audi 1997b, 182. This is an important point, since agent-based virtue ethics staunchly (and rightly) denies that benevolent motivation is merely conscientious.

Furthermore, parochialism infects intuitionism also because the intuitionist has no way of saying what facts are relevant to evaluation in the first place. Clearly, facts about what leaves other people worse off, say, are relevant to our assessment of whether a given trait counts as a virtue, but in many cases those sorts of facts—such as that the ability to love is a more important part of human nature than the ability to win prestige or earn money, say—*do* require an ethical outlook before they can even be recognized *as* facts (see Hursthouse 1999, ch. 8; Nussbaum 1990, 1992, 1993, 1995). In that case, an ethical outlook must come in to ground views about what traits are virtuous, but it is precisely this that the fundamentality thesis rules out. And it should be clear by now that the intuitionism of agent-basing also accounts for its problem with normativity. Aretaic concepts, if fundamental and intuitive, cannot be reckoned with within our broader ethical outlook, and without that supporting outlook, as Elizabeth Anscombe (1981*b*) noted, we come unstuck from our intuitions, and have nowhere left to turn.

So far I have focused on agent-based virtue ethics as a form of intuitionism about *virtuousness*, but now we should note that such intuitionism entails intuitionism about *rightness*, too. As Gary Watson has observed, virtue ethics is committed to the priority of virtue to the concept of right action, in the sense that 'the concept of proper or right conduct will be well understood only if the concept of virtue is' (1990, 454). However, if we 'hold that we can understand what the virtues are and how they are expressed without the benefit of any general theory', then such priority is 'gratuitous'—both concepts now rest on the intuitive apprehension of a virtuous motive, and so 'the distinction between virtue intuitionism and act intuitionism seems merely to be nominal' (1990, 454f). Ironically, in the twenty-first century agent-based virtue ethics has brought virtue ethics full circle to precisely the sort of view against which virtue ethics began in the twentieth century as a protest movement.[26]

3.4 Reasons for Virtue[27]

I turn now to a final problem for agent-based virtue ethics, viz. that it cannot explain why we all have reason to be benevolent rather than cruel. This problem is hardly new for virtue ethics. For instance, in her important

---

[26] It is also precisely the sort of view that Slote himself rejects (2001, 5, 7). For the idea that virtue ethics is a 'protest movement', see Louden 1990. In appreciating this irony, I have benefited from discussion with Dirk Baltzly.

[27] In thinking about the issues in this section I have been deeply influenced by Mark LeBar's excellent paper, 'Virtue Ethics and Deontic Constraints'.

paper 'Morality as a System of Hypothetical Imperatives', Philippa Foot had envisioned moral persons as bound to morality not by duty, but by their own love and benevolence towards other persons—such persons serve 'in the army of duty' but only as 'volunteers' (1978c, 167, 170). On that view, one who refuses to volunteer may be 'amoral', 'mistaken', and have his life 'most sadly spoiled', but of course whether or not these considerations are reasons to volunteer is strictly his own business (1978c, 166f). In fact, Foot not only recognized but indeed advertised this implication of her view: 'I am, therefore, putting forward quite seriously a theory that disallows the possibility of saying that a man ought...to have ends other than those he does have: e.g. that the uncaring, amoral man ought to care about the relief of suffering or the protection of the weak' (1978c, 169f; see also Anscombe 1981a, 19f). Simply put, on this view the reasons I have depend on what I desire, on what I happen to think is in my interests.

Foot has openly and honestly rejected her earlier view, particularly in her comments on 'William Frankena's Carus Lectures', and more recently in her book *Natural Goodness*. In particular, she rejects the idea that, as Frankena objected, 'the moral "ought" will not be applicable to other agents unless their desires are the right ones' (1981, 308). Her mistake, she now says, was in thinking 'that reasons had to be based on an agent's desires' (2001, 10), and she now holds that reasons of morality are reasons of 'practical rationality', which hold for all persons, regardless of what particular desires or ends they happen to have. It is, she says, 'the distinguishing characteristic' of just, charitable, courageous, and temperate persons that 'they recognize certain considerations (such as the fact of a promise, or of a neighbour's need) as powerful, and in many circumstances compelling, reasons for action. They recognize the reasons, and act on them' (2001, 12; see also Pincoffs 1986, 113f).

If anything is clear, I think it is that whether I have reasons to be benevolent rather than cruel does not simply depend on whatever desires I happen to have. Whether I have a reason to help another out of a well rather than fill it with piranha, say, is not simply my own business. Reasons to help another out of a well and not to fill it with piranha are what philosophers call 'deontic constraints'. I cannot defend the existence of deontic constraints here, but I do want to ask whether agent-based virtue ethics could countenance them, even in principle.

One way to avoid basing the reasons there are to be benevolent on mere desires is to say, with Christine Korsgaard, that reasons based on desires are one's 'personal property', whereas moral reasons are 'common property', reasons that are reasons for everyone (1993, 25f). In technical parlance, this is a distinction between 'agent-relative' and 'agent-neutral' reasons, respectively.

If the only sort of reason there were for me to be benevolent and not to be cruel were 'merely *my* property', then, as Korsgaard says (1993, 47f),

> my victim would not have the right to demand that I act on it. Consider a comparison. If you have an agent-relative reason to climb Kilimanjaro, and don't do it, I may entertain the thought that you are being irrational. I can see what your reasons are. But if I have no reason to bring it about that you climb Kilimanjaro ... then I have no reason to talk you into doing it. I have no reason to do anything about your relative reasons, even to think about them, although I may happen to. I certainly don't have a reason to complain of your conduct when you don't act on them, and if I do, you may justifiably tell me that it is none of my business. If deontological reasons were agent-relative, the same thing would hold for victims. My victim could entertain the thought that I have a reason not to treat him this way, but that would give him no grounds for complaint. Astonishingly enough, it turns out to be none of his business.[28]

Clearly, the concern here is not to suggest that people should act only 'from duty', or 'to give the moral "ought" a magic force' (Foot 1978*c*, 167)—on the contrary, this concern is not *whether* reasons can be given for being benevolent rather than cruel, but what *kinds* of reasons they are. Whatever reasons there are for benevolence, on this view, at least some of those reasons must be common property, agent-neutral reasons; otherwise, the reasons that I have not to be cruel turn out—perversely—to be no one's business but my own (Korsgaard 1996*a*, 134f; see also Stohr and Wellman 2002, 67ff for discussion of related issues). In Korsgaard's phrase, such reasons 'supervene on the relationships of people who interact with one another', on the 'I-thou' relationships that permeate all human interaction, and thus 'exist for all rational agents' (but 'would not exist in a world without them'; Korsgaard 1993, 48 and n., 28).

The view that reasons are agent-relative holds that what reasons an agent has depend on particular features of the agent. Consequently, the idea that what reasons I have depend on my particular desires, and are therefore strictly my own business, is one type of agent-relative view. But not all agent-relative views need entail that one's reasons are strictly one's own business. Mark LeBar argues that at least some moral reasons are, in Stephen Darwall's (2006) phrase, 'second-personal', holding for agents as members of a community of rational agents. That second-personal standpoint is deeply embedded in shared human existence, and recognizes the claims persons have upon each other and that persons are justified in holding each other accountable for their treatment

---

[28] See also Samuel Scheffler, who has argued what is wrong with cruelty, say, cannot be simply the fact that cruelty compromises the well-being of the perpetrator: 'Surely any adequate explanation' of what is wrong with cruelty, Scheffler says, 'must make reference to the effects of such behavior on its victims.' Scheffler 1992, 117; see also Scheffler 1988.

of each other. Virtue involves responsiveness to certain kinds of reasons, and in particular the nexus of attitudes typical of the second-person standpoint count as a virtue: virtue is part of flourishing as human beings, and the second-personal standpoint is a *sine qua non* of a life that is even recognizable as a human life. So it is not simply that it is in one's interests to take up the second-personal standpoint, but that for human beings, there is no serious alternative to doing so. But such reasons are not really 'common property', since an agent's reasons depend on his or her flourishing in a way that no one else's reasons do.[29]

The idea that moral reasons are not simply one's own business has deep historical roots as well. As Julia Annas argues, the ancient Stoics held that benevolence—indeed, a demanding form of impartial benevolence—is the result of 'the rational development of our natural tendency to other-concern', in which case reasons for benevolence are generated by our common humanity (1992*b*, 141). And so on. As we have seen, naturalists about the virtues offer different accounts of what makes reasons for benevolence real reasons, but they all agree that such reasons are real, and must be, if they are to be normative and more than parochial. They agree also that such reasons for benevolence must attach to us as the kinds of beings that we are, in virtue of 'essential features of specifically human life'. So understood, then, the reasons for benevolence are real reasons and genuine deontic constraints—reasons to which victims of others' cruelty can hold those others accountable. On such a view, understanding benevolence in the light of human flourishing or *eudaimonia* is not to restrict reasons for benevolence to whatever an agent happens to take to be in her self-interest, say, but to locate those reasons in our shared nature and form of life.[30]

What does agent-based virtue ethics have to say about reasons for benevolence? In *From Morality to Virtue*, Slote had conceived the problem of addressing 'deontological' concepts as one of showing that assessment of action using aretaic vocabulary (e.g. 'admirable' or 'deplorable') can have as much 'force' as deontological vocabulary (especially 'right' and 'wrong'; Slote 1992, ch. 10).[31] But the issue is not deontological vocabulary, but deontological ideas: whether we describe Fred's action as 'deplorable' or as 'wrong', the real question is

---

[29] LeBar, 'Virtue Ethics and Deontic Constraints'. See also the recent discussion of deontic constraints in Swanton 2003, ch. 10.

[30] And a good thing, since it is far from clear that the tie between virtue and happiness is sufficiently tight, given the possibility of bad luck, that it is reasonable to expect people to live up to the demands of virtue ethics for that sort of reason; see Annas 2005*a*, 19–21.

[31] Slote 2001, 4 continues to focus on the 'epithets' employed in agent-based virtue ethics as of special significance. See also Zagzebski 1996, 238f, 242f.

whether doing it remains, ultimately, only Fred's business.[32] Moreover, even if the use of aretaic terms is public, reasons to avoid such public 'epithets' are Fred's business, if aretaic terms are fundamental. They depend on how strongly Fred feels about being publicly labeled 'deplorable', presumably.

In *Morals from Motives*, on the other hand, Slote turns instead to the substance of deontology (rather than just its vocabulary), considered as a set of prohibitions on certain acts of sacrificing one to save another, for instance. He then argues that 'good overall motivation' includes concern for others beyond those one specially loves, so that 'anyone willing to kill in order to save (a few) extra lives has morally bad or unacceptable overall motivation (like a person who loves some human beings but has *no* concern about others)'. In that case, Slote argues, 'we also have agent-based reasons to say that it is wrong to act on (i.e., do what reflects) a willingness to kill in order to save extra lives, and this is deontology (or a part of deontology, though analogous arguments would hold for other relevant parts of deontology)' (see 2001, 79–87).[33] But the problem remains: what reasons are there for me to have a good overall motivation, that are not strictly my business? On an agent-based view, there is nothing more to say about such motivation than that it is admirable, but surely whether or not I have a reason to seek the admiration of others is strictly my own business, if anything is.

Finally, Slote sets out to answer a certain type of immoralism, arguing that we are 'rationally justified in being moral', since it is rational to care for oneself and the virtues are necessary for the enjoyment of important personal goods like achievement and intimacy (2001, ch. 7).[34] But deriving the necessity of being virtuous from 'a fundamental rational requirement to care about having a full and good life oneself' still leaves that necessity the agent's own business. The immoralist challenge under consideration here is not that one may be a fool for going in for the virtues, but that going in for the virtues at all is strictly one's own business.

Agent-based virtue ethics cannot take that challenge seriously: since it cannot give normative reasons for benevolence, *a fortiori* it cannot provide normative reasons that are deontically constraining, either. We should give up on virtue

---

[32] Overlooking this point, Slote 1992, 164 moves swiftly from 'deplorability' to 'criticizability'. Someone may deplore my taste in books for turning my nose up at their favorite novel, but can hardly criticize me for doing so.

[33] One of these 'other parts', Slote says, is sensitivity to the distinction between killing and letting die (2001, 96).

[34] It is important to note that, while Slote does agree that this relation holds between virtues and other goods, what he denies—and what agent-basing must deny—is that that relation explains why the virtues are virtues.

ethics altogether long before we give up on deontic constraints, I think, so virtue ethics has no alternative but to reject the fundamentality of virtue. In that case, virtue ethics must be, in Slote's terms, either agent-prior or agent-focused; what it *cannot* be is agent-based.

And that is significant. It has already been shown that although Slote's fundamentality thesis entails that deliberative excellence or phronesis is redundant in an account of the virtues, having a virtue necessarily involves exactly the kind of practical reasoning of which Aristotle says that phronesis is the mastery (see also Zagzebski 1996, 99). And now it is clear, second, that although the fundamentality thesis rejects any grounding of virtue concepts, virtue ethics cannot allow that the virtues are fundamental—they must be grounded in *something*. They cannot be grounded in prior views about right action, nor in theories of aretaic language as expressing attitudes and feelings, say, or as commending and recommending (see Annas 2005, 11f; Foot 2001, ch. 1; Geach 1956). They must be grounded in a reflective ethical outlook rather than in metaphysical or religious facts, say, since all facts are reason-giving only within an ethical outlook; so they must be grounded in some view of what human beings have reason to do. And since human beings are not transcendental selves outside nature, virtue ethics must turn, then, to some form of ethical naturalism. That is why the failure of agent-based virtue ethics is an important and interesting failure: it reveals why virtue ethics needs naturalism.

Conclusion

It is important to notice that the failure of agent-based virtue ethics stems entirely from the account constraint, which agent-basing accepts, even if we set aside the act constraint as agent-basing does. The account constraint requires that our serious practical concerns must all be built into an account of right action, and of course those serious practical concerns can be reckoned with because they are part of an ethical outlook that can be reckoned with—as we saw in the preceding chapter, that is why the account constraint is a minimal constraint. For agent-based virtue ethics, the 'smuggling' comes not in the account of right action, but in the fundamentality of the virtues: ultimately, what we can consider a virtue is beholden to our serious practical concerns, and thus to our overall ethical outlook. Consequently, since every account of right action must meet (at least) the account constraint, no virtue ethical account of right action can be agent-based. So for virtue ethics it is the minimal account constraint itself that, given the confines of the VE constraint, requires virtue ethical naturalism.

Does virtue ethics also need phronesis? I think that we can now see that it does, for at least two broad sorts of reasons. One, we have seen in this chapter that virtue ethics must employ the notion of specificatory deliberation in its account of the virtues: part of being a benevolent person, for instance, is the ability to make benevolent ends determinate through deliberation.[35] We have also seen that if the virtues are excellences, then since the virtues involve specificatory deliberation, intelligence in specificatory deliberation—a kind of reasons-responsiveness—must be part of what is excellent about the virtues, as traits of rational creatures. Therefore, given that the virtues are all excellences of rational creatures, the virtues must all include deliberative excellence of a specificatory sort. That is, the virtues must all include phronesis.

And two, the account constraint requires virtue ethics to make phronesis part of all the virtues. As we have seen, virtues have targets. These targets connect to the serious practical concerns to which we want a theory of right action to do justice; some of them are internal to the agent (motivations, attitudes, etc.), and some are external (consequences, states of affairs, etc.). Now I trust it is clear that the account constraint requires that, if one defines right action in terms of the virtues, then those virtues must be reliable where their targets are concerned. This is not because such reliable abilities are necessary in order for one to do a right action at all. Rather, it is because virtue ethics understands right action in terms of what is *characteristic* of the virtues, and the latter must preserve a tight connection between the exercise of a virtue and the hitting of a target, if the account is to do justice to the serious practical concerns that those targets represent. As Slote (2001, 18) himself says, if a certain kind of trait or motive turns out to be inept and unreliable, then we should question whether such a trait or motive can really be virtuous. Now, we have also seen in this chapter that reliability in hitting the targets of the virtues requires specificatory deliberation that is intelligent and flexible; and that is just what phronesis is. In order to satisfy the account constraint, therefore, the virtues in terms of which right action is defined must all include phronesis.

But something still remains. I have argued that, given the demands of a virtue ethical theory of right action, phronesis must be part of all the virtues. Doesn't this set the bar too high on what and who can count as virtuous?

[35] See also Zagzebski 1996, 99: 'It is clear that virtuous persons acting out of virtue have certain aims, and we generally think that it is not sufficient to merely have the aims in order to be virtuous, but that a virtuous person reliably produces the ends of the virtue in question. So compassionate persons are reliably successful in alleviating suffering; fair persons are reliably successful in producing fair states of affairs; generous persons are reliably successful in giving to those who are in need, and so on.'

To be sure, my argument does raise the bar high—it requires that every virtue must involve good specificatory deliberation. But why think that it must therefore require phronesis? Why not say that the specificatory deliberation involved in deliberation must be only good enough? How much phronesis is phronesis enough? These are the questions we must address now, in the next chapter.

4

Right Action and 'The Virtuous Person'

It has been said that, for virtue ethics generally, an action is right if and only if it is what an agent with a virtuous character would do in the circumstances (Oakley 1996, 129; Hursthouse 1997; Hursthouse 1999a, ch. 1). This is true, I think, although that is today a much more controversial thing to say. It is that controversy that I wish to discuss here. Virtue ethicists in recent years have increasingly retreated from ideas about what 'the virtuous person' would do, viewing such ideas as too abstract and idealized to be of much real use. In place of such ideas have come virtue ethical accounts of right action that focus on certain sorts of motives, say, or achieving the aims characteristic of the virtues. It may seem, then, that when I say that virtue ethics understands right action in terms of the virtuous person, I must be backing some particular version of virtue ethics, but in fact I think that all virtue ethical theories must ultimately understand right action and the virtues in light of 'the virtuous person', even if they need not put it quite that way.

In *one* way, the issue of 'the virtuous person' is not pivotal—in fact, that is one central point I hope to make. The issue is not pivotal in the sense that it does not in fact divide types of virtue ethics after all, on my view, so whether or not a virtue ethicist puts an account of right action into a form that speaks explicitly of 'the virtuous person' is neither here nor there; and that itself is worth noting. In another way, though, the issue of 'the virtuous person' is a very pivotal one indeed, since the major impetus for avoiding that notion is the worry that it turns virtue ethics into a theory about what perfect and ideal people do, and thus of limited interest at best for people like us, very real and inevitably imperfect. Not surprisingly, philosophers with that worry have exactly the same sort of worry about phronesis, since it is really phronesis, if anything, that seems to make a model of 'the virtuous person' an impossible and thus useless ideal. And of course the two issues come together explicitly in Aristotle, who defines virtue as a state of character concerned with choosing the mean, where this latter is determined by right reason—that is, he says, as the *phronimos*, the person with phronesis, would determine it (*NE* II.6, 1106b36–1107a2).

What I argue here is that the notion of 'the virtuous person'—as well as the notion of the *phronimos* or the *spoudaios*—is not the sort of ideal it has been supposed to be. If I am correct, then the notion of 'the *phronimos*' is nothing to be afraid of—and more than that, it is a notion that no virtue ethics can do without. I begin by reviewing some of the more common objections to the notion of 'the virtuous person', before considering an important recent account of right action that seeks to do away with it altogether.

4.1 Doing Without 'The Virtuous Person'

4.1.1 *The Usual Objections*

The main objections to talk of 'the virtuous person' have been of three basic sorts: that such talk is unrealistic of virtuous people as they actually are; that it is an inadequate heuristic for thinking about right action; and that an idealization of virtue is problematic in its own right. I shall consider these objections in that order.[1]

(1) The first sort of objection finds fault with the idea that 'the virtuous person' does what is right, because of course virtuous people do not always do what is right (e.g. Louden 1984, 230; Hurka 2001, ch. 8; Kawall 2002; Das 2003, 331). In that case, preserving the connection between what is right and what 'the virtuous person' does means making the requirements on virtue increasingly stringent; in fact, it seems we must restrict the virtuous to 'the *phronimoi*', persons of a rare sagacity indeed. As Julia Driver complains, 'Only the *phronimoi*, the wise, are virtuous' on this sort of view, 'and these people are few and far between' (2001, 53).[2] Indeed, as Driver notes, this seems quite an elitist view of the virtues. Even worse, if these *phronimoi* are the standards of right action and right opinion on moral matters, then it would seem that anyone who disagrees with one of them must be 'morally flawed', and this seems to replace reasonable moral disagreement and exchange with what Ayn

---

[1] Another objection is that 'the virtuous person' is supposed to have all the virtues, unlike any real virtuous person. For the most part I leave this sort of objection aside in this chapter, since it is an objection to the so-called unity of virtue thesis, and not to 'the virtuous person' *per se*. I shall return to the unity of virtue in Ch. 11.

[2] Schneewind 1997, 200 suggests that the 'Aristotelian theory may have been suited to a society in which there was a recognized class of superior citizens, whose judgement on moral issues would be accepted without question'. See Prior 2001, 336f for well-placed criticism of this suggestion.

Rand called 'argument from intimidation'[3] (see Driver 2001, 12; Schneewind 1997, 200; see also Adams 2006, 123).

Notice also that if the *phronimoi* are such standards, then the phronesis they have must be 'global', that is, broad enough to ensure right action no matter the context in which one finds oneself; but of course phronesis comes only with experience, and no one can have enough experience to have such 'global' practical wisdom (see Badhwar 1996; Swanton 2003, 229f). Even Rosalind Hursthouse—perhaps the leading contemporary proponent of casting right action in terms of 'the virtuous person'—has felt some unease with the idea, observing that virtuous persons do not always act 'in character'; consequently, Hursthouse has modified her earlier formula of right action as what a virtuous person would do in the circumstances, by adding that right action is 'what a virtuous person would *characteristically* (i.e. acting *in character*) do in the circumstances' (1999*a*, 28, my italics; see also Das 2003, 331).

(2) Other objections focus on 'the virtuous person' as a kind of ideal. Perhaps the most common objection of this sort is that such an ideal, whether real or imaginary, is often useless as a heuristic for thinking about right action. Objections of this sort assume that virtue ethics tells us to do what is right by thinking about what a virtuous person would do in our circumstances, and then doing that; they then point out some rather serious (and fairly obvious) problems for this sort of view.[4] For one thing, it may well be that a virtuous person would not be in my circumstances in the first place, if my circumstances are themselves the result of, say, my previous wrongdoing, or the pressing need to reform my deficient character (I discuss these sorts of cases in Chapter 2). And even when it would make sense to think of 'the virtuous person' in our circumstances, we may be utterly unable to 'fathom what the hypothetical moral exemplar would do were he in our shoes', as Robert Louden says, and again, 'sometimes even he will act out of character' (1984, 229). Indeed, if I am not virtuous, fathoming what a virtuous person would do in my circumstances may be entirely beyond my grasp. As the wizard Gandalf points out in *The Fellowship of the Ring*, the last thing that the ambitious would expect someone to do with a magic ring is try to destroy it, rather than use it to increase one's own power, since the very sensibility of such a motive is quite foreign

[3] See MacIntyre 1981, ch. 2 for discussion of just this sort of devolution of disagreement among the British intuitionists. I shall resist the temptation to raise the question whether much of the recent philosophical talk of what everyone knows about the virtues, provided one is not an *elitist*, is itself a kind of argument from intimidation.

[4] This sort of objection is very frequent, even though Hursthouse 1997, 220f has explicitly disavowed that virtue ethics considers such ridiculous questions as, 'Would Socrates have had an abortion if he were a raped, pregnant fifteen-year-old?'

to someone motivated mainly by power himself.[5] Likewise, even if I could fathom what a virtuous person would do in my circumstances, I may not be able to do what that person would do, anyway—perhaps such a person would exercise a level of courage, say, or of skill or competence, that is simply beyond me.[6] And in any case, Janna Thompson has a point when she says that it would be 'irrational for us to place our trust in what a single individual, however virtuous, thinks is right' (Thompson 1998, 73, cited in Swanton 2003, 230; cf. Wolf 1997, 93).[7] Assuming, of course, that we can even find that individual: as Louden points out, Aristotle emphasizes the importance of the *phronimos*, but he does not say 'how to track down a *phronimos*'. Louden speculates that this is because, in a more face-to-face community like the ancient *polis*, the *phronimoi* may have been easier to spot (Louden 1984, 233; cf. Louden 1997, 106; see also Schneewind 1997, 199f).

(3) A less common objection to 'the virtuous person' as an ideal—but I think one of the most important objections nonetheless—is that it may well be a mistake to aspire to such an ideal in the first place. It is tempting to suppose, with Kant, that even if I must inevitably fall short of a certain ideal, still the best thing for me to do is to try to come as close to it as I can.[8] However, as Christine Swanton has observed in her excellent book *Virtue Ethics, A Pluralistic View*, such aspirations may in fact prove ruinous (see also Wolf 1997). For instance, virtues require inner strength, and where one is lacking in such strength, trying to emulate stronger persons with virtues one lacks may lead one not closer to those virtues, but indeed further away. For instance, as Nietzsche observed, altruism without inner strength becomes distorted, and is not an excellence but a deplorable sort of self-serving or resentful *noblesse oblige* (2003, 62ff; see also Swanton 2005; Doris 2002, 150). Swanton thus adapts Nietzsche's injunction, 'Do not be virtuous beyond your strength', and argues

---

[5] See also Hursthouse 2006a for discussion of how virtue makes a difference in what one takes as premises for practical reasoning; cp. 1999a, 188–91.

[6] I recall some such observations as these from Julia Driver's comments during an 'Author Meets Critic' session on Rosalind Hursthouse at the Pacific Division meeting of the American Philosophical Association, 2002. See also Foot 1978a, 4f and Hursthouse 2006a, 300f for some of the skills that a virtuous person may need to have. I also recall that at one time, 'What would Jesus do?' was a familiar slogan. I appreciate the intent behind it, but as I once heard theologian Kerry McRoberts put the point, it is important to remember that sometimes Jesus responded to a person's blindness by spitting on the ground and rubbing mud in his blinded eyes, something it would be quite useless for any of *us* to do.

[7] Likewise, Swanton 2003, ch. 12 makes a convincing case that virtue ethical accounts of practical reasoning are better off without the 'monological' approach to virtue ethical epistemology that takes 'the virtuous person as oracle'.

[8] Kant says that virtue 'is an ideal which is unattainable while yet our duty is constantly to approximate to it'; see Kant 1964, 71, cited in Wolf 1997, 90. See also *MM* 1.11, whose author claims that even if aspiration falls short, it benefits the aspirant.

that virtue should be seen not in terms of ideals, but rather as adjusted to an individual's capacities and strength (2003, ch. 9, esp. 206ff; see also 2003, 24f, 64f; 2005, 190f). And so Swanton rids her virtue ethics of 'the virtuous person', since aspiring to such ideals can in fact do more harm than good.

Swanton herself characterizes right action in terms of the characteristic 'targets' of the virtues, rather than in terms of 'the virtuous person'. As I have suggested, it is an interesting question whether such an approach is in fact a real alternative to thinking of right action and the virtues in terms of 'the virtuous person', after all, and in particular whether it is an alternative to thinking of those things in terms of phronesis. Since Swanton's is a particularly clear and compelling virtue ethical account of right action that avoids the notion of the *phronimos*, we should look at it more carefully. What role can phronesis play in an account of right action that focuses directly on the targets of the virtues, rather than on virtuous agents?

4.1.2 Swanton's Alternative

To understand Swanton's notion of a virtue's target, we should begin by noting that virtues tend to operate on certain sorts of characteristic concerns, such as pleasure and pain, fear, the use of money, regard for authority, respect for the claims of others, and so on. Swanton (2003, ch. 1) calls the 'field' of a virtue some body of concerns with which it is characteristically (but not uniquely) involved, such as 'the bodily pleasures which are the focus of temperance'. Furthermore, virtues tend to operate on things in their field in certain characteristic ways, such as by promoting them, but also—and more interestingly—by valuing them, honoring them, respecting them, being receptive to them, and so on. Such forms of appropriate 'responsiveness' to items in a virtue's field or fields Swanton calls its 'modes', and one virtue is distinguished from others by its peculiar 'constellation' of characteristic modes of responsiveness; this constellation is what Swanton calls the 'profile' of a virtue. It is noteworthy that virtues are individuated by their profiles, and not by the individual modes themselves, since in fact some modes—most notably love, respect, and creativity—are common to all the virtues. (I take up the individuation of the virtues in Part II.) Finally, a mode of responsiveness is matched to an item in a virtue's field in terms of what it is about that item that makes the response to it an appropriate one: in particular, the item's having value, or having a certain status, or being beneficial, or the agent's having a 'bond' with it. What makes a mode of responsiveness appropriate to an item in a virtue's field is the 'basis' of that mode of responsiveness.

We can now understand the idea of hitting a virtue's 'target' as responding appropriately to items in the virtue's field. Such targets can be either internal or external to the agent; for instance, determination has as its target the making of a sustained effort, whereas magnificence has as its target a particular kind of result that is grand and tasteful, rather than vulgar or tacky. It is also worth noting that the same virtue can have several targets, since there can be many items in its field (or fields) with different bases, and thus many different modes in its profile; that hitting the target can vary with contexts, since for instance to kill an animal is, in some contexts, not cruel; and that some targets are matters of avoiding things, as for instance the target of modesty is to avoid an inflated view of oneself (see Swanton 2003, 29f and ch. 11, esp. 231–8).

It is in terms of the targets of the virtues that Swanton defines right action, and crucial to her account is her distinction between an 'act from virtue' and a 'virtuous act'. An agent does an 'act from virtue' when he or she has some virtue or other, and acts in a way that expresses that virtue. An agent who does a 'virtuous act', however, need not have a particular virtue, but may simply act in such a way as to hit the characteristic 'target' of that virtue (2003, 233, 238f, 243f; see also Aristotle, *NE* II.4, 1122b1–21, cited at 2003, 231f). Since Swanton believes that one need not be virtuous in order to act rightly, she understands right action in terms not of acts from virtue, but of virtuous acts. However, since a virtuous act may be virtuous in one respect but fail to be virtuous in other relevant respects, not all virtuous acts are right acts. Consequently, Swanton understands right action in terms of those virtuous acts that are virtuous in *all* relevant respects; such acts Swanton calls 'overall virtuous'.[9] An overall virtuous act must be the best possible act in the circumstances, although it need not be uniquely best, or obligatory (2003, 240f). According to Swanton, an act is right if and only if it is an overall virtuous act.

Swanton's account of right action is a compelling one—and note that her account makes no mention whatsoever of 'the virtuous person', much less 'what the virtuous person would do'. Of course, this is no accident, since a central theme of Swanton's virtue ethics is its rejection of 'ideals' of virtue. But despite this theme, and the fact that phronesis is usually regarded as part of what makes such ideals so remote from our experience, Swanton does hold that phronesis is an important aspect of the virtues. '[P]ractical wisdom', she says, 'is a component of all virtue, at least characteristically', and so acts from virtue express, among other 'fine inner states', that of 'practical wisdom' (see 2003, 99, 145, 293). This is what we should expect, since as the previous chapter made clear reliably hitting the target of a virtue involves correct apprehension of the

---

[9] See 2003, 243f, 252f; see also 232, 238 for the idea that some acts from a virtue may fail to hit the target of that virtue. We shall return to 'overall virtuousness' in Ch. 5.

mean. So although an act from virtue does not suffice for right action, acts from virtue will *generally* and *systematically* tend to be right acts only if virtue involves phronesis. (And I think that phronesis is a central part of Swanton's virtue ethics in an even deeper way; I shall say more about this below.)

At the same time, though, the role of phronesis in Swanton's view is complicated in at least two important ways. First, Swanton has a strong Nietzschean strain in her theory of virtue, and in particular she says that while all the 'quotidian' virtues include practical intelligence, the 'heroic' virtues do not (2003, 171f). The 'quotidian' virtues are the virtues of quotidian persons: these virtues are important for parents, administrators, policy-makers, and professionals (2003, 27f), people of ordinary talents and aspirations, while the 'heroic' virtues belong to specially talented artists, say, and zealots pursuing great causes, and in general those who are 'grandiose' in their 'life-affirming' creativity (2003, 82–4, 135).[10] The difference between these classes of virtues, Swanton notes, makes a big difference where phronesis is concerned: whereas the quotidian virtues require the 'cautionary effects of wisdom', in persons with heroic virtues creativity and zeal may properly take free reign; in fact, 'manic grandiosity' may be virtuous and 'life-affirming' in a highly creative person, even if it stems from 'lack of self-love', and even if it leads one to misery, ill health, and indeed self-destruction (2003, 27, 135, 82–4).[11] What is clear is that the 'heroic' virtues involve no phronesis—on the contrary, in such persons practical wisdom simply gets in the way of heroic virtue. Indeed, Nietzsche says his ideal philosopher 'is a "free spirit" who lives "unphilosophically" and "unwisely", above all *imprudently*' (*Beyond Good and Evil*, §205, p. 132, cited in Swanton 2003, 171). Of course, the heroic virtues are not virtues in terms of which right action is defined; but that only underscores how unlike the character virtues they are, especially since they have a completely different relation to deliberation and deliberative excellence. It is unclear, then, how the Aristotelian elements of Swanton's view are to fit alongside these Nietzschean elements.

And second, the role of phronesis even in quotidian character virtues turns out to be somewhat compromised. Swanton discusses briefly the famous Milgram experiments, in which an alarming number of subjects complied

---

[10] Slote also defends the 'admirable immorality' of great passion, as in Gauguin, when it 'is directed towards larger, impersonally valuable goods…something publicly, impersonally, valuable that people can benefit from' (1983, 102f). The case of Gauguin is interesting here, since it illustrates that some with heroic creativity may also have quotidian responsibilities. Where does phronesis fit in for them? See also Pincoffs 1986, ch. 7 for an interesting discussion of Gandhi.

[11] However, Swanton does not go as far in this direction as does Nietzsche, who sometimes suggests that there is 'no normatively required limit to the agent's expression of his creativity or benevolence', 2003, 142.

with requests to administer what they believed were very painful and even dangerous electric shocks to others, and says that while such subjects acted badly, nonetheless it may be that they acted from virtue. On the one hand, the reluctance and distress apparent in many subjects, she says, may suggest that they had virtues of benevolence; and on the other, it seems clear that benevolent agents may also have virtues of proper respect for authority, say, which were also relevant in the context of the environment. Where these subjects may have gone wrong, then, was not in lacking virtues, but that 'where virtues such as trust and fidelity appeared to conflict acutely with another—non-maleficence—many subjects gave insufficient weight to the latter', presumably 'under severe stress' (see 2003, 30–3). Obviously, Swanton denies that the subjects acted rightly or in an overall virtuous way; but she does say that their actions could nonetheless have been actions from virtue, for all we know. This analysis of the cases is therefore puzzling, since Swanton also agrees with Aristotle in that she 'regards practical wisdom as the glue which not only integrates the components of the profiles of the individual virtues, but also unites those virtues one to another' (2003, 27).[12] And indeed as we saw in Chapter 1, an essential feature of phronesis is that it discerns the mean of a virtue not in a myopic way, but in a way that meshes with the targets of the other virtues. Yet her analysis of the Milgram subjects suggests that they may have acted both virtuously, and thus presumably with practical wisdom, and yet in a surprisingly myopic way, focusing on the mean of one virtue while utterly violating others. It is unclear to me, then, how Swanton's remarks on practical wisdom (is it the same as phronesis?) are to be squared with her views about what can count as an act from virtue, and it seems that it is the former idea that is under-developed.

Swanton's position on phronesis, then, is complicated and somewhat difficult to make out. All the same, it seems clear that for the most part Swanton's theory *is* a kind of Hard Virtue Ethics—in fact, I think her theory can be viewed as a powerful and rich discussion of phronesis; I shall say more about this below. However, Swanton's discussion of Milgram's subjects is revealing, since it clearly connects with her anti-idealizing stance on the virtues. Swanton argues that virtue is a 'threshold concept': rather than 'think of virtue as an ideal state towards the realization of which one may progress, but which it is difficult or impossible to attain', Swanton maintains instead that 'in a world characterized by considerable evil, neediness, and frequent catastrophe, less than ideal states may count as virtuous'—virtue need not be perfect but only

---

[12] Swanton also seems to take a harder line on virtues of obedience elsewhere, 2003, 40, 47, and on the flexibility of practical wisdom, e.g. 246f.

'excellent or good enough' (2003, 24f, cf. 228f).[13] Now I think that Swanton must certainly be correct in thinking that virtue requires not perfection but being virtuous enough. But here a question arises. Swanton repeatedly connects this conception of virtue with her rejection of 'the virtuous person' as a useless and potentially dangerous ideal, and in particular one that is too abstract and too demanding. So where does this leave things for phronesis and the *phronimos*—are those notions too stringent, too idealized, as well? Or can one be practically intelligent 'enough' too? If one can be practically intelligent by being practically intelligent enough—if phronesis too is what Swanton calls a 'threshold concept'—then why should we suppose that 'the virtuous person' or 'the *phronimos*' is incompatible with a 'threshold' conception of virtue, with the idea that one can be virtuous by being virtuous enough? Yet if practical intelligence is not what she calls a 'threshold concept', then how could we say both that virtue is a 'threshold concept' *and* that phronesis is a 'component of all virtue', even if only 'characteristically'?

I do not know how Swanton would respond to these questions, but I want to argue that thinking of virtue in terms of 'the *phronimos*' and indeed 'the virtuous person' is not an alternative to the idea that real phronesis and virtue require only phronesis and virtue enough, but in fact is an implication of that very idea. Phronesis, like virtue, comes in degrees along a range or 'scale', and the notion of 'the virtuous person', complete with phronesis, is not necessarily an ideal for us to aspire to, but an ideal that 'calibrates' that scale and thus makes the very idea of such a scale a meaningful one. Phronesis, then, is a kind of ideal: it is an ideal of the sort of person who not only deliberates about the targets of the virtues, but actually hits them, and hits them reliably. But phronesis requires only phronesis enough: one need not be perfectly or ideally wise in order to be 'wise enough'—to 'know "what's what"', in Philippa Foot's phrase (1978a, 6). Phronesis, I argue, is a matter of degrees, and the notion of 'the virtuous person' and 'the *phronimos*' tells us what those degrees mean.

One crucial question, then, is whether the notion of 'virtuous enough' must be understood in relation to a standard or ideal, since clearly not all uses of 'enough' require any such standard. Another crucial question, as we have seen, is whether and how phronesis can be both an ideal and such that phronesis enough can be phronesis indeed. I take up these questions now—the first in §4.2 and the second in §§4.3 and 4.4—before turning to some final questions about why such locutions as 'the virtuous person' and 'the *phronimos*' are so

---

[13] Swanton seems to be rejecting the view that Pincoffs 1986, 108 calls 'brittle perfectionism', viz. the view that anything short of perfect virtue is a moral failure.

prone to misunderstanding, as I think they have been misunderstood not only by their detractors but even by some of their proponents (§4.5).

4.2 'Virtuous Enough'

In the Monty Python film *The Meaning of Life*, the board of a large American corporation has, for some unexplained reason, formed an *ad hoc* committee on the meaning of life, which is summarized in two main points: first, that people are not wearing enough hats, and second that the meaning of life lies in the development of the soul, although this is often eclipsed by more trivial concerns. Rather missing the point, the board mainly gets worked up about hats: 'What do you mean "enough"?' one of them demands, 'Enough *for what purpose?*' Being an American myself, perhaps I shall be forgiven for asking a similar sort of question: I agree that a person need only be virtuous enough to be virtuous indeed, virtuous *tout court*, but what does 'enough' mean here? Enough for what purpose?[14]

Here the question is worth asking. It seems undeniable that being virtuous enough is a sufficient condition for being virtuous *tout court*—not perfectly virtuous or even virtuous without qualification, but nonetheless virtuous in a genuine, *bona fide* sense.[15] But in general, being F *tout court* is only one 'purpose' for which we might say that someone or something is F enough. And as the purposes change, so too do the constraints on being F enough. So what are the constraints on being virtuous enough, when by 'virtuous enough' we mean virtuous enough to be virtuous *tout court*?

That is the question I want to explore in this section, and I argue that where the purpose is being virtuous *tout court*, an idealization of virtue is necessary. But we must begin with the notion of being 'F enough' more generally, since this notion turns out to require rather a lot of care and attention. Not all 'enoughs' are created equal

4.2.1 Satis Concepts

First some very important terminology. Swanton says that virtue is a 'threshold concept', by which she means that one can be virtuous without being perfectly so—it is enough for virtue that one's responsiveness to the demands of the world be 'good enough'. Although I share Swanton's view about what suffices

---

[14] I understand 'virtuous *tout court*' contrastively: not merely 'virtuous' in a degenerate sense, or as an honorific, or by analogy, etc.

[15] Wolf 1997, 95 suggests that 'morally good person' is also a concept of this type.

for being virtuous *tout court*, there is a problem with the term 'threshold concept' that will become clear shortly.[16] But there is more at stake than labels here, since getting clear on the label also involves getting clearer on just what 'virtuous enough' means.

Some concepts, like *virtue*, are such that something can be F by being 'F enough'. For ease of discussion, we can call these concepts 'satis concepts', *satis* being the Latin word for 'enough'. In this respect, satis concepts like *painful* and *bald* are unlike, say, *whole* or *perfect*, or *prime*, *positive*, and *even* in the case of numbers, which we might say are 'binary' concepts: in the case of the latter, since there are no degrees of F-ness among F things, things are either 'absolutely' F or not F at all, and so it makes no sense to talk here of something's being 'F enough'.[17] By contrast, satis concepts are such that there are degrees of F-ness among F things, and so since something need not be 'absolutely' F to be F, something can be F by being 'F enough'. The class of satis concepts is not a distinct class of concepts, but cuts across other classes (the same is true of binary concepts too, as we shall see). In particular, some satis concepts will be concepts with sharp boundaries, and some will be vague concepts. I begin by considering satis concepts with boundaries.

'Boundary' satis concepts are such that while something can be F by being F enough, there is also a boundary dividing F things from not-F things. Notice that since boundaries establish 'set-theoretically describable divisions', boundaries by definition are sharp (Sainsbury 1996, 253). For instance, we might say that *painful* is a boundary concept, since anything above a certain boundary of pressure on the skin, say, will count as painful.[18] So even though *painful* has a boundary—there are no degrees in between F and not-F things—it is still a satis concept, since there are degrees of painfulness, and something can be painful by being painful enough in degree. Consequently, it makes sense to say that something need not be 'absolutely' painful, only painful enough, to be over the boundary of painfulness.

It is important to note, however, that most boundary concepts are binary rather than satis concepts: that is, most boundary concepts are such that there are no degrees of F-ness either between F and not-F things, *or* among F things. For instance, *positive number* is a boundary concept, since there is a

---

[16] I thank Mark Colyvan for pointing this out; and I thank both him and Lynda Burns for numerous comments and suggestions that have proved invaluable to the development of my thought in this chapter (although they cannot be held responsible for its faults).

[17] In these terms, we can represent Unger 1975, 65–8 as arguing that satis concepts are apparent only, and in fact are all binary concepts; see Lewis 1979, 353f for a compelling refutation of this argument.

[18] I owe the example to Rick Benitez. As we shall see below, there are plenty of other examples as well, since we can stipulate boundaries for vague concepts, and thus treat any vague concept as a boundary concept.

boundary between positive and negative numbers, but it makes no sense to say that a number need only be 'positive enough' to be positive,[19] because that boundary concept, unlike the boundary satis concept *painful*, is not continuous but binary.[20] Boundary concepts, then, are such that there is a sharp set-theoretical boundary between F and not-F things, whether or not there are degrees of F-ness among F things (i.e. whether or not F is binary). Only where there are degrees of F-ness among F things is a boundary concept also a satis concept.

Here our earlier terminological issue resurfaces: is a 'threshold concept' a boundary satis concept? I do not think that Swanton means that virtue is a boundary concept, even of a satis variety, when she says that it is a threshold concept. For one thing, Swanton is admirably sensitive to the complex and gradual nature of moral development, and would be the first to agree that although every courageous person begins life lacking courage, there is no sharp boundary, no discrete point at which anyone makes the transition to being courageous. Likewise, a central thesis of Swanton's virtue ethics is that *virtue* (unlike *tall* or *bald*) is a multi-dimensional concept: virtue is not a single dimension along which people differ and develop, but a host of dimensions—and many vague concepts have borderline cases precisely because of their multi-dimensionality.[21] And of course her main point is that while none of us is unfailingly courageous, for all that some of us are still courageous *tout court*. So when Swanton says that virtue is a 'threshold concept', I do not think that she means it is a boundary concept.[22] Nonetheless, I think it is best to avoid the term 'threshold' here, where it could readily suggest a sharp boundary.

Since *virtue* is a satis concept, but lacks a sharp boundary, it would seem to be a vague satis concept. A classic description of vague concepts holds that a vague concept F is such that there will be 'borderline cases' of F, that is, cases in which no method of making F more precise could settle in a privileged way whether the thing is F or not. Vagueness thus arises because of the concept itself,

---

[19] I thank Neil McKinnon for the example.

[20] Are any vague concepts binary? *True* may be a vague concept, at least if there really are vague terms: in a sorites paradox, a statement like 'The first person in the sorites series is tall, so the person in the *i*th position in that series is tall' is true for some positions near the first and false for more distant positions, but there need be no position in the series that divides the true from the false instances of the statement. So if there are vague terms, *and* if there are no degrees of truth, then 'true' is both vague and binary. This is why vagueness raises its familiar problems for the Law of Excluded Middle. Fortunately, we need not take up the issue here.

[21] I thank Mark Colyvan for this point. See also Keefe and Smith 1996, 5.

[22] See also Hursthouse 1999a, ch. 7 for the idea that the *virtue*, as well as *moral motivation*, are (in our terms) vague satis concepts.

not because we happen to lack a method that would settle these cases. This account of vagueness does not go quite far enough, though, since a concept with sharp boundaries between F things, not-F things, and borderline cases is not a vague concept, despite having borderline cases; so we should say instead that a concept is vague if it lacks such boundaries (Sorensen 2006, §1; Sainsbury 1996; see also Keefe and Smith 1996, 15).[23] Concepts like *bald*, *tall*, and *heap* are vague concepts, since there are cases in which it cannot be settled whether the things in question really are bald, or tall, or heaps (except by stipulation or fiat, which is to change the subject from *bald* to *bald**), and it *also* cannot be settled just where those cases begin or end. Like a boundary satis concept, then, vague concepts admit of degrees of F-ness among F things—we can say they are 'continuous', rather than binary—but unlike all boundary concepts, vague concepts also admit of degrees between F things and not-F things.

Now that the 'vague' and 'boundary' varieties of satis concepts have been distinguished, we should take a closer look at what unites them as satis concepts, so that we might get a better grip on our quarry, the notion of being 'F enough' to be F. What do satis concepts all have in common? As we have just seen, all satis concepts are continuous—they admit of degrees of F-ness among F things, that is, some F things can be more F than other F things (e.g. Yul Brynner is balder than Mikhail Gorbachev, and impalement more painful than a pin-prick). It is therefore tempting to say that satis concepts are those for which it is possible to be F without being 'as F as can be'. For instance, *painful* is a continuous boundary concept, and to be painful enough is to be painful—it need not be as painful as can be. The same is true of some vague concepts; for instance, one need not be as bald as can be—entirely devoid of hair—to be bald enough to count as bald *tout court*. However, for such vague concepts as *heap* and *tall* it makes no sense to speak of something's being as much of a heap or as tall as can be.[24] For only some satis concepts does it make sense to talk about whether or not an F thing is as F as can be, so that is not their distinguishing feature.

---

[23] We may say, equivalently, that a concept is vague just in case the concept is such that it has borderline cases, *and* that for that concept ' "borderline case" has borderline cases'; see Sorensen 2006, §1. Sainsbury 1996, among others, claims that supervaluationism retains borderline cases, but eliminates 'boundarylessness', i.e. entails that 'borderline case' has no borderline cases; but see Keefe and Smith 1996, 34f who argue that the objection is not sufficiently sensitive to supervaluationism as conceived by Fine 1975. (I think that Sainsbury's objection does stick, however, in the case of degree theories of vagueness.) By contrast, the epistemic view of vagueness holds that while any vague term 'F' does pick out a boundaried set of F things, we lack epistemic access to that boundary, so the concept remains vague nonetheless.

[24] It is an interesting question whether there are any continuous boundary concepts for which 'as F as can be' is meaningless, but I shall not pursue it here.

This latter difference among satis concepts is instructive because it suggests different methods for telling when a thing is F or not (i.e. when this can be told), depending on whether 'as F as can be' is meaningful for that value of F. And this brings us closer to our big question: When, if ever, must 'virtuous enough' be assessed in the light of an ideal? First, consider the case in which some satis concept is such that 'as F as can be' is meaningless, for instance, the satis concept *tall*. In such cases, F-ness is usually determined in terms of central cases—for instance, 'Michael Jordan is tall'—and relations of simple resemblance (where some salient feature or features are common to all F things), family resemblance (where there is no salient feature common to all F things), and so on.[25] But central cases are not ideals.

What about those satis concepts for which 'as F as can be' does have a meaning? Here things are rather more complicated. In many of these cases, we can again use the 'central case and resemblance' method to tell, where possible, whether something is F or not. Consider, for instance, the satis concepts *painful* (a boundary satis concept) and *bald* (a vague satis concept). Doctors sometimes ask their patients to describe their pain by ranking it in relation to a merely annoying pinch on the one extreme and the most excruciating pain they can imagine on the other. Now, there is some sense to the notion of 'as painful as can be', at least in a way there is not for 'as tall as can be', even if, thankfully, most of us do not know just what it is. But because we do not know what it is, and do not really need to know in order to give a useful ranking of pain, we can simply think of some central cases of pains we have experienced, and rank our present pain by rough resemblance to them. Likewise for *bald*: perhaps Yul Brynner and Matt Lucas (the *Little Britain* TV star who suffers from alopecia) are 'as bald as can be', but again, we can use any of the central cases (Mikhail Gorbachev, say) to assess other cases in terms of their resemblance to central cases.

However, with other satis concepts for which the idea of 'as F as can be' has meaning, we may also exploit the very idea of 'as F as can be' to determine whether a thing counts as F or not (where this can be determined). In fact, in some cases we *must* try to exploit that idea. For instance, *person* is a multi-dimensional vague concept; in fact, it is a stock example of a vague

---

[25] Such a method can also be used to generate boundaries when boundaries are needed: for instance, we may take it as clear both that Jupiter and Mars are planets and that the bodies in the Kuiper Belt are not planets, and thus work towards a boundary that decides for objects like Pluto. On such triangulation, cp. Sainsbury 1996, 259f. (Is *planet* a boundary concept? Perhaps there can be borderline cases of concepts in which it is unclear whether those concepts are vague.) And recall Wittgenstein's famous observation that it is only in terms of family resemblance relations that we can speak of what counts as a game. For some difficulties involved in central cases and similarity relations, see Sainsbury 1996, 262f.

concept, since fetuses and patients in severe comas, say, fall in a zone between 'definitely a person' and 'definitely not a person' that seems disturbingly free of sharp boundaries. *Person* is also a satis concept, since one need not be a perfect or even a paradigmatic case of personhood in order to be a person. Now, one of the interesting things about *this* concept—*person*—is that we have a sense both that there is such a thing as the 'nature' of personhood, and that this nature is something we need to understand (for medical purposes, say). Even if such an understanding could not eliminate borderline cases (and I do not think it could), such an understanding would be important *before* we could use the simple central-case-and-resemblance method: perhaps there is no difficulty identifying the central cases, but *in what ways* must a person resemble the 'central cases'? We therefore need an account of what *makes* the central cases central, that is, of what makes a person a person, and therefore we need an account of the nature of personhood—of 'as much a person as can be'. This is not to deny, of course, that we may come to acquire a concept like *person* through experience of central cases; it is only to say that when we need to know what really counts as a person, as in medical cases, reliance on central cases alone is no longer enough.

When we try to say what personhood really is, we construct a theoretical model of what we take to be the essential features of personhood, in some kind of reflective equilibrium, and realized to the fullest degree, since the model must illuminate the central cases, not just join their ranks. This model, we should note, is an ideal, and therefore not merely a central case: you or I could stand as a central case of personhood, but not as a model of personhood, since particular persons always have shortcomings in some dimension or other of personhood, a shortcoming that the model is to reveal *as* a shortcoming. Of course, it is no easy matter to construct such a model, and as the debates over abortion and euthanasia make clear, a model does not magically create a boundary where none was before. But for an important range of concepts, determining what is F enough to count as F *tout court* actually *requires* an approach of this general form, and thus a fair bit of idealizing. Satis concepts that must be understood via such models I shall call 'model concepts'. And it is my thesis that *virtues are model concepts*. To see why, let's look more closely at model concepts.

4.2.2 Model Concepts

When is a satis concept a model concept—when *must* a satis concept be understood via a theoretical model? Some cases of 'F enough' require no such model because 'F enough' is purely interest-relative, and sometimes those interests permit—and even require—that we eliminate vagueness by simply stipulating a boundary. For instance, consider the children's game of racing to fill a cup by carrying water across the room in a spoon. Since the object of the game is to be the first to fill one's cup, players need to know with a fair bit of precision when a cup counts as 'full', and an easy way to solve this problem is to draw a line on the cup and stipulate, 'Full is at that line'. Notice that a cup that is 'full enough' in this stipulated sense is not necessarily full *tout court*; all we can say is that it is 'full*', full for this rather special purpose. Likewise, consider risk management experts determining a safety threshold for an electric power generating plant. One way to determine such a threshold is to correlate graduated electric utility rates with graduated levels of safety in electricity production and delivery, and set the safety threshold at that point above which area residents declare they are unwilling (or, more often, unable) to pay for safer electric utilities.[26] (Notice, then, that stipulated thresholds or boundaries need not be *arbitrary*.) Unfortunately, it is only too clear that 'safe enough', in this rather special sense, is not the same thing as 'safe' *tout court*; all we can say is that it is 'safe*', and hope for the best. Consequently, a concept is (functioning as) a model concept only if 'F enough' is not to be replaced by any 'F*'.

On the other hand, some purely interest-relative applications of satis concepts do not involve replacing the original vague concept F with a stipulated boundary concept F*. For instance, I may describe someone as 'bald', meaning that he is bald enough to play the lead role in a play about Mikhail Gorbachev that I am directing. (The example is from Graff 2000.) Here 'F enough' again fails to entail 'F *tout court*', just as it fails when I describe a piece of ground as 'flat', meaning that it is flat enough for me to park my bicycle on (perhaps in contrast to all the dramatically uneven ground around here). Since model concepts are such that 'F enough' entails 'F *tout court*', we can say that a satis concept is (functioning as) a model concept only if 'F enough' is not purely interest-relative.

What makes 'F enough' *purely* interest-relative? When we ask whether a fetus or a comatose patient is a 'person enough', we take a keen interest in the answer, but what we want to know is whether the fetus or patient is a person *tout court*, not a 'person*', or a 'person' relative to just any old interest or purpose we may have. Here our interest is in finding out whether the patient is *really* a person, and so here 'person enough' is not purely interest-relative.

---

[26] See Cassedy 1992–3 for discussion of this so-called 'willingness to pay' model of risk evaluation. I am not at all sanguine about the ethical implications of this method, but for our purposes we need consider only its methodology and not the ethical aspects of that methodology. And to be fair, it does at least *attempt* to take residents' preferences seriously, something that many models of risk evaluation cannot claim.

Depending on how the answer comes out, we may even have to revise the interests that initially prompted the question.[27]

We are getting closer to an account of model concepts, but we are not quite there yet. Some cases in which 'F enough' entails 'F *tout court*' are not purely interest-relative, but also are not model concepts. For instance, we may say that to be 'bald enough' is to be bald enough to warrant the description 'bald', interests aside, given how competent speakers use that term. Since that, presumably, just is all that 'bald *tout court*' means, 'bald enough' would therefore entail 'bald *tout court*'. This is very different, though, from the sense in which being 'person enough' suffices for being a person *tout court*: if investigation revealed that a comatose patient was in fact a person *tout court*, then the patient's residing in a community of competent speakers who do not use the word 'person' to refer to the comatose would be neither here nor there—in this case the word must fit the fact, not vice versa. We can mark this important difference by distinguishing a *de dicto* sense of being F enough to be F *tout court* from a *de re* sense. So even where there is such a thing as 'as F as can be', no model of F is required to give meaning to 'F *tout court*', where the latter notion is only *de dicto*.

Therefore, a concept F is a model concept just in case being F enough entails being F *tout court*, where 'F *tout court*' is understood neither in a purely interest-relative sense nor in a *de dicto* sense, but in terms of what it is to be F, *de re*.[28] In the case of model concepts, the possibility of error about 'F enough' is more than the possibility of being out of step with how competent speakers talk about what is F enough. It is instead the possibility that one may even be in step with everyone else about the central cases, but nonetheless be mistaken

---

[27] So I do not agree with Graff 2000 that, in cases of vagueness, whether something is F or not is always interest-relative. Graff explicitly discusses only vague adjectives, with the promissory note that the analysis could be extended to vague nouns as well, although only on a case by case basis. However, 'person' seems to be a vague noun for which being F enough is not always interest-relative (and as I argue below, there are others); so I do not think that the promissory note can be redeemed.

It is worth mentioning a recent analysis of 'enough' statements offered by Meier 2003. Meier analyzes statements like 'Bertha is old enough to (be legally permitted to) drive a car' as assigning an age-value to Bertha that is equal to or greater than that unique age-value than which there is no lower age-value at which driving a car is permitted by law (2003, 87). This example works because the law specifies such a unique age-value; for the purposes of legally driving a car, 'old enough' has a boundary. However, interestingly, Meier's other case—'She is too young to date'—presumably has no such boundary, yet the analysis is the same in both cases. (Similar problems infect related analysis of 'too' statements; e.g. 'This food is too good to throw away' is analyzed as saying that the quality-value of the food is greater than the unique maximal quality-value of food at which we will throw the food away (93). Presumably there is no such *unique* value, i.e. no boundary.)

[28] Notice, then, that boundary concepts can be model concepts, too. So if *virtue* turns out to be a model concept, it will be so even if one thinks (as I do not) that it is a boundary concept. I have benefited from discussion with Neil McKinnon on this point.

in thinking that those cases really are or are not F. That is why *person* is a model concept: when we think about abortion and euthanasia, what we want to know is whether fetuses or the comatose *are* persons. Consequently, central cases of personhood are not enough, for two reasons. One, we need to know not only *that* such-and-such is a central case, but also *why* it is so. And two, the very idea of being F *tout court*, in a *de re* sense, implies the possibility of serious error about what things are F, and even about what is a central case of F (more on this below). The form of a solution to puzzles about whether fetuses or the comatose are persons, therefore, must start with recognition of personhood as a model concept.[29] (And it is there, of course, that the hard work really begins.)

To take another example, *rational* seems to be a model concept, too. It certainly is a vague concept: there is no sharp boundary that divides a now-rational developing mind from its erstwhile non-rational stage, as if by only a moment. (And like *person*, *rational* is also multi-dimensional.) It is also a satis concept, since no one is perfectly rational or as rational as can be, and yet 'rational' is not merely an honorific. And *rational* is a model concept, because rationality *tout court* must be understood in the light of a model of rationality that involves idealized principles of rationality, such as the transitivity of preferences and the forming of all-things-considered judgments. Model concepts are therefore an important sub-class of satis concepts that are generally overlooked in discussions of vagueness, which have focused mainly on common usage of vague predicates (and, less often, of other vague locutions).

Satis concepts, being continuous, involve a scale on which some F things are more F and some less F than other F things. But to overlook the class of model concepts is to overlook an important difference in the ways that different types of satis concepts can be placed on a scale. Cups are full, power plants are safe, and men are bald by degrees that can be ordinally ranked, and in some cases we can even say by just how much one degree differs from another.

---

[29] Lewis 1979, 351–4 says that the standards for what one may call 'F enough' are determined by conversational context, which makes a certain level of precision salient in the conversation. One way to put our point, then, is that in a conversation in which it matters what is F *tout court*, in a *de re* sense, one must at least acknowledge that use of 'F enough' is constrained by the fact that F is functioning as a model concept. This way of putting the point allows that what I have called a model concept can be used in conversations with standards lower than *de re* standards. Someone might suggest that *person* is therefore not a model concept, but is an ordinary concept that can, in some contexts, be constrained by a model. However, I prefer to say that *person* is a model concept, even though it does not function as a model concept in every conversation that deploys the concept without violation. This is so because for concepts like *person* the *de re* sense of F *tout court* is prior to other uses, in terms of the direction of revision from the former to the latter.

How such scales are *calibrated*, then, depends on our interests, or perhaps on common usage of the related terms. By contrast, model concepts like *rational* and *person* also yield a calibrated scale, but here the scale requires a 'standardized' calibration: what it is to count as rational at all, and to what extent a given agent is rational, is to be determined (where it can be determined) by a scale that is calibrated by a model of ideal rationality that both sets the top end of the scale and gives meaning to the idea that a particular agent occupies a certain level on that scale. (Likewise for personhood.) Understanding what it is to be F *tout court* in a *de re* sense, then, calls for a theoretical model of 'really F'.

4.2.3 Virtue as a Model Concept

Virtue is a vague satis concept, but is it also a model concept? I think that it is. As we have seen, a satis concept F is a model concept when there is the possibility of serious error about what counts as a central case of F. The possibility of such error is nowhere clearer, I think, than in Nietzsche's critiques of certain allegedly central cases of virtues. Nietzsche argued that most of his contemporaries were wrong to think of certain character traits—commonly called 'pity' or 'charity'—as central cases of good character, since he believed that the traits so celebrated actually rested on psychological distortions, such as self-loathing and resentment (Swanton, 2003 *passim* and 2005). If Nietzsche was correct in his assessment of those traits that his contemporaries praised as central cases, then either those traits were not central or genuine cases of charity but only bastardizations (since real charity is a virtue), or they really were cases of charity but charity is not a genuine case of virtue.

Errors of the sort Nietzsche alleged are real possibilities for an important range of satis concepts, and any account of those concepts that has recourse to no more than commonsense views of F things is of course bound to preserve such errors. Satis concepts of that type, then, are model concepts, and so it is clear that virtue is a model concept. If anything, Nietzsche's discussion of charity (whether correct in detail or not) shows that virtue is a model concept *par excellence*. Therefore, *it is a mistake to suppose that the idea that one need only be 'virtuous enough' to be virtuous is an* alternative *to thinking of the virtues in terms of ideal models*. On the contrary, thinking of virtue in terms of ideals is *required* on account of the very sort of satis concept that virtue is. Likewise, it also seems indispensable for virtue ethics that all the virtues involve phronesis, since phronesis standardizes that crucial aspect of virtue that is deliberative excellence. Where virtue ethics is concerned, virtuousness not only admits of calibration, but requires a standardized calibration, and thus a model of ideal virtuousness that both sets the top end of the scale and gives meaning to the idea that a particular agent occupies a certain level on that scale.

Consequently, it seems clear that *virtue* and *phronesis* are satis concepts, and in particular are model concepts as well, at least where virtue ethics is concerned. The qualification 'where virtue ethics is concerned' is significant, because an ethical theory could stipulate that 'virtuous enough' simply means virtuous enough for right action, say, understanding the latter in some prior and independent sense. But such a theory would not be a form of virtue ethics, which must hold that 'the concept of proper or right conduct will be well understood only if the concept of virtue is' (Watson 1990, 454; this recalls the VE constraint from Chapter 2). On the other hand, a theory of the virtues could rely on little more than common usage of virtue terms, and so on, but such a theory could not, I think, make a credible link between right action and 'the virtues' so understood. For virtue ethics, then, to link right action to the virtues is to link right action to traits that really are virtues, so the latter must be understood in terms of a theoretical model of what a virtue is.[30]

Notice that in calling *virtue, phronesis, person*, and *rationality* model concepts, we do not deny that we rely on our beliefs about clear cases in arriving at that model. The model of 'the virtuous person' is constructed on the basis of a totality of evidence and beliefs in reflective equilibrium, including beliefs about psychology, well-being, reasonableness, and indeed the 'clear cases' of virtue. The point is that, as the model comes together, parts of that totality are liable to revision so as to fit with other parts (such as Nietzsche's observations about 'charity'), and the *'clear' cases are eventually as liable to revision as any other.* That is why, for concepts of this sort, their application must be determined by such a model, and not simply by the clear cases taken on their own. *Tall* and *bald* are not model concepts, because for them there is no such totality of beliefs and evidence, but only clear cases that could not in principle fail to be real cases.

Our conclusion is that virtues are model concepts, but perhaps we should look for ways to resist this conclusion. Construing virtues as model concepts reintroduces 'the virtuous person', of course, and therefore, it seems, precisely the sort of view of the virtues that prompted rejection of 'the virtuous person' and 'the *phronimos*' in the first place. To be sure, we have shown what is wrong with that class of objections that assume that the idea of 'the *phronimos*' sets ideal or exceptional wisdom as a necessary condition on one's being virtuous at all: if virtue is a model concept, then it is also a satis concept. But we are still left wondering who this '*phronimos*', this 'virtuous person' is, and talk of this

---

[30] Hursthouse 1999a, ch. 7 takes virtue to be what I have called a model concept and suggests, plausibly, that an ideal agent plays the same sort of role in Kantianism (151), although she does not develop the idea as far as we are doing here.

person as an 'ideal' and a 'standard' seems to suggest that we should all aspire to that ideal, a task that seems bound to fail and even potentially disastrous in the attempt. Furthermore, it may be possible for a virtue ethics to accept the idea that the virtues are model concepts, and thus offer an idealized model of the *virtues*, without also employing any idealized model of 'the virtuous *person*'; in fact, I think that this would be very much like (a version of) Swanton's own approach, as I explain below. I begin with the point about aspiring to ideals.

4.3 Ideals and Aspirations

Suppose that I accept that some ideal model of virtue sets the top end of the 'scale' of virtuousness, and 'calibrates' that scale so as to give meaning to the idea of someone's being virtuous to a less than ideal degree (overall, or in some respect or other). To what do I commit myself, in accepting this ideal? It is clear that I have not committed to accepting the attributes of that model as forming a set of necessary conditions on my being virtuous at all, since I accept that model as calibrating a *range* or continuum, and a range with many dimensions. But have I nonetheless committed to aspiring to become as like that ideal as possible? How can I really accept that ideal without aspiring to it—what else could accepting that ideal mean? And isn't this precisely why we should want to get by without ideals?

4.3.1 Aspiration and 'The Rational Person'

Here the parallel between *rational* and *virtuous* as model concepts is apt in a further way, since idealized models of rationality such as Donald Davidson's have come in for similar sorts of criticism as 'the virtuous person' has.[31] Davidson defended a principle (often called the 'Principle of Charity') which says that a necessary condition on interpreting the speech and behavior of another agent is one's taking that agent to exemplify certain basic features of rationality, such as 'consistency, closure, and transitivity of preferences', as well as forming and acting on all-things-considered judgments; this state of an agent Carol Rovane calls 'overall rational unity' (1999, 471f).[32] But as

---

[31] In thinking about this issue in Davidson's philosophy and its parallel in virtue ethics, I am greatly indebted to Deborah Soles for useful comments and suggestions.

[32] It is important to note that taking agents in this way is not an act of magnanimity or a good rule of thumb, but a precondition of the very possibility of interpretation; see Davidson 1984, 137, 197; Ramberg 1989, ch. 6.

Rovane notes, to some philosophers the Principle of Charity has seemed 'far too stringent. The fact is that persons hardly ever do consider *all* things before they act' (1999, 472). In other words, because Davidson takes rationality to be what we have called a model concept, his view effectively introduces a model of 'the rational person', and this has seemed to some to make rationality an unrealistic idealization. However, this reaction to the Principle of Charity and 'the rational person' is based on an important misunderstanding—the same sort of misunderstanding, I think, that prompts a similar reaction to the notion of 'the virtuous person'.

Note that in saying that 'the rational person' sets the standard for rational agents, we do not thereby say that matching that standard is a necessary condition for being rational. On Davidson's view, rationality is not all-or-nothing, but is what I have called a satis concept, allowing even rather wide degrees of slippage and imperfection (1999, 480f). The Principle of Charity has 'the rational person' set the standard for rational agents by offering a model for understanding what can count as rational, and as more rational or less, in real agents. It is also clear, though, that 'the rational person' is thus a kind of ideal, and more than that, a normative ideal, since rationality is also a normative concept. As Rovane says (1999, 473),

qua beings who are reflective as well as rational, we are able to grasp the normative force of the requirement [of overall rational unity]; and to grasp its normative force is just to recognize that we *ought* to meet it; and nothing more is required for being committed to meeting it than recognizing that we ought to meet it.

What does committing to meeting that requirement come to? Obviously, the ideal of 'the rational person'—the person with 'overall rational unity'—is 'an ideal of which we are bound to fall short', but it is my view that committing to this ideal *is not the same as committing to becoming as like it as possible*. Rather, to commit to the ideal of overall rational unity is to accept the principles of such rationality as principles one recognizes as *one's own* principles, principles to which one can be held, by which one can be criticized, and in relation to which one must frame one's response to such criticism—indeed, the very giving of such criticism presupposes the agent's ability to respond in just this way (see esp. Davidson 1985; see also Rovane 1999, 473f). In that case, Rovane notes, that ideal serves 'as an effective normative guide in our lives': for one thing, the ideal 'provides a reference point by which we can evaluate our own thoughts and actions, and count them either as rational successes or as rational failures'; and for another, the ideal 'also provides a goal towards which we can strive even as we recognize our failures to achieve it' (1999, 473). Now, it seems clear to me that accepting that ideal necessarily involves being motivated to be rational, and to improve in rationality. But even if that is so, to accept the ideal is not necessarily to aspire to become as like the ideal as possible, as I argue now.

Internalists about motivation (myself included) hold that accepting an ideal, in the sense that Davidson and Rovane discuss, necessarily motivates one to adopt that ideal as an ideal for oneself, to stand for assessment in the light of that ideal, and to improve oneself (where possible) in the direction of that ideal. However, it is perfectly consistent with internalism to say that accepting an ideal does not entail aspiring to become as like the ideal as possible. The question here is not *whether* one is motivated to do something in virtue of accepting an ideal, but *how much* that acceptance must motivate one to do. Such thorough-going aspiration, after all, is not merely a commitment to rationality in the pursuit of one's projects, not even the project of becoming more rational, but a commitment to a rather special and strange project, a project that it may well be *irrational* for one to adopt.

Take for instance the idea that 'the rational person' acts on all-things-considered judgments. As Davidson says, to accept such an ideal is to accept the rationality of all-things-considered judgments as a principle of one's own; the charge that one has violated that principle cannot be met with the response, 'So I have broken your rule; who says I should do things your way?' (Davidson 1985). By accepting the ideal, one has made the 'rule' or principle a principle to which one sees oneself as bound. But committing to making all-things-considered judgments is not the same as committing to the (rather queer) life-project of becoming the best maker of all-things-considered judgments there can be. That project, like every other, consumes resources and opportunities, and can no more be assumed to be a rational one than any other project can. That is a fact about practical rationality: when it comes to making all-things-considered judgments, at some point it is reasonable to stop considering, choose, and hope that the choice is one we can live with, or perhaps grow into (see Schmidtz 1994, 245). Indeed, trying to become persons who do consider all things before acting is something that we have all-things-considered reasons *not* to do.

Put another way, rational agents act for reasons, and this extends also to the act of taking something to be a reason for acting. This means, of course, that we can never become beings who act for reasons that go 'all the way down'. But it does not follow that someone committed to being rational in his actions is thereby committed to the project of searching for reasons as far down as possible, like computing the value of pi to yet a further decimal place. As David Schmidtz says (2001, §§I, VI),

We come as close as we can to being reasonable all the way down when we become aware of our limits, and serene about them.... At any point, we determine how much longer the chain of reason-giving needs to be by asking what purpose is served by saying more. We go back as far as we have reason to go. Then we stop. To keep going would be unreasonable.

Perhaps we should say instead that by accepting the ideal of 'the rational person' I commit to the project of becoming as rational as *I* can be—as thorough as I can be in forming all-things-considered judgments, say. But the reasonability of that project cannot be taken for granted, either. Accepting the ideal gives me a reason to be rational, and to improve where improvement is necessary and is not unreasonably costly. And where I must accept my limitations with serenity, I may reasonably reject calls to improve, but what I may *not* reasonably claim is that my limitations are anything but just that: limitations.[33] To accept 'the rational person' as an ideal commits me to living up to certain principles of rationality as principles of my own—that is what acceptance of that ideal is—but it is a further question just how far it is reasonable for me to take the project of living up to those principles. The model of reasonability itself calls me no further than is reasonable.

So, to put the point in terms of 'calibration', acceptance of 'the rational person' as an ideal is to accept the ideal of overall rational unity both as constituting the top of the scale of rationality and as giving sense to the idea that one's own rationality falls in a particular place on that scale. In this sense the ideal is a 'normative' one: a precondition of rational agency is that one accept that ideal as calibrating the scale of rationality. Just how high on the scale one ought to strive to rise, however, is a further idea—and one that is among a number of other considerations, including the fact that it may be less rational, all things considered, for certain persons to try to rise past a certain point, given their particular circumstances.[34] Considerations of rationality set constraints on one's projects, including the project of trying to become as rational as possible.

4.3.2 Aspiration and 'The Virtuous Person'

I believe that the notion of 'the virtuous person' and 'the *phronimos*' functions for virtue ethics in precisely the same fashion as 'the rational person' does in

---

[33] That is why the model must be an *ideal*. As Broadie 1991, 259 points out, 'A mixed pair of ethical terms can hold of the same subject, but then this subject is not an appropriate model, since a model should not send mixed messages. It makes sense in a work of practical ethics to shape the logic of the terms in such a way that they cannot send mixed messages.' See also Broadie 1991, 191.

[34] Note also that no single ideal could embody all the things that are worth pursuing in a lifetime; see Wolf 1997, 95ff.

a theory like Davidson's.[35] To accept an ideal model of 'the virtuous person' as a standard by which scales of virtuousness are calibrated is, for one thing, to accept certain 'principles' of character—such as 'Be honest', 'Be fair'—as principles of one's own.[36] For a person who accepts that ideal, an accusation of dishonesty cannot be met by the response 'So what if I am dishonest? "Be honest" is your rule; why should I do things your way?' To be an honest person, one must accept standards of what counts as the virtue of honesty as standards of one's own. It therefore also commits one to improving and to avoiding complacency about one's character. And since to accept that ideal is to acknowledge that virtue is what I have called a model concept, it is therefore to accept an objective and real standard of virtuousness. To accept that virtue is a model concept is to accept that one cannot in good faith adjust one's assessment of one's virtues to a merely stipulated standard, or to the standard of popular opinion and the vernacular. What it is to be virtuous, like what it is to be rational, is a standard to be *discovered*, from within our best understanding of ourselves and our reasons, in reflective equilibrium,[37] and a model of 'the virtuous person' is meant to represent our best attempts to systematize our discoveries so far.[38]

Furthermore, as in the case of 'the rational person', the notion of 'the virtuous person' is useful for thinking about the progress of such limited and developing creatures as ourselves. For one thing, that notion sets standards by which we can determine in a person who is developing towards courage, say, that what he or she is developing towards is indeed *the virtue of courage* in the first place, rather than recklessness or self-destructiveness, say. This point is crucial to virtue ethics, which must treat virtues as psychologically real entities—nexuses of emotions, desires, goals, and values—rather than as mere propensities to certain stereotypical forms of action, since only the former make one flexible enough to act well and rightly in a variety of contexts. And for another, setting standards in this way allows assessment of how well

[35] More than that, I think that it *always has* functioned that way, particularly in philosophers like Aristotle and Hursthouse, although I shall leave such exegetical questions aside for now.

[36] It should go without saying that such ideal standards need not be simplistic, such as 'Always tell the truth'. On the contrary, one reason 'the *phronimos*' is taken as an ideal is precisely that such standards are *not* simplistic. These principles, standards, or rules I take to be equivalent to what Hursthouse 1999a and others call the 'V-rules', and I take e.g. Aristotle's discussion of 'the mean'—and for that matter, Swanton's discussion of the 'targets' of the virtues—as an attempt to arrive at a philosophically best statement of those principles.

[37] See McDowell 1995a. I agree with McDowell that the outlook from which we make such discoveries about virtues is and must be an ethical outlook. See also Ch. 3.

[38] This is important, since a standard should not be arbitrary, the imposition on the rest of us of someone's personal standard; see Pincoffs 1986, 109–12. This point is, I take it, of a piece with Janna Thompson's worry that we mentioned above.

one's development is coming along: where it is excelling and where falling short, where there are strengths to build on and weaknesses that are potential developmental pitfalls, and how best to develop from here.[39]

Where improving is not possible, or the striving not reasonable, 'the virtuous person' reveals what limitations one must learn to accept. A virtuous attitude towards one's limitations in virtue is, I think, rather like a rational attitude towards one's limitations in rationality. Since virtue is a model concept that ranges over persons, to accept principles of virtuous character as normative just is to accept 'the virtuous person' or 'the *phronimos*' as a normative ideal. And just as in the case of 'the rational person', how far one ought to ascend the scale is a different issue (and it is here that serenity proves its worth). As Aristotle notes (*NE* II.9), hitting the mean is always difficult, and can be much more difficult for some persons, given their particular makeup, than it is for others. In such cases, he says, one is often better off erring on one side than another: temperance, for instance, is not abstinence, but for some people with particular weaknesses (for sex, say, or food, or alcohol), it is better to err on the side of abstinence than to aim for the mean in its ideal sense, and risk falling into indulgence which is even worse. Aristotle's discussion of these cases is too quick, and he has little to say about whether those who veer to one side of the mean are virtuous *tout court*. But I certainly want to say that they can be, even though they are far from ideally virtuous—and the *wisest* course for them may be to *remain* so. Of course, this is to acknowledge their limitations, not to pretend that they have none; but although they can be only so virtuous, that can be virtuous enough.

Therefore, as in the case of rationality, to accept an ideal of virtue is to accept the project of improving, but that leaves the question how far each of us ought to take that project. And again, as with all projects, that project requires resources and opportunities and, as Swanton is correct to observe, can pose significant risks, including risks to the very quality of one's character. How far to take that project, then, is a question of what is good for people, and for some person in particular. It is a question, that is, that requires phronesis to answer correctly. This is not to say, absurdly, that phronesis must therefore precede the virtues. As Aristotle observes, one cannot develop phronesis without having developed to some degree the particular virtues of character (*NE* VI.12); I take this to mean that phronesis can develop only where (at minimum) one

---

[39] It is important to note that it is not an implication of this view 'that we cannot understand "courageous act"...until we have (so to speak) got our hands on the exemplar, the agent with the virtuous character'; see Hursthouse 1999a, 80 who considers and rejects this view. Such a view is mistaken for the same reason as the idea that we cannot understand 'rational act' without a conception of 'the agent with overall rational unity'.

has already accepted principles of virtuous character as principles of one's own. At some point in development, however, phronesis must begin to take the reins, both to direct one's further development *and* to determine how far it is rational, and beneficial, and indeed virtuous to take the very project of developing and improving. Since virtue is a model concept, virtue requires phronesis, or at least phronesis enough.

Finally, it is important to note that 'the virtuous person' does not eradicate the possibility of reasonable disagreement on moral questions. Where there is no view that 'all right-thinking people' must have, 'the virtuous person' is not modeled as having a particular belief, although the model should refer to how it is virtuous to confront such difficult issues, and to handle the fact of disagreement among reasonable persons. 'The virtuous person' does not turn moral disagreement into moral failure (see also Pincoffs 1986, 146).

Perhaps we shall worry that this way of understanding talk of 'the virtuous person' means that such talk *per se* now introduces nothing new to a virtue ethical theory of right action. After all, I have said that 'the virtuous person', like 'the rational person', systematizes virtue ethics' best attempts at saying what it is to be virtuous, and in that case, although virtue ethicists disagree about what it is to be virtuous, that is a difference between one theory's model and another's, not a difference between theories with a model and theories without. But in fact, that is my point: understanding right action in terms of 'the virtuous person' is not to take a *special* type of virtue ethical approach to right action; it is instead to forge the *standard* virtue ethical link between right action and the virtues. Virtue ethics ties right action not to duty or to consequences but to virtues, features not of situations but of persons. To forge that link is not to say that being ideally virtuous is a necessary condition for being virtuous at all; it is not to say that right action involves fathoming what 'the virtuous person' would do; and it is not to set up an ideal to which virtuous persons are expected to aspire.

In fact, when we understand the link that way, virtue ethics can also show in a straightforward way what is praiseworthy about remedial action, such as actions taken to break one's habit of lying (I discuss such actions in Chapter 2). As Robert Johnson (2003) has pointed out, actions like these have real moral merit, even though they are acts that no virtuous person would do. However, 'the virtuous person' *does* turn out to be relevant to thinking about the merit of such acts, after all: to undertake remedial acts in good faith is admirable and praiseworthy—and even, in a sense, virtuous—because it is to (begin to) accept standards of virtue as standards of one's own.

For all these reasons, 'the virtuous person' comes as standard with virtue ethics. There is no doing without these sorts of ideals, and no reason to want to do without them. However, to say that 'the virtuous person' does not distinguish one form of virtue ethics from another is not to say that it contributes nothing distinctive to virtue ethics. I want to say now what I think its contribution is, before saying (in the final section) why that contribution is so easily missed.

4.4 Virtues, Persons, and 'The Virtuous Person'

I have argued that concepts like *virtuous* are model concepts, and thus require a model of virtue to determine what is 'virtuous enough' to be virtuous *tout court*. But perhaps I have been too quick in supposing that this means we must have a model of the virtuous *person*. Part of what makes 'the virtuous person' seem such an unattractive ideal is that it is a model of a person who is virtuous as a *whole*; but no real person is or even could be perfect in even one virtue, let alone in the virtues, in the plural. Perhaps, then, we could understand each virtue as consisting in certain sorts of states, such as modes of responding to the demands of the world (a certain constellation of modes comprising a distinctive 'profile' for each virtue), and treat each of these modes as a model concept, thus giving meaning to the idea of one's responding via that mode in a good enough way. In that case, whether a person is (say) courageous *tout court* depends on one's stable disposition to respond to the demands of the world via the modes associated with courage in a good enough way. So even though 'virtuous enough' requires a model, it need not be 'the virtuous person'.

Indeed, Swanton herself understands a virtuous mode of response as one that is (among other things) free of psychological distortions, and as she recognizes, this requires a model of healthy psychological states, since the idea of a distortion of an inner state—as when putting others' interests ahead of one's own is distorted by self-loathing—'presupposes a norm relative to which something is distorted' (2003, 180, cf. 186f; cp. Thompson 1995, 295f on the notion of 'defect' in organisms). And while this model of psychological health illuminates the notions of 'distorted' and 'undistorted' psychological states, it does not also represent a level of health that one's psychological states must attain in order for them to count as healthy at all: 'the standards of what counts as displaying a virtue need not be set by the perfectly healthy person' (2003, 63).

This last claim is ambiguous between the rejection of the very idea of 'the perfectly healthy person', and the claim that although 'the perfectly healthy person' sets the norm, states short of perfect health can still count as healthy *tout court*. In the latter case, retaining 'the healthy person' while rejecting 'the virtuous person' would require special pleading, since 'the virtuous person' would be playing exactly the same part for *virtuous* that 'the perfectly healthy person' plays for *healthy*. But perhaps we could reject 'the perfectly healthy person' altogether and replace it with a model of 'the perfectly healthy *state*'. The question, then, is whether the model of 'the virtuous person' adds anything of special importance to virtue ethics for being the model of a kind of *person*. I think that it does.

The importance of that model stems from the connection that virtue ethics makes between right action and the virtues. As all virtue ethicists agree, making that connection means that virtue ethics requires a conception of the virtues as psychologically robust rather than 'thin'. A well-known thin conception of virtue is Julia Driver's (who rejects virtue ethics and its theory of right action), on which the notion of a virtue is like the notion of 'fitness' in biology: as a biological trait is fit insofar as it facilitates the preservation of the organism in its environment, so a character trait is a virtue insofar as it 'systematically produces a preponderance of good' in the agent's environment (2001, xvii). On this view, although moral virtues supervene on mental rather than physical attributes, moral virtue requires no *particular* sort of underlying psychology, and in particular no cognitive attributes. In fact, one of Driver's central points is that one may well have certain virtues without having any idea that one does; for instance, she argues that 'modesty' is a virtue that supervenes on one's ignorance of certain facts about oneself. Whatever else we say about such a theory, it is clear that it is one that no virtue ethicist could accept, since it makes a virtue too psychologically thin to support the close connection that virtue ethics must make between being virtuous and acting rightly—not acting rightly in a perfect or universal way, but in a way that is intelligent enough to be, in Driver's terms, reliable and flexible. Here, 'reliability' concerns the regularity of one's action across situations that are contextually similar, and 'flexibility' concerns one's ability to adapt one's actions across dissimilar contexts. Each is indispensable to the tie between virtue and right action, and as Driver notes, it is flexibility that requires the virtues to be psychologically robust (so that flexibility therefore comes at too high a cost; 2001, 53f). On such a robust conception of the virtues, virtue refers not to some 'state' or 'attribute' of an agent in isolation, such as a certain form of ignorance, but to a set of practical, affective, and cognitive abilities with which a person with that virtue interacts with the world. Such sets of abilities cannot be hived off on their own, since they tend to merge with each other, and together make up a whole character.[40] In order to maintain its tie between virtue and right action,

---

[40] I take up these issues in greater detail in Ch. 10.

then, virtue ethics must adopt a robust conception of the virtues, and in that case, the virtue ethicist must understand the virtues, and modes of virtuous response, within the agent taken as a whole.

Interestingly, with respect to this 'holism' the virtues are rather like certain other biological concepts (besides fitness). In his important paper 'The Representation of Life', Michael Thompson begins by considering the common practice among writers of textbooks in biology of characterizing 'life' or 'living things' in terms of a fairly standard list of discrete traits more common among animate things than among inanimate things, such as high levels of organization, reproduction, energy conversion, and so on. Thompson worries not about the contents of such lists *per se*, but about the very attempt to classify living things from the bottom up by means of any such list of common features. For instance, while it is true of living things that they take energy from the environment and convert it into other forms of energy, it is also true that things like asphalt pavements take energy from the sun and convert it into heat (1995, 258f). The problem is not merely that converting energy is (obviously) not a sufficient condition for being a living thing. The problem is much deeper than that: a characterization of living things ought to illuminate the concept of a living thing, rather than merely give symptoms of life, so there must be something about the organism's taking of energy that marks it off from the analogous process in the asphalt. In that case, we cannot build up an account of vitality from a prior list of independently identified vital processes.

Rather, a process can be marked off as a *vital* process, Thompson argues, only by setting the process within what he, following G. E. M. Anscombe, calls a 'wider context': 'When we call something an acorn', Anscombe observes, 'we look to a wider context than can be seen in the acorn itself. Oaks come from acorns, acorns come from oaks; an acorn is thus as such generative (of an oak) whether or not it does generate an oak' (1981c, 81, cited in Thompson 1995, 272). It is this 'wider context' that reveals which kind of process of converting energy is the relevant kind of process to consider in the case of living things: it is the kind of process that, as in the acorn but not the asphalt, is part of the life of an organism. The explosion of a hydrogen bomb, for instance, interrupts the energy conversion process in both the acorn and the asphalt, but only in the former case can we say that the bomb interrupts a process that was *unfolding* or going somewhere, so to speak. In the case of the asphalt's energy conversion, answering the question 'What happens next?' by saying 'That depends on whether a hydrogen bomb goes off, say, or it starts raining' is a perfectly good answer, but this is no way to say 'what happens next' when we look at the process in the acorn. The acorn but not the asphalt has a wider context within which the process is going somewhere (Thompson 1995, 260f). Wider context is therefore crucial to discriminating between vital processes and other sorts of processes that are superficially similar but have nothing to do with life.

Likewise, wider context is also crucial for discriminating between vital processes of different sorts, as for instance 'ingesting fish' counts as part of a process of eating (in a shark, say) only in virtue of its fitting into the overall system of the shark's vital activity in a particular way. A new shark species that ingests fish only to convert them into a digested brew that it spits out to frighten off predators cannot be described as eating the fish it ingests (Thompson 1995, 272–5). And of course this role of wider context is relevant outside biology as well, since for instance the act of swinging a bat can count as 'striking out' only if the one swinging it is playing a game of baseball (Thompson 1995, 276, citing Rawls 1967, 164). So where some process or act can be understood as the process of an X only in terms of 'wider context'—as in the case of vital processes and plays in games—X cannot be adequately characterized from the bottom up by listing such processes or acts; the attempt yields at best a list of the thing's symptoms. Therefore, neither life nor a particular life-form can be characterized from the bottom up, process by process.

Can we understand virtues and virtuous states from the bottom up, process by process—or mode by mode—without 'wider context'? That depends on what the virtues are. If virtues are psychologically thin, then they may need no wider context to be understood. This is not to say that they can be understood in a vacuum—on the contrary, on Driver's view the virtues must be understood in the context of an agent's environment in which they regularly produce good results. But here the context is no wider than in the case of energy conversion in the asphalt, which must be understood in the context of the asphalt's environment in which the sun shines down on the pavement (and a hydrogen bomb does not go off, etc.). By making the social environment the context for identifying virtues, as Driver does, we focus on behaviors that we divide into groups and patterns, treating a virtue as whatever psychological features underwrite a given behavioral pattern (Driver 2001, 95; Thomson 1997, 280f). But it is possible, and I think even likely, that there may be no single psychological feature, or bundle of features, that underwrites any given behavioral pattern. Behaviors that appear to form a pattern of generosity, say, from such a perspective, may in fact be caused by sympathy on some occasions, largesse on others, or ulterior motives, weakness of will, prodigality, a good mood, and so on. 'Generosity' thus becomes a placeholder for whatever accounts for the pattern, rather than the name of a proper character trait. Such a view is not available to the virtue ethicist, who analyzes right action in terms of a prior account of psychologically thick character traits that are human excellences. (I return to this issue in Chapter 10.)

Psychologically thick virtues, by contrast, can be understood only within the wider context of the agent taken as a whole, that is, as a nexus of beliefs, attitudes, priorities, aims, commitments, and skills. Recognizing this fact, Aristotle holds that virtue is not just a matter of doing certain kinds of things, but of doing them with knowledge, from a state of character that is settled and stable, and for the right kinds of reasons (*NE* II.4). This idea is a central part of contemporary virtue ethics, as well; Michael Slote, for instance, holds benevolence to supervene on a particular kind of 'overall motivation', and Swanton and Rosalind Hursthouse hold that character traits generally (including vices like racism) are not discrete psychological states but are patterns that extend clear across one's psychology (Swanton 2001, *passim*; Hursthouse 1999*a*, ch. 5). Furthermore, the virtuousness of some mode of responding to the world connects with the whole nexus of character seen as going through time: when I must choose between honoring conflicting commitments to meet a friend and to attend a school board meeting, whether my resolution of the dilemma counts as good enough may depend on whether desegregation, the subject of the school board meeting, is an issue to which I have devoted myself (Pincoffs 1986, 22f; see also Hursthouse 1999*a*, 70).

So the psychological thickness of the virtues means that they can be understood only within a wider context, and as we have seen, virtue ethics does require that the virtues be psychologically thick. Consequently, when virtue ethics forges a link between right action and the virtues—including positing a general pattern of virtuous persons acting rightly—we must understand this as forging a link between right action and a virtuous system or nexus, and that of course is a virtuous agent or character taken as a whole. Likewise, whether or not a mode by which a given person (virtuous or otherwise) responds to the world is a virtuous one also requires situating that mode within a whole nexus of the agent's character. In that case, our understanding of a virtuous person cannot be built from the bottom up in terms of the disposition to certain kinds of virtuous modes of responsiveness, since the very idea that such modes are *virtuous* modes of responsiveness requires the wider context of a virtuous character taken as a whole—for virtue ethics, virtuous dispositions, like vital processes, make sense only within their wider context. Because virtue is a model concept, it cannot be understood without reference to an ideal of virtue. And because virtue must be understood within its wider context, that model must be that of a whole virtuous character, that is, an ideal of the virtuous *person*. There is no forging a link between right action and virtue that does not, at some point or other, rest on the model of 'the virtuous person'. 'The virtuous *person*', therefore, is an ideal that virtue ethics cannot do without.

So commitment to 'the virtuous person' does not separate different versions of virtue ethics, after all, even though not all versions need define right action explicitly in terms of 'what the virtuous person would do'. As I have understood it here, talk of 'the virtuous person' captures and indeed highlights that feature of all virtue ethics—its focus on the person as a whole—that is much of what makes virtue ethics an alternative to other types of moral theory. I have talked about 'the virtuous person' and its role in a theory of right action, but of course we could also speak of 'the utilitarian', who acts so as to promote the best consequences possible. Here 'the utilitarian' is a model of the sort of principles one commits to when one commits to utilitarian principles. But unlike 'the virtuous person', 'the utilitarian' reduces without remainder to those principles, none of which needs the sort of wider context within which virtue ethics understands the virtues.[41] 'The virtuous person' has much more to offer, and I close this chapter by considering why he has been such a frequently misunderstood figure.

4.5 Representing 'The Virtuous Person'

We have already considered Michael Thompson's view that vital processes can be understood only within a 'wider context' of a life-form taken as a whole. But Thompson also notes that our linguistic resources for representing and discussing life-forms are difficult to analyze and prone to misunderstanding. I think that talk of 'the virtuous person' is prone to misunderstanding of just the same sort, so I begin with some points about language.

Consider an ordinary phrase like 'the domestic cat'. Superficially, that phrase looks like a Russellian definite description, but while 'The domestic cat is asleep on my armchair' may be true when I point to my slumbering cat Sophie, statements like 'The domestic cat has three to five kittens in a litter' are certainly not true when I point to Sophie—not only because she has had no kittens, but more importantly because no cat has ever had three to five kittens in a litter, but only an exact number (see Thompson 1995, 282, 285).[42] (And consider Wikipedia's claim that 'The cat has been living in close association with humans for somewhere between 3,500 and 8,000 years'—surely *that* is no

---

[41] Schneewind 1997, 181f discusses a seventeenth-century Cambridge scholar, well trained in the natural law tradition, whose lecture notes on Aristotle's *NE* define virtue as 'a constant disposition of the soul to live according to law'. Such a definition of 'the virtuous person' reduces in the same way that 'the utilitarian' does.

[42] Thompson (1995, 285n.) acknowledges his debt to Anscombe 1981b, 38 for her similar observations on statements about how many teeth humans have.

definite description!) Statements of the latter sort, which are the regular fare of nature shows and biology textbooks, are what Thompson calls 'Aristotelian categoricals'. In addition to taking the apparent form of statements whose subjects are definite descriptions, Aristotelian categoricals can also assume the apparent form of universal quantifications ('domestic cats') and existential quantifications ('a domestic cat'); but again those forms are only superficial. Nor can they be understood simply as statistical generalizations, since it is possible to infer from 'Fs are G' and 'Fs are H' that 'Fs are both G and H', and thereby 'we will presumably always be able to produce a true statement of [the latter] form involving a complex conjunctive predicate that is not true of *any* member of the kind denoted by its subject, living or dead'. (As Thompson says, 'nobody's perfect'; 1995, 288.) Likewise, statements like 'The domestic cat has three to five kittens in a litter' do not imply for every female domestic cat a certain probability that it will have three to five kittens in a litter; nor are they statements about what 'most' domestic cats are like, or about what domestic cats are like *ceteris paribus*, if nothing interferes. Nor, importantly, do they imply 'ought' statements like 'If Sophie were as a domestic cat ought to be, she would have three to five kittens in a litter' (see Thompson 1995, 281–90 for careful discussion).

I am not in a position to say what the logical form of an Aristotelian categorical is (although I have said what its form is *not*), so I am not in a position to say decisively whether statements about 'the rational person' and 'the virtuous person' share that logical form.[43] But the resemblance is instructive at several important points. In all of these cases, 'the F' (or 'Fs' or 'an F') is meant not to talk about some particular F thing, or about all F things, or about F things as they ought to be. Such use of 'the F', which is in a different mode than its surface grammar suggests, is what I shall call 'model discourse': it is discourse not about *things*, but about a certain *model* of things. Of course, statements about 'the domestic cat' are based on information gathered from observations of particular domestic cats. But as we have seen

---

[43] William Stewart has suggested to me in correspondence that Aristotelian categoricals could be analyzed via Robert Goldblatt's (1983) higher-order, many-sorted, free (of existential import), intuitionistic logic with a definite-description operator. This is an intriguing suggestion, but again, more than that I am not in a position to say.

We must also note that Thompson means to restrict Aristotelian categoricals—which he also calls 'natural-historical judgments'—to life-forms, and as he is aware it is difficult to determine whether his account does in fact isolate them in that way or instead describes a broader 'class of what we may call "non-Fregean generalities" ' (1995, 292–5). It is of course well beyond the scope of our present inquiry to investigate that issue, so I shall simply point out some important similarities between Aristotelian categoricals and statements about 'the rational person' and 'the virtuous person' in hopes of casting some light on the latter two.

they are not mere generalizations about the cats observed, because from that information we can form a long conjunction about 'the domestic cat' that is not true of any particular cat. Rather, such conjunctions build up a detailed model of 'the domestic cat' considered as a unique life-form.[44] The same is true of statements about 'the rational person' and 'the virtuous person'. We do learn about virtue and about rationality from one another, but in talking of 'the virtuous person' and 'the rational person' we are not generalizing about our observations. Rather, we employ a model (or bits of a model) that we have constructed from what we have learned from our observations.

Note, though, that statements about 'the rational person' and 'the virtuous person' are not descriptive in quite the way that statements about 'the domestic cat' are. Both sorts of statements stand in for bits of theorizing about the things in question—models are theoretical items, of course—but the models of rationality and virtue stand in for parts of a normative theory, or rather a theory about a normative concept. So the difference is not a difference between types of model discourse (or between model discourse and something else), but merely a difference in the types of concepts that are being discussed via model discourse.

Our discussion of the form of talk about 'the virtuous person' has been brief, but I think that it reveals why that sort of talk is so prone to misunderstanding. Talk of 'the virtuous person' is a type of model discourse, and in particular is at least very much like model discourse employing Aristotelian categoricals, and to date the logical form of such discourse has been, at best, very difficult to analyze. But since such talk can assume the superficial form of a universal predication, it can be mistaken for a claim about what 'virtuous persons' are like, and thus as giving a set of necessary conditions for being virtuous. And since it can assume the superficial form of a definite description or an existential predication, it can be mistaken for a claim about some ideal agent, real or imaginary, whose thoughts and intentions we are supposed to work out (perhaps by asking them, if we live in a small enough city to find them), or whom we ought to aspire to be like. This is a misunderstanding; 'the virtuous person' is not someone we traipse around the *polis* to find, any more than 'the cat' that has lived with humans for as many as 8,000 years.

Getting clear on talk of 'the virtuous person' helps dispel some common worries about the sort of action guidance that virtue ethics gives. For one thing, it becomes clearer that talk of 'the virtuous person' affords a way of

[44] Indeed, Thompson 1995, 276–8 argues that life-forms or species are in fact prior to members. This is not to deny that we compile information about a species from observations of its members, but means that we perceive a world of particular members as a world of members *already* sorted into different species.

modeling practical problems, not of *solving* them.[45] The solution of any given practical problem is not to do what 'the virtuous person' would do, since many practical problems cannot be solved at all—there is no 'right thing' to be worked out in such cases—and in any case, 'the virtuous person' does not serve as a problem-solving heuristic in a theory of what it is right to do any more than 'the rational person' does in a theory of what it is rational to do. Rather, talk of 'the virtuous person' models practical problems by focusing attention *away* from a decision procedure for solving the problem and onto an approach to the problem that takes as central the way in which one makes it, carries it through, etc., including the idea that virtuous action includes skillful practical reasoning on the part of the one facing the problem.[46]

I do not intend to add to the literature on applications of virtue ethics here, but I should point out that it is an advantage of this way of modeling problems that it can make them more tractable, without giving the false appearance that such problems must be solvable, or are only technical ones of interpreting and following rules, or that how one deals with such problems can be disconnected from the agent considered as a continuing and developing whole (Annas 2004; Hursthouse 1995a; Hursthouse 1999a, chs. 1–3).[47] Such an approach to problem-modeling makes it clear that one's response to moral problems has a past and a future: one's ability to respond to such problems appropriately when they arise will depend on how one's character has developed so far (and this can serve as a word to the wise),[48] and the response one makes is itself another step in that very development (Pincoffs 1986, 60, 67, 169). Such modeling does

---

[45] Such a distinction is, I think, implicit in Foot's work on abortion and euthanasia, as well as Hursthouse's on abortion (1997; see also 1995a), and more recently in Swanton's development of a variety of virtue ethical problem-modeling that she calls 'dialogic ethics' (2003, ch. 12), one that can be used even by non-virtuous agents (267). See also Annas 1993a, ch. 1 for the idea that the virtues offer a 'framework for ethical reflection', which suggests a kind of modeling of practical issues, rather than solving the problems they raise.

[46] See also Merritt 2000, esp. 370f, who rightly observes that virtue ethics is in the first instance an ethical theory about the 'long haul', that is, about the development of virtuous agents over time, and not primarily about one-off actions.

[47] In fact, recent textbooks in applied ethics have begun to appreciate this advantage, although in some cases this is in spite of themselves. For instance, in one popular book on engineering ethics the primer chapter on ethical theories makes no mention of virtue ethics, yet when the authors turn to 'real world' cases (e.g. how to avoid avoidable accidents) in the very next chapter, they turn not to the favored procedures, algorithms, and matrices of the primer chapter, but to the idea that engineers need to have traits like responsibility, and thus that engineers need virtues. (See Harris, Pritchard, and Rabins 2000; although this textbook is the one with which I am most familiar, its failure to consider virtue ethics among the major approaches is widely shared, although things are getting better in this regard, as this textbook also shows.) Perhaps this sort of turn is not surprising, since, as Anscombe 1981b, 39 noted, modeling problems with concepts like whether someone acted responsibly or not can settle many issues of action assessment straightaway.

[48] This is a major theme in Tom Wolfe's neo-Stoic novel *A Man in Full*.

not, of course, always tell one the answer (even when there is one), but it may tell one what one really needs to know within the larger project of becoming someone who is good at finding answers (Pincoffs 1986, 15f, 30).

Understanding model discourse about 'the virtuous person' also makes clearer what sort of ideal 'the virtuous person' is. And it also clarifies Swanton's own talk of 'the perfectly healthy person'. As we have seen, Swanton understands virtue as a kind of psychic health, and notes that this requires a normative model of psychic health relative to which a distortion counts as a distortion. Psychic health, then, is a model concept, and likewise talk of 'the perfectly healthy individual' should be understood as model discourse. The notion of what I have called a model concept is neither new nor unfamiliar, but I have argued that our understanding of such concepts must extend to the notion of 'the virtuous person' and 'the *phronimos*', just as it should extend to 'the rational person' and 'the healthy person'. Otherwise, 'the virtuous person' shall remain a most misunderstood fellow.

Conclusion: Implications for Hard Virtue Ethics

Phronesis is what Swanton calls a 'threshold concept' after all. We have seen that this fact has important implications for our understanding of the role of 'the virtuous person' and 'the *phronimos*' in virtue ethics. It also has important implications for the role of phronesis in virtue ethics. As we saw in the second chapter, all forms of virtue ethics are committed, at least, to what we called the 'account constraint', which holds that an account of right action is adequate only if that account takes sufficiently into consideration all of our serious practical concerns. As we saw in the third chapter, this constraint has the result that every virtue must involve deliberation that is wise (even if not perfectly or ideally so) about such matters as what counts as genuinely helpful or benevolent and, in general, where the 'mean' or the 'targets' of the virtues lie. And as we have seen in this chapter, deliberation that is wise *tout court*—even if not perfectly or ideally so—must be understood as deliberation that displays phronesis, and which accepts 'the *phronimos*' as an ideal, that is, as deliberating according to standards that one accepts for oneself as the appropriate standards of deliberation.

In that case, any adequate virtue ethical account of right action must hold that the virtues all include phronesis—that is, phronesis enough—and therefore only forms of Hard Virtue Ethics can give an adequate virtue ethical account of right action. This means that any view of the virtues that omits phronesis cannot accept even the account constraint on right action. Since that constraint is the minimal constraint that any ethical theory must meet, for all that we may stand to learn from such views we should not consider them forms of virtue *ethics*, but a theory about virtues of some other kind.[49] The divide between Hard and Soft Virtue Ethics is therefore a *fundamental* divide. It separates those theories of the virtues that can meet the minimal formal constraints on an account of right action from those that cannot.

But of course not all of the gates at which virtue ethics can fall are matters of formal constraints; indeed, some of the main grounds for skepticism about Hard Virtue Ethics are that it has implausible implications. Our discussion of model concepts can help answer some of these objections. If we understand phronesis as a model concept, then we can view Swanton's discussion of the 'common modes' of the virtues as a discussion of several aspects of phronesis—and a particularly insightful and subtle discussion of phronesis at that. For instance, Swanton notes that phronesis regularly hits the targets of the virtues because phronesis grasps the appropriate balance or equilibrium of love, intimacy, and 'drawing close' on the one hand, and respect and 'keeping distance' on the other (2003, ch. 5). An important implication of this way of amplifying the notion of phronesis is that it discourages the common misconception of phronesis as narrowly intellectualist. Rather, phronesis is a form of practical intelligence that is far from narrow, but includes receptivity, freedom from psychological distortion, and the expression of fine inner states (2003, ch. 5); it involves an equilibrium of 'strength' and 'gentleness', that is of self-love and caring for others (153ff); it involves creativity in solving problems and expression of virtues (7); and it reveals itself in objectivity rather than bias (177).

In that case, we should not think of phronesis as a kind of intellectual prowess confined to a sophisticated elite, but rather in terms of psychic health, inner strength, balance and equilibrium, etc.; as Swanton says, 'practical wisdom is closely tied to emotional life and to one's character' (2003, 133), and so 'the description of practical wisdom as an "intellectual" virtue is misleading, for practical wisdom in its fullest sense involves right ways of seeing the world effectively and motivationally' (179). To be sure, phronesis does require a broad experience and a grasp of what is good, serious, and worthwhile (Hursthouse 1995a, 68–74; Foot 1978a, 5–8; Foot 2001, ch. 6), but this need not be philosophically sophisticated. To have phronesis is to be reliably apt both in one's grasp of the mean or 'target' of a virtue, and in one's ability to act in accordance with the virtues in a balanced, integrative way. Phronesis

---

[49] This problem for a Nietzschean virtue ethics, we should note, does not rest on our viewing Nietzsche as an immoralist, as Swanton 2005 argues convincingly we should not.

is therefore a kind of intelligence, but it is a kind that is within the reach of the 'ordinary adult human being', in Philippa Foot's phrase, and not restricted to those who are 'clever' or have 'access to special training' (Foot 1978a, 6).[50] As Julia Annas has recently put the point (2006, §A.1), the practical reasoning in question is

just what everyone does, so it is hard to see how a theory which appeals to what is available to everyone is elitist. Different virtue theories offer us differing ways of making our reflections more theoretically sophisticated, but virtue ethics tries to improve the reasoning we all share, rather than replacing it by a different kind.

Indeed, so much should be clear already from our review of deliberation and phronesis in Chapter 1.

But there are other objections too, such as that Hard Virtue Ethics implies that to have any virtue is to have them all. As I said in the first chapter, having a virtue involves 'knowing what a virtue is for', by which I mean, on the one hand, deliberating wisely and reliably about where the mean lies (cf. Swanton 2003, 236f, 288), and on the other, deliberating in a way that integrates the concerns of the diverse virtues (cf. 27).[51] These two aspects of virtue are the twin roles of phronesis. As virtue ethicists note, an act is not right simply because it is virtuous in some respect[52] but is right only if the act is virtuous overall or in all respects. It is the second, integrative role of phronesis that establishes a link between being virtuous and a regular pattern of doing acts that are virtuous *overall* and thus right. But in that case, it seems that to be courageous—and thus to be one who regularly and reliably acts rightly through one's courage—one must also be just, as well as temperate, even-tempered, etc., and surely this is too stringent a condition on courage.

In addition to this rather special problem for Hard Virtue Ethics—the problem of the 'unity of virtue'—there is also the more general problem that, as many philosophers have argued in recent years, much research in the social sciences suggests that the virtue ethicist's model of human psychology and action as involving character and traits of character is inaccurate at best and just plain false at worst. I shall take up these issues in Parts III and IV (though not in that order). First, though, I turn in Part II to another pressing problem for all virtue ethics that has received far less attention. As is by now familiar, virtue ethics understands right action in terms of action or motivation that is

---

[50] On deliberative excellence that is central to phronesis, see Swanton 2003, ch. 12.

[51] Even if one must sometimes accept that one cannot always satisfy every one of those concerns in a way that it is virtuous to want to satisfy them (see Ch. 2, §2.4.2).

[52] e.g. we sometimes say that an act, though unjust, may still be courageous. On this thorny issue, see esp. Foot 1978a; Driver 2001, ch. 4.

overall virtuous and in accordance with all the virtues, but for that reason it is somewhat surprising how little virtue ethicists have had to say about whether we can say what 'all the virtues' are. The problem is not that we do not have a definitive 'list' of all the virtues, but that many of the grounds on which virtue ethicists sometimes claim to have identified a new, distinct virtue would, if carried out, suggest that 'all the virtues' are infinitely many. In that case, it would be unclear *even in principle* what notions like 'overall virtuous' and 'in accordance with the virtues' could even mean. I take up this issue in the next three chapters, where I argue that the virtues must have some sort of unified structure, a structure that, again, requires us to understand the virtues as all involving phronesis.

PART II
The Enumeration Problem

5

The Enumeration Problem

In this chapter and the two that follow, I want to explore a problem that virtue ethicists and their critics alike have almost entirely ignored, but which if unresolved would jeopardize the very possibility of virtue ethics. This problem stems from the conjunction of a necessary feature of virtue ethics and a commonplace one. The necessary feature is that virtue ethics understands right actions and virtuous persons in terms of the virtues, in the plural; and the commonplace is that virtue ethicists tend to be so open-handed about what 'the virtues' are that on many theories there will be infinitely many of them. If right action is action in accordance with the virtues, and a virtuous person a person who has the virtues, but virtue ethics tells us that the virtues are infinitely many, then virtue ethics cannot say what right action is action in accordance with, or what it would be to be a virtuous person. This problem I call the 'enumeration problem'.

I begin in this chapter with a closer look at the enumeration problem and its implications, before working towards an outline of a way of addressing this problem in the next two chapters. Such an outline, I argue in Chapter 6, requires a kind of order or structure among the virtues that they can have only if phronesis is a central part of every virtue. In Chapter 7, I apply that structure to a test case, namely the Aristotelian virtue of 'magnificence'. Then in Parts III and IV I take up pressing questions as to how any virtues that beings like us could have, could ever have that kind of structure.

5.1 The Enumeration Problem: An Introduction

5.1.1 The Necessary Feature and the Commonplace

As I just said, the enumeration problem is a problem for contemporary virtue ethics because of the conjunction of the fact that virtue ethics must understand right action in terms of the virtues, with the fact that many virtue ethicists have been indifferent as to whether the virtues are countable. Let's take a closer look at these two issues in turn.

The Necessary Feature   Virtue ethicists give widely differing accounts of virtue, but all acknowledge that in the end 'virtue' here is in fact elliptical for *the virtues*, in the plural. This is because virtue ethics needs the notion of being 'overall virtuous', in two ways. First, virtue ethical theories of every sort must understand *right action* in terms of the overall virtuousness of action. Right action is not to be understood in terms merely of some particular virtue or other, for a number of reasons. For instance, Christine Swanton (2003, ch. 11) says that while an action is virtuous (kind, say) when it hits the 'target' of virtue—that is, roughly, when it does what it is characteristic of kindness to do—a virtuous action is right only when it is virtuous *overall*, that is, when it also meshes with the characteristic aims or 'targets' of all the other virtues as well. Such an action is not kind-but-unjust, say; rather, it both hits the specific target of kindness and also passes muster where the targets of the other virtues are concerned. Likewise, Michael Slote (2001, chs. 1–2) says that an action is right just in case in doing it the agent has expressed or acted from an inner motivating state that is virtuous overall, and therefore 'balances' various ethical considerations. Rosalind Hursthouse (1995a; 1999a, ch. 1) holds that an action is right just in case it is what a virtuous person would do in the circumstances (plus some other qualifications), where a 'virtuous person' is understood as a person who has those character traits that are 'the virtues', in the plural. And so on.

This convergence on the importance of *the virtues* in an account of right action is no accident. Different forms of virtue ethics differ as to whether an action can be a right action when bad luck, unavoidable ignorance, or tragedy interferes, but what virtue ethics cannot allow is that an action can be right even when things go badly *because* the agent has acted badly in some respect or other. As we saw in Part I, theories of right action are meant to assess actions against the backdrop of our serious practical concerns, and no theory could be taken seriously which would make the link between rightness and those concerns as loose as that. And we should also suppose that any view that made the connection between virtue and right action that loose is not really a form of virtue ethics anyway.[1] Not surprisingly, Aristotle observed that a person who acts from a naive sort of virtue may fail to act in accordance with *the virtues*, even when acting 'generously' (say) in some narrow sense, and

---

[1] These two considerations correspond to what in earlier chapters I have called the 'account constraint' and the 'VE constraint', respectively.

thus is as likely to act wrongly as rightly (*NE* VI.13). This is not necessarily to insist on the unity of virtue—that the virtues work only as a complete bundle—but it certainly is to say that a theory of right action based on the virtues cannot simply equate right action with action in accordance with some virtue or other.[2] Virtue ethics, then, must understand at least the central cases of right action as action in accordance with *the virtues*, and since all cases are to be understood in the light of the central cases, virtue ethics can say nothing about right action without the notion of the virtues, in the plural.

The second place that virtue ethicists (and many virtue theorists) employ the notion of overall virtuousness is in the idea of a 'virtuous person', that is, a person who has the virtues in the plural. The importance of this notion is clearest with those theories that understand right action in terms of what a virtuous person would do, but as I argued in Chapter 4, sooner or later all forms of virtue ethics require a theoretical model of 'the virtuous person', which models the structure or 'natural makeup' of every virtue as well as the connections that hold between them in a person considered as a whole. So the notion of being 'virtuous overall' is crucial to virtue ethics, both for talking about right actions and for talking about virtuous persons.

The Commonplace Feature   As I said at the outset, this necessary feature of virtue ethics sits uncomfortably alongside an unnecessary but nonetheless commonplace feature, namely, certain practices of identifying and individuating the virtues which, if applied consistently, would result in innumerable virtues, and thus would undermine the very idea of an action's or a person's being virtuous overall. For instance, virtue ethicists often observe that people may be intemperate about food, say, but temperate about drink and sex, and conclude that the apparently single virtue of 'temperance' must in fact be a host of smaller-scope virtues like temperance-about-sex, temperance-about-drink, etc.[3] But of course people compartmentalize character traits in all sorts of ways, and the principle generalizes; so on this sort of approach, there seems no way to escape the virtues being infinitely many. Likewise, Hursthouse asks whether there is a virtue of good parenting, or whether good parents are simply those parents who are just, honest, compassionate, etc. (1999*a*, 213f). Hursthouse notes that 'it is not unknown for people to be rather good parents but very limited in virtue outside their immediate family circle', and concludes that good parenting may be its own virtue, since it can be separated from other

---

  [2] I consider the unity of virtue in Ch. 11.

  [3] And perhaps even these are too coarse, as some may be temperate about sweets but not about savoury snacks, etc. These sorts of considerations are discussed in writers as otherwise diverse as Doris 2002, ch. 4 and Badhwar 1996.

virtues like compassion. There is no disputing the data, but if the lines we draw between the virtues match all the ways in which persons may do well despite serious shortcomings elsewhere, our theory will again posit infinitely many virtues. And *a theory with infinitely many virtues cannot make sense of the notion of overall virtuousness.*

Nor is the phenomenon of compartmentalization the only path to an open-handed conception of the virtues. For instance, Swanton argues that a virtue is a disposition to certain forms of appropriate responsiveness to the things with which it is characteristically concerned, and is identified by its peculiar 'constellation' of forms of responsiveness (what Swanton 2003, ch. 1 calls a virtue's 'profile'). This is a reasonable proposal, but what is less clear is whether such constellations or profiles are of finite number. This is even less clear in Slote's view that the virtues are those traits that we find morally 'admirable', as a matter of common sense, in certain circumstances; yet surely there is no limit to how many traits we can admire in their own distinct way, especially since on Slote's view such admirability is 'fundamental' and entirely underived (see Slote 1992, 2001; I discuss this last feature of Slote's view in Chapter 3).

But perhaps no one is more open-handed about 'the virtues' than Aristotle himself. Aristotle's discussion of the virtues is far more familiar in contemporary virtue ethics than those of other ancient Greek moral philosophers, and this can hide the fact that his view was, in its open-handedness anyway, a striking anomaly. For instance, in the fourth book of the *Republic* Plato had identified the virtues by means of a prior identification of the parts of the soul: the soul, he argued, has three parts, and so there is one virtue consisting in the healthy relation of each part to the rest of the soul, plus a fourth virtue consisting in the healthy relation between all of the parts as constituting a whole.[4] This yielded Plato's four major virtues of courage, wisdom, temperance, and justice (which supervenes on the whole). So far from being open-handed, by the time of the *Republic* Plato had in fact *shortened* his list of virtues from an already very short list of five that had included piety; Plato, like the Stoics after him, seems to have decided that piety is really a form of justice and not an independent virtue (see esp. Plato, *Gorgias* 506e–507e; Plato, *Protagoras* 329d–330b *et passim*; Arius Didymus in Stobaeus, *Anthology* II.5b2). And so it seems that at least by the time of the *Republic* Plato had arrived at the notion of a 'cardinal' virtue, that is, a virtue to which other virtues may be subordinate but which is itself subordinate to no other virtue. Later the Stoics embraced not only Plato's four virtues, but also his notion of cardinality, and went on to

---

[4] I discuss this aspect of Plato's view of the soul in Russell 2005a, chs. 4, 7.

subordinate to the four virtues a rather diverse list of other virtues (I list these later on).

By contrast, Aristotle himself seems strikingly modern in his casual approach to finding new virtues without the hierarchical organization of a cardinal theory. For instance, Aristotle (*NE* IV.2) observes that some people need to make grand expenditures, and to do so virtuously: intelligently, tastefully, discreetly, for the right reasons, from the right state of character, etc. No other virtue, not even generosity, is going to equip one to act virtuously in *just* this way, which involves unique demands, complexities, temptations, and opportunities for error. In that case, one may be even outstanding for generosity but for all that not magnificent, and so Aristotle concludes that a new virtue—'magnificence'—is involved here. The principle generalizes: where we have distinctive, new contexts and demands for virtuous action, we must also find distinctive, new virtues. But since distinctive, new contexts and demands are countless, so too will be the virtues.[5]

Aristotle seems to appreciate the point, since his discussion of the virtues takes a rather 'laundry list' approach: the virtues, Aristotle tells us, include not only courage, temperance, generosity, and justice, but also magnificence, pride, proper ambition, good temper, friendliness, truthfulness, wittiness, and—we must presume—so on.[6] It is the 'and so on' that is so striking about Aristotle's list. Even if we accept all these traits as virtues, we still get the sense that if we wanted to, we could continue Aristotle's rambling list of virtues without hindrance from anything but our imagination. And Aristotle himself suggests no general way to continue. Perhaps for this reason Aquinas later undertook to

---

[5] In answer to the question 'What Are the Virtues?', The Virtues Project (*www.virtuesproject.com/virtues.html*) offers a virtue for every week of the year. In fact, they offer more than one such list, and together these come to no fewer than 71 virtues: acceptance, assertiveness, beauty, caring, cleanliness, commitment, compassion, confidence, contentment, cooperation, courage, courtesy, creativity, detachment, determination, devotion, diligence, discernment, enthusiasm, excellence, faith, flexibility, faithfulness, forgiveness, friendliness, generosity, gentleness, grace, gratitude, helpfulness, honesty, honor, humility, idealism, integrity, joyfulness, justice, kindness, love, loyalty, mercy, moderation, modesty, obedience, orderliness, patience, peace, perseverance, peacefulness, prayerfulness, purity, purposefulness, reliability, respect, responsibility, reverence, righteousness, sacrifice, self-discipline, service, steadfastness, tact, thankfulness, tolerance, trust, trustworthiness, truthfulness, understanding, unity, wisdom, and wonder. Moreover, many of these virtues could be subdivided further; for instance, 'cleanliness', the site goes on to explain, refers to personal hygiene, one's choice of clothing, one's choice of food, one's choice of mental activities, avoidance of harmful drugs, and dealing with one's mistakes. The other virtues also unpack in similar sorts of ways. I do not mean to criticize The Virtues Project for their prolific list; they do not, after all, pretend to be philosophers or virtue theorists, but are people trying to help other people live better lives. However, their list does prompt the question, why stop at 71? Why stop at all, for that matter? And are we philosophers doing any better?

[6] Con. Reeve 1992, 169f, who says 'that Aristotle can be confident to some degree that the virtues he lists are all the virtues that there are'; I shall return to this issue in Ch. 7.

structure Aristotle's list by overlaying it with a very Stoic model of the cardinal virtues.[7]

But if the contrast between Aristotle on the one hand and Plato, the Stoics, and Aquinas on the other puts into sharp relief the importance of parsimony in a theory of the virtues, it also reveals that it is possible to think that the virtues are *too few*. The answer to an over-expansive conception of the virtues surely is not an over-restrictive one; it is no small thing to say just how many the cardinal virtues are, or which ones they are.[8] It seems undeniable that the virtues are many and diverse, and that efforts to restrict them to short, closed lists are thus bound to be controversial (see Swanton 2003, esp. 70–6; Pincoffs 1986, 82f). Furthermore, as the exponentially increasing seriousness of, say, environmental responsibility demonstrates, we must keep an open mind about just what sorts of human virtues we may come in time to discover, and to need to develop in order to live in peace and to meet the demands of our world (see Hursthouse 2006b). Nor is there any denying the overwhelming evidence that no courageous person (say) is courageous across all areas of his or her life, and it is pointless to stipulate that such a person therefore could not be 'really' courageous in any area at all.

Finally, producing a *closed* list of cardinal virtues would be more of a solution than the enumeration problem requires, anyway. That problem arises when the virtues are innumerable, making it impossible even in principle to say what 'overall virtuous' means. It would be enough to say that the cardinal virtues are in principle countable, without having to solve the very

---

[7] For an excellent discussion of Aquinas' revision of Aristotle's ethics in this regard, see Irwin 2005. Irwin also argues that Aquinas further innovated by eschewing the Stoic view that the cardinal virtues are only genera of which the particular virtues are species, and holding instead that the particular virtues are 'exercises' of the cardinal virtues. The interpretation of the Stoics on this point is controversial, however, and I shall not consider it here. The sort of cardinality that I develop in the next chapter will be of the latter kind.

Why Aristotle himself eschewed cardinality is not clear; Dalcourt 1963, 58 suggests that Aristotle rejected it because he rejected the psychology that supported Plato's version of cardinality, but that would be an extraordinary case of throwing out the baby with the bathwater, and in any case should have prompted Aristotle to jettison as well a great many more theses that Plato had supported with his model of the psyche, such as the unity of virtue.

[8] Proponents of cardinality rarely appreciate how difficult these questions are, e.g. Oderberg 1999 claims that the traditional four cardinal virtues—justice, temperance, courage, and wisdom—are all the cardinal virtues there are, but in defending this thesis he argues that these are the virtues of certain crucial moral faculties (apprehension of the good, desire for the good, etc.), without defending the pivotal assumptions that these are the only virtues of those faculties and that these are the only such morally crucial faculties there are. Note too that such arguments for short lists of cardinal virtues, as in Plato, rely on necessarily simplifying psychological models, on which the vast complexity of the psyche must be reduced to as small a number of 'parts' or faculties as possible; see also Oderberg 1999, 308. Aquinas' own defenses of the traditional list of four cardinal virtues are, alas, as simplistic as any other; see *Summa Theologiae* 2–2 q61, and Dalcourt 1963, 71 for discussion.

different (and far from special) epistemic problem of determining just how many cardinal virtues there are. The latter problem does not jeopardize the very idea of being 'overall virtuous'; it just points out that it takes hard work to say what being 'overall virtuous' comes to. One can address the enumeration problem without too much dogmatism about just which virtues are the cardinal ones. Reasonable virtue ethicists could disagree over how to address that issue; the enumeration problem, by contrast, threatens their whole enterprise. (The distinction between these two issues will be important in the next chapter.)

The challenge posed by the enumeration problem is therefore one of meeting the *twin* needs of regulating the proliferation of the virtues *and* of taking seriously the plurality of the virtues. How could a single conception of the virtues meet both needs? The problem of accounting for the virtues in a way that is both parsimonious and respectful of the plurality of the virtues is what I have called the enumeration problem.

In the next two chapters I shall try not so much to make such a full-blown accounting of the virtues *per se*, but to explain some of the most important general features of such an account. For now, I want to look further at the enumeration problem itself and its potential implications, and since no contemporary virtue ethicist seems to be in danger of making the virtues too few, my focus in the rest of this chapter will be on problems of proliferation.

5.1.2 *What is the Enumeration Problem?*

I now want to clarify the nature of the enumeration problem a bit further, in three ways. First, I examine some ways in which a few philosophers have touched on this problem, as well as other problems of an analogous sort. Second, I say a few words about the relation between the enumeration of the virtues, on the one hand, and the identification and individuation of the virtues on the other. (I return to this issue in greater detail in the next chapter.) And third, in §5.1.3 I consider a number of ways in which the enumeration problem is a general one, and applicable to diverse kinds of virtue theories. As I go, I shall also point ahead to the role that I will develop for cardinality in addressing the enumeration problem in following chapters.

The Enumeration Problem: Some Background   I said above that the enumeration problem has been almost entirely ignored; yet it has not gone *completely* unnoticed in the history of philosophy. The attention has frequently focused on the alleged oddness of the traits that may count as virtues on a sufficiently expansive view. For instance, despite the Stoics' parsimony about the cardinal virtues, Plutarch complains that the Stoic Chrysippus

unwittingly stirred up, in Plato's words, a 'swarm of virtues', both unwonted and unfamiliar. For corresponding to courage in the courageous man, mildness in the mild man, and justice in the just man, he has posited graceliness in the graceful man, nobilitude in the noble man, greatliness in the great man, goodliness in the good man, as well as other such virtues as tactfulness in the tactful man, affableness in the affable man, and wittiness in the witty man, and filled philosophy with many absurd names which it does not need.   (Plutarch, *On Moral Virtue* 441b, my translation, modifying Long and Sedley 1987, §61.B.7)[9]

Plutarch refers to Plato's *Meno* (71e–72a), where Meno says that there are different virtues for men and women, young and old, free and slave, and indeed for every task and every person. To this Socrates makes the tongue-in-cheek reply, 'I seem to be in great luck, Meno; while I am looking for one virtue, I have found you to have a whole swarm of them' (trans. Grube, in Cooper 1997).[10]

   More recently John Skorupski (2004, 12n.) has raised a similar query for certain contemporary accounts of the virtues:

Consider (i) generosity, fair-mindedness, prudence; (ii) courtesy, reliability, calmness, open-mindedness, good humour; (iii) authenticity, sincerity, spirituality, nobility, aesthetic sensibility; (iv) self-respect, chutzpah, boldness, hipness, attitude and cool. They all have something to be said for them. Are they all virtues? If not, why not?

And in her excellent recent paper 'Environmental Virtue Ethics', Rosalind Hursthouse considers with great care the very important choice between understanding environmental responsibility as involving its own distinct virtue or virtues, on the one hand, and as being an extension or outgrowth of other virtues, such as justice or temperance, on the other. Although Hursthouse opts for the former view, her discussion strongly suggests that she appreciates the seriousness of the choice. One should not introduce new virtues lightly.

   However, while philosophers have noticed (sporadically) that some theories multiply the virtues in one way or another, they have had almost nothing to say about the implications of such multiplication—and thus almost nothing to say about what we are calling the enumeration *problem*. There seems to be some resistance to taking the virtues in swarms; but we are not told what problems, exactly, would arise if there were a swarm of virtues. It is not a terribly

---

   [9] See also Cooper 1999, 96f. It is difficult in translation to capture Plutarch's focus on the oddness of the coined Stoic terms for these virtues. It is far from clear that Plutarch is being entirely fair here, though: e.g. Aristotle also speaks of 'tactfulness' at *NE* IV.8, 1128a17 and 'wittiness' at II.7, 1108a24; and in any case, there is far more structure in the Stoic list of virtues than Plutarch would have us suppose.
   [10] Cp. Aristotle, *Politics* I.13 on different virtues for men, women, and slaves.

serious problem, I think, merely that a certain view would involve a lot of virtues, or even some possibly odd-looking ones. Those may be problems, but I do not see them standing poised to undermine the very integrity of the enterprise. Rather, the enumeration problem, as I understand it here, focuses specifically on the fact that the unlimited multiplicity of the virtues jeopardizes the crucial virtue ethical notion of overall virtuousness.

Enumeration, Identification, and Individuation   Although enumeration both resembles and is connected to some rather more familiar issues bearing on how we sort the virtues, it is not exactly the same as any of them. Constructing an account of the virtues, in the plural, proceeds in two basic steps, which have already made brief appearances. First is the *identification* of the virtues, concerning questions like, 'What makes generosity (say) a virtue, and not greed? Loyalty rather than disloyalty? Temperance rather than indulgence?' As we saw in Chapter 3, answers to questions of this type come via some form or other of ethical naturalism, such as eudaimonism, which helps us determine whether some trait is a good thing or bad in the character of creatures such as we are. And second is the *individuation* of the virtues: by what criterion does each virtue differ from every other virtue? What makes generosity, say, the virtue that it is, and not the same as justice or courage or good wit?[11] These steps together give meaning to the notion of an action's and a person's being virtuous overall. So what is the relation between enumeration, on the one hand, and identification and individuation on the other?

Recall Aristotle's view that magnificence is a virtue, in particular, a virtue of large-scale expenditure. As we shall see in Chapter 7, some philosophers have complained that Aristotle should have exercised more parsimony about his virtues in this regard. One way to be more parsimonious about the virtues is to be more parsimonious about identification, and deny that anything like magnificence could be a proper virtue (Annas 1996; con. Swanton 2003, 71ff). Of course, for many traits that is just the move to make, but notice that if this approach is to bear most of the weight of halting proliferation, we shall always be fighting against the fact that the virtues are plural. We need not deny that plurality outright, but it will generally be the consideration that is made to give way. And in any case, why shouldn't we suppose that part of virtuous character is a fair bit of good will and intelligence where large donations are

---

[11] See e.g. Urmson 1980, 163 ff, who individuates virtues one per specific type of emotion, and Hursthouse 1999b for well-placed criticism of this view; see also Williams 1995a and Hursthouse 1995b, who individuate virtues according to the sorts of reasons for which the one with a given virtue acts; and so on. However, it is rarely asked of such methods how well they would fare regarding enumeration; so I consider individuation more closely in the next chapter.

concerned, at least for those in a position to make such donations? Just where is our parsimony to end? Parsimony in identifying virtues is important, but it certainly cannot be the whole story for handling the enumeration problem.

The other way to close off an over-expansive account of the virtues is to be parsimonious about individuation. For instance, we may agree that something like magnificence can have its place in virtuous character, at least for some, but argue that such a virtue is best understood as some part or aspect of another virtue. Perhaps magnificence, we might say, is an aspect of generosity, a kind of 'specialization' of generous impulses where an increase in the scale of the expenditure requires an importantly new level of sensitivity and competence. On such an approach, respecting the plurality of the virtues does not always mean making longer and longer 'laundry lists' of virtues. Rather, in some cases taking some 'new' trait to be a virtuous one can be a way of increasing our understanding of other virtues in richness and detail, as well as their potential for being given an interesting new focus. In that case, we do not end up with merely a 'longer' list of virtues, but a more subtle view of what more specific and specialized forms a virtue like generosity can take, with the appropriate means and practice, and thus what kinds of acts can be in accordance with generosity, because of our richer and more detailed understanding of generosity. Plurality, then, can become increased details, rather than just raw numbers.

In my view, while it is important not to be profligate about identifying virtues, still the weight of the enumeration problem falls mainly on how we *individuate* the virtues. If we cannot trust simply to parsimony about what attributes are virtuous, then we must look for a way to establish structure among those many attributes. This is what 'cardinal' theories of the virtues do. For instance, Aquinas and the Stoics identify rather many virtues, but by arranging them as a handful of cardinal virtues and a 'swarm' of subordinate virtues, there is no proliferation of the virtues in accordance with which an action is right and a person virtuous, but a richer picture of the various forms those virtues can take. 'Overall virtuousness' is thus understood with respect to the cardinal virtues, which are in principle countable (the job of actually counting them, you will recall, being another task). This is all very programmatic at this point. But in the next two chapters, my remarks about ways of managing the enumeration problem will focus mainly on the (extremely complex) notion of individuating the virtues, and on cardinality in particular.

5.1.3 The Generality of the Enumeration Problem

This talk of 'enumerating' the virtues may suggest a rather narrow view of what the virtues are, for instance, that they are rigid theoretical entities, perhaps floating as Forms in a philosopher's heaven, waiting for us to 'count' them properly. Likewise, talk of 'cardinal' virtues may suggest that taking the so-called enumeration problem seriously would require us to take a very restrictive view of the virtues, as all reducing to those few virtues on a very short, closed list. And how are we to arrive at such a short and authoritative list, anyway?[12] By counting Forms, or analyzing pure concepts, or what?

These appearances are deceiving, I argue, and the enumeration problem is a general one that cuts across many important differences between views of the virtues. There are three points I now wish to make in this regard. One, I want to say more about why taking the enumeration problem seriously does not mean compiling an authoritative list of virtues. Two, taking the enumeration problem seriously does not mean thinking of theorizing about the virtues as counting Forms or analyzing concepts. And three, the enumeration problem arises even for the view that virtue is one continuous thing rather than an assortment of various attributes.

Enumeration and Epistemic Modesty First, taking the enumeration problem seriously does not entail producing a very short list of virtues. This is because, as I have said, it is possible to give a manageable structure even to a rather long list of virtuous attributes, depending on how one individuates virtues. To see this, suppose that a theory of the virtues treated them all as on a par with each other—that is, no virtues are cardinal, and so no virtues are subordinate to or forms of any other virtues. In that case, such a theory could accommodate the plurality of the virtues only by allowing its very long list of virtues to get longer and longer; and that, of course, is to court the enumeration problem.

On the other hand, suppose that a theory of the virtues were structured so that some virtues were cardinal, and some virtues were subordinate to these. Consider one such list of cardinal virtues' various subordinate virtues, offered by the Stoics (Arius Didymus in Stobaeus, *Anthology* II.5b–5b2):

PRUDENCE	TEMPERANCE	JUSTICE	COURAGE
Deliberative excellence	*Organization*	*Piety*	*Endurance*
Good calculation	*Orderliness*	*Good-heartedness*	*Confidence*
Quick-wittedness	*Modesty*	*Public-spiritedness*	*Great-heartedness*
Good sense	*Self-control*	*Fair-dealing*	*Stout-heartedness*
Good sense of purpose			*Love of work*
Resourcefulness			

---

[12] It is worth noting that such lists have a long and varied history, yielding incompatibly different lists in different traditions. See MacIntyre 1981, 181ff for discussion.

This sort of list can be expanded in two ways: one, it can be expanded 'horizontally', by adding more cardinal virtues, and two, it can be expanded 'vertically', by adding more subordinate virtues. Consequently, on such an approach one's efforts to avoid the enumeration problem are not restricted to curtailing plurality along the horizontal dimension—by contrast, on a non-cardinal view, *all* plurality is horizontal. Rather, one can also allow for considerable plurality along the vertical dimension, so that such plurality is not merely 'yet more' virtues, but more detail and richness added to the cardinal virtues. And since the vertical dimension is available to release so much of the 'pressure' of the expansion of the many and diverse virtues, it now becomes far less urgent, where the enumeration problem is concerned, to worry about having 'just so many' cardinal virtues along the horizontal dimension, and therefore less urgent to try to produce a short, closed list of cardinal virtues. Of course, this does not *prove* that the virtues are finitely many along either the vertical or the all-important horizontal dimension; but it is a mistake to look for such a proof at *this* level of theorizing, anyway. The only proof there can be is to produce a plausible theory of the virtues with a finite number of cardinal virtues. Our task is not to construct a virtue theory, but to examine certain formal features of such a theory. Expansion along the vertical dimension is not problematic, since that expansion enriches our understanding of the cardinal virtues; the virtues by which we understand 'overall virtuous' do not multiply thereby. And since this decreases the impetus to expand along the horizontal plane—to expand in the way that gives rise to the enumeration problem in the first place—there is no reason to be skeptical about the prospects of a virtue theory that is finite along this dimension. At this level of theorizing, then, cardinality should give us all the confidence we need.

It is worth pausing briefly to note that such an approach is also inspiring confidence in some contemporary personality psychologists, in their efforts to classify ways in which personality and character function well. In their recent book *Character Strengths and Virtues*, Christopher Peterson and Martin Seligman write that they 'hope to do for the domain of moral excellence (character strengths and virtues) what the *DSM* [*Diagnostic and Statistical Manual of Mental Disorders*] does well for disorders', namely to classify such strengths so as to facilitate their professional recognition, assessment, and further research (2004, 7f). Although they compiled as broad a list of virtues as possible from cross-cultural surveys ranging from psychology and philosophy to literature to all forms of pop culture (even to greeting cards), nonetheless the list that resulted is not of the 'laundry list' type but of a 'Linnaean' genus-species type, and was remarkably economical to boot (14–16). In particular, their search yielded a classification of six 'core' or cardinal virtues—'wisdom, courage, humanity, justice, temperance, and transcendence'—and twenty-four 'character strengths' or (in our terms) subordinate virtues or exercises, which represent major ways in which the core virtues are exercised (13). The six core or cardinal virtues are identified as those that are universal, important for the survival of the species, and necessary for good character. The 'character strengths' (or subordinate virtues) are particular ways of being virtuous with respect to the core virtues, for instance, by being brave, being persistent, or having integrity in the case of courage, or by being hopeful, appreciating beauty, or having a sense of purpose in the case of transcendence. These strengths are identified by no fewer than ten criteria, such as their contributing to a good life, being valuable for their own sake, their exercise relative to other persons being non-zero-sum, and so on (16–28). To have a virtue, on this view, is to have at least some of the strengths (depending on cultural or social setting, say) by which it is exercised; that is, one must have the virtue in some of the characteristic ways in which it is had, although not necessarily (and probably not likely) in all of those ways, at least in a good enough way (as they put it, 'at threshold values', 13).

Although Peterson and Seligman do not pretend that their list of character strengths is exhaustive (2004, 13), there is no reason to worry about them rampantly expanding, either, for two reasons. One, the criteria for these strengths are fairly stringent, so they are not likely to expand *rampantly* in the first place (unlike the 'one virtue for every way it is good to be' sort of approach). Two, and more important, expansion at the level of strengths or subordinate virtues is not expansion of those virtues in relation to which the notion of 'overall virtuous' is given meaning. To be sure, there is no pretense of exhaustiveness at the core or cardinal level, either, but the sorts of criteria appropriate to the more stringent notion of core or cardinal virtues—such as universality, and playing an essential role in good character and a good life—make expansion here far less likely anyway. Now, we may not accept Peterson and Seligman's criteria, or their conceptions of the various virtues; our project may be fundamentally different from theirs, being much more evaluative than descriptive; and so on. But the point is that it seems reasonable to hope that a hierarchical classification of the virtues could yield a viable alternative to the 'laundry list' sorts of approaches that make the enumeration problem such a threat.

However, Peterson and Seligman also make it clear that they do not offer a 'deep theory' of the virtues and strengths that they classify—theirs is only a classification, not a 'taxonomy' (2004, 6f)—and as a result, they have somewhat less to say about the relation of subordinate to cardinal virtues than we would want for our purposes. I shall focus on that relation in the next two chapters.

For our more immediate purposes, there are three things I should point out about a cardinal approach in virtue theory. One, addressing the enumeration problem by means of cardinality does not mean producing a very *short* list of virtues. We require only that the (cardinal) virtues be countable; beyond that, there are no requirements as to how many there are. Two, it falls to each particular virtue theorist to say *which* virtues are cardinal, and this we can expect to be a matter of reasonable disagreement between theorists. And three, there is no need that the list should be *closed* in any *dogmatic* way. As the possibility of environmental virtues suggests, we must remain open-minded about what we may discover to be a virtue, along each dimension. But this just means, again, that the virtues are difficult to count, not that they are uncountable in principle. And of course it remains difficult to know when an act or person is overall virtuous, but we knew that would be difficult anyway. Our task is not to say what 'overall virtuous' means, or to make it easy to say what it means, but only to restore our confidence that it can in principle have a meaning.

Enumeration and 'Concreteness' Very roughly speaking, the enumeration problem arises when an account of the virtues fails to make them countable; but in what sense could the virtues be 'countable', anyway? Here there are two extremes to avoid. On the one hand, it would be a mistake to suppose that identifying and individuating the virtues is *entirely* down to the discretion of the theorist doing the identifying and individuating. Virtues are attributes of human beings, and what virtues there are depends on what patterns of feeling, desiring, choosing, and acting it makes sense for human beings to have. Consequently, what sorts of traits are virtues, and what is the salient difference between one virtue and another, are matters that can be determined only within a wider ethical outlook on what it makes sense for humans to do, and as we saw in Chapter 3, such an outlook must be in equilibrium with certain 'essential features of specifically human life' (Foot 2001, 14).[13] Furthermore, we also saw there, on the one hand, that to identify a virtue is to identify some attribute that we have a reason to have, to develop, and to exercise, and on the other, that such reasons must not be merely 'one's own business'. So we cannot simply 'count' the virtues in any old way we please.

At the same time, Owen Flanagan is surely correct to note that '[t]here is about traits the possibility of what Whitehead termed "misplaced concreteness"—that we take trait names as names for simple substantive things

---

[13] The sort of naturalism I endorse is best articulated by McDowell 1995a, which is different in important respects from Foot's naturalism; but I shall not pursue the differences here.

when they are in fact names for complex processes with fuzzy edges' (1991, 278). If he is right, then 'counting' may be the wrong metaphor altogether when it comes to the virtues. And so here we might suppose that the so-called enumeration problem could get off the ground only by imbuing the virtues with such 'misplaced concreteness', treating the virtues as concrete entities 'out there' somewhere, waiting for us to count them properly. Can we avoid the enumeration problem simply by eschewing such 'misplaced concreteness'?

I do not think that we can. Suppose, as I myself believe, that the virtues are not 'out there' (where?) for a theory to itemize, but are things only for a theory to *construct*, as it arrives at a view about what it makes sense for persons to feel, to choose, and to do, in equilibrium with certain 'essential features of specifically human life'. Such a theory, that is, understands both the nature of the virtues and their relationships to one another—their identification and their individuation—only from within a broader ethical outlook on human life. Notice, though, that such a view *still* individuates the virtues, and still understands right action and virtuous persons in terms of the virtues, in the plural, that it individuates. So the problem remains: such a theory must be able to attach meaning to the notion of overall virtuousness, and cannot do so if its mode of individuating the virtues it constructs makes them innumerable. The enumeration problem, therefore, presupposes no metaphysical 'Platonism' about the virtues.

Enumeration, Modularity, and Unity   Finally, we may suspect that the so-called enumeration problem arises only for a 'modular' theory of the virtues, whereas no such problem would arise for a theory on which 'the virtues' are in fact only different names for parts of a single thing, 'virtue'. Such a 'unitarian' view of the virtues has a very long tradition, going back at least to Plato's *Protagoras*, where Socrates suggests that 'the virtues' may in fact be parts of a single thing, virtue, somewhat as the various 'parts' of gold are all parts of a single thing, namely gold as a mass (329d). And as Flanagan (1991, 268–75) tells the story, such a view persisted through the European Renaissance, and in fact has come down to us through modern psychologists like Jean Piaget and Lawrence Kohlberg, who hold that moral development is a matter not of acquiring a collection of individual modules of 'moral competence', but of gradually acquiring moral competence as a whole, singular module. The enumeration problem may arise for more 'Aristotelian' theories (cf. *NE* VI.13) on which 'virtue' is a term for a diverse (but connected) set of different moral competencies, but does it also arise even for a 'unitarian' account of the virtues?

I am myself highly sympathetic to unitarian theories, but I think that such views must still reckon with the enumeration problem. The unitarian view is a view about the relation between the 'parts' of virtue and the whole. But whatever the relation of the parts to the whole, such a unitarian view still individuates those parts, that is, particular virtues like justice, courage, temperance, etc. After all, it is surely no use to limit one's action guidance to the injunction to 'be virtuous'. Elizabeth Anscombe (1981*b*) once noted that sometimes shifting from the question 'whether what we are doing is right' to 'whether we are being honest' can make the answer clear straightaway, but I do not think the same would be true of a shift to the bald question 'whether we are being virtuous'. Consequently, even a unitarian view of the virtues still requires the notion of overall virtuousness, and must attach meaning to that notion *in terms of the virtues it individuates*. We may understand 'overall virtuousness' with Plato, understanding the virtues not as discrete parts but as aspects of a unified whole, but the enumeration problem just shifts to those aspects. Granting that virtue is a whole, we still must ask what that whole is—what are its attributes? If its attributes are infinite, then there is no accounting for 'overall virtuousness' in terms of that whole.

An illustration may prove useful. Consider the Stoic virtue theory, on which it is not only the case that to have any virtue entails having every virtue, but that to have any virtue *is* to have every virtue, since all the virtues are one. Now, on the Stoic view each of the cardinal virtues is a sort of practical, ethical expertise, in two ways: primarily, each is an expertise in its own particular range of ethical considerations, and secondarily, an expertise in integrating its own considerations with those of each of the other cardinal virtues (see Arius Didymus in Stobaeus, *Anthology* II.5b–5b2). To say that virtue is one, then, is to say that all of these forms of expertise go together as a unitary whole, which is a whole expert grasp of ethical considerations. The difference between one virtue and another, then, is not a difference between separate modules, but is a difference between the various sorts of ethical considerations of which virtue as a whole is an expertise (see Cooper 1999, 88f, 99–103). On such a view, then, if the virtues are not countable, then these ethical considerations are not countable, either, so that the idea of virtue as a unified grasp of those considerations is a non-starter. And I think we can say, more generally, that even on a unitarian conception of virtue the enumeration problem still applies, since it is a problem that potentially arises in the course of attaching meaning to 'overall virtuousness' in terms of a plurality of virtues, whatever sorts of 'parts' of virtue as a whole they may be.

There is, however, an extreme unitarian view that may be able to sidestep the enumeration problem altogether, and we even find such a view among the Stoics Menedemus and Ariston. On this view, virtue is one, and the virtues in the plural do not differ at all in their internal structure. Rather, in the case of Menedemus, there are no plural virtues at all, only a plurality of names we apply to virtue. On the other hand, on Ariston's view there are differences between virtues, but these differences are not internal but purely relational, like the differences between forms of sight in the case of bright and dark objects (Plutarch, *On Moral Ends* 440a–441e; see Cooper 1999, 90–6). On either version of this view, the virtues would represent different ways of characterizing a single thing, and since the unity of the thing itself is independent of how many ways it can be characterized, 'overall virtuous' would mean simply 'in accordance with virtue'. But sidestepping the enumeration problem in this way comes at too dear a cost. As we saw in Chapter 3 (§3.2.1), acting from virtue involves deliberation that specifies and makes determinate one's virtuous end. In that case, as ends differ, so too does the practical reasoning involved in specifying them. And it seems clear that virtuous ends do differ; virtue as a whole does have an end—acting well—but of course one can act for the sake of the end of 'acting well' only by acting for the sake of some more particular end—to help another, say, or to deal fairly. Acting from virtue therefore has a different deliberative structure for different ends—and that difference just is a difference in the internal structure of the virtues. So too, it seems, thought the Stoic Zeno (see Cooper 1999, 95f, 105–7). Any *workable* unitarian theory of the virtues, therefore, will treat virtue as a unity of plural virtues with internal differences, and thus will have to take the enumeration problem seriously.

With these few points of clarification in place, we can perhaps best understand the enumeration problem by understanding the various particular problems that it has the potential to make for virtue ethics. In the rest of this chapter, I discuss three of these that I think are especially important: one, problems concerning overall virtuousness and right action (§5.2); two, problems concerning overall virtuousness and being a virtuous person (§5.3); and three, problems concerning overall virtuousness and ethical naturalism (§5.4).

5.2 Enumeration and Overall Virtuous Actions

5.2.1 The Finitude of the Virtues

One of the most serious problems that the enumeration problem makes for virtue ethics is one that has a parallel in a familiar problem in the philosophy of language. One constraint on theories of the grammar or syntax of a learnable language is that the principles of that grammar be finite, since it is not possible even in principle to learn a language if doing so involves mastering an infinite number of grammatical principles. So while the set of meaningful, grammatical sentences in any language is infinitely large, this set cannot require an infinitely large store of grammatical resources. One implication of this fact is that a learnable language can contain only a finite number of what Donald Davidson has called 'semantical primitives', where a semantical primitive is an expression for which 'the rules which give the meaning for the sentences in which it does not appear do not suffice to determine the meaning of the sentences in which it does appear' (1984, 9). The task for a theory of grammar, then, is to account for an infinite set of possible linguistic tasks in terms of a finite set of linguistic rules—that is, to 'understand how an infinite aptitude can be encompassed by finite accomplishments' (8).

One question that Davidson raises is whether quotations are semantical primitives, or whether the meaning of a quotation is instead a function of the meanings of the components of the quoted phrase and their structure. For instance, consider the view that a quotation is 'a constant individual name of a definite expression', that is, something equivalent to a proper name that names the utterance being quoted. On this view, every quotation is a semantical primitive, because its meaning is not compositional, so that the grammar of the rest of the language is not sufficient to determine its meaning. In short, there must be a new grammar for every quotation. But since in any language there can be infinitely many different quotations, no language in which quotations worked like that could be learnable, even in principle, because its grammatical rules would be infinitely many—one for each semantically primitive quotation (Davidson 1984, 10f; see also Tarski 1956, 159, cited by Davidson).

The problem for such a theory of quotation is something like an enumeration problem: if the infinite aptitude of a competent speaker of some language can be encompassed only by infinite accomplishments, then there can be no such thing as a competent speaker of that language—no matter how much any speaker has learned, there will always remain an infinite expanse of grammatical ignorance. Consequently, no theory of syntax that entails an infinite number of semantical primitives can be a legitimate theory for a learnable language. Simply put, to learn a language is to gain the grammatical ability to express an unlimited number of quotations, but if each quotation comes with a new rule determining its meaning, then such a language cannot in principle be learned.

The enumeration problem is a parallel problem for virtue ethics. The set of actions that can be done well or virtuously in different contexts is infinitely large, but the virtues by which actions are done well cannot be infinite, since in that case there could be no such thing as 'the virtuous person', an 'overall virtuous motivation', or an account of 'overall virtuous acts', and therefore no such thing as a virtue ethical account of right action or virtuous persons, even in principle.

Now in a theory of the virtues the equivalent of a semantical primitive is a virtue whose exercise is a different thing from the exercise of any other virtue. As we saw above, there are two ways of understanding these 'primitive' virtues. On a theory like Plato's, the Stoics', or Aquinas', the cardinal virtues are primitive (in fact, the Stoics call them the 'primary' virtues), while the subordinate virtues—what Aquinas calls the 'secondary' and 'derived' virtues, and the 'exercises'—are such that their exercise is not a different kind of thing from the exercise of some primitive (i.e. cardinal) virtue or virtues. On the other hand, without cardinality—as in Aristotle's and all modern theories—all the virtues are primitive, that is, the exercise of any virtue is different from the exercise of any other (even if different virtues must sometimes be exercised together). Therefore, the issue of cardinality is at the heart of the enumeration problem: for a cardinal theory, the infinity of the virtues *per se* is not really the problem, as long as that infinity comes to no more than infinitely many interesting ways of exercising or focusing a finite number of cardinal virtues. The enumeration problem, then, is a problem for any account on which there are infinitely many *primitive* or *cardinal* virtues.

Given that virtue ethics must theorize about right actions and virtuous persons in terms of the virtues, in the plural, no theory of the virtues that entails an infinite number of 'primitive' virtues can be a legitimate theory of the virtues for the purposes of virtue ethics. And given the apparent fact that persons can, in principle anyway, be virtuous overall, *no such virtue theory* could be legitimate, full stop, the purposes of virtue ethics aside. No such virtue theory could be a viable theory of what it is to be a virtuous person. Consequently, a theory of the virtues is restricted to working with a finite number of primitive virtues. Again, this does not mean that we must have ready a definitive 'list' of those virtues, or demonstrate that the primitive virtues are just so many, any more than a theory of syntax must determine just how many semantical primitives a language can have.[14] But it does suggest that the only way to halt the proliferation of primitive virtues while taking seriously

---

[14] Consider Flanagan's claim (1991, 33) that the unity of the virtues is psychologically implausible because 'there is no determinate list that includes all the virtues, and thus no clear meaning can be ascribed to the idea of possessing *every* one' (emphasis in original). Are we to suppose, by equivalent reasoning, that the notion of mastery of a language is psychologically implausible, if there is no determinate list that includes all the semantical primitives?

the plurality of the virtues is to look for structure among them, of the sort that cardinal theories propose. Virtue theories, like language theories, must include compositionality.

Again, these remarks suggest not a solution of the enumeration problem but a sketch of the broad outlines that such a solution would have to take. And it remains to be seen more precisely what the 'cardinality' of a virtue would amount to, what it would mean for one virtue to be an 'exercise' of another, and indeed whether the very idea of cardinality can survive the jump from the thirteenth century. These questions are the focus of the next two chapters. But for now I want to consider more carefully the point I made above, that the enumeration problem, if unresolved, would jeopardize the very possibility of a virtue ethical theory of right action.

5.2.2 *Was Prichard Right About the Virtues After All?*

Let me state the point again, since it bears repeating. Suppose that, as there are (say) infinitely many distinctive contexts for virtue, or infinitely many forms of appropriate responsiveness, or infinitely many forms of moral admirability, or what have you, so too there must be infinitely many primitive virtues. In that case, it would still be possible to describe an act as a virtuous act, that is, an act that hits the 'target' or 'mean' of some virtue or other. It would also be possible to describe an act as an act from virtue, that is, expressive of the virtuous inner state of the agent who does it. However, on this supposition, there could be no such thing as a virtue ethical account of right action. Such a theory of right action is meant to be a general theory for assessing actions and offering guidance, and the resources of that theory come from its account of the virtues. So it is not an option for a theory to account for the infinite range of possibly right actions by simply producing yet more virtues. Therefore, if virtue ethics makes the virtues infinitely many, it can give no general account of right action, and therefore cannot be a self-standing moral theory itself, but could at most be a complement to such a theory. Let's take a closer look at each of these steps.

First, consider right action as a matter of action guidance. As Rosalind Hursthouse has shown, the 'rightness' of an act is sometimes an action-guiding notion—a matter of what one ought to do, of what decision one ought to make—and sometimes an action-assessing notion, that is, a matter of what we can consider a 'good deed' or give a 'tick of approval' (1999a, ch. 2). Where virtues are individuated by distinctive contexts, say, virtue-based action guidance must offer a new virtue, or perhaps a new range of virtues, for each distinctive new context of action. Since action guidance depends on context, in many cases—infinitely many, in fact—it will depend on the addition of yet another primitive to the theory. In that case, virtue ethics could offer no general approach to action guidance.

Furthermore, the enumeration problem also makes it awkward to give action guidance even about this or that action. For instance, when virtue ethicists say of a scoundrel that he or she ought to put right some situation stemming from his or her earlier wrongdoing, they usually say this because it would be callous or deplorable for this person to do otherwise. Yet if there are infinitely many primitive virtues, then presumably there will be infinitely many vices as well—infinitely many ways of failing to mesh with the virtues—and so it will be impossible to characterize an action as what one ought to do, on the grounds that that action, unlike some other, involves no further vice—there always remains another vice for which the act will need to be checked. And so even when a given decision would be overall virtuous, we could never in principle be in a position to know that it is.

This result generalizes. As I mentioned above, Anscombe pointed out that putting questions about what one ought to do in terms of the virtues ('Would it be just to do such a thing?') sometimes makes the answer clear straightaway, but given the enumeration problem, there would be in principle no point at which such questions could end. We can imagine ourselves going down a list of virtues and vices and sizing up an action in terms of each of them, never coming to the end of the list. And I trust it is clear that this problem persists even though only some of the virtues are relevant to any given action, since one can never know that one has isolated all the relevant virtues from among an infinite number.

Second, the enumeration problem also blocks a virtue ethical account of right action as an action-assessing notion. As we saw in Chapter 2, many virtue ethicists hold, and are entitled to hold, that when even a well-intended action involves or results in some terrible thing that no virtuous person would ever want to bring about, the action cannot be considered a virtuous one (even if virtuously chosen), because in such an action the characteristic aims of virtue are unmet or frustrated, and therefore the action cannot be considered a right action, either. But given the enumeration problem, assessing an action as right would involve checking for the infinitely many respects in which an action can fail to be virtuous, and therefore there would be no way to tell, even in principle, that a given action has failed in none of them. On the other hand, some virtue ethicists (like Michael Slote) hold that the rightness of an action—its being a good deed—depends entirely on its being virtuously chosen, but here 'virtuously chosen' means that the action is done from an inner state that is virtuous overall (and thus 'balanced', in Slote's phrase), a property of inner states that we could not detect given the enumeration problem.

Gary Watson (1990) has shown that any theory of right action that is a form of virtue ethics must hold, at the minimum, that a virtue can be understood apart from a formula of right action, *and* that right action cannot be fully understood apart from an account of virtue. And as we have seen here, for virtue ethics to understand right action in terms of virtue is really to understand right action in terms of *the virtues*. But of course, the enumeration problem, if unsolved, would mean that no account of *the virtues* could be given, and therefore that for virtue ethics right action could not be fully understood at all. Given the enumeration problem, there could be no such thing as a virtue ethical account of right action, even in principle; a theory of right action that involves the virtues, then, could not be a distinctively virtue ethical theory. Virtue ethics, then, could not be a distinctive ethical theory, but at most a theory about the goodness of agents and self-improvement. Philosophers from H. A. Prichard to William Frankena to Robert Louden have objected for the last hundred years that that is all a virtue-based theory could ever be, and as long as the enumeration problem stands, so too does that objection.

5.3 Enumeration and Overall Virtuous Persons

5.3.1 Overall Virtuous Persons

Perhaps virtue ethics could not even offer much by way of a theory of self-improvement either, in the face of the enumeration problem. We improve by becoming (more) virtuous, but the notion of being virtuous in a given respect must bear certain counterfactuals: a just person, say, not only has an actual 'track record' of a certain sort, but also would, if confronted, be able to withstand certain temptations to injustice, to find what justice requires in new contexts, and so on, at least to an acceptable extent. It is here that the other virtues come in, since lacking even a very different virtue like temperance, for instance, may lead one to act unjustly in situations in which justice is threatened by the strength of one's appetites (see Hursthouse 1999b). This is not necessarily to say that one cannot be virtuous in any respect unless one is virtuous in every respect, but there is no denying that questions of whether and to what extent a person is virtuous in one respect can be answered only by considering how this person also stands with respect to *the virtues*, taken in the plural. Given the enumeration problem, no such answers can be forthcoming, in principle. Here, the problem is more than an epistemic one: there is no way that a finite agent can stand with respect to an infinite number of virtues.

The loss of the notion of an overall virtuous person has a couple of very important implications. For one thing, as we saw in the previous chapter, being virtuous does not mean being perfect or ideal, since *virtue* is what I there called a 'satis concept': one can be virtuous indeed if one is but 'virtuous enough'. However, the meaning of 'virtuous enough' cannot simply be stipulated; 'virtuous enough' does not mean 'virtuous enough for some other interest of ours' (such as that a certain proportion of us should all get to qualify), but must involve being virtuous enough to count as virtuous *tout court*, in fact and not merely in a manner of speaking. *Virtue* is therefore a very special kind of satis concept that I called a 'model concept': being 'virtuous *tout court*' depends not on merely how we use the word 'virtuous', but on an understanding of the real nature of virtue, and therefore on a model of 'the virtuous person'. Now as I have just argued, the question of how virtuous one is with respect to any one virtue cannot be answered in isolation from considerations of how one stands with respect to the virtues in the plural. Therefore, the model of 'the virtuous person' must be a model of the *virtues*, if it is to be a model of any virtue at all. However, there could be no such model of infinitely many virtues; therefore, given the enumeration problem, there could be no such thing as a model of any virtue at all. And since *virtue* is a model concept, the enumeration problem undermines the meaningfulness of the idea that one could be virtuous *tout court* by being virtuous enough. Therefore, there could be no sense of 'virtuous enough' except one that we stipulate relative to some other purpose, or that merely tracks common use of virtue words.

Furthermore, the loss of the notion of an overall virtuous person also undermines the notion of phronesis. One of the central roles of phronesis is the ability to deliberate so as to find the 'mean', that is, to determine what act would, in the circumstances, count as genuinely virtuous—just, say, or benevolent. Phronesis also has the role of finding the act that would be virtuous overall, striking an appropriate balance between the very diverse demands of the world. And so, as falls the notion of 'overall virtuous' action, so falls this aspect of phronesis: there could be no such thing, even in principle, as integrating the virtues in an overall way, and so no deliberative skill of doing so. Furthermore, as we saw above, hitting the 'mean' of a virtue in action cannot be understood in a one-off way, since a lack in any other virtue at all could potentially upset one's ability to hit that mean reliably. In that case, the enumeration problem threatens the possibility of phronesis in both its twin roles at once.

The enumeration problem therefore undermines the very idea of phronesis as a deliberative excellence that unifies the concerns of the various virtues in an overall way. The loss of phronesis in its integrative role, I argue now, would be particularly costly, as it would leave us with a picture of the virtues as fairly isolated, discrete, and 'myopic' behavioral dispositions. I discuss the problems associated with such a picture of the virtues in greater detail in later chapters, but in the rest of this section I shall mention two particularly distressing implications of such a view. First, such fragmentation renders practical advice framed in terms of the virtues rather trivial and powerless (§5.3.2); and second, such fragmentation also renders our understanding of the virtues too thin to be of much interest in explanations of behavior (§5.3.3).

5.3.2 Enumeration and the 'Flock of Virtues'

Since the enumeration problem would prohibit a theory of the virtues from attaching meaning to the notion of an 'overall virtuous' agent, it would also be unable to account for any ability, such as phronesis, to integrate the virtues in an overall way. One implication of this fact is that on such a theory, the virtues must be relatively myopic and isolated behavioral dispositions, and this only worsens the difficulties of providing meaningful action guidance. Let me explain why.

A classic example of such a 'myopic' conception of the virtues comes from R. B. Brandt, who considers the 'traditional' view of honesty as 'just an aversion to, say, breach of promise up to a "standard" level', and observes that the complexity of ordinary 'concrete situations' calling for honesty will require, on this view, 'a whole flock of different desires/aversions, all delicately tuned, so that their conjoint action will bring us out where a rational person would want us trained to come out' (1981, 277).[15] One clear problem with this thin, behavioral account of the virtues is that it can address a concrete ethical concern only by throwing more 'virtues' at it. Now, even if it is not to be expected of virtue ethics or indeed of any ethical theory that it should *reduce* the complexity of moral life to an elegant problem-solving procedure,[16] still the unregulated expansion of 'the virtues' threatens merely to *reproduce* that complexity in the multiplicity of what can count as a virtue. No tractability is gained.

Furthermore, throwing more virtues at a concrete ethical concern cannot address that concern, anyway. As Wittgenstein observed, rules do not include further rules for their own application, and this shortcoming cannot be remedied by adding yet further rules. The same holds for tendencies, aversions, desires, and mere behavioral dispositions, which do not include intelligent

---

[15] See also Brandt 1988 for further analysis of virtues as aversions, tendencies, etc. Brandt's 'flock' of virtues should of course bring to mind Meno's 'swarm'.

[16] On this point see Annas 2004; Hursthouse 1995a; Hursthouse 1999a, ch. 2; Louden 1990.

principles to guide them as concrete practical concerns demand, either. So the multiplication of such 'virtues' can never be enough. John McDowell (1997, 143f) has put the point this way:

> Suppose the relevant range of behaviour, in the case of kindness, is marked out by the notion of proper attentiveness to others' feelings. Now sometimes acting in such a way as to indulge someone's feelings is not acting rightly [e.g. when doing so would violate another's right]. ... In such a case, a straightforward propensity to be gentle to others' feelings would not lead to right conduct. ... Possession of the virtue must involve not only sensitivity to facts about others' feelings as reasons for acting in certain ways, but also sensitivity to facts about rights as reasons for acting in certain ways; and when circumstances of both sorts obtain, and circumstance of the second sort is the one that should be acted on, a possessor of the virtue of kindness must be able to tell that that is so. So we cannot disentangle genuine possession of kindness from the sensitivity which constitutes fairness.

And of course, this result generalizes well beyond the virtue of kindness. As a practical theory, then, such a 'flock of virtues' approach is a non-starter.

Now, I do not think that any virtue ethicist today would accept as thin a conception of the virtues as the one that Brandt suggests. But an alternative to a view like Brandt's requires a conception of overall virtuous action, and (as McDowell observes) a conception of phronesis that enables an agent to find overall virtuous action. Notice also that as the virtues multiply, the smaller the practical role that each individual virtue is called on to play in 'overall' virtuous action. In the face of the enumeration problem, then, any account of the virtues we may try to give must end up looking very much like an account of the Brandt-style dispositions, and thus have little more to offer as a practical theory than a 'flock of virtues'. And that is most unfortunate: reflection on the virtues should make the complexity of our moral experience more tractable, not simply reproduce it in an ever-expanding list of virtues; the 'flock of virtues' approach leaves practical problems exactly as they are. Such unregulated expansion of the virtues therefore threatens to render the practical advice and guidance of virtue ethics rather feeble, telling us little more than that the best way to act with respect to X is to act according to that excellent and—wouldn't you know it!—specifically X-regarding disposition (or perhaps, flock of dispositions). The notion of virtuousness in this or that respect is not enough for virtue ethics, but that is all that the enumeration problem would leave us.

5.3.3 Enumeration and the 'Situationist' Challenge

The loss of a notion of integrating the various virtues renders virtue-based guidance of action uninteresting, and as I argue now, it also threatens virtue-based explanations of action. This is therefore a problem for virtue theory generally, not just virtue ethics. As we have seen, one major impetus for a 'fragmentary' picture of the virtues is the observation that people who display one sort of virtue in certain types of contexts may not display that sort of virtue elsewhere. However, the more contextually-bound the virtues are, the less important they are as features of human psychology.

If 'situationism' teaches us anything, it is this. In contemporary social psychology, situationists hold that people's behavior very often varies more with the situations in which they find themselves than with the ordinary dispositions we commonly suppose people to have. Several philosophical psychologists have argued that this thesis can be made consistent with the view that there *are* character traits, but that such character traits would have to be very contextually-bound and narrow in their scope of operation, so that modeling human action in terms of character traits gains far less than we might have thought over modeling action simply in terms of contextual and situational factors from the beginning. For that reason, such philosophical psychologists object to the character-based model of human psychology that virtue ethics presupposes, claiming that there is little evidence that character traits are of much practical importance in the human psyche, and therefore that the notion of character is the wrong place to begin a practical ethical theory (see esp. Doris 2002).

Now, even if the empirical data of the social psychologist suggest that *behavior*, as seen by an outside observer, displays surprisingly little consistency across different sorts of situations, nonetheless we should note that social psychologists have *also* argued that *practical reasoning* (and therefore *action*, from the agent's point of view) demonstrates a considerably higher degree of consistency across situations (Ross and Nisbett 1991, 163–7). In that case, a rather Aristotelian line of defense of virtue ethics presents itself: the virtues that figure in virtue-based approaches to ethics include phronesis, by which those virtues have greater cross-situational consistency than do 'virtues' in a more naive or everyday sense (see Kamtekar 2004). In that case, it is far from surprising that, as social psychologists report, many people whom we would generally consider 'compassionate', say, may do surprisingly callous or even cruel things under certain situational pressures. In fact, it would be highly surprising if social psychology did *not* have such findings, since as Aristotle observed most of our so-called 'virtues'—what Aristotle called 'natural virtues' (*NE* VI.13, 1144b1–17)—are little more than dispositions or tendencies to act in certain stereotypical ways (*à la* Brandt, for instance), but usually without much by way of practical intelligence; in that case, he says, we may be as likely to go wrong as right when acting from such 'virtues', since those 'virtues' are not developed enough to withstand situational pressures and other sorts of variables. Rather, virtues in the strict sense—and the virtues with which virtue ethics works—involve practical reasoning, since virtue in the strict sense involves integration and balance of diverse demands, and thus a high degree of situational flexibility. Therefore, on this line of response, while situationism may have shown that the 'natural virtues' are of limited reliability in the face of situational pressures, it has not asserted anything that an Aristotelian virtue theory has ever denied. (I take up this argument in greater detail in Chapters 8–10.)

However, this sort of response requires that the virtues all include practical reasoning about the 'mean' in an overall virtuous way, and since the latter notion is threatened by the enumeration problem, this response is unavailable to most virtue ethicists writing today. For one thing, many virtue ethicists hold that the virtues tend to be specific to increasingly narrow areas of life. For instance, in her influential paper 'The Limited Unity of Virtue', Neera Badhwar argues that the virtues operate only within spheres or 'domains', where a domain is an area of practical concern that is both serious enough to warrant the operation of the virtues in them and susceptible to compartmentalization by the agent from other such areas.[17] Likewise, as we have seen, many virtue ethicists take it for granted that the possibility of being virtuous in one area of life without being similarly virtuous in other areas suggests that different virtues apply in those areas. In this fashion, as we saw above, Hursthouse argues that there is a virtue of good parenting, and against the view that good parents are simply those parents who are just, honest, compassionate, etc., on the grounds that 'it is not unknown for people to be rather good parents but very limited in virtue outside their immediate family circle' (1999a, 213f). In each case, a virtue is seen as highly bound by context. Such a view of the virtues is a recipe for precisely that model of the virtues that skeptics about character have advocated as an *alternative* to a character-based psychology.

For instance, John Doris argues that, given such a recipe, the virtues would be as narrow as, say, courage-in-the-face-of-physical-danger-on-the-battlefield-in-the-face-of-rifle-(as-opposed-to-artillery)-fire, since psychological research suggests that courage can be compartmentalized at just such fine-grained levels as that (2002, 62; see also Upton 2005).[18] The fragmentation of the virtues therefore trivializes their role in our understanding of human psychology, and

---

[17] I discuss Badhwar's view in Ch. 11.

[18] This picture also replaces virtues understood as what Pincoffs 1986, 79f calls 'dispositions'—nondeterminate tendencies, e.g. to be polite—with 'habits', determinate tendencies such as tipping one's hat in the presence of a lady. Arguably, then, this fragmentation of the virtues actually eliminates them, if virtues are dispositions in Pincoffs' sense.

jeopardizes the very conception of practical intelligence needed in order to avoid such a fragmentary alternative to the virtue ethicist's cherished notion of character as a central feature of human agency and action. There is no denying that the virtues are plural, but capturing their plurality by simply allowing them to proliferate by context is to render them uninteresting. It is also to upset the very notion of 'overall virtuous' action, and with it the possibility of phronesis—that is, the possibility of anything but 'natural virtues' in Aristotle's sense. As Aristotle saw and social psychology seems to have confirmed, the natural virtues are as likely to go wrong as right. In that case, the connection between virtue and right action would be, again, so loose that there could be no such thing as a virtue ethical theory of right action in the first place.

5.4   Enumeration and Naturalism

I turn now to a final set of implications of the enumeration problem, this time for ethical naturalism.

It is no 'misplaced concreteness' to say that virtues are real things. This follows simply from the fact that a virtue is a kind of character trait. As such, a virtue is a psychological attribute; in particular, it is a certain pattern of desires, goals, emotions, attitudes, beliefs, priorities, and so on. Furthermore, this pattern hangs together, in the sense that, one, these goals, beliefs, priorities, etc. cohere with each other; two, the pattern can be identified as such a coherent, mutually supporting bundle; and three, these patterns can be individuated from each other (even if they are not discrete). And as we have just seen, these patterns can be identified as causes of certain ranges of action, which are both stable over time and consistent across a wide variety of situations. (I look at all of these features of a virtue more closely in Part III.) What interests us, then, is an account of the virtues themselves, and not merely an account of our virtue vocabulary.

Now, ethical naturalism—for instance, eudaimonism—aspires to give an account of the virtues that is in equilibrium with certain 'essential features of specifically human life', including the nature of human psychology. Obviously, human psychology is finite: our character could not have infinitely many traits. Therefore, no theory on which the virtues are infinitely many can be a naturalistic theory of the virtues. Of course, that character can be *described* in infinitely many ways, but for the naturalist, the virtues are not ways of speaking about character, but real traits, real ways that one's character and psychological makeup are, or can become. A theory of the virtues, then, is not simply a theory of a set of terms in which persons can be described or assessed; it is a theory of virtues as real patterns of emotions, desires, goals, and values (see Hursthouse 1999a, ch. 5).[19] So ethical naturalism cannot ground any theory of the virtues (as opposed to the 'exercises' of the virtues) on which they are infinitely many.

This is ironic, because the fragmentation and compartmentalization of the virtues is usually touted as being a new, improved, and decidedly 'realistic' picture of the virtues. What is realistic is the fact that our characters tend to be spotty and inconsistent, and that we tend to compartmentalize them; but what cannot be realistic is the idea that the virtues themselves divide up along these kinds of lines. It would be better to say, I think, that the virtues, not unlike practical skills, say, develop differently from person to person, and in a spotty and uneven way in every person, but that we should not mistake these developmental patterns for the structure and boundaries of the virtues themselves. We can talk about compassion as one thing and good parenting as another, but why think, just like that, that they must really be different traits, different psychological attributes? Some people are more compassionate towards their children than towards other people; but why think that that shows separateness of *traits*, as opposed to highly uneven *development* of a single trait? Such questions concern our actual psychology, not how we talk about ourselves. (I return to this issue in Chapter 11.)

As I said earlier in this chapter, we can consider a given trait a virtue in the sorts of creatures we are only from within a broader ethical outlook. So if a trait is a virtue, we might say, then it is a trait by which one is responsive to considerations that we can judge to be real reasons from within such an ethical outlook. But of course no such outlook could encompass an infinite number of primitive virtues, or an infinite number of primitive considerations to which it is virtuous to be responsive, so likewise ethical naturalism could not ground any theory on which there are infinitely many such virtues.

Courting the enumeration problem therefore represents an abandonment of ethical naturalism. We can see this in yet another way: if traits differ contextually, then of course they will also differ cross-culturally, whether human nature differs cross-culturally or not. It is a difficult question whether, say, the courage of a Quaker is the same as the courage of a Samurai,[20]

---

[19] I am aware of the view of Driver 2001 that the virtues need involve no sort of psychological structure at all, but it seems to me that a serious point against this view is the fact that if anything should reveal something rather deep about a person taken as an agent with a practical identity, revealing their virtues should. I take up this point in Ch. 12.

[20] I owe the example to Julia Annas.

but contextualism about virtues forces an answer in advance of any closer inspection of the actual traits. That would be unfortunate; as one philosopher has noted,

Indeed, what may be regarded as especially plausible about virtue-ethics is that it offers clear criteria of moral value and virtue that precisely cut across any and all culturally grounded normative differences. Indeed, we can see that people from different parts of the world have very different—even contradictorily opposed—moral beliefs, but we are nevertheless able to recognize certain cross-cultural criteria of moral attitude and conduct. The Moslem shopkeeper down the road has different beliefs from me, but I am well able to appreciate his honesty, integrity, courage and industry; on the other hand, I may have no trouble recognizing the racist bigots who persecute him—albeit in the name of my own culture—for the liars and cowards that they are. It is also clearly important that some such cross-cultural criteria of moral value are recognizable if there is to be the possibility of holding some cultures to moral account precisely for their injustice, mendacity, intemperateness or cruelty. (Carr 2003, 231; see also Polansky 2000)

There is no denying that our *exercise* of a virtue is contextual, and that the possible distinctive exercises of the virtues are infinitely many, but there is no reason to slip from the contextuality of how we *develop* and *exercise* a trait, to the contextuality of that trait *itself*. In fact, that result would be more than unfortunate, since as these remarks suggest there is no reason to think that nature and the 'essential features of specifically human life' differ cross-culturally. And so again, no theory of the virtues that individuates the virtues by context can be grounded in ethical naturalism.

Finally, without grounding in ethical naturalism virtue ethics would be threatened as a practical, action-guiding theory, in at least two important ways. First, a major attraction of virtue ethical forays into applied ethics is the distinctive perspective it brings to applied issues, for instance by casting dilemmas not simply as quandaries to be sorted out, but as episodes in the lives of people and groups that develop over time, and thus have a life before and after the dilemma that shapes what they 'ought' to do in reaction to it (for examples, see Pincoffs 1986, ch. 1; Hursthouse 1997 and 1999a, chs. 2–3). We have already seen one way in which virtue ethical guidance, given the enumeration problem, would be in danger of becoming cheaper and less interesting. But notice that the cheapening of virtue talk would be compounded by the fact that, if the virtues are not individuated for naturalistic reasons, then it could be as good a reason as any to say that some trait is its own virtue in order to signal one's 'genuine concern' over something, as serious enough to 'warrant' a virtue of its own ('See how much I care about this thing—enough to make a special *virtue* of it!').[21] A convincing covering argument for doing so could usually be found readily enough: the virtue in question identifies a good way of acting, which can be isolated from other good ways of acting, which requires its own distinctive skills, etc. It would be most unfortunate if serious discourse about the virtues were to devolve into shibboleths. Serious ethical concepts besides the virtues, after all, frequently fall prey to such dilution; consider how notions like 'oppression', 'exploitation', and 'rape' run the risk of losing much of their real gravity when they are used merely to talk about the awfulness of other things in grave tones. (And isn't it outrageous that we should so drain those notions!) The enumeration problem therefore has serious repercussions for the identification of the virtues, which requires ethical naturalism.

And second, in the face of the enumeration problem virtue ethics may still offer rules like 'Be honest, rather than tactless or deceitful', say, but since the account of the virtues is ultimately severed from a conception of human nature, such rules come detached from a wider context of the agent as a whole, someone who needs the virtues not merely in this respect or that, but ultimately in an overall way. When virtue ethics tells us how to develop, how to improve our character, it cannot meaningfully tell us to improve in an infinite number of ways, so it must fall back on urging us to improve in this respect and that, without any possibility of a conception of overall improvement as a whole agent. A key feature of virtue ethics, and one that has often been touted as setting it apart as a distinctive and distinctively attractive alternative, is its approach to ethical theory via the notion of an agent taken as a whole, rather than as someone who follows rules or generates consequences. Given all that the enumeration problem would force virtue ethics to give up, what would virtue ethics have left, if it should fail to meet this problem?

Conclusion

There can be little question but that virtue ethics, as it now stands—and, I think, as Aristotle himself left it—has clearly courted the enumeration problem. Nor can there be any question but that the enumeration problem, if left unresolved, would be deadly for virtue ethics, and indeed for virtue theory more generally. And it also seems clear that the problem stems from undue attention to our methods for individuating the virtues, that is, for determining what virtues are primitive or cardinal virtues.

[21] Here I have benefited from discussion with Robert Feleppa.

In the next chapter, then, I take up three related issues: one, in what way it is best to individuate the virtues; two, what it would mean for a virtue to be a 'cardinal' virtue and for other virtues to be 'subordinate' to it; and three, and more particularly, what it would mean for a subordinate virtue to be 'of the same kind' as the cardinal virtue to which it is subordinate. After sketching an approach to these issues, I conclude that individuating the virtues requires a structure among the virtues that only phronesis could give them; in that case, only Hard Virtue Ethics can offer any hope of a resolution of the enumeration problem. I shall then extend my approach in Chapter 7 to the task of individuating the Aristotelian virtues of generosity and magnificence, as a kind of trial run.

6

Individuating the Virtues

The enumeration problem is the problem that while virtue ethics must understand right actions in terms of overall virtuousness, and both virtue ethics and virtue theory must understand virtuous persons in terms of overall virtuousness, the most common ways of determining what virtues there are seem to imply that there are infinitely many of them. At the same time, many ways of restricting the number of primitive or cardinal virtues seem negligent of the plurality of the virtues, and to rely on the dogmatic assumption that we already know what all the cardinal virtues are.

In the previous chapter, I argued that the best way to approach the enumeration problem is through the individuation of the virtues, and in particular by sorting the virtues into a structure of 'cardinal'—literally, 'pivotal'—and 'subordinate' virtues, as we find in the virtue theories of the Stoics and (following the Stoics) Aquinas. Because the plurality of the subordinate virtues can be seen as enriching our understanding of the 'primitive' or cardinal virtues, such a structure can accept the plurality of the virtues without merely spinning longer lists of primitive or cardinal virtues. So, I argued there, this approach seems to do both of the things we want. But I did not show that this solution is actually available to us contemporary philosophers. That issue is the concern of this chapter.

Of course, such an approach will not be a simple one for us to take, in no small part because the notion of cardinality is one we no longer encounter in contemporary virtue theories. For that matter, although virtue theories inevitably end up individuating the virtues in one way or another, individuation has rarely received much direct attention. It is well beyond my scope to construct a full-fledged cardinal theory of the virtues here, but I do wish to look at some general features of such a theory—enough anyway to show that it is worth our time thinking seriously about cardinality.

In particular, I examine three main issues. First, I discuss criteria for individuating virtues. I focus on one formal constraint on such criteria in particular, namely that individuation should not make the virtues too discrete, as (say) individuating them by their contexts of exercise does. With this constraint in mind, I then review some individuation criteria that have been offered, and settle on the view that virtues are individuated by the kinds of reasons to which the virtues are responsive (§6.1). Second, since such a criterion relies on the idea that two superficially distinct virtues may actually be responsive to reasons of the same kind, I examine the difficult idea that one virtue can be 'of the same kind' as another virtue (§6.2). And third, I suggest a way of understanding the nature of cardinality, and the relation between cardinal and subordinate virtues, such that subordinate virtues are responsive to reasons 'of the same kind' as the cardinal virtues to which they are subordinate (§6.3). I conclude by considering the implications of our discussion of individuation for the idea that phronesis must be part of every virtue (§6.4).

6.1 From Individuation to Enumeration

6.1.1 Connectivity

An important desideratum in an individuation criterion is what I shall call 'connectivity'. As we saw in the previous chapter, some criteria tend to pull virtues apart rather than together. For instance, the criterion that individuates virtues according to the tendencies of agents to compartmentalize, for instance, is perhaps the limiting case of a criterion lacking connectivity, due to its enormous potential to fragment virtues into smaller and more isolated bits. This is because such a criterion focuses on certain snapshots of agents who display a virtue in some settings but not others. It is because the virtues lack connectivity on such a view that the view openly courts the enumeration problem.

By contrast, focusing on practical reasoning can reveal connections despite superficial diversity. This fact has been clear to social psychologists for some time. For instance, to a casual observer, a waiter who is warm with some patrons, solicitous with others, haughty with others, and so on, would seem to be acting in a wide range of different ways. Nonetheless, these superficial differences can belie the underlying unity of the waiter's single goal of earning good tips, who therefore adjusts his behavior to please patrons with differing expectations (Ross and Nisbett 1991, 164, discussing Cialdini 1988). Such a criterion for 'individuating' the waiter's actions, then, finds connections between the actions where a more superficial individuation would have found only disparity and fragmentation. Such a criterion would display what I mean by connectivity.

The enumeration problem makes the importance of connectivity obvious. While an individuation criterion is meant, of course, to show the differences between different traits, some criteria also allow that different traits can still be 'of the same kind'. Just as being haughty with patrons differs from being solicitous, but both can be actions 'of the same kind'—tip-seeking actions—so too, we may suppose, being generous differs from being magnificent, but perhaps magnificence could still be a virtue 'of the same kind' as generosity, perhaps in virtue of a shared structure of practical reasoning. In that case, we could add magnificence to our 'list' of virtues, making that list richer, rather than merely 'longer'. Of course, so far this is all very sketchy, but at least we know now to be on the lookout for individuation criteria that can identify not just diversity, but also unity in the midst of diversity. And of course, much of this chapter must be occupied with the idea that virtues can be 'of the same kind'.

I now want to look at some individuation criteria, and I shall say more about connectivity in relation to the criterion that I favor. An added benefit of approaching enumeration via individuation is that, although individuation has not attracted nearly enough attention, it has still attracted far more attention than enumeration has, so we are beginning where there is also more light.[1]

6.1.2 Compartmentalization

One view that we have already seen individuates the virtues in terms of how agents can compartmentalize different character traits. For instance, we may say that the virtues involved in good parenting are distinct from the other virtues, since good parents not infrequently show compassion to their children but indifference to people outside the family circle (Hursthouse 1999a, 213f). That is true, of course, but to individuate virtues on the grounds of such phenomena could confuse the level of a virtue's *development* in a given agent with the *makeup* of the virtue itself, considered as a type.

This is an important distinction: we must distinguish how a thing develops in this or that agent from an account of what that thing is. Recall from Chapter 3 that a virtue is a character trait that is an excellence in reasons-responsive creatures such as we are. But what it is to be responsive to certain reasons in an excellent way is a different matter from how persons come to be responsive

---

[1] I make no pretence to exhaustiveness in my review of enumeration criteria. In particular, I shall consider only secular approaches, setting aside e.g. the view of Augustine that the virtues are different forms of the love of God, and among secular approaches I also set aside those, such as Plato's, that rest on outdated models of the psyche.

to them, or approximate a responsiveness to them. I do not doubt that, at least for most of us, charity really does begin at home, and that we develop compassion for near and dear before our compassion extends to more distant others. For all I know, it may be that we evolved to develop compassion in a piecemeal, modular fashion. It may even be that compassion towards near and dear and compassion towards strangers activate different parts of the brain. I do not know. But what I do know is that none of this would show that the reasons there are for being compassionate to various others are necessarily different—that would require a *normative* argument, not a biological one. In that case, we should say that one is not fully responsive to reasons for compassion as long as one remains unreflectively compartmentalized in one's compassion. This is not to say, of course, that as compassion develops, the boundary between strangers and loved ones should break down altogether. But it may be that one cannot be fully responsive to reasons for compassion until any such barriers as there are within one's compassion, are themselves responsive to reasons for treating loved ones and strangers differently. Consequently, parents who are compassionate to their children but indifferent to others need not be evidence of a developed parenting virtue distinct from compassion, rather than of a developmentally lopsided version of compassion. After all, it seems very likely that as compassion develops properly, it is naturally such as to transcend boundaries of personal connection to a far greater degree than such parents have so far managed to do. How a thing is learned is a different question from a proper understanding of what that thing is.[2]

Therefore, the lines between virtues in developing agents need not track the lines between the virtues themselves. For the same reason, such a criterion will regularly interpret the disunity of one's development of a virtue for a plurality of distinct virtues, and so will give us very little basis for identifying connections despite normatively superficial differences. For all these reasons, then, I think we should set this approach to individuation aside.

6.1.3 Emotions and the Mean

Aristotle's discussion of the virtues of character places great emphasis, and rightly so, on the fact that the virtues involve not only action but also *reaction*,

---

[2] Here there is also an analogy to Aristotle's philosophy of science in the *Posterior Analytics*. Aristotle there depicts science as having a deductive structure, and readers have often taken this as a description of the generation or development of scientific knowledge, and thus as wildly implausible (and what's more, deeply inconsistent with Aristotle's reports of his own scientific work). However, Barnes 1969 has argued convincingly that Aristotle's is instead a theory of the structure of an area of scientific knowledge, taken as a whole, organized body. Analogously, I distinguish between the structure of a virtue, considered as a type having a nature, and the structure of development of virtues in particular agents.

that is, the rich emotional life of virtuous persons. Taking this important idea as a cue, J. O. Urmson argues that the virtues should be individuated according to the emotions that each virtue specially concerns (1980; see Hursthouse 1999*b* for critique). For instance, on Aristotle's view anger is a type of emotion of which there is one virtue, namely 'even temper', and even temper is a virtue concerned with one type of emotion, namely anger. Urmson's thesis is a bold one, positing a one-to-one mapping between all virtue types and emotion types more generally.

However, despite its success in analyzing even temper, such a general approach to individuation is highly problematic. Now, we can set aside the difficulties involved in individuating emotion types. Although it is unclear whether, say, rage is a kind of anger or is a different emotion type, it seems inevitable that every attempt to individuate the virtues will do so by correlating the virtues with some other set of things that will themselves require individuation, so this is no *special* problem for Urmson's view. We can also ignore for now the problematic idea that there is a virtue for every type of emotion, since we may individuate virtues according to the emotion type (or even bundle of types) that each specially concerns, even if there is no virtue for some emotion types.[3]

Where individuation is concerned the really problematic idea is that each virtue does specially concern some emotion type (or bundle of types). Outside the virtues of good temper and, perhaps, courage, the virtues do not seem to have specific emotional ranges. For instance, it is clear that the virtue of generosity does involve a certain emotional life: surely the generous person will feel repelled by waste and vain extravagance, for instance, will act generously towards friends out of friendly feeling for them, and so on. But it is equally clear that we cannot individuate generosity from the other virtues by picking out some real emotion type that is the special concern of generosity, the 'generosity emotion', as it were.[4] Focusing on different emotions to individuate the virtues

---

[3] As Urmson 1980, 166–9 himself recognizes, in his discussion of spite Aristotle is unable to find an emotion type in respect of which spite is the bad state, but in respect of which one may be in a 'mean' or virtuous state. It is vicious to be spiteful, but it is difficult to see what the single emotion is that has gone wrong in the spiteful person but which goes right in virtuous persons. Aristotle suggests that the mean to contrast with spite is 'righteous indignation'; however, Aristotle defines righteous indignation as pain at another's undeserved good fortune, and spite as *rejoicing* at another's undeserved bad fortune, so there seems to be no single emotion that is involved in each case (*NE* II.7; cp. *EE* III.7, 1233b18–26; *MM* I.27).

[4] Swanton 2003 discusses the 'modes' by which a person with a given virtue is appropriately responsive to the demands of the world, and it is clear that many of these modes are types of emotion. But Swanton argues convincingly both that each virtue involves a plurality of modes that are emotion types, and that many of these emotional modes of responsiveness are common to all the virtues.

will therefore lead us to overlook the sameness of the virtue concerned with those emotions, and so this criterion too performs very poorly with respect to connectivity.[5]

6.1.4 Desires

The truth in Urmson's view, I think, is the idea that a virtue can be usefully individuated according to certain kinds of *attitudes* characteristic of that virtue. In this spirit, we may individuate the virtues in terms of their characteristic sorts of *desires*, understood simply as motivational states toward or away from some object. For instance, we may say either that to do a generous act, say, is to act from a type of desire characteristic of generosity, or that to be generous is to have, characteristically, desires of a certain type, or both. Such desires, then, are not simple appetites: the virtues are concerned with appetites like hunger, thirst, and so on, but there is no virtue by which one acts from a characteristic sort of hunger. As Marguerite DesLauriers has recently suggested, such a method would require individuating desires in terms of both their objects and the circumstances in which the desires are generated. For instance, justice and generosity both involve desires about the distribution of goods, differing in the circumstances in which such desires arise for the just and for the generous person. In that case, we could say that 'desires that correspond to the judgments of *phronēsis* and have to do with the distribution of goods that are the spoils of war to the citizens will be just desires, but desires that correspond to the judgments of *phronēsis* and have to do with the distribution of goods that are the property of the agent will be generous desires' (2002, 115). On this view, we individuate virtues according to types of practically intelligent desires to act, where these types are individuated according to certain characteristic object-circumstance pairs. As DesLauriers says, these desires are 'desires for different kinds of goods' (114).

Such an approach faces the obvious difficulty of individuating objects and circumstances of desires into kinds, but again, facing *some* such difficulty as this will be common to every individuation criterion. More to the point is that there are two basic ways to individuate the objects and the circumstances of a desire: from the agent's point of view, or from the point of view of some outside observer. The difference may not matter much in the case of individuating the objects of appetites (for food, in the case of hunger; for drink, in the case of thirst; and so on). But it makes a big difference for the sorts of desires by which we would individuate virtues. Return to our example

---

[5] Although the emotions do not individuate the virtues, this is not to say that the emotions are any the less important in the makeup of the virtues.

of the tip-seeking waiter: we could say that he tailors his various behaviors towards his patrons in order to satisfy his desires, but what desires does he mean to satisfy? To an outside observer, he may seem to desire in one case to be endearing and well liked, in another to desire to intimidate others, and so on; but *ex hypothesi*, the object of his desires is the same every time. Clearly, then, the waiter's desires must be individuated according to *his own* construal of the objects of those desires, his judgments about which features of the circumstances are salient given his interest in them, and so on. Consequently, individuating desires according to objects-cum-circumstances would ultimately have to rest on the individuation of different patterns of practical reasoning about those objects. In that case, the desire-based individuation criterion may be able to do well with respect to connectivity, but if so, this would only be by appeal to a more basic individuation of patterns of practical reasoning. So let's consider individuation according to the reasons to which the virtues are responsive.

6.1.5 Reasons

The truth in the desire-based approach, I think, is in the idea that a virtue can be individuated by the sorts of considerations for which persons with that virtue characteristically take themselves to be called into action. As Rosalind Hursthouse says, the 'most significant aspect' of a virtue is 'the wholehearted acceptance of a certain range of considerations as reasons for action' (2003, §2). This suggests a more promising route to individuating the virtues in terms of the sorts of *reasons* that are characteristic of the virtues. This sort of approach has largely taken its cue from Aristotle's observation that acting virtuously involves, among other things, choosing one's action 'for its own sake' (*NE* II.4, 1105a31–2). As Bernard Williams points out, we understand that someone has acted generously, say, only if we understand that the reasons for which he has acted are generous reasons, such as to help or to please another (1995a; 1985, 10f). Likewise, to have a virtue is (among other things) to be characteristically responsive to certain sorts of reasons: 'if an agent has a particular virtue', Williams says, 'then certain ranges of fact become ethical considerations for that agent because he or she has that virtue' (10).[6] Hursthouse offers several examples of such reasons: for justice, we can imagine such reasons as 'It's his', 'I owe it to her', 'She has the right to decide', 'That would mean breaking my promise'; for generosity, 'He needed help', 'He asked me for it',

---

[6] See also Williams 1995a, 17f; McDowell 1997, 142; Foot 2001, 12. It is difficult to tell whether this view is shared by Pincoffs 1986, 101f, who speaks of virtues as individuated by their respective 'considerations'.

'It was his 21st birthday', 'She'll be so pleased'; for temperance, 'I'm driving', 'I'd like you to have some', 'You need it more than I do', 'The cheaper one's fine by me'; for courage, 'I could probably save him if I climbed up there', 'Someone had to volunteer', 'One can't give in to tyrants', 'They'll suffer if I don't get to them'; and so on (1995b, 25).[7] These examples show the sorts of considerations that are characteristic of different virtues, from the point of view of a person with the virtues, and it should be clear that acting for reasons of these sorts does not necessarily involve acting with certain sorts of occurrent thoughts, or with special philosophical categorizations of one's action. And I think the examples also dispel the worry that individuating virtues in terms of their reasons necessarily involves an intellectualist or elitist conception of virtue.

It is important to understand what kind of reasons individuate virtues, on this view. Following Robert Audi (1997a, 77), I distinguish between the *reasons there are* to be generous (say), on the one hand, and the *reasons for which* one does in fact act, on the other. For instance, as Audi says, '[t]here can be reasons to keep one's promises, even if nobody wants to'. The 'reasons there are' are reasons to which everyone ought to be responsive, regardless of their other desires or aims. In this sense we say that there are reasons to be generous, even if nobody wants to be generous. 'Reasons for which' one acts, on the other hand, are those considerations for which an agent is in fact moved to act. Knowing the reasons for which someone acts makes his or action intelligible, as when we learn that Fred bought a ticket to China because he has always wanted to visit the Great Wall. The reason for which a person acts tells us, roughly, why the person sees fit to act as he does—it displays the action as an *action*, and not just a happening.[8]

The reasons for which Fred acts, then, make Fred's actions intelligible, and when those reasons coincide with the reasons there are for acting as Fred has acted, Fred's actions are not only intelligible but justifiable. This means that when one acts from a *bona fide* generous motive, the 'reasons for which' one acts coincide with the 'reasons there are' to act generously. On the view at hand, one's generosity is revealed by the sorts of considerations that one characteristically takes as reason-giving, that is, one's characteristic responsiveness to the reasons there are for being generous. Someone who helps

---

[7] See also Hursthouse 1999a, 128, and 2003, §3: 'it is part of our ordinary understanding of the virtue terms that each carries with it its own typical range of reasons for acting'. See also Tiberius 2006. I am skipping over the interesting disagreement between Hursthouse and Williams as to how to understand reasons of temperance and courage.

[8] A 'reason for which' is therefore different from a 'reason why', since the reason why someone did something may be that, e.g., he or she was on drugs. See Audi 1997a, 77.

a neighbor fix his car out of appreciation of the neighbor's need acts for a different reason than someone who helps out of appreciation of his own need of the neighbor's help on some other project. The difference provides a litmus test that we use all the time, since reasons of the first sort are revealing of the agent's generosity while the second are not.[9]

So understood, it is also clear that particular considerations in virtue of which we act generously admit of infinite diversity and variety. In this sense, there is no such thing as *the* reason for which generous persons act: a generous person will help this person because he is a neighbor, that person out of sympathy for her misfortune, and so on. As Williams puts the point, a person with a virtuous disposition 'will have a specific repertoire of considerations that operate for or against courses of action' (1995a, 18). Likewise, Christine Swanton also individuates the virtues in terms of their characteristic repertoires or 'profiles' of responsiveness to considerations regarding what she calls 'the demands of the world' (2003, 22).[10] Even so, these various 'reasons for which' can each be a case of responding to the 'reasons there are'. Consequently, to individuate virtues according to their 'characteristic reasons' must be to individuate them according to the *reasons there are* to be generous, say, or just.

Another reason to individuate the virtues by such characteristic reasons is that doing so can reveal how virtues such as generosity and magnificence are naturally related to each other. It may be the case that a person could develop a responsiveness to reasons of magnificence without developing a responsiveness to reasons of generosity, but again, we should not mistake this developmental order for a real independence between their respective characteristic reasons. Individuating the virtues by the reasons for which this or that virtuous agent acts invites just that sort of mistake. Furthermore, we also want a normative standard for the development of generosity: one need not be perfectly generous to be generous *tout court*, but we need to be able to say in what direction improved generosity would lie; and improved generosity is, on the present view, a matter of improving in responsiveness to the reasons there are for

---

[9] Notice that one can be responsive to a reason without necessarily acting on it, even when one acts virtuously; e.g. one's responsiveness to a reason can manifest itself as regret when one cannot act on it, as tempering what and how one acts instead, and so on (I return to this point in Ch. 11). It would be more correct, then, to speak of the reasons to which one is characteristically responsive rather than the reasons for which one characteristically acts; but so long as the point is understood, it will be harmless to talk in either way.

[10] Con. Aristotle, *Posterior Analytics* II.13, 97b15–25, who says that 'magnanimity' can be individuated by such responses as intolerance of insults and indifference to fortune, and that if these types of response have nothing in common, there will be two forms of magnanimity. It is unclear what Aristotle means by a 'form' of magnanimity, what commonality comes to in this context, and in particular why Aristotle thinks that (each form of) magnanimity must involve only one sort of responsiveness, rather than a repertoire or profile.

generosity. So I propose that a virtue, like generosity, is to be individuated by the reasons there are to act generously, and that having the virtue of generosity is (among other things) to be characteristically responsive to those 'reasons there are' by making them the 'reasons for which' one acts.

Notice too that this account of individuation also explains why it may seem *prima facie* plausible to individuate virtues in terms of their usual contexts of operation, since certain sorts of considerations and reasons do tend to be primary in different sorts of contexts.[11] It also explains why we so often observe that agents compartmentalize virtues between contexts, since it requires considerable experience, reflection, and maturity to realize that the same reasons apply in different sorts of contexts that one had not previously appreciated as connected. And it explains why a given virtuous person may not be equally virtuous in all respects; even though responsiveness to reasons of generosity, say, cannot be separated from responsiveness to reasons of justice, nonetheless it is a familiar feature of persons that they do tend to be more responsive to some sorts of reasons than to others.[12]

This way of individuating the virtues also seems to reflect the idea that the virtues are correctives (Hursthouse 1999b, 107, citing Foot 1978a, 8).[13] We need the virtue of generosity because there are reasons to be generous, and our natural instincts are not enough to make us responsive to those reasons in the ways we should be (see *NE* VI.13). We do not have these reasons because generosity is a virtue; generosity is a virtue because we have these reasons. It is quite fitting, then, that it should be the reasons that give the virtue its special, individuating identity.

If reasons individuate virtues, then there is an isomorphism between relations among virtues (in their internal structure or natural makeup) on the one hand and relations among the associated virtue reasons on the other. And this may

---

[11] Such a view seems similar, at least in this respect, to that developed by Plato (in the *Republic*) and the Stoics which individuates the virtues not by areas or circumstances, but by the distinctive ways in which the virtues each take up certain basic ethical considerations (which they hold to be salient to absolutely every action). See Cooper 1999, 100f, 109f. On such a view, multiple virtues will be concerned with a given action not merely because some actions fall within multiple areas—as when a single action falls within both promise-keeping (justice) and duties to parents (piety), to borrow Cooper's example—but because actions require the successful consideration of a wide range of reasons in order to be done completely well.

[12] Hursthouse 1999a, 130f attributes to Williams the thought that 'One way in which people just do vary is that they are more sensitive to the sorts of considerations cited in the [characteristic] reasons of one virtue than they are to those cited in another'.

[13] However, I do not think that this is *all* we should say the virtues are. As Irwin 1988a, 67 and n. 6 points out, construing virtues as remedies of specific tendencies to go wrong gives us no reason to expect that virtues will be reciprocal, or even that they will not come into conflict. I return to these issues in Ch. 11.

prove advantageous for purposes of enumeration, since individuating according to reasons shows connections otherwise easy to overlook. This is precisely what we see in the case of the tip-seeking waiter: the reason for which he acts with his patrons as he does, is that he is seeking large tips in each case. Since the reasons for which one acts can coincide with the reasons there are to act so, it also seems clear that seemingly different actions in different contexts can all be justifiable in terms of the same reasons there are for such actions. In other words, thinking of virtues in terms of responsiveness to characteristic reasons shows unity where other approaches merely see disparity.

In this respect, reasons are connective. In fact, it is this connectivity that motivates the idea that magnificence could be (in some sense) a special case of generosity, since it seems likely that, at some level, the reasons should turn out to be of the same basic sort, such as reasons to benefit others with one's resources. Connectivity is a complex attribute of the virtue reasons, operating at two main levels. First, the same virtue reason can obtain in situations of infinite diversity. This is apparent in the sorts of lists of virtue reasons that we looked at above: recall that for generosity, examples of generous considerations were as diverse as 'He needed help', 'He asked me for it', 'It was his 21st birthday', 'She'll be so pleased', and so on. To help one person fix his car because he needs help, and to give someone else a gift because it is his birthday, is to respond to quite different considerations in each case, but it makes sense to suppose that in each case, there is a reason to be generous, and it is ultimately to that reason that a generous person responds in these different situations (see also Hursthouse 1999a, 130f). The notion of responsiveness to the reasons there are is connective inasmuch as it can unify an infinite diversity of acts for virtue reasons.

Second, while responses to reasons of generosity can take infinitely many different shapes, and likewise for responses to reasons of magnificence, it also seems likely that reasons of magnificence could be a *species* of reasons of generosity. In other words, to respond to reasons of magnificence may in fact be to respond to reasons of generosity, much as Plato (by the time of the *Republic*) and the Stoics seem to have decided that to respond to reasons of piety is a particular way of responding to reasons of justice. The first type of connectivity, then, is the fact that very diverse 'reasons for which' can all coincide with the same 'reason there is', and the second type is that different 'reasons there are' can be related as genera and species. And of course it is with the latter notion that we come back to cardinal and subordinate virtues. So it seems that the reasons approach to individuation can give the virtues the kind of structure they need in order for us to avoid the enumeration problem.

Or rather, perhaps the reasons approach *could* give that kind of structure, *if* we knew what it meant for different reasons to be reasons 'of the same species', and what it meant for different species of reasons to be 'of the same genus'. As we have seen, a general problem for any approach to individuating virtues in terms of some X is that we must then individuate Xs, and that is as true of the reasons approach as any other. But we cannot keep putting the problem off. In the next section, then, I examine the crucial notions of reasons being 'the same' and 'of the same type'. It is beyond my scope to offer a full-blown account of these notions, but I do mean to argue that prospects for clarifying them are far from bleak.

6.2 'The Same Reasons'

6.2.1 'The Same Reasons' and Moral Theory

A theory of the virtue of generosity tells us what exactly the virtue of generosity consists in, and on the reasons view of individuation, this will include an account of the kind of reasons that are generous—that is, it will say what sorts of 'reasons there are' to be generous.[14] Since that can be said only from within a certain ethical outlook, such a theory will be substantively ethical rather than purely formal. I shall not try here to provide such a theory, which we can call a *special theory* of virtue reasons. Instead I take up the more general and *formal* question of what it means for virtue reasons to be 'of the same kind'. As we have seen, reasons have a content that makes clear the considerations in virtue of which an agent takes himself to have a reason to act, such as 'He needed help' and 'It's his 21st birthday' in our now-familiar examples. The trick for a *general theory* of virtue reasons is to show how reasons such as these, which have different contents, could nonetheless be reasons of the same kind, and how they could coincide with the same 'reasons there are' for generosity.

I said above that avoiding the enumeration problem requires virtue theory to lean rather heavily on the notion of kinds of reasons, but reliance on such a

---

[14] But it will not include only that: the view under consideration individuates the virtues by their reasons, but it need not say that the virtues just are forms of responsiveness to reasons. This is significant, as it seems that some actions—what Hursthouse 1991 calls 'arational actions'—could be intentional, but not done for a reason, and it is not unlikely that virtues may involve dispositions to perform certain sorts of arational actions. I do not think that this observation undermines the individuation of the virtues by their characteristic reasons, since such actions do seem more marginal as cases of virtuous action, and since we can explain their virtuousness in terms of the reasons there are to be disposed to them (see Swanton 2003, 132f).

notion at some point or other is hardly unique to virtue theory. For instance, it seems obviously true that people in different cultural and historical situations can and do act for the same reasons, even if they do so in response to very different sorts of considerations. We also recognize the possibility of acting for multiple reasons, and this cannot be simply a matter of responding to multiple considerations, since a single reason can be responsive to multiple considerations; rather, acting for multiple reasons is a matter of acting for reasons of different *kinds*. Likewise, one's reasons can be under-described and even misdescribed, as when we say that one person published diligently and another lied on his CV, both in order to secure a tenure-track job and therefore 'for the same reason'. We should say instead that the latter but not the former candidate's reason was perhaps to secure a tenure-track job at any cost, and therefore that the two did not act for the same kind of reason (see Schmidtz 2001, § V.d). But of course that description of their reasons takes for granted that there is such a thing as a 'kind' of reason.

Furthermore, so-called 'dialogic' theories of conflict-resolution also rely on the notion of the same kind of reasons (see Swanton 2003, ch. 12 for an excellent discussion). For instance, suppose that I have promised my children a trip to the park, only to have friends arrive from overseas on the promised day, wanting to visit the campus where I work (which has a unique outdoor sculpture collection). A dialogic approach to this conflict would involve looking for a course of action (if there be any) that would allow me to respect both the reasons there are to keep my promise and the reasons there are to be hospitable to my guests: for instance, perhaps the children could accompany us to the campus and play on the lawns there. Here my aim is to find a new course of action in which I can still act for the same kinds of reasons—such as keeping promises—even though this involves not doing what I had originally intended to do for those reasons.

Furthermore, a vigorous debate in recent years has concerned whether the rightness and wrongness of actions must be understood as involving any general principles. Generalists hold that judgments of right and wrong are possible only if those judgments are underwritten by some or other sizable set of general moral principles, and particularists deny this. This disagreement stems from a deeper disagreement: must the features of an action that bear on its rightness or wrongness bear in the same way on the rightness or wrongness of all actions in which they appear? Particularists, unlike generalists, hold both that a feature of one action may bear positively on its rightness even though the same feature need not bear positively on other actions—on the contrary, that feature may even bear negatively on other actions—and that this phenomenon is no barrier to our making competent moral judgments (see Dancy 2004, chs. 1, 5).[15] On such a view, then, the fact that I keep my promise to return your hammer when you ask for it may make my action right, even though such promise-keeping would not make my returning the hammer right if you ask for the hammer in an obvious fit of murderous rage. Where the features that bear on the rightness and wrongness of actions include the reasons for which one acts, then, generalists will affirm and particularists deny that how an agent's reason for acting bears on the rightness or wrongness of the act must be the same for every action done for the same reason. And since *ex hypothesi* such reasons must be the same despite differences in the particular considerations to which agents respond, a debate over their bearing on actions would be a debate over the bearing on actions of—again—reasons of the same kind. (I shall have more to say about this debate below.)

Perhaps the notion of kinds of reasons is nowhere more familiar than in Kantian ethics. A notorious problem surrounding Kant's notion of the 'maxim' of one's action is that the same action may described with one maxim that indicates the wrongness of the action, and with another that indicates its permissibility or perhaps even its rightness; which description of the maxim is to be the privileged one? Addressing themselves to this problem, Barbara Herman (1993, 75f, 143–5, 218–24) and Christine Korsgaard (1996b, 57f, 82) argue that a Kantian maxim must include not only a description of the action, but also the agent's actual reason for doing it (although sometimes the former makes the latter transparent). In that case, the Kantian individuates maxims by their reasons. However, not all maxims are individuated in terms of one-off reasons, but many involve the intention to act for the same reasons over time, what Kant scholars call *Lebensregeln* and what I have called characteristic reasons

---

[15] 'Bearing on' the rightness or wrongness of an action is left deliberately ambiguous here, since particularists deny both the strong claim that if a feature of an action makes it right (wrong), then all actions with that feature must also be right (wrong), and the weak claim that if a feature contributes positively (negatively) to an act, then it must do likewise in all actions in which it figures. See Dancy 2004, 79. Consequently, particularists reject an 'atomistic' theory of how features of action make actions right or wrong, in favor of a 'holistic' theory. As Dancy argues, 'A principle-based approach to ethics is inconsistent with ... holism' (77).

Virtue ethics, like many ethical theories, is party to this debate; see esp. Swanton 2003, 242–4, who argues that the virtuousness of one act may bear positively on it, while the similar virtuousness of another act may not bear positively on it, or may even bear negatively on it. Notice the difference between holism about how features of action bear on its *rightness*, and holism about how features of action bear on its *virtuousness*; e.g. Swanton embraces holism of the former sort (indeed, she seems to take a harder line here than Dancy 2004, 84 himself), but seems to reject holism of the latter sort, since she understands the virtuousness of action as dependent always on the same feature, viz. the act's hitting the 'targets' of the virtue in question. The difference is important, as I shall remain neutral on the former issue (as long as I can), leaving it to the special theory, but shall develop an account of virtue reasons that is incompatible with the latter sort of holism. However, I shall return to this issue below, which I shall suggest *seems* ultimately to rule out any such neutrality on the holism/atomism debate with respect to rightness, after all.

(see Allison 1990, 93); such an intention is, of course, an intention to act for the same kind of reasons over time. Furthermore, Herman (1993, 147ff) argues that the Categorical Imperative can rule out not only particular acts done for particular reasons, but also kinds of acts done for kinds of reasons.

And of course the notion of kinds of reasons has a long record in virtue ethics, since the virtue reasons themselves are *kinds* of reasons. Aristotle, on a very natural reading of *Nicomachean Ethics* II.4, holds that to have a virtue is (among other things) to have a firm and stable disposition to choose actions for virtuous (generous, say, or just) reasons—that is, to be stably disposed to act for a certain kind of reason as a matter of character. In fact, it is just this view of Aristotle's that has prompted the modern approach of individuating the virtues in terms of their respective virtue reasons. Furthermore, since Aristotle's view construes the possession of a virtue in terms of the stability of one's disposition to act for certain reasons, it is consistent with the clearly attractive idea that one who lacks the virtue may still act for the relevant virtue reasons, an idea that itself takes for granted that there are kinds of reasons.[16]

Clearly the notion of kinds of reasons has played a long and often pivotal role in the philosophy of action and in moral philosophy, and it is a notion we have little difficulty using. But for all that, it is far from obvious just what that notion is. We do tend to recognize reasons like 'He needed help' and 'It's his 21st birthday' as reasons of the same kind, but what makes them the same? What kind of 'kind' is a 'kind of reason'? And how would one know what other reasons are also reasons of that kind? Perhaps we could be contented to say that this notion is no more mysterious in virtue ethics than in any other theory in which it appears, but not only do *tu quoque* responses rarely satisfy, I have also indicated why virtue ethics is *especially* reliant on the notion of kinds of reasons, ultimately staking its viability as a moral theory on it, given the threat of the enumeration problem. That is why virtue ethics needs a general theory of the virtue reasons, and while I cannot fully construct such a theory here, I do wish to remark on some of its more important features, and in particular on the notion of 'the same reason'.

6.2.2 'The Same Reasons'

To individuate the virtues by their reasons, we must first individuate their reasons, but what is it to individuate reasons? Reasons have content, and it is the content of a reason that makes it the reason that it is. It seems clear, then, that content will be different for different virtue reasons. 'He needed help' can

---

[16] See also Hursthouse 1999a, 133ff (cf. 158), 146f, 152. I shall return to this idea below.

be a reason to be generous, but 'A promise is a promise' is a reason to be just, not generous; to suppose that one is being generous in keeping a promise is to understand neither generosity nor promise-keeping. To individuate virtues by their reasons, then, we must individuate reasons by their content.

Now, we have already seen that the reasons by which we are to individuate the virtues are the 'reasons there are' (to be generous, say), but sameness of content is a very difficult notion, and I think it may help to approach it in more concrete cases involving particular agents and the reasons for which they act. We could then extend our observations about sameness in such cases to the individuation of the virtues, since relations between 'reasons for which' can be mirrored by relations between 'reasons there are'.

Let's begin at the beginning, then. We often say that different persons, or the same person at different times, act 'for the same reason', and we say this even when they do rather different things. I think we are right to say this, but what could it mean? To know the reason for which someone has acted is to know the content of some sort of thought in virtue of which the agent saw fit to act. It is not easy to say exactly what sort of 'thought' that is. For instance, philosophers have often described it as the pairing of a belief that an action is of a particular sort and a 'pro-attitude' towards doing an action of that sort (see Davidson 1980, 5).[17] That thought has also been described as 'an intention with which the action was done' (Davidson 1980, 7), and it is an interesting question whether reasons are intentions. Interesting too is the question whether the content of that thought belongs to only one part of the pairing, or whether the content belongs to a single kind of thought that is no literal pairing at all, as when Aristotle says that 'decision' is a 'deliberational desire' (*NE* III.3, 1113a10).[18] Fortunately, we can side-step these difficult

---

[17] Of course, our attributions of reasons to an agent do not always refer to the pair, but those attributions can plausibly be taken as elliptical references to such a pair; see Davidson 1980, 6–8. It is also important to note that pro-attitudes are a group of attitudes of which desires are types, and indeed 'reasons for which' are sometimes described as pairs of beliefs and desires. But surely a pro-attitude need not involve the idea that one acts in order to attain something one desires; recall my comments on DesLauriers, above.

[18] As McDowell 1998, 113 puts the point, the major and minor premises of a practical syllogism

correspond to a single fact about the agent, which we can view indifferently as an orectic state or as a cognitive capacity. This explains how Aristotle can equate practical wisdom both with the perceptual capacity (*EN* 1142a23-30) and with a true conception of the end (*EN* 1142b33). It is not just that he credits each of these to the practically wise person, as if they might be independent attributes of him; he says of each that it is what practical wisdom is.

Con. Davidson 1984, 159, who says that in stating the reasons for which someone acts we 'exhibit the rationality of the action in the light of the *content of the belief* and the object of the' pro-attitude (italics added). In appreciating the significance of this difference I have benefited from discussion with Mark LeBar.

issues; whatever the psychology of such reasons, what matters for our purposes is that they have a content that fits the actions done for those reasons into a coherent pattern of behavior (Davidson 1984, 159; see also Hursthouse 1999a, 124, 129; Williams 1995a).[19] The sameness of reasons is the sameness of the content of reasons.

There are three main senses in which such contents can be the same. One of these we can call *simple* sameness: Fred and George both help the neighbor fix his car, say, and they do so for the very same reason. Here we can imagine each assenting to the same description of his reason: 'I saw him struggling out there; he needed my help', say. To say that the reasons for which they act have the same content is to say that they see fit to help the neighbor in virtue of the same considerations; the descriptions of those considerations have the same referents in each case. Of course, as we saw above, we as outside observers cannot decide for them what their reasons are, much less whether their reasons are the same. At a minimum, they would have to agree that their reasons were such-and-such, and that their reasons were the same. I shall ask below whether agreement as to the same description suffices for having the same content, but for now it is easy to imagine that their reasons do have the same content, and if they do, then those reasons are *simply* the same.[20]

Second, the idea that there are *characteristic* reasons—that to be generous, say, is (among other things) to act for certain sorts of reasons characteristically[21]—involves what we can call *specific* sameness. Let's suppose that Fred helped his neighbor fix his car yesterday, and helps his father plant his garden today, for the same reason each time, and for a generous reason in particular. Now, these reasons *could* be simply the same, if in each case Fred's reason was simply to help someone or other who was struggling with something or other. But the important point is that we need not suppose that Fred's reason is of that rather unusual sort just because we suppose he acts for the same reason in each case. So let us suppose that Fred's reason for helping his father is not simply the same as his reason for helping his neighbor; in that case, here we encounter the idea of a *kind* of reason.[22] Reasons are specifically the same when they are 'the same' in the sense of being reasons of the same kind.

---

[19] Audi 1997a, 104 makes the point by saying that we can model action done for reasons in terms of a practical syllogism, where the content of the reason is expressed in the major premise.

[20] It is important that sameness of reasons, in any sense, not require sameness of vocabulary, sophisticated concepts, etc. See Hursthouse 1999a, 126f; McDowell 1997, 142.

[21] See also Davidson 1980, 4 for the idea that the notion of 'attitude' includes 'permanent character traits that show themselves in a lifetime of behaviour', and thus what I shall call characteristic reasons.

[22] That specific sameness does not reduce to simple sameness follows also from the fact that, as Audi 1997a, 78f, 104 observes, people can act for the same reasons even if they act from different practical syllogisms, and indeed even if they act from no practical syllogism at all.

The third kind of sameness deals with kinds of a different kind. Let us now suppose that Fred helped his neighbor fix his car yesterday, and that today he makes an endowment of $100,000 to benefit the families of victims of a recent mining disaster. His endowment is not a case of plain generosity, but rather of what Aristotle calls magnificence, and yet it makes sense to suppose that, at *some* level, the reasons behind these two very different actions may not have been all *that* different. In such a case, we might say that the reasons for which Fred acted yesterday were reasons of generosity, that his reasons today are reasons of magnificence, and that magnificence is a special case or 'specialization' or 'exercise' of generosity, at a more generic level. It seems likely, then, that one kind of reasons can be a 'species' of some other kind of reasons, understood as a 'genus'. Such reasons I shall say are *generically* the same. It is generic sameness, of course, that seems most in need of clarification.

On the account of individuation that we are developing here, a virtue is (among other things) a characteristic responsiveness to certain sorts of reasons, on different occasions and in different circumstances, and so the notion of such a virtue rests on the idea of reasons having what I call specific sameness. Likewise, the idea that one virtue could be a special case of some other virtue—as magnificence may be a special case of generosity—and therefore the idea that some virtues are cardinal and others 'exercises', rest on the notion that different species of reasons can belong to the same genus. I have suggested that these two sorts of sameness are more or less commonsensical, but the present account of the virtues requires that we give these ideas a clearer meaning than common sense gives them. The way to understand these two sorts of sameness, I suggest, is to consider two ways in which an agent like Fred could understand his own reasons for his actions as converging when he reflects further on them.

Return to Fred's helping his neighbor with his car. Suppose that Fred's reason for helping is that he could see that his neighbor needed help, and suppose that he tells us so when we ask him his reason. (For purposes of our thought experiment, we should suppose throughout that Fred's answers are sincere, reflective, and true.) Now suppose that Fred reflects further, this time not on his act of helping, but on the reason for which he helped: why does he think that the neighbor's need *counts* as a reason for him to help? Before considering how Fred might answer this new question, notice how such answers will undergo a change in form. If Fred's next answer cites another reason (as opposed to a fit of akrasia, say), that reason will be more *general* than the one before: it may drop any special reference to *this* neighbor—for instance, he may now say 'I like to help neighbors when I can'—or his answer may drop special reference to this *neighbor* ('I like to help others when I can'), or to fixing the car ('I like to help my neighbor when he's struggling with something'), or even to helping ('I like to please my neighbor, when I can'), and so on. We can call this generalizing of reasons under repeated reflection the phenomenon of *conversational shift*.

Now suppose that Fred engages in similar reflections about his helping his father plant his garden, and that this conversation also shifts. It is not of course inevitable that the reasons that Fred reports here should generalize so as to converge with his answers about the neighbor, even though both actions were cases of helping; but suppose that, in this case, Fred was acting for the same reason each time, and thus that the two sets of answers converge in this way—for instance, 'I like to help others when I can'. Fred's more particular reasons for different actions therefore 'cluster' around a more general 'species' of reason. This is not to say, please note, that Fred took himself in both cases to be acting on some *general principle* or policy that he thought applied in each case; Fred may even find it surprising that his reasons should converge under conversational shift. Nor again is it to generalize the two series of answers until we arrive at a suitably general sentence that could apply in each case. The key is that Fred himself should see his reasons in the two cases as of a piece, even if that fact had not struck him prior to reflection. It is for a special theory of generosity to determine what would count as a generous reason, but conversational shift is a formal mechanism for revealing when the reasons for which one performs different actions may all be reasons of the same generous kind. Such convergence under conversational shift I shall call *clustering*.[23] Reasons that are specifically the same, then, are reasons that tend to cluster under conversational shift.

There is a second kind of convergence under conversational shift as well, which we can call *ascending*, and it takes two importantly different forms. One, suppose that Fred's reflections on helping his neighbor or his father reveal that his reasons in each case were generous. Now suppose that Fred reflects even further, asking now why he thinks that there are reasons for generosity in the first place. Suppose that Fred replies, 'I can hardly ask "why be generous"—we'd be in a rotten state if people didn't help each other!' Here Fred's answer generalizes to an answer that he may find appropriate even when asked about fair play or temperance: without taking those reasons as reasons, 'we'd be in a rotten state'. This conversation has shifted by ascending from

---

[23] Notice that I have imagined reasons clustering around just *one* kind of reason, but this is no more than a simplifying assumption. Likewise, we should not suppose that a virtue can be subordinate to only one cardinal virtue; here I agree with Oderberg 1999, 312.

reasons associated with *some* virtue to reasons associated with *virtue*, moving one level up, so to speak.[24]

And two, ascension can also occur from one particular set of virtue reasons to another set. Suppose that Fred now reflects on the endowment he made; why did he bother? He may say, 'Those poor people—someone had to do something'. He has given a reason, but again he can reflect on that reason as well, perhaps asking why he thought *he* had to do something. Suppose that as his reasons unfold, they cluster around magnificence (again, as determined by a special theory); perhaps he says, sincerely, 'In my sort of position, it is important to give something back to the community'. Now if he keeps on with his reflections, the generalization can again go to the next level up, but where is that? Well, suppose that it goes towards generosity: 'I like to help others when I can', say. Ascension of this type moves from reasons clustering around one particular virtue to reasons clustering around some other particular virtue. Generic sameness, then, obtains between two kinds of reasons when reflection on one kind ascends to reasons of the other kind.

Our discussion of the ways in which reflection on the reasons for which one acts may unfold has shown what the specific and generic sameness of such reasons amount to. But as we have seen, the virtues are to be individuated not in terms of the reasons for which this or that virtuous agent acts, but in terms of the *reasons there are* that differ from virtue to virtue. How do the phenomena of 'clustering' and 'ascending' shed light on the individuation of the virtues, and on the idea of cardinality?

6.3 Reasons, Individuation, and Cardinality

6.3.1 A Reasons-Based Approach to Cardinality

I argued in Chapter 4 that *virtue* is a special kind of vague concept that, like *person* and *rational*, must be understood via an idealized model; in the case of *virtue*, that model is 'the virtuous person'. What counts as a generous reason, therefore, requires a model of the generous person, which models an idealization of reasons of generosity as constructed by a special theory of generosity. We can therefore move easily from 'reasons for which' to 'reasons

---

[24] We should not suppose that levels go up forever, as Aristotle's discussion of a *final* end (*telos*) makes clear (*NE* 1). Also, the content of the reasons why certain traits count as reasons is a matter undertaken at another level of virtue ethics than the one we are discussing here—and an important matter it is, since differences in views about that content can lead, and historically have led, to incompatible lists of virtues; see MacIntyre 1981, 183ff. I discuss that level of virtue ethics—at which virtue ethics turns to ethical naturalism—in Ch. 3.

there are', since the reasons for which the modeled generous person acts just are the reasons there are to be generous. And as I have said in this chapter, it is the job of a special theory of generosity or justice (say) to specify the content of the reasons there are to be generous or just, a specification that is made from within a substantive and naturalistic ethical outlook. With such a specification, we can then understand the specific sameness of reasons of generosity or justice on the grounds that some of the reasons for which we imagine the virtuous person acting in particular circumstances tend to cluster (under conversational shift) around the reasons there are to be generous, and others around the reasons there are to be just. We can also individuate virtues like generosity and justice on the grounds that these two species of reasons converge (if at all) only by the mechanism of ascension to virtue-general reasons in the virtuous person. And we can understand the generic sameness of two sorts of reasons as the tendency for ascension in the virtuous person from one of these sorts to the other, as it seems likely would happen in the case of magnificence and generosity.

Consequently, such a model of the virtues would reveal not only that there are reasons to be generous and to be magnificent, but also that there are reasons to *connect* one's responsiveness to these two sorts of reasons. In fact, the model suggests that there are reasons to connect *all* the virtues, since ultimately they all ascend to a general conception of the place of the virtues in one's life—that is, because naturally they all *are* connected in this way. A further implication of this way of individuating the virtues is that a person will count as having a given virtue only if he characteristically acts for reasons that would, under reflection and conversational shift, tend to cluster around the reasons there are, and ascend towards other reasons, in a way sufficiently mirroring that modeled by the virtuous person.

This is not to say that one can act for magnificent reasons only if one thereby also acts from reasons that are (perfectly) generous as well; to what extent conversational shift must parallel that of the virtuous person is for a special theory to determine. But such a modeling of magnificence and generosity does allow us to make better sense of the idea that generosity is a cardinal virtue of which magnificence is an exercise. In the model of the magnificent person, reasons for which the magnificent person makes large-scale gifts cluster around general reasons of magnificence under conversational shift. Under further conversational shift, general reasons of magnificence ascend to general reasons of generosity.[25] And under yet further conversational shift, general reasons of

---

[25] We could then, perhaps, understand this claim as what Aristotle intends in saying that all the magnificent are generous (*NE* IV.2, 1122a28–9), i.e. as a claim about the structure of the reasons there

generosity ascend to general reasons of no particular virtue, but of virtue as a whole.

In general, then, to say that X is a *cardinal* virtue and Y is an exercise of X is to say that the model of the Y person exhibits ascension under conversational shift from the reasons characteristic of Y to the reasons characteristic of X, *and* the model of the X person exhibits ascension from reasons characteristic of X to reasons rationalizing all of the virtues simply *qua* virtues. However, since in theory cardinality chains can be more than two links long, we can also introduce the notion of *relative* cardinality: virtue X is cardinal relative to virtue Y just in case the model of the Y person models conversational shift as ascending from Y-reasons to X-reasons. Likewise, to be an 'exercise' of another virtue is to be the value of such a Y.[26] Therefore, the notions of characteristic reasons and of cardinality can be given a straightforward meaning, and this is exactly the result we wanted.

However, that result does come at a price. I do not think that it comes at too high a price, but before concluding our discussion of individuation and cardinality we should pay close attention to a couple of serious complications for the approach I have sketched here.

6.3.2 Holism About Reasons

On the approach I have sketched, a complete understanding of a virtue requires modeling the content of its characteristic reasons, which in turn must be understood in terms of the connections between those reasons and other sorts of reasons, connections understood as those between cardinal and subordinate virtues. Consequently, that account assumes that the content of virtue reasons is 'holistic', and as such, it has both the merits and the demerits of holism about the content of beliefs. Those demerits form our first complication, so we should take a closer look at content holism.

We should begin by noting what it is about content holism, at least in a moderate form, that makes it so attractive. Suppose that Fred sincerely assents to the sentence, 'Salmon are fish', and that George sincerely assents to the same sentence. Do Fred and George have the same belief that salmon are fish? That is not obvious. Suppose that each is prepared to agree that guppies are fish, that trout are fish, and that swordfish are fish, but George, unlike Fred, is

---

are for magnificence and for generosity. In any event, questions of exegesis aside, that does seem to be the best way to make such a claim come out true.

[26] Note that all cardinality relations will be transitive, non-reflexive, and asymmetric. Since they are transitive, it seems worthwhile to distinguish between the cardinality that holds between X and Y (a) when no other virtue intervenes, and (b) when X is cardinal relative to Z and Z is cardinal relative to Y; but I shall neglect this for now.

also prepared to agree that whales are fish. Fred and George are not on exactly the same page about fish, then; does this mean that they are not on exactly the same page about salmon, either? That is difficult to say; but suppose we find further that George, unlike Fred, is prepared to agree also that sea-sponges are fish, that jellyfish are fish, that silverfish are fish, that microfiche are fish.... As we get towards *this* end of the series of things George is prepared to say are fish, we lose all confidence in these fish-related beliefs of George's (indeed, we find it difficult to say that they are beliefs about fish!), and every step towards this end of the series raises questions about the content of George's belief at the previous step. And as we lose confidence in all of his fish-related beliefs, we also lose confidence in our initial impression that he and Fred had the same belief about salmon. In that case, whether or not Fred and George have the same belief about salmon depends not only on their readiness to agree with the same sentence, but also on a host of other intentional attitudes touching on the belief in question.[27] It seems clear, then, that agreement to the same statement does not suffice for sameness of belief. It therefore seems a benefit of content holism that it holds that the content of any belief depends on the content of many other beliefs, and cannot be determined one belief at a time; beliefs come in rather large groups. By contrast, atomism about content is the view that the content of a belief depends on one's other beliefs in only an attenuated way, if at all.[28]

As I have suggested, our account of individuating the virtues requires a similar sort of holism about the content of reasons. Return to our first case, in which Fred and George both help the neighbor fix his car. Suppose now that as we question Fred and George about the reasons of each, their answers tend

[27] See Schwitzgebel 2006, §3.2, whose example I have adapted here. See also Davidson 1984, 168. Despite the unfortunate terminological overlap, it is important not to confuse holism and atomism about the content of intentional attitudes, with holism and atomism about how features of action bear on rightness and wrongness, a distinction noted above.

[28] e.g. atomists agree that sameness of content involves agreement on definitions; this is significant, since it reveals that although we call physics a natural science whereas Locke does not, this does not in fact entail a difference in beliefs, since Locke is not using the term 'science' in our sense. See Soles 2004. On holism, see esp. Quine 1951, esp. 38ff, and Davidson 1984, esp. chs. 9–11. Davidson 1999, 330 puts the view very succinctly: 'We could not figure out beliefs one by one: each depends on many others to fix its content. We could not figure out a single belief unless we had some idea what motivates an agent. We could not start to guess what someone meant by his utterances unless we had a pretty good idea what he believed and wanted. And so forth.' Holism has a number of substantial implications, one of which is that, as Cavell 1999, 407 notes, rationality 'is not an optional feature of the mind but among the very conditions of its existence', since holism holds that 'the content of a mental state like a belief or a desire is constrained by its normative relations with other mental states in a holistic mental network'. Other implications are the meaninglessness of the analytic/synthetic distinction (Quine 1951), and of the distinction between conceptual scheme and empirical content (Davidson 1984, ch. 13). For a critique of holism, see esp. Fodor and Lepore 1992.

to converge, each prepared to say, for instance, 'It would have been pretty mean of me not to help'. What happens if we continue to ask why? Suppose that Fred's answers unfold as they did above, but when we ask George about why it matters to him that not helping would have been mean, he says, 'I don't want people to think I'm mean', or perhaps, 'My own car has been sounding dodgy lately, so I can't afford to be mean about helping with cars these days'. Here we find out more about George's other reasons, and it becomes clear that under conversational shift his reasons diverge from Fred's. In that case, it seems that Fred and George sincerely assent to the same sentence at one level of questioning, but further questioning seems to reveal, eventually, that that sentence does not mean the same thing in each of their mouths, as Donald Davidson would say.

The content of a reason, then, depends partially, but crucially, on the content of other reasons and attitudes. And of course the content of reasons is what conversational shift increasingly reveals: by showing how reasons at one level generalize to another level, conversational shift serves to illuminate what the reasons actually were that we were inspecting prior to the shift. Conversational shift therefore looks always in two directions: upwards towards more generalized reasons, and back downwards with a richer perspective on the content of the reasons from which the conversation has moved on. Interestingly, given holism about reasons it turns out that simple sameness of reasons is no more 'basic' than either specific or generic sameness of reasons: reasons match each other, to whatever extent they do, only taken as *bodies* of reasons. Conversational shift about reasons and holism about their content together make sense of the idea of kinds of reasons. So far, so good.

However, holism about belief content has a downside, one that troubles holism about reasons as well. I said above that holism about belief makes the content of any of one's beliefs dependent on rather many of one's other beliefs—but how many other beliefs is that? It seems plausible that beliefs depend on *some* other beliefs for their content, but extremely implausible that beliefs depend on *all* other beliefs, which would mean that we could not share *any* belief at all unless we shared *all* of our beliefs. But it is not clear where to cut off those other beliefs that are relevant to the belief in question from all the others. If there were analytic truths, then we could identify the 'relevant' beliefs as those beliefs Q such that one believes that P only if one also believes that Q, on the grounds that 'if P, then Q' is analytic. But holism traditionally has figured importantly in the case *against* the analytic/synthetic distinction;[29] and failing some such distinction, it is difficult to see how one could stop the slide from 'many other beliefs' to 'all other beliefs' (see Fodor and Lepore 1992, ch. 1; Schwitzgebel 2006, § 3.2).[30]

An analogous problem arises for holism about the content of reasons. It is, I take it, beyond question that one need not have a full-blown virtue, such as generosity, in order to do an act that is generous, and to act for reasons that are generous. However, holism about reasons leaves it unclear how much leeway a generous reason can tolerate where one's other beliefs and attitudes are concerned, and some philosophers may well object that holism does not allow nearly enough leeway. For instance, Rosalind Hursthouse goes so far as to say that people who are downright vicious or wicked can, on occasion, act for virtuous reasons. For instance, one may have recently fallen in love, or fallen prey to inverse akrasia, and thus become temporarily aware of the sorts of considerations that the virtuous characteristically find to be reasons to act, and act on those considerations (1999a, chs. 6–7 *passim*). But if the content of reasons is holistic, then the content of the reasons for which one acts will consist in its relation to a wide variety of other beliefs and attitudes; but in these beliefs and attitudes—evaluative and otherwise—the virtuous and the vicious can differ quite widely (1999a, 188–91).

Among such beliefs are beliefs about general patterns concerning virtue and well-being: 'Nice guys finish last' is not an evaluative belief, but it is a belief that involves a broader ethical outlook, one that, I take it, generous persons will not share. Suppose that George believes that nice guys finish last, but Fred does not. When George helps the neighbor fix the car, thinking it a nice thing to do, can his reason have the same content as Fred's reason? Can his reason have the content of a generous reason? It is extremely unlikely that

---

[29] e.g. Quine 1951, 40 wrote that if something like holism is true, then

> it becomes folly to seek a boundary between synthetic statements, which hold contingently on experience, and analytic statements which hold come what may. Any statement can be held true come what may, if we make drastic enough adjustments elsewhere in the system.... Conversely, by the same token, no statement is immune to revision. Revision even of the logical law of the excluded middle has been proposed as a means of simplifying quantum mechanics; and what difference is there in principle between such a shift and the shift whereby Kepler superseded Ptolemy, or Einstein Newton, or Darwin Aristotle?

[30] Davidson 1999, 307 says that on his view the content of one attitude is not as tightly tied to one's other attitudes as some of his critics, such as Fodor and, perhaps, Evnine 1999, have supposed. Rather, his holism is 'mainly a constraint. Sentences have logical relations with other sentences, and interpretation must, as far as possible, preserve these relations.' Whether this does in fact avoid the problem raised I leave as an exercise for the reader.

very many of an agent's attitudes undergo significant change or suspension, even temporarily, all at once; so on the view I have sketched, how could the virtuous and vicious come to act for the same virtuous reasons?[31]

It seems clear, then, that my holistic account of reasons does not allow nearly as much leeway as Hursthouse wants. Now perhaps about such matters there can be reasonable disagreement. But as our discussion of holism about belief should make clear, in the worst case scenario holism about reasons may entail that the model of the virtuous person is the only one who could ever act for a virtuous reason at all: can one be responsive to the reasons there are to be generous without being responsive to all the reasons there are? What is more, the content of one's reasons depends not only on one's other reasons, but also on certain of one's beliefs (for instance, about whether nice guys finish last). Put another way, this problem about holism raises yet more complexity for the notion of being virtuous enough to be virtuous *tout court* (Chapter 4). Holism about reasons, then, inherits *exactly* the same problems that plague holism about belief. I do not wish to suggest that either form of holism is therefore doomed, and it is of course far beyond my purview to consider solutions to this problem; but I do want to point the problem out as something requiring serious thought from virtue theorists.[32]

6.3.3 Holism About Rightness

Finally, the second complication for my sketch of a general theory has to do with its implications regarding particularism at the level of the special theory. Recall from §2.1 that generalism is the view that the same feature of an action determines or at least contributes to the rightness or wrongness of all acts that share that feature, in the same way, whereas particularism is the denial of that view. In my sketch of the general theory, I have tried to remain neutral regarding this debate.[33] However, it now seems apparent that if holism about the content of reasons is correct, *and* if a person's reasons for acting are among the features bearing on the rightness or wrongness of the act—as virtue ethics holds they are—then in some cases it will be most unclear, and perhaps beyond

---

[31] In thinking about this issue I have benefited from discussion with Luke Russell. See also Arpaly (2003, 8–10), who discusses the possibility that someone like George could act for generous reasons against his better judgment, so to speak, that nice guys finish last.

[32] See also Arpaly 2003.

[33] Notice that on a holistic view of the content of a reason, there need be no particular list of beliefs that one must have in order to have a reason with that content, since that content can be identified in terms of the logical, epistemic, and practical space that it occupies. (Cp. Davidson 1984, 157; 1991, 153.) We need not, then, suppose that a special theory of such content must give it the form of some general moral principle.

settling, whether the reasons for which an act is done constitute 'the same feature' in different actions.

This is an important point, since both sides in this debate take for granted the idea of different actions having 'the same feature'. For instance, Christine Swanton considers a case in which a person acts kindly to a stranger, but goes so far as to indulge the stranger needlessly at the expense of his own legitimate interests, and she concludes that the agent's kindness here detracts from the 'overall virtuousness', and thus the rightness, of the act (2003, 243f). If content holism is correct in its depiction of the content of the agent's reason for acting, then it would seem that that content depends importantly on the agent's other beliefs, attitudes, and reasons, including those about indulging others and sacrificing his own legitimate interests. Is the 'kindness' of the agent's reasons a feature of this action that would *also* be shared by the act of another agent who is *not* prepared to indulge others at the expense of his own legitimate interests? The answer to that sort of question is far from clear. It seems to me, therefore, that a debate between generalists and particularists about the relation between the reasons for which agents act and the rightness (wrongness) of their actions would be moot, pending either a more fine-grained special theory of kindness and the content of kind reasons, or an alternative to the picture of 'same kind of reason' that emerges in the general theory given content holism.[34] I am pessimistic about the latter, so I think a special theory of kindness must say rather a *lot* about the content of reasons characteristic of kindness.

What is more, it is not clear that the general theory I have sketched allows neutrality about this debate, after all. Let me say why. Jonathan Dancy considers a view of moral properties that is common in virtue ethics: at one level, certain non-ethical facts about an action (e.g. that Fred helped his neighbor fix the car for such-and-such reasons) are correlated with certain characterizations of the action involving thick ethical concepts (that Fred's act was generous), and these in turn are correlated with certain thin ethical concepts (that Fred's act was right). This picture, Dancy says, is compatible with holism about rightness, as long as it is not the case that *both* of these correlations are invariant. Now as we have seen, Swanton (2003, 242–4) rejects invariance between ethically thick and thin concepts, but content holism clearly makes her counterexamples to such invariance significantly less compelling. Dancy, on the other hand, denies invariant correlation between non-ethical facts and thick ethical concepts, holding instead that, for instance, arriving after the arranged time is not always

---

[34] Raz 2000, 228–9n raises some different worries about particularism's reliance on an undeveloped view of 'the same reasons'; see Dancy 2004, 97–9 for discussion.

a case of tardiness. But I think this is an artifact of his example. As he says, there is no invariant correlation between arriving after the arranged time and being tardy (2004, 84), but I think the correlation must be *much* tighter than this between acting for a reason with a certain content and acting generously (and likewise for the relation between hitting the target of generosity and acting generously). So *if* facts about the content of the reasons for which one acts are invariantly correlated with thick ethical concepts like 'generous' (*pace* Dancy), and *if* the generosity of an action always at least speaks in its favor with respect to thin ethical concepts like 'right' (*pace* Swanton), as content holism would seem to suggest, then virtue ethics is incompatible with holism about rightness.

I do not know how to resolve these complications—how to solve the problems raised by holism about the content of reasons, or how to settle the question of the consistency of virtue ethics with holism about rightness—and I raise them only to alert the reader to them. Even so, I think the most reasonable thing is to remain hopeful of accounting for the sameness of reasons in some way that both makes sense of cardinality and is plausible in its own right. What I take to be beyond question, in any event, is that virtue ethics cannot survive without a working account of the content of the reasons that individuate the virtues, in a way that preserves the crucial connectivity of the virtues. I have suggested one such account, and despite the problems and complications surrounding it, hopefully the prospects are not too bleak—at any rate, no bleaker than the dominant movements in philosophy of language, semantics, philosophy of social science, artificial intelligence, and cognitive psychology that rely on the idea that some form of holism about content is workable (see Fodor and Lepore 1992, 7).

6.4 Implications for Hard Virtue Ethics

I argued in the previous chapter that virtue ethics cannot survive as an alternative ethical theory unless it can avoid the enumeration problem, and I have argued in this chapter that it cannot avoid the enumeration problem without cardinality. The cardinality of the virtues yields a rich and complex model of the virtues and the relations between them, and it is worth taking stock: what implications does that model of the virtues have for virtue ethics, in terms of phronesis and the unity of the virtues?

The thesis that the virtues have a cardinal structure is the thesis that the virtues are all intimately related to each other, in two important ways. One, the virtue reasons of a cardinal virtue and the virtue reasons of its subordinate virtues are related as genus to species, as (we have supposed) reasons of magnificence are generically the same as reasons of generosity. And two, each virtue involves responsiveness to reasons that rationalize every virtue, just as such, as part of a whole life of a creature that acts for reasons. As these two forms of connectivity hold, first, between subordinate virtues as species and cardinal virtues as genera, and second between genera themselves, we can call them generic connectivity and cross-generic connectivity, respectively. Each form of connectivity has significant implications for the role of phronesis in our model of the virtues.

First, consider the implications of generic connectivity. The virtues are individuated in terms of their characteristic reasons, and therefore to have a virtue is to be properly responsive to those reasons. However, proper responsiveness involves *successful* practical reasoning about how those reasons come into play, and what they demand, in diverse sorts of situations. And that means that having a virtue involves having phronesis. As Bernard Williams puts the point, without phronesis 'one could not reliably see what [virtue] reasons could lead to, or what more specific considerations might fall into the class of [virtue] reasons' (1995a, 18). It takes phronesis, that is, to grasp connectivity between considerations as belonging to virtue reasons of a certain species, as happens in specificatory deliberation, and the same holds true at the level of a genus of virtue reasons: it takes phronesis to grasp that a commitment to be responsive to one species of reasons is also a commitment to another species of reasons. Simply put, then, where there is connectivity there must be phronesis. Therefore, a cardinal virtue, and each exercise of that cardinal virtue, requires phronesis. Since cardinality is indispensable for virtue ethics, so too is phronesis.

Moreover, it is clear that phronesis and the virtues are global across contexts in which considerations bearing on their characteristic reasons arise. Again, this is not the obviously false claim that anyone who has a virtue will display that virtue across all relevant contexts, but a claim about the nature of virtue (as modeled in 'the virtuous person'). Because it is the nature of a virtue to be responsive to reasons of certain general *kind*, a cardinal modeling of the virtues entails that the virtues are not by their nature contextually bound but rather global across contexts. Compartmentalization of one's responsiveness to virtue reasons is an all too common and very real phenomenon in imperfect and developing creatures like us, but it is not a feature of the natural makeup of the virtues themselves. The phronesis that any virtue involves, then, must be the same as that involved in every other virtue.

And second, similar conclusions follow from the fact that the cardinally-structured nexus of virtues displays cross-generic connectivity. Holism about the content of reasons implies that the content of any chain of virtue reasons, such as that comprised of generosity and magnificence, must be understood in light of (at least some of) the other chains. For instance, it seems clear that the content of the reasons of generosity depends in part on one's beliefs and other attitudes about justice, say: as I said above, someone who thinks that it is a matter of generosity rather than justice to keep a promise, for instance, may well understand neither of these virtues. Likewise, we may change our minds about a person who seems to be responsive to reasons of justice if we learn that this person is unresponsive to reasons of mercy or compassion: such a person, I think, should not be described as 'just but unmerciful' (as we often do, incautiously), because there is no *virtue* of justice where there is not also mercy. It seems clear, then, that there must be connectivity not only within but also *between* chains of virtue reasons. In that case, if any cardinal virtue involves phronesis, then they all do; and more than that, they must all involve the same phronesis, that is, phronesis must be global across the various virtues.

We can see the same point in another way as well. We have seen that conversational shift at the level of a cardinal virtue takes one to considerations of human nature and well-being that make sense of the idea that the virtue in question is a virtue in fact. But of course an appropriate grasp of those sorts of considerations is just what phronesis is. This is not the absurd idea, often attributed to Aristotle, that phronesis in responding to reasons for generosity would have Fred realizing something like 'So *that's* how helping my neighbor fix his car fits into my life as a whole!'[35] It is instead the idea that phronesis is a grasp of the reasons there are for the virtues, and therefore how the virtues do fit into one's life as a whole—how ends of acting for those reasons are themselves specifications of the end of living well as a reasons-responsive creature—a grasp that makes possible one's integration of the virtues, and therefore the possibility of reliably and flexibly acting rightly, that is, acting in a way that is virtuous overall.

Furthermore, holism about the content of reasons suggests that an agent's apparent grasp of considerations indicating that generosity and justice are virtues can come into question if that agent denies that traits like mercy or courage are also virtues: does a person really grasp what makes a trait a virtue in humans if he thinks that mercy and courage are not virtues? Therefore, again, the virtues all involve phronesis, and phronesis operates across all the virtues.

---

[35] This recalls our discussion of the 'blueprint view' controversy in Ch. 1.

And this is, I think, no more than what we should expect, given the link between right action and the virtues. As we saw in the previous chapter, a necessary feature of virtue ethics is that a pattern be established between right action and the virtues, in the plural, and this pattern is possible only if the virtues tend to work together (see also Hursthouse 1999a, 154). Our model of the cardinality of the virtues has served to make some sense of what such 'working together' amounts to.[36]

These considerations also make it clear that our model of cardinality entails some form of the so-called 'unity of virtue' thesis. In particular, on this model the unity of virtue is identical to the union of the generic and the cross-generic connectivity of the virtues. That is, the connections that hold in a cardinally structured nexus of virtues just do constitute the unity that holds among the virtues. It is in the natural makeup of each virtue to function properly only in concert with all the other virtues. This is a stronger version of the unity of virtue thesis than most virtue ethicists (not to mention virtue theorists) presently accept. It is, I think, about as strong as Aristotle's own version of that thesis, which holds that 'if phronesis, which is one, is present, the virtues will all be present along with it' (NE VI.13, 1145a1–2). But it is not nearly as strong as the thesis that is often attributed—mistakenly, I think—to Aristotle, namely that if a given person has any virtue, then that person must have all the virtues. That misattribution arises from a failure to distinguish between the natural makeup of the virtues, on the one hand, and phenomena surrounding the development of the virtues in particular virtuous persons, on the other. On my view, the unity of virtue is a thesis about the nature of the virtues as modeled in more or less the way I have sketched here: it is the nature of the virtues to be global across contexts, and to involve phronesis that is global across the virtues. It is clear already that a strong version of the unity of virtue is a standard feature of Hard Virtue Ethics. If I am right about the seriousness of the enumeration problem and what it takes to avoid it, then virtue ethics requires a model of the virtues that only Hard Virtue Ethics can offer. And in that case Hard Virtue Ethics, including its commitment to the unity of virtue, is here to stay, if virtue ethics in any form at all is to be here to stay.

Of course, that conclusion raises nearly as many questions as it answers. To what version of the unity of virtue, more precisely, does the cardinality of the virtues commit us? Is it a version we can live with, or does it require phronesis and the virtues to be global to an unrealistic degree? Why should we model

---

[36] Not surprisingly, since, as Irwin 2005 points out, a major impetus for Aquinas to introduce cardinality into the Aristotelian virtues was to show that the latter do not conflict and work independently, but rather work together.

the virtues as naturally exhibiting a level of unity that actual virtuous persons never exhibit? Furthermore, virtue ethics is committed to treating virtues as deep features of the self and not just as attributes, but on the cardinal model that depth is the depth of virtue reasons; is it plausible to suppose that the self is that much of an 'open book'? Can we have much psychological depth where our virtues, and therefore our virtue reasons, are concerned? How deep does character go? How far can 'conversational shift' go? And then there is the situationist challenge, which (some would tell us) suggests that if there are any character traits at all, they are not global but only highly compartmental and contextually bound. In that case, is a global model of the virtues and phronesis only a model of traits that creatures of our kind simply cannot possess? Has the cardinal model merely changed the subject?

I take up these questions in Parts III and IV. But first, I want to conclude this part by considering one question that my discussion of cardinality does seem to answer, namely how to understand the relation between the Aristotelian virtues of generosity and magnificence.

7

Magnificence, Generosity, and Subordination

Aristotle's discussion of 'magnificence'—the virtue concerned with grand expenditure—challenges our ideas about what can be a virtue, and why, in precisely the way that virtues like justice or courage do not. Aristotle must persuade us of his particular view of what sort of virtue courage is, but he does not need to persuade us that courage *is* a virtue. But Aristotle is aware of just this further burden in the case of magnificence, and he argues that magnificence is indeed a virtue in its own right, and in particular that it is not the same as generosity, which is a rather more familiar or 'standard' virtue (see *NE* IV.1). For whereas generosity concerns a wide range of uses of wealth, Aristotle says, magnificence concerns only 'expenditure', and also exceeds generosity in scale of expenditure (*NE* IV.2, 1122a20–2; *EE* III.6, 1233a31–8). And so Aristotle characterizes magnificent action as 'expenditure that is suitable in scale' (1122a23; see also II.7, 1107b17–21).

Not surprisingly, Aristotle's introduction of magnificence into his 'menu' of virtues has proven controversial. Many have worried that since otherwise virtuous persons often will lack the wealth required for magnificence, treating magnificence as a virtue seems in tension with Aristotle's view that 'if phronesis, which is one, is present, the virtues will all be present along with it' (*NE* VI.13, 1145a1–2; see Irwin 1988a; Irwin 1988b; Kraut 1988; Gardiner 2001; Pakaluk 2002; Aquinas, *Summa Theologiae* [= *ST*] 2–2 q134 a1 obj1, a3 obj4). Some also have worried that there seems to be little of ethical or moral significance about magnificence in the first place, which seems more like an aesthetic sensibility—a sort of 'good taste'—than a proper virtue of character (Annas 1996). Although I shall have something to say about the latter issue in the course of my discussion, neither of them is my main concern at present. Instead, I want to focus on what is so immediately startling about magnificence: its very arrival as an 'upstart' virtue, whose inclusion on a list of virtues is so novel. Aristotle's introduction of magnificence compels us to ask when a desirable trait should count as one of the virtues of character, or when we have good reason to add one more item to our menu of virtues, so to speak. The metaphor of the menu is an interesting one—we imagine such a menu growing ever longer as more and more new items are added. How long is this to go on? What constraints are there on the menu's expansion?

As we saw in Chapter 5, if right action and virtuous persons are to be understood in terms of overall virtuousness—in terms of the virtues in the plural—then the expansion cannot go on forever. More precisely, an account of the virtues must have a finite number of 'cardinal' or 'primitive' virtues. A cardinal or primitive virtue is a virtue whose exercise is a different thing from the exercise of any other virtue. Cardinal virtues contrast with 'subordinate' virtues, whose exercise is a specific kind of exercise of a cardinal virtue. For instance, Plato and the Stoics both held the view that piety is a species of justice, that is, that justice is a cardinal and piety a subordinate virtue. Since the proliferation of subordinate virtues can be treated as enriching our understanding of the items on a 'menu' of virtues, rather than merely making the menu longer, it is the proliferation of primitive or cardinal virtues that most requires our attention. Furthermore, I argued in Chapter 5 that checking such proliferation does not require anything as ambitious as a short list of cardinal virtues, since the cardinal structure of the virtues itself gives us an alternative to thinking of every 'new' virtue as yet another primitive virtue. So if we can make sense of that structure, we should have all the response to the enumeration problem we need.

Unfortunately, unlike Plato or the Stoics, Aristotle seems not to have employed any notion of cardinal and subordinate virtues; instead, he seems to treat all the virtues as on a par with each other as primitive virtues. Aristotle's introduction of the 'upstart' virtue of magnificence, therefore, is clearly relevant to the enumeration problem: what principle if any could be given for recognizing magnificence as a primitive virtue, without *also* paving the way for *infinitely* many other primitive virtues?

An interesting question, then, is whether the notion of cardinality could allow us to agree with Aristotle that magnificence is a virtue, and not identical to any other virtue, *without* therefore having to treat magnificence as a primitive or cardinal virtue. Although Aristotle denies that magnificence is the same thing as generosity, he does say that the magnificent are also generous (*NE* IV.2, 1122a28–9), so the obvious place to begin is with the thought that magnificence could be subordinate to generosity. In the previous chapter, I argued that virtues are to be individuated in terms of their respective forms of responsiveness to reasons; I argued that if one virtue is subordinate to another, then they are responsive to reasons of the same kind; and I tried to attach some meaning to the notion of reasons being 'of the same kind'. What remains, then, is to show three things about magnificence and generosity. One, I argue that magnificence does indeed seem to be a virtue, as Aristotle maintains it is. Two, I argue that reasons of magnificence are of the same kind as reasons of generosity, and thus that magnificence is subordinate to generosity. And three, I offer one way of understanding the subordination relation here, suggesting that magnificence is a 'specialization' of generosity. In particular, I argue that while magnificence and generosity give one the same ends, at a general level—to benefit others with one's resources, say—nonetheless it takes both specialized skill and cleverness to attain those ends in the case of magnificence, as well as—and more importantly—a more specialized form of phronesis to specify the *content* of those ends. This is because specifying the crucial notion of 'benefiting with resources' requires rather specialized deliberative skills, when one is seeking the public benefit through large-scale expenditures.

I begin in §7.1 with an overview of Aristotle's discussion of magnificence, with an eye particularly to his view that magnificence is indeed a virtue, and specifically as not to be identified as a kind of generosity—that is, that it is a virtue alongside generosity and the other virtues. I then make a preliminary outline in §7.2 of an alternative view of magnificence that concedes Aristotle's view that magnificence is a virtue, and not the same as generosity, but nonetheless holds that magnificence is subordinate to, and in particular a specialization of, generosity. I then develop this view further in §7.3 by considering and rejecting a number of seemingly compelling alternatives to the subordination view.

If this view of the relation between magnificence and generosity is plausible, then we shall have found at least one way to regulate the multiplication of the virtues, by identifying at least one way in which the exercise of one virtue can be an exercise of another virtue. In that case, sometimes the emergence of an 'upstart' virtue is the emergence not of yet a further virtue, but of a deeper understanding of the potential for diversification of those virtues we already know there to be. Such a finding could be a first step towards a more thorough conception of the virtues that preserves their plurality without merely letting them proliferate unchecked. It would also suggest that while virtues (like skills) are contextually-bound in their development, nonetheless the emergence of virtue in a new area of one's life need not be the emergence of a new and distinct virtue, but may be the result of the development—understood as the specialization—of a virtue that one already has in other parts of one's life.

7.1 Magnificence as a Virtue

One worry about magnificence that we have not yet canvassed is that it seems too culturally specific to count as a *human virtue*, on the grounds that it is too tightly bound up with certain institutions and customs peculiar to Aristotle's Athens.[1] The latter claim is not entirely true, since the importance of large-scale, publicly visible expenditure is hardly peculiar to ancient Athens, and will be familiar in any society with concentrations of great wealth, including those in which most of my readers will spend their lives. Nonetheless, the rather special role of such expenditure in ancient Athens does seem to explain Aristotle's particular interest in outlining a virtue specially concerned with it.[2] The expenditures Aristotle has in mind take place primarily (although not exclusively) within the Athenian institution of *leitourgia*, which legally required the wealthiest citizens to provide public goods such as dramas for public festivals or the outfitting of a trireme, in lieu of other forms of taxation.[3] *Leitourgia* thus sustained and increased a city's publicly held assets, but just as important, *leitourgia* helped to create a city's characteristic beauty and grandeur. In this respect, Aristotle compares grand expenditure to the ancient practice of depositing extravagant gifts as votive offerings (*NE* IV.2, 1122b19–21, 1123a4–5).

Two parallels between *leitourgia* and votive offerings are especially worth noting. One is that each beautified the city by establishing signs of the city's wealth, and especially the wealth and generosity of its foremost citizens. This point is easily lost on us, for whom votives are mainly small tokens of personal religious devotion. But in ancient Greece, perhaps the most common purpose of votive offerings was publicly to show gratitude for—and indeed to symbolize—the special favor and prosperity the giver had received from the gods. (Or, more cynically, they showed everyone how rich the giver was.) For the city, then, votives also served as highly visible public testaments to the prosperity of its leading citizens. Likewise, magnificent expenditures add

---

[1] Thinking about magnificence will also serve as a test-case, therefore, for the idea that the virtues are plural because they are culturally relative (e.g. MacIntyre 1981).

[2] It is also worth pointing out that Aristotle's choice of cultural examples of magnificence leads to a rather narrow conception of magnificence as necessarily involving large public gifts. This is unfortunate, since e.g. Muhammad Yunus' making of small, high-risk loans to tens of thousands of beggars in Bangladesh through the Grameen Bank is arguably a form of magnificence—it certainly goes well beyond ordinary generosity—but fits uncomfortably with Aristotle's paradigm cases of magnificence.

[3] Duties of *leitourgia* also included preparing an athletic team, hosting a public feast, and preparing a delegation to a foreign festival. Festival-related duties, however, were considered somewhat less onerous, and thus could be required of a wealthy citizen once every two years, unlike trireme duties which could be required only once every three years. See the entry on liturgy in the *Oxford Classical Dictionary* (*OCD*) (ed. Hornblower and Spawforth), 875.

ornamentation and 'status' to the city as a locale, and as a people. In this respect, Aristotle says that even the furnishing of one's own estate can be a kind of magnificence: 'It is also the mark of a magnificent person to furnish himself with a household in a way suitable to his wealth (for a household too is a kind of adornment), and to prefer to spend on things whose effects will be long-lasting (for these are the finest)—in each sort of case spending what is suitable' (*NE* IV.2, 1123a6–9).[4] A magnificent person, that is, designs even his private estate so as to beautify and thus benefit the wider city, as a testament to the wealth and prosperity of the leading citizens. For this reason, the most magnificent private expenditures, Aristotle says, are those that 'hold the interest of the whole city or of its eminent figures' (1123a1–2).

The other parallel is that each type of expenditure is, and is meant to be, a reflection of the greatness of the giver: 'But it is suitable for those who have such resources stored up through their own efforts or those of their ancestors or connections, or those of noble birth, or high reputation, or anything else of that sort; for all these things bring great expectations with them' (*NE* IV.2, 1122b29–33). Not surprisingly, votive offerings were often accompanied by an inscription indicating the giver, as well as the noteworthy event in the giver's life that prompted the offering (as when an Olympic athlete places his trophy in the temple). Likewise, many wealthy citizens performed services of *leitourgia* more frequently, and at greater expense, than legally required in order to establish a public reputation for vast wealth and bounteousness (again, more cynically, to show everyone how rich they were). So a vivid, public display of a giver's wealth is meant to reflect well on the city and its citizenry, but also on the individual giver himself.[5]

Not only are magnificent expenditures like votive offerings, but indeed Aristotle says that the giving of votive offerings is itself a *form* of magnificence (*NE* IV.2, 1122b19–23). Notice, then, that magnificence extends beyond the formal institution of *leitourgia*, and includes, besides votives and the building of houses, such 'private' expenditures as the hosting of a wedding, the reception of foreign guests, the giving of gifts, and the making of public sacrifices (1122b19–20, 1122b35–1123a5).[6] Yet not every wedding

---

[4] Cp. Isocrates, *Letters* 2.19: 'Display magnificence, not in any of the extravagant outlays which straightway vanish, but in the ways which I have mentioned, and in the beauty of the objects which you possess, and in the benefits which you bestow upon your friends; for such expenditures will not be lost to you while you live, and you will leave to those who follow you a heritage worth more than what you have spent.' (Trans. Norlin, in the Perseus database.)

[5] See the entry on votives in the *OCD*, 1612f.

[6] On the entertaining of guests, cp. Xenophon, *Economics* 2.5 where Socrates, tongue-in-cheek, pities the wealthy Critobulus for the burden of entertaining guests 'on a grand scale' (*megaloprepōs*). On public offerings and religious feasts, cp. Isocrates, *Letters* 7.29, who praises the 'forefathers' for their

or gift-giving occasion is an occasion for magnificence, since, Aristotle says, magnificent expenditures are of concern to the whole city, or at least to its most prominent members (1123a1–2). Furthermore, magnificence involves a certain magnitude of expenditure, and the attempt at such magnitude by those without the means for it is not magnificent but foolish (1122b23–9; *EE* III.6, 1233b8–14).

For Aristotle, then, magnificence would be a virtue concerned with how one performs one's socially and in some cases legally defined role as a particular type of public benefactor. In one way, being magnificent is not unlike, say, being a good parent: not all virtuous persons will occupy such roles, but those who do occupy them will need to do so in excellent ways, acting for the right reasons, in relation to the right things, and so on (see also Swanton 2003, 71). And Aristotle recognizes too that large-scale expenditure opens new and distinctive opportunities for mistaken and indeed bad actions—such as just showing everyone how rich you are. Some of these are opportunities for gaffes and bad taste, and indeed Aristotle compares the magnificent person to an expert artisan (*NE* IV.2, 1122a34), as both have an eye for perceiving what is 'suitable' and 'in good taste'.[7] Magnificence involves not merely how much one spends,[8] but also how well, how tastefully, how *skillfully* one spends.[9] If this seems a minor point for a virtue, remember that to spend magnificently is to spend for a certain beneficial *purpose*, namely to benefit and beautify one's community:

Of [magnificent] expenditures, some are of the sort we call prestigious, e.g. those relating to gods—votive offerings, ritual paraphernalia, and sacrifices—and similarly for any being that is worshipped, and all the kinds of public benefaction for which it is

observance 'on a grand scale' (*megaloprepōs*) of newly instituted as well as traditional rites. See also Diodorus, *Histories* 13.82.1 for similar praise of the ancient Acragantini for their magnificence displayed in their sacred buildings.

   [7] Cp. Isocrates, *Letters* 1.27, 'In matters of dress, resolve to be a man of taste, but not a fop. The man of taste is marked by elegance (*to megaloprepes*), the fop by excess.' (Trans. Norlin.) See also Xenophon (*Memorabilia* 3.10.5; *Constitution of the Lacedaimonians* 12.5), who takes a broader view of magnificence as a kind of greatness that is evident in one's physical bearing and expression. Magnificence clearly concerns making the right sort of appearance. However, it may be in this sense that Andronicus (*Stoicorum Veterum Fragmenta* [=.*SVF*] 3.270) describes magnificence as 'a state that swells up those who possess it, and is full of arrogance' (*phronēmata plērousa*, my trans.; cp. Aeschylus, *Prometheus Bound* 953, *phronēmatos pleōs*); cf. *SVF* 3.391 on the 'swelling' of the irrational passions. I thank Dirk Baltzly for this point.

   [8] Although this is an issue; see 1122a26, 27, 1123a19–20. But see also the odd remark on magnificence on smaller scales at 1123a14–16, and Pakaluk's 2002, 208 comment on it.

   [9] As Hursthouse puts it, 'the virtue of *megaloprepeia*, magnificence, which is contrasted with vulgarity and pettiness, is a virtue which consists in correct *judgement*. The magnificent man judges correctly that the expense is worthy of the result and the result worthy of the expense; the vulgar and the petty constantly get this judgement wrong.' Hursthouse 1999*b*, 106, italics in original.

good to compete, e.g., perhaps, if people think a play should be staged brilliantly, or a trireme fitted out, or a feast provided for the city. (1122b19–23)

To be sure, magnificent expenditure involves a high degree of aesthetic sensibility, but given the role of such expenditure in civic life and civic duty, it makes sense to say that a wealthy citizen's failure to develop that sensibility may very well constitute a serious failing in character.[10]

However, Aristotle is most concerned with the sorts of temptations to extremes that tend to arise due to the grandness and publicity of magnificent expenditure. One sort of temptation is to spend ostentatiously and in a self-aggrandizing way; a person who spends in these ways Aristotle calls 'vulgar' (*banausos*). Another is the temptation of penny-pinching and cutting corners in the wrong places, making the result tacky rather than grand; Aristotle calls one who does so 'shabby', 'niggardly', or 'mean' (*mikroprepōs*). Consequently, Aristotle characterizes vulgarity and niggardliness not in terms of the bare *amount* spent, but in terms of the *reasons* for spending inappropriately on this scale. Magnificence aims at a kind of publicly beneficent grandeur (*NE* IV.2, 1122b4–6), but vulgarity results only in a tasteless and showy expenditure, aimed merely at parading one's wealth (1122a31–3; 1123a19–20), and this spoils the benefit for the city. (Consider Aristotle's palpable scorn for the practice in Megara of dressing comic actors in gaudy purple robes, 1123a23–4.) The niggardly person also misses the point of magnificent beautification, but in the opposite direction, put off by grandness and hesitating over every cost, and even spoiling the effect by holding back in some mean way (1123a24–7). Where the magnificent person sees civic beauty, the niggardly man sees expense, and is keen to keep bringing expense downwards (1123a27–31; see also 1122b7–8; 1123a27–31). By contrast, the magnificent person 'will enjoy spending and do it readily; it is shabby to budget precisely.'[11] Again, he will be more concerned how to spend in the finest and most suitable way than with how much it will cost, and how to do it most cheaply' (1122b7–10; see also *EE* III.6, 1233a38–1233b6; *MM* I.26).

For these sorts of reasons, Aristotle holds that magnificence is a virtue, as he calls it more than once (*NE* IV.2, 1122a19; 1125b1–4; see also 1107b17–21; 1122b7, 18, 29). The magnificent person, Aristotle says, 'will incur such expenditures for the sake of the fine, since this is a shared feature of the virtues' (1122b6–7; see also Annas 1996, 243). Aristotle treats magnificence as a virtue

---

[10] Thus I do not agree with Annas' (1996, 243f) assessment that such failings are *merely* 'lapses of taste', as opposed to failings with genuine moral significance.

[11] Notice that the stock of resources needed for magnificence seems to rise rather steeply if one is to give not only grandly but even *lavishly*.

because it aims at the good, acts for the right reasons, and can be contrasted with vices representing characteristic ways of doing wrong at the same sorts of things. And I see no reason to dispute this (see also Swanton 2003, 71 ff). To be sure, the wealthy Athenian would have aimed at the public benefit in ways that seem distant from our own culture, but what makes the magnificence of such a citizen recognizable as a virtue is the nature of the *reasons* behind properly magnificent expenditure.

What is less clear, however, is why Aristotle thinks, apparently, that magnificence is a primitive virtue, alongside such virtues as generosity and courage. From the fact that magnificence is a virtue, it does not follow that it is another virtue in addition to the rest, any more than orthodontics' being a skill makes it a skill alongside or in addition to dentistry. Orthodontics is of course a skill, and a skill that requires its own special training and expertise, but it is subordinate to dentistry, not parallel to it; it is a *specialization* of the skill of dentistry. Of course, Aristotle does not consider any such relationships among virtues—an omission that was far from lost on Aquinas, for one—and one might suppose that this is because of his reluctance to model the virtues on skills (*technai*). But while Aristotle points out that virtues are unlike skills in that they aim at action rather than production (*NE* VI.5, 1140b1−4), and that actions cannot be evaluated quite as products are (II.4, 1105a26−33), he nonetheless relies on certain similarities between virtues and skills to illuminate the cognitive structure of virtues. In particular, the virtues, like skills, are learned through practice, experience, and the guidance of mentors, and when learned give one a certain practical 'proficiency' and expertise—a point that Aristotle himself makes explicit in the case of magnificence (IV.2, 1122a34). Skills can become specialized because of their cognitive structure, not their productive nature, so Aristotle's attitude about virtue and skill would seem, if anything, to put *forward* the possibility that one virtue can be subordinate to another.[12] It is therefore all the more puzzling that Aristotle should begin his whole discussion of magnificence by observing that all the magnificent are generous (but not necessarily vice versa; 1122a28−9), yet proceed to place magnificence alongside generosity nonetheless.[13]

It would seem, then, that Aristotle's own position on magnificence is not the only possible 'Aristotelian' position, since it is possible to view magnificence as a 'specialization' of generosity, much as one skill can be a specialization

---

[12] I discuss the relation between phronesis and skill in Ch. 1.

[13] See 1122a28−9; cf. similar claims about 'magnanimity' at 1123b5−6, 1125b1−8. For discussion, see Gardiner 2001, 263. See also Pakaluk 2002, 203−6, who rightly argues that theses about whether the generous will be magnificent concern generosity and magnificence as 'powers', rather than the extensions of the classes of magnificent and generous persons.

of another. In the next section I shall say more about the specialization view, and then in the final section I shall further articulate and defend that view by contrasting it with some likely alternatives. I should make it clear before starting, however, that my primary commitment here is not to the specialization view *per se*, but to the broader notion of subordination. I think that specialization is a useful type of subordination to consider, but I would not for a moment deny that there may be others.

7.2 Subordination, Specialization, and Cardinality

Treating magnificence as subordinate to generosity is not merely a possible Aristotelian alternative; given the enumeration problem, such a view would be an advance over Aristotle's actual position. For one thing, the alternative view offers a richer, more detailed picture of the relation between magnificence and generosity. Furthermore, capturing that relationship by way of 'specialization' may yield at least one way of modeling the subordination of one virtue to another more generally. In that case, to identify a 'new' virtue is not necessarily to introduce a *further* virtue. On the 'specialization' view I sketch here, to speak of magnificence is still, in one very important sense, to speak of generosity. The complexity of the demands that life can make on one's character is thus not reproduced in an ever-expanding catalogue of new virtues. Rather, we gain a better grasp of that complexity by understanding how primitive or cardinal virtues of character adapt to new and distinctive areas of demand on the virtuous person.

To think about the virtues in this way is already to appreciate more fully how little structure there is among the virtues on Aristotle's list. Now, it is of the first importance to recognize that Aristotle's view nonetheless finds far more structure among the virtues than many contemporary virtue theories do, since Aristotle holds that one of the virtues—practical wisdom or phronesis—is essential to every other virtue, and to the operation of all the virtues in a unified and mutually supporting way (*NE* VI.12, 1144a29–b1; VI.13, 1144b30–1145a6). Nonetheless, Aristotle does offer his list of virtues without indicating either that that list should be understood as complete, or how one would continue that list in a principled way from where he leaves off.

That is not to say that Aristotle is entirely silent on the issue, however, since he closes *Nicomachean Ethics* III.5 as follows: 'Now let us pick up our subject again and discuss each of the virtues individually, saying what they are, what things they relate to, and how; and it will be clear, too, at the same time, how many there are' (1115a4–5). Aristotle clearly has some interest in thinking about 'how many' the virtues are, but his highly compressed remarks raise at least two questions. First, does 'how many the virtues are' mean *how numerous* the virtues are—i.e., that they are many and diverse rather than few—or does it mean *of what number* the virtues are—i.e., that there are exactly *this* many of them (seven rather than eight, say)? I see nothing in the text or the surrounding context that suggests one interpretation over the other, and the latter is clearly the stronger of the two. We cannot assume, then, that Aristotle is addressing our problem.

And second, even if 'how many' should be read as 'of what number', what method is proposed for determining what that number should be? He says that 'how many' will become clear at the same time that we find out 'what' traits are the virtues, and what things they relate to, and 'how' they relate to them, but *how* exactly is such an inquiry supposed to clarify just what number of virtues there are? Does Aristotle hold that there is a virtue for every thing to which the virtues are related, or for every way in which they are related to them? But in that case, the virtues would be infinite, and there could be no saying 'of what number' they are at all. Or does he mean something else? Aristotle simply does not say, and so there is no reason to suppose that he is addressing precisely our sort of question here, much less that we could tell how he had addressed himself to it.[14]

As we saw in Chapter 5, Aristotle's open-handedness with his list contrasts most notably with Plato's highly economical list of four cardinal virtues of temperance, justice, courage, and wisdom (*Republic* IV, 441c–442d). Perhaps such stark economy is of dubious benefit when treating of something as complex as human character, but Aristotle's list also contrasts sharply with the standard Stoic list of virtues which includes not only Plato's four cardinal virtues, but also a multiplicity of other, rather diverse virtues that are subordinate to the cardinal virtues (see Arius Didymus in Stobaeus, *Anthology* II.5b–5b2). The

---

[14] Con. Reeve 1992, 169f, who notes that the virtues are about certain sorts of goods, and concludes that those goods indicate the number of the virtues: 'It is because the virtues of character are connected with external goods in this way that Aristotle can be confident to some degree that the virtues he lists are all the virtues that there are (1115a5).' I thank Nick Eliopoulos for bringing this passage to my attention. Reeve evidently assumes both the much stronger interpretation of 'how many' as 'of what number', and that that number is determined on the basis of the things the virtues relate to. Even granting these assumptions, however, it is far from clear that we should expect a one-to-one correspondence of good-types to virtues, or even that there should be no more than one virtue that is about any given good. And again, even if goods and virtues were so related, this would show not 'of what number' the virtues are, but quite the contrary that the virtues are simply beyond number.

notions of cardinality and subordination have largely fallen by the wayside in contemporary virtue theory and virtue ethics, even among those theories that draw their main inspiration from ancient views, in part presumably because Aristotle's view of the virtues has been by far the primary source of such inspiration. And in fact some of Aristotle's commentators have felt the need for more structure within Aristotle's list of virtues. For instance, Stephen Gardiner (2001) has argued that some of Aristotle's virtues are more 'basic' than others, since some virtues—like generosity, courage, etc.—are crucial to excellence of character for every normal adult human, while virtues like magnificence are not so universally crucial, but only for persons in special circumstances.

Of course, differentiating generosity and magnificence in terms of how basic they are in this respect is consistent with their all being primitive or cardinal virtues. After all, Gardiner's proposal is specifically aimed at making Aristotle's discussion of magnificence consistent with his discussion of the unity of virtue (which Gardiner interprets as a thesis about the 'basic' virtues), not at steering the discussion of magnificence clear of the enumeration problem. More radical, then, is Aquinas' attempt to overlay a Stoic model of cardinal and subordinate virtues onto the Aristotelian virtues, treating virtues like humility and magnanimity as particular applications or 'exercises' of the cardinal virtues, and in this sense Aquinas maintains that the various 'secondary virtues' are 'derived from' (*reduci ad*) the cardinal virtues.[15] On Aquinas' model, the introduction of a virtue like magnificence need not increase the number of primitive virtues, since such a virtue can be treated as a form or 'exercise' of a more fundamental virtue like generosity, and thus more generally the apparent multiplicity of virtues turns out to be a multiplicity of distinctive ways of acting in accordance with the cardinal virtues.[16] Although I shall propose nothing as radical as Aquinas' ambitious restructuring of the Aristotelian virtues, we should take a cue from Aquinas and try to capture the complexity of virtuous character and action without merely reproducing that complexity in a 'laundry list' of virtues. And I certainly do agree with Aquinas that some virtues are subordinate to others.[17]

---

[15] Here I have benefited greatly from Irwin 2005.

[16] I have benefited here from discussion with Toby Handfield.

[17] Interestingly, Aquinas, *ST* 2-2 q134 a4 argues that while generosity is subordinate to justice, nonetheless magnificence is subordinate to—believe it or not—courage or fortitude, dividing them in this fashion on the grounds of the different parts of the soul in which he says that generosity and magnificence reside (see esp. ad 1). Aquinas here claims to follow Cicero, *On Invention* 2.54.163; but Cicero understands magnificence (*magnificentia*) as a bold resolve to do great, lofty things, whereas Aquinas understands magnificence as specifically concerned with expenditure, and makes it

On the view of subordination that I offer here, we begin by taking seriously the Aristotelian notion that virtues are (or are like) practical skills, and treat magnificence as a 'specialization' of generosity understood as such a skill. We can therefore understand magnificence as a form of generosity, while *also* making sense of the distinctive, specialized nature and demands of magnificence.

The specialization view proceeds in two basic steps. First, magnificence is subordinate to generosity. As our discussion of magnificence has shown, magnificence is characterized, and distinguished from its opposing vices, not by the mere scale of the expenditures involved, but by its distinctive *ends*, that is, its end of materially benefiting others on a public level. Magnificence therefore involves phronesis about the broader intersection of benefits and resources—what it is to benefit others, and in particular how material resources impact our well-being. It seems clear, then, that the magnificent person shares the ends and the reasons for which the generous person also acts, as well as the generous person's phronesis about material benefit. Put in the terms of the previous chapter, a theoretical model of the magnificent person must demonstrate 'conversational shift' from specifically magnificent to more generically generous reasons, when asked why there is any reason to be magnificent in the first place.

Second, where magnificence and generosity differ is in the more particular deliberative abilities required for the *specification* of the ends that they share. As we saw in Chapter 1, Aristotle holds that while virtue makes one's end the right one, phronesis makes right 'the things towards the end' by specifying the content of the end (*NE* VI.12, 1144a7–9), for instance, determining what in fact materially benefiting others would amount to in one's particular circumstances.[18] As I said above, such phronesis involves an understanding of the human good, and the way that resources impact the human good; it is through such phronesis that one is able to specify the content of the end of 'materially benefiting others' in particular circumstances. However, in the case of magnificence the impact of resources on human well-being is an impact at a specifically *public* level. Of course, the good of a human community is not a separate thing from the human good, but aiming at the good of a community does involve a number of more specialized considerations: correctly specifying the content of the end of improving one's city requires kinds of knowledge,

part of courage on the rather feeble grounds that it involves facing the danger of losing much of one's wealth.

[18] Following the argument of Ch. 3, we could say that no motive could be a genuinely generous or magnificent one, without at least a good faith effort to get such a specification right.

skill, and wisdom that do not arise in the course of more 'garden variety' occasions for generosity.

Magnificence, therefore, is not identical to generosity. Although magnificence is subordinate to generosity, because it shares the ends and responds to the reasons characteristic of generosity, nonetheless magnificence involves a more focused and specialized set of deliberative skills for specifying the content of those ends. On my view, magnificence is best understood as a 'specialization' of generosity, on the model of one skill's being a specialization of another.

In the next section I further develop the specialization view by considering four basic alternatives to it, each of which purports to show that magnificence is instead a primitive virtue: (1) that magnificence is a distinct skill; (2) that magnificence has distinct aims; (3) that magnificence aims at goods in a distinct way; and (4) that magnificence is a mean between distinct vices. I shall spend a bit more time on the first alternative than on the other three, since that alternative concerns the nature of magnificence as a skill, which is central to the specialization view, and also because the observations we make in considering this first alternative will facilitate our treatment of the other three.[19]

7.3 Alternatives to the Subordination View

7.3.1 Magnificence as a New Skill

I trust it is clear by now that it would be a *mistake* to regard magnificence as nothing more than ordinary generosity exercised on a larger scale of sums. Let us be clear: generosity and magnificence are different virtues and involve different skills. Aristotle himself is very clear on this point, noting that magnificence not only involves very special resources, but also requires very special abilities and thus special forms of training. Some of these abilities are distinctly ethical, since the magnificent person spends well in relation to what it is appropriate to spend, for the person spending, for the things the money is spent on, and so forth, and the appropriateness of magnificent expenditure includes the appropriateness of one's reasons and deliberations. And some of the abilities are of a more 'hands on' variety since, as we have seen, the magnificent person treats public expenditure as a kind of art, an exercise in public beautification as much as in public beneficence. This is clearly the sort

---

[19] In fact, I doubt that things would change very much, for the purposes of illuminating the subordination relation, if we substituted the idea that X is a specialization of Y with the idea that, say, X is for the sake of Y.

of skill, artistry, and attitude that need not be part of simple generosity.[20] Moreover, there is no sharp division between the more ethical and the more hands-on skills, since part of what makes an expenditure 'appropriate' is that it aims at expenditures that do in fact benefit and beautify one's city.[21] The difference between magnificence and generosity is therefore much more than a matter of context or scale.

Thus I agree with those of Aristotle's readers who have remarked that large-scale expenditures confront one with 'a genuinely different set of moral circumstances', requiring 'knowledge, capacities, and habituation significantly beyond that required for the smaller-scale virtues', including generosity (Gardiner 2001, 264, following Irwin 1988a, 66).[22] This is an important point, especially given the centrality of practical competence in Aristotle's conception

---

[20] This is, I take it, one of the reasons that Aristotle says both that the magnificent person must also be generous, but that generosity alone will not make one magnificent. See also Irwin 1988a, 64–6, who notes that, on Aristotle's view, being generous and having all the right intentions when making grand expenditures is not enough to make one magnificent. And see Isocrates 7.29–30, who notes the importance for magnificence in public offerings of an awareness of one's history and heritage.

[21] On the other hand, Halper 1999, 141 argues that while the generous person would not *ipso facto* be magnificent in the 'proper' sense (i.e. having the empirical knowledge to perform the paradigmatically magnificent actions), such a person would have 'psychic' magnificence, i.e. the emotional dispositions characteristic of magnificence. But this distinction is unstable, since the magnificent person's characteristic emotional dispositions (being pleased by some sorts of displays and put off by others) can be fully acquired and refined only as one gains empirical knowledge about the right sorts of ways to make grand expenditures. A crucial part of this 'empirical knowledge' is learning what to like and dislike.

[22] On the special demands involved in being magnificent, see also Irwin 1988a, 62–4 and Gardiner 2001, 283. These special demands obtain, we should note, even outside institutions like *leitourgia*, such as making expenditures that are on a smaller scale than *leitourgia*, but still significantly larger than those regularly budgeted within one's household, like throwing a wedding (note the rather brisk business of hired wedding planners). In this respect, I think Pakaluk 2002, 207–13 does well to distinguish between central cases of large-scale expenditure ('absolutely' large, requiring wealth) and less central but nonetheless real cases ('relatively' large, requiring greater expenditure than usual), and to argue that both can be occasions for genuine magnificence. See also Pakaluk 2005, 178; Aquinas, *ST* 2–2 q134 a3 ad 4. Nonetheless, three caveats are in order. (1) As 'relatively' large expenditures become, so to speak, smaller, it becomes more difficult to support Aristotle's claim that it is the *special* virtue of magnificence that is needed to make them well. (2) Not all the virtuous may have the resources to make even these sorts of expenditures. Pakaluk 2002, 208 concedes this point, arguing only that magnificence need not be limited to the very wealthy. I should note, though, that Aristotle himself may be unwilling to concede this point, given his view that it takes a fair amount of wealth to have enough leisure for the development of high degrees of personal excellence (e.g. *Politics* III.5, 1278a8ff; VII.9, 1328b24ff; VIII.2, 1337b4ff; VIII.6, 1341a5ff; see also *NE* I.8, 1099a31–b8). Note too that, as we have seen, magnificence requires a certain magnitude of expenditure, and it is not magnificent to spend beyond one's means attempting to attain it (*NE* IV.2, 1122b23–9). (3) It would be fairly easy to mistake a distinction between (a) cases that common conceptions pick out first and cases that turn out to be probative upon further philosophical reflection, for a distinction between (b) more and less genuinely central cases. Which distinction is better suited to Aristotle's various cases of large expenditure I leave as an exercise for the reader (Pakaluk 2005, 178 opts for (a)).

of the virtues. As we have seen, Aristotle says (*NE* VI.12, 1144a6–9) that a virtue makes one's 'target' the right one—to do what is just, say, or courageous—but insists that this alone is not enough to *act* in a virtuous way. Being virtuous is much more than having one's heart in the right place. It is also a matter of knowing what to do (see also Hursthouse 1999a, 148f, 118; Foot 1978c, 165f; Russell 2005b, 116–18.). Furthermore, magnificence involves not merely a new context of action, but new skills for meeting the special demands of that context. Where there is such a substantial difference in skill, there should be a corresponding difference in virtues. So if magnificence is a virtue, then it is not the same virtue as generosity.[23]

The question remains, though, exactly how magnificence and generosity *are* related as (like) skills.[24] As we saw in Chapter 1 and again in Chapter 3, Aristotle discusses two different kinds of practical skill by which experts achieve the aims of their expertise. To act as a doctor, for instance, is already to have as one's target or aim the healing of the body, but having this target in a *doctor's* way also involves knowing what constitutes healing in the case at hand, and how best to bring that healing about (see *NE* III.3, 1112b11–20). Likewise, Aristotle says that a courageous person, say, must have not only the aim of acting courageously, but also the practical wisdom or phronesis to understand what would be the courageous thing to do in the case at hand, as well as the cleverness to know how best to do that thing (VI.12, 1144a6–b1). In the case of magnificence, then, one's aim is to make a grand, beneficial expenditure, so magnificence makes one's aim right.[25] Phronesis makes right one's choices of 'the things toward' that end, that is, what that end amounts to in the circumstances (knowing the difference between grandeur on the one hand and both vulgarity and tackiness on the other, what is really beneficial, how grandeur can be a benefit, etc.). And 'cleverness' (*deinotēs*) makes apt the particular steps one takes towards that end, once its content has been specified (knowing the best designer or architect to hire, which charitable foundations are the most efficient, etc.).

---

[23] Con. Reeve 1992, 170 n. 42, who claims that generosity and magnificence can be understood as 'the same state', which can be expressed either on a small or a large scale, and that generosity and magnificence differ only in terms of the scale on which that single state is expressed. See also Aquinas, *ST* 2–2 q134 a1 ad 1, who argues that although some generous persons lack the means for magnificent acts, nonetheless all generous persons are magnificent either in act or in disposition (cp. a3 ad 4).

[24] In the discussion that follows I have benefited greatly from discussion with Fiona Leigh.

[25] The aim should be parsed into two issues: the aim itself (say, benefiting one's neighbors) and the way of aiming (by making a grand expenditure). I shall address differences in the aim in §3.2, and differences in ways of aiming in §3.3. For now, note that neither of these is itself a difference in skill, so we must look elsewhere for that difference

Now it is undeniable that magnificence and generosity differ widely where being clever about effective means to one's ends is concerned. However, this cannot exhaust the difference between magnificence and generosity, since a person could act from the virtue of magnificence in establishing a charitable foundation, for instance, while delegating most of the actual administration to others—indeed, it will often be both necessary and wise to do so. Differences in cleverness between magnificence and generosity are significant, to be sure, but they do not reveal a *substantial* difference between them *as virtues*. The real difference, then, must come down to the different forms of practical reasoning that are involved in magnificence and generosity. Since magnificence aims at benefiting the public through large, fitting expenditure, the magnificent person must grasp the intersection of fitting expenditure and public benefit. For example, building a grand monument that valorizes one sect of a hotly divided society is not magnificent, however sublime the monument may be as an artwork.[26] And as we just saw, there is no sharp line between what a magnificent person finds a fitting, beautifying expenditure and what he or she finds a beneficial expenditure. In that case, practical reasoning in a magnificent person considers questions of public benefit, and in particular of how to benefit the public through expenditure, that go substantially beyond what generosity typically calls for. A generous person may know full well how to manage resources so as to benefit her children, without ever having had even the occasion to consider how best to benefit the public through some large endowment. She may be adept at specifying well the former kind of end but not the latter.

The difference in practical reasoning between magnificence and generosity can be seen in another way as well. A person may have the aim of making a grand public expenditure, and may even be clever about all of the nuts-and-bolts details involved in executing a grand expenditure. But such an aim is not magnificent if it is indifferent to *benefiting* the public through grand expenditure. Yet the intention to benefit the public must include at least a good faith effort to fathom the intersection of benefit and expenditure. Consequently, an aim or intention is not a magnificent one unless it includes the intention to benefit, a notion with which practical reasoning is concerned.[27] Furthermore, having

---

[26] I thank John Bigelow for this point. It seems to me that this was the salient issue surrounding the controversial sculpture of the Ten Commandments removed from an Alabama courthouse in 2003.

[27] This leads to one of the problems for agent-based virtue ethics that I discuss in Ch. 3: in short, I do not think that we can even understand what a courageous, magnificent, or benevolent aim is without the attempt to fathom the sorts of considerations that are in the sphere of practical intelligence, understood as phronesis. See also Slote 1997, esp. 240.

a magnificent aim is not sufficient for having the virtue of magnificence, since magnificence fathoms the intersection of benefit and expenditure *well* or *correctly*, as well as reliably. The magnificent person not only has magnificent aims of public benefit, but also understands what really does benefit the public, and how expenditure can help bring that benefit about. Virtue makes the aim right, but phronesis makes the virtue *the virtue that it is*. We can therefore differentiate magnificence from other virtues, including generosity, in terms of the particular sorts of phronesis that make magnificence the virtue that it is. This, then, is the difference between magnificence and generosity considered as virtues, and as (like) skills.

So the question is whether that difference is sufficient to make magnificence and generosity not only different virtues, but also virtues *on a par* with one another as *primitive* virtues. I do not think that it does. While practical wisdom makes one's virtue the virtue that it is, it is the nature of the virtuous person's reasons that make his or her virtue a virtue. A magnificent person's reasons, I think, ultimately have the form 'Just think what good I could do with these resources'.[28] Since magnificence is based on such reasons, magnificence is a kind of understanding of what resources are for. However, generosity and magnificence thus seem to *share* their reasons, and it is those reasons that make each of them a virtue where resources are concerned. Generous aims, after all, are not merely aims of sharing and conserving resources, but aims of *benefiting* by sharing and conserving resources. What distinguishes magnificence from generosity is one's understanding the kind of good one could do, the people that one could do good for, and how resources can bring about such a good. But in the end the reasons that make magnificence a virtue are the same reasons that make generosity a virtue. The connection between magnificence and generosity is therefore deeper than their concern with the same sorts of *things* (resources), and stems from their sharing of the same kinds of *reasons* where those things are concerned.[29] These reasons explain why magnificence and generosity are different from other virtues, and it is their deliberative specificity in their responsiveness to these reasons that distinguishes magnificence and generosity from each other.

So the fact that the magnificent person acts for the same sorts of virtue reasons as the generous person suggests that magnificence is to be subsumed under generosity, and thus that, while they are different virtues, they are not on a par with one another. From the fact that magnificence involves significantly

---

[28] For discussion of virtue reasons, see Williams 1995*a*; Hursthouse 1995*b*; and the previous chapter.

[29] Con. Aquinas, *ST* 2–2 q134 a3 ad 1, who distinguishes generosity and magnificence merely as general and great use of money, respectively.

new skills, in terms of cleverness and even in terms of practical wisdom, it does not follow that magnificence is a primitive virtue, alongside generosity and the others.

Moreover, recall now the enumeration problem: if we accept that magnificence is a primitive virtue alongside generosity because of their differences as skills (of either type, phronesis or cleverness), then there will turn out to be infinitely many virtues, *even if* we focus on just one area, such as generosity. A person who has all the virtues where generosity is concerned will pay bills in the right way, give the right amount to the right charities, lend to others in the right way, save, give gifts, and borrow in the right way, and so on. Each of these ways of being generous involves its own distinctive practical skills, and if virtues are enumerated in terms of distinct skills, then these must not be ways of being generous after all, but further virtues besides generosity. Moreover, some of these further virtues may need to be broken down even further: perhaps there is no single competency of 'borrowing', say, since it is one thing to borrow from a friend and another to borrow from a bank. Likewise, I may be quite capable of handling my finances and giving gifts in my own cultural setting, and yet quite out of my element in these respects within a very different sort of culture, or even at a different time in the history of my own. Before long, we shall have lost count of the many virtues that result from a closer analysis of the rather straightforward virtue of generosity. Indeed, 'generosity' itself seems to have vanished in a puff of smaller virtues. (I return in §7.3.3 to consider why it makes sense to single out magnificence as a distinctive virtue, even if it does not make sense to single out a special 'borrowing' virtue, etc.)

The problem is not only that there will be so many of these newly minted virtues. This way of minting them also does little justice to our moral experience. Surely it is not the case that a person in India, say, who occupies a certain economic class, has certain kinds of relationships, is subject to certain kinds of cultural expectations regarding lending, giving, and so on, has different virtues where these things are concerned than someone in a different position in India, or in a similar position but in a different historical period in India, or in some other culture altogether, etc. Moreover, even garden-variety acts of generosity in an industrial economy like ours require radically different skills than they do in an agrarian economy based on bartering and trading, in order to be done appropriately. And so on. There is no doubt that such persons have different skills from the others where generosity is concerned, but for all that it seems quite mistaken, and indeed pointless, to say that all of these persons have different *virtues*—as if they were responsive to different reasons. Nor is it much help to say, 'Yes, but of course we can use the same general heading—"generosity"—to describe all of them'. The problem is not one of managing our vocabulary in talking about their traits. The problem is that they can all be exercising the *same traits*, acting for the *same reasons*, despite their different competencies, and that is exactly what we cannot say on the view under consideration.[30]

Contrast this with the view that generosity is a single trait, but capable of continuous molding, adapting, and specializing. On this view, as long as different people (separated by history, culture, social station, or what have you) are managing their resources from an intelligent and stable basis of prioritizing, valuing, choosing, and feeling—so long, that is, as they are managing their resources in accordance with practical intelligence—and are doing so for the same kinds of reasons, that is enough to attribute the same character trait of generosity to *all* of them, *regardless* of the particular competencies by which they act and choose in generous ways.[31] This view affords a better description of our moral learning, as well. When a generous person tries for the first time to select a gift for someone in a very different culture, for instance, it is not the case that she needs to develop a new virtue.[32] And notice how pointless such advice would be to her: 'Clearly, what you need here is to develop the virtue of cross-cultural giving (or giving-to-persons-of-that-culture)'. That sort of 'advice' merely reproduces the complexity of moral experience in the complexity of virtue-theoretical resources. On this view, there would be a new virtue every time there was a distinctly new way to go right or wrong, and the latter are hardly in short supply. The problem is not merely that we

---

[30] Irwin 1988a, 73f considers (and rejects) the possibility that there are different virtues that emerge as we ascend to higher levels of material wealth, since people living at those levels will need those new virtues in order to live well at their level. This, the argument goes, could salvage Aristotle's commitment to the reciprocity of the virtues, if we can understand reciprocity as holding level by level. The suggestion (attributed to Roderick Long) is ingenious, but once we begin introducing new virtues according to levels of wealth—and notice that new virtues should be just as likely to emerge as we *descend* to lower levels of wealth, if new virtues emerge as we ascend—where do we stop introducing new virtues? If differences in wealth bring new virtues, what other sorts of differences will bring yet more? See also Gardiner 2001, 277f.

[31] I have taken some pains to avoid saying that the outcome of their reasoning must be the *same*—that they must prioritize in the same ways, arrive at the same choices, etc. I say only that it must be both practically intelligent and moved by the same sorts of reasons, and there is no reason to expect practical intelligence to be always the same. See also Hursthouse 1999a, chs. 2–3 on moral reasoning in dilemmas, and in particular her discussion of 'pleasant dilemmas' (66f), drawing on Foot 1983.

[32] It is easy to forget how readily even a genuinely virtuous person can lose his or her 'sea legs', so to speak. As Hursthouse 2006b says,

> Human beings are, essentially, socially and historically situated beings and their virtuous character traits have to be situated likewise. A 21st century city dweller who possessed the [environmental] virtue to some degree could hardly manifest it in just the same ways as Australian Aborigines and Amer-Indians perhaps used to when they lived as hunter-gatherers. What we need to know is what would count as living in accordance with it *now* or in the near future.

could keep on creating more and more virtues, but that we would *have* to, in order to give guidance to action in contexts requiring new abilities. If virtue ethics has *anything* to tell the person in our example, I take it, it is that she needs to learn all the facts she can about such gift-giving practices, and then try to discover *what there are reasons of generosity to do in light of those facts*. This is not, of course, to give her a ready problem-solving formula, or even advice that will determine a uniquely good course of action; but we should not expect good advice to do that, anyway. The best advice we can give her is to begin with her virtue of generosity, and learn how to extend it into this new and different area. And that is exactly how the specialization view construes the relation between generosity and magnificence.

These observations also show that while the notion of 'specialization' has been developed on the model of virtues as practical skills, this notion is continuous with familiar and very general types of moral development. For instance, although we first begin to learn about virtues and 'virtue rules' (e.g. 'Be honest', 'Be fair', etc.) at an early age, and in connection with particular sorts of examples and contexts, it seems clear that we expand on this learning as we mature. As we do so, we gradually separate more particularly conventional elements of our notion of a virtue from those elements that make the virtue a part of excellent character more generally. And as we do this, we also broaden our view of the range of contexts and concerns to which the virtue is relevant and in which it can be exercised.[33] It is no small thing, of course, to discover that one needs to develop some particular competency in order to act well in some particular way. But ultimately, we need an account of how all of these competencies are to fit into one's life, one's good, and one's identity as a whole. When we fragment the virtues into menus of competencies, we lose such an account, but we can keep it if we think of virtues as central parts of an intelligent agent that can grow and expand to handle more and more of life's demands.

An interesting and, I think, attractive consequence of the subordination view is that it will be possible for a virtuous person to be constantly challenged by his or her surroundings. Even if I am generous, I shall still find myself needing to determine what it would be best for me, as a generous person, to do here and now, in these very unusual circumstances. Surely we cannot require that one must have encountered and mastered every sort of circumstance calling for generosity, before one can be called generous in a *bona fide* sense (cp. Badhwar 1996). There is no limit to the variety of distinctive ways in which one may need to be generous. Generosity is a particular virtue, but a

---

[33] Here I have benefited greatly from Annas, 'Virtue and Nature', unpublished.

virtue whose exercise consists in continual adaptation to new contexts. One of the benefits of likening virtues to practical skills in particular is the emphasis on their flexibility and adaptability, which allows the person with the skill to be creative and innovative. In other words, the practice of any virtue will surely require the constant learning of new competencies by which to succeed in the exercise of that virtue. A virtuous person will always have much to learn about being virtuous.

For all these reasons, we should say not that generosity is one thing and magnificence another, but rather that magnificence is subordinate to generosity. And one way to understand that difference between generosity and magnificence is that it is (or is like) the difference between a skill and a specialization of that skill. A 'specialization' exists not where a virtue has new materials to work with—that is simply a virtue working in a particular context—but where the virtue must adapt to its new context by specializing the practical intelligence and deliberations involved in that virtue within its new context. Through specialization, generosity has the potential, in a very real sense, to *become* magnificence.[34]

7.3.2 *Magnificence as Having New Aims*

Recall Aristotle's statement that a virtue makes one's target or aim in acting the right one (*NE* VI.12, 1144a7–8). Perhaps, then, virtues differ as their targets do, that is, insofar as they are concerned with different sorts of goods. It seems clear that magnificence and generosity have different aims or targets. Magnificence aims not merely at wisely disposing of one's resources, but at producing a certain kind of large-scale effect, one that is neither gaudy nor tacky. That, after all, is why the magnificent person is like an expert (*epistēmōn*; IV.2, 1122a34). In that case, when a generous person acquires the resources for large expenditure, we might say (as Gardiner puts the point) that 'she recognizes *that new goods are at stake, knows that a new virtue is needed*, is motivated to acquire it, and has some idea about how to do so' (2001, 284 emphasis added). Perhaps we should say, then, that magnificence is not a kind of generosity, but its own virtue, since it has its own kind of aim.

However, difference in such narrowly construed aims is neither necessary nor sufficient for difference in virtue. For one thing, it is possible for different virtues to have the same aim of this sort. To borrow an example from Rosalind Hursthouse, consider the aim of saving Plato's library from destruction (Hursthouse 1995*b*, 28f). Depending on what is threatening Plato's library, any

---

[34] Note that this is a claim about the structure of these virtues as types, not about the order of their development in particular persons. I consider this distinction at greater length in Chs. 6 and 11.

number of different virtues may have this aim: if a fire is threatening Plato's library, then it may take courage to preserve it; if one's appetite for reading threatens to wear the books out, then it may take temperance to preserve it; and so on. For another, and more important at present, a difference in aim does not entail a difference in virtues. Clearly, it will often require courage to do the just thing, say, or the temperate thing, or the friendly thing, or the loyal thing, and we certainly should not fragment courage into multiple virtues simply because it takes such widely diverging types of aims.

However, we may say that it is in exactly this way that a virtue like magnificence differs from one like courage or temperance, since these virtues are not defined in terms of any special aim, but in terms of *how* one pursues any number of good aims,[35] while magnificence *is* defined precisely in terms of its special aim. But this seems implausible to me. The aim of magnificence is not simply to make a grand effect, but (e.g. in the context of *leitourgia*) to do so *in order* to benefit one's city, and to do what one owes to one's neighbors to do; in other contexts, a magnificent person seeks to make a grand effect *in order* to please his or her children, or to bring joy to a friend, say (see also Aquinas, *ST* 2–2 q134 a3 ad 3, a2 ad 3). Consequently, it seems rather artificial to distinguish virtues in terms of such distinct aims. Different virtues seem both to aim at different sorts of ends and to share the ends at which they aim, and to do so *all the time*.

But notice that even if we were to distinguish one virtue from another in terms of their different aims, it would not follow that those two virtues are two *primitive* virtues. To be sure, a specialization of a virtue has its own sort of aim, and magnificence in particular aims at the wise use of resources specifically for a grand effect. This gives us a reason to distinguish magnificence from patience, say, as well as from generosity. But it does not give us a reason to conclude that magnificence is a new virtue alongside patience and generosity, as opposed to a specialization of a virtue. Furthermore, if we distinguish between aims at a suitably fine-grained level to give magnificence its own distinctive aim, and if we take this to show that magnificence is a new primitive virtue alongside the others, then we must introduce such a new virtue for every such aim, and these are in no short supply. Again, the same will be true even of garden-variety acts of generosity, since the aim of leaving a nice gratuity, on this sort of approach, will be different from that of leaving enough in one's account to pay the rent; and enumerating virtues in terms of aims will simply reproduce the complexity

---

[35] See Williams 1995*a* and Hursthouse 1995*b*. Williams 1995*a*, 18f argues that the aims of virtues like courage and temperance must be the aims characteristic of other virtues, while Hursthouse 1995*b*, 27–30 argues—persuasively, I think—that the aims of the courageous need only be genuine goods, and need not also be the peculiar aim of some other virtue.

of moral experience, rather than giving us a way of making it more tractable. Better to think of virtues as specializing, both in terms of new skills and in terms of new aims.

7.3.3 Magnificence as a New Way of Aiming

As we have seen, different virtues can take the same aim. But of course they do not take that aim in the same *way*. For instance, courage is identified not with a special aim, but with aiming at real goods in a particular way, viz. by facing danger or other causes of aversion for the sake of those goods.[36] Justice aims at bringing about real goods by considering what is equitable; temperance aims at bringing about real goods by calling on the agent's emotional integration; and so on. So perhaps we should distinguish virtues in terms of their distinctive *ways* of aiming at various goods.

Even if magnificence and generosity have the same sort of very broad aim—the wise use of resources, say—surely they do not have the same ways of aiming. There are two ways in which we can capture this difference. First, we may distinguish the characteristic means by which each virtue tries to achieve its aim, and we can capture those different means with different modifying phrases: generosity aims at doing well *by using resources in responsible ways*, say, while magnificence aims at doing well *by making fitting large-scale expenditures*. Fair enough, but by now it should be obvious that even if this strategy should show that magnificence and generosity are not the same virtue, that alone would not be enough to show that magnificence stands as a primitive alongside generosity. And again, the cost of making magnificence and generosity parallel in this way leads to reproducing the complexity of moral experience by introducing a new virtue for every new and distinctive sort of means one may employ in aiming to do well.

A more interesting alternative is to distinguish instead between the different ways in which magnificence and generosity take into account importantly different sorts of considerations. For instance, if we think of magnificence as the virtuous making of a large and visible public donation, as in *leitourgia*, then we shall need to take into account what we owe to the public, what would be the best use of one's resources relative to the public good, how one's donation and manner of making it will reflect on oneself, how to avoid spending in a self-serving way, how to spend in a tasteful and appropriately grand way, and so on. The difference between magnificence and generosity, after all, is not

---

[36] Hursthouse 1995b, 27–30 suggests this approach to courage and temperance, as rather special virtues not having their own distinctive aims. However, unlike Hursthouse I think that this is the right way to approach the other virtues as well.

merely one of scale, but a difference that also brings many new and complex issues into view. Since magnificence must aim at bringing about goods in ways that incorporate a distinctive bundle of issues correctly, we should say that magnificence is not the same as generosity (cp. Swanton 2003, 22f).

True enough, but again, these specialized sensitivities involved in magnificence do not establish that magnificence is a *primitive* virtue. Every exercise of generosity will consist in some special bundle or other of various considerations, and there is no principled limit to how many such unique bundles there may be.[37] For instance, it is *usually* the case that the exercise of one virtue requires the 'collaboration' of many other virtues in order to handle the special demands of bringing about real goods in particular contexts—indeed, this interdependence and connectedness of the virtues is much of the point of Aristotle's notion of acting as the virtuous person acts, with unified practical intelligence (see *NE* VI.13). The bare fact that magnificence involves a particular bundle of collaborative virtues and dimensions of virtues does not warrant the creation of magnificence as a new, primitive virtue. After all, *every* exercise of generosity—or any other virtue, for that matter—will require the exercise of other virtues in particular bundles, in order to navigate successfully the twists and turns of the particular context in which one acts. Indeed, that is why a virtuous act must be overall virtuous in order to be a right act.

Here again the notion of a specialization seems very fitting. Specializations exist not where one merely needs to do something new, but where particular bundles of skills and concerns tend to recur regularly and systematically. And while the moral status that magnificence has as a virtue is reducible without residue to the fact that generosity is a virtue—that is, that it is a virtue to use resources in appropriate ways—the status of magnificence as (like) a particular *skill* is *not* so reducible. In this sense, magnificence does involve a particular constellation of ethical concerns, and some persons may find themselves in contexts of magnificent giving often enough that they must draw these concerns together in *this* sort of way in a reliable and stable fashion. Magnificent persons develop this specific pattern of drawing such considerations together, can teach others to do so, can go awry in ways that can be sorted into repeatable patterns, and so on.[38] And so magnificence is so specialized that it is best to speak of it in its own terms. Yet it is still a specialization of another, less specialized virtue, and not a primitive virtue.

[37] On this point, see Cooper 1999, 86 ff, 109, *et passim*, who also cites Irwin 1988a, 66–72; Annas 1993a, 73–9. See also McDowell 1997, 143f; Reeve 1992, 170.

[38] Including, e.g., an appreciation of heritage, religious piety, etc.; see Isocrates 7.29–30.

7.3.4 Magnificence as a New Mean

Finally, it is important to remember that generosity and magnificence have different contrary vices. To generosity are opposed prodigality and meanness, and to magnificence, vulgarity and niggardliness.[39] More generally, one may fail to be generous by being wasteful and not taking care to preserve resources, or alternatively by being more occupied with holding on to resources than with using them for what they are for. By contrast, one may fail to spend magnificently by spending in a vulgar and ostentatious way, or on the other hand by cutting corners in a stupid way and spoiling the effect. Since magnificence and generosity are opposed to different, distinctive sets of vices, magnificence and generosity are not the same virtue. But since magnificence and generosity are therefore different 'means', are they therefore different primitive virtues?

That is far from obvious, since there is no reason to suppose that a virtue and a virtue subordinate to it must be opposed to the same vices. Indeed, at least where subordination is understood as specialization, it would be extraordinary if the increased specificity of the specialized virtue were not matched by a similar specificity in the vices opposed to it. And in fact it seems that ostentation and niggardliness are also special cases of prodigality and meanness, respectively, after all. I do not think that we should call them specializations, as there is hardly any 'skill' of being prodigal or mean. But it seems clear that there are many foolish and inappropriate ways of handling resources, and that hemorrhaging resources for the sake of vulgar display will be one of them, and holding back in cheeseparing ways will be another. In fact, vulgarity as a general kind of vice—the vice that misuses resources so as to draw desperate attention to oneself—is obviously not restricted to the very wealthy, even though only the wealthy will be able to make the sort of large and usually public vulgar effect that is specifically opposed to magnificence. Likewise, niggardliness is clearly one among many ways of being mean; it is set apart only by its specific result of marring what should have been a large, grand, and usually public effect. Why should these be *different vices* when the poor are guilty of them and when the rich are guilty of them? There is surely no reason to think that prodigal persons and vulgar persons (or mean persons and niggardly persons) necessarily act for (or from indifference to) very different kinds of reasons. We should not say that we have identified new vices simply because we have identified new and elaborate ways of expressing other vices,

---

[39] Note Plato, *Republic* VIII, 560e, who says that it is a perverse euphemism to call prodigality by the name of magnificence. (Curiously, elsewhere in the *Republic* Plato speaks of *megaloprepeia* instead as a sort of serious-mindedness.)

even if—as here—it will make sense to speak of those particular expressions of such vices in their own terms.

It seems fitting that the same sort of approach to capturing the relation between generosity and magnificence should also capture the relation between their contrary vices. But even apart from such considerations, it is far from clear that there is a virtue for every 'mean' state (in Aristotle's sense; see Gardiner 2001, 275). It is one thing to say that for every virtue there is a particular way of doing well, and quite another to say that for every way of doing well there is a particular virtue. Specifically, magnificence on our account shows one very good reason why this is not so, since some ways of doing well are new ways of specializing other virtues. And again, introducing a new, primitive virtue for every way of doing well that we may wish to discuss in its own terms will only undercut the power of virtue ethics to offer real action guidance, by needlessly multiplying virtues.[40]

Conclusion

There is an Aristotelian alternative to Aristotle's own account of the relation between magnificence and generosity. On that account, magnificence is a virtue, and is not the same virtue as generosity, but for all that it is not another primitive virtue, either: it is subordinate to generosity, because it is responsive to reasons of generosity, and it is a specialization of generosity on account of its specialized patterns of deliberation about those reasons. In other words, the notion of cardinality offers a new way of understanding the relation between virtue pairs like magnificence and generosity. I think that this alternative is an attractive one, for a number of reasons. On the view that generosity is (or is like) a skill of which magnificence is a specialization, we can account

---

[40] Therefore I am not persuaded that how we choose to characterize the relation between generosity and magnificence is 'purely verbal', as Kraut 1988, 81 says it is. It is worthwhile to contrast the notion of one trait as a specialization of another, with the options that Kraut presents for 'individuating' skills. Kraut considers two archers, one of whom can strike a small, distant target and another who can strike only close, large targets, and asks whether these are two skills or only one. On the one hand, Kraut says, we may say that the first archer has a skill that the second does not, viz. the skill of striking small, distant targets; on the other, that both have the same skill (viz. archery), but that the first archer has it to a higher degree. Kraut insists that the difference between saying that generosity and magnificence are one virtue or that they are two is 'equally arbitrary'. I have argued here that the differentiation is neither arbitrary nor merely verbal. Nor do I agree with Kraut that 'since they differ in scale, the magnificent person has more of what the generous person has'; cp. Irwin 1988b, 87. Much better, I think, to say in the case of the generous and the magnificent that the latter represents a distinctively new way of specializing in the skill of the former (a point that the comparison of the two archers cannot capture).

for one example of the complexity and diversity of virtuous activity and character, without necessarily introducing further primitive virtues to do so. And that is an important advantage, given the seriousness of the enumeration problem.[41]

A few caveats are in order. For one thing, although magnificence is a subordinate form of generosity, it bears repeating that this is not to say that the generous person is therefore also magnificent, or even that the only thing standing between a generous person and magnificence is more wealth. For another, this fact in no way jeopardizes the genuine generosity of the person who is not also magnificent, since it is surely unreasonable to say that one cannot be a *bona fide* practitioner of a skill unless he or she is also a practitioner of every specialization of that skill. That is why a person can genuinely have a virtue, and still have more to learn about being virtuous in that way. And even if every virtue operates well only if it works as part of a package including the other virtues, it does not follow that every virtue requires mastery of all of its specializations in order for it to operate well. Of course, the generous person who comes to need the specialization of magnificence will need to develop that specialization, if she is in fact generous. Moreover, one's virtues may give one reason to branch into areas that require a new specialization, and it can be a serious deficiency of character to avoid certain kinds of actions simply because one is averse to learning a new specialty (see also Russell 2005*b*, 117 and n. 29). Finally, I have not argued that specialization is the only kind of relation by which one virtue can be subordinate to another. And this leaves us with the possibility, and the challenge, of further expanding this notion of subordination, and so coming closer to a more general account of the principled limits on introducing new virtues, and to a more structured approach to the virtues than that of merely producing longer and longer lists of them. When our notion of the virtues is so structured, recognizing virtues like magnificence does not so much add yet another virtue as make the notion of a virtue richer and more detailed. Ultimately, such a notion of the virtues still works with the same fundamental building blocks—the same virtue reasons—in giving an account of ethical character.

In closing, let us recall the view that where one virtue is instantiated in an agent in one kind of context but not in another, the virtue needed in the latter context must be different from, but on a par with, the virtue displayed in the former. We can now see why that does not follow: to say that one

---

[41] The question naturally arises whether even the cardinal virtues should themselves be understood as specializations of virtue as a whole, yielding some version of the unity of virtue. DesLauriers 2002, 123–5 considers some such view; I consider the unity of virtue in Ch. 11.

needs a virtue in this area is sometimes to say that one needs to develop further a virtue that one has in some other area. Virtues develop in people in a contextually-bound way, but we already knew that. The fragmentation of the virtues requires the further assumption that if a virtue can exist in one area without also existing in some other, then those areas involve distinct virtues. That assumption overlooks the possibility that virtues, like other practical skills, can be developed and specialized, and thus extended into very different sorts of contexts. In making that fact clearer, we have not solved the enumeration problem, but perhaps we have made a first step.[42]

[42] For useful comments and discussion on earlier drafts, I thank Eva Anagnostou-Laoutides, Julia Annas, Dirk Baltzly, Craig Barrie, John Bigelow, Nick Eliopoulos, Mark LeBar, Fiona Leigh, Constant Mews, George Rudebusch, and David Runia.

PART III

Situations, Dispositions, and Virtues

8

Situations and Broad-Based Dispositions

Philosophical psychologists have told us that 'situationism' is bad news for virtue ethics and virtue theory more generally. Situationism is a research paradigm in social psychology that holds that situational variables have an impact on behavior that tells against disposition-based explanations of behavior.[1] For instance, psychologists Darley and Batson (1973) found in a well-known experiment that their subjects' likelihood to offer assistance to someone in obvious, immediate need depended far more on how hurried they were to get to a meeting than on any alleged dispositional variables. Some philosophical psychologists have argued that since there is little evidence for psychological dispositions, and since virtue theory as such is a normative theory about such dispositions, therefore virtue theory as such is empirically misguided. And since virtue ethics presupposes some theory of the virtues, virtue ethics is empirically misguided, too, and therefore of little practical value to creatures like us.

To take an analogy, no one today could take seriously a 'four-humor' tax-onomy—a taxonomy of the sanguine, melancholic, phlegmatic, and choleric humors—as a taxonomy of the basic units of personality or the causes of beha-vior. For that reason, a normative or ethical theory of character based on such a taxonomy would also be moot for creatures like us. As we saw in Chapter 3, virtue theory is a naturalistic enterprise, constructing an account of the virtues within an ethical outlook in equilibrium with our best understanding of human nature, and that must of course include an understanding of the psychological attributes that cause our behavior (see also Doris 2002, 114; cf. Campbell 1999,

---

[1] I think that in many cases 'action' would be more appropriate than 'behavior', since the former suggests a connection with practical reasoning that the latter does not. However, I use the term 'behavior' advisedly in these chapters, both because this is the standard terminology in the psychological literature, and because the relation of such behavior to practical reasoning is, in one way, at the heart of the personality theoretical controversy I discuss here.

32–8; DePaul 1999, 142). But is virtue theory empirically adequate, given the evidence from social psychology?

Responses from virtue theorists to the situationist challenge have been of three broad types.[2] One response attacks the challenge on the level of social psychology: whereas social psychologists interpret their experimental data as telling against 'broad-based' or 'robust' dispositions—roughly, dispositions to behave in consistent ways across diverse situations—in fact they do not. Perhaps the data show that the experimental subjects did not display the dispositions that experimenters were testing for, but their behavior can be explained in terms of the consistency of their (other) dispositions nonetheless.[3]

The second response attacks the challenge on the level of philosophical psychology: even if the experimental data show that very many subjects failed to act consistently, as social psychologists allege, this does not tell against the existence of virtues of character, as some philosophical psychologists allege. What it shows, instead, is that most people are not virtuous in a strict sense, but of course no virtue theorist is committed to thinking otherwise. There could be virtuous dispositions, even if most people do not have them. In fact, the data may even buttress the virtue theorist's case, by pointing out the need for strong character virtues in order to act consistently well under various situational pressures.[4]

I do not find either of these first two types of response to be fully convincing. For one thing, as I argue in this chapter and the next, I think that the interpretations of the experimental data offered in the first sort of response are generally less plausible than those offered by social psychologists themselves. I can support this claim only by examining the data, and the competing psychological paradigms at issue, in greater detail. And for another, it should be clear already that the question for the virtue theorist is not how many people are virtuous, but whether a trait-based taxonomy lines up with empirical evidence about the psychological causes of behavior in the first place. The second type of response, then, does not take the problem seriously enough: as we saw above, if the evidence for a given general taxonomy of human personality—one based on humors, or dispositions, or what have you—really is poor, then this is a serious problem for any normative theory

---

[2] See also Campbell 1999 for discussion.

[3] Examples of this sort of response can be found in Athanassoulis 2000, 217, 219; Kamtekar 2004, 468f, 473, 474; Miller 2003, 369, 378f, 383; Sabini, Siepmann, and Stein 2001, esp. 2ff; Sabini and Silver 2005, 546f; Solomon 2003, 53, 55; Sreenivasan 2002, 60; Swanton 2003, 31; and Webber 2007a.

[4] For examples of this second sort of response, see Athanassoulis 2001, 217–20; DePaul 150ff; Kamtekar 2004, 485; Miller 2003, 378f; Swanton 2003, 31; and Adams 2006.

about such a taxonomy, as well. I shall develop these two objections in more detail in the next chapter.

This brings us to the third type of response: although the experimental data do indeed tell against a taxonomy of personality and character in terms of a certain sort of disposition, nonetheless the notion of character traits as we find it in (at least some) virtue theories is not invested in *that* sort of taxonomy anyway. This third line of response does share one feature with the second, at a fairly general level of description: both responses hold that situationist psychology does not have the implications for virtue theory that many philosophical psychologists have drawn from it. The difference, however, is that while both the second and the third responses agree with the social psychologist in rejecting a particular taxonomy of personality, this third response then shifts instead to an alternative taxonomy more consistent with the data, on which it is held that an adequate theory of the virtues can be based.

It is this third sort of response that I shall give in this part of the book. Although I have some allies in this regard, broadly speaking (see Annas 2003; Butler 1998; Kamtekar 2004, 460, 470–2, 477; Sreenivasan 2002; Adams 2006, 130–5; Fleming 2006, 38ff; Webber 2006), still my own view stands apart in three ways we should notice. First and foremost, unlike most proponents of this approach, I argue that there is a personality taxonomy suggested by situationist research in social psychology, and that it is positively friendly to virtue theory.[5] Second, and accordingly, I take a much more extensive focus on situationist psychology as suggesting a positive theory of the nature of personality, and sketch the basic outlines of a normative account of the virtues on the shoulders of that personality theory. As a result, three, my view is not merely defensive. I argue not that virtue theorists should take heart *despite* what social psychology suggests, but should take heart *because of* what social psychology suggests. It is not just that virtue theory and social psychology can be consistent, but that they can actually go together rather *well*.

One might not have guessed it from the recent philosophical literature, on either side of the debate, but situationism not only is a negative thesis about dispositions, but also suggests a *positive* theory of the nature of personality. On that positive theory, personality is one's unique network of cognitive and affective strategies for interpreting and adjusting to one's environment in one's behavior. What the situationist rejects is a 'dispositionist' theory of personality, on which personality is one's unique aggregate of psychological

---

[5] An exception here is Kamtekar (2004, 477), although she does not much develop the positive account suggested by situationism. Adams (2006, 130–5) goes a little further, but not as far as I would want.

tendencies to engage in certain types of stereotypical behaviors. Simply put, the dispositionist sees personality as one's tendency to behave in certain observable ways, while the alternative cognitive-affective theory sees personality as one's tendency to behave for certain sorts of reasons. An *Aristotelian* virtue theory, with its emphasis on practical reason and phronesis, actually takes a *firmer* footing on a cognitive-affective model of personality than on a model of behavioral 'dispositions', as social psychologists use that term of art. This alternative, positive personality theory that social psychology suggests, I argue, is one that the virtue theorist—or more precisely, the Aristotelian virtue theorist—should positively welcome. Nonetheless, I do think that the news from social psychology is still very bad for *non*-Aristotelian virtue theories, and I shall say why in due course.

Before beginning, I should underscore the difference I see between situationism in *social* psychology versus *philosophical* psychology, as this difference is often obscured in the literature. The latter, I argue, has not given enough credit to the positive implications of the former for personality theory, which I think are positively friendly to broadly Aristotelian virtue theories.[6] In that case, I must begin at the very beginning, with social psychology and personality theory. In this chapter I examine dispositionism and situationism as suggesting rival positions in personality theory. In the next chapter I size up the experimental data that social psychologists offer in evidence. Then, in Chapter 10, I examine situationism's recent translation from social to philosophical psychology and consider the implications of situationist research in social psychology, and in particular the cognitive-affective theory of personality, for the normative enterprise of virtue theory.

My overall argument, simply put, is that the empirical evidence suggests that personality can be well understood in terms of basic cognitive and affective elements, such as the possession of certain goals, certain ways of attaching salience to the various features of actions and environments, and so on. Consequently, a virtue theory can be empirically adequate as long as it understands the virtues as certain forms of responsiveness to reasons. Furthermore, a virtue theory can also be an adequate theory of the virtues as normative concepts, as long as such forms of responsiveness to reasons are practically intelligent, adopting the right goals, attaching salience correctly, and so on—that is, as long as phronesis is a crucial part of every virtue. Therefore, any viable virtue theory must be a form of what I shall call Hard Virtue Theory.

---

[6] My concern in this chapter and the next will be situationism in social psychology; I turn to philosophical psychology in Ch. 10.

I begin in this chapter by paying special attention to the contrast between situationism and the more traditional research program it means to replace, namely dispositionism (§8.1), before reviewing social psychology as motivating a positive alternative in personality theory (§8.2) and some positive evidence in favor of that alternative (§8.3).

8.1 Situationism and Dispositionism

8.1.1 Social Psychology and Personality

Situationism is a research program within a field of psychology known as social psychology, which is commonly characterized as the study of how the presence of others—whether actual, imagined, or implied—influences how people think, feel, and behave (Allport 1985). Social psychologists therefore study broad behavioral patterns, such as might emerge in studies of conformity, obedience, or group dynamics, to name just a few. Since personality theory considers not such broad patterns, but the more specific bundles of personal characteristics that underlie how persons think and act (see Ryckman 2004), social psychology does not study personality in a direct way. But for all that, social psychology does bear on personality theory in some very important, if indirect, ways. For one thing, experiments in social psychology can test various personality theories. A theory of the nature of personality, after all, is a theory about the causes of behavior, and therefore commits one to certain predictions about the broader behavioral patterns that social psychologists study. So, for instance, the thesis that personality consists largely of behavioral dispositions that transcend most situational variables, can be tested by observing whether and how behavioral patterns change in experiments in which subjects are exposed to variations in the subtle features of a given situation. And for another, the results of such experiments in social psychology can also suggest new, positive models for personality theory. For instance, it could turn out that the best explanation of certain behavioral patterns is that behavior stems from the particular ways in which individuals interpret and adjust their behavior to situational variables. This would suggest that personality must consist in characteristics that are highly sensitive to situational variables rather than transcend them.

What is familiar among philosophers by now is how social psychology bears on personality theory in the former, strictly negative way. However, philosophers have paid far less attention to how social psychology leads to positive theories of personality, and in particular the sorts of positive personality theories that situationist social psychologists regard themselves as suggesting. I shall say more about the precise structure of such a personality theory as I proceed. But for now, we should begin with two different, broad approaches to personality theory, in order to see how social psychologists take the experimental evidence to tell against the one and for the other. It should become clear as we proceed that what situationism suggests is an alternative within personality theory, not an alternative to it. We can then ask (as I do in Chapter 10) whether that alternative might serve as the basis for a theory of the virtues.

Social psychology and personality theory all embrace what psychologists call 'interactionism', the view that a person's behavior is a function of both the agent's personal attributes and the situation in which the agent behaves (Lewin 1951; Lord 1982, 1076; Gilbert 1995, 103f; Doris 2002, 25f; and Ross and Nisbett 1991, 9, who call this principle a 'truism'). This is a plausible enough idea, as we usually suppose that personality differences account for different behaviors in the same situation, and on the other hand we generally make allowances for unusual behavior in unusual situations. But despite its plausibility, this notion also raises a serious difficulty: when are behaviors and situations 'the same'? Consider an example. Suppose that Fred walks through an empty school common room and comes upon a dollar coin lying on a table; and suppose that Fred sees the coin but leaves it on the table. Now suppose that George later walks through the same empty common room, but pockets the coin. Have Fred and George behaved in opposite ways? Was each of them in the same situation?

That depends on who classifies the situations and behaviors, and it is here that personality theories divide. On the one hand, it may seem obvious to us observers that deliberately pocketing the coin is a very different behavior from deliberately leaving it alone, and that being alone with an abandoned coin in a school common room is just one situation. On one traditional theory of personality, this is all the sameness we need, since situations serve mainly as 'background' against which agents behave. On this view, behavior manifests the agent's dispositions playing out against a wide range of backgrounds, and only minimally of the agent's interaction with that background (see Mischel 1968, 281 for discussion). Situations and behaviors can therefore be characterized from the observer's point of view—it is the 'actor' that is our focus, not the 'scenery', which does not change much with perspective. Of course, situations can emerge from the background, as when one behaves under duress, say. But in cases like the present one, the subjects' dispositions are held to be relatively independent of the situational background, so the observer's classification of the situation as 'the same' in each case is as good as any other. This approach to the relationship between personality and situations—an approach that depicts personality as a set of behavioral dispositions playing out against a wide range of backgrounds—is the basis of so-called *dispositionist* personality theory.

On the other hand, perhaps situations have more to do with behavior than that. Suppose that Fred leaves the coin alone because he thinks, 'Someone lost that; it's someone else's property'; he may even classify the situation alongside opportunities for shoplifting, say. Fred therefore sees his behavior as declining an opportunity to steal. By contrast, perhaps George pockets the coin because he thinks, 'Someone lost that; bad luck, but finders, keepers!', classifying the situation alongside finding a coin in the street or in a public telephone. In that case, George sees his behavior as accepting good luck, where stealing simply has nothing to do with it. From the *subjects'* point of view, therefore, each is in a different situation, and the two behaviors are not really 'opposites' after all, even if they may have at first appeared so to the observer. So an alternative approach would classify behaviors in terms of the meanings that subjects attach to them, including the subjects' own perceptions of their situation. Since it is the *subject's* personality that is in question, it seems appropriate to classify situations and behaviors from the subject's point of view, in which case differences in observed behaviors are less interesting than differences in how subjects view their surroundings and adjust their behaviors to them. It is this idea that is at the heart of *situationist* views of personality.

The situationist holds that such differences between Fred and George tell us more about their different personalities than we could gather if we were to assume that the situation was just 'the same', and their behaviors in it 'opposites', from our own point of view (Ross and Nisbett 1991, 13). Agents 'construe' their situations and attach meaning to them, and adjust their behaviors to situations *so construed*. In that case, construed situations are important causal and explanatory factors in behavior, and construal patterns are crucial aspects of personality. Situations and behaviors, on this view, must therefore be characterized from the *subject's* point of view, not the observer's, if we are to understand the subject's personality. Indeed, on this view any sharp subject/situation distinction simply breaks down (see Lord 1982, 1076f). This approach to the relation between personality and situations—an approach that depicts personality as a set of cognitive and affective modes of construing and adjusting to one's surroundings—is the basis of the situationist's preferred personality model. I now want to turn to a closer examination of these two rival personality models, in turn.

8.1.2 Dispositionism

The paradigm in personality theory now generally called 'dispositionism' was the dominant one for much of the twentieth century. It is useful to think of dispositionism as explaining patterns of behavior in three basic steps. First, we *observe* certain behavioral signs in a subject, e.g. that Fred often copies answers from a score-key on multiple-choice tests. Second, from the observed pattern we *infer* a so-called broad-based disposition, e.g. that Fred is 'dishonest' and will act dishonestly regularly and in a wide range of contexts. (I shall say more about broad-based dispositions in a moment.) And third, because the disposition operates across a wide range of contexts, we should be able to *predict* certain future behavioral patterns in that subject across a wide range of contexts, at least over the long haul, on the basis of the inferred broad-based disposition. Perhaps we shall have to watch Fred more closely during next week's essay test, for instance, and we had better not leave any valuables lying around. As Walter Mischel puts the point, this approach 'leads one to infer enduring generalized attributes in persons' on the basis of observed behavior 'and to predict from the inferred trait to behavior in various situations' (1968, 295f; see also 1968, 4, 5, 113, 295f; 1973, 262). For simplicity, I shall call this observe-infer-predict sort of explanatory schema an 'OIP schema'.

It is this predictive aspect of dispositionism that allows for the sort of experimental testing I mentioned earlier: for instance, if we observe a student cheat in one kind of situation, we should observe the student cheat in other kinds of situations, too. And more generally, if we have evidence that a person is disposed to be 'talkative', 'dishonest', or 'messy', then we should expect to observe this person doing various talkative, dishonest, or messy things in a wide range of contexts and regardless of most situational variables. This was the stuff of countless observational studies of behavior in the early and mid-twentieth century. One of the most famous studies of this kind was conducted by Hartshorne and May (1928), who studied the moral behaviors of children—in particular, cheating, lying, and stealing—for consistency across various types of situations (for discussion see Mischel 1968, 23–5; Ross and Nisbett 1991, 96–102). I shall return to their findings below.

'Broad-based disposition' is a term of art signifying two things. One, a broad-based disposition is *stable*: it tends to produce the same kind of behavior in the same kind of situation over time, such as Fred's being disposed to copy answers from the score-key on other multiple-choice tests, as well. And two, a broad-based disposition is *consistent*: it tends to produce similar behaviors even in different kinds of situations, such as Fred's being disposed to cheat using other methods and on different kinds of tests, and perhaps even to lie or to steal. A broad-based disposition, then, is 'a disposition to behave expressing itself in consistent patterns of functioning across a range of situations' (Pervin 1994, 108, cited in Doris 2002, 18). For the dispositionist, consistency is of particular significance, because explaining a behavior in a given situation in terms of a disposition so to behave in situations of that very specific sort is hardly illuminating (see Doris 2002, ch. 4). It is also the watershed issue in this debate in personality theory, because while both sides agree that the evidence for same-situational stability is excellent, they disagree sharply over the cross-situational consistency of dispositions.

It is therefore important to note that in this debate 'disposition', as a term of art, is not a label for the behavioral pattern itself, but for an underlying psychological attribute that is purported to be the *cause* of the behavioral pattern. A term like 'dishonesty', say, could refer either to a pattern of dishonest behaviors (so that we can directly observe Fred's dishonesty), or to a psychological cause of that pattern (so that we can infer from Fred's behavior a 'dishonest' personality trait). And either use of that term could be interesting depending on one's purposes. Where one wishes to focus on the pattern itself—how frequent 'dishonest' behaviors are, how other factors vary with them, and so on—one may wish to use 'dishonesty' as a label for that pattern. For other purposes, however, we need to refer to the psychology underlying the pattern. On the one hand, one could use 'dishonesty' as a place-holder label for whatever it is about persons in virtue of which such patterns obtain. On such a use of disposition terms, one takes no position on whether there is such a psychological entity as a broad-based disposition of 'dishonesty', any more than one does when one uses 'dishonesty' to label the behavioral pattern itself. The dispositionist's purpose, however, is to *explain* such patterns by *identifying* what it is about persons in virtue of which such patterns obtain. In that case, the dispostitionist means for terms like 'dishonesty' to refer to psychological attributes—in particular, broad-based dispositions—that are purported to underlie and cause such behaviors. For the dispositionist, that is, 'disposition' refers to the explanans, not the explananda (Mischel 1968, 4, 5f, 42 and 1973, 264; see also Flanagan 1991, 279; Doris 2002, 17, 66; Kamtekar 2004, 467f; Fleming 2006, 33f).

Furthermore, broad-based dispositions are inferred from behavioral signs in two main ways. One, 'trait theorists', as that term of art is used in personality theory, infer dispositions *directly* from behavioral signs.[7] Fred's dishonest behaviors, for instance, may be taken as evidence for a broad-based disposition

---

[7] Elsewhere, I shall use the term 'trait' in a non-technical, everyday sense.

to be dishonest, and the more that Fred engages in stereotypically dishonest behavior, the stronger his disposition. Prominent twentieth-century trait theorists include Allport (1937, 1966), Cattell (1950, 1957), Guilford (1959), and Loevinger (1957). (The example I gave above of the OIP schema was an example of such a direct, trait-theoretic inference.) And two, 'psychodynamic' or 'state' theorists infer dispositions *indirectly* from behavioral signs: perhaps Fred's dishonest behavior is the result of some feature of his basic personality core—resentment, say—which is operative regardless of Fred's situation. In that case, Fred's dishonest behavior could be interpreted as a manifestation of his underlying broad-based disposition of resentment, which leads him to assert control—say, by defying the authority figures who make him sit the exam—to compensate for his perception of himself as weak and ineffective. See, for instance, Freud 1953; MacFarlane and Tuddenham 1951; White 1964. (See Mischel 1968, 4–8 for discussion of both approaches.)[8]

Something common to both of these versions of the dispositionist OIP schema, and indeed to dispositionism in general, is that variations in Fred's behaviors that do not seem to manifest the disposition when expected are to be regarded as 'errors' to be factored out of the data from which we construct a profile of Fred's broad-based dispositions. On the trait theory, Fred's occasional 'failures' to cheat on tests in certain situations are to be interpreted as evidence of the relative 'weakness' of his dishonest disposition, and thus are 'averaged out' when we assess the overall strength of that disposition. When those 'anomalies' are averaged out, differences between the situations in which those anomalies occur are left aside. On the psychodynamic theory, variants in Fred's dishonesty are to be explained in terms of the dynamics of different broad-based complexes, tensions, and core personality 'problems'. Here too situational differences are set aside so as not to obscure how Fred's behavior is a manifestation of these core personality factors: Fred's behavior is to be understood as the vector sum of such dynamic factors as his defiance, resentment, passivity, etc., rather than as Fred's adjusting his behavior to suit the situation as he construes it. Fred's situation is an occasion for the display of such broad-based dispositions, and his cheating behavior is how that disposition happens to manifest itself on that occasion. In either case, then, the theorist does not see Fred as 'interacting' with the situations

---

[8] It is controversial, I should point out, whether the kind of approach that social psychologists reject is one that is fairly attributed to personality psychologists; Peterson and Seligman (2004, 10), to take but one example, feel strongly that it is not. I am not in a position to adjudicate this dispute. However, our task here is the much more modest one of elucidating what conceptions of personality the social psychologist means to rule out, whoever may have held them (if anyone), and so we can leave this (otherwise very important) dispute over labels to the psychologists.

in which we observe his behavior, or as behaving as he does because of how he interprets or 'encodes' those situations. Rather, situations function mainly as *occasions* on which Fred's broad-based dispositions are displayed, but they have no further explanatory significance. How Fred interprets, construes, or encodes the situations is therefore assigned no theoretical significance. Notice, then, that while dispositionism holds that behavior is a function of persons and situations, nonetheless situations, and the ways in which subjects interact with situations, serve mainly as variables to be factored out, and thus the dispositionist's commitment to interactionism seems a rather abstract and minimal one (see Mischel 1968, 281).

What is definitive of dispositionism, then, is its commitment to 'broad-based dispositions' as explanatory constructs, where a broad-based disposition is a behavioral disposition that operates relatively free of situational variables. All personality theorists agree that personality, as such, must be both stable and consistent; what sets dispositionists apart is the idea that consistency should be more or less independent of contextual and situational variables. Broad-based dispositions can thus be inferred from behavioral signs as interpreted by the observer. They are then attributed to the subject, and can be used to predict future behavior across a wide range of situations, also as interpreted by the observer.

8.1.3 Four Problems for Dispositionism

Despite any intuitive appeal that dispositionism might have, in experimental settings this observe-infer-predict schema has met with mixed results, at best. As Walter Mischel made clear in his landmark 1968 book *Personality and Assessment*, a review of twentieth-century personality theory, the empirical evidence for cross-situational consistency of alleged broad-based dispositions historically has been very poor. This had become apparent in numerous observational studies, and at least as early as 1928 when psychologists Hartshorne and May had found no significant correlations between a child's tendency to cheat on one sort of test by one method, and a tendency to cheat on other tests or by other methods, much less to pocket money found unattended in the classroom. They found, that is, that the predictions that should have been warranted given the alleged existence of broad-based dispositions, were not very reliable. Since cross-situational consistency is a crucial part of what it is for a disposition to be broad-based, the evidence for broad-based dispositions seems wanting. We should, I think, be cautious in generalizing from studies of children; but also I think that even studies like this one can point to deeper *structural* problems in the dispositionist model.

There are, in particular, four main structural defects in dispositionism that we should notice. The first is that, as we have seen, dispositionism lets the *observer* decide when behaviors and situations are the same. That is, dispositionism relies on 'nominal' classifications of behaviors and situations, in Mischel's phrase, rather than 'psychological' classifications made from the subject's point of view (Mischel and Shoda 1995; Shoda 1999; Mischel, Shoda, and Mendoza-Denton 2002, 51; see Doris 2002, 76f for discussion). But a single psychological attribute may cause behaviors that look very different to an observer, but look the same to the subject. For instance, a waiter who seems to behave very differently with different patrons may in fact be doing 'the same thing' in each case, such as trying to earn tips by adjusting his demeanor to his patrons' expectations (Ross and Nisbett 1991, 164, discussing Cialdini 1988; I return to this case below). By the same token, what may seem like similar behaviors to the observer may seem importantly different to the subject. As we saw earlier, George may pocket the unattended coin, thinking it just good luck, without ever being so much as tempted to *steal* money, much less to cheat on a test. We observers may suppose that pocketing the coin is the same sort of thing as stealing or even cheating, and for some purposes of our own we may even have reason to lump them together—perhaps we are interested in a whole class of 'dishonest' behaviors, such as lying, stealing, cheating, and money-pocketing, that have been on the rise lately. But since the *subjects* we observe may not group things in the way that we observers do, it should be little surprise if our predictions about how they will behave in other contexts should prove unlikely to succeed. In that case, what Hartshorne and May found was pretty much what we should have expected them to find, in children or adults. There is therefore no warrant for the inference from observations based on nominal classifications to cross-situational dispositions (see also Flanagan 1991, 291; Sreenivasan 2002, 50, 57–60; Annas 2003, 23; Kamtekar 2004, 460, 470f, 477). Nominal classifications put the focus on situation-transcendent dispositions, but in doing so, they seem to get the focus importantly wrong.

Second, dispositionism treats personality as relatively 'situation-free', rather than as one's distinctive style of interpreting and interacting with situations, and so treats situations as at most mildly interesting backgrounds against which the 'real' action takes place. But as the case of the abandoned coin shows, for the purpose of understanding a subject's personality, it is naive to suppose that we can even say what a behavior *is* without characterizing it in terms of the subject's adjusting to situations as he or she construes them. The notion of a 'behavior' is no more transparent than that of a 'situation', yet the very idea of a broad-based disposition depends on the supposed transparency of both notions.

Third, an observer's behaviors in attributing dispositions to a subject may reveal much about how that observer categorizes behaviors, but it may not be very revealing at all of the actual causes of the subject's behavior. Again, a nominal category of 'dishonest' acts—cheating, lying, pocketing found money—may be of great interest to observers, but there is no reason to assume that there is any single, cohesive psychological attribute, a disposition, that causes all the various behaviors in our nominal 'dishonesty' category—surely not on the grounds that such a category is one that *we observers* are interested in. To focus on broad-based dispositions is to treat situations as background, and therefore to leave out of our personality theory the distinctive patterns by which individuals construe the world around them. As a result, such an approach to personality theory essentially mistakes an *observer's* behaviors in classifying what a subject does, for some set of facts about the *subject's* personality (Mischel 1968, ch. 3).

Finally, and importantly, on a dispositionist approach, variance in a subject's behaviors—for instance, cheating by copying from a score-key but *not* by copying from a neighbor—is interpreted as 'error' or 'noise', a statistical irregularity liable to mislead us as to the subject's basic disposition. As a result, on this view such 'deviation' is to be averaged out, in order to obtain a more accurate picture of the subject's personality. However, suppose that a subject thinks that copying from a score-key, unlike copying from a neighbor, is a 'harmless' and 'victimless' kind of cheating, and for that reason cheats in the former way but not in the latter. That is a fact about how the subject construes the different behaviors and situations, and clearly it seems like a vital clue about the subject's personality—surely not the sort of thing to be explained away as an anomaly within a larger aggregate.

I shall turn in Chapter 10 to consider the implications of situationism for virtue theory, but already it should be clear that, where situationism is concerned, the main question for a theory of the virtues is whether it conceives of the virtues as broad-based, situation-free dispositions. It should also be clear that such a conception of the virtues is hardly the only one available. In particular, one could understand a virtue, such as 'generosity', as a psychological attribute in virtue of which one seeks certain sorts of goals, attends to certain features of situations, attaches certain kinds of salience to those features, etc.—that is, adjusts one's behaviors to one's world—in ways that we can endorse from within an ethical outlook in equilibrium.

Of course, this personality debate is an empirical one, so the question at issue is whether the evidence supports the existence of broad-based dispositions as significant determinants of behavior. It would be rather surprising if it did. After all, people generally do not learn to be trusting, say, irrespective of situational variables—irrespective of whether one is in Central Park in the middle of the night, say—but rather in a highly discriminatory way that adjusts to situational variables (Mischel 1968, 178). And in fact, there is considerable evidence against broad-based, situation-free dispositions. Mischel himself compiles a half century's worth of evidence against such dispositions—and in particular, against the cross-situational consistency of such dispositions—and in the next chapter I shall consider a further body of evidence that seems to yield the same conclusion. But before turning to that, we should complete our discussion of these two rival forms of personality theory by considering the positive theory that situationism recommends, a positive theory that we have already begun to glimpse here.

8.2 Situationism and Personality

It seems safe to say that the school of thought in empirical psychology we now call situationism first rallied as an identifiable movement with the appearance of Mischel's landmark 1968 book, *Personality and Assessment*. That movement initially arose mainly in reaction to many popular explanations of disturbing social phenomena in the twentieth century (including the era of Nazi genocide). Although research eventually leading to this paradigm had begun as early as the 1920s, it was in the 1960s that the movement really began to take shape, prompted in no small part by the shocking murder of Kitty Genovese in Queens, New York in 1963. What was surprising about this murder was that it happened out in the open, over a period of more than half an hour, and was witnessed by at least thirty-eight neighbors, none of whom intervened and only one of whom called the police, and then only after Ms. Genovese had already been mortally wounded (see Doris 2002, 28f for discussion and references). News outlets all agreed that this terrible murder was testimony to the apathy and alienation of New Yorkers—that is, that Ms. Genovese's neighbors had stood by and done nothing because that was 'the sort of people' they were. Such an explanation attributes to her neighbors some special non-helping disposition, like indifference or apathy, to explain their surprising behavior, since people are usually not disposed to stand by and do nothing when others are clearly in danger—they would, at least, report it. Both the attribution and its rationale, of course, are empirical claims, and some psychologists began to wonder whether such claims were true.

In an important 1968 study, psychologists Bibb Latané and John Darley argued that people's willingness to intervene in an emergency seemed to vary mainly with certain situational variables. They constructed an experiment in which male undergraduates at Columbia University were assigned to fill out questionnaires, some working by themselves, some alongside two other subjects, and some working alongside two confederates of the experimenters. As subjects filled out their questionnaires, smoke began to stream into the room through a vent, eventually filling the room (unbeknownst to the subjects, the smoke was fake). Latané and Darley found that 75% of subjects working alone reported the smoke, compared with 38% of the three-subject groups and only 10% of subjects working alongside impassive confederates. This result, they argued, suggests that the subjects' likelihood to intervene—even when their *own* well-being seemed to be at stake, please note!—depended not primarily on broad-based 'heroism' or 'apathy', but on whether or not the situation included other persons who hesitated or refused to get involved (Latané and Darley 1968; see Ross and Nisbett 1991, 41–4 for discussion).

Does this suggest that Kitty Genovese's neighbors were not apathetic, after all? That is not clear, but what seems undeniable is that the various details of a situation can have more to do with how people behave than do certain alleged behavioral dispositions that remain more or less constant across different situations. For these sorts of reasons, situationism holds that situations are far more powerful determinants of behavior than either dispositionism or common intuitions would lead us to expect. Therefore, the situationist's negative claim about dispositions is both a comparative and a relative one. It is *comparative*, because it holds that situations are a greater determinant of behavior than dispositions, and it is *relative* because 'greater' here is to be understood in relation to our pre-theoretical expectations.[9] As Lee Ross and Richard Nisbett put the point in their much-discussed review, *The Person and the Situation*, 'People are prone not only to be influenced by situational factors but also to underestimate the extent of such influence' (1991, 52; see also Vranas 2003, 3).

Moreover, the situationist does not argue that situations exert causal influence on behaviors *independent* of personal attributes. On the contrary, situations are determinants of behavior because situations must be classified as the agent perceives them. (As we shall see below, situationists are not behaviorists.) Whether and how agents arrive at 'readings' of a situation makes a tremendous difference as agents adjust their behaviors to the situation. So let's take a closer look now at how situationists think agents read their situations.

---

[9] In Chapter 10 I consider why those expectations come down so regularly on the side of dispositions, why they are often mistaken, and thus why it is appropriate that situationism should offer a corrective to them.

8.2.1 The Situationist 'Tripod'

Situation and Construal   According to social psychologists Lee Ross and Richard Nisbett (1991), situationism stands on three 'legs' of a conceptual 'tripod': situations, construal, and the dynamic relation between situation and person. First, as is familiar by now, the situationist places greater emphasis on the role of *situations* in explaining behavior than his traditional dispositionist rival has done. Second, and more important, the situationist holds that situations are important to behavior, *because construal is*: agents do not act within situations as against a motionless background, but attach meaning to situations and adjust their behaviors in accordance with those meanings. We arrive at judgments about our situation by interpreting them and giving them meaning, and for this reason agents in the same 'objective' circumstances often arrive at different judgments about what their situation is. To return to our earlier example, the 'same' situation of happening upon a lost coin may be for one person a case in which lost property needs to be returned and for another an innocent bit of good luck. It is only at a very superficial level, then, that we can call this the 'same' situation for both subjects, where the adjustment of their behavior to the situation is concerned.

This is an important point, because in many cases we assume that agents 'read' their situations as we do, and thus we wrongly infer that their seemingly odd behavior stems from some rather special disposition. Furthermore, to construe one's *situation* is also to construe one's *behavior* itself: in our earlier example, George does not see his behavior as dishonest because he does not see his situation as one in which honesty is even a relevant consideration (see Ross and Nisbett 1991, 13). 'To predict the behavior of a given person successfully', Ross and Nisbett conclude, 'we must be able to appreciate the actor's construal of the situation—that is, we must be able to appreciate the actor's construal of the situation as a whole' (11).

Evidence for the reality and importance of construal in behavior is manifold, and has been a major theme of personality research. For instance, studies have shown that people construe their level of welfare not in terms of their absolute level of opportunities and resources, but in comparison with the opportunities and resources available to others, and in comparison with their own at different times. In other words, people often assess their welfare by construing their opportunities and resources within a broader context, and adjust their level of subjective satisfaction accordingly (Ross and Nisbett 1991, 64f). Likewise, other studies have shown that people who are given incentives to engage in some activity (e.g. coloring with markers) are less inclined to engage in it for its own sake than those who have been given no incentives. Moreover, subjects paid to participate in some dull task (e.g. moving pegs around on a pegboard) are less likely to describe the task as interesting the more money they are paid to do it (65–7). Interestingly, the same level of wealth can be 'much' or 'little', and the same task 'interesting' or 'tedious', depending on how one construes it. Consequently, we do not experience situations as 'objective observers', but interpret situations within a highly complex context of judgments and interests. In fact, there is evidence that humans are not the only animals that construe: in one study, rats learned to select the dimmer of two lights in order to receive a reward, even when they were moved to new pairs of lights of different wattages from the lights on which they first learned the behavior. What the rats learned, that is, was not to select a light of a particular brightness, but to select a light with a property that obtained only in comparison with other lights—a brightness that was contextually defined (62).

Construal affects not only the judgments we make *about* objects in our experience, but also our very ideas about what those objects *are*. For instance, we take very different views of objects depending on different 'Gestalt' pictures of them. In one study, subjects were asked to rank different professions in order of prestige. Some subjects were told that their peers had ranked politicians at the top of the list, and others that their peers had ranked politicians at the bottom. The experimenters found that subjects' rankings of the profession of politician tended to follow those of their peers. Since all answers on the ranking exercise were known to be anonymous, it seems unlikely that subjects were seeking approval for agreeing with the rest of the group. Rather, it seems likely that the former set of subjects had taken their peers' answers as a cue that 'politician' was to be construed as, say, a Jefferson or Roosevelt figure, and that the latter had construed 'politician' as a scheming opportunist (Ross and Nisbett 1991, 69f). Construal of an object can impact one's assessment of the object, by changing what one takes oneself to be assessing in the first place.

Construals are also highly sensitive to the *order* in which we form certain impressions. Not only can early impressions be very difficult to change, but they can also shape the meanings we give to subsequent impressions (Ross and Nisbett 1991, 70f). Such 'Gestalt' pictures vary from person to person, and in fact some studies have found that subjects of opposed partisan leanings tend to interpret exactly the same filmstrip as evidence for their own partisan view (72–5). That variation is the source not only of diversity between persons, but also of much misunderstanding of each other, as numerous studies document the practice of subjects assuming that other subjects construe situations the same way they do, and labeling other subjects as differing in personality on account of their different behaviors (82–5). (I shall return to cases of the latter sort in Chapter 10.)

Finally, there is also some early evidence suggesting that construal activities can be detected in the brain. One striking and perplexing symptom of anorexia is the patient's believing that he is overweight, however dangerously thin he becomes. Recently, researchers Perminder Sachdev and Naresh Mondraty detected remarkable differences in brain activity on an MRI when anorexic women looked at pictures of other, healthy women and when the same women looked at pictures of themselves. In particular, the areas of the brain involved in visual perception and emotional processing became significantly less active when the women viewed their own photos. One tentative conclusion to draw from this early research is that anorexic women do not construe images of their own bodies in the same way that they construe the images of other women's bodies, because they do not apply the same visual and emotional processes to those different groups of images.[10]

Dynamic Interplay   The third 'leg' of the situationist 'tripod' has to do with the *dynamic interplay* between situations and behaviors, where these are considered from the agents' point of view. For instance, in one study experimenters assigned male undergraduates to engage in 10-minute telephone conversations with female undergraduates. In some cases, the male subjects were led to believe that they had been paired with a physically attractive female, and in other cases they were led to believe their partner was unattractive. Perhaps not surprisingly, the experimenters found that male subjects tended to rate their partners more personally engaging if they believed them to be attractive, and less so otherwise. However, the experimenters also presented separate recordings of either side of the conversation to a further group of subjects, and found that in the cases where the male subject had believed his partner to be attractive, auditors judged not only his side of the conversation as more engaging, but also the *female* subject's side (see Ross and Nisbett 1991, 152 for discussion). Situationists interpret this finding as showing that our construal of a situation can actually shape the situation to fit the construal: the male subjects who construed their situation as an uninteresting conversation did little to make the conversation engaging, and their partners followed suit, so that the conversation became, in fact, uninteresting (see Gilbert 1995, 128–31; see also 116–20, 126–41). Indeed, such dynamic interplay suggests that there is no sharp line between the person and the situation in the first place: personal

[10] This story was reported by D. Williams at www.time.com, 23 Oct. 2006.

attributes are shaped by situations, even as situations are shaped by personal attributes (see Lord 1982, 1076f).[11]

It is important to note that, because of its emphasis on construal and dynamic interplay, situationism is not a form of behaviorism. The behaviorists of the mid-twentieth century had insisted that 'the inner workings of the human mind could not be the proper subject matter of a scientific psychology', and thus concerned themselves exclusively with externally observable phenomena on the one hand, and on the other with a model of the mind as the accumulated sum of situational contingencies experienced in the past (Ross and Nisbett 1991, 59; see also Mischel and Shoda 1995, 251f; Doris 2002, 25). Social psychology is not behaviorist, because of its central focus on the importance of an agent's subjective construal of his or her situation as a determinant of behavior. This is an important point. As we saw above, the irony of dispositionism is that screening out information about situations compromises the quality of information about persons. The 'flip side' of that irony is that taking careful note of situational variables may tell us rather a lot about subjective psychological processes. So far from discounting the importance of individual personal differences and focusing on situations as raw 'stimuli', the situationist counts situations as persons perceive them according to their individual differences. As Mischel has put the point, 'It would be wasteful to create pseudo-controversies that pit person against situation in order to see which is more important' (1973, 254−6).

It is this appreciation of the importance of understanding behavior from the subject's point of view, rather than from the observer's, that has been a major impetus behind the massive surge of interest in the situationist paradigm over the past forty or so years. As we saw above, this is a watershed issue dividing dispositionists and situationists. Accordingly, as we saw above, Mischel has distinguished between what he calls the 'nominal' and the 'psychological' features of situations, that is, between those features of situations that are independent of how agents construe and attach salience to their situations, and those features that obtain in virtue of how the agent construes the situation, respectively. We can therefore characterize the dispositionist version of the OIP schema as predicting the consistency of *nominally* characterized behaviors across *nominally* characterized situations, and the situationist alternative as predicting the consistency of *psychologically* characterized behaviors across *psychologically* characterized situations, even where these are nominally different. Both sides agree that personality is stable and consistent, then, but differ crucially in their conceptions of those properties.

---

[11] See also Annas 2003, 22, who charges situationists with overlooking this point.

This is an important distinction because, as we have seen, it is the key to making sense of behavioral patterns that look like mere anomalies if we attend only to nominal individuations of behaviors and situations. As Mischel and Shoda (1995, 250) observe,

if situation units are defined in terms of features salient for the researcher but trivial for, or irrelevant to, the individuals studied, one cannot expect their behaviors to vary meaningfully across them, and the resulting pattern of behavior variation therefore would be unstable and meaningless. To discover the potentially predictable patterns of behavior variability that characterize individuals, the first step is to identify those features of situations that are meaningful to them and that engage their important psychological qualities (e.g. personality constructs and goals).

The foundational elements of personality theory, given the situationist 'tripod'—situations, construals, and the dynamic relations between them—are now in place. We can now consider how these elements come together to suggest a rival theory of personality.

8.2.2 Situationism and Personality Theory

These second and third legs—how we construe situations, and how construal and situation interact—also serve as the basis for a positive theory of personality to which many social psychologists are sympathetic (including Mischel and Ross and Nisbett). *Whatever* personality is, it must be something that remains fairly constant over time (stable), and which people take with them as they move through a wide range of situations (consistent). The disagreement between dispositionists and situationists concerns whether the situations and behaviors in terms of which these criteria are defined, are to be understood in nominal or in psychological terms. As we have seen, in place of broad-based dispositions the situationist offers psychological patterns of discriminating, construing, and otherwise interacting with situations. In order to construct a corresponding theory of personality, then, one must demonstrate that people interact with situations according to certain psychological patterns that are both stable over time and consistent across a range of situations. Such *patterns* are important for personality theory, because to say that people adjust their behaviors to their construals of situations, but do so without any order or reliability, is not to offer a personality theory, but to deny that there is any personality to theorize about. What, more precisely, are these psychological patterns, and is there any reason to think that they are consistent?

The basic 'units' of personality, on such a theory, are cognitive-affective processes by which agents interact with their environment. There are many such processes, and considered as types these processes are ones that all normal adult humans share. Humans learn how to construct situations and roles—for instance, what kind of thing a 'party' is, and what it is to 'host' a party—and to adapt their behaviors to those situations so as to bring about beneficial outcomes. Humans are able to encode and categorize events and persons—as 'rude', 'aggressive', or 'kind' behaviors and persons—and thus to make inferences about the intentions of others. Humans learn to expect events to have certain outcomes, including the outcomes of their own behaviors as well as the outcomes of other sorts of events. Humans also attach values to outcomes, hoping to bring some outcomes about and to avoid certain other outcomes. And humans are able to different degrees to regulate themselves by setting standards, delaying gratification, making and executing plans over time, and so on. (See Mischel 1973, 265–76.)

While these basic processes are common to all humans, humans differ considerably with respect to them—how we construct situations and roles (e.g. how am I to behave at a party?), how we encode events and persons (e.g. what do I count as 'rude' behavior?), what we expect certain acts to produce (e.g. will I be embarrassed if I do this?), what we hope to bring about (e.g. is it important for me to be popular?), and how skilled we are at planning, executing plans, and regulating ourselves (e.g. how good am I at imagining the outcomes of certain behaviors?).

Because people differ in all these ways—for instance, in their 'social intelligence', such as their abilities to formulate plans and strategies for achieving goals—people therefore differ in how they specify the content of their superficially similar goals, as well as in what they are able to do in pursuit of them. Likewise, people differ in what goals they adopt; they also differ in how they adopt and how they pursue them, depending on differences in their ability to control aggression or delay gratification, say. People also tend to differ in their habits of construing situations and actions. For instance, people tend to construe situations and actions differently, owing to differing personal histories that have led them to make very different associations with nominally similar situations (e.g. family gatherings as enjoyable or angst-filled). People also have different self-conceptions—as leaders, followers, at the mercy of fate, etc.—that shape their construal habits; likewise, people often monitor their behavior according to group identities, such as gender, ethnicity, profession, etc. The personality differences between us, then, consist largely in the different goals and priorities we have, how we conceive of ourselves and others, the meanings we attach to different situations, our various 'executive' practical skills, features of situations to which we attend, and of course, the unique whole that is the sum of all these diverse parts and their interrelations with each other (see Ross and Nisbett 1991, 164–7 for discussion).

Do these differences fall into patterns that we can recognize as personality? Before we can begin to find psychological patterns, we must first be able to identify behavioral patterns. Let's examine these two kinds of pattern in turn.

Behavioral Patterns: 'If... Then... Signatures'   When we understand the above cognitive-affective processes as causes of behavior, *and* when we attend to the features of situations in which behaviors occur rather than factoring them out as background, behaviors that otherwise look like randomness and error begin to reveal certain intelligible patterns. This is because many actions that look dissimilar to an outside observer may in fact be regarded as instances of the same thing from the agent's point of view. As Ross and Nisbett point out, this is particularly the case for diverse actions directed towards a single goal. They note a researcher on the phenomenon of social influence who reported his observations of

the highest-earning waiter in a particular restaurant for a period of time to find out what it was that he did. What was most notable about the waiter's behavior, it turned out, was that he didn't do anything consistently—except seek to maximize his tips. With families, he was warm and homey, winking at the children and anticipating their desires. With adolescents on dates, he was haughty and intimidating. And with older women eating alone he was solicitous and confidential. The 'consistency' in these diverse behaviors lay only in the energetically and thoughtfully pursued professional goal of the waiter.   (1991, 164, discussing Cialdini 1988)

They also cite other studies suggesting that '[d]ifferences in the centrality and importance of achievement—especially career achievement'—are important 'both in trying to understand individual differences within a culture, and... in trying to understand differences between cultures', and devote considerable space to discussing the importance of such attitudes in understanding cultural differences (Ross and Nisbett 1991, 164 and ch. 7). There is also evidence suggesting that differences in needs or goals can have a significant impact on how one construes situations and actions; for instance, 'a given dinner party may be a recreational situation for most guests, a social achievement test for the nervous host, and a self-promotion opportunity for the local politician in attendance' (165). By paying attention to construal, otherwise random-looking behaviors appear to take on a kind of order and pattern.

As Mischel puts the point, inferences about psychological causes must attend to the complex interaction between behavior and situation. When situations come out of the shadows of the background, we begin to detect behavioral patterns that Mischel calls 'if... then... signatures' (see Mischel 1968, 183f, 189; Mischel and Shoda 1995, 258; Kammrath, Mendoza-Denton, and Mischel 2005; see also Mischel 1973, 278). It is important to note that an if... then ... signature is not *itself* a personality attribute (*pace* Doris 2002, 77, 85)—in which case it would of course be a rather fragmentary attribute—but is instead *behavioral evidence for* consistent personality attributes (e.g. Mischel and Shoda 1995, 258). In our simple case of the tip-seeking waiter, we can derive certain if... then ... regularities from observations of his behavior in various situations: *if* the waiter is serving a lone older woman, *then* he is solicitous; *if* the waiter is serving a family with small children, *then* he is playful and homey; and so on. If we think of behavior as primarily caused by broad-based, situation-independent dispositions, then our waiter's behaviors look puzzling and 'all over the map'. Likewise, if we regard such signatures as dispositions themselves, then with respect to these behaviors anyway our waiter is no more than a bundle of narrow and disconnected dispositions. But if such signatures can be taken as evidence of broader goals, priorities, construals, expectancies, and practical skills, then we can study such if... then ... signatures in hopes of ascertaining consistent ways in which the waiter reads such situations and hopes to bring about certain kinds of outcomes in them. Indeed, unless Donald Davidson has written in vain, interpreting the behaviors of others *must* begin with the search for such patterns. And the information we gain from studying our waiter's if... then ... patterns does seem to tell us something interesting about one aspect of his individual personality.

Psychological Patterns: A Cognitive-Affective Personality Taxonomy

I turn now, in what remains of this chapter, to evidence for thinking of personality in terms of the sorts of consistent goals and attitudes of which if... then ... signatures can be taken as evidence. Cognitive-affective personality theory shifts our focus from inferred broad-based dispositions to complex cognitive patterns, and from situation-free agents to complex interactions between situations on the one hand and cognitions and behaviors on the other (Mischel 1973, 265). Rather than inferring situation-free dispositions from nominally characterized behaviors in nominally characterized situations treated as fixed background, this approach infers cognitive-affective personality constructs from behaviors given a situation-rich characterization from the agent's own point of view. As Mischel and Shoda (1995, 246) put the point,

When personality is conceptualized as a stable system that mediates how the individual selects, construes, and processes social information and generates social behaviors, it becomes possible to account simultaneously for both the invariant qualities of the underlying personality and the predictable variability across situations in some of its characteristic behavioral expressions.

Because the evidence for the stability of basic cognitive-affective capacities is good (see Mischel 1968, 88, 281ff, and ch. 2), and because such capacities can cause nominally disparate but psychologically consistent behaviors in a wide range of situations, this personality model can therefore account for personality in terms of enduring cognitive-affective constructs. Of course, there is a world of difference between broad-based dispositions and these consistent cognitive-affective capacities. A taxonomy of broad-based dispositions is meant to categorize those personal attributes that 'spill forth', so to speak, regardless of situational variables. A cognitive-affective taxonomy, by contrast, is meant to categorize personal attributes that consist in interaction with situational variables. The situationist's positive thesis, then, is that such an approach is the key to understanding the nature of personality. As Ross and Nisbett (1991, 167) put the point,

The personality theory of the future will surely continue to stress the importance of understanding people's goals, competencies, strategies, construals, and self-conceptions. Research along these lines is likely to turn up a great many interesting facts about the determinants of human behavior and to tell us a great deal about the nature and degree of consistency to be expected of different kinds of people in different kinds of situations.

We have, then, two rival taxonomies of personality, one understanding personality in terms of broad-based, situation-free dispositions, and another in terms of practical cognitive-affective processes that discriminate situations. Which taxonomy is identifying real psychological causes of behavior? There are three main types of evidence to consider. We have already seen samples from one body of evidence that testifies to the considerable power of various cognitive-affective constructs in predicting and explaining behavior, and numerous studies have examined the power of such constructs for understanding the nature of learning, delay of gratification, personality change, and so on.[12] A second body of evidence, of which I discuss representative samples in Chapter 9, points to the failures of dispositionism to predict cross-situationally consistent behavior. And a third body of evidence suggests that when situational variables are factored into the study of behavior, and when those behaviors and situations are individuated psychologically, from the subject's point of view, we begin at last to find cross-situational consistency. I close this chapter with a discussion of one such study by Charles Lord (1982) that has proven extremely influential.[13]

---

[12] For a review of this literature, one could start with Mischel 1968; Mischel 1973; and Ross and Nisbett 1991.

[13] Examples of psychological research drawing positively on the findings of Lord 1982 include Mischel and Peake 1982; Sherman and Fazio 1983; Mischel 1984; Champagne and Pervin 1987; Cone 1991; Gould and Weil 1991; Sedikedes and Skowronski 1991; Highhouse and Harris 1993; Shoda

8.3 Idiographic Predictions of Consistency

Studies of gratification delaying in children have shown that how children imagine some enticing object (e.g. whether the child visualizes a pretzel stick as a tasty snack or as part of a tiny log cabin) has a significant impact on their ability to wait before seizing the object (Mischel 1973, 260f). Such results suggest that subjects vary in their construal of stimuli, in ways that greatly affect such 'executive' skills as gratification delaying, and thus behavior. In that case, what stimulus confronts an agent—and thus what situation an agent is in, and what behavior a subject displays—depends on how the agent construes the stimulus, and thus his situation and his behavior. Therefore, in testing the consistency of a subject's behavior across situations one should enroll the subject in the process of identifying stimulus conditions and therefore individuating situations. For instance, if I am tidy about my lecture notes but messy about my desk, then whether my behaviors are 'inconsistent' depends on my judgments about the similarity or dissimilarity about such situations, where conscientiousness is concerned, say. Perhaps I see the one but not the other as affecting my ability to do my job well, and where conscientiousness is concerned, it is job performance that I care about most. How would such a test of consistency work, and would it actually detect the consistency of personality?

Such an approach would require the researcher to measure consistency relative to the standard by which the agent himself classifies situations and behaviors. That kind of approach would therefore be an instance of what psychologists call an 'idiographic' approach: what counts as a failure to behave consistently depends on the subject's own standards; for instance, consistency of conscientious behavior is to be determined according to one's own standards about situations in which conscientiousness is important (see Ross and Nisbett 1991, 163). By contrast, a 'nomothetic' approach would factor out such individual variables. On such an approach, the observer may assume his or her own standards of consistency, or (less radically) may 'average out' different points of view about standards of consistency across a population of subjects. For instance, the relevance of desktop tidiness, where conscientiousness is concerned, could be determined by averaging the various levels of such relevance that members of the subject population assign to it. So an important question for situationist personality theory is whether idiographic or nomothetic approaches generate better predictions of consistent behavior. That is, when

et al. 1994; Williams and Cervone 1998; Tett and Guterman 2000; Ratneshwar *et al.* 2001; Alison *et al.* 2002; Griffith *et al.* 2002; English and Griffith 2004; Griffith *et al.* 2006; Church *et al.* 2008.

we factor *in* situations, *as* the individual subject construes them, can we make better predictions about that subject's behavior in those situations?

In an important 1982 study, recently discussed by Gopal Sreenivasan (2002, 64–6), Charles Lord found that idiographic measures do in fact yield better predictions of cross-situational consistency than 'averaging-out', nomothetic measures. Lord was impressed by Mischel's view that there is 'reciprocal interaction' between person and situation, on which, Lord said, 'The situation is viewed as just as much a function of the person as the person is of the situation', and drew a natural conclusion:

> The notion that behavior is a function of the situation as perceived or interpreted by the individual has, of course, long been a basic premise of social psychology. Thus, in dealing with the problem of cross-situational variability in behavior, we must discover how each individual interprets situations... (1982, 1077)

So Lord set out (1) to ascertain subjects' individual assessments of similarity, with respect to conscientiousness, for a range of simple situations, (2) to assess subjects' behaviors in those situations, and (3) to determine whether (1) provided a good basis for predictions about (2). In other words, how consistent would a subject be across different situations calling for conscientious behavior (e.g. tidiness, punctuality), where researcher and subject had *agreed* as to what situations called for conscientious behavior (see Sreenivasan 2002, 61f)?

The experiment focused on such 'conscientious' behaviors as tidiness and punctuality, and included such different, potentially conscientiousness-relevant contexts as personal appearance, tidy and thorough class notes, keeping a tidy closet, keeping a tidy desk, handing in assignments in a timely fashion, etc. The experiment ascertained the subjects' individual assessments of situational similarity by four different methods:

> a. *Direct similarity ratings*: first, subjects ranked situation pairs on a scale of similarity ranging from opposite to same, where conscientiousness is concerned. For instance, a subject might rate personal appearance and note-keeping as similar with respect to conscientiousness, but neither as similar to handing in assignments on time.

> b. *Goal satisfaction similarities*: subjects also grouped situations as similar or dissimilar according to how instrumental they took them to be in achieving certain important goals, such as being well liked. For instance, a student might consider conscientiousness about appearance and assignments, but perhaps not closet tidiness, similar as means to being well liked.

c. *Self-template similarities*: third, subjects described situations by the kinds of 'template' traits involved in them (e.g. tidy closets are for 'tidy people'), and rated themselves for possession of such traits (e.g. how 'tidy a person' a subject considered himself to be); researchers then made correlations between the template description (that a tidy person should have a tidy closet, say) and the self-ranking (how tidy a person the subject considered himself to be).

d. *Template-template similarities*: finally, subjects described situations by the kinds of template traits involved in them (e.g. tidy closets are for 'tidy people'), and researchers grouped situations for subjects according to shared template traits (e.g. what other behaviors, like keeping a tidy closet, are for 'tidy people'). (1982, 1077f)

Each method offered subjects a different way to rank the similarity of situations. The very diversity of the methods offered is especially significant, since it is an important question whether people differ in their *styles* of determining similarities between situations.

Lord and his assistants then observed subjects' behaviors over a period of months and assessed, using a standardized measure and trained assessors, subjects' 'conscientiousness' in the various situations (e.g. punctuality about handing in assignments, tidiness of closet, etc.). Lord then compared the behavioral data from these observations with the subjects' four sets of similarity rankings, in two ways. First, he compared the behavioral data for each subject with that subject's *individual* set of similarity rankings, to determine whether a subject's behaviors were similar across situations that that subject had grouped as similar. This first measurement of consistency, then, was idiographic. Second, he compared the behavioral data for each subject with the *average* of all the subjects' similarity rankings; this measurement was 'consensual' or nomothetic (1982, 1077–9).

The question for Lord, then, was whether the idiographic comparisons would be more predictive of consistency than the nomothetic comparisons—and they were. For a similarity ranking to have a predictive success, that ranking would have to be correlated with a higher level of conscientiousness across similar situations (from the individual subject's or the 'average' subject's point of view) than across dissimilar situations. Lord found that goal satisfaction similarities and self-template similarities were predictive of consistency, on average, when consistency was measured idiographically, but *not* when it was measured nomothetically. He also found that while template-template similarities were predictive in both the idiographic and the nomothetic versions, on average, still the idiographic version was the more predictive of the two.

Finally, he found that while direct similarity ratings were not predictive in the idiographic version, on average, they were not predictive in the nomothetic version either (1982, 1082f).[14] For all four ranking styles, then, an idiographic approach was at least as predictive as a nomothetic approach. This suggests that if we want to assess consistency across situations, we should enroll the subject in the identification of situations with respect to the behavioral factor in question.

That is only the beginning; there are three further points about Lord's findings that are important to note (see 1982, 1085f). One, in the goal satisfaction similarities rankings, only two goals were used, and while neither goal on its own was a good predictor of consistency, prediction improved when the two goals were *summed*. So it seems that the more goals are used to rank situations as similar with respect to goal satisfaction, and the more hierarchically organized they are, the greater the predictive power. Or, more simply, the more we know about what someone wants, the more consistency we may find, at least for individuals who subjectively individuate situations in terms of goals. Two, while a ranking's predictive success was based on its *average* success for all subjects, Lord found that the various methods of similarity ranking tended to yield strong predictions for some subjects but not for others, and this suggests that people do indeed differ in their situation-individuating styles. It is therefore very interesting that, three, each of the four similarity ranking methods was such that there were subjects for whom it predicted remarkably well. In other words, in general the more we know about a subject's individuation style, the better we can predict his behavior.

So there is evidence suggesting that idiographic approaches to cross-situational consistency outperform nomothetic approaches, and this suggests that 'similar pairs [of situations] must be tailored according to each individual's perceptions' (Lord 1982, 1083), just as the situationist expected. 'It is becoming clear' therefore, as Lord says, 'that the question of whether individuals will show consistency across situations has given way to a new interest in how individuals think about and classify situations' (1982, 1087; see also Mischel 1973, 258).

Conclusion

My aims in this chapter have been threefold. First, I have taken a fresh start by examining the basic tenets of situationism in social psychology. In particular,

---

[14] It seems interesting to me that the least successful ranking method, on average, was also the most 'abstract' one, i.e. the one that did not provide subjects with a 'frame of reference' (Lord 1982, 1085).

I have focused on the rivalry between situationism and the once-dominant dispositionist paradigm it set out to replace, which understands personality in terms of broad-based, situation-free behavioral dispositions. I have also focused on the sort of positive alternative personality theory that situationism suggests. I have thus emphasized, second, that situationism suggests, after all, a positive personality theory, and its own conception of the stable and consistent personality attributes that cause behavior. And third, I have thereby taken a step towards a virtue theory that is consistent with such theories of personality, namely a virtue theory that understands the virtues as constellations of practical cognitive-affective processes by which one acts for the right goals, etc. More precisely, I have sketched an empirical theory of personality that indicates that such a virtue theory would be in touch with psychological reality, and suggests that 'traits' as such a virtue theory conceives of them are or should be part of the social psychologist's taxonomy.

I shall say more about such a virtue theory—about which several philosophical psychologists are still skeptical—in Chapter 10. But first, I turn in the next chapter to consider a few samples from a considerable body of experimental evidence concerning the cross-situational (in)consistency of broad-based dispositions, and in particular to argue in favor of the situationist interpretation of that evidence. If I am right about that evidence, then the future for virtue theory will most likely lie in a cognitive-affective conception of the virtues.

9

Situations and Dispositions: Examining the Evidence

In the previous chapter we examined two broad rival personality theories, dispositionism and an alternative suggested by situationism. Dispositionism takes the basic unit of personality to be broad-based dispositions, that is, temporally stable dispositions to behave in certain ways across a wide range of situations, with relative independence from variables between different situations that elicit the disposition. On this theory, situations are regarded as the background against which personality displays itself, and so situations serve only as occasions on which broad-based dispositions cause one behavior or another. Situationism, by contrast, takes the basic units of personality to be a variety of practical cognitive and affective processes, such as pursuing goals, attaching salience to certain features of situations, interpreting the intentions of others, valuing certain outcomes, and so on, and adjusting one's behaviors to situations accordingly. This theory focuses on how agents construe situations and give them meaning, and therefore on the important explanatory role of such construals in the agent's adjustment of his or her behavior to the situation, as the agent 'reads' that situation. I considered two types of evidence in favor of the situationist theory: one, evidence testifying to the explanatory power of various cognitive-affective processes, and two, evidence suggesting that the consistency of personality is more apparent when we adopt the agent's own classification of his or her situations and behaviors than when we classify these from some other point of view.

In this chapter I examine a third type of evidence: a body of experiments that suggest that the notion of broad-based dispositions offers little success in predicting behavior across even apparently subtle variations between situations, and that the results of the experiments can be better understood in terms of situation construal. Recently, the interpretation of this evidence has been the subject of enormous philosophical controversy. Consequently, it would be worthwhile to begin at the beginning here as well, examining that evidence and then the competing interpretations of it. In the first section, I examine the methodology behind these experiments, in order to appreciate better the burden of proof that rests on one who attempts either to prove or to disprove the cross-situational consistency of broad-based dispositions. Then in §9.2 I review a small but representative sample of four such experiments, and in §9.3 I consider and reject a number of objections to the situationist interpretations of the findings of these experiments. I argue here that the evidence favors situationism, and a cognitive-affective personality theory over a dispositionist one. Then in the next chapter I argue for Hard Virtue Theory—on which a virtue is an *excellent* pattern of cognitive-affective processes—as part of the natural development of cognitive-affective personality theory within philosophical and moral psychology.

Because some philosophical psychologists have claimed so persistently that the situationist paradigm in empirical psychology is bad news for virtue theory, most of the alternative interpretations of the experiments that I consider have come as defensive replies from virtue theorists. However, because the situationist in social psychology understands personality in terms of individuals' distinctive patterns of cognitive-affective processes and capacities, it should be clear already that at least *some* interesting theory of the virtues should be consistent with situationist research, even *given* the situationist's interpretation of that research. But more than that, my argument in this part of the book is that virtue theory—and in particular, an Aristotelian Hard Virtue Theory—should take encouragement not in spite of the apparent findings of situationists in social psychology, but because of those findings. But first, in this chapter, we need to take a look at those findings.

9.1 How to Test Broad-Based Dispositions for Cross-Situational Consistency

In the previous chapter we considered Latané and Darley's smoke-filled room experiment, which was designed to show that situational variables have a much greater impact on behavior than we ordinarily suppose. That experiment is in fact instructive for appreciating the essential features of any well-designed experiment to test for the cross-situational consistency of allegedly broad-based dispositions. Before reviewing a further battery of such experiments, we would do well to consider just what those experiments are meant to show, and how they mean to show it (see also Sreenivasan 2002, 64). Doing so, I believe, reveals a number of problems for some recent interpretations of those experiments. In particular, I want to consider five essential features of experiments on broad-based dispositions.

First, the experiment must propose some broad-based disposition that is presumed to be widespread in the subject group, either on account of the membership of that group in particular, or (more commonly) on account of that group's being a random, representative sample of the more general population. In the former case, one may rely on previous observations of behaviors, self-reports, etc., in order to establish a hypothesis about the disposition in question; in the latter case, one may rely on intuitive suppositions about what dispositions would be likely among subjects. The experimenter can leave these suppositions intuitive, please note, as long as those suppositions are likely to be shared by dispositionists, whose theory is in question after all. For instance, recall from Chapter 8 the common opinion that Kitty Genovese's neighbors in Queens must have been exceptional, since they did not fit the intuitive supposition that there is (otherwise) a widely distributed disposition to intervene in an obvious and heinous emergency. The experimenter himself need have no view about such dispositions or their distribution; the only disposition that is needed is one that the dispositionist (lay or professional, as the case may be) would presume likely among the subject group, such as everyday compassion, say.

Because the disposition in question is presumed to be widespread in the subject group, it should not be one that takes greater heroism or specialty than we should expect in the typical member of the subject group; it should be a disposition of a fairly 'common or garden' variety for the subjects in question. The disposition in question in the Latané and Darley experiment discussed above is the presumably widespread disposition to intervene in emergencies that pose a serious risk to at least one's own well-being—not to take heroic measures, but perhaps (say) to tell someone else in the building about the smoke. It seems reasonable to suppose that if such a disposition exists, it would probably be fairly common in a random group of individuals such as those in Latané and Darley's subject groups.

Second, the experiment must present subjects with a situation that, intuitively, elicits the disposition in question, such as filling a room with smoke as if from a nearby fire. It seems reasonable to suppose that if dispositions to basic self-preserving behavior are common in a subject group, then a room's filling with smoke should be the sort of situation in which that disposition would be called into play for those subjects. These two features, then, involve giving the disposition a fair chance to show itself in the subjects' behaviors.

Third, the experiment must identify some further sort of situational factor or factors, and test for any correlation between them and the subjects' behaviors when the eliciting conditions are held constant. In the Latané and Darley experiment, these factors were the presence or absence of other naive subjects and impassive confederates. If a disposition to self-preserving behavior is broad-based, and therefore operant in relative independence of the various situational factors that serve as the background of personality and behavior, then it stands to reason that the introduction of such situational factors should have a fairly small impact on the behaviors of subjects with that disposition (presumably, most of them).

Fourth, although the situational factors *are* intended potentially to exert some pressure against the elicited behavior,[1] they should exert *less* pressure against the behavior, relative to dispositionist expectations, than the eliciting conditions exert in its favor. In the Latané and Darley experiment, the presence of other subjects, and especially the presence of impassive confederates, may exert some pressure against springing into action when the smoke pours in; after all, one does not like to seem to 'lose one's cool'. However, while none of us would deny that people may fail in large numbers to display an elicited behavior in the face of *great* pressure against it, the mere presence of others hardly seems a 'great' pressure, at least if dispositionism is true. Indeed, prior to the experiment one might have doubted that such a variable would exert any pressure at all. It is therefore reasonable to suppose that billowing smoke elicits basic self-preserving behavior—leaving the room, say, or just inquiring—more strongly than the presence of another subject or confederate exerts pressure against it. So if the broad-based disposition to self-preserving behavior is common in the subject group, and if the situation is one in which that disposition is the main one elicited, then self-preserving behavior should be the norm in the subject group, whether the subjects are observed on their own or in groups.

The third and fourth factors are important because the crucial issue is one of *proportion*: if subjects fail to display the strongly elicited behavior in the face of intuitively weaker opposing situational factors, this failure is one that we would intuitively find out of proportion to the pressure exerted by those factors (see Doris 2002, 29; 2005, 657; Gilbert 1995, 104). So if behavior varies significantly with situational factors given the same eliciting conditions, this seems to be strong evidence that the notion of a broad-based disposition is an unsound basis for predictions of cross-situational consistency of behavior.

Finally, behaviors, situations, and variables within the situations are *not* to be classified from the subject's point of view. If dispositions are broad-based,

---

[1] In technical parlance, the situational factors must be 'diagnostic'; see Doris 2002, 19.

then they should operate in relative independence of variations between different eliciting conditions, and agents are not to be viewed as adjusting their behaviors between such situations. Situations-cum-construals are therefore to be assigned no significant predictive or explanatory role. If smoke billowing into a room is reasonably considered to elicit a self-preserving disposition, and if dispositions are otherwise situation-free, then the point of view from which we classify features of the situation as being the same or held constant could just as well be that of any reasonable outside observer. That is how the dispositionist does it, and it is the dispositionist's theory that is being tested.

Of course, as we saw in the previous chapter, a situation in which smoke is billowing into a room where one is alone need not be the same situation, *from the subject's point of view*, as a situation in which the same subject is surrounded by other people who do not seem worried about the smoke. The reactions of others in the latter case could perhaps serve as a cue for the seriousness of the apparent risk, and thus could lead one to assess the risk as less serious than if one had been alone and received no such cues. The situationist wagers that a subject's construal of the situation in the light of such situational factors could exert a *greater* impact on the subject's behavior than the 'objective' eliciting conditions do. As the rats in the construal study mentioned in the previous chapter responded to the brightness of a light not as an absolute property but as a property the light has only in a context including other lights, to a far greater extent humans experience and construe the various features of situations as parts of the larger situation as a whole. That, the situationist says, is why we should expect the experiments to yield little evidence for alleged behavioral dispositions that remain more or less constant in the face of different situational variables. If the situationist's wager pays off, then it would seem that construal is a major cause of behavior. And that in turn would have crucial implications for personality theory: given the important role of construal in behavior, focusing on such cognitive-affective processes as an individual's construal styles should provide more insight into his personality than focusing on his alleged broad-based dispositions.

The experiments in social psychology that I discuss in this chapter are, in the first instance, tests of the role of alleged broad-based dispositions vs. situational factors as predictors of behavior. Social psychologists then take the results, which favor situational factors as predictors, to indicate that construal is an important cause of behavior, because what situation one is in depends on how (and whether) one construes it. Finally, personality theorists then take *that* result to suggest a theory of the personality as consisting in various cognitive-affective units.

I turn now to some further experiments of this sort. The body of such experiments is enormous, so I shall confine my discussion to four representative and much-discussed experiments. I then consider the broader interpretation of the findings of these experiments.

9.2 Putting Dispositions to the Test: Four Representative Experiments

9.2.1 What the Experiments Found

As Latané and Darley found in their smoke-filled room experiment, other experiments also have suggested that situational factors have an impact on intervention behaviors. Consider two other similar studies.

In a study by Darley and Latané (1968), subjects speaking to each other over an intercom heard another participant (a confederate) fall into what sounded like an epileptic seizure. Darley and Latané found that 85% of subjects who believed they were the only listeners intervened; however, 62% intervened when they believed that there was one other listener, and only 31% intervened when they believed there were four other listeners. Subjects who believed they were the only listeners also tended to intervene more quickly than the other subjects.

Likewise, in a study by Latané and Rodin (1969), subjects filling out a questionnaire were presented with what sounded like a female experimenter taking a nasty fall behind a partition, groaning in pain, and complaining that she was unable to get up. Seventy percent of solitary bystanders offered assistance, whereas only 7% of subjects intervened when they were in the company of an impassive confederate. Social psychologists interpret the results in these two cases as indicating that people in groups tend to pause to gather cues from one another about the appropriate course of action in the situation, and when they do so, they are faced with other people also hesitating before acting, which prompts even further delays (see Ross and Nisbett 1991, 41−4 and Doris 2002, 32f for discussion of these two studies).

I come now to the two most famous, and most controversial, experiments in this genre. One of these, conducted by Darley and Batson (1973), was deliberately modeled on popular readings of the parable of the Good Samaritan. Subjects at Princeton Theological Seminary (for the sake of extra irony) were interviewed individually and then told to report to another group awaiting their arrival, but en route, each passed a striking and very unusual sight on the beautiful Princeton campus: a confederate slumped in a doorway, clearly in distress, head down, coughing, and groaning. Now, at the end of their interviews, some subjects had been told that they had time to spare before their meeting with the other group, others that they were just on time, and others that they were already running a little behind. Darley and Batson found that 63% of subjects offered assistance to the confederate when they believed they had time to spare, whereas 45% helped when they believed they were right on time, and only 10% helped when they believed they were running late. One explanation of this controversial case is that such variables as how hurried one feels can have an important impact on how one attends to various features of one's situation, such as the presence of others who may be in distress, as well as to how one attaches practical salience to those features. Indeed, Darley and Batson reported that subsequent interviews with subjects revealed not that hurried subjects simply noticed but ignored the victim's distress, but that many of them 'did not perceive the scene...as an occasion for ethical decision' (see Doris 1998, 510f; Merritt 2000, 510; Ross and Nisbett 1991, 48–50).

Finally, Stanley Milgram (1963; see also 1974) made an alarming discovery that not even he had expected: under modest pressure, most people will deliver what they believe to be extremely painful, even dangerous electric shocks to others, if the situation is just so. In Milgram's experiment, pairs of subjects and confederates met with a psychologist claiming to be studying the effects of punishment on learning. The psychologist then 'randomly' chose the confederate to play the role of 'learner' in the study and the naive subject to play the role of 'teacher'. The confederate learner was then led into another room, where the naive teacher watched as he was strapped into a chair, dabbed with conductive gel ('to prevent burns'), and fitted with an electrode; the teacher was also given a convincing, low-level shock through a similar electrode, as a demonstration. The teacher was then led back to the other room and seated at a console with thirty switches increasing in 15-volt increments from 15 to 450 volts, with various switches labeled from 'slight shock' to 'danger: severe shock', and at 435 volts, simply 'XXX'.

The teacher was then asked to read a series of word groups to the learner as part of a memorization exercise, and to deliver an electric shock to the learner for each wrong answer, including non-replies, in increasing increments. Although the confederate learner received no shocks at all, the naive teacher heard a pre-recorded series of responses to the course of shocks, from expressions of discomfort (15–135 volts), to cries of serious distress and worries about a heart condition (150–285 volts), explicit withdrawal of consent to participate (300–315 volts), hysterical screaming about a heart condition (330 volts), and finally, complete silence (345–450 volts). Teachers who told the researcher that they did not wish to continue, or wished to check on the learner, were told, in a firm but even voice, on the first occasion to 'please continue', on the second that the experiment required them to continue, on the third that their continuing was 'absolutely essential', and on the fourth that they had no choice but must go on. Thereafter, balking teachers were considered non-compliant and released.

Before conducting the experiments, Milgram's surveys of intuitive expectations of the results showed that even professional psychologists predicted extremely low rates of compliance, if any compliance at all, with the learning 'experiment'. To everyone's surprise, approximately two-thirds of the 'teacher' subjects complied with requests to continue administering shocks to the 'learner' all the way to 450 volts. Far from a one-time result, this experiment has been duplicated with widely differing subject groups, in laboratory settings of very high and very low visible prestige, and in multiple countries around the world, yet despite these variables, roughly two-thirds compliance has remained a constant result (see Doris 2002, 45 and references).

Please note that 'compliance' here does not mean 'willing agreement'. On the contrary, Milgram's subjects showed signs of extreme anxiety and even emotional trauma: 'I observed a mature and initially poised businessman enter the laboratory', Milgram wrote, 'smiling and confident. Within 20 minutes he was reduced to a twitching, stuttering wreck, who was rapidly approaching a point of nervous collapse' (Milgram 1963, 377, cited in Doris 2002, 43). In fact, when non-compliance was made easier, or compliance made more difficult, levels of compliance declined significantly. In variations of the experiment, compliance fell to 30% when the teacher was required to shock the learner by placing his hand on an electric plate; compliance fell to 21% when the researcher gave instructions by phone rather than in person; almost no subjects gave the maximum shock when they were able to choose the levels themselves; and so on (see Ross and Nisbett 1991, 32–5, 52–8; Flanagan 1991, 298f; Doris 2002, 39–51; Vranas 2005, 6–9).

Compliance in this experiment thus seems to vary with alterations in the situation. This is an important point. Although attention often focuses on the *rates* of the behaviors in these sorts of experiments (e.g. Why did so many people behave so badly in the Milgram experiments?),[2] what really catches the situationist's attention, for the purposes of understanding personality, is how

---

[2] See e.g. Arpaly 2005.

those rates *change* with changes in situational variables (Why did moving the experimenter out of the room change the rate of compliance?).[3]

9.2.2 What do the Findings Mean?

Note that these experiments all display the essential features for such experiments that we reviewed above (§9.1). Each experiment presented subjects with a situation that elicited simple rather than heroic concern for the well-being of others, and it seems reasonable to suppose that such a broad-based disposition, if there be such, would have been widespread in the subject groups. Moreover, *ex hypothesi* such a broad-based disposition should be relatively immune to situational variables that seem to be of lower strength than the disposition-eliciting features of the situation. Therefore, given the experiments' results, it seems difficult to avoid the conclusion that broad-based dispositions performed rather badly as theoretical constructs for predicting behavior in these experiments. In that case, it becomes more difficult to believe that a taxonomy of broad-based dispositions captures the real psychological attributes that cause behavior and make up personality.

Consider the Milgram experiments in particular. Ross and Nisbett note three features—in technical parlance, 'channel factors'—of Milgram's original experiments that they take to be especially important for understanding their surprising results.[4] First, subjects were not asked all at once to deliver an extremely dangerous shock to another person, but were 'worked up to' such a request through a series of steps. Once one consents to participate in the exercise, and then to assume the role of teacher, and then to give a shock at one level, it seems to become difficult to justify refusing to give a shock at a slightly higher level.[5] As a result, a situation that one would have 'read' as cruel if one had simply been approached and asked to give a stranger a strong electric shock, now becomes much more difficult to read, even as the voltage climbs. Second, although subjects wanted to quit, and expressed their desire to quit, their quitting was not taken seriously. There was no way to 'channel' that desire into action without an awkward, embarrassing, and perhaps ugly confrontation, and subjects therefore had great difficulty

---

[3] The difference between the rates and the anticipated rates is also interesting, for the purposes of understanding the behaviors of attributing traits to others and predicting their behaviors; I consider some of these behaviors in the next chapter.

[4] For discussion of channel factors, see Ross and Nisbett 1991, 46–52.

[5] For instance, numerous studies have shown that once one has taken a first step in some direction—e.g. placing a small 'drive carefully' sign in one's car window—it is then easier to regard the second step—e.g. placing a large, ugly 'drive carefully' sign on one's lawn—as the kind of thing one might do. See Ross and Nisbett 1991, 46ff; see also Flanagan 1991, 296f, 298f.

constructing what they otherwise would have found to be the appropriate response to the situation. (Moving the experimenter out of the room, for instance, would significantly weaken one of these 'channel factors'.) And third, the experimenter clearly did not share the subjects' concerns; as often when we are with others, subjects looked to another—in this case, an authority figure—for cues about the situation, and were met with persistent ambivalence about the 'learner'. Consequently, Ross and Nisbett say, 'The events that unfolded did not "make sense" or "add up" from the perspective of the subject.... [T]here was simply no way for them to arrive at a stable "definition of the situation"' (1991, 57f; see also Flanagan 1991, 296f and references).

Of course, while these considerations show what the situational pressures were, and how they may have worked on the subjects, they do nothing to remove the thought that the subjects' behaviors were out of proportion to those pressures, given intuitive expectations. The experiment would thus seem to bolster the idea that construal is a crucial part of behavior, by illustrating the disorienting effects of keeping a person from arriving at a stable construal of his or her situation. It suggests that behavior varies with thought about situations—such as how one construes one's situation so as to arrive at a 'stable definition' of it—and that the manipulation of a situation can impact such thought, and thereby have an enormous impact on what people do. As Walter Mischel notes, subjects struggle to know how to 'encode' such highly 'ambiguous' situations; behavior in the midst of such ambiguity therefore provides important information as to whether situation-encoding processes are determinants of behavior, or whether behavior stems from more situation-free dispositions (1973, 276). Removing the experimenter from the room, say, or introducing confederate 'teachers', or requiring 'teachers' to confront 'learners' directly can change perceptions of the situation and remove some of its 'ambiguity'.

It is important to remember that the moral of these stories is not that most people are scoundrels—after all, these studies also found that, when they do not receive disorienting cues, most people will readily step in to help others (see also Vranas 2005, 12–16; Doris 2002, 35). Rather, the moral is that situations, and the processes by which agents attach meaning to situations, have more impact on behavior than the dispositionist is entitled to expect. In particular, they show two important facts about the dispositionist's conception of behavioral dispositions. First, the dispositionist's notion of broad-based dispositions seems empirically inadequate, because that notion pays insufficient attention to the various ways in which even apparently subtle variations in the details of situations can change the way people represent and think about them, and thus how people adjust their behaviors to their situations—for better or for worse (see Ross and Nisbett 1991, 96–102; Flanagan 1991, 280f; Doris 2002, 62–5).

And second, although situationists agree with dispositionists that people demonstrate considerable stability of behavior in very similar situations over time, nonetheless they argue that even such stability is rather fragile under the pressure of even apparently small situational variations. This second point follows from the first: because what an agent takes a situation to be can vary dramatically depending even on fairly subtle variations in the situation, dispositions can be regarded as stable in similar objective situations only if 'similar situations' are interpreted rather narrowly (see Ross and Nisbett 1991, 101f, 148–60; Flanagan 1991, 280f; Doris 2002, 65f). And of course, the narrower those situations, the more such a view resembles the situationist view, on which agents adjust themselves to their situations on the basis of cognitive-affective processing of their situations.

But perhaps—as many virtue theorists will allege—we are being too credulous. Do these sorts of experiments really show what situationists claim that they show? As I noted in the previous chapter, virtue theorists have made three basic types of response to the situationist challenge: one, that these experiments do not tell against broad-based dispositions; two, that these experiments tell merely against the thesis that virtues are widespread; and three, that these experiments tell against broad-based dispositions, just as situationists say they do, but virtues are not a species of broad-based dispositions. I shall develop a response of the third type in the next chapter, where I consider the broader implications of situationism for philosophical psychology and virtue theory. In the rest of this one, I argue that the other two types of response are unsatisfactory. These sorts of replies have become nearly ubiquitous, and some of them raise points worth considering; but I do not believe that they are very convincing in the end.

9.3 Interpreting the Findings

Do the experiments of which social psychologists are so fond really favor situationist rather than dispositionist conceptions of personality? I think that they do, and to support that claim I shall look at a number of anti-situationist responses to the Milgram and Princeton experiments, as these experiments are the most commonly discussed in the current literature. I then turn to two more general kinds of anti-situationist objections: one, that the data can be explained as demonstrating a widespread disposition to avoid embarrassment, and two, that behavioral data, when aggregated over multiple occasions, demonstrate greater consistency than such 'one-off' experiments can reveal.

9.3.1 Questioning the Milgram Experiments

Three broad types of doubts about the Milgram experiments are especially common: doubts about the subjects, doubts about the environment of the experiment itself, and suspicions that broad-based dispositions may be in evidence in the experiments after all. These worries all go to the first broad type of response to the situationist challenge, namely that the widespread existence of broad-based dispositions is consistent with these experiments. I shall consider them in turn before examining the other kind of response, that the scarcity of broad-based dispositions is consistent with the existence of cross-situationally consistent virtues.

Doubts about Milgram's Subjects   The thought that Milgram's experiments may be consistent with broad-based dispositions has taken many forms. For one thing, a wide range of worries about Milgram's *subjects* have been raised. For instance, it has been suggested that many of Milgram's subjects must have suspected that the whole thing was a hoax—surely no one would believe that a real scientist would ask people to do such awful things. In that case, his data show not how subjects behaved in the purported situation in which they believed they were giving painful shocks to others, but how they behaved in the very different situation, for many of them, in which they went along with the pretense of giving shocks (see Doris 2002, 43f and Vranas 2005, 6 for discussion). Perhaps, then, the experiments do not tell against broad-based definitions after all.

However, such a contention is clearly inconsistent with the wide levels of extreme distress that Milgram reported in his subjects. I do not suppose that the subjects would have begun trembling, stuttering, or tearing at their flesh while merely *pretending* to shock other subjects. Likewise, even if the subjects were not absolutely certain that the scenario was genuine, their behavior would still suggest that they must have thought that the probability of its genuineness was very high indeed. In fact, Milgram polled his subjects a year later, and found that, of the more than 600 subjects who responded, 80% felt certain or nearly certain that the shocks had been real, while 19% felt either unsure, doubtful, or certain that the shocks had been fake, only 2.4% of these expressing the latter certainty (see Doris 2002, 43). (We might also consider that an obedience study in which subjects were asked to administer extremely painful shocks to a puppy that they could actually *see* being tormented also found more than three-quarters compliance; see Vranas 2005, 7 and Doris 2002, 45 for discussion.) And even if the level of doubt had been much higher among subjects, this would change the scenario from one of behaving with near certainty that one is harming others, to one of behaving with considerable risk of harming others; data about behavior even in that scenario would still have been valid.

It has also been suggested that Milgram's subjects believed that their compliance was justified, so that the experiment does not display the crucial disproportion between their behaviors and the demands of the situation, since they did what the situation demanded (see Vranas 2005, 7 for discussion). This may suggest that whatever we think about the subjects' belief in their justification, still the experiment does not show that they did not act from broad-based dispositions. Again, though, this seems very hard to square with the extreme levels of distress the subjects displayed; it seems much more likely that the subjects were the ones *most* impressed with the disproportion of their behaviors to the demands. Furthermore, recall that at the 300–315-volt level, the 'learner' explicitly withdrew his consent to participate in the experiment any further; yet most subjects continued all the way to the 450-volt level. For subjects confident in the justification of their compliance, this would have been a most obvious point for disobedience. In fact, in a variant of the experiment the learner explicitly stated at the outset that his participation was contingent 'on the condition that the experiment be halted on his demand'; yet even there, compliance was around 70% (Milgram 1974, 64; see Vranas 2005, 8; see also Adams 2006, 149). And in any case, this type of worry concedes a crucial point to the situationist and against the dispositionist: what the subject's behavior is depends on the *subject's* construal.

Another worry might be that Milgram's subjects may have acted from broad-based dispositions, because Milgram may have somehow tapped into an unusually cruel or compliant batch of subjects. But it is very unlikely that Milgram's findings resulted from the peculiarities of his subject groups. Milgram's experiment has been repeated with subject groups of both sexes, a wide range of ages, all walks of life, and in countries all over the world, yet in every case, roughly two-thirds compliance remains the norm (see Vranas 2005, 9; Doris 2002, 47).

Now, it is important to note that there were differences between subjects in their willingness to comply. Two-thirds complied, but of course that means that one-third did not. Situationism is not embarrassed by this fact, since it allows that there are significant differences between persons that are important causal determinants of behavior. On the contrary, that fact is a central pillar of situationism, which emphasizes the idea that behavior is a function of situation *and* person, where these are *dynamically interrelated*. However, the fact that different persons responded differently cannot just as well be put down to dispositions that are cross-situationally consistent, since as we have seen, in variations of Milgram's experiment that provided more channel factors whereby subjects could turn their desire to disobey into actual disobedience, compliance declined significantly.

Doubts about the Experimental Setting   If the 'key' to the Milgram experiments does not lie in reflections on his subjects, perhaps it lies instead in the peculiarities of the *environment* of the experiments. For instance, it is tempting to suppose that Milgram's subjects were perhaps especially impressed, even intimidated, by the experiment's setting at the prestigious Yale University campus. Such intimidation, the objection goes, would have increased the strength of the compassion-opposing factors relative to the compassion-eliciting factors, thereby compromising the crucial factor of disproportion. However, researchers have tested this 'prestige factor', and found that even in variants of the experiment run in a shabby office in a low-rent district, levels of compliance did not decline significantly (see Doris 2002, 49).

On the other hand, some critics have argued that the very artificiality of the experiment context itself—the fact that subjects knew they were 'in a test', and in a contrived and unnatural environment—mitigates Milgram's findings, since they show very little about how dispositions might function outside such an environment (Miller 2003, 369; Solomon 2003, 53, 55; 2005, 650f). However, studies of the institutional pressures favoring compliance in bureaucratic organizations—such as in most companies, a very 'real life' environment—suggest that those pressures are immensely greater than those that Milgram's subjects experienced (see Jackall 1985). Are we to suppose that people are *less* compliant under threats of permanent career damage than when requested by a scientist to 'please continue'? But in any case, artificiality is of course a *situational* factor (as is being at work); to say that such factors play major roles in explaining behavior does not seem like much help for the dispositionist cause. It may be that artificiality influenced the result, but what is less clear is whether the dispositionist is in a position to explain this. Moreover, intuitively anyway such a factor as artificiality does not exert greater compassion-opposing force than the hysterical screams of an innocent person exert compassion-eliciting force. Indeed, the induced ambiguity of the test situation is part of what makes these experiments so probative for testing whether upsetting the construal process has a significant impact on behavior.

In a similar vein, Nafsika Athanassoulis has also claimed that Milgram's experiments

> were not designed to uncover differences in character traits. They examined a specific reaction to a specific situation and did not reveal much about the subjects' long-term dispositions.... [E]xperiments like those carried out by Milgram provide only very limited information about the characters of agents and their results ought to be treated with caution. (2000, 217, 219; see also Fleming 2006, 38f)

Good points all. But they seem irrelevant here: the point of Milgram's experiments is that good predictions of behavior can be made based on a knowledge of the details of the experiment scenario, without having to make judgments about the subjects' 'long-term dispositions'—and that very fact seems interesting indeed for assessing dispositions as explanatory factors.

Moreover, it is important to note that the experiments in this genre form a *body* of evidence: what about cases where the eliciting conditions appeared to subjects to be 'external' to the experiment itself? This is obvious in the smoky room experiment, the seizure experiment, the fallen researcher experiment, and even the Princeton 'Samaritans' experiment; the eliciting conditions were, from the subjects' point of view, quite outside the framework of the experiment (see Doris 2002, 36, 38).

Might Milgram's Experiments Reveal Broad-Based Dispositions After All? If the problem with the Milgram experiments lies neither in the subjects nor in the test environment, then perhaps the problem lies in their alleged *significance*: perhaps, that is, broad-based dispositions can reasonably be inferred from subjects' behaviors after all. For instance, perhaps what we see in Milgram's subjects is not merely the relative weakness of their disposition to behave compassionately, but *also* the relative *strength* of their disposition to obey persons in authority. This is not to deny that their behavior was out of proportion with the demands of the situation, but to argue that their behavior resulted nonetheless from a behavioral disposition.

What disposition would that be? Well, the most obvious candidate is a disposition to obey. John Sabini and Maury Silver suggest interpreting Milgram's results as showing 'that people value obeying authority more than we thought they did' (2005, 546f; see also Miller 2003, 369). But surely we should not suppose that what Milgram's subjects experienced was an interesting revelation about their 'values', as if they discovered that, when the moment came, they found that they would just rather go along. The extreme distress the subjects displayed is outstanding evidence that they did *not* want to go along at all. Indeed, recall that many of Milgram's compliant subjects had verbally 'quit' at some time or other during the experiment.

Perhaps the obedient disposition is not one of valuing obedience to authority, but of choosing to obey even when one would most prefer to be compassionate. In this spirit, people sometimes say that the Milgram experiments demonstrate the power of 'destructive obedience', and Athanassoulis has suggested that this destructive obedience may itself be a disposition that most people have (2000, 217; see also Solomon 2005, 653). However, the question for the dispositionist is whether such a disposition would produce similar observed behaviors over a wide range of nominally dissimilar situations; and variants on Milgram's experiment involving more favorable channel factors have made it clear that such a disposition would not be consistent. In any case, as Ross and Nisbett note, the fact that so many subjects ineffectively 'quit' the experiment suggests that 'the Milgram experiments ultimately may have less to say about "destructive obedience" than about ineffectual, and indecisive, disobedience' (1991, 57), such as the difficulty we often have in disobeying when we cannot construct a 'stable definition' of either the situation we are in or the most appropriate response to it.

Another objection of this sort is that in Milgram's experiments, both the disposition of compassion and the disposition of obedience were elicited in the circumstances—indeed, this is suggested by the fact that subjects were so disturbed by their own obedience—but since the subjects' behavior could not be both obedient and compliant, their behavior would have appeared inconsistent with *some* disposition, either way. The experiment, therefore, does not offer any probative evidence against the subjects' possession of broad-based behavioral dispositions (see Swanton 2003, 31; Kamtekar 2004, 473; Webber 2007a). On the contrary, it may even show that one of these dispositions was stronger in many subjects than the other. However, this objection assumes that the strengths of the conditions eliciting compassion and those eliciting obedience were intuitively on a par in the Milgram experiments. In that case, it ignores one of the essential features of the experiment, namely that it was designed so that the compassion-eliciting conditions would be intuitively much *stronger*. That is, after all, why a pre-experiment survey revealed predictions of either no or extremely minimal compliance. This objection also focuses on the rates of compliance, *per se*, rather than the crucial issue of the variation in those rates given situational variations. Even if the dispositionist could tell a story about why compliance rates were as they were, the real struggle is in explaining why situational variables have such a profound impact on those rates (see also Doris 2002, 35).

Doubts about the Implications of Milgram's Experiments for Virtue Theory   A different type of response to the situationist, on the other hand, is to concede that Milgram's subjects showed little cross-situational consistency, and argue that such consistency usually calls for strong virtues of character, which virtue theorists usually do not believe are particularly widespread in the population anyway. In this spirit, Christian Miller and Rachana Kamtekar have each argued recently that, while Milgram's subjects may have been representative of the wider population, nonetheless their disturbing compliance demonstrates only that most of his subjects, and presumably most of the rest of us, are not fully virtuous, a rather unsurprising fact to the virtue theorist who already supposed that truly virtuous persons would be fairly rare (Miller 2003, 378f; Kamtekar 2004, 485; Winter and Tauer 2007, 77–9). Indeed, the fact that some people do manage to do what they believe is right despite pressures—such as those who defied Milgram, or the Nazis—may be due to the persistence of their dispositions (Adams 2006, 152). Such observations would explain not only why the rates themselves are so alarming, but also why they are so variable across situations: it may be a mark of the full-fledged virtues that their possessor has cross-situational consistency, but rising to such a level of virtue is difficult and takes a lot of time, so that it is not found in the majority of persons.

This objection seeks to make the point that situationism is not incompatible with virtue theory, and at that very general level of description I agree. However, I think that this way of making that point risks overlooking something rather important. Milgram's experiments, like all the others in the genre, were designed to test not for the frequency of any *special* trait or disposition, but only for one that is presumably very *ordinary* and widespread, in this case, basic, minimal compassion, what we often call 'simple human decency'. The experiment was looking only for a presumably ordinary and widespread broad-based disposition. So the question raised by such experiments is not whether virtues are rare or common, but whether the empirical evidence supports the idea that human personality and behavior can be well accounted for using a dispositionist taxonomy of personality attributes at all. To return to an analogy from the previous chapter, if human behavior is not well explained in dispositionist terms, then there is a risk that dispositionist psychology may be in the same boat as a 'four-humors' psychology. The worry, in both cases, is that our psychology *just doesn't work that way*. That is the worry that the virtue theorist must address, and the line of response we are considering here simply fails to address it. Much more effective would be to reply that virtue theory does not rest on a dispositionist taxonomy after all, despite the assumptions of some philosophical psychologists.

9.3.2 Questioning the Darley and Batson Experiment

Critics have raised similar worries about Darley and Batson's 'Good Samaritan' experiment as well, in particular that the results were due to the peculiarities of the subjects, and that the desire to avoid lateness is consistent with helpful behavioral dispositions. I take up these two worries in turn. I spend less time on them than I spent on the objections to the Milgram experiments, since our discussion of the latter should have already clarified many of the issues at stake.

Doubts about the Subjects   Darley and Batson found that helping behavior was low in the hurried group, much higher in the on-time group, and much higher again in the ahead-of-time group. But we may worry that these groups differed not only in their available time, but also in their dispositions to avoid lateness, the non-helping group including, as it happens, more 'lateness-avoiders' than the other groups. However, this seems a rather slim hope, and in fact Darley and Batson failed to identify any significant differences between helping and non-helping subjects using standard personality tests (see Campbell 1999, 39). And in any case, such a strategy merely turns a dispute over the consistency of basic compassion into a dispute over the consistency of 'lateness-avoidance', and the body of evidence on cross-situational consistency should make the dispositionist no more optimistic about the latter dispute than about the former (see Campbell 1999, 43f).

On the other hand, we might suspect that even if there were no relevant differences between members of the three sub-groups, still there could be significant differences between Darley and Batson's group as a whole and others in the general population. For instance, perhaps seminarians, like most graduate students, are particularly aware of time pressures (see Campbell 1999, 39 for discussion). However, situationism does not reject the possibility that different populations might behave differently in the same nominal circumstances. On the contrary, the situationist insists that people differ considerably in the cognitive-affective 'styles' that make up an individual's personality. What the dispositionist would need to show is that, for rather many other populations, the situational variable of lateness would not merely have a different impact on behavior, but would have very little impact, in order to establish that Darley and Batson's findings cannot be extrapolated beyond their peculiar subjects. I know of no study that has tested this hypothesis. However, I do know that Milgram's findings have been tested in this way, and the results do not make me optimistic about this general strategy.

Might the Princeton Experiment Reveal Broad-Based Dispositions After All? Alternatively, one might argue that Darley and Batson's findings actually suggest some strong broad-based disposition. One such disposition would be the disposition to help *given* available time. For instance, some have argued that the findings are consistent with the idea that people who have compassionate or altruistic dispositions under normal circumstances may not be so disposed under the stress of being late (Athanassoulis 2000, 219; cp. Sreenivasan 2002, 60). Such an approach is part of a general strategy to save dispositions: if the situationist shows that situational variables have a substantial impact on behavior, then one should define dispositions as dispositions to behave in the same ways within the relevant objective situational parameters. For instance, there may be no such single trait as 'honesty', but rather honesty-about-truth-telling, honesty-about-test-taking, etc. (Kamtekar 2004, 468f; see also Miller 2003, 383; Adams 2006, 119, 128). Fair enough, but beyond a certain point anyway such a strategy would offer merely a pyrrhic victory for the dispositionist. As this strategy grants, the empirical evidence suggests that even apparently subtle changes in a situation can have a very significant impact on behavior. This means that the situational parameters, and therefore the dispositions defined in terms of them, become increasingly narrower, but the narrower the situational range of dispositions, the less (by definition) cross-situational consistency behavioral dispositions can have—and that, of course, is precisely the situationist's point. (I shall examine a more radical virtue-theoretic approach to fragmentation in Chapter 10, §10.4.4.)

Another objection raised against the Princeton experiment is a variation of an objection we have seen raised against Milgram's experiments: the subjects with no time to spare had to choose between helping the victim they encountered, on the one hand, and helping others who were relying on them to be on time. Since they could not have helped in both ways, it is unreasonable to suppose that the experiment presents evidence of a failing in the hurried subjects' dispositions to help (Kamtekar 2004, 473; see also Adams 2006, 154). But this objection faces the same problem here as it does in the Milgram case: the question was never whether the subjects faced conflicting pressures—the experiment was designed to *ensure* that they did—but whether their supposed behavioral dispositions would be elicited by forces that were intuitively *stronger* than the opposing forces. It is therefore simply untrue that the experiment would seem to go against the dispositionist's view whichever way it came out. And again, the body of evidence suggests that intuitively weaker disposition-opposing forces tend to overpower intuitively stronger disposition-eliciting forces with surprising frequency (Campbell 1999, 41f, 44f).

Finally, some have objected that the Princeton experiment tacitly assumes that a person can have a cross-situationally consistent behavioral disposition only if one is disposed to act on that disposition in *every* relevant occasion, an assumption that is clearly unwarranted (Miller 2003, 378f; Kamtekar 2004, 474). Fair enough; but as Doris points out, 'The situationist point is not that helping is rare, but that helping is situationally sensitive' (2002, 35). Situationists are impressed not by the fact that people may fail to exercise their alleged dispositions, but by the fact that such failures occur so often in circumstances that elicit those dispositions so forcefully, relative to the opposition, in ways that can be predicted by paying careful attention to situational variables.

9.3.3 Are We Just too Embarrassed?

I turn now to two more general types of objection to the standard experiments in the situationist tradition. In this subsection, I consider the objection that the experiments all reveal a particular behavioral disposition, and in the next that aggregating multiple data sets reveals more consistency than any datum can on its own.

John Sabini and Maury Silver have argued recently that while these experiments are surprising, this is not because of any doubt they cast on the notion of a broad-based behavioral disposition, but because they reveal the surprising power of a surprisingly widespread disposition, namely, the disposition to avoid embarrassment. For instance, they argue that Milgram's subjects behaved as they did because they looked to the experimenter—the person 'in the know' in that setting—for cues about the expected or appropriate behaviors in that context, and because they had no way to disobey without a very unpleasant confrontation; and in both cases, subjects were acting so as to avoid embarrassment (2005, 550–5). Moreover, they argue that in situations such as those in the smoky room and seizure experiments, subjects tend to fail to act when others are present because they 'do not want to embarrass themselves by looking like a fool, by losing their cool' (555–7). Likewise, they argue that Darley and Batson's subjects tended to help less the more hurried they were, because they wished to avoid the embarrassment of being late (557–9; see also Sabini, Siepmann, and Stein 2001, esp. 2ff; Adams 2006, 153f).

This intriguing strategy essentially adopts the situationist's story about the dynamic interplay between persons and situations—for instance, how agents construe and identify situations by taking cues from others—and turns it into a story about a disposition, viz. the disposition to be influenced by others, to be interested in the cues they offer, and so on. But what sort of disposition is the 'disposition' to pay close attention to such social cues? On the one hand, this strategy could amount to little more than taking generic forms of dynamic interplay and giving them a collective, disposition-like name, such as 'embarrassment-avoiding' or 'social cue-taking'. In that case, though, it would seem remarkably similar to straightforward situationism, which insists that what remain constant across situations are not behavioral dispositions inferred from observed behaviors, but just these generic forms of dynamic interplay between situations and cognitive-affective processes. After all, the situationist would be the first to agree that we tend to look to one another when deciding how to construe a situation, in part because there are epistemic pressures ('two heads are better than one') and social pressures ('go along to get along') favoring consensus, and also because the experience of being significantly out of step with others tends to create psychological tension (see Ross and Nisbett 1991, 44–6; see also Gilbert 1995, 134–6; Flanagan 1991, 300). It is therefore difficult to see how the present strategy would be a defense of dispositionism *per se*.

On the other hand, the strategy could mean to offer 'embarrassment-avoiding' as a disposition to act consistently for a certain kind of reason. I do not know of any empirical evidence to suggest that this *is* the reason for which subjects in these experiments acted, but let us suppose that it is. How could we tell when a particular person had this disposition? Well, if it is a broad-based disposition to act for the sake of a certain goal—to avoid embarrassment—then it would dispose one to engage in certain behaviors for the sake of that reason across a wide range of nominally dissimilar situations. Which behaviors are those? As we saw in the case of the tip-seeking waiter, pursuing a goal is not generally to be understood in terms of stereotypical behaviors; one may do any number of things that look quite different to an observer, all for the sake of the same goal. So it seems that we would have to focus on how a person with this disposition construed situations, adjusted behaviors to situations so construed—in a word, we would be back to the situationist's approach to personality, and thus to an alternative to dispositionism. We can call cognitive-affective bundles 'dispositions' if we want to, but we do not gain anything by doing so. The situationist's point is not that there are no consistencies in personality,[6] but that such consistencies exist only in the form of enduring patterns of adjusting behaviors to situations. Sabini and Silver tell an interesting story about channel factors (see also Sabini, Siepmann, and Stein 2001, 3), but we cannot wring dispositionism from channel factors.

---

[6] See Mischel 1973, 255f, who is explicit on this point.

9.3.4 Does Aggregation Help?

Finally, notice that all of the experiments we have examined study subjects' behaviors on a given occasion; but what if we could observe subjects' behaviors in a wide variety of situations, over a significant period of time? Psychologists began exploring the possibility that such aggregation could reveal the predictive power of dispositions after all, soon after Mischel's 1968 review of the literature on cross-situational consistency. Mischel observed that many experiments had suggested that such dispositions as, say, 'talkativeness' or 'cheating' showed considerable temporal stability in situations of the same kind (e.g. talkativeness during dinner, cheating on one kind of test), but showed little correlation with nominally similar behaviors across nominally different situations (e.g. talkativeness outside dinner, cheating on a different kind of test). Indeed, the levels of cross-situational correlation of behavior observed in the studies in Mischel's review suggest that the likelihood of predicting a behavior in one situation based on observations of behavior in another would be hardly above chance (1968, ch. 2).

What made Mischel's review so revolutionary was that he did not try to explain these results away, but suggested taking them seriously and revising our understanding of behavior and personality (see Ross and Nisbett 1991, 95–102; see also Doris 2002, 63f). However, in response to Mischel's skepticism about traditional dispositionism, Seymour Epstein suggested that dispositions are less like grades on a given exam, and more like an overall grade point average: a student may do well or poorly on any given day, but an aggregate of a student's performance to date is still a reliable predictor of future performance. Less metaphorically, aggregation shows that past behaviors can be converted into an overall or mean characterization of one's disposition (e.g. shy, introverted, or aggressive to a certain overall degree), which in turn is a reliable predictor of one's future mean characterization. Simply put, one's past average is an indicator of one's future average, and is an even better indicator if one's past average tends towards 'extreme' behaviors (for discussion, see Ross and Nisbett 1991, 107–9, 116–18; Doris 2002, 74; see also Adams 2006, 122–5, who favors this sort of approach).

Now, whatever aggregation may show, it cannot of course change the fact that the correlations aggregated are, after all, quite low. This means, for one thing, that aggregation does not substantially reduce the uncertainty involved in any particular prediction, as Epstein himself recognized (Ross and Nisbett 1991, 110; Doris 2002, 73). More importantly, because of low individual correlations, a subject's aggregated distribution of behaviors still tends strongly towards the average for the population, and therefore the difference between one subject's mean and another's remains fairly low (Ross and Nisbett 1991, 110f, 114f). Consequently, outside of subjects with patterns of very extreme behaviors, aggregations reveal differences of a mild 'sort of, for the most part' variety (Doris 2002, 75).

Nonetheless, there is no denying that aggregation reveals something very interesting indeed: the more you know about how someone has behaved in a wide range of situations in the past, the better you can predict his or her behavior in the future, over the 'long haul'. Indeed, studies of the performance-predicting power of candidate interviews as compared to letters of recommendation seem to arrive at the same conclusion, in a different way. Some psychologists have found that although interviewers are often very confident about their ability to predict a candidate's future performance based on information gathered in interviews, correlations between interview-based predictions and actual performance tend to be rather low. On the other hand, predictions based on letters of recommendation written by persons who know the candidate well have been shown to have a substantially higher rate of correlation with actual performance (Ross and Nisbett 1991, 136–8). Not surprisingly, it turns out that the better you know a person, the better you can predict that person's behavior over the long haul.

However, as we saw in the last chapter, for that very reason it would be even better if we could focus on the *psychological* rather than the *nominal* aspects of what agents do and the situations in which they act. For the situationist, better than observations of past behavior, inference to dispositions, and predictions of future behavior is an understanding of an agent's goals, competencies, and particular ways of construing situations, self, and behavior. In other words, the more we take the lessons of aggregation seriously—the more you know, the better you can predict—the more we should be dissatisfied with the traditional dispositionist model.

Finally, the reader may have already noticed what is surely the biggest problem for the aggregation approach: by averaging out a person's behaviors across a wide range of situations, it treats those situations as the mere background of behavior, and treats variance in behavior as error to be statistically washed out. In that case, it sets aside an individual's pattern of if...then...behaviors, and with it what seems good evidence for drawing inferences about how the agent interacts with and adjusts himself to his or her environment (Mischel and Peake 1982, 731–9). So it would seem that the wiser course would be to appreciate the existence of 'long haul' consistency, but account for that consistency in terms of stable if...then... patterns.

Conclusion

There is no reason to deny social psychologists in the situationist paradigm either their experiments or their interpretations of them. Of course, it is another matter where those experiments and interpretations leave us as philosophers interested in modeling the human psyche. In the next chapter, I consider whether there could be any philosophical theory of character that is consistent with situationist psychology, and whether such a theory would be of any help to virtue theory in particular.

10

From Situationism to Virtue Theory

In this chapter I turn from social psychology to philosophical and moral psychology, and to virtue theory in particular. In the preceding two chapters, I have presented situationism both as a rejection of dispositionism and as suggesting a positive theory of personality, and I have argued that there is good evidence supporting situationism on both counts. In this chapter, I argue that situationism is not a threat for virtue theory to endure, but the good news for virtue theory to *embrace*. Or rather, it is good news for those theories that hold virtues to be practically intelligent forms of responsiveness to reasons, as Hard Virtue Theories do. If I am correct, then the task for the virtue theorist is one of developing cognitive-affective personality theories into normative theories about practically intelligent character.

The road from situationism to virtue theory is roughly as follows. Situationism suggests an understanding of an individual's personality as a unique bundle of cognitive and affective processes, such as the goals one adopts and pursues; the ways that one attends to certain aspects of situations; the values one attaches to certain outcomes; how one construes and attaches 'meaning' to situations, behaviors, and the intentions of others; one's practical and self-regulatory skills; and so on. Such processes tend to form cohesive clusters or 'attributes', such as one's goal of being liked by others, the value one attaches to certain outcomes vis-à-vis that goal, the features of situations one picks out as salient vis-à-vis that goal, and so on. Adopting this personality taxonomy, the virtue theorist then considers the virtues as psychological attributes in virtue of which one pursues goals that it is good to pursue, attends well to features of situations vis-à-vis such goals, deliberates intelligently about such goals, etc. The virtue theorist thereby moves from personality to a normative notion of 'character', which can be seen as that subset of a cognitive-affective personality bundle that is particularly of ethical interest; alternatively, character could be seen as the whole personality insofar as it comes in for ethical scrutiny.[1] A 'character trait', then, would be some identifiable and cohesive cognitive-affective attribute, considered from an ethical point of view, and such a trait would be a 'virtue' when in virtue of it one pursues the right kinds of goals, attends to the right kind of saliencies in situations, attaches the right kinds of values to the outcomes of behaviors, and so on. In short, once an empirically adequate personality theory has been identified, the work of the virtue theorist is first to construct an interface between that personality theory and a conception of character, and then to engage in ethical reflection on the various attributes of character so understood.

So far my remarks have been very sketchy, but I trust it is clear that there *is* a path from empirical personality theory to normative virtue theory. Indeed, the path from a cognitive-affective personality theory to some sort of virtue theory seems difficult to miss. Unfortunately, philosophers who have translated situationism for a philosophical audience often have not had nearly enough to say about the positive implications of situationism for personality theory. For instance, Gilbert Harman, one of the most influential figures in this debate, explicitly acknowledges the consistency of goal-seeking behaviors and cognitive strategies (1999, 329; 2001, 122), but considers none of the implications that this observation has for a positive theory of personality. On the contrary, Harman gives the impression that situationism is an alternative *to* personality theory, rather than an alternative *within* personality theory.

But perhaps the philosophical debate rests on more than a lopsided account of the social psychological evidence. In particular, perhaps the problem is that the situationist's positive personality theory would not help the virtue theorist after all. Recently John Doris has argued that while taking cognitive-affective processes seriously can suggest a considerable level of behavioral consistency, still one can *always* identify consistency in behavior if one is but sufficiently creative in the choice of one's standards of consistency. In that case, he argues, even if virtue theory can avail itself of an empirically adequate standard of consistency, nonetheless such a standard would be *normatively* inadequate. Simply put, a theory of the virtue of 'honesty', say, must be a theory about a trait that produces behaviors that are consistent with the *right* standard, and not just with whatever standard any old agent reckons is 'honest enough for his purposes' (2002, 76ff).

---

[1] Since I am a holist about the content of reasons (see Ch. 6), I believe that there would be no interesting boundary between aspects of personality alleged to be salient with respect to one's responsiveness to virtue reasons and those alleged not to be salient. Therefore, I prefer to think of character as the whole personality (in the psychologist's broad sense) considered from an ethical point of view. See also Hursthouse 1999, 187–91. But I shall not pursue the issue here.

My aim in this chapter, then, is to defend the idea that virtue theory—and in particular, Hard Virtue Theory—can embrace the positive conception of personality that situationism suggests. To do this I must show that the resulting virtue theory would be both empirically adequate—based on an empirically plausible personality taxonomy—and normatively adequate, that is, plausible as an account of character that is excellent and productive of action that is good.

I begin by (further) defending the empirical adequacy of such a personality taxonomy—in particular, its crucial conception of consistency—which some philosophical psychologists have played down and others have explicitly criticized (§§10.1–10.2). In the rest of the chapter I consider three main types of virtue-theoretical responses to Doris' worry that no virtue theory embracing the situationist view of consistency could be both empirically and normatively adequate. One of these is to reject both dispositionist and situationist theories, and to focus instead on commonsense views about what traits there are and which ones are the virtues. The problem with this approach, I argue, is that the empirical evidence about our everyday practices of attributing traits to agents very strongly suggests, not that the very idea of personality or character is confused, but that many of our ways of thinking about those notions are nonetheless problematic and in need of correction. So the virtue theorist cannot simply abandon social science for 'common sense' (§10.3).

Another approach is to stipulate that a virtue is whatever psychological attribute underlies certain patterns of reliably and consistently good behavior, and to leave it to the empirical psychologist to sort out a proper taxonomy of such attributes. But the problem with this approach is that if the situationist is right, then there need be no particular correlation between nominally defined sets of behaviors and underlying psychological attributes of any cohesion at all, even within a single individual. This fact has the important implication that virtue theory must begin from an empirically adequate taxonomy of personality attributes, not from nominal behavioral patterns. Moreover, this result falsifies the common thought that one can start with one's preferred theory of right action and define virtues in terms of it. So the virtue theorist cannot focus on behaviors and leave it to social science to sort out the attributes (§10.4).

Finally, I consider the remaining approach, which is for the virtue theorist to begin with a plausible personality theory and work towards a virtue theory, rejecting the claim that normative adequacy requires nominal consistency. This approach is the sort I sketched above, whereby one defines character traits in terms of cognitive-affective personality attributes, and defines virtues as those character traits that conform to normative standards. I argue that such a view is both empirically and normatively adequate, and that it is equivalent to what I have called Hard Virtue Theory, and indeed to Aristotle's own virtue theory. I conclude that among philosophical views of character, Hard Virtue Theory is in the unique position of standing firmly on the evidence from social psychology about the nature of personality (§10.5).

10.1 Situationism: From Empirical to Philosophical Psychology

Situationism gained widespread attention among philosophers in the 1990s with the publication of Owen Flanagan's important 1991 book *Varieties of Moral Personality*, in which Flanagan offered a lengthy and careful discussion of situationism and thereby began translating situationism into a set of negative and positive implications for philosophical psychology. Situationism has gone on to become a major 'hot button' issue among philosophical psychologists and virtue theorists, largely due to the more radical interpretations of situationism offered by Gilbert Harman in a series of papers beginning in 1999, and by John Doris in his 2002 book *Lack of Character*. I consider these three contributions in turn, and how they have led to an almost exclusive focus on situationism as a negative thesis.

10.1.1 Flanagan's Ecumenicalism

Although many philosophical psychologists have distanced themselves from the positive situationist alternative in personality theory, some philosophical psychologists have been rather more impressed by that positive alternative. To be sure, Flanagan was critical of virtue theories that overlook the situational sensitivity of behavior, but he was also quick to point out that one's understanding of the cross-situational consistency of behavior depends on one's positive theory of what constitutes a 'situation' and thus a 'behavior'. In particular, Flanagan argued that for the purposes of identifying behavioral consistency as evidence of an agent's personality, behavior must be classified from that agent's own point of view (i.e. psychologically rather than nominally, in Mischel's terms). Recognizing the importance of construal and other cognitive-affective processes, then, Flanagan argued that there are psychologically real character traits, which are situationally sensitive rather than broad-based or 'global', that is, operant in relative freedom from situational variables (see esp. 1991, 280f, 291). It seems appropriate, then, that Flanagan should describe his position on the existence of personality and character traits as 'ecumenical' (305), and such ecumenicalism seems quite appropriate given our overview of the situationist paradigm in the last two chapters.

But despite Flanagan's sensibly modest approach, and perhaps because Flanagan did not develop more fully the positive conception of character he thought situationism suggested, subsequent discussions of situationism among philosophical psychologists have tended to focus on situationism mainly as a *negative* view.

Unfortunately, such a focus results in a distorted picture of situationism, in a number of ways. For one thing, such a focus dislocates the situationist paradigm from its place in the development of personality psychology and social science in the twentieth century. Situationism represents not merely the rejection of an erstwhile dominant approach to personality theory, but the outlines of a new theory of personality to replace it. After all, the body of evidence that eventually led to the situationist paradigm was evidence against one personality theory, but it was also simultaneously evidence *for* another. Moreover, to overlook the positive implications of situationism is to lose sight of what, more precisely, it replaces—namely, a taxonomy of behavioral dispositions that are relatively *situation-free*. Only by considering the alternative cognitive-affective taxonomy can we fully appreciate what sorts of psychological processes the dispositionist theory had *left out* of its theory of personality, and thus exactly why it came to be considered a failure. Accordingly, we can also better understand what alternatives situationism still leaves open.

For these reasons, overlooking those positive alternatives is likely to give the very misleading impression that situationism is an alternative *to* personality theory, full stop, rather than an alternative *within* personality theory. In fact, as we saw in Chapter 8, it is only the positive side of situationism—its focus on construal and other cognitive-affective processes as the basic units of personality—that distinguishes the situationist paradigm from behaviorism. An exclusively negative focus, therefore, not only distorts what situationism is about, but may also leave one with little alternative to simple behaviorism (see Webber 2006, 2007*b* for a similar worry).

Nonetheless, the fact that situationism suggests positive alternatives in personality theory has received very little press in its more recent translation from empirical to philosophical psychology, and we should find out why. Do philosophical psychologists find those positive alternatives more problematic than their counterparts in social psychology do?

10.1.2 Harman's Skepticism about Character

In 1999 Gilbert Harman published a very influential paper—'Moral Philosophy Meets Social Psychology'—in which he forcefully suggested a number of implications of the situationist movement for philosophical psychology and for virtue theory in particular. Harman's discussion was far more incendiary than

Flanagan's, and prompted a flurry of publications on the subject, among them a series of further papers by Harman. Simply put, Harman argued that 'there is no empirical basis for the existence of character traits' (1999, 316). This is not to say that there is no evidence for dispositions *at all*—on the contrary, he said cheekily, people seem generally disposed to over-attribute dispositions to one another (327)—but rather that there is no evidence for *broad-based* dispositions, of which he takes traditional personality and character traits, and especially the traditional virtues, to be species. Thus, Harman argued that since broad-based dispositions are crucial to the very notion of character and personality, there is therefore no evidence for character or personality, in any very interesting sense: 'There is no reason at all to believe in character traits as ordinarily conceived' (2000, 223; see also 1999, 326f).

In his papers on situationism over the past several years, Harman has consistently defended this robust skepticism about the very idea of character. Although it is sometimes difficult to tell whether this skepticism is a denial of the *existence* of character itself, or a denial of the existence of any good *evidence* for character, recently Harman has explicitly clarified his position as the latter, weaker, epistemic claim (2005, 16f). This is a relief, for as several of his critics have noted, from the fact that we tend to make unwarranted judgments about character and to be over-confident in those judgments, it of course does not follow that there is no such thing as character (Sreenivasan 2002, 53f; Miller 2003, 372f; Fleming 2006, 30).[2]

In any event, Harman's considered view is that the evidence from social psychology yields no reason at all to believe in character traits. We should appreciate by now just how radical a claim that is. Harman claims that the preponderance of the evidence offers no support either for the existence of broad-based dispositions, as the dispositionist conceives of them, *or* for the existence of personality and character, full stop. Apparently, Harman assumes that the dispositionist's conception of personality is the only game in town (see Sreenivasan 2002, 64 for a similar objection). However, this is a strange assumption for Harman to make, given his acknowledgement that 'To have different character traits, [people] must be disposed to act differently in the same circumstances (as they perceive those circumstances)' (Harman 1999, 317). Of course, the parenthetical remark, 'as they perceive those circumstances', makes all the difference in the world. As we have seen, the situationist's positive thesis about personality is that distinctive mental attributes can and do reveal

---

[2] Of course, one might be forgiven for attributing to Harman the stronger, metaphysical claim, when he publishes papers with titles like 'The Nonexistence of Character Traits' and 'No Character or Personality'.

cross-situational consistency, *if* we look at what agents do in their circumstances 'as they perceive those circumstances'. So it seems either that Harman does not take his parenthetical remark very seriously, or that he is unimpressed by its positive implications for theories of personality and character (see Solomon 2003, 52 for a similar complaint).

There is some reason to think that Harman does take the remark at least *somewhat* seriously. In a 2003 article, he quotes the following passage from psychologist Ziva Kunda (1999, 435, cited in Harman 2003, 89), as offering examples of the kind of disposition attributions he says we should avoid:

> The librarian carried the old woman's groceries across the street. The receptionist stepped in front of the old man in line. The plumber slipped an extra $50 into his wife's purse. Although you were not asked to make any inferences about any of these characters, chances are that you inferred that the librarian is helpful, the receptionist rude, and the plumber generous. Perhaps because we do not realize the extent to which behavior is shaped by situations, we tend to spontaneously infer such traits from behavior.

The sort of inference Kunda describes should now be familiar from the dispositionist's OIP schema (Chapter 8), and the problem with that schema, as we have seen, is that it attributes dispositions to agents without giving sufficient consideration to their circumstances, and in particular to how they construe their circumstances—that is, to how they 'perceive those circumstances'. To be benevolent, rude, or generous, after all, is not simply to behave in a certain stereotypical way, but to act for certain kinds of reasons, or perhaps with indifference to certain reasons. The person who steps ahead of the old man in line because he cannot see the old man, say, or because the old man gave him his place in line is not appropriately labeled 'rude'. Construal matters.

However, if Harman does take this point seriously, then he must be unimpressed by its positive implications, which social psychologists like Mischel and Ross and Nisbett take such pains to point out. Yet if he is unimpressed, he does not make it clear why. On the contrary, although Harman points out that people act from 'skills and strategies' in fairly stable ways over time, he does not consider whether this could open up new ways of thinking about personality or character—in fact, he *opposes* this point to thought about character (1999, 326). But as we have seen, social psychologists point out that understanding individuals' stable patterns of cognitive-affective skills and strategies, social intelligence, and self-control can also reveal the cross-situational consistency of an agent's superficially disparate behaviors, and thus that such an understanding just *is* a new theory of personality.

Furthermore, Harman points out in several places that people differ in the types of goals they pursue (as well as their 'strategies, neuroses, optimism, etc.'), but he does not consider whether these sorts of differences could ground a more sophisticated conception of personality or character, either; again, he opposes such differences to the notion of differences in personality or character (1999, 329; 2001, 122; see also Kamtekar 2004, 472). Finally, Harman seems to echo Walter Mischel in noting that people 'tend to be in *or think they are in different situations*' (2001, 122, emphasis added), that is, that people construe their situations in different ways that significantly impact what they do, and what they take themselves to be doing. But yet again, the obvious next step is not one he takes—that personality and character can be complex bundles of cognitive and affective processes by which individuals construe their world and adjust their behaviors to it. Instead, the point is again opposed to the very idea of personality or character.[3]

Harman's conclusions therefore stand in stark contrast to those drawn by social psychologists who also reject dispositionist taxonomies of personality. Perhaps it is little wonder that (as Harman, to his credit, relates) Lee Ross responded to a presentation of Harman's at Stanford by remarking that he (Harman) drew conclusions about character that 'were more extreme than any he [Ross] would draw' (Harman 2005, 10). More than that, it would seem that the extreme and incendiary nature of Harman's view has actually misrepresented situationism as a paradigm in personality and social psychology, with the most unfortunate result of unnecessarily polarizing philosophical discussion on the matter.[4] Mischel reported in 1973 that several personality theorists had distorted the results of his 1968 review by turning them into a polarizing 'person-situation' debate, a trend that personality psychology by now has largely outgrown (Funder 2001). So perhaps there is still hope for overcoming the current polarization of the situationist debate in philosophical psychology as well.

10.1.3 Doris on Consistency

In 2002 John Doris published an excellent book, *Lack of Character*, which to date is the only book-length discussion of the implications of situationism for philosophical psychology. Like Flanagan and unlike Harman, Doris believes that the empirical evidence does leave room for warranted belief in character—albeit

---

[3] See DePaul 1999, 144f, who also complains that Harman ignores the significance of agent's perspectives on and reasons for their actions in thinking about character.

[4] See also Doris 2002, 25f for warnings against polarization. I find myself in agreement with Sreenivasan 2002, 64 that there is 'a sense in which the confrontation between situationism and a theory of virtue over the existence of "character traits" operates at cross-purposes. I am afraid that this crossing of purposes must be laid at the door of situationsm's philosophical advocates.' See also Kamtekar 2004, 477, 485.

of a very modest sort. On the one hand, Doris is willing to concede that behavioral dispositions that are stable in similar situations but not consistent across dissimilar situations, may nonetheless be considered 'character traits' of a sort. Our evidence, Doris says, does not suggest that there is no reason to think that character and personality do not exist at all, but it does suggest that they exist only in a very 'fragmented' form, replacing 'honesty', say, with situation-specific traits like 'answer-key honesty' and 'score-adding honesty' (2002, 39, 64ff; see also Flanagan 1991, 291; Upton 2005). On the other hand, he concedes that the evidence against consistency may be compatible with the existence of some very rare 'saints' and 'monsters' at the extremes, who tend to be saintly or monstrous across a wide range of situations (2002, 60, 65).[5]

Of course, such situation-free consistency is not the sort that is of interest to the cognitive-affective personality psychologist. However, and more important for our purposes, Doris also appreciates the idea that taking an agent's point of view seriously makes an important difference for how we assess that agent's consistency across different situations. But while Flanagan does not much develop this idea (1991, 291), and Harman sets it aside altogether, Doris develops it only to distance himself from it (2002, 76–85). Here Doris self-consciously moves away from the approach to consistency advocated by Mischel and other situationists working in personality psychology. The problem with making the agent's point of view the standard of consistency, Doris says, is that such standards can make claims to consistency too easy. As I read Doris, there are two arguments here: one, that psychological (rather than nominal) characterizations of situations make cross-situational consistency come cheap; and two, that such consistency would not match the normative standards of a virtue theory anyway.[6] I consider the first argument now, and the second in the next section.

10.1.4 Consistency and Empirical Adequacy

When Spinal Tap were asked on National Public Radio in the U.S. a few years ago whether they thought they had finally become a household name, they replied, 'It depends on the household, really'. Fame can come rather cheap if

---

[5] See also Vranas 2005, who holds that while not very many people have consistent traits, there may be more of them than just these rare, marginal cases.

[6] At any rate, I *think* there are these two arguments; I confess that I do not find Doris' discussion entirely clear here. In particular, I struggle to see whether he has separated empirical worries from normative ones; in fact, I would not be entirely surprised if Doris thought that the worry was a normative one throughout. Even so, what I have classified here as an empirical worry may be worth discussing in its own right, even if I have got Doris wrong on this point.

one is free to choose one's own standard! Similarly, Doris says (2002, 80) that cross-situational consistency can come cheap, too:

While a change in context, as from nominal to psychological situations, may reveal consistency on one perspective, it cannot resolve inconsistency on the other. The real question concerns what regularities, or failures of regularity, should interest us. Consider my inconsistency in distance from the last gas station on Route 80 west before Toledo. Noting that I am consistently compassionate, or consistently less than fifty miles from the Earth's surface, does not make my gas station inconsistency go away. Yet as far as I know, most folks have no compelling interest in consistency of position relative to the last gas station before Toledo on westbound Route 80; they can therefore safely ignore the inconsistency most of us exhibit relative to this standard.

Doris' worry seems to be that the kind of consistency that we find on a psychological rather than a nominal characterization of a subject's situations and behaviors may not be a very interesting form of consistency after all. Pick any set of behaviors, and there will usually be *some* standard or other relative to which they can be assessed as consistent. The fact that an agent can generally find some standard relative to which his or her behaviors come out consistent is undeniable, but uninteresting. In that case, the only consistency that counts is that of observable behavior, that is, nominal consistency. That is the consistency that matters, but the other sorts of 'consistency' that psychologists like Mischel and others identify cannot change the fact that consistency of the former sort is still missing.

To drive the point home, Doris considers a mountain climbing team that left two other climbers for dead on Mt. Everest without offering any assistance. According to the leader of the climbing team, this was not a wrong thing to do: 'Above 8,000 meters', he said, 'is not a place where people can afford morality' (Doris 2002, 78). As Doris puts it, this climber seems to think that regions above 8,000 meters are 'morality-free zones'. By his own 8,000-meter standard, the climber's leaving-for-dead actions were consistent with his stopping-to-help actions at lower altitudes; yet somehow, most of us probably will not get excited about consistency of this sort. So here we have a case of different-looking behaviors, but without much trouble we can concoct a standard according to which the behaviors come out consistent after all. But why should we care about any 'consistency' like that? The point is not just to find consistency, but consistency *according to a meaningful standard*.

If the point holds in the case of the mountain climber, then it should hold in the case (from Chapter 8) of the waiter who behaved very differently towards his patrons but acted for the sake of the same goal in each case. The point of the mountain climber case, after all, is to cast doubt on the very idea of psychological (vs. nominal) consistency as meaningful consistency; since it is only in psychological rather than nominal terms that our waiter is consistent, the idea of his consistency should be problematic, too. If there is no relevant difference between the sorts of policies by which the climber and the waiter come out consistent, and if the climber's consistency is uninteresting, then why think the sort of consistency we attribute to the waiter is of any interest for theories of personality or character? But I want to argue now that once we understand the climber's consistency in such a way as to make it no different from the waiter's, then while those two forms of consistency clearly differ in their moral value, nonetheless they do not differ with respect to their personality-theoretical significance. This is because, in order to make sense of the idea that the climber is consistent in the same way that the waiter is, we must understand the climber's consistency in relation to certain cognitive-affective processes, and where the climber's personality is concerned, this is hardly consistency by just any old standard.

Consider the mountain climber's policy, which is to behave compassionately below 8,000 meters, but not above. What does that mean? It is tempting to suppose that this is no policy at all, but merely a cover story for morally shocking behavior; but I suppose there are a couple of ways that he could really mean it.[7] On the one hand, suppose (uncharitably) that he chose 8,000 meters as a sort of 'magic number'—there is no reason for that number, it is simply the one he chose for his standard, and thank heavens he chose it rather than sea level. However, now the climber begins to look unintelligible: we can assign no meaning to the fact that he has taken that standard as the one to act in accordance with, but can simply note that it just is the standard he has adopted. Indeed, calling his standard a 'policy' at all now begins to seem an honorific. We need not insist that one must be able to give reasons for a policy all the way down before it can count as a policy, but a 'policy' for which no reason could (even in principle) be given is one that cannot stand up under scrutiny *as* a policy. He is instead being arbitrary and capricious, and cooking up a standard to mask that arbitrariness does not make it go away. On this supposition, then, the climber is importantly unlike the waiter, whose policy at least looks intelligible rather than arbitrary. Doris is therefore correct to suppose that not all standards or policies are interesting as measurements of consistency. Some standard or other can usually be got cheap. But since the climber is so different from the waiter on this reading of Doris' thought experiment—and thus is

---

[7] And of course, following Doris, I too should point out that I write this from a place that is safe, warm, and dry.

not probative for thinking about consistency in Mischel's sense—we can set it to the side.[8]

On the other hand, suppose—as seems more likely anyway—that 8,000 meters is not arbitrary, and the climber thinks there is a *reason* to act differently at such high altitudes (whether he is correct or not). For instance, at very high and dangerous altitudes stopping to help others, and to share one's food, water, or oxygen with them, is far too risky, even deadly (at least, if one intends to proceed to the summit of the mountain). We may feel that that policy is a rotten one, and likewise for the goal of getting to the summit at any cost; but that is to say that he has a bad policy or goal, not that he does not have one. At least we can see that his policy *is* a policy, and we can find the climber's adopting that policy to be intelligible—we can at least see why he acts according to *that* policy rather than some other, or none, just as in the waiter case. On this reading of the climber case, then, the climber seems to be 'consistent' in the same sense as the waiter. So this must be the right way to read Doris' thought experiment.[9]

Notice, though, that while the climber's consistency may look morally worse than the waiter's, nonetheless it now looks no less genuine, and no less interesting, as a form of consistency. There is a very big difference between the standards that Mischel and others propose for assessing consistency and the very cheap standards that Doris rightfully rejects. As we saw in Chapter 8, Charles Lord asked his subjects, in a variety of ways, about their own views about consistency, based on their goals and self-conceptions. He might have looked for consistency in their behavior with respect to, say, the proximity of their behavior to a certain gas station on the highway outside town, but he did not. It would not have told him anything about his subjects' personalities if he had. What he was after was a standard that looked like a real standard—not a standard one cooks up for the sake of *ad hoc* consistency, but a standard in terms of the kinds of cognitive and affective patterns that are not only *intelligible* as causes in the first place, but which independent evidence suggests are *real* causes of behavior. The situationist's negative argument against broad-based dispositions as causes of behavior also suggests instead that we behave as we do because of the distinctive cognitive-affective processes we engage in. When the

---

[8] This is not, I think, the result of setting the bar too high for what counts as a policy. Robert Adams (2006, 146) tells of his own policy of giving to mendicants, despite thinking that this is an inefficient form of giving, for the sake of 'the respectful human action that it facilitates'. Consequently, he is quite willing to let himself be swayed for or against giving on particular occasions—if he has money in an outer pocket, say, but not if he has to unbutton his overcoat to take out his wallet; and so on. I see no reason not to consider this a policy, even though Adams' behaviors may well look wildly inconsistent to an outside observer.

[9] Indeed, Doris himself (2002, 78) describes the policy in terms of a 'goal'.

question is the content of someone's personality, his consistency with respect to *those* processes, then, is hardly something that the situationist can regard as cheap. For the purposes of *that* question, what other standard could there be?

It is important to note that Doris' skepticism is far from incendiary; on the contrary, his view of cognitive-affective theories of personality and character is a modestly 'skeptical wait-and-see', a view which he says 'stands refutable' by empirical evidence (2002, 85).[10] It is also important to remind ourselves that even if we are off one of Doris' hooks, the empirical one, still another awaits us—the worry that such consistency as I have just discussed is insufficient for the *normative* demands of virtue theory. After all, 'honesty' proper is one thing, and honesty 'by my lights', or 'honest enough for my purposes', is another, and it seems clear that it is only the former sort of honesty that is of interest to virtue theorists. Indeed, Doris even concedes that such a conception of consistency 'may be a boon for personality psychology', but he hastens to add that even so 'it is of little help to characterological moral psychology' (2002, 84). So I now turn in the rest of this chapter to consider whether this new avenue for thinking about personality and character is likely to be of any help to virtue theory after all.

10.2 Situationism and Virtue Theory: Normative Adequacy

As we have seen, one of situationism's central positive theses is that what look like 'random turns' to an 'objective' observer may actually belie considerable order and consistency, *if* we consider them from the agent's point of view.[11] To quote J. R. R. Tolkien, not all those who wander are lost.[12] But while situationism's positive theses may suggest a taxonomy of personality—whether one's personality be good, bad, or indifferent—what about a taxonomy of the *virtues*? Much of why we care to study the virtues in the first place is that we care about the goodness of what people do, and we associate virtue with good action—not just *consistent* action, but consistently *good* action. In that case,

---

[10] Doris also says there that he doubts that he will be refuted by further evidence, 'given the track record of empirical work on personality and moral behavior'. But I find this confusing—what 'track record' does he have in mind? Presumably, the track record of traditional personality theory based on broad-based dispositions; but what could *that* track record have to do with the prospects of a personality theory that starts from the *rejection* of the dispositionist model?

[11] I thank Mark LeBar for this way of putting the point.

[12] Tolkien, *The Fellowship of the Ring*. The line is from a poem about Strider, a ranger whom most villagers mistake for a mere vagabond.

while we can identify 'honesty by one's own lights' as some feature of one's personality, this is no way to go about defining the *virtue* of honesty. So why think that cognitive-affective personality theory can help the virtue theorist?

My being generous involves actually being generous in my actions, not just being as generous as it suits me to be. Doris' view seems to be that virtue therefore requires *nominal* consistency of the virtues—in the case of generosity, regularly giving to others across a wide range of nominally dissimilar situations. And this, Doris argues, presents the virtue theorist with the following major problem (see esp. Doris 2002, 84; see also 2005, 663–5; Adams 2006, 136–8). Perhaps virtue theory could avail itself of the social psychologist's conception of consistency, but only by standards that hold from the agent's point of view; yet 'generosity by one's own lights' surely is not the same thing as generosity proper. The alternative is a theory of certain broad-based dispositions, complete with nominal consistency, but the evidence against the existence of such dispositions is enormous. Therefore, the virtue theorist needs the social psychologist's help here, but he cannot afford to take it.

I see three broad ways that a virtue theorist might try to get past this problem. One, the virtue theorist might argue that while traditional dispositionist psychology is empirically inadequate, many 'commonsense' approaches to the virtues are a far cry from dispositionism. In fact, common sense is often highly sensitive to the situational and contextual relativity of character. For instance, we observe that people who are good parents are sometimes rather lacking in compassion towards people outside their family, and it seems a point of common sense to conclude not only that parenting virtues are distinct from the virtue of compassion, but also that such people vary in their behaviors because they attach different values to different relationships. Because commonsense views of character are not just the same as theoretical dispositionism, the virtue theorist might try to adopt some commonsense view as an alternative to the character taxonomies of the dispositionist and the situationist alike. The hope, then, is that this approach just might save virtue theory from the empirically inadequate dispositionist taxonomy, as well as from the situationist taxonomy that Doris finds so normatively inadequate.

Two, the virtue theorist could argue that by a virtue he just *means* that psychological attribute that does in fact underlie a pattern of behaving consistently well across a range of situations, nominally defined, whatever that attribute turns out precisely to be. On this response, the virtue theorist focuses on purely normative questions about what behavioral patterns are good ones, identifying a given virtue with that psychological attribute responsible for a given pattern, and leaving it to the empirical psychologist to sort out the precise nature of that attribute. For instance, one could classify actions with certain sorts of consequences as right actions or 'just' actions, say, and hold that the virtue of 'justice' is whatever psychological attribute is responsible for such actions. It would then be a job for empirical psychologists to sort out whether that attribute is a broad-based disposition, a cognitive-affective bundle, or what have you. Questions of empirical adequacy are therefore 'out-sourced' while the virtue theorist focuses on strictly normative questions. The strategy is therefore to concentrate one's efforts on normative adequacy, and get empirical adequacy for free.

And three, the virtue theorist could adopt a cognitive-affective conception of personality and of consistency, and understand a character virtue as obtaining where a person's own standard of consistency is also a normatively adequate one. This is, of course, to take on the sort of theory of the virtues that I sketched at the beginning of this chapter. Taking such a view would require, of course, offering an alternative to Doris' conception of normative adequacy as nominal consistency of certain types of 'virtuous' behavior. Such an alternative might appeal to the notion of goals, for instance: to be generous, on this view, is to be consistent about pursuing the goal of doing well by others with one's resources. In short, this response would be to embrace a cognitive-affective taxonomy of personality, and argue that a virtue is a bundle of cognitive-affective processes by which one seeks the right goals, attends to the right features of situations, and so on, and adjusts one's actions accordingly. In other words, we could argue that normative adequacy is not the same thing as nominal consistency, after all, and argue instead for a standard of normative adequacy that a cognitive-affective character taxonomy can meet.

I want to discuss the first of these alternatives now, and the other two in §10.4 and §10.5, respectively. I argue that the third approach, and only that approach, is successful, and moreover that that approach commits one to Hard Virtue Theory.

10.3 From Common Sense to Virtue Theory?

Perhaps there is a third way for the virtue theorist, besides either a dispositionist or a cognitive-affective taxonomy of personality and character. Perhaps one could first drive a wedge between commonsense psychology on the one hand and theoretical dispositionism on the other, and then construct a virtue theory upon commonsense psychology. Here the virtue theorist cuts the

Gordian knot, leaving dispositionists and social psychologists to themselves, focusing instead on what common sense may have known about character all along.[13]

There are two ways to object to this sort of approach. One would be to argue that commonsense is necessarily wedded to dispositionist ideas, despite these protests. This is the sort of argument that Harman makes, but I disagree, as I shall explain below. Instead, I argue that although common sense is indeed a far cry from the dispositionist paradigm, commonsense views of personality and character still have too many problems to inspire very much confidence in this way around the problem.

How does common sense differ from dispositionism? Consider some of the ways in which we laypersons do *not* trust in the 'broad-basedness', so to speak, of alleged broad-based dispositions. For instance, Doris considers a case in which a friend to whom one is sexually attracted invites one over for a romantic dinner while one's spouse is out of town. Someone confident in a 'broad-based' disposition to be faithful to his or her spouse may therefore suppose that taking in a good dinner with this friend should be harmless—he or she is, after all, a 'faithful spouse' (1998, 516f). But of course, common sense finds it obvious that the thing to do in such a case is to avoid the situation altogether, just as it is obvious to every dieter that it is better to keep fattening snacks out of the house than to keep them around and trust to will-power. Likewise, my father often describes locking his house or car as an act of 'keeping honest people honest'. It seems clear, then, that common sense about personality and character is nothing like flat-footed dispositionism (see also Annas 2003, 27; 2005c, 638; Flanagan 1991, 291). On the contrary, it is precisely because the traditional dispositionist's notion of 'broad-basedness' is so simplistic that such dispositionism often offends against common sense.

Nonetheless, there is a large body of research on commonsense trait-attribution behavior, and unfortunately it suggests that whatever our lay personality 'theory' is, in the final analysis it suffers from serious defects in empirical adequacy. The behavior of attributing dispositions to others is, after all, a kind of *behavior*, and studies of this behavior have discovered some rather interesting trends. (In fact, it is better to talk about attribution behavior than lay personality 'theory', since in place of any such theory we find instead, I think, an amalgam of very different sorts of attribution behaviors.) Simply put, we generally tend to divide the behaviors we observe into an agent whose actions are the focus of attention, and a situational background against which the

---

[13] One might say that this is the *de facto* approach of Slote 2001.

agent acts.[14] For instance, if we notice that Fred whistles to himself as he walks through the pet shop, we may focus more on Fred's *whistling* than on Fred's doing so *at the pet shop*. As a result, we often attribute dispositions to persons to explain their behavior without paying as much attention to the impact of their situation. We may therefore describe Fred simply as a 'whistler', someone who likes to whistle, and we may have fairly high confidence in predicting that Fred is disposed to whistle in other kinds of contexts as well. In fact, research suggests that we tend to have more confidence in these sorts of predictions than in predictions about how a high-scoring athlete in one game will score in future games (see Ross and Nisbett 1991, 122–4). But our confidence may be unjustified if, say, Fred mainly tends to whistle when he is nervous, such as when he finds himself in an aisle full of large snakes in terrariums. Following Lee Ross (1977), psychologists often call this common trend towards unwarranted attributions the 'fundamental attribution error'.[15] Ross and Nisbett describe the fundamental attribution error (henceforth 'FAE') as 'people's inflated belief in the importance of personality traits and dispositions, together with their failure to recognize the importance of situational factors in assessing behavior' (1991, 4; see also Gilbert 1995, 105f).

One body of research strongly suggests that we tend to attribute dispositions with a surprising degree of indifference to the poverty of our evidence for such dispositions. For instance, one study assigned male subjects a pair of essays to read on the same topic, one poorly and one well written, and attached to each essay a (bogus) photo of either an attractive or an unattractive female 'author'. The experimenters found that subjects tended to assess the 'authors' of the poor essays as better writers when those essays were accompanied by an attractive photo; in fact, they rated those 'authors' almost as highly as they rated the unattractive 'authors' of the good essays! (See Doris 2002, 93 for discussion.) The evidence for attributing good writing skills to those 'authors' was very poor, but biases about attractive and unattractive persons seem to have led to highly unwarranted assessments of who is a 'pretty (!) good essay writer'. (See also Mischel 1968, 58.)

What is even more surprising is a demonstrated tendency to explain behavior in dispositional terms, even when the behavior *clearly* has more to do with situational factors than with any special attributes of the agent. For instance, in one famous study researchers paired subjects as 'quizmasters' and 'contestants' for a quiz game. Each quizmaster was then asked to write ten difficult but

---

[14] See Ross and Nisbett 1991, 139–41 for a review of research on this phenomenon; see also Doris 2002, 104.

[15] Gilbert 1995 calls this phenomenon 'correspondence bias'.

not impossible questions on a topic of his or her choice, and to quiz his or her appointed contestant on them. Not surprisingly, the quizmasters knew far more of the answers (all of them, of course) than did the contestants. However, researchers found that subjects who had observed the quiz game—and even the contestant subjects themselves!—tended to rate the quizmaster as the overall 'more knowledgeable' in each pair (see Ross and Nisbett 1991, 127f). Apparently, the fact that the situation was *obviously* rigged to favor one subject over the other made little difference to their general assessments of their intellectual dispositions.[16]

Likewise, another study found that even when subjects had watched a film on the Milgram experiments that specifically emphasized how the various situational factors of the experiments had affected their outcome, subjects nonetheless predicted that Milgram's 'teachers' would still administer relatively high shocks to the 'learners' even without those situational factors in place (see Ross and Nisbett 1991, 132). Whether the subjects were persuaded of the film's thesis or not, they clearly ignored the situational variables even after they had been pointed out.

It seems clear, then, that we tend not only to look for dispositions to explain behaviors, but also to look beyond situational variables when doing so, and thus to overlook many crucial clues about agents' if…then…behavioral signatures, such as we discussed in Chapter 8. These tendencies are clear outside the laboratory, as well. For instance, when Patty Hearst was on trial as an accomplice to armed robbery, having cooperated with the extremist group that had kidnapped her, the prosecution asked jurors to consider whether she behaved as she did primarily because of the sort of person that she was, or primarily because of the situations she was in. The jury found Hearst guilty, despite knowing some rather overwhelming facts about her situation, such as that she had been bound, blindfolded, and kept in a closet for fifty-seven days, repeatedly threatened with death, repeatedly raped, and repeatedly browbeaten with extremist doctrine. More persuasive, evidently, was the prosecutor's argument that 'most of us' are the sorts of people who would do just about anything rather than participate in a dangerous armed robbery, whatever the situation (see Gilbert 1995 for discussion). The thought seems to have been that Hearst did what she did because she had a general disposition to do such unlawful acts. Her tragic situation may have given her disposition an occasion to manifest itself, but it otherwise played no causal or explanatory role in her behavior.

---

[16] I have to confess that Alex Trebek (host of the American quiz show *Jeopardy!*) has always struck me as seeming very knowledgeable; but of course, how would I know if he weren't?

Consider another, much more recent case. On 2 February 2007, Italian authorities suspended soccer matches following a literally explosive riot between rival fans in Catania, Sicily, in which a police officer was killed. Remarking on the situation, the vice director of Italy's best-selling sports paper cited an Italian cultural disposition to ignore rules. Yet two years earlier, laws had been passed in Britain requiring stadiums to adopt tougher security measures, and these laws had had considerable success in curtailing the hooliganism for which British soccer matches had previously earned such a widespread reputation.[17] Again, it seems more appropriate to focus on the situations surrounding the event—such as the quality of a venue's security measures—than on the alleged dispositions of the participants.

Not only do we tend to attribute dispositions despite faulty evidence for them, and even in the face of strong situational evidence against them, but it also seems that we tend to have much more *confidence* in those attributions than is warranted. In one well-known study, experimenters asked subjects to predict whether a particular individual—the 'target'—would comb his hair if the experimenters asked to take a photo of him. Subjects who predicted the target's behavior on the basis of an interview with the target attached an expected accuracy of 77% to their predictions, although their actual accuracy (60%) was only slightly higher than other subjects who had predicted on the basis of just the target's name and photo (57%). What is more, the latter subjects had predicted an accuracy level of 72%! Note, then, that those with less information about the subject were about equally confident in their dispositional predictions as those who had had much more information (see Ross and Nisbett 1991, 134). Furthermore, researchers have found that subjects are often just about as confident in their predictions of the *consistency* of dispositions in situations of different sorts, as they are in their predictions of the *stability* of those dispositions in future situations of the same sort (129f). This suggests that, for practical purposes anyway, we tend not to distinguish very much between stability and the consistency of the dispositions we attribute, yet research shows that such predictions differ significantly in their accuracy. In these sorts of cases, equal confidence is over-confidence.

The FAE has been observed not only in laypersons, but also in the attribution behaviors of professional psychotherapists. As Mischel reported in his 1968 review, researchers had documented the tendency of therapists to arrive at an overall picture of a patient's broad-based dispositions within the first few hours of contact (as early as the first two to four hours), a picture that not only tends to remain fixed over time, but which therapists also tend to regard

---

[17] This story was reported by I. Fisher and P. Kiefer in the *New York Times*, 9 Feb. 2007.

as repeatedly 'confirmed' by further information. However, such confidence often seems to be sustained by the therapist's minimizing and even disregarding subsequent disconfirming evidence (1968, 56–9, 126f). Furthermore, other research in Mischel's review found that even using formal personality tests to classify patients within standard disposition-based personality categories failed to increase predictive success over less formal generalizations made on biographical data alone (120). The FAE, therefore, is relatively immune to extinction by education, and translating dispositionist views about personality into formal assessment methods leaves the FAE almost exactly where it was before. In a word, the FAE is not just for laypersons.

It seems clear enough, then, that laypersons and professionals alike make a lot of mistakes in attributing dispositions and making disposition-based predictions. Research has also suggested a number of reasons why we make these mistakes as often as we do. This research suggests that instead of chalking up attribution mistakes to a single, monolithic cognitive tendency like the FAE (as e.g. Harman seems to do), we can explain those mistakes in terms of a fairly wide range of factors (see also Webber 2007b). For one thing, it seems that we tend to ignore the fact that different people view or construe their circumstances in very different ways, and therefore misunderstand what the agent takes himself or herself to be doing; for the same reason, we often fail in predicting even our own behavior in imagined situations (see Ross and Nisbett 1991, 85–9; Gilbert 1995, 115–20). Furthermore, we often tend to assume that the motivations and situations of other people even in very different walks of life are more or less uniform with our own (Ross and Nisbett 1991, 154–6),[18] and this is compounded by the familiar difficulty involved in imagining someone else's very different situation in adequate detail (Gilbert 1995, 113–15). It is also clear that much of the relevant information about a person's construal of his or her situation is often unavailable—we are not mind-readers—and need not even be concurrent with the observed behavior: a subject's construal of a situation we see the subject in today may be shaped by what he or she was told about such situations the day before (Gilbert 1995, 111–13).

Our observations of the behaviors of others also tend to be selective, in a couple of ways. On the one hand, our interactions with others tend to occur within the same context (e.g. at work, at church), and we tend to move from the observed stability of their behavior in that context to predictions about the consistency of their behavior in different contexts (Ross and Nisbett 1991,

---

[18] I remember once riding through a run-down and visibly poor neighborhood, and hearing the driver wonder aloud why the residents had not given more thought to location in their choice of real estate.

148–50; Gilbert 1995, 137f). On the other, people often realize that other people are making attributions about them, and often adjust their behavior accordingly, to sustain a particular sort of 'image' (Gilbert 1995, 138–41; Ross and Nisbett 1991, 150–4, 156–8). Likewise, one's behavior tends to generate attributions on the part of others, which in turn leads others to create for one an environment that can establish or reinforce a corresponding self-attribution, making in some cases even for considerable, lifelong behavioral stability (see Ross and Nisbett 1991, 158–60). Furthermore, our presuppositions about another person can shape how we treat them, in ways that increase the likelihood that the person will behave in ways that appear to confirm our presuppositions (Gilbert 1995, 128–34; see also Mischel 1968, 56–8).

But perhaps one of the most interesting explanations of our attribution behaviors has to do with the particular psychological processes involved in attribution behavior. While it is clear that we explain behavior by attributing dispositions (e.g. 'he is very rude'), it is also clear that we adjust our attributions in the light of mitigating situational factors ('but then he had just received a very bad piece of news'). However, these two sub-processes are not on a par psychologically: research suggests that we attribute first, and automatically, but we adjust for situations *second*, and then only *with effort* (Gilbert 1995, 120–5). The difference between these two sub-processes therefore has the result of frequently insulating our attributions against challenges from other kinds of information, especially information about clearly relevant situational factors.

The FAE therefore has a firm footing in our psychology as disposition-attributing agents, but it would be a mistake to think that the FAE is simply inevitable. Although the evidence is incomplete, there does seem to be some support for the hypothesis that tendencies to describe others in terms of general dispositions (e.g. 'he is generous'), rather than in terms of more specific behavior descriptions ('he brings me provisions') or external situational factors, demonstrate considerable cultural variability. In particular, the attribution of dispositions seems to be much more frequent in cultures with an anti-fatalistic worldview than in more fatalistic cultures, perhaps because people in more anti-fatalistic cultures are more likely to regard situations as the relatively uninteresting background against which individuals 'make their own destiny' (see Ross and Nisbett 1991, 184ff; Flanagan 1991, 281; Gilbert 1995, 107f; Doris 2002, 105f). Interestingly, the process of attribution seems to be automatic, but the frequency with which it operates should not be taken as fixed.

Furthermore, although the FAE does seem to be real, it is important not to overstate it. For one thing, when we say that someone is shy or well behaved, say, we often hasten to add that nonetheless 'she does have her moments'; and even when we do not verbalize them, such qualifications are generally understood (see Doris 2002, 97). For another, it seems that attribution also has an important epistemic role to play: attributing a general disposition to someone is a fairly economical way of storing and recalling information about his or her behavior (Mischel 1968, 54; Flanagan 1991, 311f; Gilbert 1995, 108–11; Doris 2002, 98), and the presumption of stability and consistency makes another person less of a 'moving target', and their behavior therefore easier to interpret.[19]

Moreover, as we saw in the previous chapter, studies of performance prediction have shown that predictions of a candidate's performance based on letters of reference from persons who know the candidate well are more likely to be accurate than are predictions based on interviews (Ross and Nisbett 1991, 136–8). One way to interpret such findings is that laypersons have access to substantial 'longitudinal' data, building up fairly reliable profiles of persons they know well and observe over time (see Goldie 2000, 166 and 2004, 52–69, cited in Webber 2007b; see also Solomon 2005, 651). I would propose, as seems likely and as Walter Mischel and his colleagues have argued,[20] that such profiles are usually built up from observations of those persons in various situations, allowing the observer to compile behavioral and situational evidence rather like if…then…signatures, from which inferences can be made about underlying attributes with a reasonable level of confidence. There is no reason to think, I suggest, that common sense is *very* far off from a cognitive-affective conception of personality, our undeniable attribution errors notwithstanding. And in that case there is no reason at all to think that the layperson's *very idea* of character should be rejected wholesale (see also Webber 2007b).

So attribution errors need not be stupid or unintelligible errors, and they may not be errors that we have to make as often as we do. But for all that, our everyday attribution behaviors still display a host of problems. An important implication of research on attribution behavior, therefore, is a serious warning against hastily attributing behavior to personal dispositions, and an encouragement to pay close attention to situational factors that can cast light

---

[19] Also, while lay 'personality theory' has been compared to 'folk physics' (e.g. Harman 2003, 88), this comparison is seriously misleading: the basic 'building blocks' of folk physics (e.g. the notion of objects moving through inner forces) are replaced outright by sophisticated physics, but of course empirical psychology—including, please note, situationist psychology—currently continues to operate in terms of the beliefs, desires, and so on that are the stock-in-trade of folk psychology. See Solomon 2003, 47f; 2005, 652.

[20] See e.g. Mischel and Shoda 1995, 258; Mischel, Shoda, and Mendoza-Denton 2002, 52; Kammrath, Mendoza-Denton, and Mischel 2005.

on what agents take themselves to be doing.[21] And a further implication, of particular immediate interest to us, is that even if a commonsense personality taxonomy is not the same as the theoretical dispositionist's taxonomy, still it is unlikely to offer us all the empirical adequacy we need, and could use a corrective.[22] It would seem, then, both that the virtue theorist must reckon with the empirical adequacy of the character taxonomy with which he or she begins, and that neither dispositionism nor commonsense intuitions alone will do.

10.4 Out-Sourcing the Empirical Work?

I turn now to a second possible virtue-theoretical response to Doris' dilemma between the empirical inadequacy of the dispositionist taxonomy and the purported normative inadequacy of the cognitive-affective one. One way to maintain a normatively adequate conception of the virtues is perhaps to define virtues in terms of stable and consistent patterns of good-producing behavior, from an observer's (i.e. a nominal) point of view. On this view, it is a necessary condition of having a virtue that one exhibit a consistent pattern of good stereotypical (e.g. 'compassionate') behaviors. Normative adequacy, as Doris regards it, is a given.

There are two ways to define virtue in terms of behavioral patterns. First, we could define the notion of 'having the virtue of compassion' as simply the *same* as displaying the pattern of compassionate behavior in question. But recall that, for the personality psychologist's purposes, such a pattern of behavior is the explanandum, and the explanans is some psychological attribute responsible for the pattern. So this sort of approach would not be a kind of *virtue* theory anyway, but rather a theory of the moral qualities of certain kinds of behaviors. Virtue theory is a theory of psychological attributes, whether or not a virtue must take the same psychological form in every person in which that virtue is instantiated. A preference for using virtue vocabulary as labels for other kinds of things does not a virtue theorist make.

The alternative is to define 'compassion' as whatever psychological attribute underlies the observed pattern of nominally identified 'compassionate' behavior, so that virtue remains a purported explanans. Here the virtue theorist

---

[21] See Ross and Nisbett 1991, 243. For discussion of numerous practical implications of situationism, see 1991, ch. 8.

[22] Interestingly, Annas (2005c, 639) suggests that virtue ethics itself could serve as a corrective for many conventional forms of thought about the virtues, by redirecting our attention from superficially, stereotypically 'virtuous' actions ('That was dangerous; he must be courageous') to more complex forms of practical reasoning.

attends exclusively to the ethical taxonomy of certain consistent patterns of behavior, nominally characterized, stipulating that the virtues are whatever psychological attributes turn out to underlie such patterns, and leaving it to the empirical psychologist to determine just what sorts of things those psychological attributes are—broad-based dispositions, cognitive-affective processes, or whatever. Consequently, empirical adequacy is secured by definition—a virtue is that psychological attribute of a person that underlies a behavioral pattern that just *is* nominally consistent. And since the behavioral pattern in question must be one of *good*-producing behaviors, normative adequacy is guaranteed too.

I want to consider two ways of defining virtues as attributes behind behavioral patterns that have been suggested in the virtue-theoretical literature. One of them defines virtuous character traits in terms of *right action*, and the other in terms of *virtuous action*, where in each case the actions are defined independently of the traits. I then explain why I do not think that any version of this approach is a viable solution of the dilemma.

10.4.1 Virtue in Terms of Right Action: Driver's View

One way to deploy this strategy of 'out-sourcing' the work on empirical adequacy is to construct a theory of right action—in terms of consequences, say—and define a virtue as a psychological attribute responsible for certain patterns of right action, whatever that attribute should turn out to be. For example, we could say that 'justice' is the name of some attribute or other by which one consistently produces right action (such as the production of good consequences) in the context of the distribution of resources. This deployment of the out-sourcing strategy begins from behavioral patterns classified as different sorts of right actions, defines a virtue as whatever character trait is responsible for some such pattern, and leaves it to the personality psychologist to sort out the proper taxonomy for specifying the precise nature of such traits.

This type of strategy rests on an approach to virtue theory that will be familiar to readers of Julia Driver's 2001 book *Uneasy Virtue*. According to Driver, '*x* is a virtue iff it is a character trait that produces actually good consequences overall or systematically' (2001, 95). Now, Driver distinguishes between 'virtues' and 'moral virtues', the latter being a species of the former. First, Driver understands *virtues* as traits which actually produce good consequences (and do not merely intend to), and do so directly (as opposed to being in accordance with rules or policies that tend to produce good consequences). It is worth noting that Driver's view is not a 'maximizing' consequentialism, twice over: the good consequences of a trait need not be maximized in order for the trait to be a virtue, and the trait itself need not have good consequences on every single occasion of its exercise. Finally, the regular and 'systematic' production of good consequences is to be assessed only within the agent's actual and usual environment: for instance, the same trait may have excellent consequences in nineteenth-century rural England and horrible ones in Nazi Germany, but this does not keep that trait from being a *bona fide* virtue in the Victorian farmer (2001, ch. 4). Second, a *moral* virtue, according to Driver, is a virtue which also regularly benefits others and not just oneself (as opposed, e.g., to prudential virtues, which have good consequences 'primarily for the agent'), and which stems from some 'character trait or quality of the mind' (91, 108).[23] (In what immediately follows, for the sake of simplicity, by 'virtues' I shall understand the moral virtues in Driver's sense.)

Driver also considers the important questions of the temporal stability and the cross-situational consistency of the virtues. (Roughly, Driver refers to these as the 'reliability' and 'flexibility' of the virtues, respectively.) Since Driver defines the virtues as traits that *systematically* produce good consequences, virtues are stable (or 'reliable') by definition:

[I]f the virtue is a disposition, reliability is already built into the concept … If the agent, like any object, has a disposition to behave in a certain way (or, in the case of sentient beings, has certain feelings), then she is reliable with respect to that behavior or those feelings.   (2001, 10, 54)

More importantly for us, these virtues seem to be nominally consistent by definition as well. An Aristotelian account, Driver says, aims to establish consistency (or 'flexibility') by making practical wisdom part of the virtues: 'The true usefulness of wisdom is flexibility and responsiveness to the unusual'. The Aristotelian, that is, insists that the virtues must all be underwritten by the psychological attribute of practical wisdom or phronesis, and makes this the basis of the consistency of the virtues, on the grounds that phronesis enables the agent to adjust to a wide range of situations. Driver, however, argues that neither phronesis nor any other sort of knowledge or intelligence is necessary for the consistency of the virtues. She does concede that 'sensitivity to the morally relevant features of a situation is important' (2001, 54), but since she offers no account of such 'sensitivity', it would seem that on her view consistency would have to be a matter of definition too.

On Driver's view, then, we do not begin with a theory of dispositions or other attributes and demonstrate their consistency, but we begin with consistency itself—a consistent pattern of right actions—and stipulate that

---

[23] Driver also distinguishes moral virtues from aesthetic virtues which are merely 'polite' (25) and 'merely pleasing' (91).

virtues are the psychological attributes that cause those consistent behavioral patterns, whatever those attributes turn out to be. In other words, a virtue is whatever psychological attribute underlies a particular stable and consistent pattern of good-producing behavior, where that behavior and its cross-situational consistency are characterized in nominal terms. Here we take a virtue to be the explanans of a certain behavioral pattern, rather than the explanandum, that is, the pattern itself. It then falls to the psychologist rather than to the virtue theorist to identify the psychological content or contents of that explanans. Indeed, Driver chides the Aristotelian virtue theorist for being too determinate about the nature of the virtues, since such a theorist holds that the virtues must involve phronesis.

10.4.2 Virtue in Terms of Virtuous Action: Thomson's View

Another way to deploy the out-sourcing strategy is to define virtues in terms of a prior conception of virtuous action. On this view, rather than defining virtuous actions in terms of the exercise of the virtues, we begin by classifying certain patterns of behavior as just, say, or generous, and then understand the virtue of justice as that character trait responsible for patterns of just behavior, generosity as that character trait responsible for generous behavior, and so on.

Judith Jarvis Thomson (1997, 280) takes just this sort of approach to the virtues:

> I shall take the noun phrase 'being just' to refer to what all just acts have in common, just people being just only derivatively, in the sense that they are prone to performing just acts. But I shall follow a common usage according to which the noun 'justice' refers to a character trait possessed by people, namely, the character trait that consists in proneness to performing just acts.[24]

On this approach, the virtue theorist's focus is wholly on the normative analysis of certain patterns of behavior. To be sure, there is some psychological attribute, some character trait, that is responsible for each such pattern, but it falls to the empirical psychologist to provide an empirically adequate taxonomy of such attributes. So the virtue of justice is whatever psychological attribute is the cause of patterns of just behavior.

Notice that both versions of the out-sourcing strategy share a commitment to what I shall call the Correspondence Assumption: where there is a stable and consistent pattern of right or virtuous behavior in some agent, there is some psychological attribute or other in that agent—a virtue—that is responsible for that pattern. Again, to the extent that the theories I have discussed are theories

---

[24] Thomson also extends this analysis to generosity, kindness, 'and so on' (281).

of *virtues*, they are committed to the Correspondence Assumption: a virtue is a psychological *attribute*, and not just a name given to any chance assortment of factors behind some behavioral pattern.

10.4.3 The Problem for Driver and Thomson

However, the Correspondence Assumption, so stated, is ambiguous: are the 'patterns' to which the attributes correspond defined *psychologically* or *nominally*? The difference is important. One reading of the Correspondence Assumption seems extremely safe: when we identify and individuate a behavioral pattern *psychologically*—that is, from the agent's point of view—then we are on our way towards identifying a cohesive cognitive-affective bundle, such as one's pursuing a kind of goal, attaching value to certain outcomes vis-à-vis that goal, and so on. So much is just what cognitive-affective personality theory would teach us. But such a personality theory would *also* teach that the Correspondence Assumption is false, when we identify and individuate behavioral patterns *nominally*, that is, from the observer's or theorist's point of view. For instance, a subject may exhibit a stable and consistent pattern of 'compassionate' behavior, from the observer's point of view, in one type of context because he cares deeply for another, in another because he wishes to endear himself to someone, in another out of feelings of guilt, and so on.[25] Consequently, it is possible and indeed likely that patterns of nominally 'compassionate' behavior may well have *no* single explanans. In that case, the psychology responsible for such a pattern may very well be a hodge-podge of disparate, unconnected psychological factors, rather than any proper psychological attribute or character trait that causes the 'compassionate' behavioral pattern. So the nominal reading of the Correspondence Assumption is false.

The problem for the out-sourcing strategy, therefore, is that it requires a correspondence between behavioral patterns and underlying attributes, where those patterns are *nominally* defined. But of course, *nominal consistency is no guarantee of psychological consistency*. So this out-sourcing strategy faces a dilemma. On the one hand, one could insist that a virtue is identical to absolutely *whatever* psychological factors turn out to cause certain behavioral patterns, however disparate those factors may be, that is, even if those patterns cannot be aligned with any genuine psychological attributes. But that is just to say that there is no interface between one's taxonomy of virtues, understood as character traits, and an empirically adequate theory of the psychological causes of behavior. In

---

[25] Arpaly 2004, 95 offers an interesting discussion of one such case.

other words, that is to give up on the Correspondence Assumption altogether, and therefore on that whole side of a 'virtue theory' that has to do with *character*, rather than with behavior. The resulting view would be an ethical classification of certain behavioral patterns—and more power to it, for all I can tell; it just would not be a theory of the *virtues*. Such an approach would respond to Doris' dilemma for virtue theory by merely changing the subject. Treating virtues as such purely theoretical constructs is not to construct a virtue theory, but to use virtue vocabulary to talk about something else.

On the other hand, if we understand a virtue as a genuine psychological attribute, and not just a chance assortment of disparate psychological factors, then we cannot stipulate that a virtue is whatever attribute is responsible for certain nominally classified behaviors, because there may well be no attribute of *that* sort. That is what situationism teaches us. Rather, if we hope to show that virtues are consistent traits, then we must first define virtues, understood as real psychological attributes, and (I think) as bundles of cognitive-affective processes by which agents interpret their situations and adjust their behaviors to suit them. In that case, the virtue theorist *must* take a stand on an empirically adequate taxonomy of personality and character, and work from there towards a theory about which items in that taxonomy are the virtues. Given that virtue theory is a theory about *virtues*, it cannot simply out-source labor on empirical adequacy.

More successful in this regard is the view that virtues are forms of characteristic responsiveness, in a variety of different contexts, to certain sorts of reasons, and that the melding of virtue 'modules' is really the gradual dropping away of contextual barriers in one's responsiveness to those reasons. That would mean, however, that we could not understand consistency in nominal, overt-behavioral terms, but should focus instead on psychological consistency, consistency in seeking goals and responding to reasons. And that seems more plausible on independent grounds, too. Proper development in virtue, in reasons-responsiveness, should lead to a more mature grasp of what *unifies* justice as one thing, despite the diversity of contexts in which one acts justly (see Annas 2005c, 639, 641). Moral maturity is more than just having picked up more behavioral habits. The fragmentation view is no friend of the virtue theorist—not, at any rate, if our being reasons-responsive creatures has anything to do with what is a virtue in us, as surely it must.

So it seems that virtue theorists, whether they like it or not, must be in the business of assessing the empirical adequacy of theories of personality. We cannot assume that a nominal behavioral pattern is underwritten by a proper psychological attribute, so virtue theory must begin from a theory of psychological attributes, not from a theory of right action or virtuous action.

10.4.4 Virtues as Fragmentary Dispositions: Adams' View

But perhaps this is too quick. As one virtue theorist has noticed, although there need be no coherent psychological attribute that accounts for 'courageous' or 'honest' behaviors, full stop, still there may be such an attribute for more fragmentary dispositions, such as 'physical courage' or 'law-abiding honesty'. Robert Adams has argued recently for such an account of the virtues of courage and honesty (2006, ch. 8). Adams notes that while the cross-situational correlations of behaviors across dispositions are low (the rare extreme cases aside), nonetheless such correlations do exist, and are clearer if they are aggregated over time (122–5). Thus one may have a disposition 'to exhibit a particular type of behavior', not at every or almost every opportunity, but in ways that 'amount to significant probabilities of relevant behavior', even if those probabilities are not terribly high (124). Courage and honesty, Adams argues, can be defined in terms of such dispositions, because they are highly fragmentary: they are not unified psychological traits, but rather composites of narrower, fragmentary dispositions. Indeed, 'courage' and 'honesty' are potentially misleading labels for what are really composites of separate traits like 'moral courage', 'physical courage', 'business honesty', 'law-abiding honesty', and so on (127–9; 179ff).[26] Each of these traits is itself a virtue, since to be honest about one's work is after all a good way for one to be, even if one is not honest also with one's spouse, say (127–30).

Adams rejects the Correspondence Assumption in the case of composite virtues like honesty and courage. Such a virtue is the result of similar fragmentary dispositions converging in an agent 'to form a cross-situationally consistent composite disposition [that] can rightly be regarded, in some cases, as constituting a genuine or more complete case of the particular virtue' (2006, 126f). Adams recognizes that a virtue, strictly speaking, is not a hodge-podge of disparate psychological attributes, but must hold together as a 'psychological reality' (127), so that it can realistically be regarded as one trait. We should not be misled, for instance by language, into thinking that there is such a thing as one virtue corresponding to some range of behaviors just because we describe those behaviors with one name ('honest' or 'courageous', say; 127f). I shall call this principle 'the unity of *a* virtue': however the virtues are related to one another, each virtue must at least constitute a unified psychological attribute. This is not to say that a virtue must have exactly the same psychological makeup

---

[26] In Adams' terms, virtues like courage are 'structural' virtues, virtues that consist not in having appropriate values, but only in being well oriented towards what values one has (e.g. 2006, 175). Con. Hursthouse (1995*b*), whose view is, I think, closer to the truth: courage, as a virtue, has no goods that are its particular concern, but is an orientation towards real goods, nonetheless.

in every person who has it, but only that any such psychological makeup must hang together as a real trait.

A virtue like honesty or courage is therefore taken to be the psychological composite of traits underlying the converging honesty- or courage-relevant, situation-specific patterns of overt behavior (less those behaviors that are badly motivated) (2006, 126f). But as Adams realizes, 'supposed' virtues like honesty and courage are therefore 'really rather heterogeneous groups of dispositions' (128). To say that honesty is a virtue, then, is not to say that there is some unified psychological attribute that is a virtue, but rather that there are many different, more fragmentary dispositions all 'in the neighborhood' with one another, and that each of these is a virtue.

This approach may suggest that it is possible, after all, to start with nominal classifications of overt virtuous behaviors, and define virtues in terms of these, *provided* that one is willing to make those virtues sufficiently fragmentary. Indeed, perhaps such an approach could even be extended to the other virtues, too. But I think that a view like Adams' still has a serious empirical problem. Adams recognizes that the Correspondence Assumption would be false at the level of a 'composite' virtue. But why think that that assumption would be true at the level of a fragmentary or modular virtue, either? If there is no reason to infer a single psychological attribute underlying someone's 'honest' behaviors, why think that there is such an attribute underlying his 'workplace honest' behaviors? Even if none of the motivations behind those behaviors is bad, why think that they form any kind of unit? The Correspondence Assumption is not false for broader rather than narrower consistency; it is false for any kind of *nominal* consistency. Adams' strategy is ingenious, but in the end it only moves the problem back.

Moreover, I think that this fragmentary approach suffers normative problems as well. In particular, while we may grant that it is good for a person to be honest in business, there are at least two serious complications for thinking of a fragmentary honesty 'module' as itself a proper virtue. One, surely there is no limit in principle to the number of ways in which we may describe persons as good, but if each of these is to count as a virtue, then there is in principle no limit to the number of virtues. In that case, the notion of someone's or something's being 'overall virtuous' becomes highly problematic (see Chapter 5). And two, the narrower a virtue is—the more myopically focused on some area of concern it is the more difficult it is to understand it as an excellence of reasons-responsive creatures. This is not to say that one must be honest everywhere if one is to be honest at all, but it is to say that responsiveness to reasons should lead to ever-diminishing compartmentalization (cp. Annas 2005c). Since the present view takes virtues like honesty to be inherently fragmentary, it is therefore difficult to see how such fragmentary 'honesties' could be proper excellences of reasons-responsive creatures.[27]

10.4.5 The Problem for Deflationary 'Virtue Ethics'

Finally, the falsity of the Correspondence Assumption for nominal behavioral sets has an important further implication. As I mentioned in Chapter 2, philosophers sometimes understand the virtues in terms of some prior theory of right action, holding that the virtues are just those traits that regularly produce right action (as the utilitarian conceives of it, say). In fact, such an approach has often aimed at trivializing and deflating virtue ethics: there is nothing special about moral theorizing in terms of the virtues, the idea goes, because after all, *any* moral theory can be translated into that sort of view; so virtue ethics is not really a genuine alternative to other kinds of moral theory. Julia Annas (1998, 40) describes this common thought (which she herself rejects) as follows:

> [I]f virtues are seen as dispositions to do the right thing, whatever that is, and if that is determined by the theory, then virtues can be reshaped to accommodate whatever is, according to the theory, the right thing, and their content just falls mechanically out of the theory. Thus, we get utilitarian virtues which are simply dispositions to do whatever is, from a utilitarian point of view, the right thing to do, and whose content must, obviously, be completely fluid....It is easy to see why virtue, so conceived, is not very important or serious from a theoretical point of view.

But if situationism is right about the causes of behavior, then such an approach is a non-starter: because virtues, like any other personality or character attribute, must have psychological consistency, and because nominally consistent behavior may well be caused by disparate psychological factors, we cannot define virtues in terms of the nominal consistency of behavior. *A fortiori*, we cannot define virtues in terms of nominally consistent performance of 'right action', either. Remarkably, we find that no theory of the virtues can be empirically adequate if it makes the thesis that 'an action is right just in case it is what a virtuous person would do' come out as a truism![28]

Therefore, a virtue as a character trait cannot be defined in terms of right action or virtuous action, nominally characterized, after all. Of course, one is always free to mean by 'virtuous person' someone who is disposed to do virtuous actions or right actions, nominally characterized, but what one cannot do is suppose that one thereby describes any *trait* of such a person's psychology.

---

[27] I am of course aware, however, that Adams will probably find such a view 'elitist' (123). I consider this charge in Ch. 4, and return to it in Ch. 11.

[28] See Ch. 2 (§2.4.1), and Hursthouse 1999a, 30f, for discussion of that truism.

Consequently, one cannot suppose either that one is thereby talking about the virtues in the way that virtue ethicists do.

No character trait, including virtue, can be defined in terms of nominally classified actions. That is an empirical point. It is therefore ironic that Harman specifically cites Thomson's view as an empirically adequate account of the virtues (Harman 1999, 327f).

Notice that to insist, as Doris does, that virtue theory is committed to nominal consistency is to insist that the virtues must be identified in terms of a prior conception of right or virtuous action. But if the arguments of the preceding paragraphs are correct, that would be a death sentence for virtue theory. So the crucial question is whether virtue theory really *does* require nominal consistency in order to give a normatively adequate account of the virtues. What we need, then, is to find a way to identify virtues with attributes that have psychological consistency, *and* to reject the idea that nominal consistency is the sort of consistency the virtue theorist needs. I take up these issues in the final section, and argue that an Aristotelian virtue theory—complete with phronesis—succeeds on both counts.

10.5 A Cognitive-Affective Approach to the Virtues

We are discussing different responses to an alleged dilemma for the virtue theorist, between adopting an empirically inadequate dispositionist personality taxonomy, on the one hand, and adopting a normatively inadequate cognitive-affective personality taxonomy, on the other. The first response I considered suggested an intuitive taxonomy as a third alternative, but our intuitions about dispositions seem to be in considerable disarray. The second response suggested remaining agnostic about psychological taxonomies, but this approach collapsed into a theory of good behavior patterns rather than of virtues. Since I have argued that the cognitive-affective taxonomy seems to be a reasonable model of the nature of personality, I propose that we adopt that taxonomy, and argue that that taxonomy is well suited to the normative enterprise of virtue theory, after all. I consider the empirical and the normative adequacy of such a theory, in turn.

My remarks here shall be fairly brief. It is not my aim to construct the sort of virtue theory that would be adequate in these two respects, but to argue that some such theory is a real possibility. And that there is such a possibility should already be clear from the discussion in this part of the book. Still, it will be of considerable help to sketch at least the main points outlining such a possibility.

10.5.1 Empirical Adequacy

It remains, then, to embrace situationism and define virtues in cognitive-affective rather than behavioral terms, as mental attributes by which one acts for certain kinds of reasons. On a cognitive-affective conception of the virtues, we understand behavioral consistency from the agent's point of view, and understand one's consistent character trait to be a virtue just in case one's own standard of consistency where that trait is concerned is *also* an ethically good one, in virtue of which one acts for ethically good reasons. For example, we might understand 'compassion' as a character trait in virtue of which one regularly acts for compassionate reasons, acts for the sake of certain goals (e.g. the goal of benefiting others for their own sake), attends to certain features of situations as practically salient, classifies situations as opportunities to help (rather than, e.g., to ignore or to exploit), attaches value to certain kinds of outcomes, and so on, and adjusts one's behaviors accordingly.[29] Such a character trait could be temporally *stable*, since one could of course commit to acting for such reasons over time (see also Chapter 1, §1.1.2), just as much as (say) a waiter can commit to acting for the sake of making tips over time. Such a character trait could also be *consistent*, since acting for certain reasons or goals can underwrite a wide range of psychologically similar (and nominally dissimilar) behaviors in a wide range of situations, and it is surely as possible to act consistently for virtuous reasons and goals as for any others. Consequently, character traits on such a conception would be psychologically consistent, and therefore that conception would be empirically adequate.

Such an account of the virtues would be nothing new, since it is in fact part of the Aristotelian tradition in virtue theory.[30] According to Aristotle, although virtue is gained through habituation, this process results not in a 'broad-based behavioral disposition' but in an appreciation of certain sorts of aims as appropriate and reasonable, in an intellectually and emotionally stable way.[31] As Julia Annas notes, in the 'classical version' of virtue ethics a virtue

is not a habit in the sense in which habits can be mindless, sources of action in the agent which bypass her practical reasoning. A virtue is a disposition *to act*, not an entity built up within me and productive of behaviour; it is my disposition to act in certain ways and not others. A virtue, unlike a mere habit, is a disposition to act *for reasons*, and so a disposition which is exercised through the agent's practical reasoning; it is built up by making choices and exercised in the making of further choices. When an honest person decides not to take something to which he is not entitled, this is not the upshot

---

[29] See also Butler 1998, who reviews such forms of practical reasoning in the work of Wiggins and McDowell and extends them to a theory of character traits.
[30] See also Kamtekar 2004, 481f; Webber 2006, §5.   [31] See Ch. 1, §1.2.1.

of a causal build-up from previous actions, but a *decision*, a choice which endorses his disposition to be honest.   (Annas 2006, §A.1; see also 2005c, 637)

The aims that a virtuous person adopts therefore 'color' how he responds to situations—as opportunities for generosity, say, or as situations just crying out for fairness. Likewise, Aristotle says that to act as the virtuous person acts is to act for the sake of a goal that one values for its own sake, and to which one is firmly committed (*NE* II.4, 1105a31–3). And virtue requires wisdom or phronesis because hitting the 'mean' with respect to virtue is a matter of properly adjusting one's behavior to complex situations (see *NE* II–V; *EE* II; see also Webber 2006, 206), and therefore requires reasoning well about just what achieving such goals amounts to (see *NE* VI.1, 12–13). That is why Aristotle says that virtue 'makes the goal correct, while wisdom makes what leads to it correct' (VI.12, 1144a7–9). Goal-seeking, self-direction, attending, construing, planning, adjusting—for the situationist, this the stuff that psychological consistency is made of.

But can this be right? Can an Aristotelian virtue theory really take on board the findings of social psychology? Doris' skepticism on this point is typical:

According to Aristotle (1105a27–b1), genuinely virtuous action proceeds from 'firm and unchangeable character' rather than from transient motives. The virtues are *hexeis* (1106a11–12), and a *hexis* is a state that is 'permanent and hard to change' (*Categories*, 8b25–9a9)…. These features of Aristotle's moral psychology are prominent in contemporary virtue ethics…. [V]irtues are supposed to be *robust* traits; if a person has a robust trait, they can be confidently expected to display trait-relevant behavior across a wide variety of trait-relevant situations…. An emphasis on robust traits and behavioral consistency is entirely standard in the Aristotelian tradition of character ethics.   (2002, 17f, italics in original)

Everything that Doris says here is true. But how is it supposed to tell against Aristotelian virtue theory? The crucial question is not whether Aristotelians believe in 'robust traits', but whether 'trait-relevant behavior' arising from traits is defined *nominally* or *psychologically*. Put another way, is 'trait-relevant behavior' to be understood as, say, stereotypically 'just' actions, or actions done in the practically intelligent pursuit of just goals? To be sure, Aristotle thinks that the non-virtuous can often identify the just actions of just persons; in fact, it is through such identification that they are able to imitate just persons and eventually develop a just character of their own. But for our purposes, that is the crucial point—to have the virtue of justice, Aristotle says, is to act *as the just person acts*: with knowledge and from a stable commitment to the right sorts of reasons (*NE* II.4). The sense in which a just person is stable and reliable, on an Aristotelian theory, is that a just person acts for certain sorts of ends and adjusts his behavior so as to achieve those ends in a wide range of situations. On such a virtue theory, therefore, a virtue is defined in terms of 'robust traits' that produce consistent behaviors across situations, where those behaviors are understood in psychological rather than nominal terms—as the just person would regard them, say.

Reflecting on how one comes to have a virtue, on Aristotle's view, should also remind us that to have a virtue is not to spring forth all at once fully armed to do well, no matter where and no matter what. In any particular person, the development of a virtue is always slow, laborious, and above all piecemeal. As a person develops in courage, say, he will develop it first in those areas in which he first begins to habituate himself, before expanding his responsiveness to reasons for being courageous to other areas. The same is true for phronesis: it requires a grasp of the ends of the various virtues, and since the grasp of each such end comes about in a piecemeal way, so too, necessarily, must phronesis. That is why we must accept, as I argued in Chapter 4, that to be virtuous *tout court*, it will have to be enough that one be virtuous enough. The fact that a person with a given virtue will do better in some contexts than others certainly adds further complexity to what it means to be 'virtuous enough'—how many and what sorts of situational pressures must one already be able to withstand, say, if one is virtuous enough?—but it does not undermine the very idea of being virtuous enough. Likewise, the fact that virtue and phronesis are piecemeal in their development does not undermine the idea that part of what it is to *improve* in virtue and phronesis is to overcome (with difficulty and piecemeal gains) various contextual boundaries. What is undeniable is that there are such boundaries in moral and cognitive development to overcome, not that the prospect of doing so is empirically hopeless.[32]

The fact that an Aristotelian virtue theory should be the sort that comes out strong upon inspection of the findings of social psychology is significant and indeed ironic, as it has typically been Aristotelian theories that have served as the philosophical psychologist's favorite target. In fact, not only does the Aristotelian view that I have sketched here offer an empirically adequate conception of what good character *is*, but it is also consistent with a plausible understanding of how good character is *sustained*. On the Aristotelian view, the consistency of a virtue is not the consistency of a broad-based disposition relatively free of situational variables. Rather, it is the psychological consistency of certain kinds of strategies for adjusting oneself to situations.

---

[32] On the idea that the contextual and piecemeal nature of cognitive development is a serious problem for virtue theory, see esp. Doris 2002, 69f; 2005, 659; Vranas 2005. See also Adams 2006, 155–8 for reply.

Notice, then, that part of such strategies, at least when one is practically intelligent, is to adjust one's behavior so as to avoid certain kinds of situations and to seek out others. Situationism teaches us that one cannot simply trust to 'dispositions'; one must be very careful about one's surroundings, because they can shape us even as we shape them. Not even consistent psychological attributes are immune from disruption and interference by environmental variables.

The essence of this observation is nothing new. For instance, the apostle Paul tells us not to be fooled—bad company corrupts good character (1 Corinthians 15:33). The empirical evidence seems to tell in Paul's favor. Maria Merritt has recently discussed the implications of situationism for understanding just how dependent one's character may be on the company one keeps. Merritt observes that being virtuous requires a grasp of the impact that situations can have on one, but notes that simply being sensitive to these factors may well not be enough to keep one on track: 'Perhaps the very cognitive and motivational capacities needed to adjust our ethical sensibilities and reactions to these recently discovered situational factors are, in their own operation, subject to unanticipated situational factors' (2000, 372; see also Doris 1998, 510f).

Simply put, our ways of viewing the world that make cross-situational consistency possible are 'remarkably subject to alteration' as a result of our interactions with others:

For instance, a particular relationship or setting may decline in a person's life, to the point where the situation-specific dispositions supporting his participation in it cease to be active or even cease to exist. Or in the opposite case, increased importance of a particular relationship or setting in a person's life could bring into being, or strengthen, related situation-specific dispositions. I call this the sustaining social contribution to character.   (Merritt 2000, 374)

Our values are shaped by the relationships we share with others, because in those relationships we develop habits to behave in certain ways, and how we behave has an effect on what we value. That, we might say, is *how* bad company corrupts good character.

The upshot of these observations is that a theory of the virtues has less chance of establishing the consistency of the virtues, to the extent that it downplays the 'sustaining social contribution to character'. I think that Merritt—and indeed Paul!—must certainly be right about this. However, Merritt also claims that Aristotelian theories of the virtues assume a high degree of independence of character from social sustenance, and instead base the sustenance of one's character on the strength of one's commitment to reasons (2000, 378f). Is that true?

Here we should separate two issues: it is one thing to understand the virtues as forms of responsiveness to reasons, and another to suppose that that responsiveness is independent of the company we keep. Put that way, it seems clear that an Aristotelian conception of the virtues can take on board the point that character is, among other things, socially sustained. In fact, it is a point that Aristotle himself explicitly *does* take on board, in his discussion of friendship:

[W]hatever it is that for each sort of person constitutes existence, or whatever it is for the sake of which they choose to live, it's this they wish to spend time doing in company with their friends... for wishing as they do to live a shared life with their friends, they follow and jointly engage in the occupations in which they think they are sharing life with others. The friendship of inferior people, then, has bad effects, since they take part in inferior occupations, not being possessed of stable character, and become bad into the bargain, by making themselves resemble one another; whereas the friendship of decent people is decent, and grows in proportion to their interaction; and they even seem to become better by being active and correcting each other, for they take each other's imprint in those respects in which they please one another—hence the saying 'For from good men good things come'. (*NE* IX.12, 1172a1–3, 6–14)

In a word, if there is something that you value, and if you tend to spend your time with other people who share that value, then you will probably continue to have that value, for better or worse. The same goes, I take it, for one's goals, construal patterns, and so on.[33] Even if Aristotle thinks that phronesis is necessary for all virtue, he also clearly thinks that we need each other to help keep phronesis alive.

Aristotelian virtue theories, then, can embrace empirical findings both about what character is and about how character is sustained. It is therefore ironic that Aristotle in particular has served as the philosophical psychologist's whipping boy in recent discussions of situationism. After all, the upshot of the last forty-plus years of situationist social psychology is that a cognitive-affective conception of personality would seem to be an empirically adequate one, and it is this sort of approach to character that a careful reading of Aristotle would also suggest. So much for the empirical adequacy of an Aristotelian virtue theory. But what about its normative adequacy?

10.5.2 *Normative Adequacy*

A normatively adequate virtue theory, recall, would require a plausible normative standard of consistency, and that is not necessarily the same thing as a

---

[33] See also Kamtekar 2004, 483, who says that Plato and (in all likelihood) the Stoics also held that '[m]ost people's characters are produced and sustained by a particular social situation'. See also 2004, 487–91.

psychological standard. A person with the virtue of compassion, for instance, must behave consistently not with respect to just any standard of his or her own choosing, but with respect to a correct and appropriate standard of compassion. Now, Doris assumes that such a standard would be one of compassionate behavior that is nominally consistent. In that case, the virtue theorist seems to be in serious trouble, since as I have argued, we should not define a virtue in terms of nominally consistent behavior, since the social psychologist's very plausible understanding of personality suggests that nominal consistency can be caused by very disparate psychological attributes. And of course, Doris does have a point: a virtue theory is not a theory of good intentions, but a theory of attributes that are systematically tied to good *action*.

However, to regard nominal consistency as the only adequate normative standard of consistency is to overlook the possibility that the normative assessment of a character trait, understood as a particular bundle of certain cognitive-affective processes, could be a matter of determining whether in virtue of that trait one seeks goals and in general is both cognitively and affectively responsive to reasons that can be endorsed in an overall way from within an ethical outlook in equilibrium. Surely it is clear that psychological attributes by which one adjusts one's behaviors to situations so as best to meet the goal of benefiting others for their own sake, say, are precisely the sorts of attributes we can endorse as excellences in human character. And as I argued in Part I, such attributes will be reliably and systematically tied to right action, just in case those attributes also involve phronesis. It is by phronesis that one is able to deliberate well so as to specify just what hitting that goal in the right way would amount to in the situation at hand. And it is by the same phronesis that one specifies the hitting of that goal in a way that takes the various goals or 'targets' of the other virtues into account in an overall way. Without phronesis, one may be prone to act with virtuous intentions, but for all that not well, or to act well in some respects, or for some 'good reason', but in other respects not well. With phronesis, on the other hand, the virtue that makes one's goal the right one is paired with the wisdom to get the practical specification of that goal right, as well. And that wisdom, as Aristotle argues, is also paired with the savvy or 'cleverness' to figure out how best to attain that goal, so specified. Moreover, phronesis and the virtues are inherently practical, rather than static—they all concern *what to do*.[34] It is difficult to see what more one could want by way of normative adequacy from an account of the virtues. Therefore, a virtue theory can be both empirically and normatively adequate after all—at any rate, so long as that theory is a form of Hard Virtue Theory.

[34] See also Ch. 1, §1.2.1.

So we can summarize the approach to the virtues that I have sketched in this section as one of progressing from an empirically adequate personality theory, to an empirically and normatively adequate virtue theory. This process takes place in four basic stages. First, we begin with an empirically adequate theory of *personality*, and we have good evidence for thinking that such a theory is a cognitive-affective theory of personality. Recall that on such a theory, personality is one's unique nexus of cognitive-affective patterns by which one adjusts one's behaviors to situations as one takes them to be. That means that personality includes both one's distinctive ways of attaching meanings to situations and one's distinctive ways of adjusting one's behavior to situations in light of those meanings. So our personality taxonomy should take as its basic units certain forms of practical reasoning (broadly construed) and representing one's experience.

Second, we define *character* in the terms of that personality theory. By 'character', I mean personality insofar as it is of normative significance, either as that subset of personality that is specifically ethically salient, or as the whole of one's personality considered from an ethical point of view. In either case, character can be understood in terms of personality, viewed through a normative lens. Third, we can now define a *character trait* as a cohesive bundle of cognitive-affective character attributes. Consequently, fourth, we could at last define a *virtue* as a character trait by which one regularly, and with phronesis, acts for reasons that we can take to be good reasons from within an overall ethical perspective.

It is clear, then, that the sort of conception of the virtues that can be adequate in both of these ways is the sort that I have been defending throughout this book. I have understood a virtue as a commitment to act for virtuous reasons, where this is much more than acting 'with one's heart in the right place'. In Part I, I argued that to act in good faith for, say, compassionate reasons involves serious practical thought about what would, in fact, count as compassionate, that is, about what really would benefit another in the particular circumstances. I also argued there that having the virtue of compassion requires not only committing to act for the sake of compassionate goals, but also having the phronesis that is needed to understand those goals correctly. And I argued for the importance of understanding the moral validity of those goals from within a reasonable and naturalist ethical outlook in equilibrium. Furthermore, in Part II I argued that a virtue must be individuated in terms of the reasons characteristic of it, and that the relationships between virtues must be understood as the relationships that hold between those reasons. An Aristotelian virtue theory, complete with phronesis, is one that can be happily conjoined with the cognitive-affective personality taxonomy that social psychology suggests. And as far as I can see, it is the only one that can.

Conclusion

Our review of personality theory has led to the realization that given the current state of the empirical evidence, a viable virtue theory would do well to start with a cognitive-affective taxonomy of personality and character, of just the sort that situationist social psychology suggests. Furthermore, such a theory can be normatively as well as empirically adequate, holding that such cognitive-affective repertoires are those by which one acts for the right sorts of reasons, for the right sorts of goals, attaches the right sorts of values to outcomes, and in general, those that constitute a form of deliberative excellence. That, of course, is to say that every virtue must involve phronesis.

This is a significant result, for virtue theorists and their critics alike. Because not all virtue theories think of the virtues as all involving phronesis—indeed, not all virtue theories agree that virtues even require deliberation—not all virtue theories face the implications of empirical research on personality on an equal footing (cp. Merritt 2000, 367). Virtue theory can not only survive the situationist's empirical findings, but in fact can willingly embrace them. Or rather, this is possible for just those virtue theories that are species of Hard Virtue Theory.

PART IV

Defending Hard Virtue Theory

11

Phronesis and the Unity of the Virtues

In the first three parts of this book, I have argued that virtue ethics and virtue theory must accept the proposition that phronesis is part of every virtue in the strict sense (as opposed to, say, Aristotle's so-called 'natural' virtues). In this final part of the book, I argue that this is not bad news, by addressing some worries I have not had the opportunity to address earlier. One of the main reasons that some will be pessimistic about that proposition is its association with the very controversial thesis that to have one virtue is to have them all—the so-called 'unity of the virtues' thesis (UV for short). It is with that thesis that I begin.[1]

There seems to be little question but that phronesis is tightly connected to the idea that the virtues form a unity, of some sort or other. Perhaps the classic statement of that idea is Aristotle's, in the concluding chapters of his discussion of phronesis in book VI of the *Nicomachean Ethics*. Having phronesis, Aristotle says, entails having all the virtues (in the strict sense): phronesis begins from a correct grasp of the ends of action, and in order not to be mistaken about the ends of action one must have the virtues (VI.12, 1144a29–b1). Furthermore, having a virtue in the strict sense entails having phronesis; to be sure, there are virtues without phronesis (the natural virtues), but these virtues are not the proper excellences of human character and agency—virtues without qualification—because, lacking phronesis as they do, they are prone to go astray (VI.13).[2] Consequently, Aristotle says, it cannot

---

[1] A warning about labels. It is common for scholars of ancient philosophy to call this thesis the 'reciprocity of the virtues', and to reserve 'unity of virtue' for the much stronger thesis that all the virtues are the same. See e.g. Irwin 1988a; Annas 1993a, 76. I think that this usage is preferable; nonetheless, I shall adhere to the convention current among most ethicists and speak of the 'unity of virtue' as the weaker thesis that to have one virtue is to have them all. Furthermore, I shall not be concerned with the stronger thesis here, although I think it is worth taking seriously.

[2] See also Wolf (2007, 152), who notes that natural virtues differ from the virtues in the strict sense, insofar as the former but not the latter can be described 'non-evaluatively'.

be the case that the unqualified virtues 'can be possessed independently of one another', 'since if phronesis, which is one, is present, they all will be present along with it' (1144b33–1145a2). Likewise, among contemporary philosophers it is generally agreed that the idea that all the unqualified virtues involve phronesis entails that those virtues form *some* sort of unity, although there is considerable variety in views about what sort of unity that would be (see esp. Badhwar 1996; McDowell 1997, 142–4; Hursthouse 1999a, 153–7; Swanton 2003, 286–8).

Aristotle's argument also reveals two common grounds for skepticism about UV, one corresponding to each of his main premises: on the one hand, we may deny his first premise, that to have phronesis is to have all the unqualified virtues; on the other, we may be skeptical about his second premise, that virtues in the strict sense all involve phronesis. Of course, the second premise is the thesis for which I have argued in the first two parts of this book, although I shall have more to say about it here as well. But what about the first premise—the idea that phronesis implies all the virtues? It is difficult to see why Aristotle should claim anything as ambitious as that. After all, the second premise alone establishes *some* sort of unity among the virtues: if every virtue involves phronesis, and the same phronesis as every other virtue, then every virtue involves a grasp of its own ends in a way that is intelligent and flexible rather than rigid or myopic, and so the virtues should at least be compatible with one another.[3] As we shall see shortly, even the latter thesis is a very controversial one. Why then does Aristotle try to bite off so much more, arguing as he does that phronesis requires a grasp of the ends of every virtue—and not just any sort of grasp, but a grasp that actually amounts to possessing each of those virtues?

The problem with such an ambitious claim seems obvious: we may know that Fred has the unqualified virtue of courage, and if UV is true, then this means that Fred must have every other virtue, too; but of course we know Fred, and that he does not have every virtue, any more than the rest of us do. Perhaps, if we are honest, we cannot really describe Fred as generous; but why should *that* force us to take back the assessment of him as courageous? So surely, we will conclude, UV cannot be true; in particular, it cannot be the case that having phronesis requires having every virtue. Perhaps phronesis about courage requires a basic decency where the other virtues are concerned, but as Aristotle takes pains to argue, a basic decency does not rise to the level

---

[3] This is as far as Susan Wolf goes: 'to have one virtue, one must have the knowledge required for the possession of the others, but this is not the same as the requirement that one possess the other virtues themselves' (2007, 161).

of an unqualified virtue. In fact, it is difficult to see why Aristotle should have thought he was entitled to such a strong claim about phronesis, since he shows only that phronesis is jeopardized by corruption or badness (*mochthēria*) in any area of virtue (*NE* VI.12, 1144a34–6), but the absence of vice is not the same thing as virtue.

Nonetheless, I think that UV is true, although, as I argue in this chapter, appreciating the truth of UV requires distinguishing between two very different interpretations of it. The thesis that phronesis entails all the virtues could be the thesis that, *for any agent*, that agent can have phronesis only if that agent also has all the virtues; or it could be the thesis that *any theoretical model* of phronesis must also be a model of all the virtues. On the former reading, UV implies that if phronesis where courage is concerned can be attributed to Fred, then Fred must be virtuous in every way, and this is simply false: as we saw in Chapter 4, to be wise *tout court* one need not be perfectly wise, but only 'wise enough', and this falls considerably short of being wise in every way, and thus short of being unqualifiedly virtuous in every way. However, we also saw in Chapter 4 that notions like 'wise enough' and 'virtuous enough' require a theoretical model of phronesis and virtue that reveals their 'natural makeup', so to speak, and the thesis that phronesis entails all the virtues can be understood as a claim about that model: there is no model of a virtue that is not also a model of phronesis, and no model of phronesis that is not also a model of all the virtues; so there is no model of a virtue that is not also a model of the virtues. They can be fully understood only as a package.

It is on this second interpretation, I argue here, that UV is true. So interpreted, the classic argument for UV is sound, for reasons that have not been appreciated in contemporary discussions of unity. (I shall not, however, pursue the purely historical question whether this is how Aristotle understood UV.) It has become common to distinguish the claim that virtues can be independent of, or even incompatible with each other *in this or that agent*, from the claim that the virtues are independent or incompatible *in themselves* (see esp. Walker 1989, 350–2). The latter is a claim about a theoretical model of the virtues. Such a model functions like 'models in mechanics', as A. D. M. Walker has noted: 'examples to which reality can only approximate but which nonetheless serve to illuminate the matter in hand by allowing us to argue initially on the basis of a more manageable set of assumptions' (1993, 61). In short, I argue that the thesis that phronesis entails the virtues, although false as it is commonly interpreted, is nonetheless true interpreted as a thesis about the natural makeup of virtue, that is, about the unqualified virtues as they appear on a plausible theoretical model of them. Although I focus on

UV as a thesis about an adequate model of the virtues, nonetheless that model requires that a substantial degree of unity must obtain among the virtues even of particular virtuous agents. I discuss these implications at the end of the chapter.

In the first section of this chapter, I take up a crucial question for any discussion of UV: what sorts of virtues are the ones that are to form a unity? Whether the virtues are unified depends, of course, on what the virtues are like, and much of the disagreement over UV comes down to different conceptions of what a virtue is. I shall sketch a conception of the virtues I think are unified by developing the Aristotelian idea that the relevant virtues in this context must be excellences of persons considered as rational, practical agents. Not only are these the only sorts of virtues for which UV has ever been seriously entertained,[4] but it also seems clear, I argue, that any theory of the virtues must take such virtues as its central cases.

In the second section, I discuss some different rationales for UV with respect to unqualified virtues. Although Aristotle unifies the virtues by showing their mutual connections through phronesis, other approaches unify the virtues through psychological considerations, conceptual considerations, or considerations of the immediate demands of action and choice. Here I argue that any complete rationale for UV must ultimately rest on the more Aristotelian approach of unifying the virtues through phronesis.

Finally, in the third section I discuss the distinction between the two interpretations of UV I mentioned above, and argue for a particular type of model-based analysis of the claim that phronesis entails all the virtues. In short, I defend UV for the virtues understood as excellences (§11.1), which are unified through phronesis (§11.2), where this unification is understood as a thesis about a theoretical model of the unqualified virtues, rather than about particular virtuous agents (§11.3). In the course of doing so, I also hope to make clear why such an interpretation of UV is an important and philosophically interesting one.

---

[4] For example, consider Aquinas:

> Moral virtue may be considered as perfect or as imperfect. An imperfect moral virtue, temperance for instance, or fortitude, is nothing but an inclination in us to do some kind of good deed, whether such inclination be in us by nature or by habituation. If we take moral virtues in this way, they are not connected, since we find men who, by natural temperament or by being so accustomed, are prompt in doing deeds of liberality but are not prompt in doing deeds of charity. But the perfect moral virtue is a habit that inclines us to do a good deed well; and if we take moral virtues in this way, we must say that they are connected... (*Summa Theologiae* 1–2 q65 a1, cited in Jacobs and Zeis 1990, 642)

11.1 The Unity of Which Virtues?

As Aristotle might have said, 'virtue' is said in many ways; and the idea of unity or even of compatibility between virtues seems wholly out of place on some ways of thinking of the virtues. In particular, opponents of UV often think of virtues as motivational forces that sometimes pull one in opposing ways, whereas proponents hold that, despite the conflicts that virtuous persons face, the virtues are intelligent and flexible attributes which tend to work together rather than against each other. Much of the disagreement over UV, then, stems from a deeper disagreement about what sorts of things the virtues are.

Now, there is no need to restrict the word 'virtue' to just one sort of trait, but it seems clear that at least the central cases of virtue are to be *excellences*—traits in virtue of which one fulfills one's nature as a rational and emotional creature that chooses and acts. In this first part of this chapter, I argue that the sorts of virtues that are excellences of this sort are also the sorts that work together and tend to form some kind of unity.[5]

11.1.1 'Trajectories' and 'Directions'

If the virtues form any kind of unity at all, then at the very least having and acting from one virtue must not be incompatible with having and acting from another. That compatibility depends on what the virtues are like, and on many common views of the virtues, even this much will seem like too much. Philosophers offer many considerations in support of the idea that the virtues, so far from forming any kind of unity, conflict with each other. Perhaps the most common argument against UV stems from the existence of moral conflict and dilemma. Life is only too full of situations of conflict, as for instance when one must choose between showing mercy in allowing a student to submit a late paper and exercising justice in enforcing the rules of the course; between truthfully telling a student that he would waste his time pursuing a graduate degree in philosophy, and being more tactfully evasive about his prospects; between justly keeping a promise to meet a friend, and piously rushing to the side of a parent who has suddenly fallen ill; and so on. These conflicts, it is

---

[5] This is, of course, Aristotle's own type of argument for UV in *NE* VI.13; see also Hursthouse 1999a, 153 7.

There is a further question, for one with a cardinal theory (such as myself), of whether UV applies to all the virtues or only to the cardinal virtues. For now, I shall be concerned only with cardinal virtues. For an interesting review of the relation between UV and the cardinality of the virtues in the medieval period, see Walsh 1986.

sometimes said, just are conflicts between one virtue and another: between mercy and justice, truthfulness and tactfulness, justice and piety, and so on.

Likewise, consider the irreducible diversity of good things: commitments, attachments, and obligations; liberty and freedom from coercion, interference, and assault; welfare and utility; achievement and creativity; hopes, dreams, and aspirations; and so on (see Nagel 1979b; see also Williams 1981). Different virtues have different sorts of goods as their main spheres of concern (see Swanton 2003, 20f *et passim*), and so as these irreducible goods come into conflict, the argument goes, so too must the virtues.

This conflict between virtues is not only practical, but can also take a deeper psychological form. Philippa Foot has noted that a particularly 'difficult thought' for UV is the thought that a person may be such

that he can only become good in one way by being bad in another, as if e.g., he could only rein in his ruthless desires at the cost of a deep malice against himself and the world; or as if a kind of dull rigidity were the price of refusing to do what he himself wanted at whatever cost to others.   (Foot 1983, 397; see also Swanton 2003, ch. 9)

However, A. D. M. Walker has argued that the psychological incompatibility of the virtues is even deeper than this. The problem for UV, he argues, is not merely that some particular agent's psychology may be such that moral improvement with respect to one virtue competes with moral improvement with respect to another virtue, but that those virtues are in such competition with each other in their very nature. This problem, Walker argues, stems from the relation between character and personality. The 'development of a virtue shapes, as it were, the entire personality', Walker observes, as when the virtue of kindness involves a more general way of looking at people, focusing on their particularity and vulnerability. However, Walker argues, 'the type of personality which is congenial to the development of one virtue can accommodate certain others only to a limited extent', since for instance the virtue of justice involves a sort of personality that conflicts with a kinder sort of personality. He concludes not that kindness pushes out justice altogether, or vice versa, but that the personality traits associated with such virtues are incompatible 'beyond a certain point' of the development of those virtues, so that those virtues are incompatible beyond the same point (1989, esp. 350–6).

However, UV certainly does not deny the existence of serious moral conflicts and dilemmas—on the contrary, the appeal of UV often stems from the thought that it is precisely *because* of such conflicts that the virtues must work together to find solutions, when they exist, that are good in an overall way. What the proponent of UV denies is that such conflicts arise *from the virtues themselves*: justice is not a matter of simply pushing for some value that is in competition with the value the mercy pushes for, but concerns its characteristic sort of value as part of a body of values of which mercy is also a part. Likewise, the proponent of UV does not deny the irreducible plurality of goods, only the idea that the virtues push for different goods in a myopic way (see Annas 1993*a*, 75f, 78f; Irwin 1988*a*, 68f; Telfer 1989–90, 37, citing Sorabji 1980, 207; see also Watson 1984, 63). Moreover, Gary Watson has argued that while conflicts may be such that one must choose between expressing and acting on one virtue or another, this is a conflict between opportunities for virtue, not between the virtues themselves, as if such virtues always conflicted, or were necessarily incompatible in the same character (1984, 64f).

Finally, the virtues of justice and kindness may be incompatible to some extent in the same personality, *if* each of those virtues involves a fairly exclusive focus on one sort of value, but again, that is precisely the sort of view of the virtues that proponents of UV reject. To be sure, Aristotle maintains that a virtue must be a 'firm and unshakable' disposition of character (*NE* II.4, 1105a32–3), but this 'firmness' serves only to mark off the virtues from more transitory inclinations; it does not imply a tendency to do some stereotypical sort of thing or promote some stereotypical sort of value in a rigid, myopic way (see Swanton 2003, 287f).

What seems clear, then, is that a major disagreement between proponents and opponents of UV concerns what sort of thing a virtue is: between a view of the virtues as each focusing on its own sphere of concern with little regard for the spheres of other virtues, and a view of the virtues as each focusing on its own sphere of concern as necessarily situated among the others. The former view takes a wide range of varieties. One way of focusing on just one type of concern is to have a tendency to do certain sorts of acts where that concern is relevant. For instance, as we saw in Chapter 5, R. B. Brandt says that the 'traditional' view of honesty is that it is 'just an aversion to, say, breach of promise up to a "standard" level' (1981, 277). Likewise, James Wallace takes generosity to be a tendency to give away something of value to oneself, out of concern for the good of others; and 'The stronger the tendency', he says, 'the more generous the person' (Wallace 1978, 135f, cited in Watson 1984, 57f). We may also identify each virtue with a tendency to act according to some *prima facie* duty, say, or with a tendency to fulfill some sort of socially desirable role (see Irwin 1988*a*, 67 for discussion). On such views, a virtue need not be a tendency to aim at the 'mean' with respect to some good; so one might even say that, so understood, such traits as vivaciousness and serenity, forthrightness and tactfulness, and physical courage and pacifism, can all count as virtues, and as such, their tendency to conflict with each other as virtues is immediately obvious (Flanagan 1991, 33). We should not suppose that such a view necessitates a picture of the virtues as mechanical and unthinking, because such virtues can involve deliberative adherence to certain sorts of considerations, such as the particularity and vulnerability of others, as in Walker's discussion of kindness, or the importance of showing respect to legitimate authority figures.[6]

We can perhaps further understand this sort of view, and its opposite, by considering the difference between what I shall call a 'trajectory' and a 'direction'. Suppose that two vehicles are moving down the same road, both going east; how should we describe the way in which each is moving? If we say simply that each is heading due east, this will be true even if each vehicle is unmanned and careening out of control; yet if we say that each is heading to the library and then to the stationer's, this picks out not merely the *trajectory* along which the cars are moving (even if the library, and then the stationer's, happen to be in their path along that trajectory), but a sort of intelligent *direction* that the drivers of the cars are taking. On the view of the virtues under consideration, the virtues are more like 'trajectories' than like 'directions': the virtues, that is, tend toward certain sorts of actions or considerations, and as such, exercising a virtue will result in good action if the trajectory is unobstructed and tending in what happens to be the right way, but there is not internal to a virtue an excellence by which a virtue apprehends the correct direction *all things considered*. Consequently, on the 'trajectories view' of the virtues, the fittingness of the exercise of a virtue to one's circumstances—and thus the rightness of such an action—is fortuitous, so far as the virtue itself is concerned; and so such virtues can lead to action that is positively bad, and can themselves become faults of character, just as Aristotle observes in discussing the 'natural virtues' (*NE* VI.13).[7]

The contrasting 'directions view' of the virtues holds that while each virtue operates primarily within its own characteristic sphere of concern, to have a virtue involves understanding and deliberating about things in that sphere as bearing on the spheres of concern characteristic of other virtues as well. This sort of view is perhaps best known from Aristotle, who understands a virtue as a

[6] See Swanton 2003, 30–3, who seems, in a rare moment, to think of the virtues in this sort of way.

[7] Some views of this sort are what Watson 1984 has called the 'straight view' of the virtues; however, Watson focuses on views on which the virtues are simple tendencies to action, and this focus is narrower than the class of views I am calling the trajectories view.

tendency to choose, act, and feel in accordance with 'right reason' or phronesis, which transcends all the various spheres of concern of the particular virtues (see esp. *NE* VI.1, 5). And various forms of the directions view are widely attested even among contemporary virtue ethicists with widely diverging views on what phronesis is and whether it is necessary for the virtues.[8] It seems clear, then, that the directions view is necessary for the case against the incompatibility of the virtues. In the rest of this section, I argue first in support of the directions view, and second that the directions view is also sufficient to show the compatibility of the virtues.

11.1.2 *The Directions View*

I offer four main arguments for the directions view, each of which I think is fairly decisive: one concerning the nature of the virtues as excellences, two arguments concerning the fact that to act from a virtue is to act for a reason, and an argument concerning the empirical adequacy of virtue taxonomies.

The Virtues as Excellences   The first sort of argument is a classic Aristotelian one, which begins from the idea that a virtue is a kind of human excellence, in two ways: one, the virtues make us reliable and flexible in acting well, and two, the virtues are realizations of our human nature as practically rational creatures. These points are the basis of Aristotle's so-called 'function argument' for the thesis that the human good consists primarily in the virtues:

> But perhaps it appears somewhat platitudinous to say that happiness is the chief good, and a more distinct statement of what it is is still required. Well, perhaps this would come about if one established the function of human beings.... [If] a human being's function we posit as being a kind of life, and this life as being activity of soul and actions accompanied by reason, and it belongs to a good man to perform these well and finely, and each thing is completed well when it possesses its proper excellence: if all this is so, the human good turns out to be activity of soul in accordance with virtue (and if there are more virtues than one, in accordance with the best and the most complete).   (*NE* I.7, 1097b22–5, 1098a12–18)

Simply put, because we are creatures that act, and act for reasons and on the basis of deliberation and choice, the excellence of such creatures as we are must be a kind of intelligent success in action and practical reasoning. And that is what Aristotle takes the virtues to be, without qualification (see also Hursthouse 1999*a*, 153f; Korsgaard 1986, 278).

---

[8] For instance, although Slote 2001 denies that phronesis is necessary for virtue, nonetheless he holds that an all-things-considered 'balance' in overall motivation is a necessary part of every virtue. (Although the problem for such a view, as I argued in Ch. 3, is how to establish that balance without deliberation of precisely the sort characteristic of phronesis.)

Now, as his discussion of the natural virtues in *Nicomachean Ethics* VI.13 makes clear, this is not to assert that only those virtues that are excellences in this sense can be called 'virtues' in any sense. But it is to say, one, that we must have a theory of the virtues that *are* the excellences of human character; two, that such excellences should in fact be the central cases among all the traits rightly called 'virtues'; and three, that such excellences should be the focus of ethical thought that begins from the virtues. In other words, the study of the virtues, in the first instance, must always be the study of the virtues that are excellences.

Since the virtues can be excellences on the directions view, but not on the trajectories view, approaching such topics as UV, and the relation between virtue and right action, from the perspective of the trajectories view is simply to begin from the wrong virtues.[9] The problem for the trajectories view, then, is not that it fails to talk about virtues at all, but that by focusing on the sorts of virtues it does, it simply changes the subject. This has an important further consequence: not only must virtue ethics take up some form of the directions view of the virtues, but so too must *every virtue theory*, regardless of its ethical orientation, on pains of being, at best, woefully incomplete. And since, as I argued in Chapters 3–4, the only way to account for the virtues on a directions view is as involving phronesis, not only is it the case that the only viable forms of virtue ethics are forms of Hard Virtue Ethics; it turns out that the only viable forms of virtue theory are forms of Hard Virtue Theory, that is, those theories of the virtues that hold that every virtue that is an excellence involves phronesis.

Virtues and 'Contrastive' Reasons   My second and third arguments for the directions view arise from the fact that acting from or exercising a virtue is one kind of acting for a reason. Consider the difference between acting for a reason and, say, acting from compulsion, such as flipping a light switch three times when entering a dark room. It is clear that there is no arguing a person out of a compulsion, not simply because the person *will not* be persuaded by our argument, but because the person *cannot* be so persuaded on this point. Things are just the opposite in the case of acting for a reason: perhaps the person will listen to the arguments against the action

---

[9] The strength of the connection between virtue and right action involved here is significant. As Adams (2006, 190) shows, one way to avoid the thought that the exercise of any virtue requires the balancing of it with other virtues, is to soften the connection between virtue and rightness. That is a move I think we should avoid, as it threatens to obliterate the distinction between virtue proper and 'natural virtue' (cp. Adams 2006, 187).

and still do it, but if so, this is *not* because what motivates the person to act is isolated from other sorts of considerations.

At the very least, then, reasons for acting are 'contrastive', in Robert Audi's phrase, in the sense that one who acts for a reason must at least be 'susceptible to counterinfluence' where that reason is concerned, that is, susceptible to being influenced by alternative reasons (Audi 1997a, 93–5).[10] This is not merely to say that the agent can in principle be persuaded to do something else: after all, a person could perhaps be persuaded to exercise heroic strength of will on some occasion not to do what he feels compelled to do, but this does not make the compelling motivation 'contrastive' in the relevant sense. That motivation is not rational, because it cannot take the form of a judgment that, despite whatever considerations there may be against it, still the thing to do is to flip the switch three times. Counteracting the strength of that motivation, even when one believes one has most reason to counteract it, does nothing to make that motivation any the more rational.

The significance of these observations for the trajectories view should be clear: the more myopic the virtues in their very nature, the less rational they are as sources of action and feeling. At the extreme is something like Wallace's view, that the stronger one's tendency to a certain kind of action stereotypical of some virtue, the greater the extent to which one possesses that virtue. Presumably, no such tendency would be stronger than a psychological compulsion to give whenever one perceived another's good. In that case, the very *perfection* of a trajectories virtue would consist in its absolute motivational irresistibility, which would require extinguishing any aspect of rationality in it whatsoever. So an implication of such a view is that one should be the more generous, the less rational one's motivation for giving to others; and surely that cannot be right. And even on less extreme versions of the trajectories view, it is still a standard feature of having a certain virtue that one who has it tends to focus on its sphere of concern in a way that is more or less blind to what other reasons there are. Of course, the agent as a *whole* may be susceptible to counterinfluence against acting on his motivation to do, say, a stereotypically generous act; but recall that one can be susceptible to counterinfluence in the same way about giving in to a compulsive motivation. The point is that to exercise a virtue is to act for a reason; but to the extent that a virtue is myopic about its sphere of concern, to that extent exercising a virtue is not acting for a reason, and a virtue not a form of practical rationality. If some

---

[10] I take up this issue further in the next chapter.

virtue V is an unqualified virtue, then, it must involve responsiveness to V reasons.[11]

Virtues and Normativity   Note that to act for a reason is to act for some consideration that one takes to be normative. For an animal, simply *having* an appetite or some other sort of impulse is all that is required to set the animal in motion. By contrast, we do not just behave, we *act*; and so we *act* on an impulse (rather than merely follow it) not just because we have the impulse, but only if we think there is some reason to act on it, that is, that acting on that impulse is 'the thing to do' (even if not necessarily the 'morally right' thing to do).

As Christine Korsgaard puts the point, our ability to think about our perceptions and desires, rather than merely being conscious of them,

> sets us a problem no other animal has. It is the problem of the normative. For our capacity to turn our attention on to our own mental activities is also a capacity to distance ourselves from them, and to call them into question. I perceive, and I find myself with a powerful impulse to believe. But I back up and bring that impulse into view and then I have a certain distance. Now the impulse doesn't dominate me and now I have a problem. Shall I believe? Is this perception really a *reason* to believe? I desire and I find myself with a powerful impulse to act. But I back up and bring that impulse into view and then I have a certain distance. Now the impulse doesn't dominate me and now I have a problem. Shall I act? Is this desire really a *reason* to act? The reflective mind cannot settle for perception and desire, not just as such. It needs a reason. Otherwise, at least as long as it reflects, it cannot commit itself or go forward. (Korsgaard 1996, 93, italics in original)

Clearly, part of having a virtue that is an excellence is to act in ways that one takes there to be good reasons to act.

Now, as Korsgaard points out, we can act from motivations that count as good reasons to act because we are creatures that choose acts from within a 'practical identity', that is, 'a description under which you value yourself, a description under which you find your life to be worth living and your actions to be worth undertaking' (1996, 101). Our practical identities tend to be many and various: the same person can think of her actions as worth doing under the description of herself as a parent, a sister, a daughter, a Presbyterian, a Greek, a teacher, a wife, a friend, and so on. These identities are all contingent, not in the sense that one could, say, stop being Greek, but in the sense that it is always open to us to challenge and reconsider the idea that one's ethnicity or place in a family is something that gives reasons to act.

---

[11] For the notion of 'virtuous reasons', see Williams 1995a; Hursthouse 1995b; and Ch. 6.

Consequently, we need reasons not only for our particular actions, but also for our practical identities themselves, and this involves reflecting on one's life as a whole. This means that developing a characteristic responsiveness to a certain range of reasons—including generous reasons, say, or reasons of justice—cannot be cut off from a broader conception of oneself as a whole, and thus from one's other practical identities. Again, the implications for the trajectories view are clear: that view would have us suppose that the virtues are each a tendency to focus on one sphere of concern instead of the others, whereas it seems rather that a virtue must focus on its sphere of concern as it is connected to other spheres, if there is such a thing as acting for virtuous reasons at all. Therefore, if V is an unqualified virtue, then V must involve responsiveness to V reasons, as situated within a broader range of what other practical reasons there are.

Virtues and their Empirical Adequacy   Finally, the trajectories view defines a virtue as a disposition to manifest a certain range of behavior; for instance, such a view understands the virtue of generosity as the disposition to give of one's time and belongings to others, either much of the time or on a wide range of occasions. That means that the trajectories view begins by classifying behaviors into types, from the observer's or theorist's point of view, and assigning virtue terms as placeholders for the psychological attributes responsible for behavioral patterns of the various types. Such a view therefore adopts what we called in Part III a 'nominal' classification of behaviors, rather than a classification that attends to how agents themselves perceive their situations and their behaviors.

However, we saw in Part III that the problem with such nominal classific-ations is an empirical one: we cannot infer any single psychological attribute, or even any single, cohesive bundle of psychological attributes, from behaviors so classified. Our best empirical model of the nature of personality has it that a person may give freely to others, from the observer's point of view, on some occasions out of friendly feeling, on others out of guilt, on others to curry favor, on others to put another in one's debt, and so on. Indeed, empirical research on personality has shown that often there is no attribute or cohesive bundle of attributes underlying such sets of giving behaviors that is anything like a character trait, but only a rag-bag of different aims and motives. A virtue is a *trait*, and therefore it cannot be just any old hodge-podge of psychological phenomena that underlie some set of behaviors. The trajectories view is therefore empirically inadequate as an account of virtues.

By contrast, the directions view understands virtues in terms of responsive-ness to certain kinds of reasons. On the directions view, a virtue is a cohesive bundle of cognitive and affective attributes—the goals one seeks, the outcomes one values, one's practical skills, and so on—by which one adjusts one's behavior to one's situation, for the sake of realizing some goal or outcome. As we saw in Part III, a very attractive empirical model of personality and character has it that personality and character consist of such bundles of cognitive-affective attributes. It is because personality and character are ways of adjusting behavior to situations, as one sees one's situations, that we cannot infer traits from nominally classified behaviors: what looks to the observer like a single 'type' of behavior is often a quite disparate set of behaviors, from the agent's point of view. The way to understand personality and character, then, is to understand how agents perceive their situations and their behaviors, and thus the characteristic reasons for which they act. The directions view is therefore an empirically adequate conception of the virtues, while the trajectories view is not.

For all of these reasons, therefore, it is clear that the only virtues worth discussing when it comes to UV are the virtues as the directions view describes them.[12] Still, the directions view alone may not be enough to establish the compatibility of the virtues: as Walker has argued, the opportunity cost of performing (say) a truthful action is the forgoing of a tactful action; and of course, it is by our actions that we have the virtues or not. Indeed, such a view of the opportunity costs of a virtuous action may even be suggested by Watson's defense of the compatibility of the virtues, viz. that sometimes where two virtues are both relevant, one must choose to act either on one *or* on the other. I conclude this section by arguing that, on the directions view, virtuous actions do not have such opportunity costs after all.

11.1.3 Conflicts and Correlations

In his influential paper 'The Incompatibility of the Virtues', A. D. M. Walker argues that sometimes a situation is such that two (or more) virtues are relevant in it, but one cannot act on both virtues. For instance, Walker considers 'a range of situations in which we can exercise the virtue of truthfulness only at the expense of not exercising the virtue of tactfulness, as when we are asked a question to which the straightforward answer will pain our questioner' (1993, 47; see also Watson 1984, 64f; Lemos 1993, 87f). Likewise, we can consider a case in which an otherwise responsible student has failed to turn in an assignment on time, and now asks his instructor for permission to submit the assignment late.[13] In cases such as these, the question is not which action

---

[12] Notice that the directions view would also support a eudaimonist form of naturalism about the virtues, on which the virtues are taken as constituents of the project of living a coherent, whole life.

[13] I thank David Soles for the example.

would be right or acceptable—in each case, we can concede that either option would be appropriate (*ceteris paribus*).

Nor—and this is important to see—is the question whether the same *action* could be described as virtuous in both respects, that is, as both truthful and tactful, or as both just and merciful. As we have seen in earlier chapters, an exercise of a virtue (e.g. generosity) is not the same thing as a virtuous (e.g. generous) act, even in the case of an unqualified virtue. As Robert Audi and Christine Swanton put the point, a virtuous act is one that intentionally hits the 'target' of the virtue in question, 'such as the well-being of others in the case of beneficence' (Audi 1997*b*, 180; see also Swanton 2003, 29f and ch. 11, esp. pp. 231–8). An exercise of the virtue of beneficence, by contrast, is an act that the agent chooses from his or her stable character virtue of beneficence, and such an exercise is neither necessary nor sufficient for a beneficent act: on the one hand, even a typically callous person can do something kind on occasion, and on the other, even a truly and wisely beneficent person's best attempts to help others can fail to come off as planned. So the relevant question in the cases of conflict under consideration is whether the same action could be an *exercise of both of the virtues* in question.

Walker argues that in such cases of conflict, exercising the virtue of truthfulness is to forgo the opportunity of exercising the virtue of tactfulness on that occasion. Now, this view, which Walker calls the 'Conflict Assumption', does not generate an incompatibility between the virtues straightaway, as Walker is well aware: as Watson argues, pointing out conflicts between opportunities to exercise different virtues does not itself undermine the idea that the same person could possess those different virtues. However, Walker argues that the incompatibility of the virtues does follow if we conjoin the Conflict Assumption with what he calls the 'Correlation Assumption': *ceteris paribus*, one has a virtue to a greater extent the wider the range of circumstances in which one would exercise that virtue.

Walker contrasts the Correlation Assumption with the more simplistic view that correlates one's virtuousness with the bare frequency of one's exercising of that virtue (1993, 54).[14] Rather, his view is that if I would exercise the virtue of truthfulness in a wider range of situations than I would exercise the virtue of tactfulness, then I have the virtue of truthfulness to a greater extent than I have the virtue of tactfulness: 'the greater this range' he says, 'the higher the degree to which the virtue is possessed' (54). Of course, the greatness of such

---

[14] However, as Walker is aware (54f), his view would collapse into the frequency view in the absence of a principled way of individuating situation types; although I am pessimistic about the prospects of such an individuation, I shall not press the point.

a range is not the sole determinant of the extent to which one has a virtue, but Walker argues that it certainly is *one* determinant; hence the *'ceteris paribus'* in the Correlation Assumption (see 55f). Now, if I have to choose between exercising truthfulness and exercising tactfulness in situations like the one in question, and my possession of each virtue is correlated with the range of situations in which I would exercise that virtue, then the extent to which I can have the virtue of tactfulness is inversely proportional to the extent to which I can have the virtue of truthfulness. In this sense, Walker argues, these two virtues—and many other pairs of virtues—are incompatible with each other.[15]

It is important to note that the view of the virtues on which Walker's argument rests is not *obviously* a trajectories view. On Walker's view, it may be the case that failing to exercise the virtue of tactfulness in one's answer is not blameworthy, *if* one does so in order to exercise the virtue of truthfulness instead (1993, 57). This may suggest a sort of directions view: tactfulness concerns its own primary sphere of concern, but is willing to forgo certain preferred actions when some other virtue, such as truthfulness, gives one a reason to do so. (I shall return to this question below.)

I argue now that the Conflict and Correlation Assumptions are both false, because each relies on an untenable view of what it is to 'exercise' a virtue. To see what is distinctive about that view, consider a sharply contrasting alternative. In 'The Unity of Virtue', John Cooper offers a case of conflict that is like Walker's cases in the relevant respects, but gives it a very different analysis. In Cooper's case, one has made a promise to meet a friend for lunch, but just as the time arrives one receives news that a parent has suddenly fallen very ill. Suppose that one responds to this conflict by rushing to the parent's aid, and as soon as possible, apologizing to one's friend, explaining one's actions and making amends.[16] What virtue or virtues, Cooper asks, has such a person exercised in this action?

We would, I suppose, describe this as a pious act rather than a just act, but as Cooper notes, it seems nonetheless that in so acting one *exercises* both piety *and* justice: the virtue of

justice, in the stringencies of this unusual situation, did not, after all, require keeping the promise, or else arranging in advance to obtain leave not to; justice in these

---

[15] Notice that the Correlation Assumption is much stronger than the observation that since experiences, opportunities, and talents vary, and since virtues arise from virtuous actions, virtues will develop at different rates and to different levels in any given person. The latter view is perfectly consistent with UV. See Walsh 1986, 460 for discussion of this weaker thesis in Buridan's virtue theory; see also Watson 1984, 64f.

[16] As Cooper 1999, 86f notes, in this case that would be the only right thing to do; in this way, his case differs from Walker's cases, but that difference will not matter here.

circumstances requires only explaining oneself after the fact and duly making amends. *Doesn't that mean, however, that your 'power' of justice, and not only that of piety, causes you to go to the parent's bedside—while also, of course, causing you further to contact the friend as soon as possible and explain the situation?*   (Cooper 1999, 87, emphasis added)

In this respect, the case seems no different from the cases we considered above: isn't it clear that the thing to do when telling someone a hard truth is to do so in a way that leaves them feeling more encouraged than the opposite? That the thing to do when 'sugar-coating' the painful truth is to do so in a way that does not mislead? That the thing to do when enforcing a class rule is to do so in a merciful rather than a callous way? That the thing to do when bending a class rule is to do so for reasons that one would have applied for other students in similar situations? If so, then these cases show not an agent who chooses between exercising one virtue or another, but an agent who chooses to exercise *both* of the relevant virtues so that the action is good in an overall way.

Why then does Walker treat such cases as requiring one to exercise one virtue or another? Where exactly do Walker and Cooper disagree? Cooper argues (a) that it is not simply one's action, but also one's reasons for one's action, that determine the exercise of a virtue: to break a promise in order to go to one's ailing parent's side is not unjust, although breaking a promise simply because one no longer feels like keeping it would be (1999, 88; see also Foot 1983, 397; Watson 1984, 64f). Likewise, (b) it also seems clear that in a case like Cooper's, it would not be an exercise of justice to keep a promise, when what one should do instead is to break it and go to one's parent's side. However, Walker agrees with the first claim (a), since he says that there is nothing blameworthy about failing to exercise one relevant virtue in the circumstances, provided that one does so in order to exercise another relevant virtue instead. Furthermore, a proponent of the incompatibility view could agree with the second claim (b) as well, holding that there are cases in which it would be unacceptable and blameworthy to exercise one virtue when one ought to have exercised another instead.

Rather, the difference seems to stem from differing views of what it is to 'exercise' a virtue. For instance, Walker says that one does not exercise mercy simply by feeling pity for the person one justly punishes, say, since to exercise a virtue is to exercise it '*in action*' (1993, 49f, italics in original). This seems to me an implausibly restrictive conception of exercising a virtue, but even if we accept it, why is it not to exercise two virtues 'in action' when the one 'tempers' the exercise of the other, as when one tells a painful truth in as compassionate and encouraging a way as possible, rather than simply blurting it out, or making a joke of it? There are, after all, *pro tanto* reasons both to be merciful and to be just, and whether it is better to punish or to pardon, one must be responsive to both sorts of reasons in one's choice and action.

Presumably, Walker does not count such 'tempering' as an exercise of a virtue, apparently because he thinks of exercising a virtue as doing what one, insofar as one has the virtue in question, would prefer to do. For instance, in the case of the late assignment, perhaps the instructor, as merciful, would wish to allow the late submission, and as just, would wish not to bend the rules; in the case of the ailing parent, perhaps one would, as just, wish to keep the promise, and as pious, one would wish to visit one's parent; and in the case of the painful truth, perhaps one would, as truthful, wish to make the truth plain, and as tactful, one would wish to spare the other's feelings. Walker's view seems to be that in such cases one cannot do both of the things one would wish to do, and that one therefore must choose which to do; and this Walker interprets as exercising one virtue rather than another.

On the other hand, Cooper seems to think of exercising some virtue V as acting for V reasons: on this view, one is appropriately responsive to reasons of justice, say, both when one keeps one's promise, *and* when one breaks one's promise because keeping it would leave an ailing parent in the lurch. Likewise, on this latter view of exercising a virtue, one is as appropriately responsive to reasons of mercy or tactfulness when one bends the rules or knocks the 'hard edges' off a painful truth when there is good reason to do so, as one is when one punishes or speaks frankly in a way that is compassionate rather than callous.

Which view of exercising a virtue should we prefer? We should reject Walker's view of exercising a virtue, in favor of the reasons view, for at least three reasons. First, notice that on Walker's view, to exercise a virtue is, apparently, to act so as to do the sort of thing that, as having that virtue, one would wish to do. This raises a dilemma for Walker's account of incompatibility. On the one hand, we could say that in telling a painful truth in a compassionate and encouraging way, one *has* done what, *qua* tactful, one would wish to do: tactfulness does not simply wish to avoid painful truths, but *also* to avoid any unnecessary pain when a painful truth must be told (con. Walker 1993, 47f). On the other hand, we could say, with Walker, that to exercise a virtue involves seeking to hit the target of that virtue, rather narrowly construed, such as avoiding painful truths, full stop, in the case of tactfulness.

The first line of thought is clearly much closer to the truth. We can put the point in terms of the 'targets' of a virtue. Although, as we have seen, intentionally hitting the target of a virtue is not the same as exercising a virtue, nonetheless part of having a virtue is that one has a standing wish to act so as to hit the target of that virtue. Now, it seems clear that a virtue has both primary and secondary targets: in the case of tactfulness, the primary target is to cause no pain to others in truth-telling, while the secondary target is to minimize pain as far as is consistent with the telling of a truth which, though unavoidably painful, still must be told. Of course, *qua* tactful, one would rather avoid causing pain altogether, other things being equal; but surely that does not mean that tactfulness has no target when other things are *not* equal. However, to take this line of thought is to embrace the reasons view of exercising a virtue, which is of course the view that Cooper takes. On that view, one exercises both truthfulness and tactfulness in telling a painful truth in a compassionate way—they take in each other's washing, so to speak—and consequently, the incompatibility of truthfulness and tactfulness cannot even get off the ground.

Second, Walker's view of exercising a virtue faces a further dilemma, as well. Suppose that in Walker's case one chooses to tell a painful truth rather than to be evasive. In such a case, either tactfulness tempers one's truth-telling, or it does not. If it does not, then the action is blameworthy, and one's 'truthfulness' is not a virtue, on the directions view, because it is prone to be a fault. Quite rightly, Walker rejects such a view of the virtues as potential defects (1989, 357f; 1993, 51 ff). On the other hand, if tactfulness does temper one's truth-telling, then of course that just *is* to exercise the virtue of tactfulness, in addition to the virtue of truthfulness. So if it is not blameworthy to exercise a virtue, then it must be possible to exercise multiple virtues in the same action, such as when one virtue tempers the more direct or primary exercise of another. Once again, this is to prefer the view that to exercise a virtue V is to act for V reasons, and on that view, the incompatibility thesis loses its footing.

Third and finally, on Walker's interpretation of 'exercising a virtue', his view of the virtues must be a form of the trajectories view, after all. As we saw above, the directions view of the virtues holds that each virtue considers its own primary sphere of concern, as situated among a host of connected spheres of concern. The alternative is the trajectories view, on which each virtue considers its own sphere of concern in relative isolation from the others; on this view, a virtue is a tendency to perform some range of stereotypical actions, say, or to promote some particular sort of concern. Furthermore, as we have seen, Walker holds that it is not blameworthy to forgo exercising one virtue, *when* one does so in order to exercise another, and I indicated that this may suggest a form of the directions view of the virtues: while each virtue has its own primary sphere of concern, it is willing to stand aside when this would allow the exercise of some other virtue. Now, on Walker's view, a tactful person will sometimes decide that the thing to do is not to be evasive about the truth, but to be direct and frank; however, on Walker's view, one does not make this decision *qua tactful*, but *only qua truthful*. In that case, virtues like tactfulness must be trajectories: tactfulness, on Walker's view, considers its own sphere of concern, but *not* the sphere of concern of truthfulness. Consequently, the directions view about the nature of the virtues entails the reasons view about the exercise of the virtues. Once we reject the trajectories view, then, we can no longer get the case for the incompatibility of the virtues off the ground. So much, then, for this implausibly narrow view of what it is to exercise a virtue.

Without Walker's conception of what it is to exercise a virtue, his Conflict and Correlation Assumptions fall by the wayside, as well. Consider what it would mean, on the directions view of the nature of the virtues, to become *more* virtuous. Suppose that some person exercises the virtue of generosity in Walker's sense—does what she, *qua* generous, would most wish to do—in a wide range of situations. Now suppose that although she would never do anything blameworthy in the exercise of generosity, nonetheless she does tend to give to her own needless detriment on occasion, perhaps because of insecurity about the loyalty of her friends, or because of low self-esteem. Finally, suppose that she becomes less insecure, feels better about herself, etc., and as a result becomes more intelligent about her giving, recognizing that although generosity is a virtue, this is no reason to treat herself so shabbily. The result of such a change 'in action', it seems clear, would be a tendency to give to others in need on a narrower range of occasions than before ('Yes, as a rule I would like to help out; but this time, I need the time for myself'). On the directions view of the virtues, someone who undergoes this sort of a change is becoming generous to a greater extent than before: such a person counts as improving in generosity because her generosity is becoming a *better* form of practical rationality and character. By 'more generous' here, we do not mean more prone to engage in stereotypically generous actions—and on the directions view, that is what we had better not mean. We mean that this person has the virtue, the *excellence* of generosity to a far superior degree now than before. Put another way, a tendency to give on fewer occasions may very well be one of the results of changing from being a more *profligate* person to being a more *generous* one. Consequently, the directions view of the virtues is incompatible, first of all, with the idea that moral conflicts require virtuous persons to choose between exercising one virtue or another—that is, with the Conflict Assumption. Because the directions view takes the virtues to be excellences of practical rationality, it is committed to the idea that having a virtue involves being appropriately responsive to reasons associated with that virtue. If acting from a virtue V is to act for V reasons, then one acts for those reasons even when that virtue can only temper what one does. And in that case, moral conflicts do not require one to exercise one virtue rather than another.

Furthermore, the same thought experiment also shows what is wrong with the Correlation Assumption. As we have just seen, on the directions view of the virtues it is possible for a person to become *more* virtuous despite becoming disposed to exercise that virtue in a *narrower* range of circumstances; this corollary of the directions view I shall call the Negative Correlation Thesis. If the Correlation Assumption were true, this would mean that the generous person in our thought experiment must in fact come to have the virtue of generosity to a *lesser* extent than she had before her change. Yet just the opposite is true: she has become a much *better* generous person, since her generosity is now an excellence in her character to a much *greater* degree than it was before. On the directions view, she has become *more generous*, not because she has become disposed to give to others in need in a wider range of circumstances—quite the contrary—but because she now has a better understanding of what generosity is for, that is, a better understanding of the nature of the reasons for generosity. Put another way, as she uses her improving phronesis to specify her generous ends on a wide variety of occasions, she finds that her earlier knee-jerk open-handedness is actually unfitting on very many of those occasions. So a corollary of the directions view is the Negative Correlation Thesis, and that thesis is incompatible with the Correlation Assumption. Consequently, it seems that the Correlation Assumption belies a form of the trajectories view of the virtues, yet again: because the Correlation Assumption is incompatible with the Negative Correlation Thesis, it must hold that the virtues are to be understood in terms of tendencies to engage in certain stereotypical types of actions, and that just is a version of the trajectories view.

On the directions view, therefore, it makes sense to talk about actions that are overall virtuous, about persons (real or hypothetical) that have all the virtues, and about phronesis as integrating the perspectives of the different virtues in deliberation. And, of course, on that view it makes sense to talk about the virtues as forming *some* sort of unity. In the rest of this chapter, I consider what sort of unity it makes sense to talk about.

11.2 What Unifies the Virtues?

If 'virtue' is said in many ways, so too is the idea of their 'unity'. In this section I examine the four most common strategies for unifying the virtues: that the very concepts of the virtues suggest their unity; that the virtues must be unified in a virtuous action; that the psychology of each virtue unifies it with the others; and that the virtues are unified through phronesis. I argue that the last of these four strategies is the one that must ultimately underlie any account of the idea that the virtues form a unity, whatever else we may say about the others.

11.2.1 The Conceptual Approach

The idea that the virtues form a unity sometimes rests on certain claims about the very concepts associated with the virtues: once we understand what a virtue like justice must involve, given our concept of that virtue and perhaps of virtue in general, we shall see that it must be conjoined with other virtues such as mercy, say; and so on. For instance, some of the considerations that I raised above in favor of the directions view of the virtues rested on a number of observations about the very idea of a virtue. One of these is the observation, following Aristotle, that the central virtues in any account of the virtues must be excellences, given the very idea of a virtue without qualification. Likewise, it seems part of the concept of such a virtue that to exercise a virtue is to act for certain sorts of reasons, and it seems in turn to be part of the concept of a reason that it be 'contrastive' in the sense we discussed above.

More generally, it seems paradoxical to suggest that a person can have the *virtue* of generosity, and yet be disposed to give to the wrong people, in the wrong amounts, on the wrong occasions, and so on. Rather, a virtue is not a simple tendency to do a type of thing, but to 'feel, deliberate, choose, and act *well* in certain respects' (Watson 1984, 58, emphasis added). Indeed, some have suggested on conceptual grounds that the virtues are 'reliable dispositions to do what is morally right in the relevant contexts' (see Lemos 1993, 86 for discussion). Surely this last goes too far; and in any case, no virtue ethicist—who understands right action in terms of the virtues—would define the virtues in terms of right action (see Watson 1990; Hursthouse 1999a, ch. 1; and my discussion of the 'VE constraint' in Chapter 2.). Nonetheless, the idea that virtues reliably lead their possessors to act well does seem to be part of the concept of a virtue, and since an assessment of an act as 'well done' is an all-things-considered assessment, it seems that the virtues would regularly have to work together.

But if some of the arguments in favor of UV are conceptual, so too are some of the arguments against it. Some of these too we have seen already: for instance, Walker describes his own view—that the exercise of one virtue (such as truthfulness) can exclude the exercise of another virtue (such as tactfulness)—as a conceptual argument for the incompatibility of the virtues

(1993, 46f). I have argued that Walker's particular conceptual claims are untenable, but more generally, I think that a case either for or against UV cannot rest *entirely* on conceptual grounds, for at least three reasons. First, I think a healthy dose of skepticism is in order when it comes to any attempt to draw substantial theses from a 'pure concept'. As we saw in Chapter 2, for much of the twentieth century (and earlier) it was taken for granted that the very concept of a 'right action' is such that an agent's motives and other inner states must be simply irrelevant to the rightness of action. This is no longer something that can be taken for granted about rightness, because there is no sharp boundary in the first place between a 'pure' concept of rightness on the one hand and our theorizing about it on the other.[17] Now, the idea that a virtue is an excellence *does* seem to be a deep and fairly stable part of the concept of a virtue, and it does tell against the incompatibility of the virtues (or so I and others have argued); but we need more than that to take us all the way to UV.

Second, although conceptual arguments for UV may show that having one virtue requires the support of moral *decency* and sensibility where other virtues are concerned, this does not show that each virtue requires every other *virtue* (see Watson 1984, 59f; Telfer 1989–90, 44f; Walker 1989, 359; Lemos 1993, 90–2; see also Dent 1984, 159). Being 'morally decent' in matters of giving, for instance, is not the same thing as having the unqualified virtue of generosity itself. To be sure, having a virtue does not require perfection; UV is the claim that the virtues need each other, not that nothing short of perfection in one's whole character can count as virtuous or morally decent.[18] Nonetheless, having a virtue does involve a level of stability and firmness of character, as well as practical intelligence, that simple moral decency need not (see also Hursthouse 2006a). So nothing as strong as UV is needed in order to make the point that virtuousness in any area implies coherence with moral decency in other areas.

Finally, even if strictly conceptual considerations could demonstrate the truth of UV, this would still leave us with some serious questions. It is one thing to show from first principles *that* UV is true, and another to show *how* such a thesis could be true, that is, just what it is that *unifies* the virtues. Conceptual arguments, then, can support the case for UV, but they cannot make that case on their own. What aspect of every virtue is it that unites it to every other virtue?

---

[17] See Ch. 2 for discussion.

[18] For such a charge against UV, see Geach 1977, 163f; for rebuttal, see Watson 1984, 62f, Lemos 1993, 86f. See also Ch. 4 and Swanton 2003 for the idea that to be virtuous *tout court*, one need not be perfectly virtuous, but only virtuous enough.

11.2.2 The Action Approach

Some of the very most common considerations cited in favor of UV stem from the idea that if one is to do well in a particular situation, one needs to draw upon multiple virtues in choosing and performing one's action. For instance, as we have seen, telling a painful truth requires both truthfulness and tactfulness: to be tactlessly frank is not to exercise the *virtue* of truthfulness, and to be misleadingly evasive is not to exercise the *virtue* of tactfulness.

But such considerations, though true, are hardly decisive in favor of UV. For one thing, it seems clear that there are cases in which the lack of some virtue may do nothing to hinder the exercise of some other virtue. For instance, Aristotle says that 'wittiness' is a virtue (*NE* IV.8), and while this seems plausible, it is difficult to suppose that the lack of this virtue is particularly likely to interfere with exercises of courage, say, on anything like a regular basis (cp. Jacobs and Zeis 1990, 651). Still, we should not overstate the significance of this problem: although the exercise of one virtue may not require another in a *given* situation, there is surely no predicting what combination of virtues will be necessary on different occasions in the course of a normal life.

A more serious problem for the action approach is a version of the more general problem we raised for conceptual arguments for UV: acting well, all things considered, from any virtue requires moral decency in other, related areas as well, but again, such decency need not rise to the more demanding level of possessing a virtue. And the action approach also shares another defect of the conceptual approach: even if the demands of acting well should require all the virtues to act together, we are still left with the question *how* they are able to work together in the required way. Two answers to this question come to mind: one, each virtue is a feature of a certain kind of psychology—such as what Plato's readers often call 'psychic harmony', say—such that the psychology underlying one virtue is the same as the psychology underlying all of the others; and two, each virtue involves phronesis, and phronesis unifies the spheres of concern of the various virtues in deliberation. I take up these two approaches in turn.

11.2.3 The Psychological Approach

The classic statement of a psychological approach to UV comes from Plato in book IV of the *Republic* (see Russell 2005a, chs. 4 and 7 for discussion). The soul, Plato argues, consists of three basic parts: a reasoning part, a part that is 'spirited' and emotional, and a part that is 'appetitive' or desirous. When the soul is in harmony, Plato says, the reasoning part leads the whole, and is supported in its leadership by the emotional part; and together, these two parts keep the appetites in check. The four (cardinal) virtues, Plato argues, supervene on different aspects of this psychic harmony: because reason leads the whole soul, the soul is wise; because the emotions support the judgments of reason, the soul is courageous; because the desires and appetites are in line with reason, the soul is temperate; and because the whole soul is so arranged that every part does its proper work, the soul is just (see 441c–442d).

Plato's model of the soul has few modern supporters, but there is much to be said for a psychological approach in general, nonetheless. For instance, it seems clear that one cannot have the *virtue* of truthfulness unless one also has such psychological attributes as sympathy and care, and these are, of course, the same attributes that are closely associated with the virtues of tactfulness, mercy, compassion, and so on. And it is also clear that such a view suggests not only that the virtues form a unity, but also how and why they do so.

Moreover, although there have been many psychological arguments aimed to demonstrate not the unity but the incompatibility of the virtues, these arguments have rested on variants of what I have called the trajectories view of the virtues. For instance, as we saw above, Walker has argued that the sympathetic personality that underlies the virtue of kindness is necessarily at odds with developing the virtue of justice beyond 'a limited extent' (1989; see also Flanagan 1991, 33). But while such a view of the virtues does not commit one to the grossly implausible claim that a trait can still be a virtue even when taken wrongfully to excess, it clearly rests on a myopic view of the virtues—for instance, of justice as concerned with enforcing rules *as opposed to* taking a concern for particular others. Alternatively, Walker has also argued that circumstances may require actions of an agent which exercise one kind of virtue (e.g. the 'combative virtues') but which, through no fault of the agent's, have the effect of eradicating the kinds of psychological attributes that make possible the development of other kinds of virtue (e.g. the 'domestic virtues'). Walker considers Sartre's example of the student who chooses to join the Resistance rather than pursue a more 'domestic' life, and asks, 'Is it not possible, even likely, that his frequent need to disregard his own and others' sensibilities will harden his heart and extinguish all kindly and sympathetic feeling?' (1990, 45). If so, then it would seem that virtues are such as to be incompatible, because certain forms of moral luck can call on some virtues that undermine the psychological traits necessary for other virtues. However, the problem with this view is that the proponent of the directions view, even if he accepts the details of Walker's case, will surely say that since the eradication results in a kind of myopia, none of the resulting character traits are excellences, that is, virtues without qualification.[19]

Nonetheless, a psychological approach would suffer from a version of the general problem that also infects the other approaches we have considered: even if the virtue of truthfulness requires sympathy for others, say, having the needed sympathy need not amount to possession of the virtue of tactfulness or mercy. Furthermore, while a purely psychological approach can show both that the virtues form a unity *and how* they do so, it cannot do so without recourse to an account of phronesis. The argument for this is in two steps. First, since having a virtue involves being characteristically responsive to certain sorts of reasons, not just *any* kind of mutual psychological support can ground the unity of the *virtues*. After all, a compulsive habit and a neurotic fear may support each other, and share an underlying psychological basis. And as Julia Annas has observed, many more quotidian forms of irrationality can also be 'mutually reinforcing', and form some kind of unity, such as when vanity, selective reasoning, and an unflinching self-righteousness conspire to keep one out of touch with uncomfortable truths (2005*b*, 4 ff). So what is needed is not merely mutual psychological support between the virtues, but mutual *rational* psychological support.

In that case, second, the psychological attributes that support the virtues must be such that, on the one hand, one can accept them as *good* attributes to have, and in a 'mixture' that one can accept as a good one; and this involves seeing the virtues as part of a whole self. And on the other, one must be able to judge correctly how to balance the various psychological attributes supporting the virtues, such as when sympathy should be the dominant or primary practical concern and when it should not. Consequently, a psychological attribute can support multiple *virtues*, only if those virtues are also supported, and unified, by phronesis. As Plato himself argues, the soul is wise when reason leads the whole, because only reason is capable of looking after the whole soul in the right way (see also 586e–587a; Annas 2005*b*, 1f). That is, as Plato recognized, a psychological unification of the virtues is not an *alternative* to unification through practical intelligence, since the former must be complemented by the latter.

It seems, then, that any complete account of UV must eventually appeal to the idea that the virtues are ultimately unified through phronesis, so I turn finally to that approach.

---

[19] To borrow a line from Williams 1981, divine intervention seems to be the only guarantee against such awful sorts of moral luck. See also Hursthouse 1999*a*, 85f.

11.2.4 The Approach via Phronesis

The view that the virtues are unified through phronesis is most familiar from Aristotle. Every virtue that is a proper excellence, he argues, chooses and acts in accordance with right reason or phronesis (*NE* VI.1, 13), and since phronesis grasps the end of each virtue as part of an overall view of what one has reason to do, phronesis requires every virtue (VI.12). Neo-Aristotelians like Rosalind Hursthouse and John McDowell offer similar sorts of arguments. 'Practical wisdom', Hursthouse writes, is 'the ability to reason correctly about practical matters', and although 'practical matters' span many different kinds of contexts or ranges, nonetheless 'the same sorts of judgements about goods and evils, benefits and harms, what is worthwhile and what is relatively unimportant crop up across the ranges' (1999*a*, 154), and this suggests that the virtues form some kind of unity, because phronesis unifies them. In a similar spirit, McDowell notes that 'the specialized sensitivities which are to be equated with particular virtues ... are actually not available one by one for a series of separate identifications' (1997, 143), since one does not have the virtue of generosity, say, without the practical intelligence to discern when giving to some would involve injustice to others (see also Wolf 2007, 148–50).

Such an approach makes the directions view of the virtues central to the case for UV, and this seems appropriate. On the one hand, a virtue that is an excellence must involve appropriate responsiveness to reasons, of the sort characteristic of phronesis; on the other, a virtue that is an excellence must be regularly and reliably tied to good conduct, which (as I argued in Chapters 3–4) requires good deliberation of the sort characteristic of phronesis. So it seems that, on the directions view, the virtues should form a unity precisely because of their common basis in phronesis. Moreover, such an approach shows not only that the virtues form a unity, but also *how* they do so.

Of course, this sort of approach to UV has met with considerable resistance. For one thing, we clearly develop the various virtues in a piecemeal fashion: each of us has different experiences, opportunities, and natural capacities, so that some virtues develop in each of us ahead of others, and we do not all develop in the same ways; people differ from each other in their sensitivity to certain sorts of reasons; and of course, no one can develop all of the virtues all at once (see Watson 1984, 64f; Walsh 1986, 460; Telfer 1989–90, 45; Hursthouse 1999*a*, 130f, 155, citing Williams 1995*a*, 17).[20] But if to have any virtue is to

---

[20] See also Flanagan 1991, 268–75, who discusses and defends a 'multiple-competence view' of moral learning, on which one learns multifarious sets of competencies for different moral areas or 'modules', rather than acquiring moral competence as a single module.

have phronesis, and to have phronesis is to have every virtue, does this not mean that the only way to develop the virtues at all is to develop them all at once, and that every virtuous person should be virtuous to the same extent and in the same way as every other virtuous person?

Now, these sorts of objections move a bit too quickly. We should recall that to be virtuous *tout court*, one need not be perfectly virtuous, but only 'virtuous enough'; and the same is true, *mutatis mutandis*, for phronesis—each is what I called in Chapter 4 a 'satis concept'. Consequently, having a virtue does not imply having perfect or full-blown phronesis. However, now it seems that we have met the above objections at a perilously high cost: if having a virtue does not imply full-blown phronesis, then presumably having a virtue does not imply having every other virtue, either. It is clear that full-blown phronesis entails having every other virtue, but it is not at all clear that having 'phronesis enough' entails being virtuous, or even just 'virtuous enough', in every respect. For instance, it does seem likely that a person could have phronesis enough about human goods to be generous—that is, generous enough to be generous *tout court*—even if that person is merely continent about caloric intake, say, and thus not temperate enough to be temperate *tout court*. This is of course a variant of the general problem that has plagued every approach to UV we have examined so far: having any virtue entails having an adequate level of phronesis, and thus an adequate level of moral decency where the other virtues are concerned, but not necessarily those virtues themselves, strictly speaking, even understood as satis concepts. So this approach seems to face a dilemma: either it is stuck with the implausible thesis that the virtues must come all at once, or it is unable to show that UV is true. And since I have argued that any approach to UV must ultimately rely on unifying the virtues through phronesis, this may seem the end of the line for UV.

In the final section of this chapter, I argue that the appearance of this dilemma is dispelled upon closer examination of UV: on my view, it is not in the first instance a thesis about how the virtues are in particular, developing agents, but about the natural makeup of the virtues themselves.

11.3 Attributive and Model Theses

It seems clear that on what I have called the directions view of the virtues, the virtues form *some* sort of unity or other, at least insofar as the perspective of each virtue takes in something of the perspectives of other virtues as well. It also seems clear that any attempt to explain how the virtues are able to form any sort of unity must ultimately appeal to the notion that each virtue involves the deliberative virtue of phronesis. What is less clear, however, is *what* sort of unity the virtues share, and in particular whether it can amount to anything like UV, the thesis that each virtue entails every other virtue.

To be sure, having any virtue requires moral decency in other ways as well, but since such moral decency need not rise to the level of virtue proper, it would appear that UV faces a serious general dilemma. On the one hand, the proponent of UV could hold that having a virtue requires the very robust sort of moral decency in other ways that *does* rise to the level of virtue proper; but this seems very unlikely,[21] and in any case would make the conditions on having any virtue far too demanding. And on the other, one could argue that to have basic moral decency just is to be virtuous without qualification, but this makes the conditions on having such a virtue implausibly lax, even though virtue is a satis concept. Alternatively, perhaps UV could be interpreted as holding only of those virtuous persons among us who are fully or 'perfectly' virtuous;[22] but even if such a case could be made, perfectly virtuous persons are surely only mythical creatures, and so such a form of UV would be relatively uninteresting, having very little to say about any of *us*.[23]

Furthermore, although so far we have focused on this general problem as concerning the relation between one virtue and the others, we should note that a similar problem arises with respect to any one virtue, considered across different sorts of contexts. For instance, it is only too obvious that a person who is even inspiring for her courage in standing up for what's right in the face of social pressures, may nonetheless fall short of courage when it comes to facing risk of physical harm. Yet, as Neera Badhwar points out, 'an assumption that is implicit in UV' is 'that if someone has a virtue, she must have it in all areas or domains of her life, i.e. that every virtue is global or comprehensive in scope' (1996, 308).

In this final section, I argue that although these objections hold against UV, interpreted as a thesis about what any particular person with a virtue must be like, there is nonetheless an interpretation of UV on which UV is not only plausible but attractive and philosophically interesting. I argue that UV is best interpreted as a claim about the nature of the virtues considered as

---

[21] See Hursthouse 2006*a*, who makes the excellent point that often what one needs in order to do the right thing is not virtue or phronesis proper, but simple decency and common sense. See also Wolf 2007, 162.

[22] See Telfer 1989–90, 47; see also Lemos 1993, 97–103, who argues persuasively that such a view would fall prey to the same sort of general problem that infects other versions of UV, anyway.

[23] As Walker 1990, 48 says, 'It is difficult not to feel that the "moral hero" is a chimaera [*sic*] and that with his appearance we enter the realms of fantasy'.

types, that is, about what I shall call the 'natural makeup' of the virtues. This distinction between these two ways of interpreting claims about the virtues is one that has seldom if ever been discussed very explicitly, so I begin by making it clearer. To do so, I begin by considering Badhwar's view in greater detail, since doing so will reveal that even critics of UV implicitly rely on precisely this sort of distinction, as well.

11.3.1 Virtues and Domains

Neera Badhwar argues in her important paper, 'The Limited Unity of Virtue', that

[t]he existence of a virtue in a particular domain of a person's life does not imply the existence of that (or any other) virtue in any other domains; for instance, someone may have the virtue of kindness in his relationships with friends or family members, but this does not necessarily mean that he will be kind towards strangers. (1996, 308)[24]

Badhwar makes a number of undeniable observations in support of this thesis, which we may call the 'disunity-across-domains' thesis. For one thing, human understanding in general is not an all-or-nothing affair, as if one could not be an expert in any area of science without being expert in all areas, so the simple fact that phronesis is a kind of human understanding does not show that it is all-or-nothing. Nor is there any reason to suppose that phronesis in particular must be all-or-nothing: to be sure, phronesis involves an understanding of the good, but surely the good is not such that one must either understand every part of it or understand none of it. And for another, it is of course obvious that people are anything but uniform in moral character across the different areas of their lives. After all, the development of the virtues and of phronesis differs both within and between persons, given variations in their moral upbringing, their talents, natural dispositions, and so on. Likewise, one develops phronesis and the virtues through experience and practice, and that experience is unavoidably piecemeal and selective (1996, 313–16).

So Badhwar concludes that one's possession of any given virtue is specific to some particular 'domain' of one's life, even if (as Badhwar also holds) having a virtue in one domain requires a corresponding form of moral decency in other domains. By a 'domain' Badhwar means any area of an individual's life that is *both* one that that individual is able to compartmentalize (more or less) from other sorts of areas, *and* of sufficient importance to warrant the exercise of practical wisdom in that area. It is important to notice, then, that the notion of a 'domain' is not meant to carve the areas of one's life at what we might

---

[24] See also Badhwar, 'Self-Knowledge, Character Traits, and the Milgram Experiments', unpublished.

suppose are their 'natural joints'. Rather, the issue here is what constitutes, for a given agent, an area of her life in which she may be able to develop certain virtues, without having to develop those virtues in other areas. Moreover, not every area that an agent may be able to compartmentalize will be a domain; only those areas that carry sufficient depth in their involvement with human life will be candidates for domains, in this sense (1996, 316–18).

Now, there are two different senses in which virtues may be specific to domains, and the difference between them is of great significance. First, one could hold that 'courage' in social settings is the same *in name only* as 'courage' in the face of physical danger. On this view, it is not merely the case that what is involved in learning to exercise courage is specific to a given domain, but that the virtues *themselves* are specific to these domains.[25] Hence, to speak simply of 'courage' is potentially misleading, since in fact there exists only social-settings-courage, physical-danger-courage, and so on, sharing the common label 'courage' on account of superficial resemblance and for economy of vocabulary. Or second, we could hold that courage is the same virtue in every domain in which it emerges—perhaps because courageous reasons exist across domains—and that it is only the *emergence* of courage that is piecemeal and domain-specific. On this view, there is no such thing as social-settings-courage as opposed to physical-danger-courage, only people who are better able to respond to reasons for courage in social settings than to respond to those same reasons in situations of physical danger, say.

Although Badhwar does not make this distinction explicit, it is clear that she intends the domain-specificity of the virtues in the second, weaker sense—and with good reason. For one thing, the stronger conception of domain-specificity individuates the virtues according to domains; since there seems to be no limit in principle to the number of 'domains' that different agents can compartmentalize, the virtues will be innumerable in principle as well, and that would mean that no account of 'the virtues' or 'the virtuous person' could be given, even in principle.[26] For another, this stronger view has a difficult time giving a plausible account of moral development. If a virtue in one domain is in fact a distinct trait from its namesake in some other domain, then there would be little reason to expect that moral improvement (or degeneration) in the case of the one should have any more impact in the case of the other than improvement (degeneration) in any chance virtue would. Yet consider the surprise we feel when we learn someone who appeared to be outstandingly kind in one domain has committed some act of great cruelty in

---

[25] This seems to be the view of Adams 2006, 179–84.
[26] See Ch. 5 for discussion of such problems.

another (cp. Hursthouse 1999a, 155f). In such cases, we are very strongly inclined to retract our judgment that such person has the *excellence* of kindness in any domain at all. And on the directions view, there is good reason for this: someone *that* compartmentalized, it would seem, is too myopic about 'kindness' to be genuinely responsive to reasons for kindness.

Notice also that this stronger view of domain-specificity requires one to take a version of the trajectories view of the virtues. On the trajectories view, each virtue focuses on its own sphere of concern in a more or less myopic way, where spheres of concern of the other virtues are concerned. In order for a virtue of character to overcome this myopia, it must be intimately connected to a virtue of the practical, deliberative intellect—phronesis—which serves to connect these different spheres of concern in deliberation. However, on the strong domain-specificity view, phronesis, being a virtue, would have to be domain-specific as well. In that case, phronesis would be myopic, unable to deliberate about one's ends in an integrated way. Such 'phronesis', therefore, would not be an *excellence* of deliberation, and therefore none of the other virtues of character would be excellences of character, either. The strong version of domain-specificity of the virtues, therefore, is incompatible with the directions view of the virtues, on which the virtues at the center of any account of the virtues are excellences of character and practical reasoning.

By contrast, Badhwar (1996, 320) holds that phronesis and the virtues are 'potentially general':

Just as theoretical wisdom in the realm of, say, human physiology, embodies an understanding of physiological principles that apply as well to certain other species, practical wisdom in, say, the domain of love and concern for a particular individual embodies an understanding of principles that apply as well to other human beings and other human affairs.

Consequently, Badhwar argues that having a virtue in any domain is inconsistent with having the opposing vice, or even serious moral ignorance where that virtue is concerned, in other domains. So it seems clear that Badhwar holds the far more plausible view on which the virtues are domain-specific only in their development and exercise, not in their natures.

Notice what follows from this conception of domain-specificity: although each virtue admits of disunity across domains in particular agents, nonetheless a virtue retains its *identity across domains*. To account for this identity, we require an analysis of, say, courage, on which we can say what it is the 'nature' of courage to do and to grasp in every domain. And of course such an analysis must consider courage as a type, that is, as an excellence of character with a 'natural makeup' we can model, since there need be no particular courageous person whose courage possesses such domain-generality. Therefore, since it is undeniable that courage in this or that person is domain-specific, even though the identity of courage itself is domain-general, we must distinguish two levels of discourse about the virtues: one on which to talk about this or that courageous person, and one on which to talk about the nature of courage itself.

It is this distinction that I mentioned above as the key to a proper interpretation of UV, the thesis that each virtue entails the other virtues. Before we can construct such an interpretation, however, we need a somewhat sharper understanding of these two levels and the purposes they serve.

11.3.2 The 'Model' and 'Attributive' Levels

Suppose that Fred has lately become much more prone to give of his time and possessions than he had been in the past (however we choose to gloss 'more prone' here). Does this mean that Fred has become more generous? To answer this question, we must take a step back and ask what it is to improve in generosity, that is, what it is to possess generosity to a greater extent, and therefore what generosity itself is. As we saw above, *both* the trajectories view and the directions view of the virtues take this step back, offering different conceptions of the nature of a virtue, such as generosity. On one version of the trajectories view, we might say that generosity is a proneness to perform certain stereotypical acts, and therefore that to become more generous is to become more prone to do such acts (on more occasions, say, or in a wider range of situation types). By contrast, the directions view holds that generosity is an active responsiveness to reasons of a certain sort, and thus that to become more generous is to become better in one's responsiveness to those reasons. To take this step back, then, is not to offer a particular sort of account of the virtues, but to offer *any* account of the virtues at all. This 'stepping back' is a shift from what we might call the 'attributive' level—the level at which we attribute a virtue to a particular person—to the 'model' level, at which we construct a model of a virtue so as to understand the 'natural makeup' of that virtue.

Another way to put this point is that a model of a virtue is meant to illuminate the natural course of the development of that virtue. As we have seen, the directions view of the virtues holds that the virtues are forms of responsiveness to reasons. Since the natural end-point of a virtue is excellence in responsiveness to its characteristic reasons, the natural course of that virtue's development is one that works towards that end-point—it is a process that *unfolds*. This unfolding, I argue, requires a theoretical model (see also Chapter 4).

It is important to notice that I make no 'special pleading' for this distinction; the opponent of UV relies on such a distinction every bit as much as the proponent does. In fact, this distinction between attributive and model levels is found in many places, and outside ethics. In particular, the unfolding of a virtue's course of development is, in one important respect, like such biological processes as photosynthesis in plants and eating in animals. To say that photosynthesis works and unfolds towards an end-point is not to say, of course, that the plant (or anything else) is 'pursuing' that end-point, as if it were a goal. Rather, it is to say that a process can be understood as the process of photosynthesis or eating only by understanding that nutrition and growth are the end-points of those processes. To borrow an example from Michael Thompson, we can imagine a species of shark that ingests 'food' only to spew it out to ward off predators; in such a species of shark, that process of ingestion is not a process of eating, because it does not have the end-point that eating has.[27] Likewise, we can understand certain changes in an agent's character as part of the process of developing a virtue only if that process is unfolding towards the end-point of making the agent more appropriately responsive to certain sorts of reasons. It is the end-point that makes a process both an unfolding and the particular kind of unfolding process that it is.

Processes that unfold in this way require a theoretical model to be properly understood, for two main reasons. One, processes like photosynthesis in this particular plant, eating in this animal, and moral development in this agent, can all be interrupted before they reach their natural end-point, if only because death leaves many processes unfinished. In such cases, it usually makes sense to say that the process of photosynthesis (say) was interrupted, rather than that the process was not photosynthesis in the first place; but of course, that means having a model of the process as having a natural end-point, as being *such as to* unfold in a certain way, even if it should happen to be interrupted on some occasion. And two, as our imaginary shark demonstrates, we can change our minds about processes that turned out to lead away from the natural end-point of the process we initially supposed it was. For instance, what seems on the surface to be generosity may in fact turn out to have rather little to do with appropriate responsiveness to generous reasons. For both reasons, in virtue theory, as in biology, a model of a thing's 'natural makeup' is not simply a log of how it *happens to go* with that thing in this or that case, but a model in equilibrium that reveals how it is *such as to go* with things of that kind.

The process of becoming more generous is a process that unfolds, and therefore has a makeup; and different theories of the virtues construct different

---

[27] See Thompson 1995. I discuss Thompson's paper in greater detail in Ch. 4.

models of that makeup, on which they tell different stories about how it is 'such as to go' with this virtue or that. Consequently, theses about virtues can be seriously misleading, unless we interpret them correctly as either attributive or model theses. For instance, as we saw above, it is only by distinguishing these levels that we can make sense of the idea that although the development of a virtue in particular agents is domain-specific, nonetheless the virtue itself has a domain-general identity and nature. On an attributive interpretation, the claim that a virtue is not unified across domains is the undeniable claim that people develop the virtue in a piecemeal fashion; on a model interpretation, however, it is the highly problematic claim that the virtues themselves are individuated by domains.

By now it is clear, I trust, both that the distinction between attributive and model theses about the virtues is indispensable, and that that distinction is employed left, right, and center, despite the lack of explicit attention it has received in the literature on the virtues. In the last few pages of this chapter, I explain how this distinction casts light on the case for UV.

11.3.3 The 'Limited Unity of Virtue'

We can begin by returning to Badhwar's critique of UV, as it will become clear that, as a model thesis (and not an attributive one), UV is in fact consistent with the evidence she brings against it.

In place of UV, Badhwar offers an alternative theory she calls the 'Limited Unity of Virtue', or 'LUV' for short. One thesis of LUV is one we have already seen—that possessing a virtue in one domain does not entail possessing it in any other domain—which I have called the 'disunity-across-domains' thesis. Its other thesis we can call unity-within-domains: possessing a virtue in one domain entails possessing every other (relevant) virtue in that domain as well.[28] Since 'every domain involves normative features relevant to all the virtues', Badhwar argues, 'a virtue can maintain its normative focus only in the presence of all the other virtues' within a given domain (1996, 322).

We have already seen that Badhwar, rightly, interprets the disunity-across-domains thesis as an attributive one. But what about the unity-within-domains thesis—is it an attributive or a model thesis? As an attributive thesis, unity-within-domains meets with a general problem that by now is quite familiar: even if we agree that Fred cannot possess the virtue of generosity within a domain unless he is morally decent in all other respects within that domain,

---

[28] LUV also includes a third thesis, which we noted above, '[t]he existence of virtue in one domain implies the absence of vice as well as of ignorance in most other domains', Badhwar 1996, 308. But we can leave that thesis aside here.

such moral decency need not amount to virtue proper. As an attributive thesis, then, unity-within-domains seems to be false. On the other hand, that thesis looks quite defensible as the model thesis that it is part of the natural makeup of every virtue to unfold within a domain so as to take into consideration, in an excellent way, the perspective of every other virtue within that domain, that is, that every virtue entails the others within a domain. Moreover, the qualification 'within a domain' now seems unwanted, since the virtues, *in their natural makeup*, are domain-general rather than domain-specific: as we saw in §11.3.1, virtues are domain-specific in how they develop in this or that agent, but have an identity—a natural makeup—that is general across domains. So, on a consistent model interpretation, the unity-within-domains thesis is simply that it is part of the natural makeup of every virtue to unfold so as to take into consideration, in an excellent way, the perspective of every other virtue, that is, that every virtue entails the others.

Now, recall that LUV is meant to be an *alternative* to UV. Yet, once the distinction between the attributive and model levels is in place, and applied so as to make the central theses of LUV come out true, LUV sounds for all the world like UV after all. Properly interpreted as a model thesis, the unity-within-domains thesis is the thesis that every virtue entails the others, but that just *is* UV, *if* UV is interpreted as a model thesis—and why not interpret UV that way? 'The most fundamental difference' between LUV and UV, Badhwar says, is that LUV rejects the thesis that to have a virtue in one domain, one must have that virtue in the other domains, as well (1996, 308). However, UV as a model thesis is perfectly consistent with LUV's claims about disunity across domains, where the latter is interpreted as an attributive thesis. Of course, UV accepts the thesis that virtue in one domain entails possession of that virtue in all other domains, but only as a model thesis—and on that interpretation, LUV accepts it, too.

It should now be clear, more generally, that UV has usually been interpreted as the (wildly implausible) *attributive* thesis that if someone possesses one virtue, then that person must also possess every other virtue as well. But I argue that we should take seriously the idea that UV is instead a model thesis, that is, a thesis about the natural makeup of the virtues, rather than about particular virtuous persons. It remains, then, to take a closer look at such an interpretation of UV, and to ask whether UV so interpreted remains philosophically interesting.

11.3.4 *The Model Interpretation of UV*

I argue that UV is a thesis that belongs to a model of the natural makeup of the virtues. Now, to say that UV is a thesis about 'models of virtue' is to say that UV concerns an idealization of virtue, but (as we saw in Chapter 4) such ideals require great care. For instance, J. L. Ackrill argues that UV is a kind of idealization:

This idea of the 'unity of virtue' is at first sight very strange. In real life people have some virtues and not others. However, this is because in real life we are not dealing with *perfect* examples of any virtue.... If, for theoretical purposes, we are to explain what would be involved in the perfect possession of any one virtue, we find we cannot allow defects anywhere in the character... (Ackrill 1981, 137, italics in original)

Ackrill's view is different from the view, mentioned above, that UV is about people who are 'perfectly' virtuous, I think, since he makes it clear that UV is a thesis about an ideal that is not any living, breathing person, but one conjured only 'for theoretical purposes'.[29] Nonetheless, Ackrill leaves it far from clear what his 'perfect examples' are for. Surely such an ideal is not meant to show virtue 'as it ought to be', as if to say that if Fred were 'as a generous person ought to be', then he would be fully virtuous in every way. This would be far too demanding a view of the virtues; and it would be a potentially perilous one as well, since aspiration to exceedingly demanding levels of excellence may actually leave one a morally worse character, if such excellence goes beyond one's inner strength (see Swanton 2003, ch. 9; see also Foot 1983, 397). And in any case, what are these 'theoretical purposes'? Are they relevant outside pure speculation, or does shifting UV to an idealization render it largely uninteresting?

However, in our own case we have *begun* with certain clearly pressing theoretical purposes, and found ourselves needing a model of the virtues as a result. Our discussion of the domain-specificity of the virtues suggested one such purpose: the idea that the identity of a virtue is constant between domains, despite the domain-specificity of the virtues in particular agents, requires a model on which to construe the natural makeup of the virtue. And our overview of general accounts of the virtues, such as the trajectories and directions views, suggested another: each account takes a step back to ask, on a purely theoretical level, what it is to have a virtue, and thus what it is to improve in one's possession of a virtue.

This latter point is especially apt, since on its model interpretation, UV is a direct corollary of the directions view of the nature of the virtues. On that view, every virtue is a form of responsiveness to practical reasons within its sphere of concern, where those reasons are situated within a broader range of other sorts of practical reasons. Consequently, on that view it is part of the natural makeup of every virtue to unfold so as to take into consideration the perspective of every other virtue in practical deliberation about ends.

---

[29] Thus I do not read Ackrill in the way that Telfer 1989–90 and Lemos 1993 do.

From the directions view, then, there follow two theses that by now should be quite familiar. One, it is part of the natural makeup of a virtue to unfold so as to have a broader and more intelligent grasp of what practical reasons there are for virtuous choice, action, and feeling; that is, it is part of the nature of every virtue to entail phronesis (cp. *NE* VI.13). And two, since it is in virtue of phronesis that one is responsive to practical reasons for virtue in an excellent, balanced, and integrated way, it is part of the natural makeup of phronesis to unfold so as to be fully responsive to all such reasons; that is, it is part of the nature of phronesis to entail every virtue (cp. *NE* VI.12).

Taken together, those two theses just *are* UV, interpreted as a thesis about models of virtue. The idea that the virtues are a unity, and that they are unified through phronesis, is therefore a corollary of the view that the virtues are excellences of character and practical reasoning. The classic Aristotelian argument for UV is therefore a sound one.[30]

One remaining question, then, is whether UV remains an interesting thesis about the virtues on such an interpretation. But surely it does! So interpreted, UV maintains, for one, that to improve in the possession of any virtue V is to improve in one's effective responsiveness to V reasons across the different areas of one's life, on the one hand, and to improve in one's grasp of V reasons as situated within what other practical reasons there are. Moreover, UV therefore suggests a sort of 'litmus test' for the emergence of a *bona fide* virtue in a particular agent: for instance, whether Fred's recent rise in stereotypically 'generous' behavior signals the emergence of or improvement in the excellence of generosity, depends on whether this change makes Fred more or less prone to respond intelligently and appropriately to other sorts of practical reasons—that is, whether this trait tends towards *unity* with other forms of moral goodness in Fred. If it does not, then this is a reflection of Fred's becoming *less* responsive to reasons, so that his purported 'generosity' begins to look instead like prodigality, say. Likewise, UV makes sense of the surprise we experience when a person kind in some circumstances is cruel in others: what had seemed to be a virtue of kindness, we discover, is in fact paired with a shocking lack of responsiveness to reasons of kindness; so although kindness does not require perfection, too much divergence from the natural makeup of kindness can lead us to retract our earlier attribution of that virtue.

---

[30] It is an interesting question whether Aristotle himself understood UV as a model thesis, of the sort I have described here. Charity would certainly recommend such a reading of Aristotle, unless we are to suppose that somehow he had simply overlooked the fact that there are no people who are virtuous in every way. Nonetheless, Aristotle's text on this point is too scant to determine the issue with any great certainty.

Finally, it is important to see that the model of virtue that UV describes is consistent with variations in virtuousness both within and between genuinely virtuous persons. Since UV is not an attributive thesis, it is compatible with the undeniable observation that we all differ in our experiences, natural dispositions, and upbringing, so that variations in virtuousness are a normal part of every life. UV denies not that the *development* of the virtues is piecemeal and fragmentary, only that the virtues *themselves* are piecemeal and fragmentary in their very nature. Furthermore, UV does not entail that it is a moral failing in a person to devote more time and resources to expressing generosity to others, say, than to fighting injustice, since such a focus on one sphere of concern need not be a *myopic* focus on that sphere. And likewise, UV is compatible with the fact that there are some virtues that only some people will have the need and the opportunity to develop. For instance, a very wealthy citizen may develop the rather specialized virtue of 'magnificence' in making large public gifts, but it need be no failing in another, less wealthy citizen not to develop such a virtue, since each citizen can still be virtuous in an excellent rather than a myopic way.

In sum, then, the thesis that every virtue involves phronesis does commit us to some version of the unity of the virtues. I have argued that the version of that thesis to which it commits us is a plausible one, and more than that, positively attractive for the rich model of the virtues that it offers.

12

Responsibility for Character

In previous chapters I have defended a view of the virtues as crucially involving certain forms of practical reasoning and deliberation. I now want to take stock, briefly, of that view, and in particular to focus on what that view has to say about the intuitive idea that a virtue is not just any attribute of a person, but an attribute that has a special kind of psychological 'depth'. More specifically, to have a virtue is to be committed to acting for the sake of certain ends, ends that are 'deep' in the sense both that one must give them a determinate content through practical thought, and that one must see the point of maintaining and pursuing those ends. After all, as I have argued, pursuing the ends characteristic of a virtue in an intelligent and excellent way involves seeing the point of those ends within a cohesive *body* of ends of other virtues. Consequently, to have a virtue is to have an end that one specifies and adopts—an end that one *constructs*—for oneself. And since a commitment to such ends would seem to be a part of one's very identity as a practical agent, a virtue is therefore part of an identity that one constructs for oneself.

So much for what my view commits me to. But to what extent *can* humans direct themselves and construct their identities—to what extent, that is, can humans be responsible for their character? Rather surprisingly, virtue theorists have had fairly little to say about responsibility for character.[1] Perhaps this is paired with the recent trend among virtue theorists of increasing indifference to phronesis as part of the virtues. In any case, before taking up responsibility in this final chapter, we should begin by reflecting on the connection between virtue theory and the notion of being responsible for one's character.

12.1 Depth, Self-Construction, and Responsibility

Consider the intuitive notion of psychological depth. When I tell you that Sally has the virtue of compassion, I seem to tell you something much deeper

---

[1] A noteworthy exception is Adams 2006, 158–70.

about Sally than when I say that Sally has red hair. Roughly speaking, I tell you something about *who Sally is* when I say she is compassionate, whereas I only say *what Sally is like* when I say she is red-headed. This is not simply because red hair is a physical attribute, and compassion a mental one. If I tell you that Sally can solve quadratic equations, say, or that she has a habit of flipping the light switch three times when she enters a dark room, I describe some of her mental attributes, but again tell you only what she is like. (In fact, if her switch-flipping is a kind of compulsion, then Sally herself will experience this mental attribute as something alien.) We would still be left wondering, 'But who *is* Sally—what sort of person is she? What makes her tick? What would we know if we knew her well?' Describing such mental attributes as mindless habits or arithmetical skills implies that Sally does certain things with a certain *frequency*, perhaps; whereas telling you that she is compassionate implies that she does certain things for certain *reasons*. Describing the reasons for which Sally characteristically acts, then, tells us much more about who she is, and so such a description seems to give us the 'depth' that seems appropriate to the notion of a virtue (cp. Adams 2006, 14). So the view of the virtues I have developed in this book—namely, that virtues involve certain characteristic patterns of responsiveness to reasons, which one grasps and gives specific content through the exercise of phronesis—meshes nicely with the intuitively attractive idea that virtues of character are attributes with considerable psychological depth.

The intuitive notions of 'depth', and of attributes that are part of 'who one is', are interpreted on this view as descriptions of that level of practical reasoning at which one constructs ends for oneself. Ends are 'constructed' in two respects. One, it takes practical reasoning to specify the content of one's end before one can choose a particular act for the sake of that end. As we have seen at many points in this book, the physician has the end of producing health, and the generous person the end of materially benefiting others, but it takes deliberation to determine just what, in one's particular circumstances, achieving those ends would amount to. In this sense, ends are constructed insofar as one's ends are made determinate through deliberation. And two, ends are constructed in the more radical sense that one adopts certain ends through practical reasoning, within a broader ethical outlook on what is good for human beings. As I argued in Chapter 1, when we choose ends rationally, we adopt ends (such as certain life projects) as the specification of the content of other ends (such as the end of living well). A genuinely virtuous person, I have argued in this book, must construct these ends *well*, in both of these respects, and therefore with phronesis. Phronesis is necessary for virtue, because successful practical reasoning about ends and reasons is necessary both for making a systematic connection between virtue and right action, and for making virtue an excellence of the practically rational creatures that we are.

One's characteristic ends and reasons are deep attributes of the self—of 'who one is'—and therefore crucial parts of one's very identity as a unique practically rational creature. In fact, the construction of one's ends and reasons is part of the construction of the self. As Christine Korsgaard has argued, what one constructs when one constructs one's ends and reasons is a 'practical identity', that is, 'a description under which you value yourself, a description under which you find your life to be worth living and your actions to be worth undertaking' (1996a, 101). This casts further light on the difference between 'who one is' and 'what one is like': attributes of the latter sort, such as being good with numbers, can be part of one's practical identity, not just as such, but only insofar as one may represent those attributes as being an important part of one's life and projects. The intuitive notions of 'depth' and of 'who one is', then, have led us to a more substantive notion of the self as directing and indeed 'constructing' itself—a self that is fully *one's own*. Because Hard Virtue Ethics and Hard Virtue Theory are heavily invested in the idea that practical reasoning constructs ends and reasons, they are equally heavily invested in the idea of self-construction.

A Hard Virtue Theory would therefore be the polar opposite of, say, the sort of virtue theory defended by Julia Driver, who argues that 'a virtue is a character trait that produces more good (in the actual world) than not, systematically' (2001, 82). On Driver's view, virtues are mental attributes that do in fact produce good consequences, regardless of whether one aims at those consequences or not, in a fairly regular and systematic way in the agent's actual environment of action. Notice that to have such a virtue, it is enough that one simply *have* some mental attribute that is fortuitous in this special sort of way; indeed, one can have such virtues without even knowing it.[2] Such a virtue, then, need not be a 'deep' attribute of a person, part of 'who one is', but may be no more than a sort of 'causal designation',[3] and thus simply part of 'what one is like', or (which comes to the same thing) of how things have turned out in one's case. Such virtues need be 'one's own' only in the very thin sense that they are located in one rather than in others.

---

[2] In fact, Driver 2001, ch. 2 argues that at least one virtue—modesty—is such that if one has it, then one must not know that one does. I prefer the alternative view of Swanton 2003, 237f.

[3] I owe the phrase to Pincoffs 1986, 8. For critique of a 'causal designation' view of the virtues, see Pincoffs 1986, 8, 43, 46; but con. p. 88.

Now, I have argued throughout this book that 'depth', in the form of an agent's responsiveness to reasons, is a crucial feature of the virtues: because of the tie between virtue and right action (Part I), because virtues must be individuated as forms of responsiveness to reasons (Part II), because virtue is part of one's very conception of oneself and one's environment (Part III), and because of the idea that a virtue is an excellence of a practically rational creature (Chapter 11). But if such depth, as we have seen here, goes all the way to the construction of the self understood as a 'practical identity', could such creatures as we are have *that* sort of depth of character at all? After all, none of us *literally* constructs himself or herself. I have understood 'self-construction' as a matter of constructing a practical identity through practical reasoning, but of course by the time one is able to think for oneself, one does so only within a framework of thought and affect that results from a complex mix of heredity and experience. Many philosophers have argued that this latter fact jeopardizes the notion that one's character could be 'one's own', in any richer sense than that one's character is located in one rather than in others. It is a long history of experiences and influences that has led to the particular set of values, attitudes, and goals that one has, and every stage in that history is a result of new experiences interacting with characteristics that one's history has produced, going back ultimately to infancy when one had no control over anything. In that case, we might say that *all* attributes are matters of 'what one is like', of how things have turned out in one's case; indeed, one philosopher has argued on these grounds that one's character is 'one's own' in no deeper a sense than the color of one's hair or the shape of one's face (Strawson 2003, esp. 221). Even if that goes too far, it is clear enough that the idea that the virtues are a 'deep' part of the self, in the sense in which I understand that idea, is one that we shall have to defend.

One type of defense would argue that the self transcends its causal history; but it seems clear that a self can construct itself only on the basis of its values and attitudes, and therefore only on the basis of the very sort of character we need to account for. So if a 'transcendent' self is the sort that can construct a practical identity, the question of responsibility simply gets pushed back to it. Another defense rests on the idea that there is radical indeterminacy in the world, which makes it possible to re-direct one's character. However, to many philosophers, myself included, this indeterminacy has seemed either too radical to be true, or, more often, unlikely to make character 'one's own' in a deeper sense anyway. Couldn't character still be merely a bundle of causal designations, whether those designations came about through random events or determined ones?

A third line of defense would argue that self-construction is not the 'historical' notion of having originated one's character oneself, but the forward-looking notion of being able to conduct oneself in accordance with one's stable values and preferences. In other words, having a character of one's own depends not so much on how one *came to have* one's character, as on *what one can do* with the character one has. This is much closer to the sort of 'self-construction' that, I have argued here, concerns the virtue theorist. After all, the idea that the virtues are deep attributes leads to the notions of practical identity and self-construction, not because depth requires a certain history, but because depth involves having ends one grasps for oneself. However, the 'forward-looking' line of defense has traditionally regarded an attribute as 'deep' to the extent that that attribute occupies a certain 'level' in one's motivational structure, as for instance one's basic preferences about one's desires operate at a higher level of one's overall framework of motivations than one's desires do. On one prominent version of that view, to be responsible is not merely to be able to act on one's desires, but to be able to act on one's desires because one prefers, at a higher level of reflection, to act for the sake of those desires (see Frankfurt 2003). But as critics have noted, if it is possible to be alienated from one's lower-order desires, then it should be just as possible to be alienated from one's higher-order desires, which are, after all, still desires (Watson 1975).

I trust that these remarks have made it clear that every theory of the virtues—at any rate, every theory on which the virtues are more than mere 'causal designations'—must eventually do business with the difficult idea of being *responsible* for one's character, that is, the idea that one's character can be one's own in a deeper sense than that it is located in one rather than in others. Since the third, so-called 'compatibilist' line of defense of responsibility for character allows responsibility to be a function of practical reasoning, rather than of developmental history, the view of responsibility for character I offer here shall be compatibilist in this sense. Compatibilism holds that responsibility is a forward-looking notion: to be responsible for one's character is to be a person who can take responsibility for that character, to be capable of directing oneself and one's development, rather than being merely the unfolding of prior causes. Incompatibilism, by contrast, holds that responsibility is backward-looking: to be responsible for one's character is to be responsible for how one's character came to be as it now is. Simply put, compatibilists and incompatibilists alike are interested in the notion of self-construction; but whereas incompatibilists see a self-constructor as a person with a certain *history*, compatibilists see a self-constructor as a person with a certain *power*. Since my view is a compatibilist one, I think that the notion of being responsible for character—having a character that is one's own—should be separated from questions of how one's character originated. What I must show, then, is that such a separation yields a plausible way of thinking about self-construction and responsibility for character.

Now, the more traditional compatibilist view I mentioned above looks for different levels within motivational structures as the key to understanding responsibility, but I shall argue that the real issue is freedom from alienation from that structure, whatever the level. So I begin instead with the very idea of freedom from alienation. What characterizes alienating desires, such as compulsive desires or desires that result from manipulation (such as brainwashing), is that one cannot 'engage' with them in reflection. That is, one cannot rethink such motivations, because their motivating power has nothing to do with practical reflection at all. I understand the notion of freedom from alienation as having *critical distance* from one's motivational structure, and in particular one's characteristic aims and priorities. On my view, to have critical distance from one's character is to be able to rethink one's various character traits, and I argue that to have critical distance from one's character is to be responsible for one's character, that is, to have a character of one's own.[4]

I begin in §12.2 by rejecting the view that responsibility for character is or entails responsibility for the history of one's character. I then articulate the notion of critical distance in §12.3, and argue in §12.4 that critical distance is both necessary and sufficient for responsibility for character, on a forward-looking conception. I conclude in §12.5 by considering a number of possible objections to the critical distance view of responsibility for character.

Three quick caveats about the notion of 'character' I use here are in order at the outset. One is that by 'character' I mean more than patterns of 'characteristic' or typical behavior, but the sorts of psychological attributes that underlie such patterns of behavior in a relatively stable way over time. Two, I focus in particular on such attributes as having certain aims and priorities.[5] And three, although the 'consistency' of the virtues was the focus in Part III, here I shall assume only that character is stable over time, without having to rely on more controversial theses about the consistency of

---

[4] My conception of responsibility is thus closest to Wolf's (1990), but unlike Wolf, I think critical distance is sufficient for responsibility. I discuss this issue in §12.4.2.

[5] As Trianosky 1990, 95 points out, questions of one's responsibility matter more in our estimation of a person's character traits, in this narrower sense (e.g. one's benevolence), than in other sorts of 'characteristics', such as 'dexterity in business', to use Hume's phrase.

character traits in generating certain kinds of behavior across a wide variety of contexts.

12.2 On Responsibility and 'Ultimate Responsibility' for Character

It is common to think that adult humans are usually responsible for their character, such as one's being a generous or selfish person, but it is also clear that character begins in childhood under influences for which one has no responsibility at all. So the question arises, how could we come to be responsible for our character, having begun with no responsibility at all? Why think that such an idea is even *applicable* to us, dependent creatures that we are?

Some philosophers argue that responsibility for one's character—for being the sort of person one is—is or implies 'ultimate responsibility', that is, that one must be the historical *originator* of one's character. This view seems to raise special issues for character: it is not obvious how one could originate one's character through purposive actions for which one is also responsible, since purposive actions themselves seem to stem from character. Not surprisingly, some have argued that such problems are insoluble. One sort of doubt is a conceptual one: if the concept of responsibility for character involves originating one's character, then the very fact that one starts life as a child makes such responsibility impossible. Other worries stem from the fact that one shapes oneself only on the basis of how one already is. Perhaps as we retrace an adult's history, we find that any so-called 'self-shaping' vanishes in a series of unfoldings of prior influences beyond the agent's control, so that at no point between childhood and adulthood does responsibility for character become apparent. Furthermore, any 'self-shaping' reflection would be set within a framework of more basic or 'higher order' values, but one need not be any more responsible at the level of the more basic self than at any other level. On the other hand, some have argued that such problems are soluble, but their solutions require some form of indeterminism, and as I said above, there is widespread controversy as to whether indeterminism helps.

My own view is that people can be responsible for their character, without being responsible for the *development* of their character. Before developing that view, in this section I examine two versions of the ultimate conception of responsibility. On the stronger version, responsibility for one's character means having originated it through past actions of one's own that constitute a sufficient condition for one's character. This view, I argue, raises no special issues for character, but seems to do so only because it is ill suited to handle the possibility of *joint* responsibility, of which responsibility for character is but one type. The weaker version holds that responsibility for one's character means having originated it through one's past actions that were indispensable to the sufficient condition for one's character. This view can accommodate joint responsibility, but it throws into sharp relief the 'backward-looking' focus of ultimate responsibility, which I argue rests on the false assumption that not being alienated from one's character requires that one be the historical originator of one's character.

12.2.1 *Strong Ultimate Responsibility and 'Sole Authorship'*

Ultimate responsibility—or 'UR' for short—requires that to be responsible for one's character, one must, in some sense, have *originated* one's character. In his widely read paper, 'The Impossibility of Moral Responsibility', Galen Strawson holds that to be 'truly responsible' for one's character is to be '*causa sui*' (literally, 'cause of oneself'), that is, responsible for character all the way down, apart from any antecedent external influence. According to Strawson, responsibility for your character requires that 'you *and you alone* [be] truly responsible for how you now are' (Strawson 2003, 220, italics added; see also Nagel 1979a, 35).[6] Such responsibility requires not merely self-authorship but indeed *sole* authorship, and Strawson argues (rightly, I think) that no one can be responsible for his or her character in this sense.

But not all proponents of UR are so pessimistic. Robert Kane argues that although responsibility for one's character requires having originated one's character through actions one also originated, one *can* be responsible for character in this sense, despite the fact that one is inevitably shaped by external influences. In his 1989 paper 'Two Kinds of Incompatibilism', Kane argues that one is ultimately responsible for one's character in virtue of having shaped it through choices undetermined by one's character, and for which one was ultimately responsible. According to Kane, an agent is ultimately responsible for such a choice when the only possible explanations of the agent's choosing must be expressible in terms of the agent's 'decision', or intentional termination of an effort of will (provided also that the decision meets certain minimal standards of rationality). What makes for ultimacy, on Kane's view, is a fact about possible explanations: if one is ultimately responsible for X, then the only possible explanations of X must be in terms of the agent's

---

[6] Strawson also cites Nietzsche (*Beyond Good and Evil* §12) as describing responsibility as being *causa sui*.

(minimally rational) deciding, where deciding determines a choice without being determined by anything else (1989, 227, 231f, 236; on 'decision' see also 2000a, 70).

Thus Kane focuses on purposive choices that involve an *effort* of will, such as when an agent is in conflict about what to do, and he defines UR first in terms of them. In these cases, the effort of will is terminated by a decision, which is intelligible in the light of the agent's character and antecedent circumstances, but is not determined by them. Since it is only that decision, and not the character or circumstances that explains the choice, the agent is ultimately responsible for that choice. Second, Kane says that when such choices have determined one's character, one is ultimately responsible for that character, and thus also for characteristic choices without effort of will (1989, 235f, 241, 244, 245, 251f).[7] Given the definition of ultimate responsibility for character in terms of ultimate responsibility for choices, one is ultimately responsible for his or her character just in case the only explanations of the agent's character are prior character-shaping choices for which the agent was also ultimately responsible.

This account entails that, again, one must be *wholly* responsible for one's character, to be responsible for it at all. To be sure, Kane does allow that the influence of heredity, environment, and conditioning can form the background of those character-shaping choices for which one is ultimately responsible, and thus that such influences can form, indirectly, the background of one's character (1989, 224, 248).[8] But if I am to be responsible for my character, then in the end the explanation why I have just the character I do must be in terms of what decisions *I* have made in the past, and in no other terms than those—that is what ultimacy comes down to. So notice two features of this first, strong version of UR: one, it requires 'sole authorship', and two, it is backward-looking, focusing on how one's character was formed. I want to focus on the sole authorship aspect of the strong version first, and leave its backward-looking focus until the discussion of the weak version, which also shares that focus (§12.2.2).

Not surprisingly, strong UR seems to raise special issues for character. According to Strawson, strong UR yields insoluble problems: no one can originate his or her character, and indeterminacy does not help (2003, 222–5).

---

[7] On the relation between responsibility for choice and for character, see also van Inwagen 1989, 418–21.

[8] Kane thus distinguishes 'absolute control' over choice—that is, the determination of choice by an effort in turn determined by character, such choices not being 'limited by heredity, environment, and conditioning'—which requires determinism, from 'ultimate control', which requires indeterminism.

According to Kane, strong UR is possible, but requires a dramatic indeterminacy in the act of deciding.[9] But although strong UR seems to raise special issues for character, in fact those issues stem from the inability of strong UR to handle responsibility for character as a species of the more general notion of *joint* responsibility. That is a problem for strong UR, not for the idea of responsibility for character.

Consider an ordinary case of joint action. Suppose that Fred makes a pile of bricks near a doorway, and that George makes a pile of bricks next to Fred's. Suppose also that it takes the resulting 'heap' of bricks to block the doorway. Who is responsible for blocking the doorway? On strong UR, neither of them. Fred is not responsible for blocking the doorway, since we can explain Fred's blocking of the doorway only by referring also to George's action, and vice versa. Of course, the heap consists of Fred's pile and George's pile, and each can be responsible for his own pile. But neither can be responsible for the heap, and since neither pile is sufficient to block the doorway, neither can be responsible for blocking the doorway, either. Now, *perhaps* this is what we should say if Fred and George act completely separately and the heap results by mere coincidence. However, on strong UR, neither Fred nor George could be responsible even if they should *conspire* to block the doorway, since neither Fred's nor George's action is sufficient to explain the blocking of the doorway. Of course, on strong UR it may be that some 'corporate body' of Fred-and-George can be responsible for blocking the doorway, yet it seems bizarre that neither Fred nor George can be even partially responsible for blocking the doorway, and that precisely because they *both* are responsible. And if such corporate responsibility reduces to individual responsibility, as some hold it does, then there could be no responsibility for the heap at all.

Notice that this example is actually friendly to strong UR in one important respect: since the heap can be disaggregated into Fred's pile and George's pile, there is at least *some* responsibility that each can have in this scenario. Each is responsible for his own contribution—his own pile—as a discrete, independent part that is exclusively his own.[10] But most products of joint effort

---

[9] Kane 1989, 227, 235f describes indeterminism as 'something of a nuisance', the 'high price' of incompatibilism, despite making it a 'positive feature of incompatibilist free agency'.

[10] See also Nagel (1979a, 26) who asserts that 'Where a significant aspect of what someone does depends on factors beyond his control, yet we continue to treat him in that respect as an object of moral judgment, it can be called moral luck'. One's participation in a joint effort will be, on this definition, a case of moral luck, and Nagel says that all forms of moral luck are 'opposed by the idea that one cannot be more culpable or estimable for anything than one is *for that fraction of it* which is under one's control. It seems irrational to take or dispense credit or blame for matters over which a person has no control, or for their influence on results *over which he has partial control*' (28, emphasis added).

are unlike this heap of bricks in this respect, and most contributions to joint effort—and in particular, the various contributions to one's character—are neither discrete nor exclusively one's own.[11] To be sure, it is a long-standing puzzle how to assess individual responsibilities for joint efforts, but strong UR requires such solutions to be of just one type—disaggregation—and that type looks hopeless. Perhaps neither I nor those who have influenced me are responsible for my character, but even so, surely the reason is *not* simply that we all contributed in a way that does not admit of disaggregation.

The strong version of UR, then, shows nothing worrisome about character, but only its own inability to account for the very idea of joint responsibility.[12] For the same reason, strong UR clearly is not our commonsense conception, which is constituted in part by our belief in the intelligibility of joint responsibility, partial responsibility, and differing degrees of responsibility, *without* necessarily disaggregating joint efforts. As Harry Frankfurt has said, 'There is a difference between being *fully* responsible and being *solely* responsible' (2003, 336 n. 10, italics in original).[13]

12.2.2 *Weak UR and 'Back-Tracking'*

Even if a 'sole authorship' conception of responsibility is problematic, there remains the underlying worry that our starting life with no responsibility

---

[11] As philosophers like Moody-Adams (1990, 127–9) and Homiak (1999) point out, both the development and the change of character are highly social and cooperative enterprises. No wonder that Nagel, who evidently works with the ultimate conception, says that 'The area of genuine agency, and therefore of legitimate moral judgment, seems to shrink under this scrutiny to an extensionless point.... Eventually nothing remains which can be ascribed to the responsible self, and we are left with nothing but a portion of the larger sequence of events, which can be deplored or celebrated, but not blamed or praised' (1979a, 35, 37). Consequently, our 'basic moral attitudes' are threatened 'when we see how everything we do belongs to a world that we have not created' (38). See also Strawson 2003, 221. Notice, then, that it would not help to say that, given the pile of bricks that was already there, George's stacking of his pile is sufficient to block the doorway. That turns the blocking of the doorway into a case of sole responsibility, but the point is to understand joint responsibility.

[12] It may be tempting to reply that UR was never intended to be applied to cases of joint responsibility in the first place. Fine; but then UR cannot be applied to responsibility for character either, since human character is always the product, necessarily, of joint effort.

[13] Strawson 2003, 215–18 and Kane 1996, ch. 6 each argue that the ultimate conception is central to our common understanding of responsibility. But while they succeed in showing that we commonly think that people construct themselves, I do not think that they show that we think people construct themselves *in the way the ultimate conception requires*. For instance, Strawson 2003, 217f claims to find the ultimate conception not only in the words of philosophers and public figures, but also in our ability to find intelligible the notion of eternal reward in heaven and eternal punishment in hell. But I think it is at least as likely that the thought we find intelligible is simply that people can be responsible *enough* to warrant such reward or punishment, whether they are 'ultimately' responsible or not.

at all for who we are necessarily jeopardizes any responsibility we could have for who we become. Consider this famous passage from John Rawls (1971, 104):

It is one of the fixed points of our considered judgments that we do not deserve our place in the distribution of natural endowments, any more than we deserve our initial starting place in society. The assertion that a man deserves the superior character that enables him to make the effort to cultivate his abilities is also problematic; for his character depends in good part upon fortunate family and social circumstances for which he can claim no credit. The notion of desert seems not to apply to these cases.[14]

Of course, Rawls speaks of *deserving* one's character, but it is clear that on Rawls' view we do not deserve our character because we are not responsible for it in the right way, since our character has a history that begins with things that merely happened to us.[15] Nonetheless, Rawls does think that people can deserve: people are not so responsible that institutions should be structured so as to reward desert, but people can be responsible enough for character to deserve *within* just institutions (1971, 103, 137, 140, 313f).[16] Consequently, Rawls rejects a 'sole authorship' conception of responsibility, yet Rawls' worry about responsibility remains. This brings us, then, to the 'backward-looking' focus of UR: the idea that responsibility for one's character is a function of what one has done at some point in the past to make one's character what it is. Clearly, this focus is not peculiar to UR, but is shared by many common conceptions of responsibility for character, a fact that gives Rawls' argument its polemical force. But by considering the weak version of UR we can bring that focus into clearer view.

Our discussion in §12.2.1 suggested that responsibility is what I have called a 'satis concept' (Chapter 4): one need not be responsible for everything, in

---

[14] For discussion of Rawls on indolence, see esp. Sher 1979 and Rachels 1997, 180–6.

[15] Desert and responsibility are linked; as Rachels (1997, 180) has put the point, 'if people were never responsible for their own conduct ... no one would ever deserve anything'; cf. Moriarty 2002, 134. The connection between responsibility and desert is more complex than it may seem at first, but it is undeniable that the ability to be deserving presupposes that one be a responsible agent; see Smilansky 1996, responding to Feldman 1995.

[16] While Rawls speaks in these passages of entitlements rather than deserts, his point is not merely that just institutions should reward what they announce they will reward, but that their doing so satisfies what is a legitimate expectation of reward given what those institutions have announced—in effect, they announce what will count as 'deserving'. His point, then, seems to be the preservation of a sense of one's getting what one deserves, in this special sense. See Moriarty 2002 for an excellent discussion. Rachels 1997, 181, however, seems to suggest that, on Rawls' view, no one is deserving at all. But Rawls holds that responsibility comes in degrees because responsibility can be *partial*: character 'depends in large part upon fortunate family and social circumstances for which [one] can claim no credit' (Rawls 1971, 104; see Moriarty 2002, 136), and for Rawls this does not show that no one is responsible for his or her character at all.

order to be responsible at all. Perhaps for this reason Kane has moved away from glossing ultimate responsibility as a form of sole responsibility. In his 1996 book *The Significance of Free Will*, Kane argues that ultimate responsibility requires that one be 'responsible for any sufficient reason of one's action', but not that one 'be the complete or sole cause of the sufficient reason' (1996, 73; see also 2000*a*, 66f). An agent may be responsible for an action even if other factors are part of its explanation, so long as the agent is solely responsible for something that has made a difference where that action is concerned. On this view, ultimacy requires only that one's free agency be indispensable to any sufficient explanation of the event (1996, 72–4).

Returning to our earlier example, we can see that Fred and George each meet the conditions for weak UR. Each is responsible (*ex hypothesi*) for his own contribution to the heap of bricks, and since the contribution of each is necessary to explain the blocking of the doorway, each is responsible for blocking it. Notice too that weak UR does not require us to disaggregate the heap into parts for which each is solely responsible. It requires only that each have done something for which he was responsible and which made a difference to the heap that resulted. So, weak UR is consistent with joint responsibility.

Since UR for character is understood in terms of UR for choices, a correspondingly weak UR for character would hold that an agent is ultimately responsible for his or her character when any sufficient reason for the agent's character being as it is must include actions or omissions for which the agent is also ultimately responsible. That is, one must have made an indispensable contribution to one's character, by doing something to which one had made an indispensable contribution.

Kane argues that these conditions can be met, since agents are capable of what he calls 'self-forming actions' (including omissions) for which one has 'sole authorship' and thus can claim 'underived origination' (1996, 74–80).[17] I shall not discuss Kane's proposal any further, beyond noting that it still requires a dramatic indeterminacy (see Strawson 2000; Kane 2000*b*, 163–7; see also Kane 2000*a*, 67f).[18] Instead, I want to focus on the view that the question of responsibility is a question of responsibility for origins. The ultimate

---

[17] Kane argues that agents are responsible for actions and traits by making the agent an originator in virtue of 'self-forming willings': acts of will that are undetermined by one's reasons in advance of choosing, but are explained by one's reasons when they are chosen (and are such that, if one had chosen the other alternatives, those would have been similarly explained, as well); Kane 1996, chs. 8–10. Moreover, Kane argues that that there is in fact prior responsibility in childhood in virtue of such self-forming willings, and that this contributes to responsibility in adulthood; Kane 1996, 181.

[18] Kane 2000*a*, 68–71 also argues that this version of UR 'entails alternative possibilities for at least some acts in an agent's life history'; see also van Inwagen 1989.

conception is, as Kane puts it, a 'back-tracking' view: responsibility for one's character now, requires responsibility for having formed one's character in the past. Why is ultimate responsibility a matter of my having originated my character? Why is it not enough that I be able to act in a certain way with respect to the character I have now, however I came to have it? That is, why should we take a backward-looking rather than a forward-looking approach to responsibility for character?

This question goes to the heart of Kane's rejection of compatibilism. Kane describes 'compatibilist freedoms' as freedom to act on one's ends without coercion, compulsion, etc., whereas incompatibilists add that agents must also be creators and sustainers of their ends (1996, 14f, 32f). Compatibilist responsibility is forward-looking: one is a responsible agent not in virtue of having originated one's ends, but in virtue of one's ability to direct one's will on the basis of the ends one has now. Incompatibilist responsibility, by contrast, is backward-looking: one is a responsible agent in virtue of having made oneself the agent one is.

Kane prefers the backward-looking view because he finds compatibilist responsibility too weak. Victims of manipulation—the sort of manipulation described in Skinner's *Walden Two*, in Kane's example—are not the originators or authors of their ends and desires, even if those are the ends and desires they now want to have. In that case, Kane says, such victims are alienated from their ends and desires, and thus the compatibilist must agree that they are not responsible for them. However, Kane then argues that in this respect there is no important difference between manipulation and determinism—the upshot is the same whether our motivations come from a manipulator, or just from the ordinary course of nature. Consequently, determinism is as alienating as manipulation, and thus incompatible with responsibility after all. In that case, compatibilist responsibility may be worth something, but it cannot be all the responsibility that we want (1996, 15, 64ff and ch. 6).[19] The solution, Kane says, is to require that agents be responsible not only for acting on their ends, but also for having their ends, in virtue of having originated them (67–71).[20] This is the point of the ultimacy condition, and it is that condition that makes UR specifically incompatibilist (Kane 1996, 36f, 73f, *et passim*; 1989, 224f).

---

[19] See also Mele 1999, 275, who describes 'modest' UR as the view that, while there are significant sorts of responsibility besides UR, nonetheless UR is more important or desirable than any sort of compatibilist responsibility (see also 285–7).

[20] See also Zimmerman 2003b, 642f; and Fischer 1987, 103–5, who concludes from such cases of manipulation that 'moral responsibility' just is 'a *historical* phenomenon' (italics in original).

A standard reply is to argue that manipulation is alienating in a way that determinism is not, but I share Kane's pessimism about this strategy;[21] in any case, there is another course to take. Where the incompatibilist argument breaks down, I think, is in its assumption that having originated one's motivations is a necessary condition for one's not being alienated from them. That assumption is false. For instance, none of us originates the end of surviving, but we need not be alienated from that end. After all, in a normal human being, pursuing that end involves finding further ends to live for, and as we find things worth surviving for, we can transform that end by finding reasons to survive, instead of just going on a raw survival instinct.[22] In that case, although one did not originate that end, still that end has come to be one's own, over time, and moves from being a simple instinct to survive to a kind of reason to survive. So one can engage that end in precisely the ways one cannot engage motivations one has been manipulated into having, and thus need not be alienated from that end, even though one did not originate it. More generally, a motivation that is available for that kind of assessment and transformation is one from which one is not alienated. By placing a 'back-tracking', backward-looking condition on responsibility, UR seems to identify having an end of one's own with having an end one has created. The real issue is alienation, not origination. Likewise, the problem with the forward-looking views that Kane rejects is not that we may have motivations that we have not originated. The problem is that we may be alienated from our motivations, however we came to have them.

In the next section I sketch an understanding of responsibility for character that is both forward-looking and excludes alienation. I argue that one is responsible for one's character just in case one has critical distance from one's character. On this view, the important question where responsibility for character is concerned is not whether one is responsible for having given oneself the character one has, but whether or not one is alienated from one's own character traits, that is, whether those traits are available for reflective assessment and transformation.

12.3 What is Critical Distance?

Traits that are available for us to rethink critically are traits from which we are not alienated but have critical distance. What more precisely does it mean to

---

[21] See Kane 1996, 69–71 for discussion; see also Pereboom 2001. But see Fischer 2000, 147 and references for a compelling rejoinder.

[22] Here I have benefited from Schmidtz 1994. See also Schmidtz 2001, §8.

have 'critical distance' from character? Consider the difference between two kinds of self-reflection, one in which critical distance is not possible and one in which it is. Consider first a compulsive person, for instance, who discovers that she has a compulsion—flipping the light switch exactly three times upon entering a room, say—and who discovers also that she would be better off without that compulsion. In that sense, one can realize that one has a reason not to have that compulsion, and thus to seek treatment for it, etc.[23] Now consider a non-compulsive person who discovers that she characteristically takes great offense at petty impoliteness, and that she does so because of her attitudes about impoliteness, which she thinks gives her a reason to take offense. In the former, switch-flipping case, the compulsive agent cannot engage what moves her to that behavior on a normative level. For her it is a 'black box', so to speak, and even though she decides she would be better off without the compulsion, she cannot rethink her reasons for her behavior, because there *are* no reasons motivating her behavior. But in the latter, offense-taking case the agent can engage the discovered motivation on a normative level, assessing it not 'from the outside' as how she finds herself moved to act, for better or worse, but 'from the inside' as how she interacts with the world as an agent. The second agent, unlike the first, has critical distance from what moves her.

This way of illustrating the notion of critical distance also reveals that critical distance from one's character is a normal part of life, and comes about as a result of the normal development of human reflective capabilities. As Korsgaard puts the point, beings of our kind are distinctive not for having aims and desires on which we act, but for needing our actions on our aims and desires to be ones that we can recognize as reasonable. We have this distinctive need—which Korsgaard calls 'the problem of the normative' (1996a, 93)—precisely because we are creatures who distance ourselves from our aims and desires and call them into question, that is, because our reflective nature gives us critical distance from ourselves.

Consequently, a character trait from which I do not have critical distance is a trait that has me, not the other way around. Such a trait is not a part of me as an agent; it is an area of my self into which my identity as an agent does not extend. By contrast, critical distance from one's character traits means that those traits belong to one as an agent; such a character is there for one to reckon with. Reckoning with one's character is a kind of

---

[23] But not necessarily. One may find that a brute desire is one that one would rather keep, such as the craving for tobacco; see Watson 1975, 213. Likewise, persons suffering from bipolar disorder or 'workaholism' sometimes recognize their disorders, but prefer to retain them in order to remain so highly productive.

reflecting on a broad practical framework from within that very framework, and thus one type of a process often illustrated with Otto Neurath's metaphor of sailors repairing their ship while still at sea (1959, 201), and particularly familiar from John Rawls' discussion of the process of bringing our considered moral judgments into reflective equilibrium, moving back and forth between more and less 'provisional fixed points' within our judgments (1971, 19–22; see also McDowell 1995a). Of course, one can never step outside one's own perspective, but this is precisely why such reflection is so important and interesting, offering some objectivity from within a subjective viewpoint.[24] The process is also piecemeal, as one reflects on some judgments from the perspective of other judgments, but none of these 'provisional fixed points' need be beyond questioning.[25]

Critical distance makes possible even profound changes in character, since reckoning with one's character makes possible three types of results. First, and most obviously, such reckoning may lead one to adopt, reject, or otherwise alter one's ends. Second, and perhaps more important, reckoning with one's character can change one's *relationship* to one's character and ends. By standing back from one's characteristic patterns of reasoning, choosing, and acting, and considering whether there are good reasons for them, one can develop a new sense of endorsement and 'ownership' of them, even where one decides there is no reason to change them. In reckoning with one's character, one asks whether the aims and values on which one acts are reasonable aims and values to have and to act on, and the mere fact that these *are* one's aims and values is not enough to answer that question. This is especially so in the case of one's characteristic aims, where so much more is at stake, since they are part of one's sense of who one is, along with one's attachments and relationships, and to engage those aims normatively is to ask, Am I the person I want to be? Critical distance shows one what one must accept, to the extent that one accepts what other serious judgments one has, but the latter acceptance is by no means assured. For instance, the discovery that I have the character I do merely because I have inherited a certain perspective is a *disturbing* discovery, because it now makes that very perspective vulnerable. As Rawls observes, crucial to

[24] As McDowell 1995b, 213 observes, reflection on 'one's inherited scheme of values...[goes on] from inside the ethical way of thinking that one finds oneself with'. See McDowell 1998, 118 and esp. 1995a for compelling critique of the very idea of such reflection as going on from outside an inherited ethical view. See also White 1991, 201ff, and Kupperman 1991, 54–8, who also cites Glover 1988, 135, 136, 179.

[25] As Rawls 1971, 20 says, 'even the judgments we take provisionally as fixed points are liable to revision'. It is also important to point out that neither the notion of critical distance in general, nor that of reflective equilibrium as a particular means to critical distance, implies that the self be transcendent, disembodied, or 'noumenal'. I shall return to this issue.

scrutinizing current desires and aversions is examining how they have acquired them, so as to determine what reasons, if any, one has for those desires and aversions, as one considers what plan for living one has reason to adopt now. Such reflection is forward-looking; and although it considers the origins of our character, this is because we need to know whether we have reason to *go on* being as we are, or whether doing so would needlessly perpetuate the results of mere historical accidents (Rawls 1971, §64).[26]

Reflecting on one's scheme of values, therefore, places one's 'collection of putative perceptions' of what is good and bad 'at risk', in John McDowell's phrase, and makes them 'vulnerable to being unmasked as illusory, on the ground that they do not hang together so as to be recognizable as expressing a coherent scheme for a life' (1995b, 214). Being creatures that need reasonability in what we do and what we are like, we have no choice but to accept the vulnerability that such reckoning brings. The reason that we experience this vulnerability in the first place also explains why not just anything will count as rescuing us from it: the sorts of attitudes, aims, and values that we need are ones that a creature faced with the 'normative problem' can recognize as 'expressing a coherent scheme for a life'.

The third potential result of such reckoning is that one should arrive at a greater sense of unity as a practical agent. Engagement with one's character on a normative level leads, as McDowell says, to a deeper appreciation of 'how one's hitherto separate perceptions of what situations call for hang together, so that acting on them can be seen as putting into practice a coherent scheme for a life' (1995b, 213). Likewise, Robert Audi argues that successful first-order 'self-reconstruction' (i.e. generating character traits in a way short of producing a wholly new character) normally requires efforts 'to retain some trait, say benevolence, and seek to strengthen it and to subordinate certain new traits to it' (1991, 308f). Consequently, one can reflect not only on the particular elements of one's character, but also on the *connections* between those elements that make them into a sort of whole. This is not to suggest that we step outside our framework or 'scheme of values' as a whole to reflect on it, but we do reflect on it as a kind of whole. It is important to see that the connections *between* parts of one's character need reasonability of their own, and thus can become vulnerable under reflection as well.

---

[26] Likewise, as Taylor (1982, 111) has said, part of personhood is the ability to ask 'Do I really want to be what I now am? (i.e. have the desires and goals I now have?) In other words, beyond the *de facto* characterization of the subject by his goals, desires, and purposes, a person is a subject who can pose the *de jure* question: is this the kind of being I ought to be, or really want to be?' Taylor connects this sort of query to Frankfurt's (2003) notion of the 'capacity for reflective self-evaluation'. See also Audi 1991, 309.

For all these reasons, a character that an agent can reckon with is a character that one can make one's own. A character that is one's own, in this sense, expresses not merely what one is like, but who one is. Such a character, that is, has depth: one's characteristic ends are available for construction, not only by specifying their content, but also by grasping what reasons there are to adopt them. Now, one need not have made one's character one's own in this sense, in order to have critical distance from it. Rather, the possibility of making one's character one's own, in a deep sense, reveals that *a character from which one has critical distance is a character from which one is not alienated*. And this seems extremely promising for making a case for responsibility for character, since being alienated from one's character, I think, is the main barrier to being responsible for one's character. So we must take a closer look in the rest of this chapter at whether critical distance really does make any difference where responsibility for character is concerned. I argue in the next section that one's level of critical distance from one's character and one's level of responsibility for one's character directly vary together, and then consider a number of further objections to this view in §12.5.

12.4 From Critical Distance to Responsibility

It seems clear that both critical distance and responsibility are matters of degree. Neither concept has sharp boundaries; and each is what I have called a vague satis concept.[27] The critical distance view holds that as critical distance from character decreases, so too does responsibility for character, and that as critical distance increases, so too does responsibility. For the sake of simplicity, however, I shall speak of these claims as the theses that critical distance is necessary for responsibility and that critical distance is sufficient for responsibility, respectively. I argue for the necessity claim by showing, for one thing, that where there is no critical distance from character (and thus alienation), there is also no responsibility for character. And I argue for the sufficiency claim by showing that where there is critical distance from character (and thus no alienation), there is responsibility for character.

I shall consider a number of difficult cases that test the idea that responsibility for character and critical distance from character vary together. In doing so, I

---

[27] One need not have critical distance either from all of one's character or none of it. How much critical distance, and from which of the various dimensions of character, is 'enough' to be critical distance *tout court*? How responsible must one be to be responsible *tout court*? For the character as a whole? For any part of character? These are extremely difficult questions, and I shall not attempt to give a general answer to them here.

hope to make it clearer why it is critical distance and freedom from alienation from one's character, rather than the origins of one's character, that is crucial for responsibility for one's character. These cases will be of four types: cases of lacking critical distance from character as a result of (A) the doing of others or (B) one's own doing; and cases in which a person has critical distance from his character when it arises from (C) the doing of others or (D) his own doing. We can arrange these cases as follows:

	No critical distance	Critical distance
Character changed by the doing of others	*Type A*	*Type C*
Character changed by one's own doing	*Type B*	*Type D*

Simply put, my view holds that responsibility is lacking in the left-hand column (cases of types A and B) and is present in the right-hand column (type C and type D cases); these are the necessity and the sufficiency claims, respectively. In other words, responsibility varies along the vertical dimension with the columns, not along the horizontal dimension with the rows as backward-looking views would have it. Disagreements are most likely to focus on cases of type B and cases of type C.

I shall also give closer attention to the claim that critical distance is sufficient for responsibility than that it is necessary, because it is the sufficiency claim that is of the greater interest for Hard Virtue Theory. As we saw in §12.1, a character with phronesis is a character that is fully one's own. It seems clear that a person with phronesis has critical distance from his character; so if critical distance suffices for responsibility for character, for having a character that is 'one's own', then character can have the sort of depth that Hard Virtue Theory says it has in the *phronimos*.

12.4.1 *The Necessity of Critical Distance for Responsibility for Character*

Traditional 'Real Self' Views   We have spoken of critical distance as obtaining within a framework of practical reasoning. The role of such a framework is also central in those accounts of responsibility that Susan Wolf has called 'deep self' or 'real self' views (2003; 1990, ch. 2). Traditional compatibilists like Harry Frankfurt, Gary Watson, and Charles Taylor disagree over the nature of our reflective framework and its role in an account of responsibility, but they agree both that reflection takes place within a framework of serious commitments, and that that very fact somehow helps the case for responsibility. Frankfurt argues that responsibility stems from the capacity to transcend 'first-order' desires and to formulate the 'second-order volition' or preference that one have a certain desire, and that it be from that desire that one act. On Frankfurt's view, persons can be responsible because of their capacity to reflect in a structured way, moving 'back' from one's momentary desires to the perspective of one's more fundamental ends. However, as Watson (1975) has argued, second-order volitions are still only sorts of desires, and there is no reason that the higher order alone should be particularly revealing of responsibility. As Susan Wolf has pointed out, 'an agent who is alienated from her first-order choice may be alienated from her higher-order choices as well' (1990, 30).[28] In that case, the very fact that reflection is hierarchical does not help the case for responsibility either for action or for character. The problem with this view is that it does not make critical distance from one's character necessary for responsibility for character.

Watson's own view is that responsibility is based on the capacity to act on one's 'values', desires not of a different level but of a different *kind*, since it is in virtue of one's values that one construes certain things as good and worth pursuing, something that need not be true of ordinary desires. Furthermore, values and (mere) desires can conflict in the sense that what one most values may not also be what one most strongly desires, and in such cases 'a person may be obstructed by his own will' (1975, 213). A free agent, by contrast, is one who acts without obstruction, and thus one who acts from his values, in Watson's sense.

This is an improvement, because a value, by definition, is not alienating. The question, though, is whether values are widespread enough in one's character for one to be responsible for one's character overall. Even if a 'value' is necessarily non-alienating, it is far from obvious that to have any value at all is to have values all the way down.[29] In fact, Watson argues that 'the value placed upon certain activities depends upon their being the fulfillment of desires that arise and persist independently of what we value'. Watson offers the examples of erotic desire, hunger for food, and 'the craving for tobacco' as desires that are presupposed by certain values. What sets valuing sexual activity,

---

[28] See also Wolf 2003, 379–85, who argues that in one's deepest self, even when it is the self one wants to have, one may be unable to tell right from wrong, and thus be incapable of taking responsibility for oneself. Frankfurt 1987 answers Watson's charge that it is arbitrary to cease reflecting simply because one has ascended to some higher-order desire or volition. It is not arbitrary to cut off deliberation, Frankfurt argues, when one reasonably foresees one would arrive at the same conclusion each time one were to deliberate further, any more than it is arbitrary to stop checking one's arithmetic once one reasonably foresees arriving at the same answer in each further checking episode. After all, we check under pressure, not for the sake of it. This is an important point, but of course it is consistent with one's foreseeing the redundancy of further deliberation on the grounds that those ends of one's that will always drive one to the same conclusion are beyond reckoning anyway.

[29] This is the point at issue between Herman 1993 and Schmidtz 2001. Note that Watson 1975, 212f explicitly denies that values can rest only on further values.

dining, or smoking apart from merely desiring those activities, on Watson's view, is the judgment 'that to cease to have such appetites is to lose something of worth' (1975, 212f; see also Wolf 1990, 43–5). But in that case, denizens of Walden Two can have and act on values in Watson's sense, even if they are alienated from their most fundamental aims and desires. And one may find even a compulsion most convenient, and its loss a loss of something of worth. In that case, one may be able to have and to act on values from which one is not alienated, while nonetheless being alienated from fundamental parts of one's motivational hierarchy. 'Valuing' thus seems to be compatible with being alienated from one's character on balance. It seems clear, then, that not just localized but fairly *widespread* critical distance is necessary for responsibility for character. (I return to this point in §12.5.3.)

Finally, Taylor argues that at the highest level we reflect in terms of fundamental 'evaluations' which, though unchosen, take a definite shape only as we articulate them for ourselves, and thus 'shape our sense of what we desire or what we hold important in a certain way'. Here Taylor recognizes that the most basic volitions and values of a responsible agent must not be fixed beyond revision (1982, 122–6). Taylor is correct, I think, but it remains somewhat obscure on his view how through such 'articulation' and 're-evaluation' one can become responsible for ends and evaluations that start out as basic and as yet 'unarticulated'. Perhaps what Taylor means by 'articulation' is what we have discussed as specifying the content of one's goals; but surely it seems possible to specify the content of a goal from which one is alienated. For instance, I may be able to specify the content of the goal of respecting authority figures, say, even when I have been brainwashed by cult leaders to have this goal. The problem, then, is one of showing that one is not alienated from but has a rational grasp of one's goals, not just that one can 'articulate' them and make them determinate. Perhaps this is where 're-evaluation' comes in; if so, this is to put the issue onto what I have called critical distance. Yet again, we find the real issue to be that responsibility for character requires critical distance from character.

The problem with traditional versions of the 'real self' view, and thus with traditional forward-looking conceptions of responsibility, is that they do not take seriously enough the necessity of critical distance for responsibility for character. So precisely that necessity, then, must be built into any forward-looking view.

Objections to the Necessity Claim   But is critical distance really necessary for responsibility for character? That, after all, is to deny that responsibility is necessarily a historical notion, and to say that as long as one has no critical distance from one's character, one is not responsible for one's character, *regardless* of how one came to lack that critical distance. It is easy enough to see, in a Walden Two-type case, that a person is not responsible for a character that has been fixed beyond critical distance as the result of manipulation by others (a type A case); so a forward-looking, compatibilist conception of responsibility gives a plausible answer in such a case, *pace* Kane. But what about an agent who has put his own character beyond critical distance, as a result of his own past actions and choices (type B)? Is it really the resulting alienation from character that is the issue, or is the issue who caused the alienation—whose past actions make him to blame for it?

Here we need to examine more closely what it means to lack critical distance. In particular, lack of critical distance jeopardizes the very possibility of acting for a reason. If I am motivated to act by some inner state X, and X is a reason, then necessarily I have critical distance from X (see Audi 1997a, 93–5; Wallace 1997, 324; Smith 1997, 307f). This is so because, if X is a reason, then X is 'integrated' into my other reasons so that I am 'susceptible to counterinfluence' where X is concerned, in Audi's phrase (1997a, 93–5). To act for a reason is not necessarily to act with certain sorts of thoughts, but as Audi has observed, the reasons for which one acts are 'contrastive' in the sense that other considerations can be brought to bear on one's assessment of the reason for which one acts. Likewise, R. Jay Wallace notes that 'reasons for action just are considerations that have deliberative significance' (1997, 324), and Michael Smith that brainwashing makes one immune from responsibility not by making one incapable of acting on one's desires, but by giving one desires that are 'beyond revision', diminishing 'the capacity an agent has rationally to evaluate alternative hypotheses' (1997, 307f).[30]

Therefore, to lack critical distance from character is to be incapable of acting for characteristic reasons that are *contrastive* (in Audi's sense), that is, incapable of acting for characteristic *reasons* at all. Such a person, I believe, is no more a responsible person than someone who has come to be in the same position as the result of manipulation. To be sure, there is a difference in who is *to blame* in these two cases; but that is just to make the obvious statement that there is a difference in who brought the agent into that unfortunate state. The real question is the nature of that unfortunate state itself, in virtue of which one is now incapable of taking any responsibility for oneself. It seems to me perfectly possible that a person may be able to rob himself of the opportunity to be a responsible agent, an agent with a character of his own. Why should other

---

[30] See also Sher 2001, 151, who characterizes vice as a lack of responsiveness to (some range of) moral reasons.

people, or just ordinary nature, have such an ability over a person, but not the person himself? And this is the spirit of the following compatibilist principle: to be responsible for one's character, one must be able to take responsibility for one's character. Since taking responsibility requires real scrutiny and thus critical distance, critical distance is necessary for responsibility for character.

It is plausible to say, then, that a person without critical distance from his character does not have a character that is really his own, and is thus not a responsible agent where that character is concerned, regardless of who has made him so (i.e., in both type A and type B cases). But what about the sufficiency of critical distance for responsibility: can it really be the case that there is responsibility for character wherever there is critical distance, regardless of how that character came to be? I turn to that thesis now, and then consider several further objections to it in §12.5.

12.4.2 The Sufficiency of Critical Distance for Responsibility for Character

My basic argument that critical distance is sufficient for responsibility for character is a straightforward one: there is no reason that it shouldn't be. As we have seen, a character from which one has critical distance is a character from which one is not alienated. In that case, it is difficult to see what more that responsibility for character could require, *unless* we think that responsibility just is *ultimate* responsibility, responsibility for origins. But there is no reason to think that. Furthermore, self-construction in the sense of constructing reasons for oneself and thus one's practical identity, is not a matter of one's history, but of developing a self that represents 'who one is', and not merely 'what one is like', or how things happen to have turned out in one's case.

Nonetheless, I wish now to consider several kinds of cases that challenge the sufficiency thesis. First, Susan Wolf has argued that a person can have critical distance from a feature of her character but be unable to revise that feature of her character in accordance with 'the true and the good', and thus fail to be responsible for that trait. Moreover, David Zimmerman has offered some thought experiments in which a person is imagined to have a 'new' character, as if by implant, which is radically severed from her prior character. Such persons seem not to be responsible for the new character, even though it is otherwise like an 'ordinary' person's character. These thought experiments yield several difficult cases for the critical distance view that are worth considering carefully. I argue that the critical distance view gives a positively attractive analysis of each of these cases.

Objections to the Sufficiency Claim: Wolf's View   Consider Susan Wolf's 'reason view' of responsibility. According to Wolf, responsibility requires that the agent have the 'ability to form or revise her deepest values in light of the truth', and that the agent 'also have at least the ability to consider' the reasonability of those values (1990, 141). Wolf therefore seems to agree that critical distance is *necessary* for responsibility. What Wolf denies, though, is that critical distance is *sufficient* for responsibility. Wolf holds that an agent who has a bad character trait but believes that it is a reasonable one, is not responsible for that trait, since she does not evaluate that trait 'in accordance with the True and the Good', in Wolf's phrase. Is having a bad character a barrier to being responsible for one's character?

Wolf considers a person who passes up opportunities to be generous to friends, because she is too self-centered or mercenary a person to be bothered. If we suppose that this person 'does not mind being the kind of person she is', and perhaps thinks it is 'quite a reasonable ... way to be', then, Wolf says, she is 'unable to have different and better values—she is unable to change her real self in accordance with the True and the Good' (1990, 83–6). In this case, the imagined person presumably has critical distance from some feature of her character—she is able to find it 'a reasonable way to be'—but because her reflection on this feature of her character is flawed, Wolf argues, she is not responsible for that feature, and thus not 'responsible for her failure in friendship'.

Why does Wolf say that such a person is 'unable' to have different and better values? On Wolf's view, such a person is not blameworthy, and thus she either cannot understand that she acts badly, or could not govern her actions even if she were to understand that she acts badly (or both; 85f). Presumably the stingy agent is not 'unable' in the latter sense—what she does, after all, is what she believes it is reasonable to do—but why think that she is *unable* to understand that she acts badly? Perhaps the idea is that this person would not in fact be put off her stingy ways by attempts to persuade her. That may be, but the important question is *why* she would not be put off. After all, being open to rational influence on some point does not mean that one may *in fact* be talked out of one's position on it. It means that one can genuinely consider the reasons for and against one's position. For instance, when Plato's Socrates is asked about what appear to be reasons against being just, he responds by taking those apparent reasons seriously (and Plato spends ten books of the *Republic* doing so), as if he thought it reasonable that a just person should consider them. It seems clear, then, that a just person is open to rational influence, even if he or she will not *in fact* be put off being a just person. Steadfastness need not be stubbornness. If Wolf's case is one of steadfastness, then the woman in her case would seem both to have critical distance from her character (i.e., she is a type D case), and to be responsible for it.

On the other hand, if the stingy person will be not put off because she is not susceptible to rational influence on this point, then she does not have critical distance from her stinginess, after all (a type B case). And if she will not be put off her stinginess because it ultimately rests on some deeper motivation from which she is alienated, then what critical distance she may have from her stinginess (if any) will be highly localized. However, we have already seen (§12.4.1) that the critical distance necessary for responsibility is not localized, but widespread (I shall consider how widespread it should be in §12.5.3). In that case, this is no counterexample to the thesis that such critical distance is sufficient for responsibility.[31] Thinking a bad trait good is itself no obstacle to being responsible for it.

But is Wolf's case now a counterexample to the necessity claim? On this second way of reading Wolf's example, it is rather like the type B case we considered in §12.4.1, in which a person lacks critical distance from his character as a result of his own doing. If it is through her own actions that the woman in Wolf's case (on this second reading) has become insusceptible to rational influence, should we say that she is responsible for her character? As I argued above, whether such a person is responsible for her character depends on whether she can act for characteristic reasons, which are necessarily contrastive. A person lacking such reasons is no longer capable of taking responsibility for her character, even if she is the cause of this inability of hers. Now, we need not suppose that the woman in this case is in as extreme a situation as that. But the general point still holds: the degree of one's responsibility for character depends on the degree to which one is capable of reckoning with oneself. Simply put, the less contrastive her reasoning is, the less she is a responsible agent. Her character is that much less her own, even if it is her own doing that has made it so.

Objections to the Sufficiency Claim: Zimmerman's 'Self-Abnegation' Case

Now consider a different kind of case, in which an agent acquires a 'new' character that is like yours or mine, except that it is so severed from the agent's prior character that the agent no longer seems responsible for her character. If so, and if such an agent has critical distance from her new character, then critical distance is not sufficient for responsibility for character. On the critical distance view, then, the real issue here is whether the agent has critical distance from her new character. Can the critical distance view give a satisfactory analysis of this sort of case?

---

[31] I have benefited here from discussions with Simon Roberts-Thomson and Jason White.

In a couple of recent papers, David Zimmerman has imagined some different agents who undergo radical shifts in character. In one case, Zimmerman imagines a young woman who has spent years working in a sweatshop, and has undertaken meditative practices to replace her agony and despair over her servitude with serenity and indeed willing acceptance. Such a shift in character is a case of what Zimmerman calls 'self-abnegation'. After the shift, the agent has a profoundly different set of attitudes, goals, and values, and thus a profoundly different character. Furthermore, we can suppose that after the shift, this agent regards her character as a reasonable, perhaps the only reasonable way (for her) to be (2003a; see also 2003b, 642). This agent, then, has not lost her mind, but changed it profoundly.

Zimmerman argues that such a case resists attempts to assess responsibility. The problem, he says, is that the new character is the result of the actions and choices of another person, namely the agent prior to her sea-change. So we face a dilemma when we try to assess her responsibility for her new character. On the one hand, if we say that she is responsible for her character, then that would suggest that before her sea-change she was responsible for having had a character susceptible to self-abnegation. However, Zimmerman argues, it seems unlikely 'that people generally cultivate in themselves the tendency to such lapses of self-knowledge over the years, to such an extent that' they are blameworthy for those lapses. In any case, the profoundly revised agent would surely find it very strange that she ought to identify her *former* self as the responsible agent. But on the other hand, if we say that she is not responsible for her character, then it must be the case that while her former character made her susceptible to self-abnegation, that was no fault of hers. But the revised agent, *ex hypothesi*, is rational, and thus remains susceptible to rational influence, so why deny that she is a responsible agent where her character is concerned? Why say that her character now is just what she is like, but not who she is?

Notice, however, that this dilemma arises only if we assume, as Zimmerman does, that the question of her responsibility for the character she now has is a matter of her responsibility for her having brought that character about in the past; that is, that responsibility for character is a matter of responsibility for originating character. If responsibility for character were backward-looking, then without a doubt there would seem to be nothing to say about the responsibility of self-abnegating agents. But if we deny that responsibility is responsibility for origins, as I have argued we should, then the interesting question is how this agent is related to her character *now*—whether or not she is alienated from the values and attitudes she has developed. I do not suppose that that question is an easy one to answer, but what matters, I think, is *why* that question is so difficult. Let me explain.

As we saw above (§12.3), reckoning with one's character, and deciding what to make of one's character from here, involves reflecting on how one has got where one is now. Reckoning with oneself involves reckoning with one's history and provenance, since in such reckoning we seek 'to see our life as one whole, the activities of one rational subject spread out in time' (Rawls 1971, 420). It is the discontinuity between the agent's present and former character that makes it so difficult to tell whether she is really capable of reckoning with the character she has now. Even if we set aside the question whether she was responsible then for making the shift she made, the question remains whether the shift has left her, now, in a position to have a character of her own. The real question, then, is whether the discontinuity resulting from the sea-change has undermined the agent's present ability to have critical distance from her new character. If that ability has been undermined (a type B case), then it is plausible to think that her character is not now her own and she is not a responsible agent; but if that ability is intact (a type D case), then it is plausible that she is now a responsible agent—her character is her own. The case is therefore no counterexample to the thesis that critical distance is sufficient for responsibility for character. More than that, the issue seems to turn just where the critical distance view says it does.

Objections to the Sufficiency Claim: Zimmerman's 'Implant' Case
The importance that discontinuity makes is even more apparent in an even more radical case of character shift. Zimmerman imagines another agent in whom someone else has 'implanted' a wholly new character—a new set of desires, attitudes, aims, and values (2003*b*, 644ff; the case is from Mele 2001). For instance, imagine a studious person who receives a new character, such as that of a light-minded person, say.[32] Surely, Zimmerman argues, we could not hold her responsible for this new character of hers. Now, a light-minded, non-studious person can have critical distance from her character, so if there is only a historical difference between our imagined, post-implant agent and an 'ordinary' light-minded person, then it would seem that critical distance from character is not sufficient for responsibility for character. Perhaps, then, this is a type C case in which one lacks responsibility for character, *pace* the critical distance view.

I agree that this agent is not responsible for her newly implanted character, but I do not agree with Zimmerman that the reason is her lack of responsibility

---

[32] Zimmerman himself imagines the implanted character to be that of a bloodthirsty killer, but I prefer an example free of such moral differences in character before and after implant.

for its history. Rather, the reason is that such an agent, I think, could not have critical distance from her newly implanted character after all (i.e. it is really a type A case). To see this, notice that in this case, either such aspects of the agent's personal identity—her memories, and in general her sense of herself as extending 'backwards' in time—are preserved, or they are not. Suppose first that they are not. Again, reckoning with one's character involves reckoning with the history of one's character. So if the character implant does not leave such personal history intact, then the critical distance view holds that the new agent lacks a sufficient personal context for reckoning with her new character, and is thus alienated from it in a very real way.

On the other hand, suppose that the agent's personal identity does survive the implant, so that the new agent retains as her own certain relevant memories from her former life. But in that case, the new agent will be bewildered as to why she now has the radically different character she finds herself, mysteriously, to have (see Zimmerman 2003b, 644f). Once again, then, she cannot reckon with how she has got where she is—the history she can reflect on does not seem to be the history of the character she now has—and is therefore alienated from her new character; she cannot make it her own. So whether personal identity survives a character implant or not, the implant so disrupts the agent's sense of a continuous self that she lacks the resources to reckon with her character, and therefore lacks critical distance.

This is an important result: such cases suggest that an agent's history has *something* to do with responsibility, yet they do *not* show that responsibility is necessarily backward-looking. The significance that the agent's history seems clearly to have is also the significance that the critical distance view assigns it: namely, an agent's need to reflect on that history in order to reflect critically on the character she has now.[33] As we saw above (§12.3), part of engaging one's character on a normative level is *to examine how that character has come to be*, as part of the process of determining whether one has reason to go on as one is (see Rawls 1971, §64). This is not, please note, to locate responsibility for character in its history, but in what one can do with one's character now; it is just that part of what one must be able to do now is to scrutinize that character, *including* its provenance. In other words, it follows from the compatibilist principle that to be responsible, one must be able to take responsibility. Therefore, such sea-changed agents, so to speak, are not counterexamples to the thesis that critical distance suffices for responsibility for character. On the contrary, that

---

[33] In this sense, I agree with the view, so stated, that 'responsibility-grounding autonomous agency develops with the appropriately *continuous and active participation of the emerging person herself*'; Zimmerman 2003b, 647, italics in original, summarizing Daniel Dennett and Wright Neely.

thesis seems to handle such cases in exactly the right way, and so it emerges as a positively attractive view.[34]

Objections to the Sufficiency Claim: A Variation on Zimmerman's Implant Case Lastly, we might suppose that the appearance of a lack of critical distance in the implanted character case is due merely to the *suddenness* of the character change, which leaves the agent unable to 'keep up' reflectively with the change. But what if the 'implant' were instead a slow, gradual process—instead of a sudden implant, imagine having small doses of a character-altering drug secreted into one's tea. Would one be responsible for the different character one has at the end of this process? If the process is gradual, the objection goes, then the agent may remain critically distant from her character throughout the change (thus, a type C case); but surely such an agent would not be responsible for her resulting character, regardless.

I think that her responsibility will depend on how we flesh out the details of the process. On the one extreme, the gradual process merely replaces a big, alienating shift with a series of smaller alienating shifts. Instead of a drastic overnight change, one is presented with a series of smaller changes, each one of which presents itself as a black box. Such a case seems no different from the original implant case (a type A case), where alienation is concerned, for the compatibilist. To be responsible, one must be able to take responsibility; this latter, I have argued, requires critical distance, which can be missing from a small change as much as from a big one. At the other extreme, though, each of the changes may be subtle, allowing one to reflect on them and to determine whether one has reason to go on that way (a real type C case). At this end, the change is rather of the garden-variety sort that we experience throughout our lives. New experiences, new relationships, changes in body chemistry, and so on, all incline us in new directions in the development of character, but ordinarily they do so in ways that critical distance can keep up with. This does not excuse the manipulation, of course, but it is to say that they do not rob one of the ability to act for reasons. At this second end of the range, then, regarding the agent as responsible for the resulting character seems very plausible.

Now, there is of course a range of ways of describing the shift between the two extremes I have considered here—between clear type A and clear type C cases—but it seems plausible that responsibility for character is still

---

[34] We can also consider a variation, in which the agent is aware that the character change is owing to an implant. Here I think our verdict must be the same as in the self-abnegation case: the person she now is is not the one historically, causally responsible for the character change; but it is still an open question whether she might now be a responsible agent nonetheless.

possible at the latter extreme, and falls away (perhaps sharply) as we move towards the former extreme. And notice that critical distance seems to fall away in just the same way, too. The more the small change leaves intact one's framework for reflecting on such changes, the more ownership one can have in the results.

Again, recall that the incompatibilist's objection to the compatibilist principle is that it is indifferent as to whether one's character results from manipulation. But that is not so: the compatibilist is highly concerned with manipulation, not because the crucial question for responsibility is who does the manipulating, but because manipulation, whoever does it, is so very likely to leave one incapable of taking responsibility for oneself. And that, I think, is why manipulation is such a terrible invasion.

The critical distance view holds that the degree of responsibility for character varies directly with the degree of critical distance from character, however character was brought about, and I have argued that in a wide range of cases, the forward-looking critical distance view yields plausible results. But of course, there are more objections to that view to consider. So I turn in the final section to three further types of objections to the critical distance view. One objection is that critical distance is irrelevant to responsibility for character, because critical distance from character always (and necessarily) goes on within the broader framework of that very character. Another is that bad luck, such as having a bad upbringing, can leave one incapable of critical distance from much of oneself, and in that case, basing responsibility on critical distance is to base responsibility on something that depends on luck, and thus for which we are not responsible. The final objection I consider is that even if critical distance could be sufficient for responsibility for character, nonetheless responsibility would require a far greater degree of critical distance from ourselves than we are capable of having.

12.5 Objections to the Critical Distance View

12.5.1. Could Critical Distance make any Difference?

Many arguments against responsibility for character claim that the very fact that we judge our character 'from within' necessarily compromises the responsibility we can have for our character. However, it is not always clear whether that claim is about the very *possibility* of real critical distance from one's character at all, or about the *efficacy* of critical distance, namely that although reflection does result in critical distance from one's character, that critical distance does not gain any ground with respect to responsibility for one's character.[35] So I shall consider each version of this objection in turn.

Against the Possibility of Critical Distance   Consider the first objection: it is a moot point whether critical distance could make any difference regarding responsibility, since critical distance is impossible—the very fact that reflection on a framework takes place within that framework makes it too bound by that framework to permit real critical distance. This would tell against the necessity of critical distance for responsibility: if responsibility implied critical distance, there would be no such thing as responsibility, since there is no such thing as critical distance.

To be sure, each of us begins with a framework that is not his or her own, and however much that framework may change, what results is always a descendant of a framework that was nothing of our own doing. However, whether one is incapable of critical distance from one's character traits depends not on the bare fact that reflection goes on within the character one has, but on what a particular agent's character traits are like. Agents incapable of critical distance from themselves are incapable of normative engagement with what motivates them, and immune to prompts—even the cumulative effects of repeated prompts[36]—to reflect on their characteristic perspective, regardless of the type and source of feedback on that perspective. Agents who fit this description do so not merely because their reflection starts from within some framework or other,[37] but because of the particular framework that they have—or rather, that has them. But the more that agents fit this description, the less they are appropriate targets for the 'reactive attitudes' in the first place.[38] Responsibility for *their* character was not on the table anyway.

---

[35] See Levy 2002 for both sorts of worries.

[36] For, as Kupperman 1991, 57 points out, 'we generally can control our immediate reactions to changes in circumstances and how we act on various particular occasions, and these cumulatively do have a lot to do with changes in character'.

[37] See Moody-Adams 1990, 127f, who argues persuasively that formative experiences are 'a condition of the possibility of responsible agency', since human social interaction both shapes 'our constitutive ideals and purposes' (consider the ends that those 'raised' in the wild would be incapable of), and gives a framework of parameters within which choice can be made. However, Moody-Adams points out that these influences are not like other factors (e.g. ignorance, coercion) that constrain responsibility, since one can overcome the limitations of the former by 'self-evaluation and self-correction'.

[38] i.e. at least where those incorrigible traits are concerned. The notion of 'reactive attitudes' derives of course from Peter Strawson's seminal 1974. Levy 2002 argues that since the 'truly bad' person is incapable of effective reflection in these sorts of ways, that person is not responsible for his or her traits. I think Levy and I shall disagree over his analysis of the 'truly bad' person, but not over what an agent would have to be like to be incapable of critical distance from, and thus of responsibility for, character. Sher 1979 considers a similar defense of a strong view of indolence as blocking self-construction: every form of self-construction, the defense goes, will require effort, but the indolent person, being indolent, cannot make such an effort; so the indolent person is not responsible for the self that he or she has.

Even worse, if the very fact that critical distance would have to take place within a framework makes critical distance impossible, then we must also abandon the possibility of acting for a reason. This is because, as we saw above, reasons are necessarily contrastive. Perhaps we could strengthen a person's desires by eliminating her capacity to evaluate alternatives to them, but to eliminate such a capacity would not strengthen a person's reasons, but destroy them as reasons. Agents without any genuine capacity for critical distance are agents who do not and cannot act for reasons, so to deny the possibility of genuine critical distance is therefore to deny the reality of acting for reasons.

Against the Efficacy of Critical Distance   So the real question must be not whether critical distance is real, but whether it can gain any ground with respect to responsibility. This is a different sort of objection to the sufficiency of critical distance for responsibility. One form of this objection charges that 'both the particular way in which one is moved to try to change oneself, and the degree of one's success in one's attempt at change, will be determined by how one already is as a result of heredity and previous experience' (Strawson 2003, 214).[39] Reckoning with one's character, the objection goes, is nothing more than the unfolding of how one already is, seen merely in greater detail. But this worry hangs on the 'nothing more', which now seems rather mysterious given that this alleged 'unfolding' actually holds out the possibility not just of changing one's character, but of changing one's very relationship to one's character. As we have seen, reckoning with one's characteristic aims can lead both to aims that are importantly different—a difference that can be surprising, powerfully informative, and even highly revisionary—and to a newfound sense of the normative force for us of one's characteristic aims and values and the sort of unity they comprise. To be sure, reflection on one's character goes on within the framework one already has, but the polemical force of that claim rests on hinting that the results of reflection are 'nothing more' than the unfolding of how one already is. So understood, the claim seems simplistic, if not obtuse.

However, the interesting question is not whether anyone can be so indolent as to be incapable of critical distance, but whether such incapacity is a standard consequence of indolence. As Sher points out, the defense depends on appealing to indolence at every opportunity for reflection and change, but the more the appeal is made, the more expansive the scope of the inability to make effort, and so the more desperate and implausible the defense becomes (370).

[39] Strawson 2003, 226 says that an account of self-shaping behavior 'adds another layer of description to the human decision process, but it cannot change the fact that human beings cannot be ultimately self-determining in such a way as to be ultimately morally responsible for how they are, and thus for how they decide and act'.

Notice also two assumptions that are crucial to this sort of objection. One is that in order to become responsible, there must be some *point* at which one breaks free enough of one's history to emerge newly responsible. The other assumption is that to be responsible one must bring it about *oneself* that one is responsible; that is, if I am responsible for my character, then I must also be responsible for that in virtue of which I am responsible for my character. If at first these two assumptions seem obviously true, notice that each of them asserts that those features of a person in virtue of which one is responsible for character could not arise *naturally*, as part of normal human development. After all, natural developments—such as that from childhood to adulthood—do not occur at any point (see also Moody-Adams 1990, 128f), and we do not bring such developments about ourselves. By accepting either of these assumptions, we assume away—rather early in the day!—the very possibility that responsibility for one's character could be the result of capacities that mature in the course of one's natural development. Seen that way, these assumptions are, I think, far less compelling.

Critical distance from oneself emerges with the natural development of human reflective capacities, and therefore on the critical distance view the notion of responsibility for character becomes applicable to beings of our kind as part of normal human development, even though—just like most developmental events—it cannot be traced to any distinct point in that development. There is no such distinct point, because there is no point at which one becomes a mature, reflective agent who can reckon with one's character. Not every change takes place at a point, and in particular developmental changes usually do not. On the critical distance view responsibility is a product of natural development, a process for which no one is responsible.

12.5.2 Must We be Responsible for Responsibility?

The preceding response leads to a further objection: there is no guarantee that one's development will leave one capable of critical distance from oneself, and so the capacity for critical distance depends on moral luck; consequently, while critical distance is real, again it gains no ground with respect to responsibility. The opportunity to be responsible, in this sense, is a matter of fortunate family, social, and even biological circumstances. That opportunity can be taken away by deliberate manipulation, or merely by a bad upbringing. If responsibility for character is a developmental event, then like other developmental events, it is not guaranteed.

There are two issues here. One is the idea that one's character may develop so as to leave one incapable of critical distance from it, through no fault of one's own. The other is that responsibility for character cannot depend on good luck. If both of these claims are true, then since critical distance depends on good luck, critical distance cannot be sufficient for responsibility for character. Let's consider these two claims in turn.

So far from denying the possibility that starting-points may compromise the responsibility a given agent can have, I positively insist on it. Responsibility for character can be frustrated or stunted, because critical distance from oneself can be frustrated or stunted. Not all agents are capable of genuine normative engagement with those motivational factors for which they act. We all have burdens to bear, but some burdens are much heavier than others, and some of us get far less preparation to bear them. And Rawls is surely correct to note that perhaps the worst burden of all is to be unprepared to bear burdens. If not everyone is responsible for his or her character, as seems undeniable, then an account of responsibility for character should at least tell us some of the reasons why not. A consequence of the critical distance view is that opportunities to become responsible for one's character are not equal, and differences in such opportunities often are a matter of moral luck.

However, and this is the second point, one can be responsible for one's character without having been responsible for the opportunity to be responsible. Inequality of opportunity to become responsible for character does not jeopardize the possibility of such responsibility in those who have been given the opportunity. One can be responsible for what one does, creates, earns, etc., without having been responsible for the opportunity to do, create, or earn it.[40]

Consequently, not all of us shall be responsible for our character. Come to that, those of us who are responsible for character shall not all be equally responsible as one another, and none of us shall be equally responsible for all the parts of character for which he or she is responsible. Some of the ways we turn out leave us less capable of taking responsibility for ourselves. Furthermore, character is extremely complex, including attitudes and judgments as well as patterns of emotional response, desires, and feelings, and not all aspects of

---

[40] See Schmidtz 2002 for a similar observation about desert and opportunity. Wolf 1990, 147 goes further: 'We are not, then, and never can be fully responsible for whether and how much we *are* responsible.' These observations bring us back to Rawls' worry about responsibility and deserving, which we can now see is ambiguous between the stronger claim that someone with a 'superior character' is not responsible for that *character*, and the weaker claim that someone with a superior character is not responsible for that *superiority*. (For an excellent discussion see Sher 1979, who argues convincingly that Rawls should be read as making the latter, weaker claim.) The stronger claim is clearly implausible. A person who has taken responsibility for his or her character and made it an excellent one is responsible for the character that he or she has made, even if he or she is not responsible for having had the opportunity to make it. By contrast, the weaker claim seems undeniable, and I think it is a benefit of my view that it explains why opportunities for responsibility are unequal.

character need be equally accessible to critical reflection.[41] Here we should recall that responsibility is a satis concept: one need not be thoroughly responsible for some aspect of one's character to be genuinely responsible for it, and one need not be (equally) responsible for every aspect of one's character to be responsible for one's character—for who one is—on the whole.

12.5.3 Can Critical Distance Go Far Enough?

Responsibility is a satis concept: one need not be perfectly responsible to be responsible enough. But can we be 'responsible enough'? I have argued that fairly widespread critical distance from one's character is necessary and sufficient for responsibility for one's character, but it still remains to be shown that humans normally *do* have sufficiently widespread critical distance from their character to be responsible for their character on the whole. There is after all a long tradition of thinking that practical reasoning cannot extend to our most fundamental desires or aims,[42] and of course we can be manipulated as to our fundamental desires. So there is the risk that, despite critical distance in this or that corner of the overall scheme, one's framework ultimately may remain parochial and constraining on the whole. Of course, we may not be disappointed if we have unalterably fixed aims that turn out to be the 'right' ones to have. But I agree with David O'Connor that while such a picture of our aims suggests that one may be the object of a sort of aesthetic appreciation for one's goodness, responsibility for oneself nonetheless seems absent from that picture (2005, §1.3). Character should be part of who one is, not just what one is like.

So the question is whether humans are capable of critical distance from even their basic, fundamental aims, or if not, whether (more weakly) such aims are consistent with responsibility for character on the whole. I think that even the stronger claim can be established on multiple grounds, and I now shall discuss one of these grounds that I think illuminates especially well both how reckoning with one's character takes place within a framework, and how one can reckon with the framework itself. Here we must avoid a pyrrhic victory, however, and be sure that reckoning with one's fixed aims does not presuppose a transcendent self that is prior to its aims.

---

[41] On the complexity of character, see esp. Hursthouse 1999a, ch. 5 and Swanton 2003. I have benefited here from discussion with Bronwyn Finnegan and Fiona Leigh.

[42] Frankfurt (1992, 17f) himself argues that one can deliberate about ends only if one already has some ends that are not merely fixed but 'fixed unalterably'. See also Williams 1985, 113. Both are cited in Schmidtz 1994, 234, 237. See also Hubin 2001, 467, cited in LeBar 2004, 508. According to Hubin, an agent's 'ultimate ends' are 'the brute facts about the agent's psychology in virtue of a relationship to which policies, plans, and actions can be rationally advisable or inadvisable'.

It is true that certain 'fixed points' give practical reasoning its framework, since one can reckon with oneself only by taking as given certain fundamental ends and facts about oneself. And we have seen that even fundamental aims and 'fixed points' need not be alienating, since critical distance can extend even as far as to one's very desire for survival, as agents can find (and, given the 'normative problem', need to find) reasons to survive. Motivations we have not originated can be motivations we transform to be parts of ourselves.

We can extend this point to other fundamental aims and 'fixed points' as well. Consider the Aristotelian view that our end of living well or flourishing is a fundamental end, an end to which our other, more particular ends are ultimately referred. This is not an end that agents originate; on the contrary, caring about what becomes of one's existence seems a prerequisite for being an agent with any ends at all. Nonetheless, I believe that this fixed end can be reckoned with, and in that case, the bare fact that an end is a 'fixed' one, and one that we do not originate for ourselves, does nothing to alienate one from it. On the contrary, such ends could open up a perspective that is *salient* for the kind of being one is—they could be what makes the very prospect of a character of one's own a real possibility.

How can one have critical distance from the 'fixed' human end of living a flourishing life? Consider what Aristotle says about this end. As Aristotle recognizes, it is our nature to have, to seek, and to need reasons for our actions, choices, and beliefs, and even for our emotions and desires—it is our nature, that is, to have a 'normative problem'.[43] Aristotle understands that reflection as ultimately carried out within a framework made possible by the notion of a 'final end' (*telos*), that is, an end for which no further reason need be sought, and which can potentially organize and unify our other goals and ends (*NE* I.1–2).[44] This final end, Aristotle argues, is *eudaimonia*, which is often rendered as 'happiness' or (perhaps better) as 'flourishing', and is generally used interchangeably with 'living well' (*NE* I.4–5).[45]

---

[43] Aristotle believes that what is distinctive of human nature and activity is our ability to shape and direct our activity by reason, that is, to live 'an active life of the element that has a rational principle'; see *NE* I.7, 1097b23–1098a20, the so-called 'function argument'. For an excellent discussion of this argument, see Korsgaard 1986, who understands the force of this argument to be the idea that the fulfillment of our capacities for practical rationality is what makes us fully human. Accordingly, Aristotle says, good human activity is 'the good and noble performance of…activity or actions of the soul implying a rational principle' (1098a13–14), which is action done in accordance with human 'excellence', or virtue.

[44] For a discussion of a final end as an end that unifies and organizes other ends, see Annas 1993a, ch. 1 and references.

[45] We can recognize with Watson 1975, 215 the 'fiction' of the assertion that people generally do display the level of hierarchy and structure within their goals and reasons that such reflection would

One advantage of this specification of the final end, Aristotle says, is that it is sufficiently formal and perspective-neutral to capture the basic concept of a final end that is shared by various schools of thought that offer widely diverging conceptions of it. For instance, some people say that flourishing comes from business and money-making, Aristotle notes, and some that it comes from pleasure and enjoyment, but all are agreed that the point of offering such conceptions is to get a better understanding of what flourishing involves. But, Aristotle says, while there is broad agreement that the final end is a flourishing life, that construal of the final end also brings with it a number of formal constraints that are informative enough to adjudicate between these many competing descriptions of flourishing.[46] For instance, the problem with a money-making account of flourishing, Aristotle says, is not the content of that account *per se*, but the fact that the good life depends on what I do and what sort of person I am, while a money-making life is too fundamentally bound up with my circumstances. Such a life could simply be given to me; it doesn't involve my agency and my character—it doesn't involve *me*—in the right way. Those circumstances are also much more unstable than I need the basis of the goodness in my life to be. And of course money-making is not a sufficiently 'final' kind of goal, since money is always for the sake of something else. For all these reasons, reflection even at the formal level both demands and facilitates informative reassessment of taking money-making as a reason for organizing one's life, given that a final end should unify one's other goals, and keep one from being too dependent for one's flourishing on external circumstances.

The fixed end of *eudaimonia*, therefore, can be reckoned with, insofar as one can specify the content of that end for oneself. But more importantly, one can also reckon with that end by finding reasons to pursue it. Because that end is a formal one, one can satisfy it only by finding further ends to live for. Once I have such further ends, I can ask whether living for the sake of those ends will indeed satisfy my end of living a life worth living. But I can also reflect on how my life is going with respect to those ends for which I live, and from that perspective I can ask whether I now have a *reason* to pursue a life worth living. Perhaps I find that my projects and relationships are greatly rewarding and fulfilling, and thus that I have a reason to continue with the end of living a life worth living. At this point, the 'fixed' end of *eudaimonia* is transformed; it

---

make possible. But the point of Aristotle's talk of the systematization of one's goals and reasons under eudaimonist reflection is, I think, rather to elucidate the structure of that sort of reflection.

[46] This is the notion of formal constraints on the concept of *eudaimonia*, which Aristotle introduces in *NE* I.5 and develops more fully in I.7. See also *EE* I.3.

becomes an end for which an agent can find reasons or, tragically, find reasons wanting. Even the final end is one that can come under pressure, and when it does, it is an end for which we need reasons, since like any non-alienating motivation, it does not survive such pressure if we come to find that we have no reasons for it.

So the fixed end of *eudaimonia* can be reckoned with—it is not fixed unalterably (see also LeBar 2004, 530). One's end of living a good life as a whole, given what humans and their lives are like, can be the sort of fixed end in a framework for reflecting on one's other reasons that is both informative enough to be pertinent to reflection on one's ends, and formal enough to leave one free to reflect for oneself. Of course, to say that such a framework is informative is not to say that it settles all questions, or should.[47] Responsibility does not require that reflection must take every reasonable person to the same conclusions.[48] All we require is a framework for gaining critical distance from our character, including our characteristic ends, without being held in the grip of the fixed points that constitute the framework. A eudaimonist framework takes as fixed the end of *eudaimonia*—of living a life worth living—but this does not make reflection unfree within that framework. Rather, that end makes reflection salient for the kind of being that is doing the reflecting. Such ends are fixed, but not alienating.

I should point out that the case for responsibility for character depends not on our accepting eudaimonism in particular as a theory of practical reasoning, but only on the existence of fixed points in practical reasoning that do not undermine our capacity for genuine critical distance from ourselves. Any such framework must share the eudaimonist framework's 'structural' virtues of formality and informativeness. The point is that there is at least one plausible characterization of the fixed points that has those structural virtues. So there is ample reason to believe that one's critical distance from one's motivational framework can be both widespread and attainable.

---

[47]   Even Aristotle, who argues that the formal constraints on flourishing pick out a unique conception of flourishing (activity in accordance with excellence, provided with adequate external goods, *NE* 1.10, 1101a14–16), does not seem to think that the formal constraints close all debate on what flourishing is. In fact, his own view is not so much concluded as proposed: 'Why then should we not say that...'.

[48]   Con. Smith 1997, 316 who argues that 'Reflection can confer a special status on a desire only if the desire so formed is special relative to that reflective process. But the only way in which desires could be special relative to a reflective process is if, on the basis of such reflection, agents would all converge on the very same desires'. This is so, Smith argues, because without this 'rationalistic gloss' on reflection, 'the desires agents end up with after reflection are a function of the desires they actually have to begin with, the desires they were caused to have by the forces of socialization and enculturation that made them what they are'. The notion of critical distance from one's reasons within a eudaimonist framework for reflection shows that this dichotomy is a false one.

Does critical distance from one's fixed ends require that the self be transcendent and independent of its ends? No. Fixed ends—such as the ends of surviving and of living well—can be transformed, through reckoning with them, to ends that are affirmed. One can reckon with those fixed ends once one has developed other ends that give one reasons to live, since from the perspective of those other ends we ask whether we have reasons to affirm those ends that previously had been merely fixed. The reflective framework I have described here therefore reveals that the critical distance view of responsibility for character requires not a transcendent or disembodied self, but only a reflecting and reasoning one.

Conclusion

The view that responsibility is ultimate responsibility looks for responsibility in the origins of character. This is not entirely surprising, since often what leaves one beyond the pale of responsibility is something that happened in one's origins. But the real question is not who has done what. The real question is whether what has been done has left one in a position to take ownership of the character one has. Having a starting-point for which we are not responsible is no obstacle to becoming responsible. The obstacle could be only a starting-point which left us incapable of critical distance from ourselves.

Hard Virtue Theory takes the virtues to have psychological depth, in the sense that the virtues are forms of responsiveness to reasons that one correctly specifies and grasps through phronesis. Since such operations of phronesis construct much of a virtuous person's practical identity, Hard Virtue Theory is committed to the notion of self-construction. I have argued that it is critical distance from one's character that makes such self-construction possible, and that such critical distance both is attainable and can be widespread across one's motivational framework. Virtues that are excellences of practically rational creatures require depth, but no more depth than normal human beings are capable of.

Works Cited

Ackrill, J. L., 'Aristotle on *Eudaimonia*', in A. O. Rorty, ed., *Essays on Aristotle's Ethics* (University of California, 1980).
—— *Aristotle the Philosopher* (Oxford, 1981).
Adams, R. M., *A Theory of Virtue: Excellence in Being for the Good* (Oxford, 2006).
Alison, L., C. Bennell, A. Mokros, and D. Ormerod, 'The Personality Paradox in Offender Profiling', *Psychology, Public Policy, and Law*, 8 (2002), 115–35.
Allan, D. J., 'Aristotle's Account of the Origin of Moral Principles', *Actes du XIe Congrès international de philosophie*, 12 (1953), 120–7.
—— 'The Practical Syllogism', in *Autour d'Aristote: Recueil d'études offert à Mgr Mansion* (Louvain, 1955).
Allison, H. E., *Kant's Theory of Freedom* (Cambridge, 1990).
Allport, G. W., *Personality: A Psychological Interpretation* (Holt, 1937).
—— 'Traits Revisited', *American Psychologist*, 21 (1966), 1–10.
—— 'The Historical Background of Social Psychology', in G. Lindzey and E. Aronson, eds., *The Handbook of Social Psychology* (McGraw Hill, 1985).
Annas, J., *Hellenistic Philosophy of Mind* (University of California, 1992a).
—— 'The Good Life and the Life of Others', *Social Philosophy and Policy*, 9 (1992b), 133–43.
—— *The Morality of Happiness* (Oxford, 1993a).
—— 'Virtue and the Use of Other Goods', *Apeiron*, 26 (1993b), 53–66.
—— 'Aristotle and Kant on Morality and Practical Reasoning', in S. Engstrom and J. Whiting, eds., *Aristotle, Kant, and the Stoics: Rethinking Happiness and Duty* (Cambridge, 1996).
—— 'Virtue and Eudaimonism', *Social Philosophy and Policy*, 15 (1998), 37–55.
—— 'Should Virtue Make You Happy?', in L. Jost and R. Shiner, eds., *Eudaimonia and Well-Being*, special edn. of *Apeiron* (Academic Printing & Publishing, 2002).
—— 'Virtue Ethics and Social Psychology', *A Priori*, 2 (2003), 20–34.
—— 'Being Virtuous and Doing the Right Thing', *Proceedings and Addresses of the American Philosophical Association*, 78 (2004), 61–75.
—— 'Virtue Ethics: What Kind of Naturalism?', in S. Gardiner, ed., *Virtue Ethics, Old and New* (Cornell, 2005a).
—— 'Wickedness as Psychological Breakdown', *Southern Journal of Philosophy*, 43 suppl. (2005b), 1–19.
—— 'Comments on John Doris' *Lack of Character*', *Philosophy and Phenomenological Research*, 71 (2005c), 636–42.
—— 'Virtue Ethics', in D. Copp, ed., *The Oxford Companion to Ethical Theory* (Oxford, 2006).
—— 'Virtue and Nature', unpublished manuscript.

Anscombe, G. E. M., 'Thought and Action in Aristotle', in J. Walsh and H. Shapiro, eds., *Aristotle's Ethics: Issues and Interpretations* (Wadsworth, 1967).

—— 'On Promising and its Justice, and Whether it Need be Respected *in Foro Interno*', in *The Collected Philosophical Papers of G. E. M. Anscombe*, vol. 3. *Ethics, Religion and Politics* (Blackwell, 1981*a*).

—— 'Modern Moral Philosophy', in *The Collected Philosophical Papers of G. E. M. Anscombe*, vol. 3. *Ethics, Religion and Politics* (Blackwell, 1981*b*).

—— 'You Can Have Sex without Children: Christianity and the New Offer', in *The Collected Philosophical Papers of G. E. M. Anscombe*, vol. 3. *Ethics, Religion and Politics* (Blackwell, 1981*c*).

Arpaly, N., 'Comments on *Lack of Character* by John Doris', *Philosophy and Phenomenological Research*, 71 (2005), 643–7.

—— *Unprincipled Virtue* (Oxford, 2003).

Athanassoulis, N., 'A Response to Harman: Virtue Ethics and Character Traits', *Proceedings of the Aristotelian Society*, 100 (2000), 215–21.

Audi, R., 'Responsible Action and Virtuous Character', *Ethics*, 101 (1991), 304–21.

—— 'Acting for Reasons', in A. R. Mele, ed., *The Philosophy of Action* (Oxford, 1997*a*).

—— *Moral Knowledge and Ethical Character* (Oxford, 1997*b*).

Badhwar, N., 'The Limited Unity of Virtue', *Nous*, 30 (1996), 306–29.

Barnes, J., 'Aristotle's Theory of Demonstration', *Phronesis*, 14 (1969), 123–51.

—— translation and commentary, *Aristotle: Posterior Analytics* (Oxford, 1975).

Bentham, J., 'The Nature of Virtue', in B. Parekh, ed., *Bentham's Political Thought* (Croom Helm, 1973).

Bostock, D., *Aristotle's Ethics* (Oxford, 2000).

Brandt, R. B., *Ethical Theory* (Prentice Hall, 1959).

—— 'W. K. Frankena and the Ethics of Virtue', *Monist*, 64 (1981), 271–92.

—— 'The Structure of Virtue', *Midwest Studies in Philosophy*, 13 (1988), 64–82.

Broadie, S., *Ethics with Aristotle* (Oxford, 1991).

—— *Aristotle and Beyond* (Cambridge, 2007).

—— and C. Rowe, *Aristotle, Nicomachean Ethics: Translation, Introduction, and Commentary* (Oxford, 2002).

Burnyeat, M., 'Aristotle on Learning to be Good', in A. O. Rorty, ed., *Essays on Aristotle's Ethics* (University of California, 1980).

Butler, D., 'Character Traits in Explanation', *Philosophy and Phenomenological Research*, 49 (1998), 215–38.

Campbell, J., 'Can Philosophical Accounts of Altruism Accommodate Experimental Data on Helping Behavior?', *Australasian Journal of Philosophy*, 77 (1999), 26–45.

Carr, D., 'Character and Moral Choice in the Cultivation of Virtue', *Philosophy*, 78 (2003), 219–32.

Cassedy, E. S., 'Health Risk Valuations Based on Public Consent', *IEEE Technology and Society Magazine*, 11 (Winter 1992–3), 7–16.

Cattell, R. B., *Personality: A Systematic Theoretical and Factual Study* (McGraw-Hill, 1950).

—— *Personality and Motivation: Structure and Measurement* (World Book, 1957).

Cavell, M., 'Reason and the Gardener', in L. E. Hahn, ed., *The Philosophy of Donald Davidson* (Open Court, 1999).

Champagne, M., and L. A. Pervin, 'The Relation of Perceived Situation Similarity to Perceived Behavior Similarity', *European Journal of Personality*, 1 (1987), 79–91.

Church, A. T., M. S. Katigbak, J. A. S. Reyes, M. G. C. Salanga, L. A. Miramontes, and N. B. Adams, 'Prediction and Cross-Situational Consistency of Daily Behavior Across Cultures', *Journal of Research in Personality*, 42 (2008), 1199–1215.

Cialdini, R. B., *Influence: Science and Practice* (Allyn and Bacon, 1988).

Cone, J. D., 'Behavioral Assessment with Children and Adolescents', in M. Hersen and V. B. Van Hasselt, eds., *Behavior Therapy with Children and Adolescents* (Krieger, 1991).

Cooper, J., *Reason and Human Good in Aristotle* (Harvard, 1975).

—— 'Some Remarks on Aristotle's Moral Psychology', *Southern Journal of Philosophy*, 27 suppl. (1988), 25–42.

—— ed., *Plato: Complete Works* (Hackett, 1997).

—— 'The Unity of Virtue', in *Reason and Emotion* (Princeton, 1999).

Copp, D., and D. Sobel, 'Morality and Virtue: An Assessment of Some Recent Work in Virtue Ethics', *Ethics*, 114 (2004), 514–54.

Dahl, N., *Practical Reason, Aristotle, and Weakness of the Will* (University of Minnesota, 1984).

Dalcourt, G., 'The Primary Cardinal Virtue: Wisdom or Prudence?', *International Philosophical Quarterly*, 3 (1963), 55–79.

Dancy, J., *Ethics Without Principles* (Oxford, 2004).

Darley, J., and C. D. Batson, 'From Jerusalem to Jericho: A Study of Situational and Dispositional Variables in Helping Behavior', *Journal of Personality and Social Psychology*, 27 (1973), 100–8.

—— and B. Latané, 'Bystander Intervention in Emergencies: Diffusion of Responsibility', *Journal of Personality and Social Psychology*, 8 (1968), 377–83.

Darwall, S., 'From Morality to Virtue and Back?', *Philosophy and Phenomenological Research*, 54 (1994), 695–701.

Das, R., 'Virtue Ethics and Right Action', *Australasian Journal of Philosophy*, 81 (2003), 324–39.

Davidson, D., *Essays on Action and Events* (Oxford, 1980).

—— *Inquiries into Truth and Interpretation* (Oxford, 1984).

—— 'Incoherence and Irrationality', *Dialectica*, 39 (1985), 345–54.

—— 'Three Varieties of Knowledge', in A. P. Griffiths, ed., *A. J. Ayer: Memorial Essays* (Cambridge, 1991).

—— various replies, in L. E. Hahn, ed., *The Philosophy of Donald Davidson* (Open Court, 1999).

Dent, N. J. H., *The Moral Psychology of the Virtues* (Cambridge, 1984).

DePaul, M., 'Character Traits, Virtues and Vices: Are There None?', in B. Elevitch, ed., *Proceedings of the World Congress of Philosophy 9: Philosophy of Mind* (Bowling Green, 1999).

DesLauriers, M., 'How to Distinguish Aristotle's Virtues', *Phronesis*, 47 (2002), 101–26.

Devereux, D., 'Particular and Universal in Aristotle's Conception of Practical Knowledge', *Review of Metaphysics*, 39 (1986), 483–504.

Donagan, A., *The Theory of Morality* (University of Chicago, 1977).

Doris, J., 'Persons, Situations and Virtue Ethics', *Nous*, 32 (1998), 504–30.

—— *Lack of Character* (Cambridge, 2002).

—— 'Replies: Evidence and Sensibility', *Philosophy and Phenomenological Research*, 71 (2005), 656–77.

Drefcinski, S., 'Can Continent People Have Practical Wisdom?', *Ancient Philosophy*, 20 (2000), 109–18.

Driver, J., 'The Virtues and Human Nature', in R. Crisp, ed., *How Should One Live?* (Oxford, 1996).

—— *Uneasy Virtue* (Cambridge, 2001).

English, A., and R. L. Griffith, 'Trait Consistency and the "Big Five"', Society for Industrial Organizational Psychology Conference, April 2004.

Evnine, S., 'On the Way to Language', in L. E. Hahn, ed., *The Philosophy of Donald Davidson* (Open Court, 1999).

Feldman, F., 'Desert: Reconsideration of Some Received Wisdom', *Mind*, 104 (1995), 63–77.

Fine, K., 'Vagueness, Truth and Logic', *Synthese*, 30 (1975), 119–50.

Fischer, J. M., 'Responsiveness and Moral Responsibility', in F. Schoeman, ed., *Responsibility, Character, and the Emotions* (Cambridge, 1987).

—— '*The Significance of Free Will* by Robert Kane', *Philosophy and Phenomenological Research*, 60 (2000), 141–8.

Flanagan, O., *Varieties of Moral Personality* (Harvard, 1991).

Fleming, D., 'The Character of Virtue: Answering the Situationist Challenge to Virtue Ethics', *Ratio*, 19 (2006), 24–42.

Fodor, J., and E. Lepore, *Holism: A Shopper's Guide* (Blackwell, 1992).

Foot, P., 'Virtues and Vices', in Foot, *Virtues and Vices and Other Essays in Moral Philosophy* (University of California, 1978a).

—— 'Goodness and Choice', in Foot, *Virtues and Vices and Other Essays in Moral Philosophy* (University of California, 1978b).

—— 'Morality as a System of Hypothetical Imperatives', in Foot, *Virtues and Vices and Other Essays in Moral Philosophy* (University of California, 1978c).

—— 'William Frankena's Carus Lectures', *Monist*, 64 (1981), 305–12.

—— 'Moral Realism and Moral Dilemma', *Journal of Philosophy*, 80 (1983), 379–98.

—— *Natural Goodness* (Oxford, 2001).

Fortenbaugh, W., *Aristotle on Emotion: A Contribution to Philosophical Psychology, Rhetoric, Poetics, Politics, and Ethics* (Duckworth, 1975).

—— 'Aristotle's Distinction Between Moral Virtue and Practical Wisdom', in J. P. Anton and A. Preus, eds., *Essays in Ancient Greek Philosophy IV: Aristotle's Ethics* (SUNY, 1991).

Frankena, W., 'Prichard and the Ethics of Virtue', *Monist*, 54 (1970), 1–17.

—— 'Conversations with Carney and Hauerwas', *Journal of Religious Ethics*, 3 (1975), 45–62.

—— *Thinking About Morality* (University of Michigan, 1980).

Frankfurt, H., 'Identification and Wholeheartedness', in F. Schoeman, ed., *Responsibility, Character, and the Emotions* (Cambridge, 1987).

—— 'On the Usefulness of Final Ends', *Iyyun*, 41 (1992), 3–19.

—— 'Freedom of the Will and the Concept of a Person', in G. Watson, ed., *Free Will*, 2nd edn. (Oxford, 2003).

French, P., *The Scope of Morality* (University of Minnesota, 1979).

Freud, S., 'Analysis of a Phobia in a Five-Year-Old Boy', in *Collected Papers*, vol. 3 (Hogarth, 1953).

Funder, D. C., 'Personality', *Annual Review of Psychology*, 52 (2001), 197–221.

Garcia, J., 'The Primacy of the Virtuous', *Philosophia*, 20 (1990), 69–91.

—— 'The Right and the Good', *Philosophia*, 21 (1992), 235–56.

Gardiner, S., 'Aristotle's Basic and Nonbasic Virtues', *Oxford Studies in Ancient Philosophy*, 20 (2001), 261–96.

Geach, P., 'Good and Evil', *Analysis*, 17 (1956), 33–42.

—— *The Virtues* (Cambridge, 1977).

Gilbert, D. T., 'Attribution and Interpersonal Perception', in A. Tesser, ed., *Advanced Social Psychology* (McGraw-Hill, 1995).

Glover, J., *The Philosophy and Psychology of Personal Identity* (Allen Lane, 1988).

Goldblatt, R., *Topoi: The Categorial Analysis of Logic*, revised (North-Holland, 1983).

Goldie, P., *The Emotions: A Philosophical Exploration* (Oxford, 2000).

—— *On Personality* (Routledge, 2004).

Gómez-Lobo, A., 'Aristotle's Right Reason', *Apeiron*, 25 (1995), 15–34.

Goodin, R., *Reasons for Welfare* (Princeton, 1988).

Gorr, M., 'Motives and Rightness', *Philosophia*, 27 (1999), 581–98.

Gould, S. J., and C. E. Weil, 'Gift-Giving Roles and Gender Self-Concepts', *Sex Roles*, 24 (1991), 617–34.

Graff, D., 'Shifting Sands: An Interest-Relative Theory of Vagueness', *Philosophical Topics*, 28 (2000), 45–81.

Greenwood, L. H. G., *Aristotle, Nicomachean Ethics, Book VI* (Cambridge, 1909).

Griffith, R., A. English, Y. Yoshita, A. Gujar, M. Monnot, T. Malm, and M. Graseck, 'Individual Differences and Applicant Faking Behavior', Society for Industrial Organizational Psychology, symposium paper, 2002.

—— T. Malm, A. English, Y. Yoshita, and A. Gujar, 'Applicant Faking Behavior', in Griffith, M. H. Peterson, and D. Syvantek, eds., *A Closer Examination of Applicant Faking Behavior*, vol. 1 (Information Age, 2006).

Guilford, J. P., *Personality* (McGraw-Hill, 1959).

Halper, E., 'The Unity of Virtues in Aristotle', *Oxford Studies in Ancient Philosophy*, 17 (1999), 115–43.

Hardie, W. F. R., *Aristotle's Ethical Theory* (Oxford, 1968).

Harman, G., 'Moral Philosophy Meets Social Psychology: Virtue Ethics and the Fundamental Attribution Error', *Proceedings of the Aristotelian Society*, 99 (1999), 315–31.

—— 'The Nonexistence of Character Traits', *Proceedings of the Aristotelian Society*, 100 (2000), 223–6.

—— 'Virtue Ethics Without Character Traits', in A. Byrne, R. Stalnaker, and R. Wedgwood, eds., *Fact and Value: Essays on Ethics and Metaphysics for Judith Jarvis Thomson* (MIT, 2001).

—— 'No Character or Personality', *Business Ethics Quarterly*, 13 (2003), 87–94.

—— 'My Virtue Situation', www.princeton.edu/~harman/Papers/Situ.pdf, 2005.

Harris, C. E., M. S. Pritchard, and M. J. Rabins, *Engineering Ethics: Concepts and Cases*, 2nd edn. (Wadsworth, 2000).

Hartshorne, H., and M. A. May, *Studies in the Nature of Character*, vol. 1. *Studies in Deceit* (Macmillan, 1928).

Herman, B., *The Practice of Moral Judgment* (Harvard, 1993).

Highhouse, S., and M. M. Harris, 'The Measurement of Assessment Center Situations', *Journal of Applied Social Psychology*, 23 (1993), 140–55.

Homiak, M., 'On the Malleability of Character', in C. Card, ed., *On Feminist Ethics and Politics* (University Press of Kansas, 1999).

Hubin, D., 'The Groundless Normativity of Instrumental Rationality', *Journal of Philosophy*, 98 (2001), 445–68.

Hurka, T., *Virtue, Vice, and Value* (Oxford, 2001).

Hursthouse, R., 'Arational Actions', *Journal of Philosophy*, 88 (1991), 57–68.

—— 'Applying Virtue Ethics', in Hursthouse, G. Lawrence, and W. Quinn, eds., *Virtues and Reasons: Philippa Foot and Moral Theory* (Oxford, 1995a).

—— 'The Virtuous Agent's Reasons: A Reply to Bernard Williams', in R. Heinaman, ed., *Aristotle and Moral Realism* (University College London, 1995b).

—— 'Virtue Theory and Abortion', in R. Crisp and M. Slote, eds., *Virtue Ethics* (Oxford, 1997).

—— *On Virtue Ethics* (Oxford, 1999a).

—— 'A False Doctrine of the Mean', in N. Sherman, ed., *Aristotle's Ethics: Critical Essays* (Rowman and Littlefield, 1999b).

—— 'Virtue Ethics', in *The Stanford Encyclopedia of Philosophy*, 2003.

—— 'Practical Wisdom: A Mundane Account', *Proceedings of the Aristotelian Society*, 106 (2006a), 283–307.

—— 'Environmental Virtue Ethics', in P. J. Ivanhoe and R. L. Walker, eds., *Working Virtue* (Oxford, 2006b).

Inwagen, P. van, 'When is the Will Free?', *Philosophical Perspectives*, 3 (1989), 399–422.

Irwin, T., 'Aristotle on Reason, Desire and Virtue', *Journal of Philosophy*, 72 (1975), 567–78.

—— 'First Principles in Aristotle's Ethics', *Midwest Studies in Philosophy*, 3 (1978), 252–72.

—— *Aristotle: Nicomachean Ethics* (Hackett, 1985).

—— 'Disunity in the Aristotelian Virtues', *Oxford Studies in Ancient Philosophy*, suppl. (1988a): 61–78.

—— 'Disunity in the Aristotelian Virtues: Reply to Richard Kraut', *Oxford Studies in Ancient Philosophy*, suppl. (1988b): 87–90.

—— 'Virtue, Praise and Success: Stoic Responses to Aristotle', *Monist*, 73 (1990), 59–79.

—— 'Do Virtues Conflict? Aquinas' Answer', in S. Gardiner, ed., *Virtue Ethics, Old and New* (Cornell, 2005).

Jackall, R., 'The Bureaucratic Ethos and Dissent', *IEEE Technology and Society Magazine*, 4 (1985).

Jacobs, J., and J. Zeis, 'The Unity of the Vices', *The Thomist*, 54 (1990), 641–53.

Jacobson, D., 'An Unsolved Problem for Slote's Agent-Based Virtue Ethics', *Philosophical Studies*, 111 (2002), 53–67.

Johnson, R., 'Virtue and Right', *Ethics*, 113 (2003), 810–34.

Kakoliris, G., 'Refuting Fortenbaugh: The Relationship between Ethike Arete and Phronesis in Aristotle', *Philosophia* (Athens), 33 (2003), 183–93.

Kammrath, L. K., R. Mendoza-Denton, and W. Mischel, 'Incorporating *If… Then…* Personality Signatures in Person Perception: Beyond the Person-Situation Dichotomy', *Journal of Personality and Social Psychology*, 88 (2005), 605–18.

Kamtekar, R., 'Situationism and Virtue Ethics on the Content of Our Character', *Ethics*, 114 (2004), 458–91.

Kane, R., 'Two Kinds of Incompatibilism', *Philosophy and Phenomenological Research*, 50 (1989), 219–54.

—— *The Significance of Free Will* (Oxford, 1996).

—— 'The Dual Regress of Free Will and the Role of Alternative Possibilities', *Nous*, 34 suppl. (2000a), 57–79.

—— 'Responses to Bernard Berofsky, John Martin Fischer and Galen Strawson', *Philosophy and Phenomenological Research*, 60 (2000b), 157–67.

Kant, I., *The Doctrine of Virtue*, trans. M. J. Gregor (Harper and Rowe, 1964).

Kawall, J., 'Virtue Theory and Ideal Observers', *Philosophical Studies*, 109 (2002), 197–222.

Keefe, R., and P. Smith, 'Introduction: Theories of Vagueness', in Keefe and Smith, eds., *Vagueness: A Reader* (MIT, 1996).

Korsgaard, C., 'Aristotle on Function and Virtue', *History of Philosophy Quarterly*, 3 (1986), 259–79.

—— 'The Reasons We Can Share: An Attack on the Distinction between Agent-Relative and Agent-Neutral Values', *Social Philosophy and Policy*, 10 (1993), 24–51.

—— 'Rawls and Kant: On the Primacy of the Practical', *Proceedings of the Eighth International Kant Congress*, Memphis 1995, vol. 1 pt 3 (Marquette, 1995).

—— *The Sources of Normativity* (Cambridge, 1996a).

—— *Creating the Kingdom of Ends* (Cambridge, 1996b).

Kraut, R., 'Comments on "Disunity in the Aristotelian Virtues"', *Oxford Studies in Ancient Philosophy*, suppl. (1988), 79–86.

Kraut, R., 'In Defense of the Grand End', *Ethics*, 103 (1993), 361–74.

Kunda, Z., *Social Cognition: Making Sense of People* (MIT, 1999).

Kupperman, J., *Character* (Oxford, 1991).

Latané, B., and J. Darley, *The Unresponsive Bystander: Why Doesn't He Help?* (Appleton-Century-Crofts, 1968).

——and J. Rodin, 'A Lady in Distress: Inhibiting Effects of Friends and Strangers on Bystander Intervention', *Journal of Experimental Social Psychology*, 5 (1969), 189–202.

LeBar, M., 'Ends', *Social Theory and Practice*, 30 (2004), 507–33.

——'Virtue Ethics and Deontic Constraints', unpublished manuscript.

Lemos, J., 'The Unity of the Virtues and its Recent Defenses', *Southern Journal of Philosophy*, 31 (1993), 85–106.

Levy, N., 'Are We Responsible for Our Characters?', *Ethica*, 1 (2002), 115–32.

Lewin, K., *Field Theory in Social Science: Selected Theoretical Papers*, ed. D. Cartwright (Harper and Row, 1951).

Lewis, D., 'Scorekeeping in a Language Game', *Journal of Philosophical Logic*, 8 (1979), 339–59.

Loevinger, J., 'Objective Tests as Instruments of Psychological Theory', *Psychological Reports*, 3, monograph suppl. 9 (1957), 635–94.

Long, A. A., and D. N. Sedley, eds., *The Hellenistic Philosophers*, vol. 1 (Cambridge, 1987).

Lord, C., 'Predicting Behavioral Consistency From an Individual's Perception of Situational Similarities', *Journal of Personality and Social Psychology*, 42 (1982), 1076–88.

Louden, R., 'On Some Vices of Virtue Ethics', *American Philosophical Quarterly*, 21 (1984), 227–36.

——'Virtue Ethics and Anti-Theory', *Philosophia*, 20 (1990), 93–114.

——'Aristotle's Practical Particularism', in J. P. Anton and A. Preus, eds., *Essays in Ancient Greek Philosophy IV: Aristotle's Ethics* (SUNY, 1991).

——'What is Moral Authority? Εὐβουλία, σύνεσις, and γνώμη vs.φρόνησις', *Ancient Philosophy*, 17 (1997), 103–18.

McAleer, S., 'An Aristotelian Account of Virtue Ethics: An Essay in Moral Taxonomy', *Pacific Philosophical Quarterly*, 88 (2007), 208–25.

McDowell, J., 'Two Sorts of Naturalism', in R. Hursthouse, G. Lawrence, and W. Quinn, eds., *Virtues and Reasons: Philippa Foot and Moral Theory* (Oxford, 1995a).

——'Eudaimonism and Realism in Aristotle's Ethics', in R. Heinaman, ed., *Aristotle and Moral Realism* (University College London, 1995b).

——'Virtue and Reason', in R. Crisp and M. Slote, eds., *Virtue Ethics* (Oxford, 1997).

——'Some Issues in Aristotle's Moral Psychology', in S. Everson, ed., *Companions to Ancient Thought, 4: Ethics* (Cambridge, 1998).

MacFarlane, J. W., and R. D. Tuddenham, 'Problems in the Validation of Projection Techniques', in H. H. Anderson and G. L. Anderson, eds., *Projective Techniques* (Prentice-Hall, 1951).

MacIntyre, A., *After Virtue* (Notre Dame, 1981).

——*Whose Justice? Which Rationality?* (Notre Dame, 1988).

Meier, C., 'The Meaning of *Too, Enough,* and *So … That*', *Natural Language Semantics,* 11 (2003), 69–107.

Mele, A., 'Ultimate Responsibility and Dumb Luck', *Social Philosophy and Policy,* 16 (1999), 274–93.

—— *Autonomous Agents* (Oxford, 2001).

Merritt, M., 'Virtue Ethics and Situationist Personality Psychology', *Ethical Theory and Moral Practice,* 3 (2000), 365–83.

Milgram, S., 'Behavioral Study of Obedience', *Journal of Abnormal and Social Psychology,* 67 (1963), 371–8.

—— *Obedience to Authority* (Harper and Row, 1974).

Miller, C., 'Social Psychology and Virtue Ethics', *Journal of Ethics,* 7 (2003), 365–92.

Milo, R., 'Contractarian Constructivism', *Journal of Philosophy,* 92 (1995), 181–204.

Mischel, W., *Personality and Assessment* (John Wiley and Sons, 1968).

—— 'Toward a Cognitive Social Learning Reconceptualization of Personality', *Psychological Review,* 80 (1973), 252–83.

—— 'On the Predictability of Behavior and the Structure of Personality', in R. A. Zucker, J. Aronoff, and A. I. Rabin, eds., *Personality and the Prediction of Behavior* (Academic, 1984).

—— and P. K. Peake, 'Beyond Déjà Vu in the Search for Cross-Situational Consistency', *Psychological Review,* 89 (1982), 730–55.

—— and Y. Shoda, 'A Cognitive-Affective System Theory of Personality', *Psychological Review,* 102 (1995), 246–68.

—— Y. Shoda, and R. Mendoza-Denton, 'Situation-Behavior Profiles as a Locus of Consistency in Personality', *Current Directions in Psychological Science,* 11 (2002), 50–4.

Monan, J., *Moral Knowledge and its Methodology in Aristotle* (Oxford, 1968).

Moody-Adams, M., 'On the Old Saw that Character is Destiny', in O. Flanagan and A. O. Rorty, eds., *Identity, Character and Morality: Essays in Moral Psychology* (MIT, 1990).

Moriarty, J., 'Desert and Distributive Justice in *A Theory of Justice*', *Journal of Social Philosophy,* 33 (2002), 131–43.

Murdoch, I., *The Sovereignty of the Good* (Routledge, 1970).

Nagel, T., 'Moral Luck', in T. Nagel, *Mortal Questions* (Cambridge, 1979a).

—— 'The Fragmentation of Value', in T. Nagel, *Mortal Questions* (Cambridge, 1979b).

Natali, C., *The Wisdom of Aristotle,* trans. G. Parks (SUNY, 2001).

Neurath, O., 'Protocol Sentences', in A. J. Ayer, ed., *Logical Positivism* (The Free, 1959).

Nussbaum, M., 'Aristotelian Social Democracy', in R. B. Douglass, G. M. Mara, and H. S. Richardson, eds., *Liberalism and the Good* (Routledge, 1990).

—— 'Human Functioning and Social Justice: In Defense of Aristotelian Essentialism', *Political Theory,* 20 (1992), 202–46.

—— 'Non-Relative Virtues: An Aristotelian Approach', in M. Nussbaum and A. Sen, eds., *The Quality of Life* (Oxford, 1993).

Nussbaum, M., 'Aristotle on Human Nature and the Foundations of Ethics', in J. E. J. Altham and R. Harrison, eds., *World, Mind, and Ethics: Essays on the Ethical Philosophy of Bernard Williams* (Cambridge, 1995).

——'Virtue Ethics: A Misleading Category?', *Journal of Ethics*, 3 (1999), 163–201.

Oakley, J., 'Varieties of Virtue Ethics', *Ratio*, 9 (1996), 128–52.

O'Connor, D., 'Free Will', in *The Stanford Encyclopedia of Philosophy*, 2005.

Oderberg, D. S., 'On the Cardinality of the Cardinal Virtues', *International Journal of Philosophical Studies*, 7 (1999), 305–22.

Owens, J., 'Aristotle's Notion of Wisdom', *Apeiron*, 20 (1987), 1–16.

Pakaluk, M., 'On an Alleged Contradiction in Aristotle's *Nicomachean Ethics*', *Oxford Studies in Ancient Philosophy*, 20 (2002), 201–20.

——*Aristotle's Nicomachean Ethics* (Cambridge, 2005).

Pereboom, D., *Living Without Free Will* (Cambridge, 2001).

Pervin, L. A., 'A Critical Analysis of Current Trait Theory', *Psychological Inquiry*, 5 (1994), 103–13.

Peterson, C., and M. E. P. Seligman, eds., *Character Strengths and Virtues: A Handbook and Classification* (Oxford and the American Psychological Association, 2004).

Pincoffs, E., *Quandaries and Virtues* (University Press of Kansas, 1986).

Polansky, R., '"Phronesis" on Tour: Cultural Adaptability of Aristotelian Ethical Notions', *Kennedy Institute of Ethics Journal*, 10 (2000), 232–36.

Price, A. W., 'Aristotelian Virtue and Practical Judgment', in C. Gill, ed., *Virtue, Norms, and Objectivity* (Oxford, 2005).

Prichard, H. A., 'Does Moral Philosophy Rest on a Mistake?', *Mind*, 21 (1912), 21–37.

Prior, W. J., 'Eudaimonism and Virtue', *Journal of Value Inquiry*, 35 (2001), 325–42.

Quine, W. V. O., 'Two Dogmas of Empiricism', *Philosophical Review*, 60 (1951), 20–43.

Rachels, J., 'What People Deserve', in Rachels, *Can Ethics Provide Answers?* (Rowman and Littlefield, 1997).

Ramberg, B. T., *Donald Davidson's Philosophy of Language* (Blackwell, 1989).

Ratneshwar, S., L. W. Barsalou, C. Pechmann, and M. Moore, 'Goal-Derived Categories: The Role of Personal and Situational Goals in Category Representations', *Journal of Consumer Psychology*, 10 (2001), 147–57.

Rawls, J., 'Two Concepts of Rules', in P. Foot, ed., *Theories of Ethics* (Oxford, 1967).

——*A Theory of Justice* (Harvard, 1971).

Raz, J., *Engaging Reason* (Oxford, 2000).

Reeve, C. D. C., *Practices of Reason: Aristotle's Nicomachean Ethics* (Oxford, 1992).

Richardson, H., 'Rescuing Ethical Theory', *Philosophy and Phenomenological Research*, 54 (1994), 703–8.

Ross, D., *Aristotle* (Routledge, 1923).

Ross, L., 'The Intuitive Psychologist and his Shortcomings: Distortions in the Attribution Process', in L. Berkowitz, ed., *Advances in Experimental Social Psychology 10* (Academic, 1977).

—— and R. E. Nisbett, *The Person and the Situation: Perspectives of Social Psychology* (Temple University, 1991).

Rovane, C., 'Rationality and Identity', in L. E. Hahn, ed., *The Philosophy of Donald Davidson* (Open Court, 1999).

Russell, D. C., *Plato on Pleasure and the Good Life* (Oxford, 2005a).

—— 'Aristotle on the Moral Relevance of Self-Respect', in S. Gardiner, ed., *Virtue Ethics, Old and New* (Cornell, 2005b).

Ryckman, R., *Theories of Personality* (Thomson/Wadsworth, 2004).

Sabini, J., M. Siepmann, and J. Stein, 'The Really Fundamental Attribution Error in Psychological Research', *Psychological Inquiry*, 12 (2001), 1–15.

—— and M. Silver, 'Lack of Character? Situationism Exposed', *Ethics*, 115 (2005), 535–62.

Sainsbury, R. M., 'Concepts Without Boundaries', in R. Keefe and P. Smith, eds., *Vagueness: A Reader* (MIT, 1996).

Santas, G., 'Does Aristotle Have a Virtue Ethics?', *Philosophical Inquiry*, 15 (1993), 1–32.

Scanlon, T., 'Contractualism and Utilitarianism', in A. Sen, ed., *Utilitarianism and Beyond* (Cambridge, 1982).

Scheffler, S., 'Agent-Centred Restrictions, Rationality, and the Virtues', in Scheffler, ed., *Consequentialism and its Critics* (Oxford, 1988).

—— *Human Morality* (Oxford, 1992).

Schmidtz, D., 'Choosing Ends', *Ethics*, 104 (1994), 226–51.

—— 'Reasons for Reasons', http://web.arizona.edu/~phil/faculty/extra/dschmidtz/dschmidtz_reason.htm, 2001.

—— 'How to Deserve', *Political Theory*, 30 (2002), 774–800.

—— and R. Goodin, *Social Welfare and Individual Responsibility* (Cambridge, 1998).

Schneewind, J., 'The Misfortunes of Virtue', in R. Crisp and M. Slote, eds., *Virtue Ethics* (Oxford, 1997).

Schwitzgebel, E., 'Belief', in *The Stanford Encyclopedia of Philosophy*, 2006.

Sedikedes, C., and J. J. Skowronski, 'The Law of Cognitive Structure Activation', *Psychological Inquiry*, 2 (1991), 169–84.

Sher, G., 'Effort, Ability, and Personal Desert', *Philosophy and Public Affairs*, 8 (1979), 361–76.

—— 'Blame for Traits', *Nous*, 35 (2001), 146–61.

Sherman, N., 'Character, Planning, and Choice in Aristotle', *Review of Metaphysics*, 39 (1985), 83–106.

—— *The Fabric of Character* (Oxford, 1989).

Sherman, S. J., and R. H. Fazio, 'Parallels between Attributes and Traits as Predictors of Behaviors', *Journal of Personality Research*, 51 (1983), 308–45.

Shoda, Y., 'Behavioral Expressions of a Personality System', in D. Cervone and Shoda, eds., *The Coherence of Personality: Social-Cognitive Bases of Consistency, Variability, and Organization* (Guilford Press, 1999).

Shoda, Y., W. Mischel, and J. C. Wright, 'Personality Processes and Individual Differences', *Journal of Personality and Social Psychology*, 67 (1994), 674–87.

Skorupski, J., 'Externalism and Self-Governance', *Utilitas*, 16 (2004), 12–21.

Slote, M., *Goods and Virtues* (Oxford, 1983).

—— *From Morality to Virtue* (Oxford, 1992).

—— 'Virtue Ethics', in M. Baron, P. Pettit, and Slote, *Three Methods of Ethics: A Debate* (Blackwell, 1997).

—— *Morals from Motives* (Oxford, 2001).

Smart, J. J. C., and B. Williams, *Utilitarianism: For and Against* (Cambridge, 1973).

Smilansky, S., 'Responsibility and Desert: Defending The Connection', *Mind*, 105 (1996), 157–63.

Smith, M., 'A Theory of Freedom and Responsibility', in G. Cullity and B. Gaut, eds., *Ethics and Practical Reason* (Oxford, 1997).

Soles, D. N., 'Locke's Account of Natural Philosophy', Presidential Address, Southwestern Philosophical Society, 2004.

Solomon, R., 'Victims of Circumstances? A Defense of Virtue Ethics in Business', *Business Ethics Quarterly*, 13 (2003), 43–62.

—— ' "What's Character Got to Do with It?" ', *Philosophy and Phenomenological Research*, 71 (2005), 648–55.

Sorabji, R., 'Aristotle on the Role of Intellect in Virtue', in A. O. Rorty, ed., *Essays on Aristotle's Ethics* (University of California, 1980).

Sorensen, R., 'Vagueness', in *The Stanford Encyclopedia of Philosophy*, 2006.

Sreenivasan, G., 'Errors about Errors: Virtue Theory and Trait Attribution', *Mind*, 111 (2002), 47–68.

Stocker, M., 'Values and Purposes: The Limits of Teleology and the Ends of Friendship', *Journal of Philosophy*, 78 (1981), 747–65.

Stohr, K., and C. H. Wellman, 'Recent Work on Virtue Ethics', *American Philosophical Quarterly*, 39 (2002), 49–72.

Strawson, G., 'The Unhelpfulness of Indeterminism', *Philosophy and Phenomenological Research*, 60 (2000), 149–55.

—— 'The Impossibility of Moral Responsibility', in G. Watson, ed., *Free Will*, 2nd edn. (Oxford, 2003).

Strawson, P., 'Freedom and Resentment', in Strawson, *Freedom and Resentment* (Methuen, 1974).

Swanton, C., *Virtue Ethics: A Pluralistic View* (Oxford, 2003).

—— 'Nietzschean Virtue Ethics', in S. Gardiner, ed., *Virtue Ethics, Old and New* (Cornell, 2005).

Tarski, A., 'The Concept of Truth in Formalized Languages', in A. Tarski, ed., *Logic, Semantics, Mathematics* (Oxford, 1956).

Taylor, C., 'Responsibility for Self', in G. Watson, ed., *Free Will*, 1st edn. (Oxford, 1982).

Taylor, R., 'Ancient Wisdom and Modern Folly', *Midwest Studies in Philosophy*, 13 (1988), 54–63.

Telfer, E., 'The Unity of Moral Virtues in Aristotle's *Nicomachean Ethics*', *Proceedings of the Aristotelian Society*, 91 (1989–90), 35–48.

Tett, R. P., and H. A. Guterman, 'Situation Trait Relevance, Trait Expression, and Cross-Situational Consistency', *Journal of Research in Personality*, 34 (2000), 397–423.

Thompson, J., *Discourse and Knowledge: A Defence of Collectivist Ethics* (Routledge, 1998).

Thompson, M., 'The Representation of Life', in R. Hursthouse, G. Lawrence, and W. Quinn, eds., *Virtues and Reasons: Philippa Foot and Moral Theory* (Oxford, 1995).

Thomson, J. J., 'The Right and the Good', *Journal of Philosophy*, 94 (1997), 273–98.

Tiberius, V., 'How to Think about Virtue and Right', *Philosophical Papers*, 35 (2006), 247–65.

Trianosky, G., 'Natural Affection and Responsibility for Character: A Critique of Kantian Views of the Virtues', in O. Flanagan and A. O. Rorty, eds., *Identity, Character and Morality: Essays in Moral Psychology* (MIT, 1990).

Tuozzo, T., 'Aristotelian Deliberation is Not of Ends', in J. P. Anton and A. Preus, eds., *Essays in Ancient Greek Philosophy IV: Aristotle's Ethics* (SUNY, 1991).

Unger, P., *Ignorance* (Oxford, 1975).

Upton, C., 'A Contextual Account of Character Traits', *Philosophical Studies*, 122 (2005), 133–51.

Urmson, J. O., 'Aristotle's Doctrine of the Mean', in A. O. Rorty, ed., *Essays on Aristotle's Ethics* (University of California, 1980).

——*Aristotle's Ethics* (Blackwell, 1988).

Vranas, P., 'The Indeterminacy Paradox: Character Evaluations and Human Psychology', *Nous*, 39 (2005), 1–42.

Walker, A. D. M., 'Virtue and Character', *Philosophia*, 64 (1989), 349–62.

——'Character and Circumstance', *Moral and Social Studies*, 5 (1990), 39–53.

——'The Incompatibility of the Virtues', *Ratio*, 6 (1993), 44–62.

Wallace, J. D., *Virtues and Vices* (Cornell, 1978).

Wallace, R. J., 'Reason and Responsibility', in G. Cullity and B. Gaut, eds., *Ethics and Practical Reason* (Oxford, 1997).

Walsh, J. J., 'Buridan on the Connection of the Virtues', *Journal of the History of Philosophy* (1986), 453–82.

Walter, J., *Die Lehre von der praktischen Vernunft in der griechischen Philosophie* (Jena, 1874).

Watson, G., 'Free Agency', *Journal of Philosophy*, 72 (1975), 205–20.

——'Virtues in Excess', *Philosophical Studies*, 46 (1984), 57–74.

——'On the Primacy of Character', in O. Flanagan and A. O. Rorty, eds., *Identity, Character, and Morality: Essays in Moral Psychology* (MIT, 1990).

Webber, J., 'Virtue, Character and Situation', *Journal of Moral Philosophy*, 3 (2006), 193–213.

——'Character, Global and Local', *Utilitas*, 19 (2007a), 430–4.

——'Character, Common Sense, and Expertise', *Ethical Theory and Moral Practice*, 10 (2007b), 89–104.

White, R. W., *The Abnormal Personality* (Ronald, 1964).

White, S., *The Unity of the Self* (Cambridge 1991).

Wiggins, D., 'Weakness of Will, Commensurability, and the Objects of Deliberation and Desire', in A. O. Rorty, ed., *Essays on Aristotle's Ethics* (University of California, 1980).

Williams, B., 'Conflicts of Values', in *Moral Luck* (Cambridge, 1981).

—— *Ethics and the Limits of Philosophy* (Harvard, 1985).

—— 'Acting as the Virtuous Person Acts', in R. Heinaman, ed., *Aristotle and Moral Realism* (University College London, 1995a).

—— 'Replies', in J. E. J. Altham and R. Harrison, eds., *World, Mind, and Ethics: Essays on the Ethical Philosophy of Bernard Williams* (Cambridge, 1995b).

Williams, S. L., and D. Cervone, 'Social Cognitive Theories of Personality', in D. F. Barone, M. Hersen, and H. B. Van Hasselt, eds., *Advanced Personality* (Plenum, 1998).

Winter, M., and J. M. Tauer, 'Virtue Theory and Social Psychology', *Journal of Value Inquiry*, 40 (2006), 73–82.

Wolf, S., *Freedom within Reason* (Oxford, 1990).

—— 'Moral Saints', in R. Crisp and M. Slote, eds., *Virtue Ethics* (Oxford, 1997).

—— 'Sanity and the Metaphysics of Freedom', in G. Watson, ed., *Free Will*, 2nd edn. (Oxford, 2003).

—— 'Moral Psychology and the Unity of the Virtues', *Ratio*, 20 (2007), 145–67.

Woods, M., 'Intuition and Perception in Aristotle's Ethics', *Oxford Studies in Ancient Philosophy*, 4 (1986), 145–66.

Zagzebski, L., *Virtues of the Mind* (Cambridge, 1996).

Zimmerman, D., 'Sour Grapes, Self-Abnegation and Character Building: Non-Responsibility and Responsibility for Self-Induced Preferences', *Monist*, 86 (2003a), 220–41.

—— 'That was Then, This is Now: Personal History vs. Psychological Structure in Compatibilist Theories of Autonomous Agency', *Nous*, 37 (2003b), 638–71.

Index Locorum

AESCHYLUS
Prometheus Bound
  953: 214 n.
ANDRONICUS
SVF 3.270: 214 n.
SVF 3.391: 214 n.
AQUINAS
Summa Theologica (ST)
  1–2 q65 a1: 338 n.
  2–2 q61: 150 n.
  2–2 q134 a1 ad 1: 223 n.
  2–2 q134 a1 obj1, a3 obj4: 209 n.
  2–2 q134 a2 ad 3: 230
  2–2 q134 a3 ad 1: 225 n.
  2–2 q134 a3 ad 3: 230
  2–2 q134 a3 ad 4: 222 n.
  2–2 q134 a4: 219 n.
ARISTOTLE
Categories
  8b25–9a9: 325
De Motu Animalium
  7: 6 n.
Eudemian Ethics (EE)
  I.3: 411 n.
  II: 325
  II.1, 1219b25ff: 14
  1220a5ff: 14
  II.2, 1220b5ff: 8 n.
  II.5: 16
  II.10: 5
    1225b24–31: 5
    1226a1–17: 4
    1226a6–17: 4
    1226a11–13: 4
    1226a20–6: 5
    1226a28–30: 5
    1226a31–3: 5
    1226b5–9: 12
    1226b9–12: 5
    1226b13–20: 5
    1226b13–17: 12
    1227a5 ff: 5
    1227a18–21: 7
  II.11: 30

III.6, 1233a31–8: 209
  1233a38–1233b6: 215
  1233b8–14: 214
III.7, 1233b18–26: 181 n.
Magna Moralia (MM)
  I.11: 106 n.
  I.17: 4, 5, 12
  I.18: 8
  I.26: 215
  I.27: 181 n.
  I.34: 14, 15, 16, 19, 24, 26 n.
  II.3: 19, 24
  II.10: 16
Metaphysics
  I.1, 981a12–24: 10 n.
  VII.7, 1032b18–29: 6 n.
Nicomachean Ethics (NE)
  I.1–2: 410
  I.2, 1094a22–b11: 18
  I.3: 1, 23
    1094b11–27: 18
  I.4–5: 410
  I.5: 1, 411 n.
  I.7: 411 n.
    1097b22–5: 343
    1097b23–1098a20: 410 n.
    1098a12–18: 343
  I.8, 1099a31–1099b8: 222 n.
  I.10, 1101a14–16: 412 n.
  I.13, 1102a26–1103a10: 14
    1102a28–32: 14
    1102a32–b12: 14
    1102b13–1103a3: 14
    1102b14–25: 14
    1102b25: 14
    1102b25–33: 14
    1102b30–1: 8
  II–V: 325
  II.1: 1
    1103a18–23: 20 n.
  II. 4: 1, 2, 17, 23, 84, 85, 134, 191, 325
    1105a26 33: 1, 14, 216
    1105a27–b1: 325
    1105a28–33: 6

Nicomachean Ethics (NE) (cont.)
    1105a31–3: 325
    1105a31–2: 183
    1105a32–3: 341
  II.5, 1106a11–12: 325
  II.6: 2, 85 n.
    1106b18–1107a8: 14
    1106b21–3: 30
    1106b36–1107a2: 104
    1106b36–1107a6: 30
    1107a8–27: 15
    1107a9–12: 19
  II.7: 183 n.
    1107b17–21: 209, 215
    1108a24: 152 n.
  II.9: 55 n., 128
    1109b1–7: 15
    1109b12–23: 19
  III.2, 1111b4–11: 4
    1111b9–10: 12
    1111b10–19: 14
    1111b13–16: 5
  III.3: 8
    1111b19–30: 4
    1111b18–19: 5
    1111b30–1112a1, 3–5: 4
    1112a1–13: 4
    1112a7–13: 5
    1112a13–17: 5
    1112a21–7: 5
    1112a28–34: 5
    1112a30–31: 5
    1112a34–b11: 5
    1112b11–20: 79, 223
    1112b11–12: 5
    1112b12–14: 7
    1112b14–31: 8
    1112b20–3: 12
    1112b34–1113a2: 10
    1113a2–7: 5
    1113a2–5: 5
    1113a9–14: 5
    1113a9–12: 5
    1113a9–11: 16
    1113a10: 192
  III.5, 1115a4–5: 217f
    1115a5: 218 n.
  III.8, 1117a17–20: 12
    1117a17–22: 6 n.
    1117a20: 12
    1117a20–22: 12, 13 n.
  IV.1, 1122a26, 27: 214 n.
  IV.2: 8 n., 149
    1122a19: 215

    1122a20–2: 209
    1122a23: 209
    1122a26, 27: 214 n.
    1122a28–9: 197 n., 210, 216
    1122a31–3: 215
    1122a34: 214, 216, 229
    1122b1–21: 108
    1122b4–6: 215
    1122b6–7: 215
    1122b7, 18, 29: 215
    1122b7–10: 215
    1122b7–8: 215
    1122b19–20: 213
    1122b19–23: 213, 215f
    1122b19–21: 212
    1122b23–9: 214, 222 n.
    1122b29–33: 213
    1122b35–1123a5: 213
    1123a1–2: 213, 214
    1123a4–5: 212
    1123a6–9: 213
    1123a14–16: 214 n.
    1123a19–20: 214 n., 215
    1123a23–4: 215
    1123a24–7: 215
    1123a27–31: 215
  IV.3, 1123b5–6: 216
  IV.4, 1125b1–4: 215
    1125b1–8: 216 n.
  IV.8: 358
    1128a17: 152 n.
  IV.9, 1128b29–31: 53
  VI.1: 2, 19 n., 343, 361
    1138b18–34: 18
    1138b18–25: 16, 18, 30
    1138b25–32: 18
    1138b35–1139a17: 14
    1139a6–11: 14
  VI.2, 1139a21–31: 15
    1139a23: 16
    1139a23–6: 16
    1139a29–31: 15
    1139a32–3: 5
    1139b5: 5
    1139b5–11: 5
  VI.3: 15
  VI.4, 1139b29–31: 22 n.
    1140a10: 17
    1140a10–16: 16
    1140a20–21: 17
  VI.5: 343
    1140a25–31: 18, 30
    1140a25–28: 10, 29
    1140a28: 17

1140a31–b4: 5
1140b1–4: 1, 216
1140b4–7: 16
1140b5–6: 80
1140b6–7: 17
1140b7: 17
1140b7–10: 17
1140b21–4: 16
1140b21–2: 17
VI.6: 15
VI.7: 5, 10, 17
1141b3 ff: 33
1141b8–12: 5
1141b12–14: 17
1141b14–22: 10
VI.8, 1141b23–4: 18
1141b24–33: 18 n.
1142a11–5: 10
1142a23–30: 19, 192 n.
VI.9: 24
1142a31–b15: 12
1142b2: 12
1142b2–5: 12
1142b20–8: 24
1142b27–8: 24
1142b28–33: 8
1142b29–31: 24
1142b31–3: 24
1142b33: 192 n.
VI.10, 1143a5–b5: 19
1143a8–10: 21
1143a10–11: 21 n.
1143a11–16: 21
1143a12–18: 21
1143a16–18: 21
VI.11: 21
1143a19–20: 21
1143a25–32: 23
1143a32–b5: 22
1143b13–14: 22
VI.12: 7, 79, 128, 361, 372
1144a1–3: 17, 28 n.
1144a3–6: 17
1144a6–b1: 223
1144a6–9: 223
1144a7–8: 229
1144a7–9: 8, 30, 79, 220, 325
1144a21–2: 25
1144a23–8: 7
1144a24–6: 79
1144a26–8: 24
1144a28–9: 25
1144a29–b1: 25, 217, 335
1144a34–6: 337

VI.13: 2, 17, 31, 81, 147, 159, 186, 232, 335,
    339 n., 342, 344, 372
1144b1–17: 17, 25, 170
1144b1–9: 19
1144b3–6: 19
1144b6–9: 20
1144b8–12: 32
1144b8–9: 20 n.
1144b12–14: 32
1144b17–18: 26 n.
1144b18–30: 26 n.
1144b25–30: 19
1144b30–1145a6: 217
1144b30–1145a2: 26
1144b33–1145a2: 336
1145a1–2: 207, 209
1145a2–6: 17, 20, 28 n.
1145a2–4: 32
IX.8, 1169a26–34: 50
IX.12, 1172a1–3, 6–14: 328

Politics
I.13: 152 n.
III.5, 1278a8 ff: 222 n.
VII.9, 1328b24 ff: 222 n.
VIII.2, 1337b4 ff: 222 n.
VIII.6, 1341a5 ff: 222 n.

Posterior Analytics 15 n., 180 n.
II.13, 97b15–25: 185 n.
II.19: 22 n.

Rhetoric
II.1–11: 14 n.
II.12: 19

ARIUS DIDYMUS, in Stobaeus, *Anthology* II
5b–5b2: 4 n., 155, 160, 218
5b2: 148

CICERO
de Finibus
III.23–5: 16 n.
On Invention
2.54.163: 219 n.

DIODORUS
Histories
13.82.1: 214 n.

ISOCRATES
Letters
    I.27: 214 n.

Letters (cont.)
  2.19: 213 n.
  7.29: 213 n.
  7.29–30: 222 n., 232 n.

PAUL
1 Corinthians 15: 33, 327

PLATO
Euthydemus
  288d–293a: 16 n.
Gorgias
  456c–461b: 17 n.
  506e–507e: 148
Meno 90–1
  71e–72a: 152, 168 n.
Republic 14, 98, 186 n., 187, 398
IV: 148, 358
  441c–442d: 218, 359
VIII, 560e: 233 n.

Protagoras
329d: 159
329d–330b: 148

PLUTARCH
On Moral Virtue
440a–441e: 161
441b: 152

SENECA
Letters
  113.23: 63 n.

XENOPHON
Constitution of the Lacedaimonians
  12.5: 214 n.
Economics
  2.5: 213 n.
Memorabilia
  3.10.5: 214 n.

General Index

Ackrill, J. L. 6, 371
Adams, R. M. 88 n., 105, 344 n., 365 n.,
  374 n., 375
  on situationism 240 n., 241, 280, 284, 286,
    287, 289, 303 n., 305, 320–2, 326 n.
Aeschylus 214 n.
Allan, D. J. 8 n., 19 n.
Allison, H. E. 191
Allport, G. W. 243, 248
Anagnostou-Laoutides, E. 236 n.
Andronicus 214 n.
Annas, J., 63 n., 67 n., 88 n., 89, 153, 173 n.,
  228 n., 232 n., 236 n., 322, 335 n., 341,
  360, 410 n.
  on Aristotle 6 n., 7, 16 n., 18, 20, 23, 26,
    29, 209, 215
  on situationism 241, 250, 257 n., 307,
    314 n., 319, 321
  on virtue ethics 3, 61, 66, 98, 100, 138,
    141, 168 n., 324f
Anscombe, G. E. M. 8, 95, 96
  on naturalism/nature 87 n., 132, 135 n.
  on rightness 40 n., 160
  on virtue 87 n., 138 n., 162, 165
Aquinas, 64 n., 216, 338 n.
  on cardinality 149–50f, 154, 163, 177,
    207 n., 219
  on magnificence 209, 221 n., 222 n.,
    223 n., 225 n., 230
  areteic concepts 62, 65, 76f, 86–90, 92–5,
    98–102
Ariston 161
Aristotle
  on deliberation Ch. 1 passim, 73, 75f,
    79–88, 192, 324f, 343, 410
  and enumeration of the virtues 148–50,
    217–19
  on 'natural' virtues 19f, 146f, 170, 172,
    335, 342, 344
  on parts of soul 14f
  on phronesis Ch. 1 passim, 79f, 82, 103f,
    128f, 207, 209, 217, 220, 223, 325–8,
    335f, 337, 338, 343, 361, 372
  on right action 1f, 44 n., 50, 53
  and situationism 324–9

on unity of virtue 25f, 31, 207, 335–7,
  339 n.
on virtues of character 13f, 19f, 25f, Ch. 7
  passim, 343, 358, 361
on virtues of practical reason 1f, 13–31
on virtues of theoretical reason 14f, 21f
Arius Didymus 4 n., 148, 155, 160, 218
Arpaly, N. 202 n., 275 n., 318 n.
Athanassoulis, N. 240 n., 282, 283, 286
atomism
  about content 199
  about rightness 190 n.
Audi, R. 82, 85 n., 94 n., 391
  on reasons 184, 193 n., 345
  on targets of virtue 69, 84, 349, 396
Augustine 75, 179 n.

Badhwar, N. 48, 105, 147 n., 228
  on the unity of the virtues 33, 171, 336,
    363–70
Baltzly, D. 95 n., 214 n., 236 n.
Barnes, J. 22, 180 n.
Barrie, C. 236 n.
Batson, J. 239, 273f, 285–7
Benitez, R. 113 n.
Bentham, J. 66
Bigelow, J. 224 n., 236 n.
Bostock, D. 15 n., 17, 20 n., 24, 29n.
Brandt, R. B. 60, 168–70, 341
Broadie, S. 3, 5 n., 11 n., 16, 20 n., 26, 30 n.,
  33, 126 n.
  on practical reasoning in Aristotle 7 n.,
    8 n., 9, 12f, 17, 18 n., 19, 22, 24,
    27 n., 28–9
Buridan, J. 350 n.
Burnet, J. 8 n.
Burns, L. 113 n.
Burnyeat, M. 6 n.
Butler, D. 241, 324 n.

Campbell, J. 239, 240 n., 285, 286
Carr, D. 174
Cassedy, E. S. 118 n.
Cattell, R. B. 248
Cavell, M. 199 n.

character, *see also* psychology, empirical;
    psychology, moral; responsibility for
    character; virtue
    compartmentalization of 147f, 173, 179f,
        364–6
    depth of 133f, Ch. 12 *passim*
    and non-evaluative beliefs 4 n., 90 n., 201
    and personality 156f, 241, Ch. 10 *passim*,
        340, 348
    revealed in decision 4–6, 7, 29–30
Chrysippus 63 n., 152
Cialdini, R. B. 178, 250, 260
Cicero 16 n., 219 n.
Cleanthes 63 n.
cleverness 2, 7, 24f, 79–81, 90 n., 141, 211,
    223f, 225, 329
Colyvan, M. 113 n., 114 n.
compatibilism 378f, 381, 387f, 393, 396f, 402,
    403f; *see also* responsibility for character
compulsion 344f, 375, 387, 389, 395
Cooper, J. 152, 160, 161, 186 n., 232n
    on Aristotle 8 n., 10 n., 14, 19 n., 27
    on the unity of the virtues 350–3
Copp, D. 45, 47 n., 48, 63 n., 66 n., 67 n.,
    68 n., 91
critical distance 379, 388–413

Dahl, N. 6 n., 20 n., 21, 24 n.
Dalcourt, G. 150 n.
Dancy, J. 190, 203f, 394 n.
Darley, J. 239, 252f, 269–74, 285–7
Darwall, S. 92, 97
Das, R. 44 n., 45, 58, 66 n., 75 n., 104, 105
Davidson, D. 261
    on action 86, 192f
    on content 199 n., 200, 201 n., 202 n.
    on compositionality of language 162
    on standards of rationality 55 n., 123–7
deliberation, *see* Aristotle on deliberation
Dennett, D. 402 n.
Dent, N. J. H. 357
deontology, deontic constraints 62, 69 n.,
    95–100
DePaul, M. 240, 299 n.
DesLauriers, M. 182, 192 n., 235 n.
development, moral 20 n., 23, 55f, 114,
    127–9, 138, 159, 228, 319, 340; *see also*
    responsibility for character
    piecemeal nature of 173f, 180, 211, 326,
        361f, 364f, 369f, 373
    piecemeal nature of, contrasted with nature
        of virtue 173f, 179f, 205, 207, 211,
        366–70, 373
    in virtue ethics 2, 175

Devereux, D. 9, 10 n.
dilemmas, moral 21, 49, 51, 53, 61, 134, 174,
    227 n., 339–41
dispositions, *see* psychology, empirical
Donagan, A. 61 n.
Doris, J. 106, 147 n., 170, Chs. 8–9 *passim*,
    294, 295
    on the Darley and Batson experiment 274,
        287
    on empirical inadequacy of virtue
        theory 293, 300f, 325
    on fragmentation of character 147 n., 171,
        300
    on fundamental attribution error 308, 312f
    on Milgram experiment 275, 277–84
        passim
    on normative inadequacy of virtue
        theory 293, 300, 305f, 314, 323, 329
Drefcinski, S. 26 n.
Driver, J. 106 n., 141 n.
    on phronesis 32f, 104f, 131
    and situationism 315–17, 318f
    on virtue 131, 133, 173 n., 376

Eliopoulos, N. 218 n., 236 n.
elitism 3, 33, 104f, 140f, 184, 322 n.
enumeration of the virtues Chs. 5–7 *passim*
Epstein, S. 289
eudaimonia 11 n., 15 n., 17, 27–8, 29f, 75, 88,
    98, 410–12
eudaimonism 73, 90 n., 153, 172, 348 n.,
    411n., 412; *see also* naturalism
Evnine, S. 201 n.
excellence, *see* virtue

Feldman, F. 385 n.
Feleppa, R. 175 n.
Fine, K. 115 n.
Finnegan, B. 409 n.
Fischer, J. M. 387 n., 388 n.
Flanagan, O. 158f, 361 n.
    on fundamental attribution error 307, 312,
        313
    on situationism 247, 250, 275, 276 n., 277,
        278, 288, 295–300
    on the unity of the virtues 163 n., 342, 359
Fleming, D. 241, 247, 282, 297
flourishing 11 n., 17, 75, 88 n., 92, 98,
    410–12
Fodor, J. 199 n., 201, 204
Foot, F. 25, 41, 45, 55, 60–1, 106 n., 138 n.,
    183 n., 186, 223, 340, 351, 371
    on goodness 92f, 100
    on moral dilemma 63, 69 n., 227 n.

on naturalism 87, 88 n., 91–2, 158
on obligation 96f
on phronesis 2, 31, 82, 83, 111, 140f
Fortenbaugh, W. 6 n.
Frankena, W. 39, 40 n., 50, 96, 166
Frankfurt, H. 42, 378, 384, 391f, 393–4,
    409 n.
French, P. 40 n.
Freud, S. 248
Funder, D. C. 299

Gandhi, M. 32, 109 n.
Garcia, J. 39, 40 n., 42, 43, 45, 50, 51, 62, 64,
    74 n.
Gardiner, S. 209, 216 n., 219, 222, 227 n.,
    229, 234
Gauguin, P. 32 n., 109 n.
Geach, P. 50, 64 n., 91, 100, 357 n.
generalism 202
Gilbert, D. T. 244, 256, 271, 288, 308, 309,
    311, 312, 313
Glover, J. 390 n.
Goldblatt, R. 136 n.
Goldie, P. 313
Gómez-Lobo, A. 15 n., 19, 27 n.
Goodin, R. 82
Gorr, M. 39, 40 n., 64
Graff, D. 118, 119 n.
Greenwood, L. H. G. 6 n.
Guilford, J. P. 248

Halper, E. 222 n.
Handfield, T. 219 n.
happiness 17, 27, 29n., 67 n., 89, 98 n., 343,
    410
Hardie,W. F. R. 8 n., 15, 27 n.
Harman, G.
    on fundamental attribution error 311,
        313 n.
    on situationism 293, 295, 296–9, 300, 307
    on virtues 47, 323
Hartshorne, H. 246, 249–50
Herman, B. 78, 190f, 394 n.
holism
    about content 198–204, 206, 293 n.
    about rightness 190 n., 202–4
Homiak, M. 384 n.
Hubin, D. 409 n.
Hume, D., 379 n.,
    Humean 6, 8 n., 49, 75
Hurka, T. 45, 58, 59 n., 68 n., 104
Hursthouse, R. 20 n., 62, 63, 69, 72, 77,
    87 n., 91, 92, 176, 181, 190, 229 n., 231,
    295 n., 362 n., 366

on action guidance and assessment 2,
    46–54 passim, 62, 69, 138, 164
on compartmentalization 33, 147f, 171,
    179
on goodness 91
on nature/naturalism 87, 95
on phronesis 2, 7, 11, 18, 19f, 21, 23, 24,
    41, 55, 82, 83, 106 n., 140, 223, 357,
    361, 363 n.
on right action 1 n., 2, 37, 38, 42 n., 45,
    62, 63, 64 n., 65f, 67 n., 103, 105,
    127 n., 128 n., 146, 207, 322 n., 356
on virtue 114 n., 122 n., 134, 147f, 150,
    152, 166, 171, 173, 179, 186, 214 n.,
    230 n., 231 n., 320 n., 343, 361, 409 n.
on virtue reasons 68, 153 n., 183f, 187,
    191 n., 193, 201f, 225 n., 293 n.,
    346 n.

ideal, see model concepts
incompatibilism 378, 381, 383 n.; see also
    Kane; responsibility for character;
    Strawson, G.; ultimate responsibility
indeterminism 377, 380, 382f, 386
intelligence, see phronesis
intuition, intuitionism 22, 73, 75 n., 83,
    105 n.
    about rightness 22, 95; see also Prichard
    about virtuousness 79, 93–5
Inwagen, P. van 382 n., 386 n.
Irwin, T. 16 n., 186 n., 335 n., 341
    on Aquinas 150 n., 207 n., 219 n.
    on Aristotle 6 n., 8 n., 12, 20 n., 26 n.,
        27 n., 64 n.
    on magnificence 209, 222, 227 n., 232 n.,
        234 n.
Isocrates 213 n., 214 n., 222 n., 232 n.

Jackall, R. 281
Jacobs, J. 338 n., 358
Jacobson, D. 58, 74 n.
Jaeger, W. 8 n.
Johnson, R. 47f, 51–7, 84 n., 129

Kakoliris, G. 6 n., 27 n.
Kammrath, L. K. R. 260, 313 n.
Kamtekar, R. 170, 240 n., 241, 247, 250, 283,
    284, 286, 287, 299, 324 n., 328 n.
Kane, R. 381–8, 396
Kant, I., Kantian 41, 62 n., 106, 122 n., 190f
Kawall, J. 45, 53, 68 n., 104
Keefe, R. 114 n., 115
Keynes, J. M. 94

Kohlberg, L. 159
Korsgaard, C. 39, 190
  on Aristotle 17 n., 87 n., 343, 410 n.
  on moral reasons 96f
  on practical identity 61, 376
  on problem of the normative 346, 389
Kraut, R. 27 n., 28 n., 29, 209, 234 n.
Kunda, Z. 298
Kupperman, J. 390 n., 405 n.

Latané, B. 252f, 269–71, 273
LeBar, M. 63 n., 68, 95 n., 97f, 192 n.,
  236 n., 304 n., 409 n., 412
Leigh, F. 223 n., 236 n., 409 n.
Lemos, J. 348, 356, 357, 363 n., 371 n.
Lepore, E. 199 n., 201, 204
Levy, N. 405 n.
Lewin, K. 244
Lewis, D. 113 n., 120 n.
Loevinger, J. 248
Lord, C. 244, 245, 257, 262, 264–6, 303
Louden, R. 1 n., 48
  on Aristotle 10 n., 19, 21, 24
  criticisms of virtue ethics 37, 40 n., 69 n.,
    104–6 passim, 166
  on nature of virtue ethics 1 n., 3, 38,
    60–1f, 66, 95 n., 168 n.

McAleer, S. 67 n.
McDowell, J. 41, 42, 55, 66, 80 n., 183 n.,
  232 n., 324 n., 336, 361, 390
  on Aristotle 6, 7, 8, 13, 18f, 22, 26 n., 29,
    30, 31, 192 n.
  on naturalism 87 n., 88 n., 158 n.
  on reasons 92f, 127 n., 169, 193 n., 391
MacFarlane, J. W. 248
MacIntyre, A. 27 n., 41, 94, 105 n., 155 n.,
  196 n., 212 n.
McKinnon, N. 114 n., 119 n.
McRoberts, K. 106 n.
Meier, C. 119 n.
Mele, A. 387 n., 401
Mendoza-Denton, R. 250, 260, 313 n.
Menedemus 161
Merritt, M. 138 n., 274, 327, 331
Mews, C. 236 n.
Milgram, S. 109f, 274–6, 278–87, 309
Miller, C. 240 n., 281, 282, 284, 286, 287, 297
Milo, R. 40 n.
Mischel, W. 244, 246–66 passim, 277, 288 n.,
  289, 290, 295, 298–303 passim
model concepts, models
  and aspiration to ideals 123–30
  discourse about 135–9, 367–9

nature of 117–21, 130–5, 147, 362–9
  of virtue/phronesis Ch. 4 passim, 167,
    196–8, 202, 220, 337f, 362–73
Monan, J. 8 n.
Mondraty, N. 256
Moody-Adams, M. 384 n., 405 n., 407
Moriarty, J. 385 n.
Murdoch, I. 40 n.

Nagel, T. 340, 381, 383 n., 384 n.
Natali, C. 19, 24
naturalism 73, 77, 86–100, 153, 158 n.,
  172–5, 197, 348 n.; see also eudaimonism
Neely, W. 402 n.
Neurath, O., Neurathian 88 n., 93, 390
Nietzsche, F., Nietzschean 32, 89 n., 90f, 93,
  106, 109, 121f, 140 n., 381 n.
Nisbett, R. E. 170, 178, Chs. 8–9 passim,
  298, 308–13, 314 n.
Noddings, N. 88
normativity 139, 180, 185, 242, 410
  and commitment to ideals 124–6, 128
  problem of, see Korsgaard
  and reflection 389–91, 402, 405f
  and virtue/virtue theory 92f, 95, 98–100,
    292–4, 304–6, 328–31, 346f
Nussbaum, M. 43, 67, 95

Oakley, J. 65, 103
O'Connor, D. 409
Oderberg, D. S. 150 n., 195 n.
ought, contrasted with right, 47–59; see also
  normativity
Owens, J. 15 n.

Pakaluk, M. 7, 19, 209, 214 n., 216 n., 222 n.
parochialism 90–5
particularism 189f, 202f
Peake, P. K. 262 n., 290
Pereboom, D. 388 n.
personality, personality psychology, see
  psychology, empirical
Pervin, L. A. 247, 262 n.
Peterson, C. 156–7f, 248 n.
phronesis Ch. 1 passim, Ch.11 passim
  and deliberation 78, 79f, 82, 100f, 103f,
    108f, 141, 167, 169, 205–7, 211, 220,
    223, 325, 329f, 355
  as general/global 105, 205–7, 343, 366
  in modern virtue ethics/theory 73, 78, 101,
    103f, 108–11, 140f, 316f
  as part of all the virtues 101, 108, 121, 139f,
    205–7, 217, 220, 316, 325, 329, 335f

Piaget, J. 159
Pincoffs, E. 23, 32 n., 70 n., 96, 109 n.,
    111 n., 127 n., 129, 150, 171 n., 183 n.,
    376 n.
  on right action 40 n., 50, 61, 134, 138f, 174
Plato 17 n., 74, 75, 90, 152, 186 n., 233 n.,
    398
  on cardinality 148, 150, 163, 187, 210, 218
  on skill 16 n., 17 n.
  on the soul 14, 74, 88 n., 148, 150 n.,
    179 n., 358f
  on the unity of virtue 158f, 358–60
Plutarch 152, 161
Polansky, R. 174
practical intelligence, see phronesis
practical wisdom, see phronesis
Price, A. W. 6, 7, 9, 15 n., 16
Prichard, H. A. 40 n., 79, 93f, 166
Prior, W. J. 104 n.
psychology, empirical Chs. 8–10 passim; see
    also Lord; Mischel; Nisbett; Ross
  and attribution errors 307–14
  cognitive-affective personality theory
    258–66
  on consistency 246f, 258, 260–2, 269–73,
    293
  consistency experiments 246, 250, 252f,
    Ch. 9 passim
  dispositionism Chs. 8–9 passim
  idiographic vs. nomothetic
    measures 263–6
  Milgram experiments, see Milgram
  nominal vs. psychological
    classifications 249–53, 257–9, 261–6
  Princeton 'Good Samaritan' experiment, see
    Batson
  situationism 170, Chs. 8–10 passim
  on stability 246f, 249, 257, 258, 261, 278,
    289
  virtue theoretical replies to social
    psychology 170–2, 240f, Chs. 9–10 passim
psychology, moral/philosophical Ch. 10
passim; see also Doris; Flanagan; Harman

Quine, W. V. O. 199 n., 201 n.

Rachels, J. 385 n.
Ramberg, B. T. 123 n.
Rand, A. 104–5f
Rawls, J. 42, 66, 133, 385, 390f, 401, 402, 408
Raz, J. 203 n.
reasons
  agent-neutral and agent-relative 96–8
  content of 191–202, 204, 206

contrastive nature of 344–6, 356, 396–9,
    406
  sameness of Ch. 6 passim
Reeve, C. D. C. 6 n., 11 n., 14 n., 27 n.,
    149 n., 218 n., 223 n., 232 n.
reflective equilibrium 117, 122, 127, 390
responsibility for character Ch. 12; see also
    critical distance; Frankfurt; Kane;
    Strawson, G.; Taylor, C.; ultimate
    responsibility; Watson; Wolf;
    Zimmerman
Richardson, H. 91, 92
rightness, right action Ch. 2 passim
  account constraint Ch. 2 passim, 72, 100f,
    139f, 146
  act constraint Ch. 2 passim, 72, 100
  and consequences/outcomes 67–70
  contrasted with ought, see ought
  relevance of inner states to 39–44
Roberts-Thomson, S. 399 n.
Rodin, J. 273
Ross, L. 170, 178, Chs. 8–9 passim, 298, 299,
    308–13, 314 n.
Rovane, C. 123–5
Rowe, C. 5 n., 9, 11 n., 16, 17, 18 n., 20 n.,
    22, 24, 26 n., 33
Rudebusch, G. 236 n.
Runia, D. 236 n.
Ryckman, R. 243

Sabini, J. 240 n., 282, 287f
Sachdev, P. 256
Sainsbury, R. M. 113, 115, 116 n.
Santas, G. 66 n.
satis concepts 112–24 passim, 167, 362f, 385f,
    392, 409
Scanlon, T. 40 n.
Scheffler, S. 97 n.
Schmidtz, D. 9 n., 82, 125, 189, 388 n.,
    394 n., 408 n., 409 n.
Schneewind, J. 33, 39, 104 n., 105, 106,
    135 n.
Schwitzgebel, E. 199 n., 201
Seligman, M. E. P. 156f, 248 n.
Seneca 63 n.
Sher, G. 385 n., 396 n., 405 n., 406 n., 408 n.
Sherman, N. 6 n., 8, 9, 10, 22
Shoda, Y. 250, 257, 258, 260f, 262 n., 313 n.
Sidgwick, H. 58
Siepmann, M. 240 n., 287, 288
Silver, M. 240 n., 282, 287, 288
situationism, see psychology
Skorupski, J. 152

Slote, M. 32 n., 66 n., Ch. 3 *passim*, 109 n.,
134, 148, 224 n., 307 n., 343 n.
and Aristotle 22 n., 73, 75f, 79–88
and intuition 22 n., 75 n., 83, 89f, 93–5
on right action 2, 32, 41, 45, 51, 57–65,
passim, Ch. 3 *passim*, 146, 165
Smart, J. J. C. 39
Smilansky, S. 385 n.
Smith, M. 396, 412 n.
Smith, P. 114 n., 115
Sobel, D. 45, 47 n., 48, 63 n., 66 n., 67 n.,
68 n., 91
social psychology, *see* psychology, empirical
Socrates 17 n., 26 n., 91, 104 n., 152, 159,
213 n., 398 n.
Soles, D. N. 199 n., 348 n.
Soles, D. H. 123 n.
Solomon, J. 240 n., 281, 283, 298, 313
Sorabji, R. 6, 10, 12, 19, 27 n., 341
Sorensen, R. 115
Sreenivasan, G. 240 n., 241, 250, 264, 269,
286, 297, 299 n.
Stein, J. 240n., 287, 288
Stewart, W. 136 n.
Stocker, M. 85 n.
Stohr, K. 45, 58, 59 n., 65, 75 n., 97
Stoicism, Stoics 16 n., 152, 186 n., 328 n.; *see
also* Ariston; Chrysippus; Menedemus;
Seneca, Zeno
on action 62f, 64 n.
on cardinality 4 n., 148–50, 154, 155f, 160,
163, 177, 187, 210, 218, 219
Strawson, G. 377, 381, 382, 384 n., 386, 406
Strawson, P. 405 n.
Swanton, C. 11 n., 25, 41, 63 n., 87, 88 n.,
89 n., 98 n., Ch. 4 *passim*, 148, 150,
181 n., 185, 188 n., 189, 336, 340, 341,
341 n., 376 n., 409 n.
on magnificence 153, 214, 216, 232
on Milgram experiments 240 n., 283
on moral ideals 33f, 48, 106–11, 112f, 128,
130f, 139, 357 n., 371
on Nietzsche 32 n., 102f, 109, 121
on particularism 190 n., 203f
on phronesis 108–11, 140
on right action 2, 44 n., 45, 49 n., 51, 68f,
107f, 146
on targets of the virtues 84, 85 n., 107f,
127 n., 146, 349

Tarski, A. 162
Tauer, J. M. 284
Taylor, C. 391 n., 393, 395
Taylor, R. 40 n.

Telfer, E. 20 n., 33, 341, 357, 361, 363 n.,
371 n.
Thompson, J. 106, 127 n.
Thompson, M. 130, 132–7, 368
Thomson, J. J. 91 n., 133, 317–23
Tiberius, V. 56 n., 184 n.
Tolkien, J. R. R. 105, 304
Trianosky, G. 379 n.
Tuddenham, R. D. 248
Tuozzo, T. 6 n.

ultimate responsibility 380–8; *see also*
responsibility for character; Kane;
Strawson, G.
Unger, P. 113 n.
Upton, C. 171, 300
Urmson, J. O. 7, 19, 21, 24, 153 n., 181–2

vagueness 113–21, 196, 392; *see also* model
concepts; satis concepts
virtue ethics
action, action-guidance Ch. 2 *passim*
agent-based form of Ch. 3 *passim*
applied 2, 138 n.
categorizing 74f
constraints upon Ch. 2 *passim*, 72, 100f,
122, 139f, 146, 356
deflationary forms of 65f, 322f
and naturalism, *see* naturalism
and right action, *see* rightness
virtue theory; *see also* psychology, moral
Aristotelian Ch. 1 *passim*, 323–31
empirical adequacy Ch. 10 *passim*
normative adequacy Ch. 10 *passim*
virtue, virtues
attributive vs. model theses about 362–73
cardinal and subordinate, *see* cardinality
cognitive-affective taxonomy of 323–31
conflicts among 339–43, 348–55
cooperation between 339–55
cultural variation in 156f, 173f, 189, 212,
216, 226f
and domains 169, 361–9
and ends/goals/targets Ch. 1 *passim*, 79,
84–6, 101, 107f, 223, 229–32, 329,
349, 352f
enumeration of, *see* enumeration of the
virtues
as excellences 20, 31, 32, 56f, 87, 101, 106,
133, 179f, 321f, 329, 335, 338–67
passim, 372
heroic vs. quotidian 32, 109; *see also*
Nietzsche
identification of 153f, 159, 175

individuation of 153f, 159, Ch. 6
'limited unity' of, *see* Badhwar
natural makeup of 147, 172–4, 179f, 186f,
    205, 207, 211, 320f, 337, 364–72, 373
'natural' virtues, *see* Aristotle
as satis concept, *see* satis concepts
and stereotypical behavior 20, 30, 127, 170,
    241, 298, 314, 325, 341, 345, 353–5,
    367, 372
thin vs. thick conceptions of 374–80
trajectories vs. directions views of 339–55
unity of Ch. 11
virtue reasons, V reasons 68f, 186–208
    passim, 225f, 345, 293 n., 347, 352–5,
    372
'virtuous person', the, Ch. 4; *see also* model
    concepts
virtuousness Ch. 3 *passim*
overall virtuousness 4, 18, 20, 25, 62, 72, 99,
    108, 110, 141, Ch. 5 *passim*, 202, 206,
    232, 321, 329, 340, 351, 355
Vranas, P. 253, 275, 277, 279, 280, 300 n.,
    326 n.

Walker, A. D. M. 337, 340–59, 363 n.
Wallace, J. D. 341, 345
Wallace, R. J. 396
Walsh, J. J. 339 n., 350 n., 361
Walter, J. 6 n., 8 n.
Watson, G.
    on naturalism 87
    on responsibility 378, 389 n., 393–5,
        410 n.

on virtue ethics 2f, 42 n., 65–68, 77, 95,
    122, 166
on the unity of the virtues 341, 342 n.,
    348–51, 356, 357, 361
Webber, J. 240 n., 241, 283, 296, 311, 313,
    324 n., 325
Wellman, C. 45, 58, 59 n., 65, 75 n., 97
White, J. 399 n.
White, R. W. 248
White, S. 390 n.
Wiggins, D. 7 n., 11 n., 27, 28 n., 324 n.
Williams, B. 39, 40 n., 41 n., 42, 43 n., 47 n.,
    230 n., 340, 360 n., 361, 409 n.
    on virtue reasons 68, 85 n., 153 n., 183–5,
        193, 205, 225 n., 346 n.
Winter, M. 284
wisdom, *see* phronesis
Wittgenstein, L. 116 n., 168
Wolf, S.
    on moral ideals 30, 33, 106, 112 n.,
        126 n.
    on responsibility 379 n., 393–9, 408 n.
    on the unity of the virtues 335 n., 336 n.,
        361, 363 n.
Woods, M. 7, 26 n., 29

Xenophon 213 n., 214 n.

Zagzebski, L. 53 n., 69, 75 n., 84, 89 n.,
    90 n., 94 n., 98 n., 100, 101 n.
Zeis, J. 338 n., 358
Zeno 161
Zimmerman, D. 387n, 397, 399–403

Milton Keynes UK
Ingram Content Group UK Ltd.
UKHW022057260424
441605UK00011B/355